THE COLLECTED WORKS OF
SAMUEL TAYLOR COLERIDGE · 15

OPUS MAXIMUM

General Editor: KATHLEEN COBURN

THE COLLECTED WORKS

1. Draft of the "Proposed Preface" in Coleridge's hand. Berg Collection of English and American Literature, The New York Public Library, Astor, Lenox and Tilden Foundations; reproduced by kind permission

THE COLLECTED WORKS OF

Samuel Taylor Coleridge

Opus Maximum

EDITED BY

Thomas McFarland

WITH THE ASSISTANCE OF

Nicholas Halmi

✿ BOLLINGEN SERIES LXXV
PRINCETON UNIVERSITY PRESS

*The Collected Works, sponsored by Bollingen Foundation,
is published by Princeton University Press,
Princeton, New Jersey*

Library of Congress Cataloging-in-Publication Data

*Coleridge, Samuel Taylor, 1772–1834.
Opus Maximum : the collected works of Samuel Taylor Coleridge / edited by
Thomas McFarland, with the assistance of Nicholas Halmi.
p.   cm. — (Bollingen series ; 75) (The collected works
of Samuel Taylor Coleridge ; 15)
Includes bibliographical references and index.
ISBN 0-691-09882-4
I. McFarland, Thomas, 1926–   II. Halmi, Nicholas.
III. Title.   IV. Series.
PR4470 .F69 vol. 15   [PR4472]   821'.7—dc21
2002025150*

*The Collected Works constitutes
the seventy-fifth publication in Bollingen Series*

The present work is number 15 of the Collected Works

*Princeton University Press books are printed on acid-free paper
and meet the guidelines for permanence and durability
of the Committee on Production Guidelines for Book Longevity
of the Council on Library Resources
Printed in the United States of America*

1 3 5 7 9 10 8 6 4 2

0012942797

cl

THIS EDITION

OF THE WORKS OF

SAMUEL TAYLOR COLERIDGE

IS DEDICATED

IN GRATITUDE TO

THE FAMILY EDITORS

IN EACH GENERATION

CONTENTS

LIST OF ILLUSTRATIONS

EDITOR'S FOREWORD

THIS INTRODUCTION, as compared to others in the *Collected Coleridge*, will be dramatically brief. For it will promptly be succeeded by a long Prolegomena that takes over the usual function of the Editor's Introduction at the same time that it establishes, more copiously than an ordinary introduction would do, the intellectual coordinates without which the text must seem perplexing and barren.

These lengthy prolegomena exist because the editing of the fragments of Coleridge's *Opus Maximum* presents problems that are culturally unique and that differ radically from the other problems of the series. First, the texts themselves have appeared uniformly baffling and inconclusive for the better part of two centuries. And second, these texts can usefully be contemplated only in the context of a larger and more ambitious work that does not exist, the fabled *magnum opus*.

In addition to the commentary generated by the fragments as they stand, therefore, there is an even lengthier commentary extricating, as far as possible, the emphases and philosophical problems of the *magnum opus*. Why is it necessary to discuss a work that does not even exist, and to do so at great length? Without the contextualization supplied by the concerns of the *magnum opus*, the residue of Coleridge's endeavour known as *Opus Maximum* would lack intelligibility and point. Moreover Coleridge himself considered the *magnum opus* to be the chief intellectual event, and the final goal, of his life. It is, indeed, hardly possible to overestimate the centrality of the *magnum opus* in Coleridge's own view of his existence. And *Opus Maximum* takes its being only from the being of the *magnum opus*, however inferential the larger entity necessarily is.

It does not follow, however, that the reader is obliged to take on the burden of the entirety of the commentary provided; on the contrary, he or she can turn directly to the fragments of *Opus Maximum*. If the fragments in themselves do not readily reveal their meaning or urgency, the reader might turn back and seek assistance from the Prolegomena.

The Prolegomena facilitates individual access to any Coleridgean emphasis that may prove troubling. If, for instance, the reader feels competent to cope with a Coleridgean term such as "*logos*" but is vague about the importance or meaning of "will", it is easy to bypass the commentary on the former term and concentrate attention on the latter. If the origins and foundations of the *magnum opus* are already familiar but the reader has never understood why the existing fragments were not published, here too it is easy to tailor the use of the Prolegomena to actual needs.

On the other hand, should the reader prefer a consecutive discussion the Prolegomena has been designed to be read as a continuous exposition. Its thirty-three sections are interlinked to provide as seamless a flow of elucidation and thought as is possible. In short, it is hoped that the Prolegomena will prove a flexible and rewarding aid to the comprehension of Coleridge's undertaking.

ACKNOWLEDGMENTS

M Y MOST GENERAL ACKNOWLEDGMENT is to the great scholar Kathleen Coburn, who set both *The Collected Coleridge* and this individual edition in motion. It was her hope that Coleridge's most ambitious but fragmentary work, by being presented as fully as possible within multiple contexts of intellectual history, might be reclaimed from philosophical oblivion; the special editorial structure of the present edition was adopted in an attempt to honour that hope. Sharing in my primary gratitude, as he did in the originating of *The Collected Coleridge*, was George Whalley, who was treasured as man and scholar by all who knew him.

My most important specific debt is to J. R. de J. Jackson, who went over the manuscript with the scrupulous care that characterises his scholarship. He directed me to its palpable improvement; whatever its defects now, they are far fewer than they were before he turned his keen attention to my text and commentary. His comments were sometimes stinging, but they were almost always justified; and he not only criticised what I had done but also, from his vast knowledge of Coleridge and of editorial procedure, saved me from numerous mistakes and provided me with frequent and invaluable information.

Others read and criticised the manuscript at various stages of its evolution, and I wish to record my gratitude for early readings to Walter Jackson Bate, John Beer, James Engell, and Heather Jackson. Christopher Drummond supplied me with material for a baffling footnote. My friend Albert Cook contributed a large part of the translations from Greek and Latin; after the typescript was completed, Lorna Arnold went over it completely and supplied meticulous attention and correction throughout, especially in regard to Coleridge's Greek. Elizabeth Powers, of the Princeton University Press, stood loyally and wisely by the edition through all its vicissitudes. I did not want her to retire, but Mary Murrell, her successor, has to my delight carried on the high standard of her supervision.

Finally, I take pleasure in acknowledging the unflagging support, with respect not only to this edition but to all aspects of my career, of my admired friends M. H. Abrams and the late Walter Jackson Bate.

Princeton, New Jersey   T. M.

MY TASK in assisting the editor of this volume has consisted in writing the statement of editorial practice; revising the texts and textual notes of the Preface, Fragments 1–4, and the Appendixes according to the principles elaborated in that statement; describing and dating the manuscripts; and choosing the illustrations. As the statement of editorial practice explains, the manuscripts comprising the *Opus Maximum* are divided among the British Library and three North American libraries. I have personally examined the manuscripts at the North American locations, and am grateful for the courtesy and assistance I have received from the staffs of the Berg Collection at the New York Public Library, of the Henry E. Huntington Library and Art Gallery in San Marino, and especially of the Victoria College Library at the University of Toronto. Among the editors of the Bollingen editions of Coleridge, John Beer, James Engell, Anthony Harding, and Raimonda Modiano gave me much-needed counsel in the early stages of my work; at the Coleridge Office in Toronto, Marion Filipiuk and the late Rea Wilmshurst offered unstinting practical assistance and a sympathetic ear. Rick Tomlinson generously checked some of my transcriptions against his own and gave me additional information about the manuscripts. Mary Murrell of Princeton University Press has been a patient taskmaster. Allyson May has provided exemplary copyediting, and Gail Copeland has contended bravely with incomplete, incompatible, and occasionally non-existent computer files. Shalender Jolly assisted expertly with the proofreading, and Janet Shuter ably compiled the index on short notice. Laury Egan, the series designer, solved formidable problems of presentation in the volume. The Composing Room translated the complicated typescript into printed text, and Alice Calaprice and Lauren Lepow saw the volume through the press. I am most indebted to Heather Jackson, who graciously took time out from her work on the *Marginalia* to transcribe the *Opus Maximum* fragments in the British Library (printed here in Appendix B), and to Robin Jackson, who helpfully provided photocopies of manuscripts and other materials relating to the edition. Both have been extraordinarily generous in sharing the wisdom of their experience as editors of the most interesting and exasperating of authors.

Toronto	NICHOLAS HALMI

EDITORIAL PRACTICE

THE MANUSCRIPTS gathered under the title *Opus Maximum* do not constitute a finished work and were never prepared by Coleridge or his executors for publication. As in the case of the *Logic*, these manuscripts are, for the most part, uncorrected transcripts of a dictated text. They are inconsistent in spelling and capitalisation; erratic or simply lacking in punctuation; abounding in cancellations, insertions, and misheard or mistranscribed words. To present only a "reading text", from which all the untidiness of the manuscripts is discreetly expunged, would be false to the nature of the text; but to present only a "diplomatic text", in which all that untidiness is scrupulously translated from handwritten to printed form, would be a severe trial to the reader—and one that could still not claim the degree of textual fidelity that a photographic facsimile of the manuscripts would offer. The present edition, therefore, is intended as compromise between editorial intrusiveness and restraint. But no attempt is made, for example, to fashion main clauses for sentences consisting entirely of subordinate and relative clauses. Unrevised as they are, the texts of the *Opus Maximum* exhibit to an even greater extent than Coleridge's published writings that digressiveness to which he adverted memorably in a letter of 28 Apr 1818 to his friend William Sotheby: "my Thoughts are like Surinam toads—as they crawl on, little Toads vegetate out from back & side, grow quickly, & draw off the attention from the mother Toad" (*CL* III 94–5).

In accordance with the principle observed in earlier volumes of *The Collected Coleridge*, manuscripts or passages known or likely to be in Coleridge's hand are printed literatim, recording faithfully his spelling, capitalisation, punctuation, and cancellations. Such passages, usually insertions in the dictated text, are indicated in the textual notes. Throughout the edition the following practices apply. The foliation (or, in Fragment 3, the pagination) of the manuscripts is indicated by insertions in square brackets ([*f 1*], etc). The text of each major fragment and chapter begins flush left, regardless of how it appears in the manuscript. Possessives are standardised ("it's" and "its'", for example, becoming "its"). Words underlined once in the manuscripts are printed in italics, words underlined twice or more in small capitals. Square brackets in the manuscripts are printed as parentheses to avoid confusion with editorial insertions.

Because the spelling and punctuation of the dictated manuscripts reflect the habits of the amanuenses rather than Coleridge's own practice, and because the elementary nature of some of the mistranscriptions (particularly in Greek phrases) suggests strongly that Coleridge did not look over the text carefully after dictating it, greater liberty is taken in the editing of these manuscripts, although emendation is still kept to a minimum. Obvious misspellings, as opposed to variant spellings accepted in Coleridge's day (e.g. "opake") and excluding misspellings of proper names, are corrected silently; other obvious mistakes (e.g. the accidental repetition of words) are corrected in the text and recorded in the textual notes. The capitalisation (or lack of it) in the manuscripts is preserved (e.g. "christian"). Punctuation is altered silently when departures from the manuscripts are necessary, the changes consisting primarily in the addition of commas, semicolons, and (less frequently) dashes and colons; but changes in sentence structure (e.g. the division of a single sentence into two sentences) are recorded in the textual notes. Ampersands and ligatures (as in "phænomenon") are expanded (thus "&c." becomes "etc."), as are "y^e" (to "the") and "y^t" (to "that"); other contractions are preserved. Greek diacritics, which Coleridge and his contemporaries commonly neglected, are neither supplied where they are lacking nor corrected where they are incorrect. Passages presented explicitly as quotations (including hypothetical conversations) and philosophical terms singled out for discussion are placed within quotation marks where these are lacking in the manuscripts. (The exceptions to this rule are quotations of verse and especially long quotations of prose, which are indented from the margins of the rest of the text and printed without quotation marks.) Emendations of any kind that alter the sense or could be regarded as doubtful are recorded in the textual notes.

Coleridge's own footnotes are indicated by symbols (*, †, etc) and printed full measure. Editorial notes (written by Thomas McFarland) are indicated by numerals and printed in double columns. The order of the editorial notes assumes that a reader will read Coleridge's notes as well as his text, and the sequence of footnote numbers in the text may be interrupted from time to time as footnotes are provided to Coleridge's notes. Textual notes are indicated by superscript italic letters ($^{a-b}$, etc) and are printed above the editorial footnotes.

CONVENTIONS USED IN TRANSCRIPTION

[Logos]	A word or passage supplied by the assisting editor
[? Logos]	An uncertain reading
[? Logos/pogos]	Possible alternative readings
[? ~~Logos~~]	An uncertain reading of a cancelled word

[. . .]	An illegible word or phrase (illegible phrases of more than three words are noted in the textual notes)
⌜. . .⌝	An illegible cancelled word or phrase (single letters are not recorded, and cancellations of more than three words are recorded in the textual notes)
⟨Logos⟩	A word or passage inserted between the lines, or marked for insertion from elsewhere (in which case a textual note is provided)
⟨~~Logos~~⟩	A word or passage inserted between the lines and cancelled
~~togas~~Logos	A correction written over, or an alteration formed from, the letters of the original word

MANUSCRIPTS INCLUDED IN THE PRESENT EDITION

Listed below, in the order in which they are printed, are the manuscripts (and sets of manuscripts that have been catalogued under a single title or shelf-mark by the institutions to which they now belong) from which the texts included in the present edition are taken. Fuller information about these manuscripts will be found in the headnotes to the individual fragments and Appendixes. (A complete census of Coleridge's located manuscripts, excluding letters, is printed in *SW & F—CC*—Appendix B and Index s.v. Coleridge, S. T., MSS). The Preface and the unassigned fragments printed in Appendix B are the only manuscripts solely in Coleridge's hand; the remaining manuscripts are in the hands of Joseph Henry Green and a second amanuensis, almost certainly John Watson.

1. NYPL (Berg Collection): 4° copybook, 72 pages, 223 × 187 mm, stitched in marbled paper covers, containing transcript of letters "To Mr Justice Fletcher" and twelve other items. The relevant text is printed here as the Preface.
2. VCL S MS 29: three clasped vellum notebooks, each with a page size of 194 × 123 mm; printed here as Fragments 1, 2, and 4 (see the respective headnotes for details of each volume).
3. HEHL HM 8195 ("Divine Ideas" notebook): 4° notebook, 754 pages, measuring 165 × 155 mm, bound in thick (and now very worn and detached) boards; used by Coleridge Jan 1799–Jul 1822 or later (see *SW & F—CC*—85–92, 259–60, 871, 992–3). The notebook was sold at auction to Henry Huntington (Anderson Galleries 25 Nov 1919 lot 100), having previously been in the collection of George S. Hellman.[1] The relevant text is printed here as Fragment 3.

---

[1] This information about the provenance of the manuscript was kindly provided by Rick Tomlinson.

4. VCL S MS 28: three pocket notebooks catalogued under the collective title "Magnum Opus"; printed here in Appendix A.
5. BL MS Egerton 2801 f 84: a single leaf, 185 × 110 mm, watermarked "[18]19"; printed here in Appendix B.
6. BL MS Egerton 2801 f 123: a single leaf, 225 × 180 mm; printed here in Appendix B.
7. BL MS Egerton 2801 ff 130–1: a single sheet folded in half to make two leaves, each c. 180 × 110 mm; printed here in Appendix B.
8. BL Add MS 43225 ff 153–4: two leaves, each 220 × 180 mm. The second leaf has been mended with a strip of paper (152 × 177 mm; no watermark) attached below the text. Printed here in Appendix B.
9. VCL LT 32: last leaf of an extract from the *Bhagavadgita* with Coleridge's commentary, all in the hand of John Watson; divided here between Fragment 3 and Appendix C (see the respective headnotes for an explanation).

ARRANGEMENT OF THE MANUSCRIPTS IN THE PRESENT EDITION

The manuscripts of what was supposed to be the *Opus Maximum*—the Preface and Fragments 1–4—are presented in the order preferred by the senior editor, although it is not the order of composition, insofar as that can be determined from physical evidence (e.g. watermarks) and textual evidence (e.g. borrowings from Coleridge's other writings). Although none of the manuscripts can be dated with precision, Fragments 1–4 were dictated mostly likely between 1819 and 1823, while the holograph Preface was written no earlier than 1828 and more likely in 1832. More specific information about the dating of the manuscripts is provided in the headnotes to the individual fragments; those who wish to read the manuscripts in their probable chronological order should begin with Fragment 4, proceed to Fragments 1, 2, and 3, and conclude with the Preface. The remaining manuscript fragments, which are thematically related to Fragments 1–4 but cannot be assigned unequivocally to the *Opus Maximum* itself, are presented in the Appendixes.

ABBREVIATIONS

Abrams	M. H. Abrams *The Mirror and the Lamp; Romantic Theory and the Critical Tradition* (New York 1953)
Agassi	Joseph Agassi *Farady as a Natural Philosopher* (Chicago & London 1971)
Allsop	[Thomas Allsop] *Letters, Conversations and Recollections of S. T. Coleridge* (2 vols London 1836)

Ameriks	Karl Ameriks *Kant's Theory of Mind: An Analysis of the Paralogisms of Pure Reason* (Oxford 1982)
AR (1825)	S. T. Coleridge *Aids to Reflection* (London 1825)
AR (1848)	S. T. Coleridge *Aids to Reflection* ed H. N. Coleridge (6th ed 2 vols London 1848)
Arnold *Poems*	Matthew Arnold *Poetical Works* ed C. B. Tinker and H. F. Lowry (London, New York & Toronto 1950)
Baader	*Franz von Baader's sämmtliche Werke* ed Franz Hoffmann and others (16 vols in 9 Leipzig 1850–60)
Baeumker	Clemens Baeumker *Studien und Charakteristiken zur Geschichte der Philosophie* (Münster 1927)
Barfield	Owen Barfield *What Coleridge Thought* (Middletown CT 1971)
Barnes	Sam G. Barnes "Was 'Theory of Life' Coleridge's 'Opus Maximum'?" *Studies in Philology* 55 (1958)
Bate	Walter Jackson Bate *Coleridge* (New York 1968)
Beer	John Beer *Coleridge the Visionary* (London 1959 repr 1970)
Beer *Intelligence*	John Beer *Coleridge's Poetic Intelligence* (London 1977)
Beres	David Beres "A Dream, a Vision and a Poem: A Pscyho-Analytic Study of the Origins of the *Rime of the Ancient Mariner*" *International Journal of Psycho-Analysis* 32 (1951)
Berg & Germann	Hermann Berg and Dietrich Germann "Ritter und Schelling: Empirie oder Spekulation (mit Ritters Briefen an Schelling)" in *Die Philosophie des jungen Schelling: Beiträge zur Schelling-Rezeption in der DDR* ed Erhard Lange (Weimar 1977)
Bernoulli & Kern	Christoph Bernoulli and Hans Kern *Romantische Naturphilosophie* (Jena 1926)
BL (*CC*)	S. T. Coleridge *Biographia Literaria* ed James Engell and W. Jackson Bate (2 vols London & Princeton 1983) = *CC* VII
BM	British Library, Reference Division (formerly British Museum Library)
Boeckh	August Boeckh *On Interpretation & Criticism* tr and ed John Paul Pritchard (Norman OK 1968)
Boethius	*Boethius: The Theological Tractates* tr H. F. Stewart,

	E. K. Rand; *The Consolation of Philosophy* tr E. J. Tester (LCL 2 vols Cambridge MA & London 1973)
Boulger	James D. Boulger *Coleridge as a Religious Thinker* (New Haven 1961)
Bowlby	John Bowlby *Charles Darwin; A Biography* (London 1991)
Brinkley	*Coleridge on the Seventeenth Century* ed Roberta Florence Brinkely (New York 1968)
Buber *Between Man*	Martin Buber *Between Man and Man* tr Ronald Gregor Smith (London 1947)
Buber *Ich und Du*	Martin Buber *Ich und Du* (Leipzig 1923)
Bultmann	Rudolph Bultmann *The Gospel of John: A Commentary* tr G. R. Beasley-Murray et al (Oxford 1971)
Burnet *Theory*	Thomas Burnet *The Theory of the Earth* (London 1684)
Butler	Joseph Butler *The Analogy of Religion, Natural and Revealed, to the Constitution and Course of Nature* (London 1736)
B Works	*The Works of George Berkeley* ed A. A. Luce and T. E. Jessop (9 vols London 1949–57)
C	Samuel Taylor Coleridge
C&S (CC)	S. T. Coleridge *On the Constitution of the Church and State* ed John Colmer (London & Princeton 1976) = *CC* x
Carlyle	*The Works of Thomas Carlyle in Thirty Volumes* ed H. D. Traill (London 1896–99)
CC	*The Collected Works of Samuel Taylor Coleridge* gen ed Kathleen Coburn (16 vols in 34 London & Princeton 1969–2002)
CCD	J. Robert Barth, S.J. *Coleridge and Christian Doctrine* (Cambridge MA 1969)
CH	*Coleridge: The Critical Heritage* ed J. R. de J. Jackson [Vol I] (London 1970)
CIS	S. T. Coleridge *Confessions of an Inquiring Spirit* ed H. St. J. Hart (Stanford CA 1967)
CL	*Collected Letters of Samuel Taylor Coleridge* ed Ernest Leslie Griggs (6 vols Oxford 1956–71)
C Life (G)	James Gillman *The Life of S. T. Coleridge* (London 1838)

C Life (JDC)	James Dykes Campbell *Samuel Taylor Coleridge: A Narrative of the Events of His Life* (London 1894)
Clough	*The Poems of Arthur Hugh Clough* ed F. L. Mulhauser (2nd ed Oxford 1974)
CM (*CC*)	S. T. Coleridge *Marginalia* ed George Whalley and H. J. Jackson (6 vols London & Princeton 1980–2001) = *CC* XII
CN	*The Notebooks of Samuel Taylor Coleridge* ed Kathleen Coburn (5 vols in 10 New York, Princeton & London 1957–2002)
CPT	Thomas McFarland *Coleridge and the Pantheist Tradition* (Oxford 1969)
Cranston	Maurice Cranston *John Locke: A Biography* (London 1968)
Critical Annotations	*Critical Annotations by S. T. Coleridge* ed William F. Taylor (Harrow 1889)
CRB	*Henry Crabb Robinson on Books and Their Writers* ed Edith J. Morley (3 vols New York 1967)
C Talker	*Coleridge the Talker* ed R. W. Armour and R. F. Howes (2nd ed New York 1969)
Cudworth	Ralph Cudworth *The True Intellectual System of the Universe* (London 1678)
Darwin *Descent*	Charles Darwin *The Descent of Man; and Selection in Relation to Sex* (2nd ed 2 vols New York & London 1919)
Darwin *Life*	*The Life and Letters of Charles Darwin* ed Francis Darwin (2 vols New York & London 1979)
Darwin *Origin*	Charles Darwin *The Origin of Species by Means of Natural Selection* (New York 1979)
Darwin *Papers*	*The Collected Papers of Charles Darwin* ed Paul H. Barnett (Chicago & London 1977)
DC	Derwent Coleridge
De Q Works	*The Collected Writings of Thomas De Quincey* ed David Masson (14 vols Edinburgh 1889–90)
Deschamps	Paul Deschamps *La Formation de la pensée de Coleridge (1772–1804)* (Grenoble 1964)
De Vleeschauwer	Herman J. De Vleeschauwer *The Development of Kantian Thought: The History of a Doctrine* tr A. R. C. Duncan (London 1962)

Diderot	Denis Diderot *Oeuvres philosophiques* ed Paul Vernière (Paris 1956)
DL	*Diogenes Laertius: Lives of Eminent Philosophers* tr R. D. Hicks (LCL 2 vols Cambridge MA & London 1980)
Dodd *Fourth Gospel*	C. H. Dodd *The Interpretation of the Fourth Gospel* (Cambridge 1953)
Dodd *Tradition*	C. H. Dodd *Historical Tradition in the Fourth Gospel* (Cambridge 1963)
Doughty	Oswald Doughty *Perturbed Spirit: The Life and Personality of Samuel Taylor Coleridge* (Rutherford NJ 1981)
Du Vair	*The Moral Philosophie of the Stoicks; Written in French by Guillaume du Vair, Englished by Thomas James* [1598] ed Rudolf Kirk (New Brunswick NJ 1951)
DW	Dorothy Wordsworth
Eliot *Poems*	T. S. Eliot *Collected Poems, 1909–1935* (New York 1936)
EOT (CC)	S. T. Coleridge *Essays on His Times* ed David Erdman (3 vols London & Princeton 1978) = *CC* III
E. R. Dodds	Proclus *The Elements of Theology* ed and tr E. R. Dodds (2nd ed Oxford 1963)
Feuerbach	*Ludwig Feuerbach's sämmtliche Werke* (11 vols Leipzig 1846–66)
Fichte	Johann Gottlieb Fichte *Ausgewählte Werke* ed Fritz Medicus (6 vols Darmstadt 1962)
Fletcher	Angus Fletcher "'Positive Negation': Threshold, Sequence, and Personification in Coleridge" in *New Perspectives on Coleridge and Wordsworth* ed Geoffrey H. Hartman (New York 1972)
Frag	Fragment of *Opus Maximum* (used to refer to passages in the five major fragments in the present edition, e.g. Frag 2 f 193^v, Frag 3 p 267, etc)
Friedrich Schlegel	*Kritische Friedrich-Schlegel-Ausgabe* gen ed Ernst Behler (Paderborn 1958–)
Friend (CC)	S. T. Coleridge *The Friend* ed Barbara E. Rooke (2 vols London & Princeton 1969) = *CC* IV
Fromm-Reichmann	*Psychoanalysis and Psychotherapy; Selected Papers of Frieda Fromm-Reichmann* ed Dexter M. Bullard and Edith V. Weigert (Chicago & London 1959)
Froude *Carlyle*	James Anthony Froude *Thomas Carlyle: A History of His Life in London* (2 vols London 1897)

Gaquère	François Gaquère *Le Dialogue irénique Bossuet-Leibniz: La Réunion des églises en échec, 1691–1702* (Paris 1966)
Gedenkausgabe	Johann Wolfgang Goethe *Gedenkausgabe der Werke, Briefe und Gespräche* ed Ernst Beutler (27 vols Zürich 1948–71)
"German Literature"	"Traits and Tendencies of German Literature" *Blackwood's Edinburgh Magazine* 50 (1844)
Gilson	Etienne Gilson *History of Christian Philosophy in the Middle Ages* (New York 1955)
G Mag	*Gentleman's Magazine* (London 1731–)
Green *Dynamics*	Joseph Henry Green *Vital Dynamics: The Hunterian Oration . . . 14th February 1840* (London 1840)
Grosart	*The Prose Works of William Wordsworth* ed Alexander B. Grosart (3 vols London 1876)
Guthrie	W. K. C. Guthrie *A History of Greek Philosophy* (5 vols Cambridge 1967–78)
Haeger	J. H. Haeger "Coleridge's 'Bye Blow': The Composition and Date of *Theory of Life*" *Journal of Modern Philosophy* 74 (1976) 20–41
Hankins	Thomas Hankins *Sir William Rowan Hamilton* (Baltimore 1980)
Havelock	Eric Havelock *The Liberal Temper in Greek Politics* (New Haven 1957)
Haydon	*The Diary of Benjamin Robert Haydon* ed Willard Bissell Pope (5 vols Cambridge MA 1960–3)
HC	Hartley Coleridge
HCR	Henry Crabb Robinson
Hegel	*G. W. F. Hegel: Werke in zwanzig Bänden* ed Eva Moldenhauer and Karl Markus Michel (21 vols Frankfurt-am-Main 1967–71)
Hegel: The Letters	*Hegel: The Letters* tr Clark Butler and Christiane Seiler (Bloomington IN 1984)
HEHL	Henry E. Huntington Library and Art Gallery, San Marino CA
Heidegger *Metaphysics*	Martin Heidegger *An Introduction to Metaphysics* tr Ralph Manheim (New Haven 1959)
Heidegger *Sein und Zeit*	Martin Heidegger *Sein und Zeit* (7th ed Tübingen 1953)

HNC	Henry Nelson Coleridge
Holmes	Richard Holmes *Coleridge: Early Visions* (New York 1990)
Hoskyns	Clement Hoskyns *The Fourth Gospel* ed Francis Noel Davey (London 1947)
Humboldt	*Wilhelm von Humboldts gesammelte Schriften* ed Königlich Preussische Akademie der Wissenschaften (20 vols Berlin 1903–20)
Hume	David Hume *A Treatise of Human Nature* ed L. A. Selby-Bigge and P. H. Nidditch (2nd ed Oxford 1978)
H Works	*The Complete Works of William Hazlitt* ed P. P. Howe (21 vols London 1930–4)
Ingleby	C. M. Ingleby "On the Unpublished Manuscripts of Samuel Taylor Coleridge" *Transactions of the Royal Society of Literature of the United Kingdom* 9 (1870)
IS	*Inquiring Spirit* ed Kathleen Coburn (New York 1951)
JAAC	*Journal of Aesthetics and Art Criticism* (Madison WI 1941–)
Jackson	J. R. de J. Jackson *Method and Imagination in Coleridge's Criticism* (London 1969)
Jacobi *Werke*	*Friedrich Heinrich Jacobis Werke* ed Friedrich Roth and Friedrich Köppen (6 vols in 7 Leipzig 1812–25)
Jacobi's Briefwechsel	*Friedrich Heinrich Jacobi's auserlesener Briefwechsel* ed Friedrich Roth (2 vols Leipzig 1825–7)
Jaspers "Autobiography"	Karl Jaspers "Philosophical Autobiography" in *The Philosophy of Karl Jaspers* ed Paul Arthur Schilpp (New York 1957)
JEGP	*Journal of English and German Philology* (1903–)
JG	James Gillman
JHG	Joseph Henry Green
Kant *GS*	Immanuel Kant *Gesammelte Schriften* ed Königlich Preussische (later Deutsche) Akademie der Wissenschaften (Berlin 1902–)
Keats *Letters*	*The Letters of John Keats, 1814–1821* ed Hyder Edward Rollins (2 vols Cambridge MA 1958)
Kelber	Wilhelm Kelber *Die Logoslehre von Heraklit bis Origenes* (Stuttgart 1958)
Kierkegaard	Søren Kierkegaard *Kierkegaard's Concluding Unscientific Postscript* tr David F. Swenson and Walter Lowrie (Princeton 1944)

Kirk & Raven	G. S. Kirk and J. E. Raven *The Presocratic Philosophers* (Cambridge 1971)
Kittel	*Theological Dictionary of the New Testament* ed Gerhard Kittel tr Geoffrey W. Bromley (5 vols Grand Rapids MI 1967)
Knights	L. C. Knights "Coleridge: The Wound without the Bow" *New York Review of Books* 18 (4 May 1972)
LCL	Loeb Classical Library
Leeuwenhoek	*Anthony van Leeuwenhoek and His "Little Animals": A Collection of Writings* ed Clifford Dobell (New York 1960)
Leibniz	*Gottfried Wilhelm Leibniz sämtliche Schriften und Briefe* (Darmstadt 1923–)
Levere	Trevor H. Levere *Poetry Realized in Nature: Samuel Taylor Coleridge and Nineteenth-century Science* (Cambridge 1981)
L&L	*Coleridge on Logic and Learning* ed Alice D. Snyder (New Haven & London 1929). In the headnotes to Frags 1–3, this abbreviation is followed by Synder's designations B1, B2, etc, which have been widely adopted to distinguish the *Opus Maximum* manuscripts in VCL
Lindop	Grevel Lindop *The Opium-Eater: A Life of Thomas De Quincey* (New York 1981)
LL (L)	*The Letters of Charles Lamb, to Which Are Added Those of His Sister Mary Lamb* ed E. V. Lucas (3 vols London 1935)
LL (M)	*The Letters of Charles and Mary Anne Lamb* ed Edwin Marrs Jr (3 vols Ithaca NY 1975–8)
Locke	John Locke *An Essay Concerning Human Understanding* ed Peter H. Nidditch (Oxford 1975)
Logic (CC)	S. T. Coleridge *Logic* ed J. R. de J. Jackson (London & Princeton 1981) = *CC* XIII
Long & Sedley	A. A. Long and D. N. Sedley *The Hellenistic Philosophers* Vol I (Cambridge 1987)
Lowes	John Livingston Lowes *The Road to Xanadu: A Study in the Ways of the Imagination* (New York & Boston 1927)
LS (CC)	S. T. Coleridge *Lay Sermons* ed R. J. White (London & Princeton 1972) = *CC* VI
Luther	*Luther's Works* ed Jaroslav Pelikan and Helmut T. Lehman (55 vols St Louis and Philadelphia 1955–86)

McFarland *Originality*	Thomas McFarland *Originality and Imagination* (Baltimore 1985)
McFarland *Rousseau*	Thomas McFarland *Romanticism and the Heritage of Rousseau* (Oxford 1995)
McFarland "Wordsworth"	Thomas McFarland "Wordsworth on Man, on Nature, and on Human Life" *Studies in Romanticism* 21 (1982)
McKusick	James C. McKusick *Coleridge's Philosophy of Language* (New Haven & London 1986)
Medwin	Thomas Medwin *Journal of the Conversations of Lord Byron* (New York 1824)
Mendelssohn	*Moses Mendelssohn's gesammelte Schriften* ed G. B. Mendelssohn (7 vols in 8 Leipzig 1843–5)
Merlan	Philip Merlan "Emanationism" *Encyclopedia of Philosophy* ed Paul Edwards Vol II (New York 1967)
Michelet	Jules Michelet *Histoire de la Révolution française* (Pléiade ed Paris 1952)
Mill Works	*Collected Works of John Stuart Mill* ed J. M. Robson et al (33 vols Toronto & London 1963–91)
Miller	Craig W. Miller "Coleridge's Concept of Nature" *Journal of the History of Ideas* 25 (1964)
Misc C	*Coleridge's Miscellaneous Criticism* ed T. M. Raysor (London 1936)
Modiano	Raimonda Modiano *Coleridge and the Concept of Nature* (London 1985)
Monboddo	James Burnet, Lord Monboddo *Of the Origin and Progress of Language* (6 vols Edinburgh 1773–92)
Monod	Jacques Monod *Chance and Necessity: An Essay on the Natural Philosophy of Modern Biology* tr Austryn Wainhouse (London 1972)
Muirhead	John H. Muirhead *Coleridge as Philosopher* (London 1930 repr 1956)
Needham	Joseph Needham "S. T. Coleridge as a Philosophical Biologist" *Science Progress in the Twentieth Century* 20 (1926)
Nietzsche	*Friedrich Nietzsche: Werke in drei Bänden* ed Karl Schlechta (3 vols Munich 1954–6)
Novalis	*Novalis Schriften: Die Werke Friedrich von Hardenbergs* ed Paul Kluckhohn and Richard Samuel (5 vols Stuttgart 1960–88)

NYPL	The New York Public Library
Op Max	S. T. Coleridge *Opus Maximum*
Orsini	Gian N. G. Orsini *Coleridge and German Idealism* (Carbondale IL 1969)
Paley	William Paley *Principles of Moral and Political Philosophy* (2 vols London 1814)
Pascal	Blaise Pascal *Oeuvres complètes* ed Louis Lafuma (Paris 1963)
Perkins	Mary Anne Perkins *Coleridge's Philosophy: The Logos as Unifying Principle* (Oxford 1994)
Petry	*Hegel's Philosophy of Nature* ed and tr M. J. Petry (3 vols London 1970)
Pfleiderer	Otto Pfleiderer *Religionsphilosophie auf geschichtlicher Grundlage* (Berlin 1878)
P Lects (1949)	*The Philosophical Lectures of Samuel Taylor Coleridge* ed Kathleen Coburn (London & New York 1949)
Priestley *Disquisitions*	Joseph Priestley *Disquisitions Relating to Matter and Spirit* (London 1777)
Priestley *Doctrine*	Joseph Priestley *The Doctrine of Philosophical Necessity Illustrated* (London 1777)
PW (EHC)	*The Complete Poetical Works of Samuel Taylor Coleridge* ed Ernest Hartley Coleridge (2 vols Oxford 1912)
Ramsay	Andrew Michael Ramsay *The Philosophical Principles of Natural and Revealed Religion* (2 vols Glasgow 1748–9)
Randall	John Herman Randall Jr *The Career of Philosophy* Vol II *From the German Enlightenment to the Age of Darwin* (New York & London 1965)
RFR	Thomas McFarland *Romanticism and the Forms of Ruin: Wordsworth, Coleridge and Modalities of Fragmentation* (Princeton 1981)
Rist	J. M. Rist *Plotinus: The Road to Reality* (Cambridge 1967)
RS	Robert Southey
Robson	W. W. Robson *Critical Essays* (London 1966)
Samay	Sebastian Samay *Reason Revisited: The Philosophy of Karl Jaspers* (Dublin 1971)
Saunders	Jason Lewis Saunders *Justus Lipsius: The Philosophy of Renaissance Stoicism* (New York 1955)

SC	Sara Coleridge
Schelling *SW*	F. W. J. Schelling *Sämmtliche Werke* ed K. F. A Schelling (14 vols Stuttgart & Augsburg 1856–61)
Schleiermacher	*Friedrich Schleiermacher's sämmtliche Werke* (30 vols Berlin 1835–64)
Schlegel *Lucinde*	Friedrich Schlegel *Lucinde: Ein Roman* (Berlin 1799)
Schopenhauer	Arthur Schopenhauer *Sämtliche Werke* ed Arthur Hübscher (3rd ed 7 vols Wiesbaden 1972)
Shaffer	E. S. Shaffer *'Kubla Khan' and The Fall of Jerusalem: The Mythological School in Biblical Criticism and Secular Literature, 1770–1880* (Cambridge 1975)
Shaftesbury	Anthony Ashley Cooper, 3rd Earl of Shaftesbury *Characteristics of Men, Manners, Opinions, Times* ed John M. Robertson (2 vols in 1 Indianapolis IN 1964)
Shedd	S. T. Coleridge *Complete Works* ed W. G. T. Shedd (7 vols New York 1853)
S Letters (Curry)	*New Letters of Robert Southey* ed Kenneth Curry (2 vols New York & London 1965)
SM (*CC*)	S. T. Coleridge *The Stateman's Manual* in *Lay Sermons* ed R. J. White (London & Princeton 1972) = *CC* VI
Smart	Ninian Smart "Hinduism" *Encyclopedia of Philosophy* ed Paul Edwards Vol III (New York 1967)
SP	*Spiritual Philosophy: Founded on the Teaching of the Late Samuel Taylor Coleridge* ed John Simon (2 vols London & Cambridge 1865)
Spinoza	*Spinoza Opera* ed Carl Gebhardt (4 vols Heidelberg 1972)
Steffens *Beyträge*	Heinrich Steffens *Beyträge zur innern Naturgeschichte der Erde. Erster Theil* (Freiberg 1801)
Steffens *Grundzüge*	Heinrich Steffens *Grundzüge der philosophischen Naturwissenschaft* (Berlin 1806)
Stephen *Eighteenth Century*	Leslie Stephen *History of English Thought in the Eighteenth Century* (2 vols New York 1962)
Stephen *Library*	Leslie Stephen *Hours in a Library* (3 vols London 1909)
Sterling	John Sterling "Characteristics of German Genius" in *Essays and Tales of John Sterling* ed Julius Charles Hare (2 vols London 1848)
Strowski	Fortunat Strowski *Pascal et son temps* (2nd ed 3 vols Paris 1907–8)

SW & F (CC)	S. T. Coleridge *Shorter Works and Fragments* ed H. J. Jackson and J. R. de J. Jackson (2 vols London & Princeton 1995) = *CC* xi
TL (1848)	S. T. Coleridge *Hints Towards the Formation of a More Comprehensive Theory of Life* ed Seth B. Watson (London 1848)
TT (CC)	*Table Talk of Samuel Taylor Coleridge* ed Carl R. Woodring (2 vols London & Princeton 1990) = *CC* xiv
Tuell	Anne Kimball Tuell *John Sterling: A Representative Victorian* (New York 1941)
Urmson	J. O. Urmson *Philosophical Analysis: Its Development between the Two World Wars* (Oxford 1965)
VCL	Victoria College Library, University of Toronto
Whalley	George Whalley "The Bristol Library Borrowings of Southey and Coleridge, 1793–98" *The Library: Transactions of the Bibliographical Society* 5th ser iv no 2 (Sept 1949)
Whitney	Charles A. Whitney *The Discovery of Our Galaxy* (New York 1971)
WL (E)	*The Letters of William and Dorothy Wordsworth: The Early Years, 1787–1805* ed Ernest de Selincourt rev Chester L. Shaver (Oxford 1967)
WL (M)	*The Letters of William and Dorothy Wordsworth: The Middle Years, 1806–1820* ed Ernest de Selincourt rev Mary Moorman and Alan G. Hill (2 vols Oxford 1969)
wm(s)	watermark(s)
Wolff	Christian Wolff *Preliminary Discourse on Philosophy in General* tr J. Blackwell (Indianapolis IN 1963)
Wolfson *Philo*	Harry Austryn Wolfson *Philo: Foundations of Religious Philosophy in Judaism, Christianity, and Islam* (rev ed 2 vols Cambridge MA 1962)
WPW	*The Poetical Works of William Wordsworth* ed Ernest de Selincourt and Helen Darbishire (5 vols Oxford 1940–9)
WW	William Wordsworth

CHRONOLOGICAL TABLE
1772–1834

1772   (21 Oct) Birth of C at Ottery St Mary, Devon, to the Rev John and Ann (Bowdon) Coleridge—youngest of their 10 children

1775   American War of Independence

1778   C to Ottery Grammar School

1781   Death of C's father   Kant *Critik der reinen Vernunft*

1782   (Jul) Enrolled at Christ's Hospital, Hertford   Priestley *Corruptions of Christianity*   Rousseau *Confessions*
(Sept) To Christ's Hospital, London (until 1791)

1783   Pitt's first ministry (–1801)

1785   Paley *Principles of Moral and Political Philosophy*

1789   (14 Jul) Fall of Bastille
Bowles *Sonnets*
Darwin *Loves of the Plants*

1790   First published poem (in *World*)   Burke *Reflections on the Revolution in France*

1791   (Oct) To Jesus College, Cambridge: Exhibitioner, Sizar, Rustat Scholar   Anti-Jacobin riots at Birmingham
Boswell *Life of Johnson*
Darwin *Economy of Vegetation*
Mackintosh *Vindiciae Gallicae*
Paine *Rights of Man* pt 1 (pt 2 1792)

1792   Wins Browne Medal with Greek Sapphic *Ode on the Slave Trade*, read at Commencement 3 Jul

1793   (2 Dec) Enlists in 15th Light Dragoons as Silas Tomkyn Comberbache   (21 Jan) Louis XVI executed
(1 Feb) France declares war on England and Holland
(16 Oct) Marie-Antoinette executed
Godwin *Political Justice*
Wordsworth *An Evening Walk* and *Descriptive Sketches*

1794   (9 Apr) Returns to Cambridge
(Jun) Sets out on walking tour with Joseph Hucks; meets RS in Oxford and plans pantisocracy; Welsh tour
(Aug–Sept) Joins RS and G. Burnett in Bristol; meets Poole; is engaged to Sara Fricker
(Sept) To London and Cambridge; with RS publishes *Fall of Robespierre*   (23 May) Suspension of Habeas Corpus
(28 Jul) Robespierre executed; end of the Terror
(Oct–Dec) State Trials; Hardy, Tooke, and Thelwall acquitted of charge of treason
Darwin *Zoonomia*
Godwin *Caleb Williams*
Paine *Age of Reason* (–1795)

(Cambridge); *Monody on Chatterton* pub with *Rowley Poems* (Cambridge)
(Dec) To London

1795 (Jan) RS brings C back to Bristol
(late Jan–Feb) Political lectures
(Feb) *A Moral and Political Lecture*
(May–Jun) Lectures on revealed religion
(16 June) Lecture on the slave-trade
(Aug) Quarrel with RS; pantisocracy abandoned; meets WW
(4 Oct) Marriage to Sara Fricker
(26 Nov) Lecture on the Two Bills
(3 Dec) *Conciones ad Populum*
(Dec) *An Answer to "A Letter to Edward Long Fox"*; *The Plot Discovered*

1796 (Jan–Feb) Tour to Midlands and north to sell *Watchman*
(1 Mar–13 May) *Watchman* in 10 numbers
(16 Apr) *Poems on Various Subjects*
(19 Sept) Birth of HC
(Sept) Reconciliation with RS
(Dec) Move to Nether Stowey

1797 (summer) *Poems, to which are Now Added, Poems by Charles Lamb and Charles Lloyd*
(14 Oct) *Osorio* finished
(13–16 Nov) Walk with Wordsworths to Lynton; *Rime of the Ancient Mariner* begun

1798 (Jan) C's Unitarian sermons at Shrewsbury; C accepts £150 Wedgwood annuity
(14 May) Birth of Berkeley Coleridge
(Sept) *Lyrical Ballads*
(19 Sept) WW, DW, Chester, and C to Hamburg
(30 Sept) C to Ratzeburg

1799 (10 Feb) Death of Berkeley Coleridge
(Feb) C to Göttingen
(May) Ascent of Brocken
(29 Jul) In Stowey again
(Sept) Devon walking tour with RS
(Oct) Meets Sara Hutchinson
(27 Oct) Arrives in London

1800 (Jan–6 Apr) *Morning Post* writer; translating *Wallenstein*
(6 Apr–4 May) At Grasmere with WW
(May–Jun) Stowey and Bristol

Paley *Evidences of Christianity*
Radcliffe *Mysteries of Udolpho*

(26 Sept) WW and DW to Racedown
(Nov) Directory established in France
(3 Nov) Treason and Convention Bills introduced
(18 Dec) Two Acts put into effect
Lewis *Ambrosio, or the Monk*

(Sept) Mary Lamb's violent illness
England treating for peace with France
Threats of invasion of England

(Feb) Bank of England suspends cash payments
(Apr–Jun) Mutinies in the British fleet
(17 Oct) France and Austria sign peace treaty
(Nov) *Anti-Jacobin* begins (to Jul 1798)

(Feb–Oct) Irish rebellion
(12 Jun) Malta taken by French
(Jul) Napoleon invades Egypt
(1–2 Aug) Nelson's victory in Battle of the Nile
Bell introduces Madras system of education in England
Lloyd *Edmund Oliver*
Horne Tooke *Diversions of Purley* vol I (vol II 1805)
(Nov) Directory overthrown
(Dec) Constitution of year VIII; Napoleon First Consul
(Dec) Wordsworths at Town End (later Dove Cottage), Grasmere
Royal Institution founded
RS ed *Annual Anthology*
Schiller *Die Piccolomini* and *Wallensteins Tod*
(14 Jun) Battle of Marengo
(Aug) Union of Great Britain and Ireland
(5 Sept) Malta falls to English after long siege

	(Jul) Move to Greta Hall, Keswick	Kant *Logik*
	(14 Sept) Birth of DC	Schelling *System des transcendentalen Idealismus*
1801	(Jan) *Lyrical Ballads* (1800)	(Mar) Pitt resigns over Emancipation
	(21 Jan) Returns to London	Addington ministry (–1804)
	(Jul–Aug) At Gallow Hill with Sara and Mary Hutchinson	(Jul) Napoleon signs Concordat with Pope
	(15 Nov) To London	RS *Thalaba*
	(28 Dec–c 19 Jan) At Stowey	
1802	(21 Jan–Mar) In London, attends Davy's lectures at Royal Institution; writing for *Morning Post*; to Gallow Hill	(25 Mar) Peace of Amiens
		(8 May) Napoleon Consul for life
		(4 Oct) WW marries Mary Hutchinson
	(From 19 Mar) At Greta Hall; severe domestic discord	(Oct) French army enters Switzerland
		Ed Rev founded
	(1–9 Aug) Lakes tour and Scafell climb	Paley *Natural Theology*
	(late Aug) Visit by Lambs	Spinoza *Opera* ed Paulus (1802–3)
	(4 Oct) *Dejection* pub *Morning Post*	
	(Nov–Dec) Tour of south Wales with Tom and Sally Wedgwood	
	(23 Dec) Birth of SC	
1803	(Jan–Mar) In West Country with Wedgwoods, Poole; in London with Lamb; makes will	(Feb) Act of Mediation in Switzerland
		(18 May) England declares war on France
	(Jun) *Poems* (1803)	Chatterton *Works* ed RS and Cottle
	(summer) Visits by Hazlitt, Beaumonts, S. Rogers to C in Lakes	Cobbett *Parliamentary Debates* (later Hansard)
	(15–29 Aug) Scottish tour with WW and DW	Malthus *Principles of Population* (2nd ed)
	(29 Aug–15 Sept) Continues Scottish tour alone	
1804	(9 Apr–14 Jul) In convoy to Malta	(Mar) Code Napoléon
	(Jul) Under-secretary to Sir Alexander Ball, British High Commissioner at Malta	(Apr) 2nd Pitt ministry (–1806)
		(18 May) Napoleon made Emperor
		(12 Dec) Spain declares war on Britain
	(Aug–Nov) Sicily, ascent of Etna; stays with G. F. Leckie	
1805	(Jan) Acting Public Secretary in Malta	(Apr) Third Coalition against France
	(5 Feb) John Wordsworth drowned in loss of *Abergavenny*	(26 May) Napoleon King of Italy
		(17 Oct) Napoleon's victory at Ulm
	(Sept–Nov) In Sicily	(21 Oct) Nelson's victory at Trafalgar
	(mid-Nov) To Naples	(2 Dec) Austerlitz
	(Dec) Calabria and Naples	RS *Madoc*
		Scott *Lay of the Last Minstrel*
1806	(Jan) In Rome, meets Humboldt and Tieck, stays with Washington Allston	(Jan) Pitt d; "Ministry of all the Talents" under Grenville, who resigns (Mar 1807) after rejection of Bill to open all commissions to Roman Catholics
	(18 May) To Florence, Pisa	
	(23 Jun) Sails from Leghorn	(6 Aug) End of Holy Roman Empire
	(17 Aug) Lands in England; London, job-hunting and recovering his books and papers; at Parndon with the Clarksons and to Cambridge	
	(26–8 Oct) In Kendal with Wordsworths and Sara Hutchinson	
	(30 Oct–7 Dec) Keswick, determines on separation from Mrs C	

(21 Dec) Joins Wordsworths and Sara Hutchinson at Coleorton: (26 Dec) crisis of jealousy

1807 (Jan–Apr) Coleorton; (late Jan) hears WW read *Prelude*; writes *Lines to William Wordsworth*
(4 Apr) To London with Wordsworths
(Jun) To Stowey with family; remains, alone, until Sept
(Sept–Nov) Bristol and Stowey
(23 Nov) To London

(Mar) Portland ministry (–1809)
(25 Mar) Abolition of slave-trade
(Jul) Treaty of Tilsit
(2 Sept) Bombardment of Copenhagen by British fleet
(Dec) Peninsular War begins
C. and M. Lamb *Tales from Shakespeare*
RS *Letters from England by Don Espriella*; *Specimens of the Later English Poets*
WW *Poems in Two Volumes*
Bell-Lancaster controversy
(1 May) Wordsworths move to Allan Bank

1808 (13 Jan–Jun) In rooms at *Courier* office, Strand; lectures at Royal Institution on poetry and principles of taste
(Jul) Review of Clarkson *History of the Abolition of the Slave Trade* in *Ed Rev*
(Aug) Leeds and the north
(Sept) At Allan Bank; asks Mrs C to send his books
(Nov) First prospectus of *Friend* issued at Kendal

(30 Aug) Convention of Cintra
(Dec) Napoleon invades Spain
Lamb *Specimens of English Dramatic Poets*
Scott *Marmion*

1809 (1 Jun) Starts *Friend* in 27 numbers plus supernumerary
(7 Dec–20 Jan 1810) "Letters on the Spaniards" in *Courier*

(Feb) *Quarterly Review* founded
(9 Mar) Byron *English Bards and Scotch Reviewers*
(May) Napoleon captures Vienna
Perceval ministry (–1812)
Schlegel *Über dramatische Kunst*
WW *Convention of Cintra* pamphlet
(May) First Reform Bill since 1797 introduced

1810 (Mar) Sara Hutchinson leaves Grasmere for Wales
(15 Mar) *Friend* last number
(May–Oct) Keswick
(Oct) to London; quarrel with WW; C stays with Morgans in Hammersmith
(Nov) Meets HCR

(Jul) Napoleon annexes Holland
RS *Curse of Kehama*
Scott *Lady of the Lake*
WW *Guide to the Lakes*

1811 (20 Apr) First table-talk recorded by John Taylor Coleridge
(May–Sept) Contributions to *Courier*
(18 Nov–27 Jan 1812) Lectures on Shakespeare and Milton at Scot's Corporation Hall attended by Collier, Byron, Rogers, HCR

(5 Feb) Prince of Wales made Regent

1812 (Feb–Mar) Last journey to the Lakes
(Apr) Lives with Morgans, Berners St, Soho
(May–Aug) Lectures on drama in Willis's Rooms
(May) Lamb and HCR patch up WW quarrel

(11 May) Perceval shot
(18 Jun) US declares war on Great Britain
(22 Jun) Napoleon opens war on Russia
(Oct–Dee) Retreat from Moscow
Byron *Childe Harold* Cantos I and II

(Jun) Reissue of *Friend*
(3 Nov–26 Jan 1813) Lectures on Shakespeare at the Surrey Institution
(Nov) Half Wedgwood annuity withdrawn; contributes to RS *Omniana*

1813 (23 Jan) *Remorse* opens at Drury Lane and runs 20 nights
(summer) Morgan's financial affairs worsen; he flees to Ireland by Oct
(Oct–Nov) Lectures in Bristol on Shakespeare and on education, in Clifton on Milton and on poetry
(Dec) With Mary Morgan and Charlotte Brent at Ashley near Bath

1814 (Apr) Lectures at Bristol on Milton, Cervantes, taste; lecture on French Revolution and Napoleon; under medical care for addiction and suicidal depression
(1 Aug) *Remorse* performed in Bristol
(Aug–Sept) Allston portrait of C and Bristol exhibition; "On the Principles of Genial Criticism" pub *Felix Farley's Bristol Journal*
(Sept–Dec) Letters "To Mr Justice Fletcher" in *Courier*
(Dec) Moves with Morgans to Calne, Wilts

1815 (Jun) *Remorse* performed at Calne
(Jul–Sept) Dictating *BL* to Morgan
(Aug–Sept) Printing of *BL* and *Sibylline Leaves* begins at Bristol

1816 (Feb) Grant from Literary Fund and gift from Byron
(Mar) To London
(10 Apr) Sends *Zapolya* to Byron
(15 Apr) Accepted as patient and housemate by James Gillman, surgeon, Moreton House, Highgate
(25 May) *Christabel, Kubla Khan, the Pains of Sleep*
(Nov–Dec) Composes "Theory of Life"
(Dec) *Statesman's Manual*

1817 (Mar) Second *Lay Sermon*
(Apr) Revival of *Remorse*

(1 May) Wordsworths move to Rydal Mount
(Jul–Aug) Peace Congress at Prague fails
(10 Aug) Austria declares war on Napoleon
(Sept) RS Poet Laureate
(autumn) Wellington successful in Peninsula; Switzerland, Holland, Italy, Rhineland, Spain, Trieste, Dalmatia freed of French rule
RS *Life of Nelson*
(1 Jan) Invasion of France by Allies
(1 Mar) Castlereagh's treaty with Austria, Prussia, and Russia against Napoleon
(6 Apr) Napoleon abdicates
(May) First Treaty of Paris; Napoleon exiled to Elba; Restoration of the Bourbons
(Sept–Jul 1815) Congress of Vienna
(24 Dec) Peace of Ghent signed by Britain and US
Inquisition re-established in Spain
Cary's *Dante* completed
Scott *Waverley*
WW *Excursion*
(Mar–Jun) The Hundred Days: Napoleon escapes from Elba, returns to France
(18 Jun) Waterloo
Restoration of Louis XVIII
(20 Nov) Second Treaty of Paris
Scott *Guy Mannering*
WW *Poems* of 1815; *White Doe of Rylstone*
(24 Apr) Byron leaves England
(21 Jun) Motion for the Relief of Roman Catholics rejected in the Lords
(2 Dec) Spa Fields Riot

(4 Mar) Habeas Corpus suspended
(Apr) *Blackwood's Magazine* founded

(late Apr) "Prospectus" to *Encyclopaedia Metropolitana* issued
(13 Jun) Meets L. Tieck at house of JHG
(Jul) *BL, Sibylline Leaves*
(Nov) *Zapolya*; C's tr of H. Hurwitz's *Hebrew Dirge* for Princess Charlotte

1818 (Jan) "Treatise on Method" pub *Encyclopaedia Metropolitana*
(27 Jan–13 Mar) Lectures on principles of judgment, culture, and European literature
(Feb) *Zapolya* runs 10 nights at Surrey Theatre
(Apr–May) Pamphlets supporting Peel's Bill to regulate the working hours of cotton-factory children
(Nov) *Friend* (3 vols)
(Dec–Mar 1819) Alternating lectures on history of philosophy and on literature

1819 (Mar) Financial losses from bankruptcy of publisher Rest Fenner
(Apr) Begins occasional (to 1822) contributions to *Blackwood's*

1820 (May) HC is refused renewal of Oriel fellowship; C intervenes unsuccessfully through summer

1821

1822 (Jan) Dictating "Logic"
(25 Feb) Announces weekly class on philosophical subjects
(Dec) First record of table-talk by HNC

1823 (3 Jan–5 Mar) Mrs C and SC at Highgate; SC secretly engaged to HNC
(Nov) Gillmans move to 3 The Grove, Highgate

1824 (Mar) Elected Royal Associate, Royal Society of Literature, with annuity of 100 guineas

as *Edinburgh Monthly Magazine*
(May) Motion for the Relief of Roman Catholics rejected in the Lords
Hazlitt *The Characters of Shakespeare's Plays*
RS *Wat Tyler*
Scott *Antiquary*
(28 Jan) Habeas Corpus restored and never again suspended
(1 Jun) Parliamentary motion for universal suffrage and annual parliaments defeated
Hazlitt *Lectures on the English Poets*
Lamb *Collected Works* (vol II dedicated to C)
Peacock *Nightmare Abbey*

(May) Grattan's Motion for the Relief of Roman Catholics defeated

(29 Jan) George III d; accession of George IV
Cato Street Conspiracy
(Feb) Parliament dissolved
Revolution in Spain and Portugal
(Aug–Nov) Trial of Queen Caroline
Lamb *Essays of Elia*
RS *Life of Wesley*
WW *River Duddon*
(Feb) Plunkett's Motion for the Relief of Roman Catholics passed by Commons, rejected in the Lords
De Q *Confessions of an English Opium Eater*
Hazlitt *Lectures on Elizabethan Drama*
RS *Vision of Judgment*
(30 Apr) Canning's Catholic Peers Bill passed by Commons, rejected in the Lords
(Nov–Dec) Faction-fights between Orangemen and Catholics in Ireland
Byron *Vision of Judgment*
WW *Ecclesiastical Sketches*
War between France and Spain
Hazlitt *Liber Amoris*
RS *History of the Peninsular War*

RS *Book of the Church*

1825	(18 May) "On the Prometheus of Aeschylus" read before the Royal Society of Literature (c 25 May) *Aids to Reflection* (30 Jun) Partnership of C's publishers Taylor and Hessey dissolved	(Feb–May) Burdett's Bill for the Relief of Roman Catholics passed by Commons, rejected in the Lords Hazlitt *Spirit of the Age*
1826		General Election with Corn Laws and Catholic Emancipation as main issues HNC *Six Months in the West Indies* RS *Vindiciae Ecclesiae Anglicanae*
1827	(Dec) DC marries Mary Pridham	(Mar) Burdett's Bill for the Relief of Roman Catholics rejected in Commons; Canning PM (8 Aug) Canning d (Aug) Goderich ministry
1828	(21 Jun–7 Aug) Netherlands and Rhine tour with Dora and WW (Jun–Jul) *Poetical Works* (3 vols)	(Jan) Wellington ministry (Apr) Repeal of Test and Corporation Acts (May) Burdett's Bill passed by Commons, rejected in Lords (Jun) Russia goes to war with Turkey Hazlitt *Life of Napoleon* vols I–II
1829	(Jan–Feb) Refuses to sign petition against Catholic Emancipation (May) *Poetical Works* (2nd ed) (3 Sept) SC marries HNC (Dec) *On the Constitution of the Church and State*	Meetings held throughout the country to petition against Catholic Emancipation (10 Apr) Catholic Relief Bill passes 3rd reading in Lords (31 Apr) George IV gives assent RS *Sir Thomas More*
1830	(c Apr) *On the Constitution of the Church and State* (2nd ed)	(Jun) Death of George IV; accession of William IV (Nov) Grey ministry
1831	*Aids to Reflection* (2nd ed) (May) Royal Society of Literature annuity withdrawn; C refuses personal grant from Lord Grey	(Mar) Lord John Russell introduces Reform Bill in Commons Dissolution of Parliament Second Reform Bill rejected in Lords Final Reform Bill introduced
1832	Legacy of £300 from Steinmetz	Grey resigns; Wellington fails to form ministry; Grey recalled (May) Reform Bill passes
1833	(24 May–9 Jun) At Cambridge for meetings of British Association	Lamb *Last Essays of Elia*
1834	(Mar–Aug) *Poetical Works* (3rd ed) (25 Jul) Death of C at Highgate (2 Aug) Funeral: C interred in vault in Highgate church	

PROLEGOMENA

I. THE GREAT WORK: *MAGNUM OPUS* AND *OPUS MAXIMUM*

Coleridge, throughout the course of his intellectual life, was ridden by "an intense craving after a resting-place for [his] Thoughts in some principle, that was derived from Experience, but of which all other Knowleges should be but so many repetitions under various limitations, even as circles, squares, triangles, &c are but so many positions of space".[1] What was urged upon him by inner need was also urged by outside expectations. "Lord Egmont", recalls De Quincey, "spoke of Coleridge in the terms of excessive admiration, and urged Mr. Poole to put him upon undertaking some great monumental work, that might furnish a sufficient arena for the display of his various and rare accomplishments; for his multiform erudition on the one hand, for his splendid power of theorizing and combining large and remote notices of facts on the other". De Quincey continues: "And he suggested, judiciously enough, as one theme which offered a field at once large enough and indefinite enough to suit a mind that could not show its full compass of power unless upon very plastic materials—a History of Christianity, in its progress and in its chief divarications into Church and Sect, with a continuous reference to the relations subsisting between Christianity and the current philosophy . . . ."[2]

In accordance with such inner and outer promptings, Coleridge projected a plan for what he called his "GREAT WORK", which, under various tentative titles and evolving schemes of content, was increasingly the beacon light of all his hopes. It was "the principal Labour",[3] "the great Object",[4] of Coleridge's life.

Although the "Great Work" (like the Cartesian *mathesis universalis* that preceded it) was never completed, and although its thought was constantly siphoned off into parallel but smaller works, parts of it do exist. These parts are identified only inferentially, for they do not bear the title either of *Magnum Opus* or of *Opus Maximum*. Indeed, no work actually entitled *Opus Maximum* was produced by Coleridge himself or by his

---

[1] *CL* v 239. To Thomas Allsop, 29 June 1822.
[2] *De Q Works* ii 148.
[3] *AR* (1825) 152.
[4] *CL* vi 861, 28 May 1831. See also *CL* vi 541, Jan 1826.

xli

amanuenses; the connected fragments here presented under that name[5] are merely the most coherent and sequential arguments that clearly and unmistakably belong to the "Great Work", though other fragments almost certainly belong to that work as well.

Coleridge at different times called the "Great Work" both his *Magnum Opus* and his *Opus Maximum* (as well as according it other designations); nevertheless, a tradition has grown up by which scholars refer to the sequential fragments presented here as the *Opus Maximum*, reserving *Magnum Opus* to identify the larger entity, both achieved and projected, that dominated his aspiration during the last twenty years of his life.[6]

Coleridge had wanted "to reduce to an intelligible if not artistical form" the results of his "religious, biblical and ecclesiastical lucubrations".[7] He had hoped that if he were unable to complete the *Magnum Opus*, his executor might make available "the substance at least" of the results of his "logical, physiological, philosophical, theological, biblical, and" he hoped he was entitled to add, "religious and Christian studies and meditations" over the last twenty years of his life.[8] To honour Coleridge's wishes, more copious and ramified prolegomena are required for an edition of the *Opus Maximum* than for more self-contained and less fragmentary utterance; these draw upon letters, marginalia, and notebooks as well as upon formal publications. As he mused in 1803, Coleridge seemed to have determined to write his metaphysical works as in his Life, "intermixed with all the other events or history of the mind & fortunes of S. T. Coleridge".[9]

II. THE FOUNDATIONS OF THE *MAGNUM OPUS*

The *magnum opus*, before all else, was a work in the service of the Christian religion. Coleridge's work on the philosophy and history of Christianity[10] was intended to be comprehensive in its scope, the "Reservoir" of a lifetime's accumulation of reading and thought, the "Harvesting" of his "Life's Labours".[11]

The conceptions of "Reservoir" and "Harvesting" were essential to

---

[5] A number of passages from these fragments have been published from time to time, notably by W. G. T. Shedd, in his *Complete Works of Samuel Taylor Coleridge* (New York 1853) and by Alice D. Snyder, in *Coleridge on Logic and Learning* (New Haven 1929), as well as in various secondary studies up to the present time.

[6] See Bate 182n, 212.
[7] *CL* vi 722–3, 25 Jan 1828.
[8] *CL* vi 734.
[9] *CN* i 1515.
[10] *CL* vi 691, 9 June 1827.
[11] *CL* v 160; vi 714, 18 Nov 1827.

Coleridge's procedure. Accumulated learning was necessary to the *magnum opus* because Coleridge, like Hegel on the continent in his own time, or Jaspers in our century, considered all past thought as in some measure a contribution to the larger structure of truth. As a commentator on Coleridge's preoccupation with the seventeenth century observes: "he believed that the truth might lie in a synthesis of what was true in all other philosophical systems," and thus "undertook a stupendous amount of critical reading, not only in Latin and Greek but also in German, French, and English philosophical writing".[12]

A third unchanging characteristic of the *magnum opus* was an insistence on uniqueness; it was to have been, as Coleridge said in 1799, "the one work" to which he hoped "to dedicate in silence" the prime of his life.[13] In 1834, through the agency of his friend J. H. Green, it remained "the sole Depositarium of his Mind & Aspirations".[14]

Finally, the *magnum opus* was a conservative venture, a reaction against the intellectual currents emanating from the French Enlightenment (hence Coleridge's pervasive involvement with the seventeenth-century theological modes displaced by the Enlightenment). As early as 1796 we find Coleridge asserting a need "to rescue this *enlightened age* from general Irreligion".[15] In 1815, in *The Statesman's Manual*, he announces "We hear, at least, less of the jargon of this *enlightened age*"; but in an appendix to that tract he assails at length the characteristic thought of the French *philosophes*.[16]

Although, as shall presently appear, the *magnum opus* erected its strongest fortifications against the materialistic pantheism of Spinoza, on the one hand, and the materialistic theories of evolution that culminated in Darwin's triumph in 1859, on the other, what the French Enlightenment stood for in general not only reinforced these formal assaults but also saturated public attitudes in a way that threatened all the values Coleridge held dear: "Prurient, bustling, and revolutionary, this French wisdom has never more than grazed the surface of knowledge . . . . As the process, such the result! a heartless frivolity alternating with a sentimentality as heartless—an ignorant contempt of antiquity—a neglect of moral self-discipline—a deadening of the religious sense, even in the less reflecting forms of natural piety . . . and as the *caput* mortuum of human nature evaporated, a French nature of rapacity, levity, ferocity, and presumption".[17]

Thus Coleridge, in his own estimation, spent twenty-five or thirty

[12] Brinkley 39.
[13] *CL* I 519.
[14] *CL* VI 977.

[15] *CL* I 248.
[16] *LS (CC)* 39, 73–5.
[17] *LS (CC)* 76.

years "resolutely opposing the whole system of modern illumination, in all its forms of Jacobinism, and Legitimation, Epicurean (in our country Pelagian) Christianity, Pelagian morals, Pelagian politics."[18]

III. THE EPICUREAN AND STOIC BACKGROUND

The nomination of "Epicurean" Christianity in the passage quoted above indicates an important feature of Coleridge's defence of religion. While the French Enlightenment—"modern illumination"—provided the explicit focus of what he opposed, Coleridge identified a less evident but deep-seated threat to Christianity in the doctrines of the ancient Epicureans, which he saw as intertwined with those of the Enlightenment. Throughout the *Opus Maximum*, as well as in statements ancillary or corollary to it, there is a continuing subtext of concern with Epicurean and Stoic conceptions. Both orders of thought (which had a distinct currency in his day) threatened the Christian view; both had originated about the same time in ancient Athens; and, though differing radically from one another, the two were joined together in subsequent intellectual history by their anti-Christian implications. After all, both Stoics and Epicureans had sceptically confronted St. Paul in Athens.[19]

The Epicurean and Stoic philosophies were formulated in the aftermath of the philosophical hegemony of Plato and Aristotle, about twenty years after Aristotle's death, and vied for dominance in the later Greek world and in the heyday of the Roman Empire. Thus Cicero, in *De finibus* and *De natura deorum*, describes both doctrines at length. Neither Stoicism nor Epicureanism died when the ancient world collapsed; rather, each was revived and each became a tenacious and formidable opponent of Christianity. Where Stoicism threatened Christianity by asserting an uncomfortably similar ethical doctrine however, Epicureanism threatened Christianity by asserting an ethical doctrine and cosmology entirely different.

That vital difference in the moral status of the two doctrines accounts for Coleridge's mentioning Epicureanism more frequently and censoriously than he does Stoicism. But Coleridge kept the two modes of thought simultaneously in mind, and he was steeped in the history and doctrine of both. As early as 1795 he explicitly contrasted the doctrines of the Stoics and Epicureans;[20] late in life, in his table talk, he said that he was not interested in possible new manuscripts of Epicurus because

---

[18] *CL* v 453, 14 May 1825.   [20] *Lects 1795 (CC)* 156–7.
[19] Acts 17.18.

a complete view of Epicurus's system is preserved in Lucretius, but that he did regret the loss of the works of the old Stoics.[21] The depth of Coleridge's knowledge of the Epicurean tradition is attested by his extensive involvement with the two volumes of Gassendi's work on the tenth book of Diogenes Laertius, where Epicurus is most fully presented.[22]

Despite his relatively benign attitude towards the Stoics, Coleridge was well aware of the hidden threat posed by their doctrine, and a section in his *Aids to Reflection*, in 1825, is entitled "THE CHRISTIAN NO STOIC".[23] The rubric is formulated not to repel a radical difference, but to ensure that the true believer is not misled by a seductive similarity. As Coleridge goes on to say, "the Stoic attaches the highest honour (or rather, attaches honour *solely*) to the person that acts virtuously in spite of his feelings, or who has raised himself above the conflict by their extinction; while Christianity instructs us to place small reliance on a Virtue that does not *begin* by bringing the Feelings to a conformity with the Commands of the Conscience".[24]

Stoicism crowded hard upon Coleridge's most cherished beliefs. Indeed, Immanuel Kant, who, as Coleridge testifies in *Biographia Literaria*, had taken possession of him with a giant's hand, was, as Coleridge had to admit, virtually a Stoic himself.[25] Coleridge, in brief, was threatened by Stoicism not because it was an ethical philosophy far distant from his values, but because it was so extremely close to those very values.

The widespread social growth achieved by Stoic principles in the eighteenth century (Addison's *Cato* was an especially important vehicle) had been preceded, and seeded, by an explicit revival of Stoic doctrine in the sixteenth and early seventeenth centuries.[26] Two figures stood out in this revival, which exerted enormous influence on the European cultural scene: the Flemish scholar and humanist Justus Lipsius and the French scholar and statesman Guillaume du Vair.

Lipsius presented Stoic doctrine in three works, the first of which, in 1584, was *De constantia libri duo*, "his most famous work, which, in Latin, went through more than eighty editions and was translated into all the principal languages of Europe".[27] That was followed, in 1604, by

---

[21] *TT (CC)* I 202–3.
[22] E.g. *CN* IV 4715 and n. Significantly, along with quotation of Gassendi there is quotation of "the Christianized Stoic" Limborch.
[23] *AR* (1825) 91.
[24] Ibid.
[25] For discussion of the extent to which Kant was similar to and different from Stoic ethical thought, see Long & Sedley 398–9.
[26] See Strowski I 18–125; and, departing from Strowski, Léontine Zanta *La Renaissance du stoicisme au XVIe siècle* (Paris 1914).
[27] Saunders 22.

Manuductio ad stoicam philosophiam and its sequel *Physiologia stoico-rum*. Scarcely less resonating in their effect than the works of Lipsius were those of Du Vair. The latter's *La Philosophie morale des Stoïques* (1585) was translated into English by Thomas James in 1598 and by Charles Cotton in 1664, the latter translation being reprinted in 1667 and 1671. Du Vair's work was devoted primarily to the practical Stoicism of Epictetus rather than the theoretical work of the Early Stoa or the uni-versally popular Stoicism of Seneca, although elements of Seneca, along with Cicero and Plutarch, appear in the treatise. Du Vair, like Lipsius, specifically urged the similarity of Stoicism and Christianity: "no kinde of philosophie", said Du Vair's translator, Thomas James, "is more prof-itable and neerer approching unto Christianitie (as *S. Hierome* saith) than the philosophie of the Stoicks".[28] Indeed, "combining of two great tra-ditions appeared" when Du Vair wrote *La Saincte Philosophie. La Philosophie des Stoïques* (1584?), "in which for the first time he brought the theories of Stoic and Christian doctrines together".[29]

It was this powerful tradition, fortified by noted thinkers and scholars of the Renaissance and disseminated through the entire culture of the eighteenth century, that caused Coleridge to be on his guard against the pertinence of the Stoic moral system: "It is one of my Objects to prove the difference of the Christian Faith from Platonism even in its purest form—but so is the Xtn Moral System different from the Stoic—but as no one on this account denies the resemblances and coincidences in the latter, so neither ought we to do so in the former".[30] Coleridge in that passage speaks somewhat respectfully of Stoicism. But he extended no such respect to Epicureanism, which he, along with an entire tradition stemming from antiquity, openly despised. Though Epicurus himself did not advocate hedonism, but rather the avoidance of pain,[31] he was charged from antiquity onward with advocating a life of selfish pleasure as contrasted to the moral austerity and communal concern of the Stoics (the conception, highly respected in the eighteenth century, of "citizen of the world" was an offshoot of Stoic doctrine).[32] Thus the famous ep-

---

[28] Du Vair 45.

[29] Ibid. 8n.

[30] *CN* III 4316.

[31] Epicurus emphasised that "When we say, then, that pleasure is the end and aim, we do not mean the pleasures of the prodigal or the pleasures of sensuality, as we are understood to do by some through ignorance, prejudice, or wilful misrepre-sentation. By pleasure we mean the ab-sence of pain in the body and of trouble in the soul. It is not an unbroken succes-sion of drinking-bouts and of revelry, not sexual love, not the enjoyment of the fish and other delicacies of a luxurious table, which produce a pleasant life" (*DL* II 657). Epicurus's opponents, however, seizing upon the statement that pleasure was the good, chose to ignore its qualifi-cations.

[32] For the phrase in Epictetus see Long & Sedley 364. See also 435.

ithet of Horace, "the sty of Epicurus",[33] vividly painted Epicureans as human hogs wallowing self-indulgently in mud and filth. As Plotinus tersely said, "Epicurus denies a Providence and recommends pleasure and its enjoyment, all that is left to us".[34]

For his view that the gods, though they existed, had no care for human life, and his accompanying contention that reality was formed by a chance coming together of atoms rather than by providential design, Epicurus was stigmatized, especially in the Christian context, as preaching open atheism. And where Epicurus had said "I know not how to conceive the good, apart from the pleasures" of four things, the first of which was "taste",[35] his opponents (and actually his adherents) gleefully rendered this standpoint into the famous exhortation, "eat, drink, and be merry, for tomorrow we die".[36] As Coleridge said, "It appears that at least ninety-nine out of a hundred of Epicurus's adherents were Cyrenaics or voluptuaries in the grossest sense".[37]

Coleridge's observation attests his close attention to Epicureanism throughout his adult life. In 1795, after a censorious account of Stoicism, he says:

Far different from these were the Epicureans yet like them built all their moral Doctrines on the principle of gross self-interest. Epicurus taught that Pleasure was the final Good of Life, and by his own Life seemed to believe that Temperance and well managed Passions were the only means of true Pleasures. He taught that the world was formed by the blind Play of Atoms—that there was no Providence—and no future State—These Doctrines his Disciples fully embraced but his moral precepts they forgot or perverted.[38]

Like Stoicism, philosophical Epicureanism too experienced a revival in the late Renaissance and the seventeenth century.[39] The chief figure here was Pierre Gassendi, a philosopher whom Coleridge respected[40] and knew thoroughly.[41] Gassendi, the friend of Mersenne and opponent of Descartes (the fifth set of objections to the Cartesian *Meditations* were by him) wrote three treatises that brought Epicureanism squarely before

[33] Horace *Epistles* I iv 16.
[34] Plotinus *Enneads* II 9.5.
[35] *DL* II 585.
[36] In the book of Ecclesiastes, which was written under the direct influence of Epicureanism, the exhortation takes this form: "a man hath no better thing under the sun, than to eat, and drink, and to be merry" (Eccles 8.15).
[37] *P Lects* (1949) 217.
[38] *Lects 1795* (*CC*) 157.

[39] See Thomas Franklin Mayo *Epicurus in England (1650–1725)* (Dallas 1934).
[40] See *CN* IV 3824.
[41] E.g.: "I am acquainted with no Treatise on the discipline of the reasoning powers that I could recommend in preference to the two first Books of Gassendi's Works in Sorbière's Edition in 6 Vol. Folio at Lyons 1652" (*CN* IV 5123).

the European intellectual community. The first was *De vita, moribus, et doctrina Epicuri libri octo* (1647); the second was a commentary on the tenth book of Diogenes Laertius, in which most of extant Epicureanism is contained, *De vita, moribus, et placitis Epicuri, seu Animadversiones in X. librum Diog. Laert.* (Lyons 1649); the third and most important was *Syntagma philosophiae Epicuri* (Lyons 1649).

But it was even more as a popular tradition of behaviour known as libertinism than as an explicit intellectual position that Epicureanism saturated the seventeenth and eighteenth centuries. The *libertins* were what a writer of 1623 had called "beaux esprits", jaunty young freethinkers mainly of Epicurean descent.[42] Prominent among them were Julius Caesar Vanini and Pierre Charron, whose *De la Sagesse* became a kind of bible for the beaux esprits. In England, Shadwell's play *The Libertine* became the equivalent, in the Epicurean tradition, of Addison's *Cato* in the Stoic. *Les liaisons dangereuses* of the late eighteenth century was a classic representation of libertinism. Indeed, the libertine philosophy received its supreme expression in Mozart's *Don Giovanni* of 1787, where in glorious song Don Giovanni asserts, against patriarchy and another world, that sensual pleasures in the form of wine and women are the glory of humanity: "Vivan le femine!/ Viva il buon vino!/ Sostegno e gloria/ D'humanita!"

Coleridge may not have known Mozart's opera, but he knew the libertine tradition of Don Juan. Indeed, he discusses the Don Juan tradition at length in the twenty-third chapter of the *Biographia Literaria*, and that discussion set in motion no less a work than the *Don Juan* of Byron. Coleridge speaks of an "old Spanish play, entitled *Atheista Fulminato*, formerly and perhaps still, acted in the churches and monasteries of Spain, and which, under various names (*Don Juan, the Libertine* &c.) has had its day of favour in every country in Europe".[43] He quotes at length from Shadwell's *The Libertine* as preliminary to a critique of Maturin's *Bertram*, because the "modern drama is taken, in the substance of it, from the first scene of the third act of the *Libertine*".

But whether as moral libertinism or in its more specifically philosophical context, Epicureanism seemed to Coleridge to be a threat, explicit, inexplicit, and often intertwined with more modern philosophies, that permeated the entire intellectual spectrum of his time. He opposed himself to "the modern Epicurean, whether under its more plausible religious dress, as it presents itself in the writings of Paley, Priestley and the other masters of the school which began, or rather obtained the pre-

[42] Strowski I 129.　　[43] *BL (CC)* II 212.

dominance, from the ascension of Charles the First to the death of his son and successor".[44] As he said in the *Friend*, "If we would drive out the demons of fanaticism from the people, we must begin by exorcising the spirit of Epicureanism in the higher ranks, and restore to their teachers the true Christian *enthusiasm*".[45] That, if one wishes, is one way of describing the entire agenda of the *magnum opus*.

In the same vein Coleridge refers to "that system of disguised and decorous *epicureanism*, which has been the only orthodox philosophy of the last hundred years";[46] Locke was "the presumed father of the system, who raised it to its present 'pride of place' and almost universal acceptance throughout Europe".[47] But Epicureanism infected not only the rationalism of Locke but the religiosity of the Catholic church as well: "Ever & ever think of that deep Epicureanism of the Papists, which now spreads as *Rationalism*, Unitarianism, &c";[48] "Romanism and Despotic Government in the larger part of Xtendom; and the prevalence of Epicurean Principles in the remainder—these do indeed lie heavy on my heart!"[49]

In sum, the Enlightenment currents that so bothered Coleridge were for him almost an alternate form of, and in a sense virtually interchangeable with, the ancient threats emanating from the Epicurean and Stoic schools of antiquity: "the diffusion of Materialism and the Epicurean philosophy, in a more decorous shape, by the followers of Gassendi . . . fought in close alliance with the French taste".[50] Epicureanism (and less insistently, Stoicism) was in truth part of "the whole system of modern illumination" that he opposed: "Since the Revolution in 1688 our Church has been chilled and starved too generally by Preachers & Reasoners, Stoic or Epicurean—".[51] It was Coleridge's task to stand not only against the clamorous new voices of the Enlightenment, but also against this ancient, insidious, and protean foe.

IV. PALEY AND MORALITY

In such massive opposition, Coleridge found himself confronting opponents as varied as the fields of concern in which he was trying to defend Christianity. In theological philosophy he was opposing pantheism, and the greatest of pantheistic thinkers, Spinoza. In the conception of life, he was opposing the evolutionary trends that led to Darwin. In psychology,

---

44 See below Frag 1 f 62ᵛ.
45 *Friend* (*CC*) I 432.
46 *LS* (*CC*) 108.
47 Ibid. See also *CL* II 701.

48 *CN* II 2717.
49 *CM* (*CC*) I 105.
50 Brinkley 418.
51 Ibid. 291.

he was opposing Locke, and the French Lockean tradition of Condillac, and Hartley. In Christian morality he was opposing Paley;[52] in Christian community, Unitarianism. Espousing the tradition of Plato and Pythagoras,[53] he opposed materialism and its concomitant, mechanism. He rejected "the cheerlessness, vulgarity, and common-place character of the mechanical philosophy, and Paleyan Expedience".[54] "A nation," he said, "that substitutes Locke for Logic, and Paley for Morality, and both this and that for Polity, Philosophy and Theology, cannot but be slaves."[55]

Of the various opponents against whom Coleridge aligned himself, all except Paley still maintain visible roles in the history of thought. Since Paley has virtually disappeared from cultural consciousness, it will be useful to recall him to mind. The task is the more urgent because it is the moral sense, the conscience, from which Coleridge departs in the exposition of his co-inhering concerns. "The Sum of the Philosophy which I receive as the only true Philosophy may be thus exprest. 1. Con*science* is not a Result or Modification of Self-Consciousness; but its Ground and Antecedent Condition. (*Conditio sine quâ non*.)"[56] Conscience is thus a fundamental and exalted element in the *Opus Maximum*: "the supreme Will, which is one with the supreme intelligence, is revealed to man through the Conscience".[57]

The exponent of morality whom Coleridge rejects, as unfitted for setting forth the high meaning of conscience, is William Paley. As early as April 1801, for instance, Coleridge wrote to Poole that "even our most popular Books of Morals, (as Paley's for instance) are the corrupters and poisoners of all moral sense & dignity, without which neither individual or people can stand & be men".[58] From this position he never deviated.

---

[52] He speaks at one point of "the antimoralism of Paley" (*CN* III 3565), and in a vivid passage he laments Paley's prominence in the thought of the time: "O place before your eyes the Islands of Britain & Ireland in the reign of Alfred, its wide Morasses & dreary Heaths, its bloodstained and desolate Shores, its untaught & scanty Population/—and then behold the Monarch listening now to Bede, now to Joannes Erigena—/& then behold the same Realm, a mighty Empire, full of motion, full of Books . . . and behold them, yea, their Rules & their wise men, listening to Paley, and Malthus—/—O it is mournful" (*CN* III 3560). For the role of Paley in the complex of topics C opposed, see Fulford,

189–91. For C's assertion, in reference to *The Friend*, that "the principles of morality taught in the present work will be in direct opposition to the system of the late Dr. Paley", see *Friend* (*CC*) I 313–25.

[53] E.g. "we shall return to the School of Pythagoras & Plato even as runaway youths who after long travels & various adventures return at length to their Father's Mansion, but yet enriched & with diverse Jewels & precious things to fill & furnish & enlarge it—" (*CN* III 3819).

[54] *CL* V 464–5, 28 May 1825.

[55] *CN* IV 4800.

[56] *CN* IV 5167.

[57] See below, Frag 2 f 20.

[58] *CL* II 720.

Paley, Archdeacon of Carlisle, published in two volumes in 1786 *The Principles of Moral and Political Philosophy*, a work that in its time had an enormous currency. By 1814 it had gone into no fewer than twenty editions. What made the work so popular in its own day was perhaps the very factor that led ultimately to its disappearance from the philosophical canon: it did nothing more than reflect the decent beliefs of the country gentleman or bourgeois *paterfamilias* of the late eighteenth century. In 1794 Paley published an, if possible, even more influential work, his *View of the Evidences of Christianity*, which cemented his status as the most popular moral thinker of his age. Coleridge placed this work with the work of Grotius as the object of his animadversions against "evidences" in Christianity (for Coleridge, as a commentator says, "apart from all question of historical evidence, the essential doctrines of Christianity are necessary and eternal truths of Reason").[59] *The Principles of Moral and Political Philosophy* received the brunt of his rejection of Paley as a moralist.

The absence of intense thought and profound moral seriousness in Paley's work infuriated young intellectuals. One may gauge the situation by considering, alongside Coleridge's unceasing barrage of disparaging references, a scathing dismissal by Hazlitt:

This same shuffling Divine is the same Dr. Paley, who afterwards employed the whole of his life, and his moderate second-hand abilities, in tampering with religion, morality, and politics,—in trimming between his convenience and his conscience,—in crawling between heaven and earth, and trying to cajole both. His celebrated and popular work on Moral Philosophy, is celebrated and popular for no other reason, than that it is a somewhat ingenious and amusing apology for existing abuses of every description . . . . It is a very elaborate and consolatory elucidation of the text *that men should not quarrel with their bread and butter.* It is not an attempt to show what is right, but to palliate and find out plausible excuses for what is wrong. It is a work without the least value, except as a convenient common-place book or *vade mecum*, for tyro politicians and young divines, to smooth their progress in the Church or the State.[60]

A good example of what Hazlitt found despicable is provided by Paley's attitude towards slavery and the slave trade: while he does not morally approve of it, Paley is loathe to demand the abolition of slavery because of the issue of property rights.

Neither Hazlitt's brilliant attack nor Coleridge's related objections are entirely fair to Paley, whose attitudes are not so much craven or dishonest as they are, in a word, comfortable. There is no hint of the sublime

[59] *SP* I xliii.   [60] *H Works* VII 252–3.

chords struck by Kant's reverence for "the moral law within". That is not to say, however, that Paley's first work on morality is either foolish or without merit. It is written in a clear though orotund eighteenth-century style, and it exhibits a very considerable organisational ability in its exhaustive taking up of almost every category of personal and social moral obligation. It does not aspire to learning (though Paley was not without learning) but rather refers for the most part to a single extrinsic source, the Bible, and otherwise to practical examples and illustrations. An ordinary eighteenth-century citizen would find little to disagree with in Paley.

But that does not mean that Paley is devoid of cogent opinions. For instance, he provides a tart account of "honour". "The Law of Honour", he says, "is a system of rules constructed by people of fashion, and calculated to facilitate their intercourse with one another; and for no other purpose."[61] Again, he calmly advances the socio-economic observation that "Among men, you see the ninety-and-nine toiling and scraping together a heap of superfluities for one (and this one too, oftentimes the feeblest and worst of the whole set, a child, a woman, a madman, or a fool), getting nothing for themselves all the while, but a little of the coarsest of the provision, which their own industry produces; looking quietly on, while they see the fruits of all their labour spent or spoiled; and if one of their number take or touch a particle of the hoard, the others joining against him, and hanging him for the theft".[62]

But whatever Paley's merits, he offered an intellectual surface far too soft to serve as foundation for Coleridge's Great Work. That work had to reside on a foundation of granite, for it was the sole agent of morality, the conscience, that was to connect man with God and ultimately to validate Christian hope: "because we have a Conscience, we know that there is a God".[63] Conscience was therefore for Coleridge a keystone in the arch of rational thought: "Above all things it is incumbent on me who lay such a stress on Conscience, & attach such a sacredness to it, to shew that it is no Socratic Daimon which I mean, but the dictate of universal Reason, accompanied with a feeling of free Agency—that it is *Light*—that an erring Conscience is no Conscience, and as absurd as an erring Reason—i.e. not Reason".[64] What Paley could offer not only did not help in this project but, by its intellectual flaccidity, actually tended to depress its possibility (Coleridge even speaks at one point of "the anti-

---

[61] Paley ɪ 2.   [63] See below, Frag 1 f 110[v].
[62] Ibid. ɪ 107.   [64] *CN* ɪɪɪ 3591.

moralism of Paley").[65] Indeed, an entire brief section in a later edition of *Aids to Reflection* was accorded the rubric, "Paley Not a Moralist".[66]

V. REASON AND UNDERSTANDING

The "universal Reason" Coleridge invokes in his statement about the sacredness of conscience is a significant Coleridgean emphasis; in truth, it is without doubt the most important single term in his entire arsenal of ideas. "Reason" shares with "Will" the role of the most important of his positive assertions about meaning and life, and it stands alone as the focal conception and chief agent of his defence of Christianity.

For it was against the whole cultural fabric of the late eighteenth century, as represented by the French "Age of Reason", that Coleridge aligned himself. He condemned "the bran, straw and froth which the Idols of the age, Locke, Helvetius, Hume, Condillac, and their Disciples have succeeded in passing off for metaphysics".[67] With anxious scorn he asked "What then must be the fate of a nation that substitutes Locke for Logic, and Paley for Morality, and one or the other for Polity and Theology?"[68] The *magnum opus* was to be his "(Anti-Paleyo-grotian) Assertion of Religion as necessarily implying Revelation ["The Grotian Paleian Defence of X[tianity] how injurious to X[tianity]", he observes in 1805],[69] and of Xtianity as the only Revelation of universal validity".[70] Grotius and Paley, separated both in time and in ability, were linked together and rejected as proponents of external evidence for Christianity rather than of the internal witness that Coleridge espoused.[71]

---

[65] *CN* III 3566.
[66] *AR* (1848) 236.
[67] *CM* (*CC*) III 877.
[68] *CL* v 138.
[69] *CN* II 2640.
[70] *CL* v 134, 8 Jan 1821.
[71] Although Grotius was a far greater scholar than Paley, his effect, in C's view, conjoined with that of Paley in a manner deleterious to Christianity. The whole complex—what C rejected along with what he espoused—is revealed in a convoluted letter of 4 Oct 1806 to George Fricker: "An extract from a letter which I wrote a few months ago to a sceptical friend, who had been a Socinian, and of course rested all the evidences of Christianity on miracles, to the exclusion of grace and inward faith, will perhaps surprise you, as showing you how much nearer our opinions are than what you must have supposed. 'I fear that the mode of defending Christianity, adopted by Grotius first; and latterly, among many others, by Dr. Paley, has increased the number of infidels;—never could it have been so great, if thinking men had been habitually led to look into their own souls, instead of always looking out, both of themselves, and of their nature. If to curb attack, such as yours on miracles, it had been answered:—Well, brother! but granting these miracles to have been in part the growth of delusion at the time, and of exaggeration afterward, yet still all the doctrines will re-

Coleridge unremittingly opposed them both as ultimately exponents of the Epicureanism against which he contested. A single passage may be quoted—one that aligns the "prudential" morality of Paley, the "Paleyo-Grotian" reliance on "evidences" in religion, and their intertwinement with Epicureanism: "What then can we think of a theological theory, which adopting a scheme of prudential legality, common to it with 'the sty of Epicurus' as far at least as the *springs* of moral action are concerned, makes its whole *religion* consist in miracles!"[72]

But even more important than rejecting flawed defences of Christianity was the necessity of resisting its overt attackers: the French. Coleridge stood foursquare against "French Philosophy and modern Materialism".[73] Indeed, as indicated above, the very word that served as the emblem of the French Enlightenment, "reason", became the focal point of his resistance. The Enlightenment, in Coleridge's view, was guilty of "usurping the name of reason" and thereby it "openly joined the banners of Antichrist".[74] How pertinent such an opinion was to the demonstrable historical truth may be gauged from a single locus in Diderot, one of the triumvirate—"Voltaire, D'Alembert, Diderot"—singled out by Coleridge as leading the defection to Antichrist. In a series of jolting attacks on Christianity entitled "Addition aux Pensées philosophiques" and appended in 1762 to the *Pensées philosophiques* of 1746, Diderot uses "la raison" virtually as a sledgehammer to batter open a door to scornful mockery. By section xv Diderot is saying, "S'il y a cent mille damnés pour un sauvé, le diable a toujours l'avantage, sans avoir abandonné son fils à la mort."[75] By section xxiv he asks, "Pourquoi les miracles de Jésus-Christ sont-ils vrais, et ceux d'Esculape, d'Apollonius de Tyane et de Mahomet sont-ils faux?"[76] By section xxxi he is asserting, "La religion de Jésus-Christ, annoncé par des ignorants, a fait les pre-

---

main untouched by the circumstance, and binding on thee. Still must thou repent and be regenerated, and be crucified to the flesh; and this not by thy own mere power; but by a mysterious action of the moral Governor on thee; of the Ordo-ordinians, the Logos, or Word. Still will the eternal filiation, or Sonship of the Word from the Father; still will the Trinity of the Deity, the redemption, and the thereto assumption of humanity by the Word ... remain truths: and still will the vital head-and-heart FAITH in these truths, be the living and only fountain of all true virtue ...'." (*CL* ii 1189–90).

[72] *CL* ii 1190. As C said in the same letter, he believed in building "the miracle on the faith, not the faith on the miracle".

[73] *CL* v 8, 4 Jan 1820.

[74] *LS* (*CC*) 75.

[75] Diderot 60. Tr: "If there are a hundred thousand damned for every one saved, the devil always has the advantage, without having abandoned his son to death".

[76] Ibid. Tr: "Why are the miracles of Jesus Christ true, and those of Esculapius, Apollonius of Tyana, and Mohammed false?"

miers Chrétiens. La même religion, prêchée par des savants et des doc-
teurs, ne fait aujourd'hui que des incrédules".[77] The tone of these scorn-
ful thrusts has been prepared by the first nine sections, which constantly
invoke the efficacy of "la raison", concluding, in Section IX, with the
statement, "If my reason comes from on high, it is the voice of heaven
that speaks to me by it; it is necessary that I listen to it".[78] But "la rai-
son" has figured in all eight preceding sections.

Reason or "la raison", in short, was for Diderot, as for all the formu-
lators of Enlightenment argument against which Coleridge set himself,
precisely the faculty whose use discredited the validity claimed by Chris-
tianity. In this sense, as characteristically employed—or "usurped"—by
the French thinkers, reason was in truth the instrument of Antichrist.
Hume ("the same Scotch philosopher", said Coleridge, "who devoted his
life to the undermining of the Christian religion"[79]) makes it the basis
for a brilliant sarcasm that was certainly worthy of "Antichrist": ". . .
upon the whole, we may conclude that the *Christian Religion* not only
was at first attended with miracles, but even at this day cannot be be-
lieved by any reasonable person without one. Mere reason is insufficient
to convince us of its veracity: and whoever is moved by *Faith* to assent
to it, is conscious of a continued miracle in his own person, which sub-
verts all the principles of his understanding, and gives him a determina-
tion to believe what is most contrary to custom and experience".[80] In that
passage alone we may see, at least by implication, the urgency of Cole-
ridge's distinction of reason from understanding.

Hume, though a Scotsman, was almost as much at the centre of the
French Enlightenment as was Diderot himself, and he shared with
Diderot and Voltaire a defining hostility to religion. Indeed, the upsurge
of religiosity so closely associated with the rise of Romanticism had as
the very condition of its emergence to reject the thought of the French
Enlightenment. For a single significant example, the seminal German
Romantic, Schleiermacher, who subsequently became the most influen-
tial theologian of the nineteenth century, in his epoch-making *Reden
über die Religion* of 1799 specifically turned away from French think-
ing: ". . . I turn myself away from the French, whose sight can scarcely
be borne by one who reverences religion, because in every action, in
every word almost, they tread its holiest laws under foot. The coarse in-
difference with which millions of their people, no less than the witty jests

---

[77] Diderot 63. Tr: "Proclaimed by ig-
noramuses, the religion of Jesus Christ
created the first Christians. Preached by
learned men and doctors, the same reli-
gion today creates only unbelievers".
[78] Ibid. 59.
[79] *LS* (*CC*) 22.
[80] Hume 131.

with which individual brilliant minds among them, regard the most sublime act of history . . . suffices to prove how little they are capable of a holy awe and a true devotion".[81]

Coleridge, in his attempt to wrest "reason" from the hands of Antichrist, characteristically split the conception of reason into "reason" and "understanding" instead of jettisoning the term, precisely as he split the conception of imagination into "imagination" and "fancy".[82] Thus French "raison" became what Coleridge called "understanding", and Coleridgian "reason" resumed the thread of seventeenth-century theologising to become the guarantor of Christianity.[83] Coleridge's "Reason", at the antipode from Diderot's, was "the only supreme Reality, the only true *Being* in all things visible and invisible! the Pleroma, in whom alone God loveth the World!"[84] Though the distinction between *Vernunft* (reason) and *Verstand* (understanding) was an essential of Kantian analysis (and according to De Vleeschauwer was derived by Kant from Tetens),[85] and perhaps almost as pertinently to Coleridge's own position, an essential of Jacobi's thought, there can be little doubt that the distinction was for Coleridge not nearly so much a simple echo of Germanic currencies as it was a defensive tactic against "la raison".[86]

Coleridge's campaign against "la raison", however, was conducted in the terms established by Kant, who himself, in his monumental inspection and analysis of the human mind, was impelled by the Enlightenment's admiration for "la raison". In assessing the functioning of the mind, Kant, steeped in the tradition of Locke and of the faculty psychology of his eighteenth-century predecessors and contemporaries, realised that ramified distinctions had to be made if the subject were not

---

[81] *Schleiermacher* Erste Abtheilung I 153.

[82] For C's characteristic dichotomising of problems, see e.g. *RFR* 289–341, esp 340–1.

[83] C habitually insisted that the distinction between reason and understanding was present in Milton and in other seventeenth-century thinkers, e.g.: "Take one passage among many from the posthumous Tracts (1660) of John Smith, not the least Star in that bright Constellation of Cambridge Men, the contemporaries of Jeremy Taylor. 'While we reflect on our own idea of Reason, we know that our own Souls are not it, but only partake of it; and that we have it κατα μεθεξιν and not κατ᾽ ουσιην [by participation

only]. Neither can it be called a Faculty, but far rather a Light, which we enjoy, but the Source of which is not in ourselves, nor rightly by any individual to be denominated *mine*.' This *pure* intelligence he then proceeds to contrast with the *Discursive* Faculty, i.e. the Understanding" (*AR*—1825—246 n.)

[84] *CL* VI 600, 27 July 1826.

[85] De Vleeschauwer 85–8.

[86] The hegemony of the "Reason" was established during the first half of the seventeenth century by Descartes (see e.g. McFarland *Rousseau* 258–9); by the second half Boileau's exhortation, "aimez donc la raison", served as epigraph for an entire age.

simply to remain on the surface. Thus he departed from a distinction supplied to him by "general logic", which "is built up on a plan that coincides accurately with the division of the higher faculties of knowledge. These are, *understanding, judgment*, and *reason*."[87]

From this initial division an entire network of related distinctions emerged: inner and outer, subject and object, transcendental and transcendent, intuition and concept, concept and idea, analytic and dialectic, these and more, and most important of all, understanding (*Verstand*) and reason (*Vernunft*).[88] Moreover, since Kant customarily translated the Latin *intellectus* as *Verstand*, the word *Vernunft* from the outset was partially freed from its "ordinary language" implications.

Coleridge knew Kant's work in precise and thorough detail; indeed, it would be difficult to overestimate his saturation in not merely the three great Critiques, but even the least known pre-critical writings. He speaks only the simple truth when he says, in the *Biographia Literaria*, that

The writings of the illustrious sage of Königsberg, the founder of the Critical Philosophy, more than any other work, at once invigorated and disciplined my understanding. The originality, the depth, and the compression of the thoughts; the novelty and subtlety, yet solidity and importance of the distinctions; the adamantine chain of the logic; and I will venture to add (paradox as it will appear to those who take their notion of IMMANUEL KANT from Reviewers and Frenchmen) the *clearness* and *evidence* of the "CRITIQUE OF THE PURE REASON"; of the "JUDGEMENT"; of the "METAPHYSICAL ELEMENTS OF NATURAL PHILOSOPHY"; and of his "RELIGION WITHIN THE BOUNDS OF PURE REASON," took possession of me with a giant's hand. After fifteen years' familiarity with them, I still read these and all his other productions with undiminished delight and increasing admiration.[89]

One of the persisting hindrances to a proper understanding of Coleridge has been the simple fact that he knew Kant's work in far more detail than have any of the Coleridgean commentators; as a result, the critical picture is clouded with incorrect and sometimes ludicrous formulations.

What Coleridge found of most pressing importance in his enormous investment in reading and understanding was logical instrumentalities, not a final position with which he agreed. Chief among these instrumentalities was what Kant also emphasised: the all-pervading distinction

---

[87] Kant *GS* IV 95.

[88] Kant, as early as 7 June 1771, and again on 21 Feb 1772, wrote to Markus Herz and said that he was engaged on a work called *Die Grentzen der Sinnlichkeit und Vernunft* (Kant *GS* X 117, 124).

The significance of this title, a decade before the *Kritik der reinen Vernunft* appeared, is that it reveals the dichotomy of reason and sense-data as informing the very foundations of Kant's work.

[89] *BL (CC)* I 153.

between reason and understanding. Understanding, for Kant, was "a non-sensuous faculty of knowledge".[90] It came into play subsequent to the formation of the data of immediate awareness (intuition) but was itself under the sway of the faculty of principles (reason). As Kant says in the *Kritik der reinen Vernunft*:

> As without sensibility we cannot have any intuition (*Anschauung*), it is clear that the understanding is not a faculty of intuition. Besides intuition, however, there is no other kind of knowledge except by concepts (*Begriffe*). The knowledge therefore of every understanding, or at least of the human understanding, must be by means of concepts, not intuitive (*intuitiv*), but discursive (*discursiv*). All intuitions, being sensuous, depend on affections, concepts on functions. By this function I mean the unity of the act of arranging different representations under one common representation. Concepts are based therefore on the spontaneity of thought, sensuous intuitions on the receptivity of impressions. The only use the understanding can make of these concepts is to form judgments by them.[91]

When Kant refers to "every understanding, or at least . . . the human understanding", he virtually invites Coleridge to adopt a distinction by which "the human understanding" becomes a faculty subsidiary and inferior to reason (which Kant does not mention in the foregoing passage). Coleridge was resolutely opposed to the implications of the thought of Locke and Hume; the title of Locke's incredibly influential treatise of 1690 had been *An Essay Concerning Human Understanding*, and Hume's treatise of 1748 had been named *An Enquiry Concerning Human Understanding*. By Kant's distinction, Coleridge was, as it were, able to concede to Locke and Hume the "understanding" on which they had discoursed so acutely and copiously while retaining for his own religious purposes the superior conception of "reason". It was a solution exactly in accord with his reconciling and including temperament. As Carlyle said, Coleridge was willing to concede that "Hume and Voltaire could on their own ground speak irrefragably for themselves against any Church: but lift the Church and themselves into a higher sphere of argument: *they* died into inanition, the Church revived itself into pristine florid vigour".[92]

In another part of the reasoning function Kant discerned an activity that he called "reason" as such, which had a double function of dealing in illusion (*Schein*) and of supplying meaning to the understanding: "All our knowledge begins with the senses, proceeds thence to the understanding, and ends with the reason, than which nothing higher can be met

---

[90] Kant *GS* iii 85.
[91] Ibid.

[92] *Carlyle* xi 59.

with in us for working up the material of intuition and bringing it under the highest unity of thought. And as it here becomes necessary to give a definition of that highest faculty of knowledge, I begin to feel considerable misgivings."[93] Kant's misgivings about an actual definition of that highest faculty, it seems apparent, allowed Coleridge latitude in his own conceptions. But Kant had no difficulty in defining, if not the essence, at least the schematic function of "reason":

> If the understanding is a faculty for producing unity among phenomena, according to rules, reason is the faculty for producing unity among the rules of the understanding, according to principles. Reason therefore never looks directly to experience, or to any objects, but to the understanding, in order to impart *a priori* through concepts to its manifold kinds of knowledge a unity that may be called the unity of reason, and is very different from the unity that can be produced by the understanding.[94]

Reason therefore does not deal with objects or with nature, but generates ideas that relate solely to the rules of the understanding. There is an absolute break between reason and the outer world. This break was of the greatest consequence in Coleridge's own use of the distinction.

To find a guarantee for the autonomy of the mind itself, free from the reign of objects, or the "it is", was the primary goal in Coleridge's intellectual agenda. "Reason", which as Kant says, "goes far beyond anything sensibility can offer", frees the sense of "I am" from the tyranny of the external—a tyranny, in Coleridge's view, most devastatingly espoused by the thought of Locke and Newton. "The pith of my system", Coleridge once said, "is to make the senses out of the mind—not the mind out of the senses, as Locke did."[95] The need to counter the philosophies of Locke and Newton, which asserted the hegemony of outer reality, was a constant and never-fading urgency in Coleridge's thought. One of his plans for Wordsworth's *Recluse* was that it should refute "the sandy Sophisms of Locke, and the Mechanic Dogmatists" by "demonstrating that the Senses were living growths and developements of the Mind & Spirit in a much juster as well as higher sense, than the mind can be said to be formed by the Senses".[96] Like Blake, who was forever trying to cast off Bacon, Locke, and Newton from Albion's covering, Coleridge aligned the position of Locke and that of Newton as the absolute focus of his opposition to the rule of objects over spirit: "Newton was a mere materialist—*Mind* in his system is always passive—a lazy Looker-on on an external World. If the mind be not *passive*, if it be in-

---

[93] Kant *GS* III 237.
[94] Ibid. III 239.
[95] *TT (CC)* II 179.
[96] *CL* IV 574.

deed Made in God's Image, & that too in the sublimest sense—the Image of the *Creator*—there is ground for suspicion, that any system built on the passiveness of the mind must be false, as a system."[97]

The faculty of "reason", as elucidated by Kant, totally freed mind from being a "lazy looker-on" on an external world. Understanding was restricted to "sensuous ideas", but reason was free. "The pure concepts of understanding can *never* admit of *transcendental* use, but always only of *empirical* employment"[98] (hence Coleridge's concession, as reported by Carlyle, that the atheism of Hume and Voltaire was true "on their own ground", but lifted into a "higher sphere"—that of the transcendental use of reason—their arguments "died into inanition").[99] Kant is insistent upon the limitation of the objects of "understanding" to the sensuous world of empirical experience; reason, in contrast, "contains within itself the source of certain concepts and principles which it does not borrow either from the senses or from the understanding".[100] And he uncompromisingly insists on the absolute difference of the two faculties, despite their coordination:

Understanding may be regarded as a faculty which secures the unity of appearances by means of rules, and reason as being the faculty which secures the unity of the rules of understanding under principles. Accordingly, reason never applies itself directly to experience or to any object, but to understanding, in order to give to the manifold knowledge of the latter an *a priori* unity by means of concepts, a unity which may be called the unity of reason, and which is quite different in kind from any unity that can be accomplished by the understanding.[101]

The connection of reason with unity was especially suggestive for Coleridge, whose principal purpose was to seek rational ground for the belief in God. As Coleridge said, "The Reason first manifests itself in man by the tendency to the comprehension of all as one. We can neither rest in an infinite that is not at the same time a whole, nor in a whole that is not infinite. Hence the natural Man is always in a state either of resistance or of captivity to the understanding, which cannot represent totality without limit."[102]

Kant's other point in the preceding passage, that "reason never applies itself directly to experience or to any object", could also be extrapolated for Coleridge's intent of establishing rational grounds for belief in God: "This primal act of faith is enunciated in the word, GOD: a faith not derived from experience, but its ground and source, and without which the

---

[97] *CL* II 709.
[98] Kant *GS* III 207.
[99] *Carlyle* XI 59.

[100] Kant *GS* IV 191.
[101] Ibid. III 239.
[102] *LS* (*CC*) 60.

fleeting *chaos of facts* would no more form experience, than the dust of the grave can of itself make a living man".[103]

Kant was perhaps ultimately as concerned with faith in God as was Coleridge; a major difference between them, however, was that Kant sought the grounding of that faith through the existence of morality—his beloved "moral law within"—and not through reason as such. ("It was the moral ideas that gave rise to the concept of the Divine Being which we now hold to be correct—and we so regard it not because speculative reason convinces us of its correctness, but because it completely harmonizes with the moral principles of reason").[104]

To be sure, in the *Kritik der reinen Vernunft* Kant makes it clear that reason, though absolutely unable to prove the existence of God, nonetheless—and this is the great paradox—moves inexorably towards the idea of God. In a culminating moment near the end of the *Kritik*, he says "The ultimate aim toward which the speculation of reason in its transcendental employment is directed concerns three objects: the freedom of the will, the immortality of the soul, and the existence of God".[105] Coleridge unequivocally concurred: "God created man in his own image . . . gave us REASON . . . gave us CONSCIENCE—that law of conscience, which . . . unconditionally *commands* us attribute *reality*, and actual *existence*, to those ideas and to those only, without which the conscience itself would be baseless and contradictory, to the ideas of Soul, of Freewill, of Immortality, and of God!"[106]

And yet the two passages, despite their common alignment of freedom of the will, the immortality of the soul, and the existence of God, are not identical. Coleridge's is patently more affirmative about the existence of God. It is as though Kant directs reason tantalizingly close to the realisation of God, and then at the last moment snatches it away. He will allow reason to proceed as far as to open an "empty space" (*leerer Raum*),[107] which God might (or might not) fill. Speaking of the "noumenon", he says: "But since we can apply to it none of the concepts of the understanding, the representation remains for us empty, and is of no service except to mark the limits of our sensible knowledge and to leave open a space which we can fill neither through possible experience nor through pure understanding".[108] Kant, however, in his first *Kritik* did say that

The argument of our Critique, taken as a whole, must have sufficiently convinced the reader that though metaphysics cannot be the foundation of religion, it must

[103] *LS (CC)* 18.
[104] Kant *GS* III 530.
[105] Ibid. III 518.

[106] *Friend (CC)* I 112.
[107] Kant *GS* IV 169.
[108] Ibid. IV 185.

always continue to be a bulwark of it, and that human reason, being by its very nature dialectical, can never dispense with such a science, which curbs it, and by a scientific and completely convincing self-knowledge, prevents the devastations of which a lawless speculative reason otherwise would quite inevitably be guilty in the field of morals as well as in that of religion.[109]

But what Kant seemed to proffer, he also seemed to take back.

Thus Kant did not wholly satisfy Coleridge's requirements. The distinction between reason and understanding, which pointed so alluringly to God, did not actually arrive there. Despite Kant's seeming comfort to religion, the antinomic nature of the critical enterprise made it offer the same comfort to the opposed possibilities. Indeed, as a commentator acutely observed of the great German thinker, "it is doubtless true that his vast influence comes from the very fact that he sympathetically agrees with the fundamental contentions of everybody."[110]

Kant insisted at the outset that reason had a double function: to prescribe rules to the understanding but also to deal in illusion (*Schein*). It was this second tendency of reason that caused him to declare it unfit for the task of filling the empty space with God. In a section of the *Kritik* called "Criticism of all Theology out of Speculative Principles of Reason", Kant declared rational theology a species of illusion: "reason, in its purely speculative application, is utterly insufficient for this great undertaking, namely, to prove the existence of a Supreme Being (*eines obersten Wesens*)".[111] "What I maintain then", said Kant, "is that all attempts at a purely speculative use of reason, with reference to theology, are entirely useless and intrinsically null and void, while the principles of their natural use can never lead to any theology, so that unless we depend on moral laws, or are guided by them, there cannot be any theology of reason".[112]

Such a conclusion was unacceptable to Coleridge. Having gone so far with Kant, he could accompany him no longer. He did not entirely share Kant's consuming fascination with moral law, even though the moral figures importantly in the *Opus Maximum*; Coleridge once said that he was inclined "to believe that morality is conventional". He was instead interested in clearing the rational ground to a point where a philosophical approach could be made to the entire realm of Christian faith, a faith in which even someone as morally tattered as he could find safe haven. Reason had to do that, or there was no point in valuing it so highly. "Man alone was created in the image of God", said Coleridge, "a position groundless and inexplicable, if the reason in man do not differ from the

[109] Kant *GS* III 548–9.
[110] Randall 110.
[111] Kant *GS* III 423.
[112] Ibid. III 425.

understanding."[113] "Reason and Religion are their own evidence";[114] "Reason and Religion differ only as a two-fold application of the same power."[115] Indeed, at one point Coleridge says with unequivocal explicitness that he is attempting to make "the reflecting Reader apprehend", and thus to feel and know, "that CHRISTIAN FAITH IS THE PERFECTION OF HUMAN REASON".[116] The defiant casting of the statement into small capitals, one can hardly doubt, serves as a throwing down of the gauntlet to the claims of Kant.

Coleridge therefore gravitated to some extent away from Kant, or at least from this aspect of Kant, towards the conception of reason advanced by Kant's opponent, Friedrich Jacobi.[117] Jacobi, who had first alerted the philosophical world to the full meaning of Spinoza, who had first detected the Achilles heel in Kant's reasoning about the "thing-in-itself", who had availed himself of Hume's scepticism to denounce all our knowledge as fragmentary piecework (and who had set against even that claim to knowledge what he called his "Unphilosophie"), who had argued that all systematic demonstration in philosophy led to fatalism, was one of the most tenacious, consistent and penetrating of opponents of the Enlightenment's "raison".

Where for Kant understanding worked with materials supplied by the senses while reason had no separate source of material and could work only with what understanding supplied to it, Jacobi radically urged a different formula. Reason, like understanding, had direct access to intuitive knowledge, but in this instance not intuitive knowledge of sense data but intuitive knowledge of God: "Just as there is a sensible intuition, an *intuition* through sense, so there is a rational intuition through *reason*".[118]

Thinking along lines parallel to those of his much older contemporary, Rousseau, Jacobi elevated the role of "feeling" to great heights: "I appeal to an imperative, unconquerable feeling as the first and immediate ground of all philosophy and religion; to a feeling, which allows man to become inwardly aware and to perceive this: he has a sense for the supersensible. This sense I call *reason* (*Vernunft*), in distinction from the senses for the visible world".[119] Impregnated by the new emphasis on feeling, "reason" took on an added aura: "Human reason is the symptom of the highest life that we know".[120] Divested of the coldness that the word implied in Diderot, the new warmth of the term "reason" in Jacobi

---

[113] *LS (CC)* 19.
[114] Ibid. 10.
[115] Ibid. 59.
[116] *AR* (1825) 52.
[117] For a brief conspectus of Jacobi's criticisms of Kant, see Wilhelm Wei-

schedel *Streit um die göttlichen Dinge* (Darmstadt 1967) 8–20.
[118] Jacobi *Werke* II 59.
[119] Ibid. IV–1 xxi.
[120] Ibid. VI 91.

made it a welcome presence as the highest faculty of knowledge: "We all call reason that which makes us certain in ourselves—that which with highest power affirms and denies in us. Without certainty, no reason; without reason, no certainty".[121]

Reason, for Jacobi, was on the one hand the Kantian reason pushed farther than Kant himself could countenance[122] and on the other a re-statement of the "heart's reason" of Pascal. "Le coeur a ses raisons", said Pascal, "que la raison ne connait point"—"the heart has its reasons that the reason does not know".[123] Immediately after this famous aphorism Pascal says that "the heart naturally loves the universal being and naturally loves itself".[124] Elsewhere he claims that "we know the truth not only by the reason but by the heart",[125] a statement in which Jacobi's *Verstand* could easily substitute for reason, and Jacobi's *Vernunft* for heart.

The influence of Pascal[126] seems equally apparent in Jacobi's bold avowal of "feeling" as the foundation of philosophy. Jacobi was reputed to know French more perfectly than any German thinker since Leibniz, and among all French writers he loved Pascal most. Almost equal to his saturation in Pascal was a saturation in Rousseau. The combined influence of his French predecessor and of his older French contemporary, however, allowed the assignment of the greatest importance to "heart" or feeling:

And so we admit without timidity, that our philosophy arises from feeling, objective and pure, that it recognizes feeling's authority as an ultimate, and grounds itself, as doctrine of the supersensible, upon this authority. The faculty of feel-

---

121 Jacobi *Werke* II 314–5.

122 As Jacobi said, "The course of Kantian doctrine leads necessarily to a system of absolute subjectivity; it pleases thereby the explaining understanding that is called the philosophical understanding, and that ultimately certainly does not explain but only destroys. This understanding is opposed only by a *natural reason-faith* (*Vernunftglauben*), which warns away from that course, and which is not an explaining, but rather a positively revealing, unconditionally deciding reason. The course of Jacobian doctrine, whilst it leads with equal necessity to a system of absolute objectivity, is unpleasing to the understanding that rests solely upon concepts (one might call it the philosophizing reason),

and has for itself only the not-explaining, immediately revealing reason, or the *natural reason-faith*" (Jacobi *Werke* II 36–7).

123 Pascal 552.

124 Ibid.

125 Ibid. 512.

126 Cf Jacobi: "I will hold to my great theme—those words of Pascal: La nature confond les Pyrrhoniens et la raison confond les Dogmatistes.—Nous avons une impuissance à prouver, invincible à tout le Dogmatisme. *Nous avons une idée de la vérité, invincible à tout le Pyrrhonisme*" (Jacobi *Werke* IV-1 230). The same words also serve as the epigraph to Jacobi's *David Hume* (II 1) and are quoted by C in 1799 (*CL* I 478–9).

ing, we maintain, is the faculty in human beings elevated above all others. It is the one that alone specifically differentiates man from animal, in kind, not merely in degree, i.e., raises him above the animal *beyond comparison*. The faculty of feeling, we maintain, is one and the same with reason (*Vernunft*), or, as also can properly be said, that which we call reason and raises us above the mere understanding, which is applied to nature alone, arises solely and singly out of the faculty of feeling.[127]

Coleridge was thoroughly acquainted with Jacobi's major writings, from the *Ueber die Lehre des Spinoza* (1785; second edition 1789) and the *David Hume über den Glauben, oder Idealismus und Realismus* (1787), to the *Jacobi an Fichte* (1799) and the *Von den göttlichen Dingen und ihrer Offenbarung* (1811). He knew and came to agree with Jacobi's insistence that "the true God is a living God, who knows and wants, says to himself that I am THAT I am; not a mere I and absolute Not-I".[128] "My philosophy asks: who is God; not, what is he?"[129]

Coleridge was most especially congenial to Jacobi's insistence upon "person" and "faith" as components of reason and to his rejection of pantheism. He did not, however, accept Jacobi's "radikale Unwissenheit" (radical unknowingness) or Jacobi's rejection of system; his own view of reason and understanding consists accordingly of something of an amalgam of Jacobi and Kant rather than an exclusive adherence to either. For a single instance, where Jacobi says that "reason (*Vernunft*) affirms, what understanding (*Verstand*) denies",[130] Coleridge maintains that "reason is the irradiative power of the understanding, and the representative of the infinite".[131] Coleridge's closeness to Jacobi is especially evident in *The Friend,* in which he says, while writing on tolerance, "And here I fully coincide with Frederic H. Jacobi, that the only true spirit of Tolerance consists in our conscientious toleration of each other's intolerance".[132] He is referring to a passage in *Von den göttlichen Dingen*; on the next page Coleridge produces a statement permeated with Jacobi's (and Pascal's, and Wordsworth's) generic emphasis on heart: "There is one heart for the whole mighty mass of Humanity, and every pulse in each particular vessel strives to beat in concert with it."[133]

But it is in Coleridge's discussions of reason and understanding, which constitute so important a part of his discourse in *The Friend*, that Jacobi appears insistently. For instance, Coleridge says: "If further confirmation be necessary, it may be supplied by the following reflections,

---

[127] Jacobi *Werke* II 61.
[128] Ibid. III 334.
[129] Ibid. IV–1 xxiv.
[130] Ibid. IV–1 xliv.

[131] See below, Frag 2 f 12.
[132] *Friend (CC)* I 96.
[133] Ibid. I 97.

the leading thought of which I remember to have read in the work of a continental Philosopher. It should seem easy to give the definite distinction of the Reason from the Understanding, because we constantly imply it when we speak of the difference between ourselves and the brute creation."[134] Coleridge is here referring to Jacobi's *David Hume*. He continues his discussion of the existence of understanding in animals with an overt naming of Jacobi:

> But Reason is wholly denied, equally to the highest as to the lowest of the brutes; otherwise it must be wholly attributed to them, with it therefore Self-consciousness, and *personality*, or Moral Being.
>
> I should have no objection to define Reason with Jacobi, and with his friend Hemsterhuis, as an organ bearing the same relation to spiritual objects, the Universal, the Eternal, and the Necessary, as the eye bears to material and contingent phaenomena. But then it must be added, that it is an organ identical with its appropriate objects. Thus, God, the Soul, eternal Truth, &c. are the objects of Reason; but they are themselves *reason*. We name God the Supreme Reason; and Milton says, "Whence the Soul *Reason* receives, and Reason is her being."[135]

This important passage has been quoted at length because it illustrates so well the intertwinement of Coleridge's emphasis with that of Jacobi. Kant's steel-edged analysis of reason probably played the deeper role in Coleridge's commitment to that function, but his tantalizing way of proffering and then withdrawing reason as a basis for belief in God had less appeal. Coleridge needed a conception of reason that allowed him the basis for a rational belief in the Redeemer he so desperately felt he required ("Christianity and REDEMPTION are equivalent terms".)[136] Jacobi's conception could supply that basis, though Jacobi himself was in many ways a radical sceptic.

Indeed, it is important not to confuse Coleridge's fellow-feeling with Jacobi on the issues of reason and personality with a similarity in other respects. Coleridge's commitment to external nature and to science found no counterpart in Jacobi, who was interested only in abstractions and moral feelings. "The secret of the moral sense and moral feeling is the secret of lasting life", said Jacobi, "Faith and experience are therefore the only way by which we can attain to knowledge of the truth".[137] Goethe's green and golden world of life in nature is entirely absent in Jacobi. "God," wrote Goethe once to Jacobi, "has punished you with metaphysics . . . he has, on the other hand, blessed me with physics".[138]

---

[134] *Friend (CC)* I 154.
[135] Ibid. I 155–6.
[136] *AR* (1825) 303.

[137] Jacobi *Werke* VI 138.
[138] *Gedenkausgabe* XVIII 924.

The discussion of reason and understanding in *The Friend*, cited above, continues:

> Whatever is conscious *Self*-knowledge is Reason; and in this sense it may be safely defined the organ of the Super-sensuous; even as the Understanding wherever it does not possess or use the Reason, as another and inward eye, may be defined the conception of the Sensuous, or the faculty by which we generalize and arrange the phaenomena of perception: that faculty, the functions of which contain the rules and constitute the possibility of outward Experience. In short, the Understanding supposes something that is *understood*. This may be merely its own acts or forms, that is, formal Logic; but real objects, the materials of substantial knowledge, must be furnished, we might safely say revealed, to it by Organs of Sense. The understanding of the higher Brutes has only organs of outward sense, and consequently material objects only; but man's understanding has likewise an organ of inward sense, and therefore the power of acquainting itself with invisible realities or spiritual objects. This organ is the Reason.[139]

Coleridge's intense need to discriminate reason from understanding, so that his hope in a Redeemer might receive a rational basis, leads him into more finely fingered illustrations than are to be found in either Jacobi or Kant, let alone Diderot, for whom "la raison" is monolithically simply a given. Coleridge continues in his quest for compelling distinction:

> Again, the Understanding and Experience may exist without Reason. But Reason cannot exist without Understanding; nor does it or can it manifest itself but in and through the understanding, which in our elder writers is often called *discourse*, or the discursive faculty, as by Hooker, Lord Bacon, and Hobbes: and an understanding enlightened by reason Shakespeare gives as the contra-distinguishing character of man, under the name *discourse of reason*. In short, the human understanding possesses two distinct organs, the outward sense, and "the mind's eye" which is reason: wherever we use that phrase (the mind's eye) in its proper sense, and not as a mere synonyme of the memory or the fancy. In this way we reconcile the promise of Revelation, that the blessed will see God, with the declaration of St. John, God hath no one seen at any time.[140]

Coleridge anxiously attempts to exploit every consideration by which, at one and the same time, reason is the reason we all mean by that word, and something radically different from "la raison". He carefully isolates the use of the term as a groundwork of scientific thought:

> If the reader therefore will take the trouble of bearing in mind these and the following explanations, he will have removed before hand every possible difficulty

[139] *Friend (CC)* I 156.   [140] Ibid. I 156-7.

from the Friend's political section. For there is another use of the word, Reason, arising out of the former indeed, but less definite, and more exposed to misconception. In this latter use it means the understanding considered as using the Reason, so far as by the organ of Reason only we possess the ideas of the Necessary and the Universal; and this is the more common use of the word, when it is applied with *any* attempt at clear and distinct conceptions. In this narrower and derivative sense the best definition of Reason, which I can give, will be found in the third member of the following sentence, in which the understanding is described in its three-fold operation, and from each receives an appropriate name. The Sense, (vis sensitiva vel intuitiva) *per*ceives: Vis regulatrix (the understanding, in its own peculiar operation) *con*ceives: Vis rationalis (the Reason or rationalized understanding) *comprehends*. The first is impressed through the organs of sense; the second combines these multifarious impressions into individual *Notions*, and by reducing these notions to Rules, according to the analogy of all its former notices, constitutes *Experience*: the third subordinates both these notions and the rules of Experience to ABSOLUTE PRINCIPLES or necessary LAWS: and thus concerning objects, which our experience has proved to have *real* existence, it demonstrates moreover, in what way they are *possible*, and in doing this constitutes *Science*. Reason therefore, in this secondary sense, and used, *not* as a spiritual *Organ* but as a *Faculty* (namely, the Understanding or Soul *enlightened* by that organ)—Reason, I say, or the *scientific* Faculty, is the Intellection of the *possibility* or *essential* properties of things by means of the Laws that constitute them. Thus the *rational* idea of a Circle is that of a figure constituted by the circumvolution of a straight line with its one end fixed.[141]

Coleridge's commitment to his own version of reason is summoned against Rousseau as well as against the more glaringly rationalistic of the *philosophes*. In *The Friend* he discusses Rousseau at length in an essay entitled "On the Grounds of Government as Laid Exclusively in the Pure Reason; or a Statement and Critique of the Third System of Political Philosophy, Viz. The Theory of Rousseau and the French Economists". In that chapter appears a notable apostrophe to reason and its theological efficacy:

REASON! best and holiest gift of Heaven and bond of union with the Giver! The high title by which the majesty of man claims precedence over all other living creatures! Mysterious faculty, the mother of conscience, of language, of tears, and of smiles! Calm and incorruptible legislator of the soul, without whom all its other powers would "meet in mere oppugnancy." Sole principle of permanence amid endless change! in a world of discordant appetites and imagined self-interests the only one common measure![142]

The magnificent apostrophe continues, with scarcely diminished flow and pertinence, to isolate the crucial fact that whereas all other mental

---

[141] *Friend (CC)* I 157–8.   [142] Ibid I 190.

attainments are found in varying degrees in different men, reason is whole and complete in every man: "Thrice blessed faculty of Reason! all other gifts, though goodly and of celestial origin, health, strength, talents, all the powers and all the means of enjoyment, seem dispensed by chance or sullen caprice—thou alone, more than even the sunshine, more than the common air, art given to all men, and to every man alike!"[143]

Coleridge's campaign to reclaim "reason" from *la raison* is founded on the Germanic distinctions between *Vernunft* and *Verstand* discussed above. Thus in Carlyle's famous and wickedly denigrating portrait of Coleridge there appears, underneath the hilarity, an entirely accurate assessment of the central factor of Coleridgean thought that moved him towards the *magnum opus*:

> The constant gist of his discourse was lamentation over the sunk condition of the world; which he recognised to be given up to Atheism and Materialism, full of mere sordid misbeliefs, mispursuits and misresults. . . . Men's souls were blinded, hebetated; and sunk under the influence of Atheism and Materialism, and Hume and Voltaire: the world for the present was an extinct world, deserted of God. The remedy, though Coleridge himself professed to see it as in sunbeams, could not except by processes unspeakably difficult, be described to you at all. On the whole, those dead Churches, this dead English Church especially, must be brought to life again . . . . But how, but how! By attending to the "reason" of man, said Coleridge, and duly chaining-up the "understanding" of man: The *Vernunft* (Reason) and *Verstand* (Understanding) of the Germans, it all turned upon these, if you could well understand them—which you couldn't.[144]

The distinction of reason and understanding is the focal point of Coleridge's thought. One of the aims of the *Aids to Reflection*, in 1825, for instance was to "substantiate and set forth at large the momentous distinction between REASON and UNDERSTANDING", and this is preliminary to the intent to "exhibit a full and consistent scheme of the Christian Dispensation."[145] Indeed, it is hardly possible to overestimate the centrality of the distinction between reason and understanding in Coleridge's thought.

Why was the distinction crucial? Because "From the Understanding to the Reason there is no continuous *ascent* possible".[146] It may be sufficient partly to gloss the statement by summoning a passage from *The Friend*:

> The ground-work, therefore, of all true philosophy is the full apprehension of the difference between the contemplation of reason, namely, that intuition of things

[143] *Friend (CC)* i 191.
[144] *Carlyle* xi 58–9.
[145] *AR* (1825) viii–ix.
[146] *CL* v 138.

which arises when we possess ourselves, as one with the whole, which is substantial knowledge, and that which presents itself when transferring reality to the negations of reality, to the ever-varying framework of the uniform life, we think of ourselves as separated beings, and place nature in antithesis to mind, as object to subject, thing to thought, death to life. This is abstract knowledge, or the science of the mere understanding. By the former, we know that existence is its own predicate, self-affirmation, the one attribute in which all others are contained, not as parts, but as manifestations.[147]

The *magnum opus* was to be Coleridge's attempt at establishing that vital diversity. Its overriding purpose was "the reconcilement of the moral faith with the Reason".[148] Under the aegis of understanding, it was to render atheism and materialism, Locke and common sense, their due, and under that of reason it was to preserve the conception of self and soul and God. "All we can or need say is, that the existence of a necessary Being is so transcendently Rational, that it is Reason itself".[149]

In this view, reason looked not only backward to Plato and Pythagoras[150]—to mathematical theorems and archetypal forms found not in experience but in the functioning of the mind itself—but proleptically incorporated some of the analytical subtleties later elaborated by Husserl: "First, in Reason there is and can be no *degree*. Deus introit aut non introit.—Secondly in Reason there are no *means* nor ends: Reason itself being one with the ultimate end, of which it is the manifestation. Thirdly, Reason has no concern with *things* (i.e. the impermanent flux of particulars) but with permanent *Relations*; & is to be defined, even in its lowest or theoretical attribute, as the Power which enables man to draw *necessary* and *universal* conclusions from particular facts or forms—ex gr. From any 3 cornered thing that the 2 sides of a Triangle are & must be greater than the third.[151]

VI. THE HIGHER CRITICISM

The enormously valued distinction between "reason" and "understanding" assumed added centrality in Coleridge's thought because it enabled him to cope with the gathering pertinence of the Higher Criticism of the Bible. Always culturally prescient, Coleridge was not only well informed as to the state of Biblical studies in his own time, but saw clearly

[147] *Friend (CC)* I 520–1.
[148] See below, Frag 3 p 19.
[149] Brinkley 128.
[150] C hoped that his thought when fully preserved would be seen to be "no other than the system of Pythagoras and of Plato revived and purified from impure mixtures" (*BL—CC—*I 263).
[151] *CL* v 137–8, 12 Feb 1821.

the devastating effects the Higher Criticism would later wreak upon those who were committed to fundamentalist understandings of the Christian *kerygma*. But for Coleridge, fortified by "reason", the increasing attacks on the integrity of the Biblical accounts did little damage to his own view of Christianity. He finds no difficulty in speaking, in the *Opus Maximum*, to "those who have yet to acquire a belief in the authority of those writings [i.e. the books of the Bible], which [were] composed by so many different men, in ages so different, and under such different circumstances", because those writings "do yet contain so uniform a correspondence to the prescript of pure reason".[152] Reason relegated both the Higher Criticism and the texts it decomposed to the realm of understanding, while Coleridge himself remained secure in "the distinction between the *Reason*, as the source of principles, the true celestial influx and porta Dei in hominem internum, and the *Understanding*".[153]

Some of the more widely known works of Higher Criticism have become landmarks in the history of culture. David Strauss's *Das Leben Jesu* of 1835, translated into English by no less a figure than George Eliot, contributed greatly to the "melancholy, long withdrawing roar" of the sea of Christian faith; Ernest Renan's *La Vie de Jésus* of 1863 wrought still more destruction.

Works such as these, however, are only the tip of the iceberg in Higher Criticism; they are all, to one extent or another, popularisations of more unremitting and less heralded decompositions of the authority of the Bible. The Higher Criticism, as such, began in the seventeenth century, although adumbrations of its methods were current as far back as the headwaters of Christianity itself. That Trypho, whom Justin Martyr summoned all his powers to try to refute, was a determined and effective Higher Critic, as were Celsus, the opponent of Origen, and Origen himself. Still, it was in the seventeenth century that the Higher Criticism became an unmistakable component of the intellectual landscape. Grotius's *Annotationes in Vetus et Novum Testamentum* (1642) substituted philological criticism for assumptions of divine inspiration; Spinoza's *Tractatus philosophico-politicus* (1670) devastatingly noted the many internal contradictions of the Old Testament; Richard Simon's *Histoire critique du Vieux Testament* (1678) denied that the Pentateuch had been authored by Moses (although Simon, a devout Catholic, was opposed to Spinoza).

---

[152] See below, Frag 2 f 23. Again: "The fruits and attainments of the Reason are at hand to compensate, and make indemnification for, whatever diminution, either of the proofs, or their influence on the mind, may be inherent—in the nature of all historical testimony—by the ravages, or even the mere lapse, of time" (Frag 1 f 21).

[153] *CL* v 137, 12 Feb 1821.

The eighteenth century witnessed ever-augmenting criticism of the integrity of the Bible and of its circumstances of composition. Johann David Michaelis, at Göttingen from 1746 to 1791, published *Einleitung in das Neue Testament* in 1750, and in his *Mosäisches Recht* (6 vols, 1770–5) argued that the legislation of the Pentateuch was a human, not a divine, achievement. Robert Lowth's *Lectures on the Sacred Poetry of the Hebrews*, delivered in Latin in 1749–50. considered the Old Testament not as theology but as literature. Hermann Samuel Reimarus, whose life was written by David Strauss, wrote a work entitled *Apologie oder Schutzschrift für die vernünftigen Verehrer Gottes*, which, though not fully published until the nineteenth century, served as the basis for Lessing's sceptical *Wolfenbüttel Fragmente* of 1774–5, which rejected miracles and revelation and accused the authors of the Bible of contradiction and conscious fraud. Coleridge called Lessing "the most formidable Infidel".[154]

The most formidable of the Higher Critics in Britain was the Catholic scholar Alexander Geddes, who, beginning in 1786, planned a new translation of the Bible, the first volume of which was published in 1792. Coleridge met Geddes and carried a letter of introduction, which still exists, from him to Dr. Paulus at Heidelberg.[155]

Elinor Shaffer notes that Coleridge had a good knowledge of the tendencies of the Higher Criticism before he went to Germany; his "knowledge of German textual criticism of the Bible dated in all probability from his earliest Unitarian contacts at Cambridge". Once he arrived in Germany and began to learn German, Coleridge took special interest in the work of Johann Gottfried Eichhorn, who came to Göttingen in 1788, was a considerable presence there during Coleridge's student days, and published widely and influentially. Eichhorn distinguished the "Jehovist" from the "Elohist" sources in Genesis, and the popular mode of Deuteronomy from the priestly law in Exodus, Leviticus, and Numbers.

Coleridge knew Eichhorn's writings in thorough detail. Indeed, he extensively annotated Eichhorn's *Einleitung ins Alte Testament* (3 vols), his *Einleitung in die apokryphischen Schriften des Alten Testament*, two sets of his *Einleitung in das Neue Testament* (3 vols), and two sets of his *Commentarius in Apocalypsin Joannis* (2 vols).[156] Eichhorn, as others have noted, "was probably the greatest single source in Coleridge's exegetical background".[157]

The Higher Criticism was particularly destructive of Protestant belief

---

[154] *CL* I 197.
[155] Shaffer 27–8.
[156] See *CM* (*CC*) II 369–520.
[157] Shaffer 22.

(notwithstanding the fact that it had been chiefly espoused by Unitarians attempting to discomfit the Anglican establishment), which depended on the acceptance of those very Biblical texts that this criticism—by demonstrating multiple authorships, chronological anomalies, similarities to other writings, and internal contradictions—so successfully decomposed. Its effect was not quite so deleterious on Catholic doctrine, which depended more on the great church synods of early Christianity and less on a fundamentalist reading of the Bible.

It bothered Coleridge not at all. His deep faith was never allowed to ground itself—or misground itself—on the shifting and unstable sands of "the Jewish Literarity" in which the books of the Bible were composed; rather, his faith was firmly planted in the ground supplied by that "reason" to which he was so comprehensively committed. He, accordingly, found no difficulty in conceding that the Biblical writers were "inspired", but at the same time realising that, as fallible mortals bound by their own time and situation, they were not necessarily always perspicuous or correct. Thus in 1826, he writes:

It was by an effort of Self-denial that during my late severe indisposition I withdrew my especial study and meditation from the 4th Gospel and the Epistles of the Apostles John and Paul I. to a free examination of the first three Gospels, and a review of the Controversy respecting their authority & necessity begun by Lessing, and their authenticity and origin which commenced with Eichhorn's Theory of a Proto-euagglion and continued to Schleiermacher's Counter-theory unfolded in his Essay on the Gospel of Luke which is the last work, that I at least have seen; and II. to a careful continuous perusal of the Apocalypse in the original Greek and the Commentary of Coccëius (b. 1603, d. 1669), to whom long before Janus and Heumann the credit belongs of expunging the Nicolaitans from the list of Heresies, and evincing the little reliance that can be placed on the assertions of Irenaeus and the Fathers generally, taken apart from their authorities—while even these are too often of a very suspicious character, from the want of all sound principles of Criticism in the discrimination of Spurious from genuine Works.—My motive for the former investigation was furnished by the translation and publication of Schleiermacher's Essay with a full account of the Controversy and all the controversial Works of any Note, that have appeared in Germany since Eichhorn's Introduction to the New Testament, and Bishop Marsh's Modification of Eichhorn's Theory in this Country.[158]

Coleridge could lend himself so fully to the criticism of the ancient testimony because to him religion did not depend on their imperfect glimpses of the truth but rather on reason itself. His acceptance of this view was enabled by the true meaning of "inspiration". The word can-

[158] *CN* IV 5323.

not mean that God literally dictated to the Biblical writers, for then they would be mere automatons; rather, it must mean that the light of truth shone behind and through their time-bound and dimly perceived efforts. As Coleridge said:

> On the subject of Inspiration, I will only say thus much—that if my scheme does not satisfy every moral, and every spiritual purpose, that has or can be pretended for the popular belief, which reducing the Sacred Writers to passive instruments, *pens* in the hands of an invisible Agent, might be called the *Automaton* Scheme; and if it do not increase, rather than diminish, the reverence and deep spiritual interest, in relation to the Canonical Books collectively;—I will be myself the first to renounce it. I too contend for their *Inspiration*; but I contend that πνευμα and λογος are distinct operations, that may or may not be united in the same act, and that Inspiration is not in *all* cases accompanied by, much less the same with, *Miraculous dictation*.[159]

The comfort and correction always available from "reason" allowed Coleridge both to revere the ancient Biblical writers and to believe it possible to understand religion better than they did. As he says in a luminous qualification:

> It does seem to me a very mean & false view of Christianity to suppose that even the Apostles themselves had the degree of clearness & enlargement which a philosophic Believer of the present day may enjoy—Think only of the vast inferiority of the other Apostles to John & Paul—and the distinct marks in the writings of the latter that he was becoming more and more doubtful of the Jewish Literarity in which he as well as the rest had understood the Second Coming of our Lord. What is Christianity at any one period?—The Ideal of the Human Soul at that period.[160]

A fundamentalist reading of the Bible, therefore, was entirely irrelevant to Coleridge's Christianity. He considered "the New Testament as a collection of contemporary yet separate works by several and independent authors, each of whom may furnish available evidence in behalf of the others, subject to no greater caution than would be required in weighing & collating the testimony of *any* six or seven contemporary historians and advocates of presumptive respectability, who were the professed partisans of the same cause".[161]

His faith, in consequence, was immune to the ravages of the Higher Criticism. Christianity rested, first and foremost, on "reason"; and what it had to provide, to be believable for Coleridge, were only a very few essentials: "I am secure of my faith, in the main points—a personal God,

---

[159] *CL* VI 617.
[160] Ibid. VI 552.

[161] App A Frag (*a*) f 6ᵛ.

a surviving principle of Life, & that I need & that I have a Redeemer—
But in one I have attained to a conviction which till of late I never had
in any available form or degree—namely, the confidence in the efficacy
of Prayer. I know by experience, that it is Light, Strength, and Com-
fort.—"[162] Secure in all the main points of his faith, Coleridge could ap-
proach the ancient Biblical writers and exegetes with as much discrimi-
nation as the most sceptical Higher Critic.

I am not ashamed to say, that a single Chapter of St Paul's Epistles or St John's
Gospel is of more value to me, in light & in life, in love & in Comfort, than the
Books of the Apocalypse, Daniel & Zachariah, all together. In fact I scarcely
know what to make even of the second Coming of our Lord. Is he not "my Lord
and my God"? Is there aught good in the Soul, and he not a Dweller there?—
I am aware of the necessity of a mid course between Quakerism & a MERELY
historical Christianity—But I dare not conceal my conviction, that on certain
points we may have had clearer views of Christianity than some of the Apostles
had—[163]

Coleridge, in sum, was not in bondage to the Bible. "My principle has
ever been, that Reason is *subjective* revelation, Revelation *objective* rea-
son—and that *our* business is not to *derive* Authority from the *mythoi* of
the Jews and the first Jew-Christians (i.e. the O. and N. Testament) but
to *give* it to them."[164] But even though, for Coleridge, Christianity was
suspended inviolate, above the melting ice-floes of "Jewish Literarity",
by the golden chain of "reason", an eventual regrounding became all the
more desirable, and that grounding the *magnum opus* was designed to
supply.

VII. THE *MAGNUM OPUS* AS SYSTEM

The fact that Coleridge divided the reasoning function into "reason" and
"understanding", and thereby retained rather than dismissed those ele-
ments against which he fought, is definitive of his mental procedure. He
was by temperament an includer and a reconciler, not a rejecter. "To rec-
oncile", he once said is "truly the work of the Inspired".[165] "The great
Maxim of Leighton", he wrote approvingly, "intellectual or political, is
Subordinate, not exclude. Nature in her ascent leaves nothing behind; but
at each step subordinates & glorifies."[166]
This attitude set Coleridge aside from many who might otherwise be

---

[162] *CL* vi 577.
[163] Ibid. vi 550.
[164] Ibid. vi 895.

[165] *CN* ii 2208.
[166] Brinkley 339.

at least partly aligned with him in rejection of what the Enlightenment represented. Blake, for instance, was as concerned as was Coleridge to free himself from the rationalism of the Enlightenment, but his procedure was simply to denounce what he could not accept. For Coleridge, on the other hand, the solution was not simply to reject association psychology and affirm a theory of imagination against it. Blake candidly admits that men and works such as "Locke on Human Understanding" inspire his "Contempt & Abhorrence"; "they mock Inspiration & Vision Inspiration & Vision was then now is & I hope will always Remain my Element my Eternal Dwelling place. How then can I hear it Contemned without returning Scorn for Scorn."[167]

Coleridge too regarded Locke with "Contempt & Abhorrence". The crucial difference, however, was that where Blake could simply assert his disagreement, Coleridge found it essential not merely to abuse Newton and Locke but to argue against them on their own cognitive ground. In his phrasing, it was necessary to remove "the sandy Sophisms of Locke, and the Mechanic Dogmatists" by "demonstrating that the Senses were living growths and developements of the Mind & Spirit in a much juster as well as higher sense, than the mind can be said to be formed by the Senses—".[168]

Coleridge's desire for logical demonstration, along with his passion for reconciling and his love of connecting (he laments that Addison "produced a passion for the unconnected in the mind of Englishmen"[169]), together impelled him towards system as the necessary form of his intellectual aspiration. His mental activity was always characterised by "a striving after connected insight".[170]

My system, if I may venture to give it so fine a name, is the only attempt, I know, ever made to reduce all knowledges into harmony. It opposes no other system, but shows what was true in each; and how that which was true in the particular, in each of them became error, *because* it was only half the truth. I have endeavoured to unite the insulated fragments of truth, and therewith to frame a perfect mirror. I show to each system that I fully understand and rightfully appreciate what that system means; but then I lift up that system to a higher point of view, from which I enable it to see its former position, where it was, indeed, but under another light and with different relations;—so that the fragment of truth is not only acknowledged, but explained.[171]

---

[167] William Blake *Complete Poetry and Prose* ed David V. Erdman (2nd ed Berkeley CA 1982) 650.
[168] *CL* iv 574.

[169] *CL* iii 279.
[170] See below, Frag 1 f 37.
[171] *TT (CC)* ii 147–8, 12 Sept 1831.

The irreducible fact about the *magnum opus*, accordingly, is that it was to be a systematic enquiry, or, as he called it in 1827, "a voluminous System of Philosophy and Divinity".[172]

In his emphasis on system Coleridge not only honoured his own primary intellectual attitudes of reconciliation and connection, he also showed himself an authentic participant in the thought of his time: system was in the ascendant in the minds of the deepest thinkers in that German culture he so much admired.[173] The greatest of these, Kant, had laid down in 1781 the dictum that "human reason is by its nature architectonic, and looks upon all knowledge as belonging to a possible system".[174] He had said that "The unity of reason is the *unity* of a system".[175]

Indeed, Kant projected, though he did not achieve, a "system of metaphysics" (*System der praktischen Weltweisheit*).[176] What he did achieve, his great *Kritik*, he considered as "propadeutic" or preliminary to system, to the "system of pure reason", which exhibits "in systematic connection the whole body . . . of philosophical knowledge arising out of pure reason".[177]

Fichte followed Kant. As he said in his *Ueber den Begriff der Wissenschaftslehre überhaupt* (1794), "philosophy is a scientific procedure . . . a scientific procedure has systematic form; all propositions in it hang together in a single basic proposition and unite themselves in it into a whole—this is generally conceded".[178] The science of knowledge, he reiterates, "must have *systematic form*".[179]

The concept of the *magnum opus*'s uniqueness as a vast harmoniser of knowledge, an effort "to unite the insulated fragments of truth", finds a parallel in the vision of Novalis, who did not himself achieve system : "The philosopher who can transform all single philosophemes into one single one . . . achieves a maximum in his philosophy. He achieves the maximum as a philosopher if he unites all philosophies into a single philosophy."[180] Hegel, who did achieve a philosophical system, projects much the same vision of true philosophy as retaining rather than rejecting the "diversity of philosophical systems":

---

[172] *CL* vi 705.

[173] As he wrote to his young friend James Gillman, Jr, "The main thing, however, next to your health is your acquiring a sound solid *foundation* for a thorough Knowledge of the German Language—in order to a command over the treasures of historical & critical Learning, packed up therein" (*CL* vi

810, 10 Aug 1829).

[174] *Kritik der reinen Vernunft* (Kant *GS* iii 329).

[175] Ibid. iii 448.

[176] Kant *GS* x 441.

[177] Ibid. iv 543–4.

[178] *Fichte* i 38.

[179] Ibid. i 48.

[180] *Novalis* ii 586.

The more the ordinary mind takes the opposition between true and false to be fixed, the more it is accustomed to expect either agreement or contradiction with a given philosophical system . . . . It does not conceive the diversity of philosophical systems as the progressive evolution of truth; rather, it sees only contradiction in that variety. The bud disappears when the blosson breaks through . . . when the fruit comes, the blossom may be explained to be a false form of the plant's existence . . . . These stages are not merely differentiated; they supplant one another as being incompatible with one another. But the ceaseless activity of their own inherent nature makes them at the same time moments of an organic unity, where they not merely do not contradict one another, but where one is as necessary as the other; and this equal necessity of all moments constitutes alone and for that reason the life of the whole.[181]

It followed, for Hegel as for Coleridge, that "knowledge is real only as science or as system and can be represented only in that way".[182] "Truth is realized only as system."[183]

For Coleridge, system was not a fashion but almost an obsession. Indeed, at one point he says that "All system so far is power", and illustrates the contention by pointing out that "a systematic criminal, self-consistent and entire in wickedness, who entrenches villainy within villainy, and barricadoes crime by crime, has removed a world of obstacles by the mere decision, that he will have no obstacles, but those of force and brute matter".[184]

His total commitment to system went hand in hand with a rejection of eclecticism. It is a common mistake of commentators on Coleridge to infer from the fragmentary nature of his utterance and the heterogeneous range of his concerns that at most he should be seen as endorsing a body of thought rather than a system. But that is totally to misconceive the character of his mentation, where everything was connected to everything else. "Eclectic Philosophy", he notes scornfully at one point, "'Syncretism'; 'Adoption of the Best', or by whatever other phrases the same process of intellect may be represented, is the Death of all Philosophy. Truth is one and entire, because it is *vital*."[185] "O! This picking & choosing is a grievous evil."[186] As a final example, one projection of what must surely be an alternate though highly idiosyncratic version of the *magnum opus* emphasises as its very title the omnipresence of system in Coleridge's intellectual procedure:

[181] *Hegel* III 12.
[182] Ibid. III 27.
[183] Ibid. III 28.

[184] *LS (CC)* 66.
[185] *CN* III 4251.
[186] Ibid.

THE SYSTEM
conveyed in discourses
and Dialogues concerning Science,
Philosophy and Religion.
In ~~three~~ four Parts
by
S. T. Coleridge

———

Part the first.—entitled
    The Library
Part 2nd—entitled
    The Holly Grove in the Winter Garden.
Part 3rd—entitled
    The Cavern on the Sea-Shore
Part 4th—entitled
    Travel Talk in Autumn: or Dialogues among the Lakes and
Mountains.[187]

The *magnum opus* was to contain Coleridge's "system of Philosophy and Faith", the result of all his "researches and reflections concerning, God, Nature and Man".[188] Coleridge lamented "the contrast between the continuous and systematic character of [his] Principles, and the occasional & fragmentary way, in which they have hitherto been brought before the Public",[189] And we must guard against mistaking the fragmentary nature of the *magnum opus* as in any way implying doubt about the necessity of system.

VIII. THE *MAGNUM OPUS* AND NATURAL SCIENCE

The systematic nature of the *magnum opus* was a product on the one hand of Coleridge's urge towards inclusion and reconciliation, and on the other of his passion for connecting. But a systematic understanding of reality had necessarily to account for the structure and relation of the external world as well as for those human and religious conceptions that it was Coleridge's primary aim to validate. It had to account not only for

---

[187] *CN* III 4416.
[188] *CL* VI 714, 28 Nov 1827. See also *CL* VI 539–40, Jan 1826; 715, 28 Nov 1827; 781, 19 Jan 1829; 864, undated fragment of about 1831.
[189] *CL* VI 847–8, 29 Nov 1830.

consciousness, but also for the objects of consciousness, and, to adapt Jasper's term, for "the Encompassing" of consciousness. That is to say, any comprehensive system had to take notice of the reality and relationship of three focal entities: mind, nature, and whatever stands above or subsists beneath both: God. That requirement had been specifically formulated by Christian Wolff, in his programmatic *Discursus praeliminaris de philosophia in genere* (1728); but the requirement rested on logic, not authority.[190]

The taking into account of the external world was necessary to Coleridge's plan for a philosophical system. Although he was most concerned to defend the idea of man's relation to God, that defence willy-nilly involved him in the structure of the objective world. Coleridge had no scientific training (he frequently lamented his lack of mathematics[191] and would doubtless have been pleased had he lived to know that his principle of the "divine Tetractys" probably led to the discovery of algebraic quaternions by the great mathematician William Rowan Hamilton),[192] but he had a strong scientific interest. By temperament as well as by need, moreover, Coleridge was drawn to scientific inquiry. Indeed, as a commentator has said, "the most striking trait in the personality of Coleridge is incontestably the universal curiosity that impelled him to interest himself in the most diverse subjects with the same passion, the same desire to know, the same intense capacity of attention and reflection".[193] His notebooks provide ample justification for such a conclusion.

Despite his lack of formal scientific training, Coleridge was not temperamentally averse to the systematic requirements by which the *magnum opus* had to involve itself in natural science.[194] The general character of Romanticism, too, urged him in this direction, for the intensified awareness of external nature was an irreducible component of the Romantic shift in sensibility. It is characteristic of the whole tendency of his thought, therefore, that Coleridge reproves the Cambridge Platonists for their "ignorance of Natural Science, their Physiography scant in fact and stuffed out with fables, their Physiology embrangled with an inapplicable Logic and a misgrowth of Entia Rationalia". He continues: ". . .

[190] Wolff 33.
[191] See e.g. a marginal note of 1824: "O my most unhappy unwise neglect of Mathematics at Jesus College, Cambridge! No week passes, in which I do not groan for it!" (*CM—CC—*III 349.)
[192] See Hankins, e.g. 247, 432 n 2.
[193] Deschamps 69.
[194] For perhaps the most comprehensive overview of Coleridge's relation to the science of his time, see Trevor H. Levere *Poetry Realized in Nature: Samuel Taylor Coleridge and Early Nineteenth-century Science* (Cambridge, 1981). In this admirable work, however, there is a tendency to overestimate the validity of Coleridge's scientific lucubrations.

if Christianity is ⟨to be⟩ the Religion of the world . . . if this be true, so true must it be, that the ~~Scheme~~ Book of Nature and the Book of Revelation with the whole history of Man as the intermediate Link must be the integral & coherent Parts of one great Work. And the conclusion is: that a Scheme of the Christian Faith which does not arise out of and shoots its beams downward into, the Scheme of Nature, but stands aloof, as an insulated After-thought, must be false or distorted in all its particulars."[195]

Even without the formal systematic requirements of the *magnum opus*, Coleridge's concern for inclusion and connection of themselves led him towards scientific interests. As he himself said, the totality of his convictions would constitute a system such "that of all Systems that have even been presented, this has the least of *Mysticism*, the very Object throughout from the first page to the last being to reconcile the dictates of common Sense with the conclusions of scientific Reasoning".[196] The systematic attempt to "reconcile" elements of his experience with the "conclusions of scientific Reasoning" accounts for the scientific involvement of the *magnum opus*.

IX. THE *MAGNUM OPUS* AND *NATURPHILOSOPHIE*

Of the scientific materials Coleridge encountered in his voluminous reading, those most pertinent to his systematic accounting were unfortunately not the best available. Although he read in various scientific areas, his attention was largely focused on a body of German scientific speculation called *Naturphilosophie*, a mode soon to be discredited by the work of rigorous scientists such as Liebig, Faraday, Helmholtz, Maxwell, Virchow and others, but that enjoyed a considerable standing in the speculative intoxication of early Romanticism.

At that time, the strict division that obtains today between formal science and amateur speculation did not exist. It was, after all, the journalist and statesman Benjamin Franklin who gave the initial scientific impetus to the understanding of electricity,[197] And the journalist, theologian, and general gadfly Joseph Priestley can largely be credited with the discovery of oxygen.[198] The *littérateur* Goethe devoted immense ef-

---

[195] CM (*CC*) III 919–20.
[196] *CL* IV 706, 27 Feb 1817.
[197] See *Franklin's Experiments: A New Edition of Franklin's Experiments and Observations on Electricity* ed I. Bernard Cohen, with a critical and historical introduction (Cambridge MA

1941).
[198] Priestley was also in the thick of contemporary investigations of electricity. See his *The History and Present State of Electricity, with Original Experiments* (3rd ed 2 vols London 1775).

fort to biological and optical research,[199] while a true scientific genius like Faraday possessed almost none of the formal training that would be necessary today in order to be a scientist.[200] In this fluid situation, amateurism flourished, and the claims of empiricism versus those of mere speculation had not as yet been decisively adjudicated.

The leading idea of *Naturphilosophie* was to see nature and mind as twin aspects of a common unity, and its characteristic method was to present schematic wholes that accounted for all reality. The enabling concept and the program for all subsequent development in *Naturphilosophie* were supplied by Schelling's formula of 1797: "Die Natur soll der sichtbare Geist, der Geist die unsichtbare Natur seyn. Hier also, in der absoluten Identität des Geistes in uns und der Natur ausser uns muss sich das Problem, wie eine Natur ausser uns möglich sey, auflösen" (tr: "nature is to be regarded as visible mind, mind as invisible nature. Here therefore, in the absolute identity of the mind in us and of the nature outside us must the problem of how a nature outside us is possible resolve itself").[201]

Coleridge was well acquainted with the treatise that incorporated this initiating formula (he read it in the second edition of 1803), and in September 1817 he writes that "Man separates from Nature only that Nature may be found again in a higher dignity in Man. For as the Ideal is realized in Nature, so is the Real idealized in Man."[202] This statement, cited by a commentator as the apogee of Coleridge's scientific thought, is clearly little more than a restatement of Schelling's programmatic formula.[203]

By the time he began dictating the actual content of the *magnum opus*, however, Coleridge was perhaps even more involved with later exponents of *Naturphilosophie* than with Schelling himself, although so many common emphases exist among the *Naturphilosophen* that it is not

[199] See, e.g. Frederick Burwick *The Damnation of Newton: Goethe's Color Theory and Romantic Perception* (Berlin & New York 1986).

[200] Faraday had virtually no mathematics, and his original interest in electricity arose not from formal training but merely from reading the article "Electricity" in the *Encyclopaedia Britannica* of 1797 (Agassi 13). His genius, however, was channelled by the exigencies of the laboratory, his method being not so much one of strict induction as one of constant testing of intuitive hypotheses, a continuing process of trial and error and rectification.

[201] *Schelling* II 56.

[202] *CL* IV 769. As late as 1823, even though he was by then well aware of the flaws of *Naturphilosophie*, C clung to his hopes for this wonderful formula: "Now when the Ideal is realized in Nature, and the Real idealized in the Mind, there is the sum and content of SPECULATIVE PHILOSOPHY" (*CN* IV 5094).

[203] Miller 96.

always easy to speak with certainty. These later exponents, the chief of whom were Lorenz Oken, Gotthilf Heinrich von Schubert, Heinrich Steffens, Ignaz Paul Vital Troxler, and Gottfried Reinhold Treviranus, were well known to Coleridge[204] and he annotated a number of their treatises.[205] Perhaps Steffens was the *Naturphilosoph* Coleridge held in highest regard during his later years—certainly he is the one most praised in the *Opus Maximum*. There he is called "a still more Orphic mind" than Schelling.[206] Coleridge criticised all of them, however, for their pantheism (for instance, he rejects "Oken's Monstrosities, and semi-blasphemies or confusion of God with the World");[207] and as will subsequently appear, he attempted not so much to copy them as to pursue a parallel path that would eventually diverge into his own systematic philosophico-theological preoccupations.[208]

It is important to remember, however, that all the *Naturphilosophen* followed their leader, Schelling. Haym notes that one of the most remarkable characteristics of Schelling was his extraordinary quickness in seeing the metaphysical possibility of the discoveries made in late eighteenth-century physics and chemistry.[209] "Schelling" summarised Novalis succinctly in about 1798, "is the *philosopher of modern chemistry*".[210] Synthesising the tendencies of scientific involvement in the late eighteenth century—notably the emphases of Goethe, Kant, Herder, Franklin, Lavoisier, Galvani, Volta, and Kielmeyer—Schelling produced a model for *Naturphilosophie* as follows:

Schelling begins his construction of nature with the deduction of matter, the substratum of all appearances. Matter pulsates in eternal motion; repulsion and attraction are its driving forces, and their synthesis produces the phenomenon of gravity. Thus "universal matter" is constructed out of three elements: repulsion, attraction and gravity. This universal, undefined matter rises on the next step of

---

[204] As were "Johann Friedrich Blumenbach, Adam Karl August Eschenmayer, Kant, Fichte, Schelling, Hegel, Georg August Goldfuss, Johann Christian Heinroth, Hans Christian Oersted, Oken, Gotthilf Heinrich von Schubert and Steffens. Of these Kant, Schelling and Steffens had the greatest impact on Coleridge's emerging views of nature" (Modiano 139). Not all of those figures, however, are customarily classed among the *Naturphilosophen*.

[205] See *CM* (*CC*) III for C's annotations on Oersted and Oken, *CM* (*CC*) IV for those on Schelling and Schubert, and *CM* (*CC*) V for those on Steffens.

[206] See below, Frag 4 f 92.

[207] *CN* III 2249.

[208] For a single characteristic example, in the midst of the accumulated *naturphilosophischen* echoes in the letter of Sept 1817 cited below (nn 212, 213), C comments that these arguments are "under the disadvantage of beginning (as far as the mere *science* is concerned) with the lowest, per ascensum: whereas the only true point of view is that of Religion, namely per descensum" (*CL* IV 769).

[209] Haym 578.

[210] *Novalis* III 266.

the great process of nature to "qualitatively distinct matter" (dynamic process). The levels of the dynamic process represent a repetition of the original process of universal matter. Nature, reproducing its original productivity, raises itself to the second potence, as its levels: *magnetism, electricity,* and *chemistry,* are perceived. The linking bond of these three levels is light. Galvanism forms the transition from the second to the third potence, from inorganic to organic nature (plants, animals and men). The levels of the organic are: *reproduction, irritability,* and *sensibility.* The linking bond is called life; it encompasses the whole of nature, but possesses the greatest "energy" (*Schwungkraft*) in the realm of the organic. *Gravity, light,* and *life* are the three fundamental forces of nature. Above all, the pervasive splitting of the potences into three—(a) repulsion, attraction, gravity; (b) magnetism, electricity, chemistry; and (c) reproduction, irritability and sensibility—implies an organizing world soul. (A thought by the way that comes from Steffens).

To this point we may know only one side of the structure of reality: the three potences. Each new potence is a higher product of nature, each individual level within the potence is at any given time higher than the preceding one. Man represents the highest level, and when he achieves knowledge, nature, which is unconscious (more precisely: pre-conscious) mind, finds itself in him.

The second side of the structure of reality is called *polarity* . . . . Matter, with its forces of repulsion, striving, and inhibition, reveals to us a polar dynamism that works through the whole of nature. The life of the universe rests upon this duality of forces. The absolute is active, therefore it can never entirely be at its destination, since otherwise all activity would be canceled. Accordingly, each level and further each organic type is the result of the inhibition of a force striving to reach infinity; for nature ascends (*steigert sich*) ceaselessly, posits ever new, higher levels and types. Each individual level is a miscarried attempt of nature to represent the whole. This whole is, however, as noted above, constructed in a polar form. "It is the first principle of a philosophical doctrine of nature, in all nature to start from polarity and duality." Attraction and repulsion in matter (Kant), positive and negative magnetism, positive and negative electricity (Volta), acids and alkalis (Lavoisier), plants and animals, which relate themselves to one another as deoxydation and oxydation (Steffens), and in the animal world the polar tension of the sexes. This, in outline, is the *Naturphilosophie* of Schelling.[211]

None of the elements of this model was original, and in its emphasis on process and movement, growth and ascent, it took up the deepest motifs of Romanticism as such. Indeed, both the initial attractiveness and the eventual uselessness of *Naturphilosophie* rested upon the almost uncanny way in which Schelling was able to synthesise scientific modernities with the metaphorical urgencies of the Romantic sensibility and use the resulting structure for philosophical formulation.

[211] Bernoulli & Kern vi–viii.

It was this synthesising tendency that made *Naturphilosophie* so attractive a beacon for Coleridge's systematic hopes. The outline of *Naturphilosophie* provided above, with its manipulations of attraction, repulsion, and gravity, its "second potence" of magnetism, electricity, and chemistry, as well as its play with light, galvanism, reproduction, irritability, and sensibility and its emphasis on polarity, may be juxtaposed with Coleridge's remarks in the letter of September 1817 quoted above: "But when I take what is Length in the first power, Breadth in the second, and Depth in the third; when I take these, I say, as corresponded to by Attraction, Repulsion, and Gravitation, and these again by Magnetism, Electricity, and Galvanism or Chemismus—these by an X, a Y, and Z—& these & whatever else may intervene, as corresponded to by Sensibility, Irritability, and Reproduction . . . ."[212] and further down: ". . . the two Poles of the material Universe are established, viz. Light and Gravitation. But observe that Poles imply a null punct or point which being both is neither, and neither only because it is the Identity of Both. The Life of Nature consists in the tendency of the Poles to re-unite, and to find themselves in the re-union . . . .[213] It is evident that the materials of Coleridge's formulations, along with their scientific context, are supplied by *Naturphilosophie*. And this is true a fortiori for the specific cosmogonic formulations of the *Opus Maximum*.

X. THE *MAGNUM OPUS* AND THE PRINCIPLE OF POLARITY

The two fundamental principles for the development of *Naturphilosophie* as promulgated by Schelling and his followers, were evolutionary ascent (*Steigerung*) and polarity (*Polarität*). The *magnum opus* was involved with both principles.

Polarity was endemic to all manifestations of *Naturphilosophie*, and indeed the initiating idea that nature is visible mind and mind invisible nature is itself a polar construct. As Schopenhauer noted in retrospect, a chief characteristic of the "*Naturphilosophen* of Schelling's school" was their universal emphasis on the fact that "*polarity*, that is, the splitting of a force into two qualitatively different and opposite activities striving for reunion . . . is a basic type of almost all the phenomena of nature, from the magnet and crystal up to man".[214]

Such an emphasis was accepted by Coleridge. "All, that is finite", he says, "is conceivable only as a balance or unition of opposite Activities".[215] Indeed the scientific commitment of the *magnum opus*, as dictated

[212] *CL* IV 768–9, Sept 1817.
[213] Ibid. IV 771.
[214] Schopenhauer II 171.
[215] *CN* III 4186.

by the requirements of system, found natural expression and happy vitality in the principle of polarity, for by this means Coleridge's primary preoccupation with the human being came into alignment with the preoccupation with nature: "In my literary Life you will find a sketch of the *subjective* Pole of the Dynamic Philosophy; the rudiments of *Self*-construction, barely enough to let a thinking mind see *what it is like* . . . while the enclosed Scrawl contains a very, *very* rude and fragmentary delineation of the *Objective* Pole, or the Science of the Construction of Nature".[216] It was entirely to be expected, therefore, that in his longest projection for the actual contents of the *magnum opus*, under "Part the Second, Division Second", Coleridge presents the rubric "Polar Forces".[217]

But polarity was much more for Coleridge than a mere echo of the *Naturphilosophen*. Four qualifications must be added to an understanding of the role of polarity in the thought of the time and of Coleridge in particular. Polarity is a defining component for the entire Romantic movement; it is not limited to the *Naturphilosophen,* but occurs with equal urgency in major figures such as Hegel and Goethe and relatively minor ones such as Adam Müller.[218] It is everywhere; it participates in the structure of what can only be called the spirit of the age.[219] Schleiermacher's important theological lectures of 1799, *Ueber die Religion*, for instance, are based on an explicit summoning of polar contrasts.[220] For Coleridge, polarity was not merely nor even primarily an importation from the *Naturphilosophen* but "an ineradicable characteristic and compelling urgency of his thought".[221] It was endemic in antiquity; indeed, as Coleridge wrote in 1820: "In all subjects of deep and lasting interest, you will detect a struggle between two opposites, two polar Forces, both of which are alike necessary to our human Well-being, & necessary each to the continued existence of the other".[222] Accordingly, as another commentator has emphasised, "the apprehension of polarity is itself *The basic act of imagination*".[223] "Dichotomy, or the primary Division of the Ground into Contraries", said Coleridge, "is the necessary form of reasoning".[224] The polar involvement of the *Naturphilosophen* thus dovetailed neatly with prior and deeper Coleridgean attitudes.

Coleridge was not only intellectually but also psychologically committed to polarity. His fundamental approach to reality was dyadic:

---

[216] *CL* IV 767.
[217] See below, p. ci.
[218] See "A Complex Dialogue: Coleridge's Doctrine of Polarity and Its European Contexts" *RFR* 289–341.
[219] Ibid. 301–8 et passim.
[220] *Schleiermacher* Erste Abtheilung I 146.
[221] *RFR* 289.
[222] *CL* V 35.
[223] Barfield 145, 26.
[224] Brinkley 118.

imagination had to be split into imagination and fancy; reason had to be split into reason and understanding; imitation was split into imitation and copy, fame into fame and reputation. The One and the Many, "I am" and "it is", subject and object, God and man, father and son, mother and child, those and other dyadic forms—he even distinguished between "re-more" and "regret"—were charged with great significance by Coleridge, and they testify to a "mighty split in his allegiance and concern".[225] The idea of "alterity" came to dominate the subtlest levels of his theological thinking.

But if the dyadic commitment was psychological in its urgency (he even said that "The Dyad is the essential form of Unity"),[226] It was also openly intellectual in its elaboration, and Coleridge devoted much thought to its mysteries:

Yester morning, my dear Hartley! you appeared to agree with me on the truth of the first universal principle of the Polar Logic, as far as it is *Logic*, i.e. confined to the Objects of the Sense and the Understanding, or (what is the same) to the Finite, the Creaturely. You agreed with me, that *One* could not manifest itself or be wittingly distinguished as One, but by the co-existence of an *Other*: or that A could not be affirmed to be A but by the perception that it is *not* B; and that this again implies the perception that B *is* as well as A. We can become CONSCIOUS of *Being* only by means of *Existence*, tho' having thus become conscious thereof, we are in the same moment conscious, that Being must be prior (in thought) to Existence: as without seeing, we should never *know* (i.e. know ourselves to have known) that we had Eyes; but having learnt this, we know that Eyes must be anterior to the act of seeing.[227]

Finally, his dyadic instinct led Coleridge to realise that polarity did not simply exist as such, but led to conceptions of triplicity, and in the last period of his life, to those of fourness and even fiveness. "Year after year, yea, day after day, I see more clearly or feel more livelily the importance of the Noetic Tetrad and the Logical Pentad, as the fundamental Form of all Thinking—and of Trichotomy in all *real* definition—".[228] It was not merely that ideas and things existed in polar form, but that this dyadic fact in its own logic led to triad, tetrad, and so on.[229] "Thus the Monas,

---

[225] *RFR* 240.

[226] *CN* IV 4829.

[227] *CL* V 97. C is here utilising terms employed in Fichte's *Wissenschaftslehre*. For C's judgment of Fichte, see *BL* (*CC*) I 157–60. For C's debt to Fichte, see Daniel Stempel, "Revelation on Mount Snowdon: Wordsworth, Coleridge, and the Fichtean Imagination,"

JAAC 29 (1971) 371–84. See also Orsini 172–91.

[228] *CM* (*CC*) I 231.

[229] How inevitable such progressions are may be guaged from a tract of Franz von Baader, *Ueber dans pythagoräische Quadrat in der Natur oder die vier Welt-gegenden* (Tübingen 1798), where he attempts to show that the universal dual-

the Dyas, the Trias, and the Tetractys are one."[230] The One became not merely the two, but in truth the Many. "What is affirmed of A is equally affirmed of B: and what is true of A relatively to B, is no less true of B relatively to C. In other words, Alterity leads to *Plurality*."[231]

As clearly as did Hegel, Coleridge saw that the thesis that implied its antithesis already postulated a third form by that very fact: "We know A by A: and B by A. We know, that between A and B there is, first, a something peculiar to each, *that*, namely, by which A is A and *not* B, and B is B and *not* A: and secondly, a something common to them, a one in both; namely, that which is expressed in the copula, *is*: and thirdly, that the latter, = Being, is in order of thought presupposed in the former."[232] If twoness led to threeness, threeness led to fourness:

I have not indeed any distinct memory of Giordano Bruno's *Logica Venatrix Veritatis*; but doubtless the principle of Trichotomy is necessarily involved in the Polar Logic: ~~this~~ which again is ~~in~~ the same with the Pythagorean *Tetractys*— i.e. the eternal Fountain or Source of Nature; & this being sacred to contemplation of Identity, & prior in order of Thought to *all* division, ~~it~~ is so far from interfering with Trichotomy, as the universal form of Division (more correctly, of distinctive Distribution in Logic) that it implies it.—Prothesis being by the very term anterior to Thesis can be no part of it—Thus in

Prothesis

Thesis   Antithesis

Synthesis

we have the tetrad indeed in the intellectual & intuitive Contemplation; but a Triad in discursive Arrangement, and a Tri-unity in Result.[233]

Again, and much like Hegel, he "attempted to represent the periods of the human Race hitherto, as a Line with two opposite Poles—the patriarchal Period, best represented and longest preserved in the Hebrew nation as the primary or mid point from which both were produced, the Greeks as the Ideal Pole, and the Romans as the Real—and I observed that the synthesis or Union of Both was in Christendom".[234]

---

ism of nature posited in Schelling's *Naturphilosophie*—specifically in the treatise of 1798 called *Von der Welt-seele, eine Hypothese der höheren Physik zur Erklärung des allgemeinen Organismus*—actually must be conceived of as a threeness, and that in turn as a fourness.

[230] *CN* III 4427.

[231] *CL* v 99.

[232] C partly annotated Hegel's *Wissenschaft der Logik*, where the triadic logic receives its most comprehensive exposition. See *CM* (*CC*) 988–97. For C's priority to the formulations in Hegel's treatise, see *RFR* 294, 302.

[233] *CM* (*CC*) I 347–8.

[234] *CN* III 4378.

It was Kant who had set Fichte, and after him Schelling, onto schematisms in terms of thesis, antithesis, and synthesis. In the opening paragraph of the preface to the first edition of the *Kritik der reinen Vernunft* in 1781, Kant had said that "human reason has the special fate . . . of being troubled by questions that cannot be ignored, because they spring from the very nature of reason, but that cannot be answered, because they transcend all power of human reason".[235] In due course, accordingly, he highlighted the limitations of reason by showing "scenes of discord and confusion produced by the conflict of the laws (antinomy) of pure reason";[236] and he did so by a method that he called "*thesin cum antithesi*": "If every collection of dogmatical doctrines is 'thetic', I may denote by 'antithetic', not indeed dogmatical assertions of the opposite, but the conflict between different kinds of apparently dogmatical knowledge (*thesin cum antithesi*), to none of which we can ascribe a superior claim to our assent".[237] He then set up a series of arguments on facing pages, as for example, the "Thesis" that "The world has a beginning in time, and is limited with regard to space", and the "Antithesis" that "The world has no beginning and no limits in space, but is infinite, in respect to both time and space", and showed that reason had to argue for the correctness of both, though both could not be correct.[238]

Fichte, in his *Grundlage der gesammten Wissenschaftslehre* (1794), which saw itself as "completing" Kant, took up Kant's repeated use of the concept of synthesis and used it to resolve the thesis-antithesis dichotomy. Specifically, Fichte responded to the Kantian question, "How are synthetic judgments *a priori* possible?" by invoking the argument that "no synthesis is possible without a preceding antithesis"; "As little as antithesis without synthesis, or synthesis without antithesis, is possible; just as little possible are both without thesis".[239]

Schelling then took up Fichte's thesis-antithesis-synthesis relation and in his *Vom Ich als Princip der Philosophie* (1795) arranged the terms schematically in pyramidal form.[240] The distinction was subsequently utilised by Hegel as the dynamic underpinning of his entire philosophy (though he rarely uses the actual words "thesis", "antithesis", "synthesis").

Coleridge, for his part, looked further back and found the method in the seventeenth-century English theologian Richard Baxter as well. Commenting on Baxter's declaration that he had been "Twenty Six Years convinced that Dichotomizing will not do it; but that the Divine

[235] *Kant GS* iv 7.
[236] Ibid. iii 282.
[237] Ibid. iii 290.
[238] Ibid. iii 294–5.
[239] *Fichte* i 308–9.
[240] *Schelling SW* i 224–7.

Trinity in Unity, hath exprest it self in the whole Frame of Nature and Morality", Coleridge says:

Among Baxter's philosophical merits we ought not to overlook, that the substitution of Trichotomy for the old & still general plan of Dichotomy in the Method and Disposition of Logic, which forms so prominent & substantial an excellence in Kant's Critique of the Pure Reason, of the Judgement, &c belongs originally to Richard Baxter, a century before Kant—& this not as a Hint but as a fully evolved & systematically applied Principle. Nay, more than this! Baxter *grounded* it on an absolute Idea *pre*-supposed in all intelligential acts; whereas Kant takes it only as a *Fact* of Reflection—[241]

In the same vein, in a marginal note on Kant's *Vermischte Schriften* he says: "This page is worth noticing as an instance of the false conclusions inevitable on the Logic of Dichotomy: to the exchange of which for that of Trichotomy Kant owed his greatness".[242]

Like other thinkers of the Romantic era, Coleridge was totally committed to a trichotomic procedure, that is, to seeing the dichotomy of thesis and antithesis under the third conception of synthesis. It was this triadic development that allowed for process and progress in thought. Furthermore, the implication of trinal logic residing within the very idea of polar logic was especially important for Coleridge, for the whole course of his religious development was from theological Unitarianism to theological Trinitarianism.[243] Even on his death bed he "repeated his formula of the Trinity".[244] And if the Trinity was Coleridge's final theological bastion, it was no less important to his ultimate philosophical position. The largest task of the *magnum opus* was to extricate and validate the idea of the Trinity against pantheism and evolutionary materialism. "The Trinity", said Coleridge, "is the only Form, in which an Idea of God is possible—Unless indeed it be a Spinozistic or World-God".[245]

Because the polar preoccupation took such protean forms, and related to so many different urgencies of Coleridge's awareness, its importance is much greater than the *naturphilosophischen* contexts in which Coleridge often invokes it. Indeed, it is for him more like the whole ramified system of arteries, veins, and capillaries that, hidden from external view, sustains the organism as a whole. In fact, at one point he speaks of a "quinquarticular Dialectic (Prothesis, Thesis, Antithesis, Indifference, & Synthesis) which from its ordinary application, as Thesis, Antithesis, and Synthesis has been called the Logic of Trichotomy".[246]

---

[241] *CM* (*CC*) I 347. And see below, Frag 2 f 38ᵛ–39ᵛ.
[242] *CM* (*CC*) III 363.
[243] For extended discussion see "The Trinitarian Resolution" *CPT* 191–255.
[244] *CL* VI 992.
[245] Brinkley 146.
[246] *CN* IV 5086.

XI. THE EARLIEST PLANS FOR THE *MAGNUM OPUS*

As is no doubt customary with authors, Coleridge seems to have broached the possibility of the *magnum opus* in conversation before he did so in writing. At any rate, the earliest reference to the work appears to be Lamb's question in a letter of 10 January 1797: "You sometimes since exprest an intention you had of finishing some extensive work on the Evidences of Natural & Revealed Religion. Have you let the intention go? Or are you doing any thing towards it?"[247] Lamb's remark about "sometimes since" seems to place Coleridge's own statement a while earlier, and as the question is asked in early January, it would seem safe to conclude that Coleridge was talking about plans for the *magnum opus* in the previous year, 1796.

Certainly the outline of the *magnum opus* was present to his mind as early as that year. On 2 May 1796 Coleridge entertained the possibility of having "Robinson, the great London bookseller" pay his way to and from "Jena, a cheap German University where Schiller resides". "If I could realize this scheme", he continues,

I should there study Chemistry and Anatomy, and bring over with me all the works of Semler & Michaelis, the German Theologians, & of Kant, the great German metaphysician. On my return I would commence a School for 8 young men at 100 guineas each—proposed to *perfect* them in the following studies in order as follows—

1. Man as Animal: including the complete knowledge of Anatomy, Chemistry, Mechanics & Optics.—
2. Man as an *Intellectual* Being: including the ancient Metaphysics, the systems of Locke & Hartley,—of the Scotch Philosophers—& the new Kantian [S]ystem—
3. Man as a Religious Being: including an historic summary of all Religions & the arguments for and against Natural and revealed Religion.[248]

Though this is not a plan for a huge published philosophical system, the difference is not historically so great as might at first glance seem. For as Jaeger has comprehensively demonstrated, not only the Socratic philosophy but the whole substance of Greek culture developed as *paideia*—the education of young men.[249] Indeed, the interchangeability of education and philosophy under the aegis of *paideia* is indicated by

[247] *LL* (M) I 89.
[248] *CL* I 209.
[249] See Werner Jaeger *Paideai; The Ideals of Greek Culture* tr Gilbert Highet (2nd ed 3 vols New York 1969). The translator's version of the subtitle does not very happily render the pedagogic shaping implicit in the German: *Die Formung der griechischen Menschen.*

Coleridge some three years later, after he has actually gone to Germany. He write to Josiah Wedgwood in 1799 from Germany: "I shall have bought 30 pounds worth of books (chiefly metaphysics/ & with a view to the one work, to which I hope to dedicate in silence the prime of my life)".[250] With the phrase, "the one work", we are perhaps justified in seeing the first appearance of a specific commitment to a *magnum opus*.

The comprehensiveness of "the one work" of 1799, however, is clearly an outgrowth of the paideutic commitment of 1796. In the earlier projection, Coleridge's three divisions, "Man as Animal", "Man as an *Intellectual* Being", and "Man as a Religious Animal", denominate the idiosyncratic amalgam of scientific investigation, psychological philosophy, and theology that characterises both Coleridge's general commitment of thought and the detailed content of the *Opus Maximum* as we have it. It is intriguing witness to the constancy of Coleridge's concern that in one of the late plans he projected he gave an alternative title for the "Opus Magnum": "God, Nature and Man: A System of Theosophy, Physiogony, and Anthropology". The embryonic tripartite scheme of 1796, though in developed, altered, and more focused terminology, is more than thirty years later still discernible (with "Man as Animal" corresponding to the realm of "Nature" or "Physiogony", "Man as an *Intellectual* Being" corresponding to the realm of "Man" or "Anthropology", and "Man as a Religious Animal" corresponding to the realm of "God" or "Theosophy").[251]

By 1801 the Great Work had become firmly lodged in Coleridge's aspiration. To Poole on 16 March of that year he speaks of plans for a "work on the originality & merits of Locke, Hobbes, & Hume", and he specifically says that this work is intended "as a *Pioneer* to my greater work".[252] The commitment to comprehensiveness that signalised the scheme of 1796 is also present in a ramified proposal of 1803, although the paideutic intent has been wholly transformed into a plan for a philosophical work. In a list of "names of Works that I have planned", there appears "Eidoloclastes.———6th". Underneath this, placed within and emphasised by a rectangle, is the following specification: "On Man, and the probable Destiny of the Human Race.—My *last & great* work—always had in mind". Underneath this, "The History of Logic with a Compendium of Aristotelean Logic prefixed. 7th. History of Metaphys. in Germany. 8th". Underneath that, crossed out: "Organum vere Organum". And still further down:

---

[250] *CL* I 519.
[251] Notebook 65.

[252] *CL* II 707.

Revolutionary Minds, Thomas Aquinas, Scotus, Luther, Baxter as represent. of the English Presbyterians & as affording a place for the Church in England— Socinus, G. Fox.—9th.

Giordano Bruno, Jacob Boehmen, Spinoza. 10th.

The work which I should wish to leave behind me, or to publish late in Life, that On Man, and the probable Destiny of the Human Race, followed & illustrated by the Organum vere Organum, & philosophical Romance to explain the whole growth of Language, and for these to be always collecting materials.[253]

This projection of 1803 is the *magnum opus*.

XII. THE CONTENT OF THE *MAGNUM OPUS*

Certain elements were constant in the plan of the *magnum opus*; others passed out of the scheme as they received formulation in various published tracts. In the more comprehensive plans of his system's content, however, Coleridge repeatedly urged four distinct though interrelated subject matters: (1) a history of philosophical backgrounds, (2) a logical prolegomenon, (3) a setting forth of his own interpretation of Christianity, and (4) a consideration of viewpoints antithetical to his own, represented chiefly by pure atheism (Spinoza) and by perverted Christianity (Unitarianism). All were necessitated, in Coleridge's conception, by the twin interests of demonstration and system.

Thus in a projection of 27 September 1815, communicated to John May, his "most important work" was described as containing "six Treatises", and its plan had become scrupulously detailed:

My highest object in writing for the stage is to obtain the means of devoting myself, *a whole and undistracted man*, to the bringing forth a work, for which I have all the materials collected & ready for use; a work, which has employed all my best thoughts & efforts for the last twelve years and more, and on which I would ground my reputation, that is, the proof, that I have labored to be *useful*. The work will be entitled Logosophia: on the LOGOS, divine and human, in six Treatises. The first, or preliminary treatise contains a philosophical History of Philosophy and it's revolutions from Pythagoras to Plato & to Aristotle—from Aristotle to Lord Bacon, including the scholastic metaphysicians of what are *called* the dark ages—from Bacon to Des Cartes and Locke—and from Locke to the revival of the eldest Philosophy, which I call *dynamic* or constructive as opposed to the material and mechanic systems still predominant. (A perspicuous Compendium of the Hist. Of Phil. has been long wanted: for Enfield's is a mere Bookseller's *Job* Abridgement of BRUCKER, a man of great Learning & unwearied industry, but scantily gifted with the true philosophic insight.)

---

[253] *CN* I 1646.

The second Treatise is (Λόγος κοίνος) on the science of connected reasoning, containing a system of Logic purified from all pedantry & sophistication, & applied practically to the purposes of ordinary life, the Senate, Pulpit, Bar, &c—I flatter myself that I have not only brought together all the possible Forms of Deception and Delusion in Reasoning, from the grossest Bull which raises the laughter of a Taproom to the subtlest Sophism which has set nation against nation, illustrated by instances from writers of the highest name; but have likewise given some rules for the easy detection of false reasoning. I have labored to make it not so much a Novum Organum, as an Organum verè Organum. The III. (Logos Architectonicus) on the Dynamic or Constructive Philosophy—preparatory to the IV. or a detailed Commentary on the Gospel of St John—collating the *Word* of the Evangelist with the Christ crucified of St Paul—

The Vth. (Λόγος ἀγωνίστης) on the Pantheists and Mystics; with the Lives and Systems of Giordano Bruno, Jacob Behmen, George Fox, and Benedict Spinoza.—

The VIth. (Λόγος ἄλογος), on the Causes & Consequences of modern Unitarianism.

Previously to its being sent to the Press I mean to submit the work to some one or more learned and dignified Divines of the Church of England, the defence of whose articles I have most at heart, next to that of the Gospel Truth, which in all but some inessential and comparatively trifling points I sincerely believe coincident with our Articles & Liturgy.—[254]

It is interesting to note that this detailed projection is in all respects an outgrowth of the scheme of 1803 adduced above (the phrase "the last twelve years or more" accurately enough refers back from 1815 to 1803, and in 1803 the idea for the *magnum opus* had been said to have been "always" in mind). The "second Treatise" in the 1815 projection, "on the science of connected reasoning, containing a system of Logic", is evidently an expansion of the proposal of 1803 with regard to "The History of Logic with a Compendium of Aristotelean Logic prefixed". Its aim of being "not so much a Novum Organum, as an Organum verè Organum" repeats the rubric of the earlier plan: "Organum vere Organum". The "first, or preliminary treatise" of the plan of 1815, which "contains a philosophical History of Philosophy", takes up the "8th" proposal of 1803: "History of metaphysics in Germany". The first section of the 1815 plan, "on the Pantheists and Mystics; with the Lives and Systems of Giordano Bruno, Jacob Behmen, George Fox, and Benedict Spinoza", expands the "10th" proposal of 1803: "Giordano Bruno, Jacob Behmen, Spinoza".

Another aspect of the 1815 projection, the compendium of the history of philosophy, seems to maintain the paedeutic commitment of the ad-

[254] *CL* IV 589–90.

umbrative version of 1796, for Coleridge notes that the compendium "has long been wanted". The same educational commitment seems to be implied in the statement that he has "labored to be *useful*".

The plan of 1815, although it is perhaps the most comprehensive of Coleridge's serious visions of the *magnum opus*, is only one of a spate of statements that occurs about the same time. On 17 October 1815 Coleridge wrote to Daniel Stuart in much the same detail he had to John May. In this projection he speaks rather poignantly of the work on which he would wish to ground his "reputation with Posterity" and for which he had been collecting the materials "almost incessantly" for fifteen years. The third of the treatises is here called "the Science of Premises, or transcendental Philosophy" and is introductory to the fourth, "a detailed Commentary on the Gospel of St. John". The fifth is on the Mystics and Pantheists and is to include not only the lives of "Giordano Bruno, Jacob Behmen, George Fox and Benedict Spinoza", but also "an analysis of their systems". Coleridge concludes by saying that the *magnum opus* "will comprize two large Octavo volumes, 600 pages each".[255]

Earlier, on 27 August 1814, his first published plan for the *magnum opus* appeared, in the essay called "On the Principles of Genial Criticism" in *Felix Farley's Bristol Journal*: "I am about to put to the press a large volume on the LOGOS, or the communicative intelligence in nature and in man, together with, and as preliminary to, a Commentary on the Gospel of St. John".[256] In 1817 the *Biographia Literaria* came off the press, and it contained the second published notice of the *magnum opus*. Rejecting "materialism" because in order "to explain *thinking*, as a material phaenomenon, it is necessary to refine matter into a mere modification of intelligence", Coleridge says the subject "will (if God grant health and permission), be treated of at large and systematically in a work which I have for many years been preparing, on the PRODUCTIVE LOGOS human and divine; with and as the introduction to, a full commentary on the Gospel of St. John".[257]

We are beginning to see the truth of what Coleridge had said in 1803, that the plan for his "*last & great* work" was one he "always had in mind". On 12 September 1814, he had written with great fullness to Stuart of the work, which he disingenuously announced as actually in the process of "printing at Bristol". In this lengthy projection the title is not *Logosophia* but "Christianity the one true Philosophy", and it is to contain, as the subtitle says, "5 Treatises on the Logos, or communicative Intelligence, Natural, Human, and Divine". Here the third treatise is to

[255] *CL* IV 591–2.
[256] *BL* (1907) II 230.
[257] *BL* (*CC*) I 136.

be "a full Commentary on the Gospel of St John, in development of St Paul's doctrine of preaching Christ alone, & him Crucified", and the "4th, on Spinoza, and Spinozism with a life of B. Spinoza—this entitled, Logos Agonistes". Coleridge concludes by saying, "The purpose of the whole is—a philosophical Defence of the Articles of the Church, as far as they respect Doctrine, or points of Faith.—If Originality be any merit, this work will have that at all events from the first page to the last."[258]

If we leave aside for a moment a consideration of the historical and logical discussions that were to frame the positive assertions of the *magnum opus*, we see that these assertions took the form of a reconciliation of the polar opposites of Christianity (Paul and John) and atheism (Spinoza), and thereby resolved the great polar tension that Coleridge retrospectively described in the *Biographia Literaria* as dominating his entire intellectual history: "For a very long time indeed I could not reconcile personality with infinity; and my head was with Spinoza, though my whole heart remained with Paul and John".[259] The thought of Paul and John was to be presented in the form of commentaries on their doctrines, a mode necessary to the idea of a "Defence" of Christianity, where the validation of statements already in existence had to take precedence over merely *ad hoc* formulation. It was also a form that might well have activated Coleridge's legendary prowess as a critical commentator. That such a manner of presentation could have led to intellectual urgencies of a higher order might be easily granted if we imagine Coleridge's ideal production to be something like, say, a conflation of Karl Barth's *Der Römerbrief* and C. H. Dodd's *The Fourth Gospel*.

The other pole of assertive concern, Spinozistic atheism, also included as a sub-category perverted Christianity, or Unitarianism. "Unitarianism in its immediate intelligential . . . consequences, is Atheism or Spinosism."[260] Having passed through the crucible of Unitarian commitment himself, Coleridge spoke with special intensity on the defects of that supposed form of Christianity: "I make the greatest difference between *ans* and *isms*. I should deal insincerely with you, if I said that I thought Unitarianism was Christianity. No; as I believe and have faith in the doctrine, it is not the truth in Jesus Christ; but God forbid that I should doubt you, and many other Unitarians, as you call yourselves, are, in a practical sense, very good Christians. We do not win heaven by logic."[261]

The thought that Unitarianism, as an invalid form of Christianity, was actually a less consequent form of Spinozism, was one to which Cole-

[258] *CL* III 533–4.
[259] *BL (CC)* I 201.
[260] *CL* II 1196.
[261] *TT (CC)* I 278.

ridge frequently returned. In a note in the margin of Andrew Fuller's *Calvinistic and Socinian Systems Examined and Compared* he linked Fuller with the Unitarian bellwether Priestley: "in both systems [that is, of Fuller and of Priestley] man is annihilated . . . it is all God . . . —in brief, both systems are not Spinosism, for no other reason than that the logic and logical consistency of 10 Fullers + 10 × 10 Dr. Priestleys, piled on each other, would not reach the calf of Spinoza's leg. Both systems of necessity lead to Spinozism."[262] The high esteem in which he here holds Spinoza is also a constant in his thought: "It is a duty which we owe to truth, to distinguish Spinoza from . . . the whole nest of *popular* infidels, to make manifest how precious a thing is sincere thirst of truth for the sake of truth . . . . Now I affirm that none but an eminently pure and benevolent mind could have constructed and perfected such a system as that of the ethics of Spinoza."[263] In Coleridge's final vision, however, which was to be the *magnum opus*, Spinoza's atheism would somehow be reconciled with Christianity:

you will, therefore, perhaps, be aware that though I deem Unitarianism the very *Nadir* of Christianity, and far, very far worse in relation either to the *Affections*, the *Imagination*, the Reason, the Conscience, nay even to the UNDERSTANDING, than several of the forms of *Atheism*—ex.gr. than the Atheism of Spinoza— whose pure spirit may it be my lot to meet, with St. John and St. Paul similing on him and loving him—yet I make an impassable chasm between *an* and *ism* . . . ."[264]

.

XIII. THE TRANSFORMATIONS OF THE *MAGNUM OPUS*

Though the plan of the *magnum opus* underwent gradual but continual metamorphosis, its elements were constants in Coleridge's concern. The transformations of its projected contents were in the main simply correlatives of the fact that Coleridge began publishing in separate form various constituents of the whole scheme, with the result that the fragmentary remainder known as *Opus Maximum* is merely the unpublished residue of his total project. Later reading and meditation caused him to project extensions or ramifications of various emphases, but in largest outline the project never changed.[265] Paradoxically, in order to under-

---

[262] *CM (CC)* II 803.
[263] *C Life* (G) 321–2.
[264] *CL* VI 893.
[265] For instance, the very first reference to the *magnum opus*, that of Charles Lamb in Jan 1797, calls it "an extensive

work on the Evidences of Natural and Revealed Religion (*LL*—M—I 89), while Coleridge's first adumbrative scheme of 5 May 1796 refers to "a historic summary of all Religion & the arguments for and against Natural & re-stand what Coleridge really thought on the most urgent matters of his intellectual agenda, the *Opus Maximum* must be augmented by his other published and unpublished prose, letters, and notebooks, as well as formal treatises. Certainly it does not render his total theological and philosophical enterprise, nor does it constitute his *magnum opus*.

The projections of 1814 and 1815 surveyed above, therefore, are perhaps the most satisfactory descriptions of the content of the *magnum opus*: they are the ones least tapped by subsequent publication. After Coleridge took up residence in the house of the physician James Gillman at Highgate in 1816, the work actually began to be composed. At that time its conceptions began to be fragmented into more limited vehicles, and both projections and the names of the *magnum opus* began to differ. The "one work" referred to in 1799[266] had by 1803 a specific title, *Eidoloclastes*.[267] By August 1814 it was "a large volume on the LOGOS, or the communicative intelligence in nature and in man, together with, and as a preliminary to, a Commentary on the Gospel of St. John";[268] By September of that year it was called "Christianity the one true Philosophy".[269] By September 1815 it had another specific title, *Logosophia*.[270] This title preoccupied Coleridge's projections for some time, and in an interesting passage in his notebooks he sets out three possible versions:

Logosophia
or the System and
the Method: by S. T.
Coleridge, conveyed in Discourses
and Dialogues, concerning
~~Religion~~ Science, Religion & m
Philosophy

———

or
Logosophia:
or the System and
the Method by S. T.

---

vealed Religion" (*CL* I 209). A long descriptive title of the late 1820s—one of the last C conceived—refers to the *magnum opus* as an "assertion and demonstration of the Position, that Religion implies Revelation, and that Christianity is the only Revelation of universal and permanent validity" (Notebook 65.3), while the Extended Plan of 1828 states that

"Religion *implies* Revelation or Religion and Revelation are synonymous Terms and Revealed Religion a Pleonasm".

[266] *CL* I 519.
[267] *CN* I 1646.
[268] *BL* (1907) II 230.
[269] *CL* III 533.
[270] Ibid. IV 589.

Coleridge in four Parts consisting
of Discourses, Disquisitions, &
~~and Dialogues concer~~
Dialogues concerning
Science, Philosophy
& Religion

———

Logosophia
Or the System and
the Method by S. T.
Coleridge: in four parts consisting
of Discourses & Dialogues concerning
Science, Philosophy and
Religion[271]

In a note of 1820, under the title "The Logosophic System and Method by S. T. Coleridge", Coleridge produced an attempt at a kind of prospectus, and after considerable crossing-out starts again with "The L. S. and M. by S. T. C. On the inherent imperfection of all systems exclusively intellectual—i.e. profession to be *grounded* in Reason or in the Understanding", and continues into the formula of "Organum verè organum", concluding with a reference to the new vitality given the enterprise by the dialogical help of Green: "the whole forming a series of Discourses and Dialogues held with a fellow-enquirer during a succession of Tours at home and abroad during the years 1817[272]–1820".[273]

The project continued throughout Coleridge's career to be referred to by him indeterminately as his "Great Work", his "Magnum Opus", "Opus Magnum", and "Opus Maximum". The name *Logosophia*, which was at the forefront around the time of the *Biographia Literaria*, gradually faded away. In early 1820 the *magnum opus* began to be described in phrases like "an assertion of the ideal truth & the *a priori* probability and a posteriori internal and external evidence of the historic truth of the Christian Religion",[274] and at this period a third specific name emerged: *Assertion of Religion*.[275] By the late 1820s a fourth title appeared: *Philosophy of Epochs and Methods*,[276] also projected as "ΜΕΘΔΑΙ ΚΑΙ ΕΠΟΧΑΙ *or God, Nature, and Man: A System of Theosophy, Physiogony, and Anthropology*".[277] In 1829 appeared a fifth title: *Estesismos,*

---

[271] *CN* III 4440.
[272] 1816 first entered and then the 6 crossed out and replaced by a 7.
[273] *CN* IV 4673.

[274] *CL* v 177, 24 Sept 1821.
[275] E.g. *CL* v 120, 127.
[276] *L&L* 3.
[277] Notebook 65.2. On another page

or as Coleridge transliterated it into Greek capitals: ΕΣΤΗΣΙΣΜΟΣ, *or the System of the Faith & Philosophy of S. T. C.*[278] As the names changed, so did the number of treatises envisioned. The scheme of 1803 listed five headings.[279] In the plan communicated to John May on 27 September 1815, the "LOGOSOPHIA" was to be divided into "six Treatises".[280] A late notebook, more than a dozen years afterward, speaks of "Seven integral Parts" and "7 volumes".[281] Perhaps the most constant of these possibilities is contained in the plan communicated to Daniel Stuart on 17 October 1815, in which five treatises would "comprize two large Octavo Volumes, 600 pages each".[282] To Stuart on 12 September 1814 the plan was also envisioned as containing "5 Treatises on the Logos, or communicative Intelligence, Natural, Human, and Divine".[283] This division of five treatises into three topics is maintained in the "Preface" in the Berg Collection, where Coleridge says that his "System is divided into three unequal parts, each of which is an independent work—the whole comprized in five volumes".[284]

Perhaps the least reliable of the projections is the longest and most detailed plan dated 24–27 May 1828. This plan divides the *magnum opus* into six parts and contains information about its scheme not to be met with elsewhere. Its unreliability stems from the fact that it was produced at a moment when Coleridge, realising that time was running out, had virtually ceased work on the *magnum opus*; one suspects that the plan became more grandiose in inverse ratio to its likelihood of fulfilment. To this editor, at any rate, it seems not so much an outline of what he would (or could) do, as a compensation, an historical promissory note, for what he had not quite managed to achieve. Whatever the validity of this editorial surmise, the projection, henceforth referred to as the "Extended Plan", is unquestionably Coleridge's most detailed:

May 24, 1828. It may be well to place on record the Synopsis of the Coleridgian (*Mem.* more euphonious it will be to name it the Estesean, or Estecian) Methodology, or Philosophy of Epochs and Methods, By S. T. C., R.A. R.S.L. &c. &c.

Coleridge tentatively changed the title back and forth between "ΕΠΟΧΑΙ ΚΑΙ ΜΕΘΔΑΙ ῾Η ΜΕΘΔΑΙ ΚΑΙ ΕΠΟΧΑΙ— or the Redemption of the World, it's Method and it's Epochs: a System of Theosophy, Physiogony and Anthropology, in assertion and demonstration of the Position, that Religion implies Revelation, and that Christianity is the only Revelation of universal and permanent validity" (Notebook 65.3).

[278] *CL* VI 781n.
[279] *CN* I 1646.
[280] *CL* IV 589.
[281] Notebooks 65.1, 65.3.
[282] *CL* IV 591–2.
[283] *CL* III 533.
[284] See below, p 4.

Author of the Tomes, whereof, tho' not in Dutch, The Public little knows, the Publishers too much.
or rather of its principal Divisions.

Remaining Divisions.

Animal Life from the Polyp to primaeval Man—Ends with the physiological & the rational Grounds for the Assumption, that Man is not in the state, in which the original Family must have been both constituted and circumstanced: or a Fall of Man shewn to be a necessary Postulate of Science, I, on grounds of Pure Reason, i.e. by deduction a jam demonstratis in Parte Prima hujus Methodologiae and from the finality, or common final Cause implied in the Law and Order of Ascent of Nature inorganic or organic, as *sketched in Outline* in Part the Second: II, on theoretical Grounds, or as the only Hypothesis adequate to the Solution of the existing Circumstances.—The exhibition however of this IInd Ground is deferred to the *third Part* or (probably) the fourth Volume of the Methodology: because tho' capable of proof independent of positive Revelation and History, it will be presented in a stronger light of evidence and more convincingly for the General Reader as well as more easily to be understood, in combination with them

P.S. This Second part comprizes the prior half of the Exposition of the Idea, first enunciated in the Estecean Philosophy, that Life begins in detachment from Nature and ends in union with God:—and as the First or Ideal Part concludes with the Fall of Angels (Τῶν Λόγον Ἀριθμῶν, καὶ Δυνάμεων) so the Second Part (which, I trust, will have an equal right to be named the J a h a g ë an, as the Estecëan System (J. H. G.—Jäaitchigëan too cacophonous Y a h a h, the Ya pronounced as the last syllable in *mama* concludes with the *Fall of Man*.

PART THIRD

Introduction AA

Proof *a priori* of a Revelation—(n.b. this already given in and to be transcribed from the Gillmano-recipe or Pharmacopoeian Memorandum Book.) & that Religion *implies* Revelation or Religion and Revelation are synonymous Terms and Revealed Religion a Pleonasm . . . . BB *or Second Chapter* of the Introduction to the Third Part.

The superior Authority and Historical Reliability of the Hebrew Origines Gentium, or earliest History contained in the Mosaic Writings, proved by their exclusive coincidence with the principle canons of Historic Credibility . . . .

Section the first

The Fall of Man, in connection with Revelation, and, in relation to the Anastasis of Redemtivial Scheme (Here the views contained in my Mem Books, & in the Jahagean Ult. et Penult.) . . . An attempt to establish a philosophical & religious Supra-Copernican ? view of the Fall.

Section 2nd.

Of the two first Relations of the Redeemer to our first Parents, as comprehending the Individual and the Kind . . . .

3rd

Probable final Cause of the existence and catastrophe of the Antediluvians.

Section Fourth.

Jahagean Ult et Penult with great augmentations—as filling the interspace from Noah to the Building of Babel . . . .

P.S. Here I end the third Part or integer which in harmony with both the former closes with a Fall or Apostasy . . . the apostasy of the Families of the Earth from the Setho-Noetic Faith and Worship . . . . Had there occurred no Apostasy of the Tribes and Families, the Scheme would have stood thus

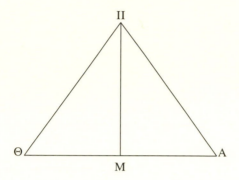

II or Prothesis Noah—of which the Base Line is to be regarded as the Production—the Thesis or + Pole [and so on through masses of detail here omitted by Snyder].

PART THE FOURTH

Commences with the exposition of the two-fold Name and Office of the Eternal Son, for which Preparation has been made in Part the First—namely as 1. the Jehovah-Person, the revealed Word, the Author and the Object of the saving Faith. Lux actualis and secondum:—2. as the Providence of the World, the energetic Sphere of Reason (Lux, Lex et Pulchritudo Rerum) and Ground . . . of (the normal) Humanity—Lumen potentiale in omnibus—and briefly and generally applies this principle to the consideration of the Races relatively to the Goodness of God and the Redemption of Men as before in relation to the Depravity of Man . . . . The second Half of the Fourth Part, or rather perhaps the second Tertia . . . goes back to Egypt and traces the course of Paganism, Greek Art, Science, Philosophy & Roman Realization and Fixture of Greek Ideas, with the History of the Jews from Ezra to John the Baptist—comprizing the substance of my Course of Lectures on the History of Philosophy—shewing the completion of the Cycle of Philosophy just before the Coming of Christ—Then, the Origin of the conversion of the Idea of the Redeemer into the expectation of a Messiah.—

The Incarnation of the Logos in Jesus—the character and purpose of the

Morals of the Gospel and the specific Object of the brief Mission of Jesus, as the Elias (See the Day-books) The Miracles of Christ—the two-fold Essence of his Death, Resurrection and Ascension into Glory—the commencement of the invisible Church, and the exposition in full of the whole Scheme of Christian Faith in all it's articles, whether as everlasting Truth or as progressive realization—in short, the Revelation of the Eternal in Time, with the gradual thinning, defecation and final transparency of the Medium, with the restoration of the Pleroma by the perfection of the personality as the Distinctity and the Union with God, in through and with the Son of God & the Divine Humanity as the Unity—Eternal Life and that last profoundest Mystery and Triumph of Love and Goodness, Eternal Death as the Pledge of it's immutability—these are the Contents of this, the completing Division of the Fourth Part.

THE FIFTH PART

Takes up the inquiry (already instituted by me in my Eight Letters on the right and the superstitious Estimation of the Scriptures) whether the infallibility &c of the Jewish & Christian Canons is or ought to be an additional & distinct Article of Faith—examines each book in succession—In short, it will be, I trust, a compleat Substitute for the German Introduction to the Old & New Testaments— This Part is critical throughout & includes various strictures on the Translation. It will be a real History of the Bible—not a flat new-wording of the Bible History—the great Object to restore the Bible to it's due place in the Love & Veneration of Christians by at once establishing it's Homopneumaty yet asserting it's Humanities . . . .

THE SIXTH AND LAST PART

aa Gives the Philosophy, and a philosophic Abstract, of the History of the Visible Church & of Christendom from the Apostles to the present times—and ends with a view of the Church of England as an Estate of the Realm (—λυσία) and the two-fold Function of it's Ministers, as Preachers & Members of the Church of Christ (εκκλησια) Trustees & Functionaries of the States—with the equal and opposite Evils of Confounding and of dividing the Functions—Closes with an Exhortation to the Clergy and a solemn Appeal to the (orthodox) Dissenters.—

If the completion of this Great Work, the main Labor of my Life, would be to the Glory of God in the advancement of the Truth in Christ, may God grant me Space and Grace to write Finish on it's last Leaf.

S. T. Coleridge
27 May 1828[285]

Grove, Highgate

The archaic elements in this projection, with their attempts to combine history with theology and philosophy, will be pointed to in the discus-

---

[285] From eleven pages of a notebook   *L&L.* in the Huntington Library, printed in

sion of the "genre" of the *magnum opus*, especially with relation to such ventures as Bossuet's *Histoire universelle*. The infusion of *naturphilosophischen* emphases reflects Coleridge's investment of reading from about 1815 on; such an emphasis was not present in the comprehensive schemes of 1814 and 1815, although it is also true that responsibility for an accounting of nature was systematically dictated by the very nature of the enterprise and present from the first. One can recall simply from portions of its title, in varying formulations, the omnipresence of the systematic triad of man, nature, and God: "researches and reflections concerning God, Nature and Man";[286] "System of Truths respecting, Nature, Man, and Deity";[287] "reason & revelation, the life of Nature and the history of Man";[288] "God, Nature and Man: A System . . . ".[289]

While the Extended Plan may seem by its extreme commitment to archaic elements to desert the essential scheme of the *magnum opus*, in fact the fundamentals are all there: "the Tetractys, and Tri-unity", "Will", "Redemption", "Polar Forces", "Fall of Man", "Ascent of Nature", "System", "the Logos", "Revelation", all as subjects of examination by reason.

More than any other projection, however, the Extended Plan seems to pertain to a psychological tendency pointed out by a commentator who speaks of "the impossible *Magnum Opus*. Its chief yearning is sublimity and unbounded power over vast domains. The *Magnum Opus* drove Coleridge to plot endless impossible projects, most of which envisage the ultimate transformation of some vast labyrinthine body of inchoate materials into an equally vast, but now perfectly lucid in structure, temple of ideal order."[290] and yet, as it is hoped that this edition will demonstrate, what exists of the *magnum opus* is both more extensive and far more consequent than legend would have it.

XIV. THE *MAGNUM OPUS* AND THE *LOGOS*

In the vast scheme of 1828 just noticed, the Fourth Part was to have dealt among other things with the "Incarnation of the Logos in Jesus".[291] The word and conception of "Logos" were at the centre of Coleridge's plans for his great work, for "Logos" not only stood historically at the fountainhead of the Christian religion, the defence of which was the great purpose of Coleridge's endeavour, but it also united an emphasis on the personality of Jesus with the philosophical conceivings that to Coleridge,

---

[286] *CL* vi 714.
[287] Ibid. vi 864.
[288] Ibid. vi 539.

[289] Notebook 65.2.
[290] Fletcher 149.
[291] See above, p. ciii.

though not to all theological thinkers, were necessary to the proper acceptance of Christianity. Such philosophical conceivings, indeed, were "reason" itself. As Coleridge said in a gnomic jotting of 1819: "No Christ (Logos, Son eternal) no God".[292] And he speaks to a correspondent in 1818 of "uniting thy energy with the Holy *Word* (Logos in the same sense as in John I.1. = intelligential Energy, distinguishable (tho' not separable even in thought) from the energic WILL").[293]

Thus in the conception of the Logos, which was, as it were, a diamond bearing on which the whole of Christianity turned, Coleridge was able to summon a rich tradition of theological conceptualisation. Moreover, Logos was a pregnant term in the whole of the ancient philosophical tradition outside of Christianity. Indeed, as a commentator has emphasised: "*Logos* is perhaps the most difficult term in Greek philosophy".[294] And it is the term Mary Anne Perkins uses in *Coleridge's Philosophy: The Logos as Unifying Principle* (1994) to marshal all aspects of Coleridge's thought.

Logos moved easily and inevitably to the centre of Coleridge's meditation. "I have in my head some floating ideas on the *Logos*, which I hope, hereafter, to mould into a consistent form", he writes to Joseph Cottle in April 1814.[295] Accordingly, as seen above, one of the favoured names of the *magnum opus* became simply "Logosophia", the wisdom of the Logos. Likewise in the various projections of the content of the great work the word "Logos" repeatedly figured, as, for instance, in the scheme of 27 September 1815, where it is said that "This work will be entitled LOGOSOPHIA: or on the LOGOS, divine and human, in six Treatises".[296]

In the lengthy project from which that declaration is taken, the fourth treatise is to be "a detailed Commentary on the Gospel of St. John—collating the *Word* of the Evangelist with the Christ crucified of St. Paul". The "*Word* of the Evangelist" was the λόγος of John, and a commentary on the Gospel of St John, especially one dealing with John 1.1, would accordingly have to be a focal point of the *magnum opus*: "In the beginning was the Word, and the Word was with God, and the Word was God". The famous statement opens up theology to philosophy, for "logos", meaning "word" or "thought" or "reason", implies rational discourse. As Schopenhauer notes: "the Greeks called word, concept, relation, thought, idea, and reason (*Vernunft*) by the name of the first, ὁ λόγος".[297] Again, Coleridge speaks of Reason (ὁ Λόγος) as "the only

---

[292] *CN* III 4489.
[293] *CL* IV 884.
[294] Rist 84.

[295] *CL* III 480.
[296] *CL* IV 589.
[297] Schopenhauer III 67.

true *Being* in which all things visible and invisible! The Pleroma, in whom alone God loveth the World!"[298] "Christ has been revealed in his identity with the Logos, i.e. as the Substantial personal Reason in whom Life is—the universal communicative Reason 'who lighteth *every* Man.'"[299] Although at one point in the *Aids to Reflection* Coleridge equates Logos with "understanding", he does so merely to keep the slate clean for his own Johannine inscribings of "reason": "In Greek Logos (Anglicé, Word), means likewise the Understanding".[300] It was specifically the philosophy of the Logos in the Gospel of John that led Coleridge, as it has others, to value that Gospel more highly than its three synoptic brethren, and to make a commentary on it a central part of his plans for the *magnum opus*. As a commentator points out, "Where the Fourth Gospel differs from the others is that its interpretation is not only in different thought forms, but is also deliberate, coherent, and in the full sense theological, as theirs is not".[301]

Coleridge's address to the Fourth Gospel was undertaken with full awareness of the Higher Criticism, and with exemplary discrimination of likelihoods and probabilities:

> Is the fourth Gospel authentic? . . . I have studied with an open and fearless spirit the attempts of sundry learned Critics of the Continent, to invalidate the authenticity of this Gospel, before and since Eichhorn's Vindication. The result has been a clearer assurance, and (as far as this was possible) a yet deeper conviction of the genuineness of *all* the writings, which the Church has attributed to this Apostle. That those, who have formed an opposite conclusion, should object to the use of expressions which they had ranked among the most obvious marks of spuriousness, follows as a matter of course.[302]

The equation of Logos and deity in the Fourth Gospel opens up religion to philosophy in another way. Bultmann says curtly that "*The Greek philosophical tradition*, in which the *Logos* is first encountered as a cosmic-divine potency in Heraclitus, and then achieves its historically most important role in *Stoicism*, is not relevant to our purpose".[303] And yet in the course of his authoritative analysis, Bultmann proceeds to ascribe to Gnostic thought a significant role in the development of "Logos", concluding, "If Logos is to be translated, the translation can only be '*Word*', the meaning already given to it through the Gnostic myth. It is nevertheless the appropriate translation."[304]

Moreover, not all commentators agree with Bultmann's exclusiv-

[298] *CL* vi 600.
[299] *CM* (*CC*) iii 23.
[300] *AR* (1825) 25.
[301] Dodd *Tradition* 5.

[302] *AR* (1825) 379.
[303] Bultmann 24.
[304] Ibid. 36.

ity.[305] The almost equally authoritative C. H. Dodd says flatly: "The opening sentences of the Prologue are clearly intelligible only when we admit that λόγος, though it carries with it the associations of the Old Testament Word of the Lord, has also a meaning similar to that which it bears in Stoicism as modified by Philo, and parallel to the idea of Wisdom in other Jewish writers. It is the rational principle in the universe, its meaning, plan or purpose, conceived as a divine hypostasis in which the eternal God is revealed and active."[306] We may with considerable confidence infer that Coleridge's own view was similar to that of Dodd. His scattered remarks frequently mention the philosophy of Philo as bearing directly upon the λόγος of John.[307] "I should use Philo (who has not been used half enough) to demonstrate that the Socinian interpretation of John's Gospel *must be false*."[308] Again, Coleridge mentions a fragment in Stobaeus in terms suggestive of the syncretisms that always occur in his projections of the *magnum opus*: "I refer to the passage in which we are told that the intelligential powers, by the Pythagoreans and Anaxagoras called the *Nous*, (the *Logos* or the *Word* of Philo and St. John) is indeed indivisibly united with, but yet not the same as the absolute principle of causation, THE PATERNAL".[309]

Coleridge liked to think of himself as adhering to the mainstream of Anglican theology, and we can hardly imagine that he would have had any difficulty subscribing to the theological scholarship of Dodd. That the Fourth Gospel presented the Logos as the focal node of meaning for all of existence was precisely the point of Coleridge's commitment to a system that argued philosophically towards a theological outcome and attempted to account under one network of argument for God, man, and world. Indeed, Coleridge's conviction that religious truth must be amenable to and saved by philosophical reasoning made him sympathetic not only to the theological approach of a scholar like Dodd, but allied him as well with the more free-wheeling and purely philosophical argumentation of Heidegger.

Though Bultmann rejects the pertinence of Heraclitus's doctrine of Logos for Christianity, Coleridge, who was less interested in historical connection as such than, as was the Marburg School of philosophy that

---

[305] For a brief conspectus of leading lines of interpretation in the nineteenth and early twentieth centuries, see Hoskyns 21–47.

[306] Dodd *Fourth Gospel* 230.

[307] C's beloved Plotinus also used (*L*)*ogos*, and in terms remarkably similar to those of Philo. For a comparison of the Plotinian *logos* with the Philonian *logos* (both use the phrase *logos gegonos*), see Rist 99–102, with the conclusion, however, that despite the similarity, Plotinus had not read Philo (101).

[308] *CL* IV 803.

[309] *P Lects* (1949) 175.

preceded Bultmann at that university, in *"erkenntnis-theoretische Legitimierung"*, that is, connections by the necessary forms of thought, welcomed Heraclitus on the Logos:

> The very same truth is found in a fragment of the Ephesian Heraclitus, preserved by Stobaeus [Coleridge found the citation in Schleiermacher], and in somewhat different words by Diogenes Laertius . . . .
> TRANSLATION:—To discourse rationally (= if we would render the discursive understanding *"discourse of reason"*) it behoves us to derive strength from that which is common to all men: (= the light that lighteth every man.) For all human understandings are nourished by the one Divine Word, whose power is commensurate with his will, and is sufficient for all and overfloweth (= shineth in darkness, and is not contained therein, or comprehended by the darkness.)
> This was Heraclitus, whose book is nearly six hundred years older than the Gospel of St. John, and who was proverbially entitled the Dark (ὁ σκοτεινός).[310]

Heidegger, who was not interested in furthering the Christian religion, finds not John, but Heraclitus, the central figure for an understanding of Logos. Though Bultmann, as noted above, dismisses the relevance of Heraclitus for the Christian Logos, Coleridge was willing to call a sketch of part of his own system by the pregnant title *"Heraclitus redivivus"*.[311] No doubt he would have agreed with Bultmann that Heraclitus's Logos was not precisely the same as that of John. For Heidegger Logos is important in Heraclitus not because it anticipates Christianity, but because it penetrates to the essential nature of being. Instead of "logic" in the modern sense, Heidegger contends, Logos actually carries the significance of "gathering together".[312]

An emphasis on Logos as a principle of "togetherness" would be congenial to Coleridge's harmonising and reconciling temperament; how well "to put one thing with another", "to bring together", "to gather", describe the twin characteristics of inclusiveness and system that mark his endeavour. How well, in short, Logos, in all its ramifications, theological, philosophical, and etymological, served the deepest purposes of the *magnum opus*. That Heidegger's etymologies are in the main sound, and that their subliminal influence could have been available to Coleridge, with his own preoccupations with Greek and with grammatical principles, are attested by a standard theological dictionary:

> λόγος in the sense (for which there is no direct evidence) of "collection" . . . .[313]
> Both in general and in detail the development of λόγος is exactly parallel to the of λέγω

[310] *LS (CC)* 97.
[311] *CL* IV 775. To C. A. Tulk, Sept 1817.
[312] See Heidegger *Metaphysics* 123–4, 128, 130–1.
[313] Kittel IV 282.

a. The sense "collection" (cf. 1b) is attested only of a number of compounds and derivatives . . . .[314]
1b. λέγω is very common in the sense "to gather" . . . .[315]
A. *The Words* λέγω, λόγος, ῥῆμα, λαλέω *in the Greek World.*
1. . . . a. The Basic Meaning of the Root. The basic meaning of *leg-* is "to gather".[316]

A final aspect of the Johannine Logos served Coleridge perhaps even more centrally than the considerations just adduced. In the fourteenth verse of the first chapter of John it is said: "And the Word was made flesh, and dwelt among us". The *logos sarx egeneto* serves to set the Christian nexus apart from all its sources and analogues. As Dodd says: "In tracing the various lines of thought, and comparing them with analogous ideas in contemporary theology, we have time and again been led to recognize the *differentia* of Johannine teaching in the fact that it finds the eternal reality conclusively revealed and embodied in an historical Person, who actually lived, worked, taught, suffered and died, with actual and direct historical consequences. The concise formula for this fact is ὁ λόγος σάρξ ἐγενετον."[317] Logos of the Fourth Gospel, in short, in melding to the idea of rational structure the reality of person, fused the deepest and most habitual concerns of Coleridge. Especially in the insistence upon person did it open a philosophical-theological highway to Coleridge, for it was in meditating on the uniqueness and deficiency of his own personhood that Coleridge came to develop the abstact principles of person that are at once the deepest and the most idiosyncratic emphases of the *magnum opus.*

Finally, the conception of Logos served Coleridge in still another essential way. Not only, as a word meaning "reason", did it coordinate with the central agenda of Coleridge's philosophical activity; not only, as the Christian word for God and Christ, did it coordinate with his overriding theological concern; but also, as the Greek word for "word", it provided a focal centre for a lifelong attention to precision in language. In October 1826 Coleridge wrote to the young James Gillman, Jr that "it is the fundamental Mistake of Grammarians and Writers on the philosophy of Grammar and Language to assume that words and their syntaxis are the immediate representatives of *Things,* or that they correspond to *Things.* Words correspond to Thoughts; and the legitimate Order & Connection of words to the *Laws* of Thinking and to the acts and affections of the Thinker's mind."[318]

[314] Kittel IV 73.   [317] Dodd *Fourth Gospel* 444.
[315] Ibid. 72.   [318] *CL* VI 630.
[316] Ibid. 71.

Indeed, so important are words and their linguistic structures to Coleridge that Logos as word may be almost as important for him as Logos as reason. Hegel comments approvingly that "λογος is defined as word. It is a beautiful ambiguity of the Greek word,—reason and at the same time language (*Sprache*). For language is the pure existence of the mind (*Geistes*)".[319] Thus the doctrine of the logos, what a commentator calls a "sunken continent" of ancient thought and a "millennium-long doctrine of the logos which has satisfied the most significant minds, especially those writing in Greek"[320] served to coordinate important elements among Coleridge's philosophical emphases.

XV. THE ORIGINATING PROBLEM AND EXISTENTIAL MOTIVE OF THE *MAGNUM OPUS*

Coleridge's emphasis on the conception of *logos* enabled him to focus simultaneously on the concerns of the Christian religion and his own philosophical preoccupations, especially as pertaining to "reason" and "communication", either of which in truth could be rendered by the single Greek word. But *logos* in the final accounting was a superficial rhetorical option rather than an indicator of the truth that lay behind Coleridge's urge towards the *magnum opus*. The *magnum opus* originated as an attempt on Coleridge's part to come to terms with the meaning of human life, a question that he saw as having a bearable answer only if the soul is immortal: "When Death shall have closed my eye-lids, must I then bid my last farewell to the streams whose murmurs have soothed me, to the fields and woodlands, where I have delighted to wander? Must yonder blue Region and all this goodly scene darken upon me and go out? . . . Have I moved and loved and reasoned and all this that I may at last be compressed into a Clod of the Valley?"[321] These questions are framed in the context of what Coleridge calls "natural longings after Immortality" and an "ardent *desire* of a future state", and both here (a sermon of 1795) and in the ramified conceptions of the *magnum opus* they obsessed Coleridge for forty years and more.

The answer to these questions determined his choice of opponents and supporters in his intellectual strivings. Thus on 27 January 1796 he proleptically identifies the evolutionary materialist Erasmus Darwin as representing the vanguard of all those strains of thought against which the *magnum opus* was later to be designed as bulwark and defence: ". . . *but*

---

[319] *Hegel* xx 106–7.
[320] Kelber 5.

[321] *Lects 1795* (*CC*) 349.

all at once he makes up his mind on such important subjects, as whether we be the outcasts of a blind idiot called Nature, or the children of an all-wise and infinitely good God; whether we spend a few miserable years on this earth, and then sink into a clod of the valley, or only endure the anxieties of mortal life to fit us for the enjoyment of immortal happiness".[322] The question of immortality was the originating problem of the *magnum opus* and Coleridge's intensely personal need for "immortal happiness" was its existential motive.

The idiosyncratic intensity of the need was the correlate of a devastating experience of the "anxieties of mortal life". Coleridge's stake in Christianity, though intellectually ramified, was not historical or theological; it arose from the misery of his own existence and the feeling that there must be something better than the torment in which he so mysteriously found himself. As I have written elsewhere, Coleridge failed to take his degree at Cambridge; he married the wrong woman; he was unable to capture the lasting respect of the women he did love; . . . he became estranged from his dearest friend; he was humiliated by the abject failure of his first born, which seemed a repetition of his own disasters; he reneged on his aspirations as a poet and did not adequately realise those as a philosopher . . . he lived a life of desperation made unquiet by interminable self-justifications and hypochondriac fancies, by a querulous inability to accept criticisms or anything less than uncritical affection. He plagiarised; he procrastinated; he spent a dismaying amount of effort, as Dorothy Wordsworth said, "in deceiving himself, and seeking to deceive others."[323]

Over these problems arched two especially mysterious disasters: an inability to work and the nightmare of opium addiction. Coleridge's intellect, noted Southey in 1815, was "as clear and powerful as ever was vouchsafed to man", but "he labours under a disease of the volition".[324] Earlier, in May 1809, Wordsworth had in a moment of intense exasperation informed Thomas Poole of his "deliberate opinion" about Coleridge: "Neither his talents nor his genius mighty as they are nor his vast information will avail him anything; they are all frustrated by a derangement in his intellectual and moral constitution—In fact he has no voluntary power of mind whatsoever, nor is he capable of acting under any constraint of duty or moral obligation".[325]

Coleridge's inability to work at self-assigned tasks was devastating and his opium addiction filled him with self-loathing. In this massive

[322] *CL* i 177.
[323] "Coleridge's Anxiety" *RFR* 105–6.
[324] *S Letters* (Curry) ii 117–18.
[325] *WL* (*E*) 352.

context of woe, Coleridge found only one hypothesis that made sense of
his situation: the Christian essential of the Fall of Man: "I profess a deep
conviction that Man was and is a *fallen* Creature, not by accidents of
bodily constitution, or any other cause, which *human* Wisdom in a course
of ages might be supposed capable of removing; but diseased in his
Will".[326] He placed the Fall of Man at the very summit of Christian
truths, second only to faith in God himself: "Now next to the know-
lege—for in this case Faith is Knowlege—of an Almighty God, the Fa-
ther of Spirits . . . the most momentous truth is the Fact of a FALL, and
that all the miseries of the World are the consequences of this Fall
. . . ."[327] If the dogma of the Fall of Man corresponded exactly to the
facts of life as Coleridge himself experienced them, another Christian es-
sential, that of redemption into a future blessedness, was equally in-
eluctable: "My Faith is simply this—that there is an original corruption
in our nature, from which & from the consequences of which, we may
be redeemed by Christ. . . . and this I believe—not because I *understand*
it, but because I *feel*, that it is not only suitable to, but needful for, my
nature.[328]

Indeed, few thinkers can have placed so much emphasis on the need
for redemption as did Coleridge. "I have prayed with drops of agony on
my Brow, trembling not only before the Justice of my Maker, but even
before the Mercy of my Redeemer. 'I gave thee so many Talents. What
hast thou done with them'?"[329] He speaks of "the two great Moments of
the Christian Faith, ORIGINAL Sin (i.e. Sin, as the *Source* of sinful ac-
tions) and Redemption; that the *Ground*, and this the *Superstructure*, of
Christianity".[330] In July 1825 Coleridge says that "the Redemption of
the World must needs form the best central Reservoir for all our knowl-
eges, physical or personal."[331] Certainly it formed the central reservoir
that watered the conception and necessity of the *magnum opus.*

While his commitment to Christian fundamentals was deeply existen-
tial, Coleridge was intellectually aware that the truth of those funda-
mentals alone led to any theoretical meaning in human existence, and
that they depended on the postulate of immortality. "If in this life only",
said St. Paul in a passage quoted by Coleridge, "we have hope in Christ,
we are of all men most miserable";[332] "If there be no resurrection of the
dead then is Christ not risen: And if Christ be not risen, then is our
preaching vain, and your faith is also vain."[333] "I cannot conceive a

[326] *AR* (1825) 136.
[327] *CL* vi 940.
[328] Ibid. ii 807, 1 July 1802.
[329] Ibid. iii 476.
[330] Ibid. v 406.
[331] Ibid. v 481.
[332] 1 Cor 15.19.
[333] Ibid. 15.13–14.

supreme moral Intelligence", agreed Coleridge, "unless I believe in my own immortality".[334] It was the general human concern with the immortality of the soul, on the one hand, and the especially intense need for redemption from his own miserable existence, on the other, that made Christianity so satisfying for Coleridge and the necessity of defending it, with all the forces at his intellectual command, so compelling. The "main points" of his faith, as he said, were only three: "a personal God, a surviving principle of Life, & that I need & that I have a Redeemer".[335]

XVI. THE CONCEPT OF PERSON

Coleridge based his defence of the meaning of his own fallen existence, and his hope for redemptive validation in a future life, on the concept of "person", and in his ruminations on the meaning of person that the *Opus Maximum* mines its deepest, richest, and most authentic vein. "Person" for Coleridge was an idea intensely charged, because he found its reference most tormentingly ambiguous in his own inner experience. He felt "self-deserted and bereft",[336] that he was "a crumbling wall, undermined at the foundations".[337] It was the agony in his own personhood that caused the concept of person to glow in his theoretical formulations. "From my Youth upward", he wrote late in life, "the most unpleasant if not the most worthless Object of direct Thought has ever been my individual Self".[338] "I feel, with an intensity unfathomable by words, my utter nothingness, impotence & worthlessness, in and for myself—."[339] Yet in this instance his individual situation found correlates in theological issues as well as in larger philosophical problems that occupied the age. Person, he and others understood, must somehow contain a structure grounded not in nature and its transformations but in a realm compatible with the Christian heaven and its invulnerability to change and dissipation.

The concept of person had a special theological relevance for Coleridge in that it allowed him to extricate the Christian idea of God from the pantheism that attracted him even as it threatened to engulf him. For Coleridge, "the perfection of person is in God, and . . . Personeity differing from personality only as rejecting all commixture of imperfection associated with the latter is an essential constituent in the Idea of

[334] *IS* 142; *CM* (*CC*) III 317.
[335] *CL* VI 577.
[336] Ibid. II 1054, 1 Feb 1804. "I know, I feel, that I am weak—apt to faint away inwardly, self-deserted and bereft of the

confidence in my own powers—."
[337] Ibid. II 929, 17 Feb 1803.
[338] Ibid. VI 984, 7 June 1834.
[339] Ibid. III 498.

God".[340] "God therefore must be at once the absolute person and the ground of all personality."[341] Accordingly, one of Coleridge's theological tasks was "to reconcile the doctrine of the Tri-personality, as deduced from the New Testament, with the unity of the Godhead as enforced in both Testaments".[342]

The concept of person was essential to Coleridge's conversion to the doctrine of the Trinity, and hence essential to his final thought. The conception of God as extramundane ground was joined, logically and emotionally, by the conception of God as "I am". In this discovery of "person" at the heart of Christian conceiving, the doctrine of the Johannine "Logos", as argued above, was of special and felicitous efficacy for Coleridge's mixture of philosophy and religion. Indeed, Coleridge, in his later thinking, maintained that "The most important speculative Theorem in the theology of a Christian is beyond doubt the Personeity of the Godhead, & the consequent Personality of the Father, the Son, and the Spirit".[343]

Person was essential to Coleridge's conceptions, moreover, in that it related to philosophical currencies of the age. Like his somewhat older contemporary, Friedrich Jacobi, Coleridge realised that only the existence of "soul" could guarantee that redemption he so ardently sought in a future life, as well as any meaning in the distraught life he actually lived ("every one, who calls himself a Christian, holds himself to have a Soul as well as a Body").[344] But soul seemed, under the progressive arguments of seventeenth- and eighteenth-century rationalism, more and more a metaphorical conception, or at least one that could not be used in cognitive argument.[345] It was thus necessary to reconceive the meaning of soul under less shopworn titles, such as "personal identity" and "personality", in order to connect the conception with other philosophical distinctions. "Since we have no greater certainty than the certainty of our existence, our Identity and Personality", said Jacobi, "we weigh all other knowledge by this fundamental truth". Person or personal identity could be inserted into philosophical schematisms; soul could not. For instance, the "reason" cherished as a philosophical conception by both Coleridge and Jacobi directly connected itself with the conception of "personality". Coleridge agreeing with and possibly echoing Jacobi, says that animals cannot be granted reason without being granted personality: ". . . we distinguish various *degrees* of Understanding there . . . . But Reason is

[340] See below, Frag 2 f 191.
[341] Ibid. f 189.
[342] Ibid.
[343] *CN* IV 5222.

[344] *AR* (1825) 386.
[345] See e.g. McFarland *Originality* ix–xii, 148–200.

wholly denied, equally to the highest as to the lowest of the brutes; otherwise it must be wholly attributed to them, and with it therefore Self-consciousness, and *personality*, or Moral Being."[346]

Soul, and therefore personality and moral being, had undergone serious conceptual vicissitudes as the result of certain tendencies in Renaissance awareness. Descartes, in the first half of the seventeenth century, had understood that the impact of Renaissance science made it necessary to jettison the Thomist synthesis; that the human essence, if it were separated from nature, must ultimately be conceived as merely an accidental form of nature, with none of the guarantees of continuity and purpose so necessary to those who thought as Coleridge did. In a radical stratagem, Descartes sought by the argument and formula of *cogito ergo sum* to place the idea of person beyond the possibility of sceptical erosion. But the *cogito*, a radical surgery of which it might be said that Descartes amputated at the hip when to other doctors only the toe seemed infected, gained logical protection for the self at the expense of imagination and feeling, and above all of external nature—those very things that later became crucially important for the Romantic sensibility in which Coleridge participated.

Moreover, though Descartes was as dominant in later seventeenth-century thought as Kant was in that of the later eighteenth and early nineteenth century, what happened to the Cartesian position was closely analogous to what would happen to the Kantian: in both instances the thinking of the master was undermined by disciples arguing in its name. Just as the post-Kantian disciples of Kant were in fact all Spinozists, Spinoza and Locke, though utilising Cartesian distinctions and approaches, developed philosophies antithetical to that of Descartes. They formulated philosophies that located reality in external nature and abrogated the independent existence of person, and thus ultimately of soul—Spinoza openly, Locke by implication.[347]

Locke and Spinoza differed considerably in method and in influence. Locke was as it were the godfather of the Enlightenment; Spinoza, on the other hand, was largely scorned by the eighteenth century.[348] In the Romantic era the situation was reversed: Locke was vilified and Spinoza apotheosised. Coleridge rejected both thinkers, Locke with contempt, Spinoza with reverence.[349]

---

[346] *Friend (CC)* I 155.
[347] Cf Crabb Robinson's report that C "assented to my remark that atheism might be demonstrated out of Locke" (*Misc C* 390).
[348] See Paul Vernière *Spinoza et la*

pensée française avant la révolution (2 vols Paris 1954); Max Grunwald *Spinoza in Deutschland* (Berlin 1897); "The Reaction Against Spinoza" *CPT* 261–6.
[349] "Of Locke he spoke as usual with great contempt", reported Crabb Robin-

Spinoza was the deeper thinker of the two. Locke, personally a Christian believer, was both less openly disturbing to established opinion and more immediately understandable, and his psychological approach did not, except to thinkers who followed unexpressed implications, seem to attack Christian guarantees. But in conceiving "the Mind to be, as we say, white Paper, void of all Characters, without any *Ideas*", and to be furnished by "*Experience*",[350] Locke not only made the mind dependent on external reality but emptied it of those conceptions necessary to maintain the conception of "soul". "The Senses at first let in particular *Ideas*, and furnish the yet empty Cabinet."[351] As Coleridge said, in Locke's tradition (in this instance the scheme of Locke's disciple, Hartley), "the soul is present only to be pinched or *stroked*, while the very squeals or purring are produced by an agency wholly independent and alien".[352] Spinoza's attack on "person" was more direct. Persons, and by implication immortal souls, are merely "finite modes" of infinite substance and possess only temporary existence; indeed, deity itself has none of the attributes of person but is rather "res extensa"—an extended thing.[353]

Much of the argument about "soul" in the century preceding Coleridge revolved around the phrase "personal identity", given currency by Locke and later re-argued by thinkers like Joseph Butler and David Hume. Locke, under the rubric "Personal Identity", said in part that "This being premised to find wherein *personal Identity* consists, we must consider what *Person* stands for; which, I think, is a thinking intelligent Being, that has reason and reflection, and can consider it self as it self, the same thinking thing, in different times and places, which it does only by that consciousness which is inseparable from thinking, and, as it seems to me, essential to it: It being impossible for any one to perceive, without perceiving, that he does perceive".[354] Locke, however, warned early on that it was "not easy to resolve" what "makes the same Man, or wherein *Identity* consists".[355]

Butler, one of the most acute of the eighteenth-century thinkers devoted to a defence of Christianity (Coleridge in his youth planned an edition of Butler's *Analogy* as a work that "aided by well-placed notes would answer irresistably all the objections to Christianity founded on a priori reasonings")[356] took up Locke's term and argued, in a tract of

---

son of a conversation with C (*Misc C* 390). For C's reverence for Spinoza, see above, Section XI, and below, Section XXV.
[350] Locke 104.
[351] Ibid. 55.

[352] *BL* (*CC*) I 117.
[353] *Spinoza* II 86 (*Ethica* Pars II Propositio II).
[354] Locke 335.
[355] Ibid. 86.
[356] *CL* I 385–6.

1736 appended to the *Analogy* and called "Of Personal Identity",[357] against the view that "Personality is not a permanent, but a transient thing: That it lives and dies, begins and ends continually: That no one can any more remain one and the same Person two Moments together than two successive Moments can be one and the same Movement: That our Substance is indeed continually changing".[358] Butler on the contrary asserted "that certain Conviction, which necessarily and every Moment rises within us, when we turn our thoughts upon ourselves, when we reflect upon what is past, and look forward upon what is to come".[359] He argued that "by reflecting upon That, which is my Self now, and that which was my Self twenty Years agoe, I discern they are not two, but one and the same Self".[360] Significantly, he understood from the outset that the whole controversy ultimately bore upon the problem of the immortality of the soul.

Three years later Hume, also under the rubric of "Personal Identity", sardonically rejoined: "What then gives us so great a propension to ascribe an identity to these successive perceptions, and to suppose ourselves possessed of an invariable and uninterpreted existence through the whole course of our lives?"[361] "After what manner therefore do they belong to self, and how are they connected with it?"[362] Although someone else "may, perhaps, perceive something simple and continu'd, which he calls *himself*" Hume was convinced there was no such principle in him: "I may venture to affirm of the rest of mankind, that they are nothing but a bundle or collection of different perceptions, which succeed each other with an inconceivable rapidity, and are in a perpetual flux and movement".[363] We "feign the continu'd existence of the perceptions of our senses . . . and run into the notion of a *soul*, and *self*".[364] Thus Hume enters the lists in decisive opposition to Butler.

Matters were further complicated when Kant, in his complex examination of the powers and limitations of the human reason, in 1781 took up the problem of personal identity, and in the first and third paralogisms of pure reason, in the second book of the section on Transcendental Dialectic in the *Kritik der reinen Vernunft*, argued the impossibility of ex-

[357] Butler 301–8. Butler treats Locke politely, but suggests that "Mr. Locke's Observations upon this Subject appear hasty; and he seems to profess himself dissatisfied with Suppositions, which he has made relating to it. But some of those hasty Observations have been carried to a strange Length by Others" (305). It is against those "Others" that Butler argues.

[358] Ibid. 305.
[359] Ibid. 306.
[360] Ibid. 302.
[361] Hume 253.
[362] Ibid. 252.
[363] Ibid.
[364] Ibid. 254.

tending the "I think" or the *cogito ergo sum* to a certainty that "I, as a thinking being (Soul), am *Substance*"[365] or that "the Soul is a person".[366]

In resting his philosophical and theological hopes on the concept of person Coleridge was thus building on a shifting and unstable base. To use person as a true foundation, he needed convincing elucidations and complications that would enable him to extricate the argument of Butler and at the same time deny the "finite modes" of Spinoza, withstand the scepticism of Hume, and dismiss the ambivalences of Kant.

XVII. THE CONCEPT OF WILL

The concept of person required reinforcement if it were to serve as a reliable foundation for Coleridgean thought. Locke had correctly identified the problem of personal identity as one "not easy to resolve", and it became even more beclouded by the paralogisms of Kant and the sceptical attacks of Hume, one of the most formidable of the thinkers against whom the *magnum opus* was designed as defence (Coleridge once described Hume as the "Scotch philosopher, who devoted his life to the undermining of the Christian religion").[367] Coleridge therefore sought to introduce a new factor into the argument, or rather to make the concept of person stronger by laminating to it, as it were, the concept of will: "we become persons exclusively in consequence of the Will . . . a source of personality must therefore be conceived in the Will, and lastly . . . a Will not personal is no idea at all but an impossible conception".[368]

Will became essential to Coleridge's thought for a number of interlocking reasons. First, will was a dynamism, not a static thing, and it accorded with the defining emphasis of Romanticism whereby process and current were substituted for fixity and classification. Will was to Locke's categories of mind as organism was to mechanism. Will could not be compartmentalised, divided, pinned down, or explained away; its seamless current unified once again Hume's discrete "bundle or collection of different perceptions" into a new and powerful reconstitution of "person". Will was "incapable of explication, or explanation";[369] "there can be nothing like it or analogous to it".[370] Will was the counterpart, in the sphere of the subject, of electricity in the sphere of the object; and both metaphorically underlay the very existence of Romanticism. As a dynamism, will also stood outside and above both the pantheism and the "mechanico-corpuscular" conceptions that posed such a threat to Cole-

---

[365] Kant *GS* iv 220.
[366] Ibid. iv 227.
[367] *LS (CC)* 22.

[368] See below, Frag 2 f 161.
[369] Frag 1 f 26.
[370] Ibid. f 27.

ridge's interests. He argued that "there is more in man than can be rationally referred to the life of Nature and the mechanism of Organization; that he has a Will not included in this mechanism; and that the Will is in an especial and pre-eminent sense the spiritual part of our Humanity".[371] It followed that "These Views of the Spirit, and of the Will as Spiritual, form the ground-work of our Scheme".[372]

As an incommensurable dynamism located at the very heart of Romantic commitments to metaphors of current and flow, the emphasis on will was one Coleridge shared with other thinkers, notably Kant, Fichte, Schelling, and, later on, Schopenhauer and Nietzsche. One might even go so far as to say that the apotheosis of the concept of will was the chief criterion of nineteenth-century thought as distinct from earlier thought. The source and font for all of these thinkers, with the exception of Kant, was the emphasis on will supplied by Jacob Boehme.

Coleridge knew Boehme's thought from early adolescence on;[373] for in the late eighteenth century a collection of English translations of Boehme's tracts had been made available by William Law and Coleridge extensively annotated a set of these volumes given him by De Quincey.[374] He held Boehme in the highest intellectual regard. Boehme "was indeed a stupendous human being. Had he received the discipline of education, above all had he possessed the knowledge which would have guarded him against his own delusions, I scarcely know whether we would have had reason to attribute greater genius even to Plato himself".[375]

Boehme's emphasis on "will" was hardly less important for Coleridge than his analysis of the Trinity. Though "will" was brought into the philosophical foreground through Kant's discussion of the moral will in the *Kritik der praktischen Vernunft* of 1788, the more truly Romantic will—the dark, mysterious "will" of Schopenhauer's *Die Welt als Wille und Vorstellung* and Nietzsche's *Der Wille zur Macht*—owes more to Boehme than to Kant. Romantic "will" derives in large part from Boehme's conception of God as "the Will of the Abyss".[376] "We rec-

[371] *AR* (1825) 132.
[372] Ibid. 245.
[373] E.g.: "Before my visit to Germany in September, 1798, I had adopted (probably from Behmen's Aurora, which I had *conjured over* at School) . . ." (*CL* iv 751, 4 July 1817).
[374] *The Works of Jacob Behmen, the Teutonic Theosopher . . . with Figures, illustrating his principles*, left by the Reverend William Law, M. A. (4 vols London 1764–81). There are fourteen

tractates in the collection, and C's set is at present in the British Library. His marginal annotations, which occupy approximately 150 pp, were apparently made over a period of time—1808–1827 might be a reasonable supposition. The annotations are now available in print in the first volume of C's *Marginalia*.
[375] *P Lects* (1949) 329.
[376] Boehme *Mysterium Magnum* i 2.

ognize the will as the eternal Omnipotence", says Boehme.[377] "The unground is an eternal nothing, but makes an eternal beginning as a craving. For the nothing is a craving after something . . . though this craving is also a nothing, that is, merely a will."[378] "The life of man is a form of the divine will, and came from the divine inbreathing into the created image of men."[379]

For the emergence of Boehme's "eternal unfathomable will of life"[380] into nineteenth-century preoccupations, two works were of special importance: Fichte's *Bestimmung des Menschen* and Schelling's *Ueber das Wesen der menschlichen Freiheit*. Schelling's treatise, which appeared in 1809, used "will" as a lever to move his philosophy from Spinozistic pantheism to a dynamic Boehmean variant. "The first beginning of creation", said Schelling, "is the longing of the One to give birth to itself, or the will of the depths".[381] "In the final and highest instance", he insisted, "there is no other being than will; will is primordial being, and all the predicates of being apply to it alone—groundlessness, eternity, independence of time, self-affirmation".[382]

Though such dramatic statements are indisputably Boehmean, they are also competitive with, and doubtless to a significant extent suggested by, Fichte's *Bestimmung des Menschen*, published in 1800. In this intense discussion of freedom and necessity, Fichte recognises that "there is a forming power in nature" that produces "flowers and plants and animals"[383] and that he is "an expression, defined through the universe, of a self-defining natural force":[384] "I myself with everything I call mine am a link in the chain of strict necessity".[385] But the system of necessity deadened him, so he asks what can be invoked against it. His answer is "will"—the force that rolls through both nature and man is not a material but a spiritual force. "The will is the living principle of reason, is reason itself",[386] "the source of true life and eternity".[387] Just as in Fichte's earlier thought the individual ego was merely an expression of the absolute ego, so now the individual will becomes a single expression of an "infinite will", which is the mediator between the spiritual world and the individual.[388]

A third conditioning factor in Coleridge's emphasis on will was, as in the instance of person, supplied by his own personal life. In that life, will seemed to be mysteriously compromised. "The *Will* of my Life is poi-

[377] Boehme *The Earthly and the Heavenly Mystery* iii 1.
[378] Ibid.
[379] Boehme *The Divine Intuition* ii 2.
[380] Ibid. ii 8.
[381] Schelling *SW* vii 395.
[382] Ibid. vii 350.

[383] *Fichte* iii 273.
[384] Ibid. 285.
[385] Ibid. 275.
[386] Ibid. 384.
[387] Ibid. 385.
[388] Ibid. 395.

soned", he laments,[389] and outside observers concurred. As noted above, Southey spoke of his "disease of the volition" while Wordsworth observed that "he has no voluntary power of mind whatsoever".[390] Hazlitt, more bluntly still, said that Coleridge was "a man without a will".[391] Coleridge's own understanding of Original Sin focused on the phenomenon of a diseased will. [392]

With so many and such powerful motives exerting pressure towards its use, will became a central element in Coleridge's system and a chief bulwark of the idea of person:

> In the New Testament I have observed that wherever *the Father* is spoken of, not as inclusive of the Word and the Spirit, or as synonymous with the Godhead but *distinctively*, the WILL, as the source of Being, and therefore in the order of thought antecedent to Being itself (Causa Sui) is meant—And not a week passes, in which some incident or other does not recall to my mind our Saviour's words—No man cometh to me unless *the* FATHER leadeth him. In vain the informing Reason, in vain the inspiring Life, the fecundating Love, if there be not that germ in the *will*, which is the Individual in his essential individuality, which is deeper than all understanding—& till it have been stirred and actualized by that ineffable *Will*, which is the mysterious Ground of all things visible and invisible.[393]

If will in this late letter "is the individual in his essential individuality", in *The Friend*, much earlier, "Will" is the "true and only strict synonime of the word, I, or the intelligent Self".[394] Thus, in the *Biographia Literaria*, "the free-will" is "our only absolute self";[395] in the *Aids to Reflection*, "If there be aught *Spiritual* in Man, the Will must be such. *If* there be a Will, there must be a Spirituality in Man."[396] The "Will" is the "condition" of "Personality".[397] "Will" is "strictly synonymous with the individualizing Principle, the 'I' of every rational Being".[398]

The refrain becomes almost a symphony in the *Opus Maximum*: the "individual Will" is "the principle of personality and free-agency".[399] Man's "responsible Will, is the essential indispensable ground & condition of his Personality".[400] "My own Will is the ground and sufficient cause of my own existence."[401] "Will is even conceived to underlie being itself: though the idea of a Will had been necessary to the idea of

[389] *CN* IV 5235.
[390] See above, Section XV: The Originating Problem and Existential Motive of the *Magnum Opus*.
[391] *CRB* I 11.
[392] See the penultimate note above.
[393] *CL* VI 641.
[394] *Friend (CC)* II 279.

[395] *BL (CC)* I 80.
[396] *AR* (1825) 131.
[397] Ibid. 279.
[398] *CN* III 3708.
[399] See below, Frag 2 f 1.
[400] Ibid. f 158.
[401] Ibid. f 226.

being and though the idea of being is necessarily contained in the idea of Will, yet they are not the same . . . . Our first position therefore is that in the order of necessary thought the Will must be conceived as anterior to all, or that which supports the being".[402]

Indeed, in the *Opus Maximum* Coleridge treats of will in two aspects: the moral will, and the absolute will. The "Absolute Will" is "essentially causative of Reality";[403] the "absolute Will" is "the universal *Ground* of *all* Being".[404] In a note elsewhere Coleridge expands on this contention to include, in utmost abstraction, the entire dialectic of his philosophico/religious schematism:

Position

I.

The Absolute Will.

Synonimes or *Appellations*: Abyss Βυσσος αβυσσος. Τὸ Ὑπερούσιον. *Asei-tatis principium ineffabile. Natura* Dei. Identitas Absoluta. Prothesis absoluta.

Position

II.

The eternal Act of Ipseity, or the Self-realization of the Absolute Will. Synonimes. Asëity. Personëity. *Alfader* (in the Gothic) The Father Almighty. Identitas εν θεσει. Mens absoluta.

Position

III.

The co-eternal *Act* of Alterity, or the Begetting of the Identity in the Alterity. The causative Conception and Utterance of THE WORD—or adequate Expression of the paternal Personëity in the Person of God . . . [405]

Will related itself not merely to being, and not merely to person, but also to idea and to reason: "in the *idea* we have found the reason one with the absolute Will".[406] "It can only be from the want of one or other, or both, of two attributes, which are not in that same sense wanting in man, that we withhold the name of Person from the higher order of animals and these are the Reason & the responsible Will."[407] Even in the structure of social law, Coleridge pointed out, "whether an individual is

[402] Frag 2 f 236.
[403] *CN* IV 5298.
[404] *AR* (1825) 328.

[405] *CN* IV 5256.
[406] See below, Frag 2 f 13.
[407] Ibid. f 166.

a person or not" is "determined by the presence of the Reason in refer-
ence to the Will, and of the Will in its bearings on the Reason".[408] But
despite their co-agency, will is even deeper than as well as prior to rea-
son: Coleridge considered that "Will is no less a real & essential Princi-
ple of Things than Reason, yea, that the Will is deeper than Reason".[409]

As with will and reason, so with will and idea. "It is this presence of
the Will, as an equally essential Co-factor with the intellective Faculty,
that distinguishes an *Idea* from a Conception, and removing the poetic
drapery constitutes the true import of the Platonic Term—for without an
act of the Will it is not possible to contemplate the Particular in the Uni-
versal, the Finite in the Absolute."[410]

Reason and will, though intertwined in their definition of person, are
not the same thing. Not only is will prior and deeper, but as Coleridge
points out, "A Will that does not contain the power of opposing itself to
another Will is no Will at all; and a Reason that did contain in itself a
power of opposing a Reason or of not being one without it, would be no
Reason at all".[411] Reason declares to us that the square of the hypotenuse
of a right-angled triangle is equal to the sum of the squares of the adja-
cent sides; from this there can be no appeal, and to this there can be no
opposition. To deny the theorem would be to be irrational. But, though
different, reason and will reciprocally function to define the human:
"there, & there only, where a reason & a Will are co-present distinctly,
but in relations either of union or oppugnancy, a personality is af-
firmed".[412]

Such interconnections were essential to Coleridge's thinking, and they
followed the prescription of Kant: ". . . there is among the transcenden-
tal ideas themselves a certain connection and unity by which pure rea-
son brings all its knowledge into one system. There is in the progression
from our knowledge of ourselves (the soul) to a knowledge of the world,
and through it to a knowledge of the Supreme Being (*Urwesen*), some-
thing so natural that it looks like the logical progression of reason from
premises to a conclusion."[413] Ultimately, for Coleridge more concretely
than for Kant, the interconnections of these ideas converged on the idea
of a living, personal God, who, to guarantee the requirements of the
Christian soul, must be conceived of as transcendent and supramundane,
not the world-god of pantheism: "This, *this*, is what I have so earnestly
endeavored to shew, that God is Ens super Ens, the *Ground* of all Being,
but therein likewise absolute Being, in that he is the Eternal Self-Affir-
mant, & the I AM in that I AM. And that the key of this mystery is given

---

[408] Frag 2 f 185.
[409] *CN* IV 5144. See also 5298.
[410] *CL* VI 533.

[411] See below, Frag 2 ff 180–1.
[412] Ibid. f 188.
[413] Kant *GS* IV 213.

to us in the pure idea of the WILL, as the alone *causa sui*".[414] Will was the most indispensable factor in the idea of the supramundane God: "by *spiritual* I do not pretend to determine *what* the Will *is* but what it is *not*—namely, that it is not Nature. And as no man who admits a Will at all . . . will suppose it *below* Nature, we may safely add, that it is super-natural".[415]

However inevitable such reciprocities, interconnections, and final focusings might be, however, they could be confusing to those not privy to Coleridge's systematically connected undertaking. As Emerson perplexedly reports of a conversation with him: "He went on defining, or rather refining: "Trinitarian doctrine was realism; the idea of God was not essential, but super-essential"; talked of *trinism* and *tetrakism* and much more, of which I only caught this, "that the will was that by which a person is a person; because, if one should push me in the street, and so I should force the man next me into the kennel, I should at once exclaim, I did not do it, sir, meaning that it was not my will".[416]

XVIII. SUBJECT AND OBJECT

Emerson was not the only one who had the uneasy sense of overhearing a private conversation when in the presence of Coleridge's continuing orchestration of his deeply examined distinctions. "His voice, naturally soft and good", reported Carlyle, "had contracted into a plaintive snuffle and sing-song; he spoke as if preaching,—you would have said, preaching earnestly and also hopelessly the weightiest things. I still recollect his "object" and "subject," terms of continual recurrence in the Kantean province; and how he sang and snuffled them into "om-m-mject" and "sum-m-mject," with a kind of solemn shake or quaver, as he rolled along. No talk, in this century, or in any other, could be more surprising."[417] Carlyle seems to have been fascinated by Coleridge's insistence on the distinction between subject and object: "He had knowledge about many things and topics, much curious reading; but generally all topics led him, after a pass or two, into the high seas of theosophic philosophy, the hazy infinitude of Kantean transcendentalism, with its 'sum-m-mjects' and 'om-m-mjects'".[418]

Though we may share Carlyle's hilarity, we must also understand,

---

[414] *CM (CC)* II 324.
[415] *IS* 132.
[416] *C Talker* 209.
[417] *Carlyle* XI 54–5. Carlyle's report of C's "snuffle and sing'song" seems to be confirmed by an anecdote C tells of himself: "The abominations of Tiberius at Capreae".—These were the words, I dictated. My Amanuensis wrote them down exactly thus—'The burning Nations of Tibby Harris and Cap. Ray.'" (*CN* III 4240.)
[418] *Carlyle* XI 56.

first, that subject and object were merely the most primary logical form
of the dyadic characteristic of Coleridge's thought; second, that they
were terms necessary to his systematic purpose; and third, that they were
then and are yet terms in the mainstream of philosophical discourse.
Coleridge sometimes invokes them outside his explicitly systematic en-
deavour. For instance, in discussing the difference between ground and
condition, he says: "The *ground* of Consciousness, i.e. that which every
act of Consciousness supposes, is the Identity or Indifference of Object
and Subject, but the indispensable Condition of becoming conscious is
the Division or Differencing of the *Subject* and *Object*—."[419]

Subject and object as logical polarity are abstractions from the exis-
tential immediacy of our feeling of "I am" in its relation to our feeling
of "it is", the adjudication of the conflicting claims of which was the con-
suming topic of Coleridge's lifetime of thought.[420] As such, they stand
in for two of the three entities that Christian Wolff had identified as the
necessary and irreducible starting points of philosophy: "human souls"
and "bodies or material things".[421] The third of the necessary entities
was "God", and the specific nature of God depends entirely on the na-
ture of the adjudication of the relationship between the subject, or the
sense of our own "I am", and the object, or our awareness of the "it
is".[422]

Thus all three elements, subject, object, and the conception of God,
were intertwined in Coleridge's thought, and their mutual implications
permeated the conception of each individual element: "Now the very
purpose of my system is to overthrow Pantheism, to establish the diver-
sity of the Creator from the sum Whole of his Creatures, deduce the per-
soneity, the I Am of God, and in one and the same demonstration to
demonstrate the reality and originancy of Moral Evil, and to account for
the fact of a finite Nature".[423] To attain this desired distribution it was
logically necessary, as Coleridge came to realise, to postulate the subject
as preceding all other awareness, but without giving up its relationship
to the object. As he said in 1832, "the pith" of his system was "to make
the senses out of the mind—not the mind out of the senses, as Locke
did".[424]

It was easier said than done, however, particularly to a mind as re-
sponsive as Coleridge's to all the variegated data of experience. In a let-

[419] *CM (CC)* IV 5276.
[420] See *CPT* 53–72, 107–25, 230–55.
[421] See above, Section VIII: The Magnum Opus and Natural Science.
[422] See *CPT* 54–70.
[423] Notebook 35, f 25ᵛ. Printed in Boulger 129.
[424] *TT (CC)* II 179, 25 July 1832.

ter of 1825 he vividly evokes the sense of the ever-continued struggle for ascendancy between subject and object:

In Youth and early Manhood the Mind and Nature are, as it were, two rival Artists, both potent Magicians, and engaged like the King's Daughter and the rebel Genie in the Arabian Nights' Enternts., in sharp conflict of Conjuration— each having for it's object to turn the other into Canvas to paint on, Clay to mould, or Cabinet to contain. For a while the Mind seems to have the better of the contest, and makes of Nature what it likes; takes her Lichens and Weather-stains for Types & Printer's Ink and prints Maps & Fac Similes of Arabic and Sanscrit Mss. on her rocks; composes Country-Dances on her moon-shiny Ripples, Fandangos on her Waves and Walzes on her Eddy-pools; transforms her Summer Gales into Harps and Harpers, Lovers' Sighs and sighing Lovers, and her Winter Blasts into Pindaric Odes, Christabels & Ancient Mariners set to music by Beethoven, and in the insolence of triumph conjures her Clouds into Whales and Walrusses with Palanquins on their Backs, and chaces the dodging Stars in a Sky-hunt!—But alas! alas! that Nature is a wary wily long-breathed old Witch, tough-lived as a Turtle and divisible as the Polyp, repullulative in a thousand Snips and Cuttings, integra et in toto! She is sure to get the better of Lady MIND in the long run, and to take her revenge too—transforms our To Day into a Canvass dead-colored to receive the full featureless Portrait of Yesterday; and alone turns the mimic Mind, the ci-devant Sculptress with all her kaleido-scopic freaks and symmetries! into clay, but *leaves* it such a *clay*, to cast dumps or bullets in; and lastly (to end with that which suggested the beginning—) she mocks the mind with it's own metaphors, metamorphosing the Memory into a lignum vitae Escritoire to keep unpaid Bills & Dun's Letters in, with Outlines that had never been filled up, MSS that never went farther than the Title-pages, and Proof-Sheets & Foul Copies of Watchmen, Friends, Aids to Reflection & other *Stationary* Wares that have kissed the Publisher's Shelf with gluey Lips with all the tender intimacy of inosculation!—Finis![425]

Because of the difficulty of adjudicating the claims of the two realms without doing violence to either, Coleridge took help where he could find it, and for a time he thought he had found it in Schelling. The dialectic of subject and object seemed, in Schelling's *System des transzendentalen Idealismus* of 1800, to be most harmoniously intermeshed and developed; accordingly, Coleridge translated the opening portions of Schelling's demonstration, without specific acknowledgement, into the twelfth chapter of the *Biographia Literaria*. By way of rather disingenuous disclaimer Coleridge had said early in the ninth chapter that "In Schelling's 'NATUR-PHILOSOPHIE,' and the 'SYSTEM DES TRANSCENDENTALEN IDEALISMUS,' I first found a genial coincidence with much

[425] *CL* v 496–7, 9 Oct 1825.

that I had toiled out for myself, and a powerful assistance in what I had yet to do."[426] He then went on to say that

> It would be but a mere act of justice to myself, were I to warn my future readers, that an identity of thought, or even similarity of phrase will not be at all times a certain proof that the passage has been borrowed from Schelling, or that the conceptions were originally learnt from him . . . . many of the most striking resemblances, indeed all the main and fundamental ideas, were born and matured in my mind before I had ever seen a single page of the German Philosopher . . .[427]

A few pages later, rather in contradiction to this, Coleridge says that

> to SCHELLING we owe the completion, and the most important victories, of this revolution in philosophy. To me it will be happiness and honor enough, should I succeed in rendering the system itself intelligible to my countrymen, and in the application of it to the most awful of subjects for the most important of purposes. Whether a work is the offspring of a man's own spirit, and the product of original thinking, will be discovered by those who are its sole legitimate judges, by better tests than the mere reference to dates. For readers in general, let whatever shall be found in this or any future work of mine, that resembles, or coincides with, the doctrines of my German predecessor, though contemporary, be wholly attributed to *him*: provided, that the absence of distinct references to his books, which I could not at all times make with truth as designating citations or thoughts actually *derived* from him; and which, I trust, would, after this general acknowledgment be superfluous; be not charged on me as an ungenerous concealment or intentional plagiarism.[428]

After these bizarre and psychologically convoluted explanations, which have much exercised Coleridgean commentators from De Quincey in 1834 to scholars in our own day,[429] Coleridge in Book Twelve embarks on a discussion of the subject/object relationship that is a verbatim translation from Schelling.[430]

Near the end of his life Coleridge repudiated "the metaphysical disquisition at the end of the first volume" of the *Biographia Literaria* as "unformed and Immature", though it contained "the fragments of the truth".[431] We may suppose that he was not so much spurred by embar-

---

[426] *BL (CC)* i 160.
[427] Ibid. i 161.
[428] Ibid. i 163–4.
[429] See *De Q Works* ii 142–6; James Ferrier "The Plagiarisms of S. T. Coleridge" *Blackwood's Edinburgh Magazine* 47 (1840) 287–99; McFarland "The Problem of Coleridge's Plagiarisms" *CPT* 1–52; Norman Fruman *Coleridge the Damaged Archangel* (New York 1971); Thomas McFarland "Coleridge's Plagiarisms Once More: A Review Essay" *The Yale Review* 63 (1974) 252–86.
[430] See *BL (CC)* i 252–7.

rassment over his verbatim translations (although presumably that fact can be accorded some weight, despite a lifetime of self-deception) as by his realisation that the promising beginning of Schelling led to pantheism, which it was the whole purpose of his own striving to avoid.

Schelling's beginning promised a reconcilement of Coleridge's perplexities about the relationship of "I am" and "it is" and neatly tied up the whole matter in a unified system. As Coleridge said, in echo of Schelling, in Chapter Twelve: "the true system of natural philosophy places the sole reality of things in an ABSOLUTE . . . . in the absolute identity of subject and object, which it calls nature, and which in its highest power is nothing else than self-conscious will or intelligence".[432] But this recension of Schelling's *Identitätssystem*, though it offered a completed system, led directly to pantheism: Schelling's Absolute was not the living God of Christianity but a blind force of nature. Coleridge came to realise that Schelling's thought, "as a System" was "little more than Behmenism" and "like Behmen's it is reduced at last to a mere Pantheism".[433] Of one of Schelling's treatises Coleridge wrote in 1818 that he could "see clearly the rotten parts and the vacua of his foundation".[434] He finally termed Schelling's thought a "Hylozoic Atheism",[435] a "sort of Plotinised Spinozism".[436] In 1825 he referred to Schelling as "the reviver of pantheist Atheism with Romish Pseudo-Catholicism for its mythologic Drapery".[437]

The harmonious interplay of subject and object in Schelling's disquisition initially seemed to promise a systematic resolution of the struggle between mind and nature, but it is not difficult to see where in that disquisition a wrong turning occurred for Coleridge's own destined path. In fact, we can see him struggling almost blindly towards that path. His *proton pseudos*, as it were, was to take at face value Schelling's "either/or": the assumption that it made no difference whether one began with the subject or the object, and that one therefore could and must begin interchangeably. Coleridge came to realise that it was precisely here that all ultimate difference originated. Even as he is repeating Schelling's identity-formula of the coalescence of subject and object in the absolute, he is also struggling to extricate his own authentic line: "We begin with the I KNOW MYSELF, in order to end with the absolute I AM. We proceed from the SELF, in order to lose and find all self in GOD."[438]

But this understanding is still liminal in the *Biographia Literaria*; it

[431] *TT (CC)* ii 293, 28 June 1834.
[432] *BL (CC)* i 285.
[433] *CL* iv 883, 24 Nov 1818.
[434] Ibid. iv 873, 30 Sep 1818.

[435] *CL* iv 874.
[436] Ibid. iv 883.
[437] *CN* iv 5262.
[438] *BL (CC)* i 283.

occurs in the same paragraph in which Coleridge expressly adheres to Schelling's "either/or": "it must be remembered, that all these Theses refer solely to one of the two Polar Sciences, namely, to that which commences with and rigidly confines itself within, the subjective, leaving the objective (as far as it is exclusively objective) to natural philosophy, which is its opposite pole".[439] Coleridge here seems to be fascinated, in high Romantic fashion, by the idea of a polar reciprocity; he needed to learn and would learn the truth enunciated in our own day by French post-structuralist theory, that in every nominal polarity one term is actually superior (plus as opposed to minus, major as opposed to minor, etc.).

In any event, his own line of thought was struggling to emerge from the Schellingian polar pattern: "In the third treatise of my *Logosophia*, announced at the end of this volume", he says in the *Biographia Literaria*, "I shall give (deo volente) the demonstrations and constructions of the Dynamic Philosophy scientifically arranged. It is, according to my conviction, no other than the system of Pythagoras and Plato revived and purified from impure mixtures".[440] That system, as shall presently appear, would lead to something quite different from Schelling. Indeed, in a note in the *Biographia Literaria*, Coleridge adumbrates his eventual realisation that though subject and object are both necessary, the object must always follow the subject: "The impossibility of an absolute thing (substantia unica) . . . as well as its utter unfitness for the fundamental position of a philosophic system, will be demonstrated in the critique of Spinozism in the fifth treatise of my Logosophia".[441] Spinoza was his greatest opponent, and Schelling, he came eventually to realise, was merely an avatar of Spinoza.

By the time of the *Opus Maximum*, therefore, Coleridge was firmly convinced that "the recent writings of Schelling and his followers" were "an attempt to clothe the skeleton of the Spinozistic pantheism & breathe life thereinto".[442] He was equally convinced "that the notion of objects as altogether objective, begins in the same moment in which the conception is formed that is wholly subjective".[443] In a note of 1825 he muses on the priority of the subject in the subject/object relationship: "Subject = Object, i.e. the Identity of S. and O. or a Subject which is itself the Object to and for itself. And this antecedent we find in the Fact of an I Am, or Self-conscious Being./ Thus in the Science of Grammar."[444]

Coleridge's dawning realisation that the subject must precede the ob-

[439] *BL* (*CC*) I 281–2.
[440] Ibid. I 263.
[441] Ibid. I 271*.

[442] See below, Frag 2 f 266.
[443] Ibid. f 98 (note).
[444] *CN* IV 5215.

ject drew him away from Schelling towards the position of Schelling's opponent, Jacobi, who repeatedly argued that "If reason can be only in person, and the world is to have a rational originator, mover, ruler, then this being must be a *personal* being".[445] On the other hand, Jacobi's lack of interest in external nature and the world of science, and his rejection of system, prevented Coleridge from establishing any extensive congruence with his thought. Indeed, the very fact that the interrelation of subject and object was so urgent for Coleridge indicated that Jacobi could provide him no complete base.

XIX. MOTHER AND CHILD

As Schelling's special adjudication of the dialectic of subject and object was first accepted and then repudiated by the English thinker, Coleridge likewise transferred his dyadic preoccupation from the Schellingian "either/or" to the, for him, more authentic and fruitful conception of the "I am", thereby resuming his deeper preoccupation with the concept of person. It is in Coleridge's extended musings on the structure of the "I am", in which he characteristically proceeds by dyadic discriminations, that the most distinctive emphasis of his thought emerges, and this emphasis is most fully developed in the *Opus Maximum*.

The dyadic combinations take three forms: the relation of mother and child, the relation of father and son, and, as culmination of Coleridge's systematic endeavour, the relation of I and Thou. All combine to supply Coleridge with an empirical accounting of the ineluctable "alterity" of human personality, and thereby validate the idea of the logical alterity of God and Christ so necessary to the maintenance in his own mind of Christianity as "reason" and not merely speculation.

His ruminations on the relationship of mother and child seem peculiarly modern, occupying as they do an area staked out by the most advanced psychoanalytical theorists of our own day, notably Heinz Kohut, Margaret Mahler, Otto Kernberg, René Spitz, H. W. Loewald, and D. W. Winnicott, among others. Logically, Coleridge's investigation stems from the authority of origins: to find what a human is, one should begin at the beginning and ask what is the situation at birth (Coleridge once presciently suggested that what happens in the nine months in the womb could be as psychologically important as everything that happened afterwards). Furthermore, the relationship of mother and child specifically involved the dialectic of subject and object that was of such moment in his thought.

[445] Jacobi *Werke* IV – 1 xlv.

There can be little doubt, moreover, that the dyadic relationship of mother and child took on added weight by becoming one of the topics of symbiotic conversation between Coleridge and Wordsworth.[446] Indeed, Wordsworth's inspired musings in the second book of "The Prelude" seem as modern as do those of Coleridge.[447] Coleridge was as fascinated as was Wordsworth by the creation of love from the dyadic relationship of mother and child, and by the creation of the infant's self as a reflection from the mother. The "first dawnings" of a baby's "humanity will break forth in the Eye that connects the Mother's face with the warmth of the mother's bosom, the support of the mother's Arms. A thousand tender kisses excite a finer life in its lips & there first language is imitated from the mother's smiles. Ere yet a conscious self exists the love begins & the first love is love to another. The Babe acknowledges a self in the Mother's form, years before it can recognize a self in its own."[448] Coleridge has here proleptically grasped the importance of that "mirroring" that has become an important element in modern psychoanalytic theory about the development of an infant (Lacan appears to have been the first to use the actual word).

Coleridge was well aware that his attention to the earliest dawnings of humanity in the mother-child relationship was outside the mainstream of developmental theory in his time: "With few exceptions, few notwithstanding the numerous works in behoof of education, founded on the principles of Mr. Locke and Drs Hartley, Priestley, Edgeworth &c.— with a few exceptions, I say, even in the schooled & educated ranks of society the first three or four years of life have been abandoned to the delusions of nature".[449] He himself, on the contrary, returns in the *Opus Maximum* again and again to the portentous importance of the dyadic development of the self, at the beginning of life, out of the initial sense of oneness with the mother. Although his emphasis differs from that of modern psychoanalytic theory in that he undertook the investigation primarily to find underpinnings for Trinitarian Christian theory, Coleridge's conclusions are often close to modern understanding:

The infant follows its mother's face as glowing with love and dreaming protection it is raised heavenward, and with the word God it combines in feeling whatever there is of reality in the warm touch, in the supporting grasp, in the glorious countenance. The whole problem of existence is present as a sum total in the mother; the mother exists as a One & indivisible something, before the outlines of her different limbs and features have been distinguished by the fixed and yet

---

446 For the existence of such conversation, see "The Symbiosis of Coleridge and Wordsworth" *RFR* 56–103.

447 *Prelude* 1850 version, II 232–48.
448 See below, Frag 2 ff 66–7.
449 Ibid. f 87.

half vacant eye, & hence through each degree of dawning light the whole remains antecedent to the parts, not as composed of them but as their ground and proper meaning; no otherwise than as the word or sentence to the single letters, which occur in spelling.[450]

Coleridge here describes in conscious schematism what Wordsworth, unconsciously, transmutes into sublime poetry. If for Wordsworth the "workings of one mind, the features / Of the same face" implied "the great Apocalypse, / The types and symbols of Eternity",[451] for Coleridge, with equal urgency and equal finality, the "whole problem of existence is present as a sum total in the mother", and this primal experience leads irresistibly to the idea of "God". We are reminded that for the greatest of nineteenth-century theologians, Schleiermacher, religion grew simply out of *Abhängigkeitsgefühl*, the feeling of absolute dependence. Nowhere is dependence more absolute than in the relation of infant and mother.

Coleridge's extrapolation of the dyadic origin of self in the mother-child relationship served his needs in the attempt to validate the three-personed God of Christianity—that is to say, a dyadic relationship of God and Christ, with the Holy Ghost as the binding principle. His argumentation was slow and painstaking, mixing the abstract and the concrete, as disparate samples will illustrate:

The alterity must have some distinctive from the original absolute identity or how could it be contemplated as other, and yet this distinctive must be such as not to contradict the other co-essential term, it must remain in some sense the Self, though another Self".[452]

... The child now learns its own alterity, & sooner or later as if some sudden crisis had taken place in its nature, it forgets henceforward to speak of itself by imitation . . . . It becomes a person, it is and speaks of itself as I; and from that moment it has acquired what it may loosen and deform, but can never eradicate—a sense of an alterity in itself which no eye can see, neither his own or others.[453]

As sure as ever the heart of man is made tender by the presence of a love that has no self by a joy in the protection of the helpless, which is at once impulse, motive, and reward, so surely is it elevated to the universal Parent.[454]

... the living truth is there, that which the mother is to her child, a someone unseen and yet ever present is to all. The first introduction to thought takes place in the transfer of person from the senses to the invisible. The reverence of the

---

[450] Frag 2 ff 88–9.
[451] *Prelude*, 1805 version, VI 569–72.
[452] See below, Frag 2 f 246; see also f 148.
[453] Ibid. f 92.
[454] Ibid. f 78.

Invisible, substantiated by the feeling of love—this, which is the essence and proper definition of religion is the commencement of the intellectual life, of the humanity. If ye love not your earthly parent, how *can* ye love your father in heaven?[455]

Because he based so much on the creation of self and love out of the dyadic relation of mother and child, which both prefigured and recapitulated the relation of God to man, Coleridge was painstaking in his imaginative recreation of that earliest human relationship. Without the truly dyadic relationship no adequate self could emerge:

. . . compare a child, insulated even from its birth, by the high rank and sullen pride of its parents, who had never fed at the bosom of a mother, say rather who had had no mother . . . . Whose servile nurse mute & joyless is forbidden to press its lips with kisses and finally one who instead of playmates is surrounded with an endless variety of playthings. Compare, I say, a creature thus denaturalized with the healthful child of a cottage, whose first playthings were its mother's lap or father's knee, who had no enjoyment that was not at the same moment seen in the form of another . . .[456]

The passage compellingly points to the stanza in Wordsworth, Coleridge's soulmate, that bids us

> Behold the Child among his new-born blisses,
> A six years' Darling of a pigmy size!
> See, where 'mid work of his own hand he lies,
> Fretted by sallies of his mother's kisses,
> With light upon him from his father's eyes![457]

The spontaneity of the infant's enjoyment of the mother was for Coleridge a warrant, or a benchmark, of the holiness of the relationship, and therefore of its symbolic foreshadowing of religious truths:

When the little Being newly nourished or awakening from its heaving pillow begins its murmuring song for pleasure & for pleasure leaps on the arm begins to smile & laugh to the moving head of the Mother who is to it, its all the World, it knows not what the Mother is, but still less does it know what itself is. If I have to put the question & to have returned the answer be to know, the babe knows nothing. But it clings to the Mother & has a right, an unutterable right, to cling to her. Behold the sweet innocent lies before thee on thy arm, looks up towards thee & towards thee stretches forth with all its limbs, has the present & yet seeks thee, unutterably thanks thee . . . . Why have Men a Faith in God, there is but one answer: the Man & the Man alone has a Father & a Mother.[458]

[455] Frag 2 f 79.
[456] Ibid. ff 74–6.
[457] *WPW* iv 281–2.
[458] See below, Frag 2 ff 66–7.

Coleridge clearly understood the phenomenon of touching as essentially bound up with the earliest awareness of being, and in this he anticipated a strong current of modern psychoanalytical emphasis. He speaks of "the three years child" that "has awoke during the dark night" in the crib by the mother's bed, and can be heard to "entreat in piteous tones 'Touch me, only touch me with your finger.' A child of that age, under the same circumstances I myself heard using these very words . . . . 'I am not here, touch me Mother, that I may be here!' The witness of its own being has been suspended in the loss of the mother's presence by sight or sound or feeling. The father and the heavenly father, the form in the shape, and the form affirmed for itself are blended in one, and yet convey the earliest lesson of distinction and alterity".[459]

As the psychoanalyst David Beres has emphasised, Coleridge himself as an infant was subjected to a "failure in maternal care".[460] Whether such experience had anything to do with his philosophical examination of the mother-child relationship can only be conjectured. In any case, his extended rumination on that relationship constitutes one of the most idiosyncratic, and in view of the weight he attached to it, one of the most important aspects of his thought: "for the infant the mother contains his own Self and the whole problem of existence as a whole, and the word *God* is the first and one solution of the problem".[461] "With the awakening of self consciousness, the first sign or representative of which is not its own bodily shape, but the gradually dawning presence of the mother's, the conception of life is elevated into that of personeity: and as particular shape is beheld only in the higher and freer conception of form, so again this form itself . . . is taken up into & becomes one with the yet higher or rather deeper & more inward principle of person."[462] In short, "If there be an awful moment in the life of Man it is that in which the yearling babe is seated on its Mother's knee".[463] This is one of the finest moments and certainly the most original emphasis in Coleridge's thought.

XX. COLERIDGE'S PHILOSOPHICAL FULCRUM: I AND THOU

Despite the emotional power of Coleridge's cognizance of the origin of religious feeling in the mother-child relationship, and of the origin of the

---

[459] Frag 2 ff 90–1.
[460] Beres 97–116. For a biographical description of the way in which the "failure of maternal care" in his childhood underlay C's adult misery, see "Cole-

ridge's Anxiety" *RFR* 104–36.
[461] See below Frag 2 f 89.
[462] Ibid. f 98.
[463] Ibid. f 69.

sense of self in alterity—perhaps even to some extent because of that emotional power—the mother-child relationship could adumbrate but not wholly or cognitively justify the theological conclusions towards which he argued. The final theological goal was the father-son relationship, and the pre-Oedipal arena of mother-child relationship, while it perhaps suggested the father-son relationship, could not directly be converted into it. Coleridge ultimately wanted to transfer the concept of alterity, so patiently extricated from the universal relationship of mother and child, to that of father and son:

That the filial Word is the intelligibile et mens altera, the Father the mens absoluta; but then in relation to the idea of himself the Intellective Word, he is both the Mens absoluta &c & is intelligibile reciprocum; as the Father knoweth the Son even so the Son knoweth the Father. Hence the synonyms for the Logos . . . & by Philo Judaeus, in writings anterior & certainly independent of the New Testament, the Logos which we are anxiously forbidden to consider as attribute, personification or equivalent term is described as Deus alter et idem.[464]

It is important to understand that the closer Coleridge approached to a rational disposition of the idea of the Trinity, that is, one that he could accept as conforming to human reason as well as to human need, the more urgent became his investigations into the structure of human personality, which was to be extrapolated into the Trinitarian truth:

. . . God is Love. But how can there be love without communication? And how can there be a communication without presupposing some other with . . . the communicant? And again how can there be love without life, or communication without act, or an act . . . . Next therefore to the eternal act . . . is the co-eternal act of alterity or the begetting of the identity in the alterity. Difficult indeed or rather impossible is it to render this idea intelligible if we turn from it & in its place substitute any production of thing from thing, or propagation of image from image, but if we pass inward on our mind and know that it is truths of minds, acts of spirits, & unities transcendent & indivisible, of which we are discoursing, we shall discover . . . .[465]

It was thus not in the relation of "thing to thing" that Coleridge came to base his hopes for the philosophical validation of Christianity, but in the realm of "the mind, exerting its powers, unaided, on such facts alone as are found within its own consciousness".[466] The relation of "thing to thing", as Jacobi had argued and Coleridge realised as well, led to fatalism, pantheism, and atheism. Accordingly, the "unities transcendent" and "truths of minds" had to be cognized and sorted out with great pre-

---

[464] Frag 2 ff 254–5.   [466] See below Frag 2 f 1.
[465] Ibid. ff 252–3.

cision, and this requirement prevented Coleridge from a loose juxtaposition of mother-child with father-son. What he needed was a principle more abstractly universal even than mother-child, and one not tied to origins. It had to be a principle that would accord with the distinctions he had extricated in his consideration of mother and child, but at the same time it had to be complete in itself and thus capable of application to the dyad of father and son. This principle he evolved in the concept of I and Thou, which may well constitute the apex, as well as the fulcrum, of his philosophical effort.

The I and Thou has become a respected dichotomy in modern thought through the agency of Martin Buber, whose classic treatise, *Ich und Du*, published in Berlin in 1922 and in Leipzig in the succeeding year, has had wide influence in various cultural fields. For Buber the true nature of the "I" is expressed by its dimension as "Duwelt", while the formal "I" of science and philosophy (and in Coleridge's day of Fichte and Schelling) implies a different meaning in a different realm, the "Eswelt".[467] It is the "dusagenkönnen" (the capability of saying "Thou") that marks the truly human; we experience things, but we encounter a "Thou"—and "all real life is encounter".[468] To Buber, this fundamental principle finds its culmination in the concept of God, not as a final "it", but as an eternal "Thou":

> The eternal Thou cannot become It, because it cannot be posited in measure and bound, not even in the measure of unmeasurableness and the bound of boundless being; because it is not a sum of qualities—cannot even be conceived as an infinite sum of qualities raised to transcendence; because it can be met with neither in nor outside the world; because it cannot be experienced, cannot be thought; because we err when we say, "I believe, that He is"—even "He" is a metaphor, but not "Thou."[469]

To Buber the testimony of the real locus of human life as I-Thou rather than I-it arises from the phenomenon of speech: "Geist ist Wort"—spirit is word. "Geist ist nicht im Ich, sondern zwischen Ich und Du"[470]—but just as words do not arise from the confrontation of I and it, but only from the encounter of I and Thou, so too does the human spirit find its only fulfilment in the Thou that alone expresses the meaning of I:

> I perceive something (*etwas*). I sense something (*etwas*). I represent something (*etwas*). I feel something (*etwas*). I think something (*etwas*) . . . . All this, and of this order, together underlies the realm of the "it."
> But the realm of the Thou stands on other ground. He who says Thou has no

---

[467] Buber *Ich und Du* e.g. 42.
[468] Ibid. 24, 18.

[469] Ibid. 129.
[470] Ibid. 49.

Etwas as his object .... He who says Thou has no *Etwas*, has nothing. But he stands in relation (*Beziehung*) ... In the beginning is relation .... The *Eswelt* has connection (*Zusammenhang*) in time and space.

The *Duwelt* has no connection in either .... Without "it" the human cannot live. But he who lives with "it" alone, is not human.[471]

Some such understanding Coleridge came to for himself. Like Buber (and also like Jaspers, who links "love" and "communication"), Coleridge realised that the phenomenon of speech implies a dyadic structure for humanity: "God is Love. But how can there be love without communication? and how can there be a communication without presupposing some other with ... the communicant?"[472] Like Buber, too, Coleridge recognised that this dyadic structure can be expressed only as the necessary reciprocity of I and Thou:

Now the third person could never have been distinguished from the first but by means of the second. There can be no He without a previous Thou .... This is a deep meditation, though the position is capable of the strictest proof,— namely, that there can be no I without a Thou, and that a Thou is only possible by an equation in which I is taken as equal to Thou, and yet not the same .... I do not will to consider myself as equal to myself, for in the very act of constituting myself *I*, I take it as the same, and therefore as incapable of comparison, that is of any application of the will ... the equation of Thou with I, by means of a free act, negativing the sameness in order to establish the equality, is the definition of conscience ... the conscience is the root of all consciousness ... the precondition of all experience,—and ... can not have been in its first revelation deduced from experience.[473]

A complicated and somewhat different version of this reasoning occurs in Coleridge's notebooks. He queries

Whether in the Dynamic Construction of Grammar the second person ought not to be advanced to the Third, and the Third retracted to the second place?—It is an evident Trichotomy, consequently, Thesis, Antithesis, and Synthesis—Now I and It are evidently the antitheses—he, She are It potenziated by the original ... Thesis—but Thou seems clearly to be

$$I + it + i = h = Thou.$$

It must never be forgotten that I is a perpetual, i.e. ever recurring Thesis.

I   It. But It is I[†] modified—I make a duplicate of I, and combining it with It or Not-I—I have the notion of a Spirit = He, or She—Then I again modify it by I—and I have Thou—

[471] Ibid. 10, 11, 25, 42.   [473] Shedd v 559–60.
[472] See below, Frag 2 f 252.

† i.e. I being = Subject-Object, I contemplate exclusively as *Object*. Thence It.—To this I substern or subadd the Subject-Object—and have He or Masn. This I modify by I taken exclusively as Subject—and the result is Thou.—[474]

It is apparent that Coleridge's formulations, though similar to that of Buber, are not identical. The I-Thou of Coleridge is a deduction from the nature of consciousness rather than an axiom of experience.

The polarity arose in the individual personality by the evolution of conscience as a condition of consciousness.[475] As Coleridge said, "I rather think that conscience is the ground and antecedent of human or (self-) consciousness, and not any modification of the latter . . . for if I asked, How do you define the human mind? the answer must at least contain, if not consist of, the words, 'a mind capable of conscience'".[476] He meditated constantly on this doubleness: "Does not personality necessarily suppose a *ground* distinct from the Person . . . ? Conscire, = scio me quasi alterum. The *Me* in the objective case is clearly distinct from the *Ego*."[477] And he eventually says, "This is the corner-stone of my system, ethical metaphysical, and theological—the priority, namely, both in dignity and order of generation, of the Conscience to the Consciousness in Man—No I without a Thou, no Thou without a Law from Him, to whom I and Thou stand in the same relation. Distinct Self- Knowledge begins with the Sense of Duty to our neighbor: and Duty felt so, and claimed from, my Equal supposes and implies the Right of Third, superior to both because imposing it on both."[478] This kind of argumentation is really about as close to Heidegger and to Freud as to Buber.

Buber himself was unaware that he had been preceded in I-Thou formulation by Coleridge. He did know that he was not the first to set forth the principle, but not until more than thirty years after the publication of *Ich und Du* did he realise that the formulation had been expressed earlier than by Feuerbach in 1843,[479] and it was to Feuerbach alone that Buber granted precedence.[480]

But Feuerbach was not in any sense the thinker who "introduced that discovery of the *Thou*, which has been called the 'Copernican revolution' of modern thought". Indeed, not only was he preceded by Cole-

---

[474] *CN* III 4426.

[475] "It appears then that even the very first step . . . the becoming conscious of a conscience . . . is likewise the commencement of experience . . ." (Shedd v 559).

[476] Shedd I 185. Cf *AR* (1848) 92.

[477] *CL* IV 849.

[478] Notebook 26, as printed in App I to Boulger 227.

[479] For the I-Thou distinction in Feuerbach see *Grundsätze der Philosophie der Zukunft* para 58–60, 62–3, in *Feuerbach* II 344–5.

[480] Buber *Between Man* 147–8.

ridge, but the distinction was very much "in the air" among the German Romantics who also preceded him. Friedrich Schlegel, in 1799, had said that "Nur in der Antwort seines Du kann jedes Ich seine unendliche Einheit ganz fühlen"—only in the answer of its Thou can every I wholly feel its infinite unity.[481] Novalis, in one of his cryptic fragments in the late 1790s, said that "the principle of 'I' is the true common and liberal, universal principle . . . also the principle of the highest manifoldness—(*Thou*) (Instead of not-I—Thou)".[482] And Franz von Baader, in 1797, argued "The requirement of unity (self-maintenance) of consciousness makes it a law of the spirit-forming power always to maintain itself in juxtaposition and reciprocity to a similar unity (a Thou). If such a Thou is not set up or is lost, the I . . . strives . . . to lay hold of it."[483]

Much more comprehensive than these hints and foreshadowings were the conceivings of the polymath and linguistic theorist, Wilhelm von Humboldt, who in 1827, in an essay on "the dual", spoke of the I-Thou principle in the same grammatical form as did Coleridge, although other aspects of his emphasis are somewhat different. "In the invisible organism of the spirit", wrote Humboldt, ". . . the concept of duality roots itself in a much deeper and more original way in thesis and antithesis, in positing and negating, in being and not-being, in the I and the world. Even where concepts divide into threes or more, the third term stems from the original dichotomy."[484]

It is not clear that Coleridge read Humboldt's essay, and in any event it was written after the Coleridgean formulations had already been made. But Humboldt's musings are of special interest as an indication of the dissemination of ideas within the Romantic world of thought, for both Coleridge's emphasis on the origin of the I-Thou out of the forms of grammar and his emphasis on the implications of this fact for communal feeling are elements of Humboldt's projection. Coleridge's argument that "Self-Knowledge begins with the Sense of Duty to our neighbor" parallels Humboldt's asseveration that "thinking is essentially accompanied by the inclination toward social existence". Indeed, Coleridge in the *Opus Maximum* observes that "Unlike a multitude of tygers, a million of men is far other and more than one man repeated a million times. Each man in a numerous society is not simply coexistent, he is virtually co-organized with, and into, the multitude of which he is an integral part . . . ."[485] Interestingly, and indicative of the multi-sourced complexity of all these medi-

[481] Schlegel *Lucinde* 221.
[482] *Novalis* II.
[483] *Baader* III 227.

[484] *Humboldt* VI 24–5.
[485] See below, Frag 2 f 15.

tations, Coleridge here not only proleptically asserts the position of Durkheim, which in itself has become the bedrock and foundation of modern sociology, but echoes a thought that he had enunciated as early as 1806, when, speaking of the personality and its relationship to the divine, he had mused about a "reflex consciousness" and said that it was not conceivable without the action of kindred

souls on each other, i.e. the modification of each by each, and of each by the Whole. A male & female Tyger is neither more or less whether you suppose them only existing in their appropriate wilderness, or whether you suppose a thousand Pairs. But Man is truly altered by the co-existence of other men; his faculties cannot be developed in himself alone, & only by himself . . . . Hence with a certain degree of satisfaction to my own mind I can define the human Soul to be that class of Being, as far as we are permitted to know . . . which is endued with a reflex consciousness of it's own continuousness . . . .[486]

Coleridge's thinking was therefore probably a compound of continuing meditation on long-held views evolving out of his own experience of life and hints from the very wide reading he had done in various philosophical sources. Although it is not clear that he was aware of such hints as supplied by Humboldt, he was undoubtedly privy to those supplied by Jacobi. For Jacobi, who for forty years and more stood in brilliant and dauntless opposition to the whole progress of philosophical thought in Germany, was as much at the forefront in the formulation of the I-Thou principle as he was in criticising the thought of Spinoza and of Kant, Fichte, and Schelling. Indeed, Jacobi may have been the first of the German thinkers to expound the I-Thou principle. In a letter of 16 October 1775, which he quotes to Lavater in 1781, Jacobi says: "I open eye or ear, or I stretch forth my hand, and feel in the same moment, inseparably, Thou and I; I and Thou . . . . Thou, thou! givest life".[487] The I-Thou principle in fact runs throughout Jacobi's works, and it is a major factor in his insistence on the primary importance of "personality".

Where Jacobi, like Buber, takes the I-Thou as an immediate awareness given in experience ("I stretch forth my hand, and feel in the same moment, inseparable, Thou and I"), for Coleridge the I-Thou must first evolve from the unity of the individual self before it can extend to the social dimension of humanity: "in the development of the mind, the consciousness itself has the appearance of another";[488] "The infant loving & exalting over its own form & features in the looking glass as over that

---

[486] *CL* II 1197.
[487] *Jacobi's Briefwechsel* I 330.

[488] See below, Frag 2 f 81.

of another is a symbol of the soul in its best & highest states";[489] the "equation of Thou with I by means of a free act by which we negative the sameness in order to establish the equality—this I say is the true definition of Conscience".[490]

Having satisfied himself that the relationship of I and Thou arose naturally in the individual awareness and accounted for both conscience and consciousness, and that it further constituted the principle of human community, Coleridge could then proceed to extricate the reasonableness of the Trinity. As we have seen, trinal conceptions arise inevitably from dyadic conceptions, so Coleridge's real task was to apprehend the possibility of the sameness (the *homoousia*) of Christ and God along with their discreteness. Both problems were solved by the I-Thou structure of personality. It only remained to understand the reciprocal necessity of Christ and God under the aegis of Son and Father. As early as 1805 Coleridge realised that "No Christ, No God!"[491] and after much reading in ancient and more recent theology, by 1810 he could say that "No Trinity, no God—is a matter of natural Religion as well as of Christianity, of profound Philosophy no less than of Faith".[492]

The logical crux, Coleridge came to realise, resided in the fact that a son could be a son only on condition there was a father; and a father a father only on condition there was a son. A "father" cannot be a father unless he has progeny, and although a "son" *in tempore* follows a father, in logic, a "person" could not be conceived with the predicate "father" except under the prior condition of our thinking of "son". The "son" existed for Coleridge with as much necessity as did the "father" and the Trinitarian problem was thereby resolved.[493] The foregoing considerations, one can hardly doubt, are what underlie Coleridge's cryptic statement in 1819: "No Christ (Logos, Son eternal) no God".[494]

Coleridge, carrying his dyadic instinct and preoccupation through polar abstractions, like subject and object, into polar concretenesses, like mother and child, found in the dyadic principle of I and Thou the means of setting Christian Father and Christian Son, God and Christ into perfect reciprocity as *alter et idem*. The "Trinity" could therefore be regarded as "the supreme Being, his reflex act of self-consciousness and his love, all forming one supreme mind".[495] "In the Trinity there is, 1. Ipseity, 2. Alterity, 3. Community."[496]

[489] Frag 2 f 246ᵛ (note).
[490] Frag 1 f 116.
[491] *CN* II 2448.
[492] *CL* III 283–4.

[493] See *CPT* 242–3.
[494] *CN* III 4489.
[495] Shedd v 398.
[496] *TT* (*CC*) II 65, 8 July 1827.

XXI. WHY THE EXISTING FRAGMENTS OF THE *MAGNUM OPUS* WERE NOT PUBLISHED

In view of the richness of the I-Thou lode Coleridge was mining, with its ramifications into subject and object, mother and child, father and son, and in view of the depth and power of those nineteenth-century currents the *magnum opus* was designed to dam up or at least channel into harmless shallows, the question presents itself, why were the existing fragments of the work not published? After all, the *magnum opus* represented, in Coleridge's own repeated assertion, the most important endeavour of his life, and unfinished and fragmentary as it was, it should, one would think, have been published shortly after his death. Probably no other single manuscript of such declared import, by a figure who occupies a major place in the canon of established authors, has so long remained unpublished.

Moreover Coleridge's mind, whatever the vicissitudes of his character and experience, was held in the highest estimation by thinkers in a position to judge. Hazlitt at one point called him "The man of perhaps the greatest ability now living"[497]—and Hazlitt was no friend. Elsewhere Hazlitt says that Coleridge was "the only person" he ever knew "who answered to the idea of a man of genius".[498] While John Stuart Mill called him "one of the subtlest intellects of this or of any age".[499]

To be sure, parts of the manuscript here presented, recorded by an amanuensis palpably almost swamped by the dictational flow, and dictated off the top of his head by a Coleridge whose opium dosage we can only guess at, ooze murkily through a swamp of near-unintelligibility—especially as encountered in a form virtually unpunctuated and unparagraphed. But still, there was every ordinary and usual reason to suppose that the fragments of this particular work, whatever their condition, would be posthumously published. The more puzzling the non-publication, the more extraordinary and unusual the reasons for such non-publication may be presumed to have been.

It would, of course, have made no sense for Coleridge himself to publish the *Opus Maximum* in its incomplete and fragmentary state, although he did discuss, several years before his death, plans for publication on the supposition of the work's completion.[500] Completion was not to be, and Coleridge left to his disciple, Joseph Henry Green, not only the

---

[497] *H Works* xii 198.
[498] Ibid. v 167.
[499] Mill *Works* i 424n.

[500] See e.g. *CL* v 294, 323–4, 337; vi 781–2.

manuscripts involved but almost entire discretion as to whether and how they should be published:

I hereby give and bequeath to Joseph Henry Green, of Lincoln's Inn Fields, Surgeon, all my books, manuscripts, and personal Estates and Effects whatsoever . . . . And my Will is, that notwithstanding any thing herein and before contained, & it is my desire, that my Friend, Mr. Joseph Henry Green, shall in lieu of selling my Books have the option of purchasing the same at such price as he shall himself determine, in as much as their chief value will be dependent on his possession of them. Nevertheless, it is my Will, that in case the said Joseph Henry Green should think it expedient to publish any of the Notes or Writing made by me in the same Books, or any of them; or to publish any other manuscripts of mine, or any letters of mine, which should any be hereafter collected from, or supplied by, my Friends & Correspondents, then my Will is, that the Proceeds & all benefit accruing therefrom, shall be subject to the same Trusts, and to be paid to or amongst such Persons as shall be entitled to my said personal Estate . . . . And further I hereby tell my Children, Hartley, Derwent, & Sara, that I have but little to leave them; but I hope and indeed confidently believe, that they will regard as a part of their inheritance, when I thus bequeath to them my affection & gratitude to Mr. & Mrs. Gillman, and to the dear friend, the companion, partner and help-mate of my worthiest studies, Mr. Joseph Henry Green.[501]

Coleridge's confidence in Green was generally shared by his other disciples and sympathisers. Although John Sterling had hoped to be allowed to publish the "theological manuscripts", such a *"magnum opus"*, wrote F. D. Maurice shortly after Coleridge's death, "is in the hands of Green, from whom it will, of course, receive every justice".[502] Maurice's correspondent, Richard Chenevix Trench, shared his approbation of Coleridge's choice: "You will be glad to hear", he wrote to W. B. Donne on 5 September 1834, "if you have not already heard, that a large body of Coleridge's manuscripts are in the hands of Mr. Green, from whom they will, of course, receive ample justice".[503]

Why were the manuscripts entrusted to Green rather than to Gillman? The latter was as much and possibly even more Coleridge's devoted friend than was Green; had, like Green, been a Coleridgean amanuensis; and had, also like Green, collaborated on some of Coleridge's work (*Theory of Life*). But it was Green who had been the special Coleridgean confidant in the evolution of the *magnum opus*: nineteen years younger than Coleridge, he was "the companion, partner, and help-mate" of Coleridge's "worthiest studies". Green's special relationship to the *magnum opus* would prove to be a significant factor in its eventual non-publication.

[501] *CL* vi 998–9.
[502] *Trench* i 164.
[503] Ibid. i 165.

For the rest, Green knew German, and Gillman did not; Green had more time at his disposal than did the hard-pressed Gillman; Green had discussed every aspect of the *magnum opus* with Coleridge and had written down almost the whole of the extant fragments in dictation from Coleridge. Green, finally, was of superior social and financial position to Gillman, and his intellectual aspirations were greater as well. "You will meet likewise, I hope, my Friend, Mr. Green, of Lincoln's Inn Field", writes Coleridge in 1824 in words typical of his enthusiasm for his collaborator: "whose lectures on Life, Form and Instinct introductory to his Course on Comparative Physiology, at the Royal College of Surgeons, have deservedly attracted so much attention. He is a remarkably well-informed Man—and as good as he is tall, being six feet 3 inches high."[504] Coleridge was undeviating in his admiration of Green and Green's powers. To another correspondent he says that Mr. Green is "the Nephew of Mr Cline, and one of the Surgeons at St Thomas's Hospital, and who has lately distinguished himself so greatly by his Lectures on Animated Nature & the Laws of Life, Instinct &c at the College of Surgeons. He is an incomparable German Scholar, in addition to his other powers and attainments—above all, he is among the very best men, I know."[505]

Along with moral probity, scientific attainment, knowledge of German, and philosophical interests, Green possessed another virtue that undoubtedly made him seem important to Coleridge. For, in stark contrast to Coleridge's own tormented indolence and procrastination, the tall disciple was a man of scrupulous habits of work and discharge of obligation. He was indeed, if we accept the admiring and affectionate remembrance of his surgical apprentice, John Simon—later Sir John Simon, F. R. S., Medical Officer of Her Majesty's Privy Council and Surgeon to St. Thomas's Hospital—a decent, true, and wholly admirable man. Green was a worthy embodiment of that ideal brother-figure for whom Coleridge searched all his life.[506]

As further testimony, one may note that in 1838 Gillman, who was perhaps the most loyal of all Coleridge's friends and supporters ("Dear Friend—and Brother of my Soul—", said Coleridge to him in 1822, "God only knows! how truly and in the depths you are loved & prized by your affectionate / friend S. T. Coleridge"),[507] dedicated his *Life of Samuel Taylor Coleridge* to Green with these unequivocal words: "To Joseph Henry Green . . . The Honoured Faithful and Beloved Friend of

[504] *CL* v 369–70.
[505] Ibid. 367.
[506] For C's psychological problems with brother-images see e.g. *RFR* 118– 29; Donald H. Reiman "Coleridge and the Art of Equivocation" *Studies in Romanticism* 25 (Fall 1986) 325–50.
[507] *CL* v 255.

Samuel Taylor Coleridge, These Volumes Are Most Respectfully and
Affectionately Inscribed". In the work itself Gillman spoke of Coleridge,
and of Green's editing of the Coleridgean remains, in these words: "His
character will form a part in the Philosophical History of the Human
Mind, which will be placed in the space left for it by his amiable and
most faithful friend and disciple, whose talents, whose heart and ac-
quirements make him most fit to describe them, and whose time was for
so many years devoted to this great man".[508]

Why then did this good man and loyal friend not publish Coleridge's
Opus Maximum? The answer seems to divide itself naturally into three
separate but related parts. First of all, the whole point of Coleridge's
"Great Work" was that it should be a system, that is, a "Whole, having
a Beginning, Middle, and End".[509] "Many a fond dream have I amused
myself with", writes Coleridge to Sterling in October 1833, "of your re-
siding near me or in the same house, and preparing with you & Mr.
Green's assistance, my whole system for the Press, as far as it exists in
writing, in any *systematic* form".[510] To publish it as a fragmentary heap,
especially in an English context much awed by the systematic triumphs
of Hegel and other German philosophers, would have seemed to invite
ridicule.

It is almost impossible to overestimate the intimidating nature of
German achievement on British (and American) culture during the mid-
dle and later portions of the nineteenth century. John Sterling wrote in
1842: "Still more remarkably than in poetry, the philosophical specula-
tions of all Europe are daily learning obedience to the example of Ger-
many . . . . In that country,—poor as Germany is compared with England
and France,—there may now probably be found the greater part of the
generous knowledge and earnest meditation extant on earth".[511] In the
previous year a writer for *Blackwood*'s asserted that "German, in par-
ticular, we *must* study; for, like Goethe's magical apprentice, having set
the imp agog after waterbuckets, he threatens to swamp and drown us al-
together, unless we get hold of the word which he will obey. Nor is it
from Germany only by external importation that the deluge floods in; we
have a sort of indwelling Germanism at home, which is very powerful,
and has many names. Undeniably Coleridge was a German, and that not
only in the grand healthy speculative and imaginative excellencies, but
in the excess and disease of these . . . ."[512]

There was thus a mystique of things German, to which Coleridge was

[508] *C Life* (G) 107.
[509] *CL* v 143.
[510] Ibid. vi 966–7.

[511] *Sterling* i 385, 404.
[512] "German Literature" 160.

inextricably linked in the minds of the British intelligentsia. Carlyle re-called that

> He had, especially among young inquiring men, a higher than literary, a kind of prophetic or magician character. He was thought to hold, he alone in England, the key to German and other Transcendentalisms . . . . The practical intellects of the world did not much heed him, or carelessly reckoned him a metaphysical dreamer; but to the rising spirits of the young generation he had this dusky sub-lime character; and sat there as a kind of *Magus*, girt in mystery and enigma; his Dodona oak-grove (Mr. Gilman's house at Highgate) whispering strange things, uncertain whether oracles or jargon.[513]

Participating as he did in the German mystique, Coleridge could scarcely be represented to the world by an *Opus Maximum* that fell short of the systematic rigour associated with the philosophical triumphs of that tradition—particularly in view of the unsettled opinion about his achievement. What was to be published must be neither: it must be a complete and coherent system.

The German systems not only suggested intimidating parallels to the Coleridgean documents with which Green was entrusted, but they also loomed portentously behind the charges of plagiarism with which Cole-ridge's reputation began to be assailed, and which constitute, one can scarcely doubt, the second part of the answer as to why Green did not publish the *Opus Maximum*. An increasingly important medical practi-tioner, Green did not have unlimited time at his command; doubtless he wished to discharge his obligations to Coleridge's thought much earlier than he did, but as his biographer says, in such work as the editing and completing of Coleridge's writings, "especially when it is frequently in-terrupted by avocations of a different nature, years glide away like weeks. And as Mr. Green continued, even till the end of his career, to hold him-self to a considerable extent at the call of his profession, so, occasion-ally, there were long spells of time when he could make but little progress at home."[514] In the meantime, Coleridge had in 1834, some months after his death and Green's acceptance of the trust, been publicly charged by De Quincey with plagiarism.[515]

---

[513] *Carlyle* XI 53.

[514] Simon "A memoir of the Author's Life" *SP* I xli.

[515] *De Q Works* II 142–8. The essay originally appeared in four parts in *Tait's Edinburgh Magazine* in 1834 and 1835, and first served to make the general pub-lic aware of C's neurotic predilection for plagiarism. It was not, however, the first printed notice of the matter, which seems to belong rather to C himself (*BL—CC*—I 160–4). Hazlitt, in his review of the *Biographia Literaria* for the *Edin-burgh Review*, next mentioned the pos-sibility, and in 1823 John Wilson, in *Blackwood's Edinburgh Magazine*, had a character in the role of ":the Opium-Eater", i.e. De Quincey (the informa-

Although this first substantial attack was loyally answered by Julius Hare,[516] in 1840 a second attack was launched. In an anonymous article in *Blackwood's Edinburgh Magazine,* "The Plagiarisms of S. T. Coleridge", the Scottish philosopher James Ferrier savagely assailed Coleridge's reputation.[517] This assault was much fuller and more convincing than De Quincey's rather casual charges, and there seems to be little doubt that it severely damaged Coleridge's philosophical reputation and shook the confidence of his disciples. Although Sara Coleridge published in 1847 a dignified rebuttal,[518] or attempted rebuttal, of Ferrier's explicitly documented charges, she seems actually to have been rather seriously thrown off balance by the emerging scandal about her beloved father. Henry Crabb Robinson notes, on 31 July 1846, "I called on Mrs. Coleridge with a volume of Landor's etc. She is in the press with a new edition of his *Biographia Literaria.* She is perplexed by the charge of plagiarism from Schelling. I gratified her by the assurance of my belief that he was unconscious of it".[519]

Sara Coleridge, despite her perplexity, was bound to loyalty by filial ties; others were not, and some accordingly defected. John Sterling, for example, performed a virtual somersault of opinion in response to the plagiarism charges. In 1828, before plagiarism was in the air, Sterling had written of "Coleridge, the brave, the charitable, the gentle, the pious, the mighty philosopher, the glorious poet".[520] In 1844, however, after Ferrier's article had appeared, and very much under the anti-Coleridgean influence of Carlyle, Sterling wrote to his son Edward as follows:

[Coleridge] was a most lazy and heedless Thinker & Student. His books are full of the most unhappy repetitions omissions mistakes and thefts from German au-

tion was undoubtedly supplied by De Quincey), say that "I have traced him through German literature, poetry, and philosophy; and he is, sir, not only a plagiary, but, sir, a thief, a *bona fide* most unconscientious thief . . . . Coleridge has stolen from a whole host of his fellow-creatures . . . . If he plead to the indictment, he is a dead man—if he stand mute, I will press him to death, under three hundred and fifty pound weight of German metaphysics" (*CH* 305, 484). See further Lindop 314–7. For a more extended discussion of C's plagiarisms see "The Problem of Coleridge's Plagiarisms" *CPT* 1–51; McFarland "Coleridge's Plagiarisms Once More: A Review Essay" *The Yale Review* 63 (1974)

252–86. For the currency and ambivalent nature of plagiarism, see Thomas McFarland "The Originality Paradox" *New Literary History* 5 (Spring 1974) 447–76.

[516] "Samuel Taylor Coleridge and the English Opium-Eater" *The British Magazine and Monthly Register of Religion and Ecclesiastical Information* 7 (1835).

[517] *Blackwood's Edinburgh Magazine* 47 (1840) 287–99.

[518] "Mr. Coleridge's Obligations to Schelling, and the Unfair View of the Subject Presented in Blackwood's Magazine," in *BL* (1847) I v–clxxxiv.

[519] *CRB* II 659.

[520] Tuell 237.

thors, hardly anything sufficiently unfolded, many things earnestly maintained & soon after denied, nothing but confusion, breaks, materials unsorted & heaps of ruin. Yet mingled with all this Ideas, sometimes his own, oftener borrowed from foreign writers, that shine out like diamonds among bricks and mud, & let us see what the man was capable of doing had it been merely as a translator of the Germans. In his conversation he was just the same. He often plunged into discussions or rather discourses which it was impossible for anyone to follow unless it had been written down & given him to study. Often he was playful ingenious wise & with all the imagery of Nature about him at his command, like the young fresh world attendant on Innocent Adam. But often too he was flat or absurd or self-contradictory or still worse retailed perhaps for a whole hour & with all the pomp of an original discovery what in after years I found had been plundered wholesale from some German book. And all this because he would not take the trouble to earn honest fame, & yet could not bear to live without admiration & notoriety. When I remember all that I owe to him, I feel a sort of ache at writing these things.[521]

The plagiarism matter seems for Sterling to lead to an impeachment and general disillusionment with all aspects of Coleridge's intellectual status.

The effect of the perplexity that settled over Sara Coleridge, and of the disillusionment that beset Sterling, was augmented in the general intellectual public by a typically Anglo-Saxon willingness not to have to take seriously Coleridge's theological and metaphysical preoccupation. When C. A. Ward, in the 1890s, came into possession of a portion of the Coleridge papers that Green had held, he announced his acquisition in a proud letter to *The Athenaeum*.[522] "To my astonishment", he later wrote,

there was not a reply of any sort, from reader, student, or publisher. I sat down contentedly, saying, "A cloud is across the moon, perhaps" . . . . Still, making all allowance possible, the apathy of students remains inexplicable to me. But I can start a further problem yet in wonder. Dr. Murray, of Oxford, in the midst of his labours of Hercules, found room and time to devote a generous interest to this. He made me send the manuscript to him at Oxford, and when all the bigwigs were in residence, he personally introduced it to the notice of those who might be the most likely to feel some interest in such a matter. Some of them kept it several weeks in hand, and after about three months' absence it came back to me without one single word of comment from anybody, either combative or appreciative.[523]

In other words, there was very little demand for the publication of Coleridge's nearly unintelligible "Great Work", either on the part of the loyal *cognoscenti*, who were embarrassed by the plagiarism charges, by the

[521] Tuell 262–3.
[522] *The Athenaeum* No 3427 (1 July 1893) 35.
[523] Ibid. No 3548 (26 Oct 1895) 571.

Hegelian epigones then reigning at Oxford, or by general English read-
ers, who were bored by metaphysics.

The latter attitude, indeed, had been the received view of Coleridge
even in his own lifetime. As Hazlitt said, in 1817, "Mr. C., with great
talents, has, by an ambition to be every thing, become nothing. His meta-
physics have been a dead weight on the wings of his imagination—while
his imagination has run away with his reason and common sense. He
might, we seriously think, have been a very considerable poet—instead
of which he has chosen to be a bad philosopher and a worse politi-
cian."[524] Byron's opinion as expressed to Medwin was that "If Cole-
ridge had never gone to Germany, nor spoilt his fine genius by the tran-
scendental philosophy and German metaphysics, nor taken to write lay
sermons, he would have been the greatest poet of the day . . . . Coleridge
might have been any thing: as it is, he is a thing 'that dreams are made
of'."[525]

Wordsworth himself shared this prevailing opinion as to the super-
fluity and even harmfulness of Coleridge's philosophical commitment:
"Wordsworth, as a poet [reported an interlocutor] regretted that German
metaphysics had so much captivated the taste of Coleridge, for he was
frequently not intelligible on this subject; whereas, if his energy and his
originality had been exerted in the channel of poetry . . . he might have
done more permanently to enrich the literature . . . than any man of the
age".[526]

It is not surprising, therefore, that Coleridge's own attempts to arrange
for the publication of his philosophical work ran afoul of this same atti-
tude. In 1825, he writes to John Taylor Coleridge concerning his relation
with the publisher, John Murray: "It was . . . understood by me, that Mr
Murray was to be my Publisher for my Works generally—The Sale of
the Christabel sadly disappointed Mr. Murray . . . . In this mood Mr Mur-
ray expressed himself in such words, as led me . . . to suppose that he
had no pleasure in this connection—at least, that he would have nothing
to do with what he called *my Metaphysics*—which were in truth my
all."[527] The situation was (and still is) that "the English have been ready
to stand up and fight for Coleridge the critic, for Coleridge the English
man of letters, but have been content—even relieved—to lay the ghost
of Coleridge the metaphysician by repeating Ferrier's incantation, 'that
Coleridge is indebted to Schelling for most of his philosophy'".[528]

The third and perhaps the most decisive of the reasons for Green's fail-

---

[524] *H Works* XVI 137.
[525] Medwin 121–2.
[526] Grosart III 469.

[527] *CL* V 437.
[528] *CPT* 16.

ure to publish the *Opus Maximum* probably grew out of the first two. He believed he had to complete what was incomplete (he thought himself obliged, says his editor, to put forth "the Coleridgian philosophy, in utmost elaboration, as a complete and coherent SYSTEM; and that, in purposing, if possible, to deliver as Coleridge's legacy to the world a SYSTEM of Coleridgian philosophy he accepted the words 'system of philosophy' in their most exactive and obligatory sense"[529]) and also to protect Coleridge and himself from the possibility of still further humiliation on the score of plagiarism. With so large a commitment, Green came unconsciously to involve his own philosophical egotism in his endeavours ("In this spirit," continues his editor, "he set to work to systematise the Coleridgian doctrines; and in this spirit . . . he for well-nigh thirty years, was at work with them").[530] In brief, the *magnum opus*, over a long course of time, gradually became not Coleridge's but Green's.

In this process of appropriation there were, in addition to the claims of a normal egotism, perhaps two additional factors at work. First, Green had been not only Coleridge's confidant, but to an extent quite unusual in intellectual collaboration, his amanuensis as well. As Lucy C. Watson recalled, her father, James Gillman, affirmed that Mr. Green was constantly writing from Coleridge's dictation, and there was also "a vast quantity of written matter in Mr. Green's handwriting for him to work on".[531] Thus an overwhelming portion of the manuscript documents of which Green was made guardian paradoxically were composed in his own handwriting; he may well have had some residual psychological sense that he had in fact originated them.

Secondly, Coleridge himself spoke of Green in terms of such enthusiasm as to install Green as virtual co-author. As is apparent from the Extended Plan, Coleridge made authorial acronyms not only from his own, but also from Green's, initials.[532] Coleridge's praise may well have led Green to an overestimation of his own philosophical abilities, and it was characteristic of Coleridge to dispense such praise. As an unfriendly commentator wryly noted, "Coleridge transfigured all he touched . . . . The merest sticks of humanity loom heroic to his charmed imagination. Alexander Ball and Andrew Bell were great men as Coleridge portrayed them".[533] Dykes Campbell commented more charitably that Coleridge "possessed in an extraordinary degree the invaluable faculty of making friends"[534] while Leslie Stephen remarked that Coleridge even in his

[529] *SP* I xl.
[530] Ibid.
[531] *The Athenaeum* No 3552 (23 Nov 1895) 719.
[532] See above, Section XII.
[533] Ingleby 108–9.
[534] *C Life* (JDC) 11.

early years "had won . . . the true sympathy and cordial affection of young men who were the distinct leaders of the next generation".[535] A virtuoso skill in personal relationship was undoubtedly lavished on Green, and it must have aroused a heady feeling of special worth and intellectual ability in the young surgeon.

In any event, instead of *The Opus Maximum of Samuel Taylor Coleridge*, edited by Joseph Henry Green, appearing in due course, in 1865, more than thirty years after Coleridge's death, a two-volume work entitled *Spiritual Philosophy; Founded on the Teaching of the late Samuel Taylor Coleridge*, by the late Joseph Henry Green, F. R. S., D. C. L., edited by . . . John Simon was published. That, and not *The Opus Maximum*, has until now resided on library shelves.

The accuracy of these conjectures as to why Green did not publish the existing fragments may be gauged by considering an exchange that appeared in the pages of *Notes and Queries* in the early 1850s. On 22 November 1851, a correspondent calling himself THEOPHYLACT posed the following question: "Are we ever likely to receive from any member of Coleridge's family, or from his friend Mr. J. H. Green the fragments, if not the entire work, of his *Logosophia*? We can ill afford to lose a work the conception of which engrossed much of his thoughts, if I am rightly informed, towards the close of his life."[536] There was no answer. On 4 December 1852, C. Mansfield Ingleby noted in the same journal that Sara Coleridge had said with reference to the "doctrine of *Aids to Reflection*", that her father, "in his latter years, added something to it, on the subject of ideas," which she trusted would appear "hereafter". Ingleby then asked: "Has this 'something' ever been published? If not, who has the MS.?"[537]

Ingleby, who would subsequently publish one of the bitterest and most scornful of all diatribes against Coleridge's philosophical use of Schelling,[538] appears to have been in his own estimation something of a gadfly to the intellectual establishment. Certainly he was a snapper-up of unconsidered trifles, for the pages of *Notes and Queries* about this time teem with questions and responses over his name. Seemingly, in this query, he is actuated not by malice but by a genuine desire to know. But on 9 July 1853, he restates his question in a way that makes his earlier query seem less than candid, enquiring again about the "fragment on Ideas" as "a sequel to the *Aids to Reflection*":

[535] Stephen *Library* II 324.
[536] *Notes and Queries* 1st ser 4 (1852) 411.
[537] Ibid. 5 (1852) 533.
[538] "On Some Points Connected with the Philosophy of Coleridge" *Transactions of the Royal Society of Literature of the United Kingdom* 9 (1870) 396–429.

Whether this fragment be identical with the *Logosophia*, or, as I suspect, a distinct essay, certain it is that nothing of the kind has ever been published.

From an interesting conversation I had with Dr. Green in a railway carriage, on our return from the Commemoration at Oxford, I learned that he has in his possession, (1) A complete section of a work on *The Philosophy of Nature*, which he took down from the mouth of Coleridge, filling a large volume; (2) a complete treatise on *Logic*; and (3) if I did not mistake, a fragment on *Ideas*. The reason Dr. Green assigns for their not having been published, is, that they contain nothing but what has already seen the light in the *Aids to Reflection*, *The Theory of Life*, and the *Treatise on Method*. This appears to me to be a very inadequate reason for withholding them from the press. That the works would pay, there can be no doubt. Besides the editing of these MSS., who is so well qualified as Dr. Green to give us a good biography of Coleridge?[539]

There was still no reply. On 27 May 1854, Ingleby, abandoning all pretense either of courtesy or lack of information, and referring to the three previous queries, quotes some statements made by Coleridge in 1820 and 1821 about the result of his dictation to Green. He then asks:

How has Mr. Green discharged the duties of this solemn trust? Has he made any attempt to give publicity to the *Logic*, the "great work" on *Philosophy*, the work on the Old and New Testaments, to be called *The Assertion of Religion*, or the *History of Philosophy*, all of which are in his custody, and of which the first is, on the testimony of Coleridge himself, a finished work? We know . . . that the *Logic* is an essay in three parts, viz. the "Canon," the "Criterion," and the "Organon;" of these the last only can be in any respect identical with the *Treatise on Method*. There are other works of Coleridge missing; to these I will call attention in a future Note. For the four enumerated above Mr. Green is responsible. He has lately received the homage of the University of Oxford in the shape of a D.C.L.; he can surely afford a fraction of the few years that may still be allotted to him re-creating the fame of, and in discharging the duty to, his great master. If, however, he cannot afford the time, trouble, and cost of the undertaking, I make him this public offer; I will, myself, take the responsibility of the publication of the above-mentioned four works, if he will entrust me with the MSS.[540]

Strong words indeed. So searing a thrust could hardly be ignored (especially since Ingleby had concluded by saying, "The Editor will, I doubt not, be good enough to forward to the learned Doctor a copy of the Number in which this appeal is published"). Green, accordingly, on 10 June 1854, in a reply entitled "Coleridge's Unpublished Manuscripts", undertook a public justification of his failure to publish the material. He begins in the classic tone of an English gentleman snubbing a bounder:

[539] *Notes and Queries* 1st ser 8 (1853) 43.   [540] Ibid. 9 (1854) 497.

In an article contained in the Number of "N. & Q." for May the 17th last, and signed C. MANSFIELD INGLEBY, an inconsiderate, not to say coarse attack has been made upon me, which might have been spared had the writer sought a private explanation of the matters upon which he had founded his charge.

Stung by Ingleby's question as to how he had "discharged the duties of his solemn trust", and by Ingleby's assertion that Green was "responsible" for the works enumerated, Green said:

... though, by the terms of Coleridge's will, I do not hold myself "responsible" in the sense which the writer attaches to the term, and though I have acted throughout with the cognizance, and I believe with the approbation of Coleridge's family, yet I am willing, and shall now proceed to give such explanations as an admirer of Coleridge's writings may desire, or think he has a right to expect.

The *Logic*, he said, was on Coleridge's own testimony "as yet *unfinished*". Of that work, "the *Criterion* and *Organon* do not to my knowledge exist; and with regard to the other parts of the manuscript, including the *Canon*, I believe that I have exercised a sound discretion in not publishing them in their present form and *unfinished*". Of *The Assertion of Religion* Green denies all knowledge:

There exist, doubtless, in Coleridge's handwriting, many notes, detached fragments and marginalia, which contain criticisms on the Scriptures. Many of these have been published, some have lost their interest by the recent advances in biblical criticism, and some may hereafter appear; though, as many of them were evidently not intended for publication, they await a final judgment with respect to the time, form, and occasion of their appearance. But no work with the title above stated, no work with any similar object—except the *Confessions of an Inquiring Spirit*—is, as far as I know, in existence.

Of the work now known as *The Philosophical Lectures*, first published by Kathleen Coburn in 1949 and re-edited for this collected edition of Coleridge's writings by J. R. de J. Jackson, Green says:

The work to which I suppose the writer alludes as the *History of Philosophy*, is in my possession. It ... consists of notes, taken ... by an eminent shorthand writer, of the course of lectures delivered by Coleridge on that subject. Unfortunately, however, these notes are wholly unfit for publication . . . . If this *History of Philosophy* is to be published in an intelligible form, it will require to be rewritten; and I would willingly undertake the task, had I not, in connexion with Coleridge's views, other and more pressing objects to accomplish.

As to the "fourth work, the 'great work' on *Philosophy*", Green says:

I have to state, for the information of Coleridge's readers, that, although in the materials for the volume there are introductions and intercalations on subjects of speculative interest, such as to entitle them to appear in print, the main portion of the work is a philosophical *Cosmogony*, which I fear is scarcely adapted for scientific readers, or corresponds to the requirements of modern science. At all events, I do not hesitate to say that the completion of the whole would be requisite for the intelligibility of the part which exists in manuscript.

I leave it then to any candid person to decide whether I should have acted wisely in risking its committal to the press in its present shape. Whatever may be, however, the opinion of others, I have decided, according to my own conscientious conviction of the issue, against the experiment.

But should some farther explanation be expected of me on this interesting topic, I will freely own that, having enjoyed the high privilege of communion with one of the most enlightened philosophers of the age—and in accordance with his wishes the responsibility rests with me, as far as my ability extends, of completing his labours,—in pursuance of this trust I have devoted more than the leisure of a life to a work in which I hope to represent the philosophic views of my "great master" in a systematic form of unity—in a form which may best concentrate to a focus and principle of unity the light diffused in his writings, and which may again reflect it on all departments of human knowledge, so that truths may become intelligible in the one light of Divine truth.

Meanwhile I can assure the friends and admirers of Coleridge that nothing now exists in manuscript which would add materially to the elucidation of his philosophical doctrines; and that in any farther publication of his literary remains I shall be guided, as I have been, by the duty which I owe to the memory and fame of my revered teacher.[541]

The three conjectures adduced above as to the reason why the fragments of the *magnum opus* were not published seem to be substantiated. What has been ascribed as the chief reason, that is, Green's gradual appropriation of the *magnum opus* as his own, under the belief that its ruinous elements would not redound to Coleridge's credit, seems clearly enough revealed ("the responsibility rests with me . . . of completing his labours").

The discomfiture occasioned by awe of the German intellectual scene is also suggested; the fragments of the *magnum opus* were "scarcely adapted for scientific readers", did not correspond to "the requirements of modern science", and some had "lost their interest by the recent advances in biblical criticism". And while Green does not mention the added possibility of further embarrassment on the matter of plagiarism, we may judge of its presence in his mind by noting Alice D. Snyder's comment, in 1929, à propos his decision not to publish the *Logic*: "It

[541] *Notes and Queries* 1st ser 9 (1854) 543–4.

takes only a cursory glance to make one realize what would have hap-
pened if he had published it as it now stands. The bulk of the second vol-
ume, and parts of the first, would have been condemned as plagiarized
from Kant, and (by those who knew him) from Mendelssohn . . . ."[542]
A third conjectured reason, that the work was not systematically com-
plete, is suggested by Green's assertion that "the completion of the
whole would be requisite for . . . . intelligibility".

Green may also, when after some years had passed he reread the
manuscripts, have found them somehow less exciting than he had at first
thought. Occasional pencilled comments on empty verso pages (possi-
bly by Charles A. Ward) seem to indicate the possibility of such a reac-
tion. Irritation, however loyally suppressed, might have constituted for
Green a fourth reason for holding back from the task.

All these reasons together, juxtaposed against Green's reverence for
Coleridge, resulted in the compromise known as *Spiritual Philosophy*
rather than the bold publication of the fragments that constituted the
Opus Maximum. We may, indeed, see still more clearly, from some of
Sir John Simon's remarks, the adverse estimation of Coleridge that al-
most certainly played a role in Green's decision, however loyal remained
his public insistence on Coleridge's philosophical pre-eminence. Con-
trasting starkly with Green's decorous written pronouncements, Simon's
remarks, one can hardly doubt, represent his master's private and un-
guarded statements, or at the very least, an amalgam of the prevailing
public view with Green's own opinions:

Coleridge had not left any available written material for setting comprehensively
before the public, in his own language and in an argued form, the philosophical
system with which he wished his name to be identified. Instead of it there were
fragments—for the most part mutually inadaptable fragments, and beginnings,
and studies of special subjects, and numberless notes on the margins and fly-
leaves of books. True, that in unambiguous terms he had sounded the key-note
of his philosophy. And there was a tradition of his oral teachings. And many of
the written fragments were in the highest degree interesting and suggestive . . . .
But here was no system of philosophy, nor even the raw materials for a system.
In that point of view Coleridge's written remains could have no value except in
their relation to a general plan and in methodical correlation among themselves.
Evidently if they were to be made conducive to a system of Coleridgean philos-
ophy, it could but be in a very subordinate degree. The system itself must first
exist in a logical form. And in order to its existence in that form, Mr. Green must
himself thus produce it;—he, with his indefatigable industry, guided by an
unique knowledge of Coleridge's conceptions and purposes.[543]

[542] *L&L* 68.   [543] *SP* I xxxviii–xxxix.

So that, for all intents and purposes, was the end of nineteenth-century possibilities for the publication of Coleridge's *Opus Maximum*. Ingleby continued to call for its publication;[544] C. A. Ward attempted, unsuccessfully, to find financial backing to set it before the public; Lucy Watson expressed the interest of loyal Coleridgeans in seeing it in print. But the opportunity had really been Green's, and Green had chosen to publish *Spiritual Philosophy* instead.

XXII. THE INCOMPLETENESS OF THE *MAGNUM OPUS*

The incompleteness of the *magnum opus* was an embarrassment to Green and was a major factor in his reluctance to publish it. But in our own day, when fragments are beginning to receive theoretical understanding, and when the completed wholes of speculative systems are no longer much respected, there need be no such embarrassment.[545] Indeed, the work's incompleteness has significance in and of itself.

The primary and most unavoidable fact about the *magnum opus* is that it was never finished. During Coleridge's lifetime, which for him as for all of us was "possible existence" (to use the conception of Jaspers), the incompleteness of the venture was tentative and adventitious, and in no way part of its essence. When death closed the gates of possibility, however, a paradox supervened: the incompleteness of the work became its completeness. Henceforth no assessment of it could be divorced from this reality.

This aspect of the meaning of the *magnum opus* expands into concentric circles of significance. First of all, the incompleteness of the work is an emblem of Coleridge's "foundering". It is also necessary to remind ourselves that despite the palpable ruin and incompleteness of Coleridge's endeavour, that endeavour is unique and it is massive in its attainment. Only now, through the modern editions set in motion by the great scholar Kathleen Coburn, are the true outlines of Coleridge's achievement becoming clear. That achievement is nothing short of gigantic. The *Collected Coleridge* will amount to thirty-four volumes when completed. Six are devoted to his marginalia, unparalleled in their range, depth, and acumen; six, from a man who could not bear to open

[544] *Notes and Queries* 1st ser 9 (1854) 591; *Transactions of the Royal Society of Literature of the United Kingdom* 9 (1870) 11.

[545] A recent biographer of C says: "Green worked on the *Magnum Opus* during the rest of his life, but was unable to coordinate its fragments into any coherent whole. There are some who still think this task may one day be accomplished" (Doughty 544n). The aim of the present ed, however, is merely to present and interpret, not to transform fragments into a coherent whole.

letters or to answer them, to correspondence. Though for the Romantics in general letters were an important cultural form, and in the hands of Byron and Keats attained great heights, it is no exaggeration to say that Coleridge's letters, in their philosophical depth, their existential vitality, and their testimony to an indefatigably active intelligence, are richer and more significant still. A further five volumes (made double volumes by the commentary they necessitate) are devoted to his amazingly vital notebooks. As De Quincey asked, after an admiring survey of the range of Coleridge's reading and concern, "Where is the man who shall be equal to these things?"[546] Coleridge, himself his own most severe critic and calumniator, ventured to say timidly, in 1828: "I dare believe that in the mind of a competent Judge what I have performed will excite more surprize than what I have omitted to do, or failed in doing".[547]

The incompleteness of the *magnum opus,* while emblematic of the larger nature of human life, is peculiarly authentic in terms of the unique life of the individual known as Samuel Taylor Coleridge, in which neurosis, frustration, and failure played so large a role. Two of his three greatest poetic productions remained incomplete as well. That his philosophical aspirations achieved no completeness stamps them with the hallmark of his entire existence. It is conventional to remark on the sadness of Coleridge's life; it might ultimately be more true simply to accept that that was the way it was.

The incompleteness of the *magnum opus* also marks it out as an intellectual edifice representative of a dominant theme in the Romantic sensibility as such.[548] The *"progressive Universalpoesie"* of Romanticism, as stipulated in Friedrich Schlegel's famous definition, "can never be completed" (*nie vollendet sein kann*).[549]

Finally, the fragmentary state of the *magnum opus,* so damaging from conventional perspective, is in terms of the two great general philosophical drifts of our time, analytic philosophy and philosophy of existence, an irrelevance. Analytic philosophy developed from a theory of "logical atomism" in which system was repudiated and discrete propositional analysis substituted.[550] The philosophies of existence, for their part, not only disown completeness, but recognise incompleteness as a necessary mark of the authentic. "Am Dasein", insists Heidegger, "ist eine ständige 'Unganzheit', die mit dem Tod ihr Ende findet, undurchstreichbar"—in existence a standing incompleteness, which comes to an end only at death, is not to be evaded.[551]

---

[546] *De Q Works* v 183.
[547] *CL* vi 770.
[548] See *RFR* 3–55.

[549] *Friedrich Schlegel* ii 182.
[550] See Urmson e.g. 14–6, 186–7.
[551] Heidegger *Sein und Zeit* 242.

From the crucial standpoints of our own time, therefore, as well as in its relationship to Romantic sensibility, the *magnum opus* in its very ruin, its "Unganzheit", achieves a special status. As Lucien Goldmann has said of attempts to systematise the fragments of Pascal's *Pensées*, such efforts do violence to the inner truth of the work.[552]

XXIII. THE GENRE OF THE *MAGNUM OPUS*

The *magnum opus* and Pascal's *Pensées* are both fragmentary. But they share another similarity of equal if not greater importance: both are representatives of the same genre. Coleridge's *magnum opus*, despite its uniqueness in his own endeavour, is not unique in its larger cultural matrix. To scholars preoccupied with literary study alone, more confinedly to Romanticism, and still more narrowly to English Romanticism, the *magnum opus* may seem almost grotesque in its Coleridgean idiosyncrasy. But *magna opera* of various intensities and configurations bespangle the cultural skies for centuries before Coleridge's own contribution.[553] To be sure, the phrase *magnum opus* can be and often is used to refer to any major work, usually with the implication that the work constitutes the apex of its author's aspiration and achievement, but the designation may be restricted in the present discussion to those works bearing a generic similarity to Coleridge's own use of the term. Though one might prefer a more limited term, such as *theodicy*, such a term would be overly restrictive.

What is the common factor that defines the genre? Any philosophical work that defends in extended rational argument the concept of ultimate meaning in human life belongs to the genre of which Coleridge's *magnum opus* is a participant. More specifically, the genre can be conceived either in an historically limited or an historically expanded description. In the former, a work in the genre is characteristically a defence of Christianity against atheism, that is, against any conception that takes away the guarantee of ultimate meaning. Such is of course the declared intent of Coleridge's *magnum opus*; it is also the declared intent of Pascal's *Pensées*, the fragments of an unfinished work to have been called *Apologie de la réligion chrétienne*.

In the expanded definition of the genre, the work might not necessar-

---

[552] Goldmann 220.

[553] Indeed, in the first half of the eighteenth century alone at least three *magna opera* appeared: Leibniz's *Théodicée* (1713), Joseph Butler's *Analogy of Re-* *ligion Natural and Revealed, to the Constitution and Course of Nature* (1736), and Andrew Ramsay's *The Philosophical Principles of Natural and Revealed Religion* (1748).

ily be a defence of Christianity, but then it must be a defence of soul or some other idea that guarantees ultimate meaning in life: one might identify Plato's *Laws* as the first example. In the narrower definition, one might say that the first instance is Aquinas's *Summa contra Gentiles*.

The generic category of *magnum opus* must satisfy two requirements. First, there must be an *assertion* of Christianity or some other doctrine of ultimate meaning, but second, there must be a *defence* against alternate possibilities. (Thus Coleridge notes that "one main object" of his own work is that of "invalidating the most plausible objections of infidels").[554] The double requirement follows from the intrinsic nature of the genre: a *magnum opus* always purports to be a true description of reality. Accordingly, as awareness of reality's components historically changes, the structure of a *magnum opus* will tend to change as well.

Thomas Aquinas characteristically brings forward the most plausible objections to his exposition of Christian faith and then argues as to the error of those objections. But the objections are mainly those of Christian heresy or of pagan philosophy; there is no threat from anything like natural science. The same is true, in another way, of a somewhat later *magnum opus*, Ficino's *Theologia Platonica*, perhaps the earliest example of the genre to figure decisively in Coleridge's own orientation towards the form.[555] Ficino, like Coleridge after him, syncretises philosophy and religion to defend Christianity, but he sees no particular threat in science.

With the Renaissance, however, such a threat began to develop. Bacon's *Great Instauration*, although not particularly a defence, nor wholeheartedly committed to Christianity, exhibits key adumbrations of Coleridge's own form: Bacon's work too is incomplete; it too is characterised by the ambition to account for the whole of reality; and it too is preoccupied with science. The *Instauratio Magna*, indeed, is a watershed in the development of the form, for henceforth scientific accounting increasingly attains equal status with religious defence.

We may see both the older version of Aquinas and the newer version of Bacon in works that appeared almost simultaneously in the early 1680s: Bossuet's *Histoire universelle* is representative of the former mode, Burnet's *Telluris Theoria Sacra* is representative of the latter. Both works were known to Coleridge. They have in common the defence of Christianity, and both works syncretise the secular and the sacred. Bossuet's book, though purporting to be a history, begins with the Garden of Eden, accepting quite literally the chronologies contained in the

---

[554] See below, Frag 1 f 21.   [555] See e.g. *BL (CC)* I 144.

Bible, and continues from Biblical accounts down into those of the Roman historians to conclude eventually with the reign of Charlemagne. This mixing of fact and what we would now call myth adumbrates Coleridge's Extended Plan.[556]

The idea of process or development in human affairs is conspicuously absent in this treatise; instead, the course of history is conceived in dramatic terms as the unfolding of a divine play. Nor is the attitude of defence very apparent; the treatise is notable rather for its certainty. The chief threat to Christianity here is identified as the splintering action of the Protestant Reformation, and Bossuet is serenely confident that the variations of such diversity constitute their own repudiation.[557]

Burnet's *Telluris Theoria Sacra*—or *Theory of the Earth*, for it is the author's own English version to which we shall refer—was immensely popular. The first Latin edition was published in 1681, the second in 1689, the third in 1702; the English translation (which Burnet says is "the same in substance with the Latin, though, I confess, 'tis not so properly a Translation, as a new Composition upon the same grounds") appeared in 1684, a second edition in 1691, a third in 1697, a fourth in 1719, a fifth in 1722, a sixth in 1726, and further editions appeared into the nineteenth century. As M. H. Abrams, among others, has shown, it was a work very much in the background for Wordsworth and Coleridge. In important respects the *Theory of the Earth* can be seen as a counterpart to Bossuet's work, but in others it represents a departure. Like Bossuet, Burnet accepts Biblical accounts as historical fact. But here science, no matter how wildly visionary by modern standards, is given a voice in the religious arguments of a *magnum opus*.

Where the *Histoire universelle* is an unquestioning application of the spirit of Augustine to the explanation of the disharmonies and ruptures of existence, Burnet specifically takes issue with Augustine: " 'Tis a dangerous thing to ingage the authority of Scripture in disputes about the Natural World, in opposition to Reason; lest Time, which brings all things to light, should discover that to be evidently false which we had made Scripture to assert".[558] To be sure, Burnet is scarcely less confident than Bossuet that Christian doctrine is in fact The Truth. Indeed, the throwing the topic open to the inquiries of natural science is conceived

---

[556] See above, Section XIII: The Transformations of the *Magnum Opus*.

[557] Or at least he seems confident in this work. Actually, he felt himself embattled against the forces of atheism. See e.g. Paul Hazard "Bossuet at Bay" *The European Mind (1680–1715)* tr J. Lewis

May (London 1953). For further study of the seething undercurrent of religious deviation and divagation in the seventeenth century, see D. C. Allen *Doubt's Boundless Sea* (1964).

[558] Burnet *Theory*, Preface to the Reader, p a iv.

by him as actually a strengthening of the Biblical case; it will be "a great satisfaction . . . to see those pieces of most ancient History, which have been chiefly preserv'd in Scripture, confirm'd a-new, and by another Light, that of Nature and Philosophy".[559]

Perhaps the most important *magnum opus* of all, at least as it figured as background for Coleridge's development, was Cudworth's vast treatise of 1678, *The True Intellectual System of the Universe: The First Part; wherein, All the Reason and Philosophy of Atheism is Confuted; and its Impossibility Demonstrated*. This daunting work occupies a huge volume of 899 folio pages, and at that it is only the first third of what Cudworth projected. A most important study could be written—it has not been accomplished so far—on the varied effects of Cudworth on Coleridge's mentation. Furthermore, because Cudworth customarily quotes fully from Greek and Latin sources and supplies translations, his work was for Coleridge and everyone else virtually an encyclopaedia of ancient thought. Cassirer even uses the designation *magnum opus* in referring to this historically important tome. Coleridge appears to have studied Cudworth early and often. Among other opportunities, he borrowed Cudworth's work (in an edition of 1743) from the Bristol Library from 15 May to 1 June 1795,[560] and from 9 November to 13 December 1796.[561]

The advent of the Age of Reason, and the scoffing of the French *philosophes* of the eighteenth century generated even more *magna opera* in defence of the Christianity they attacked. As the most telling attacks on Christianity occurred in France, so the preponderance of the eighteenth-century *magna opera* appeared in France as well. To conclude this exceedingly brief conspectus, note may be taken of a single example, that of Andrew Ramsay, a Scottish expatriate living in France. A protegé and biographer of Fénelon, he was known as the Chevalier Ramsay. In his religious beliefs Ramsay provided a worthy contrast to his countryman Hume. In 1748, after Ramsay's death in 1743, a work by him entitled *The Philosophical Principles of Natural and Revealed Religion*, a cogent and powerful defence of traditional Christianity against all the Enlightenment currents, was published. Although published in Glasgow, it emanated from the French milieu.

Ramsay aligns himself against "Deists, Unitarians, and Socinians", as well as "Locke, and the English Newtonian philosophers", but his chief opponent is Spinoza, whom he foresees as posing the most coherent and

---

[559] Burnet *Theory* a 3.
[560] Whalley 120.

[561] Ibid. 124.

devastating of all threats to Christian orthodoxy. Indeed, so squarely does he confront the Spinozistic threat, that, like Spinoza in his *Ethica*, he utilises the geometric method of presentation; the subtitle of Ramsay's work states that it is "Unfolded in a Geometrical Order". Ramsay attacks Spinoza's understanding of "infinite", asserting that "All Spinoza's errors on this head came originally from the dangerous definitions of the schoolmen, whom he had studied carefully in his youth".[562] Indeed, in his vigorous defence against all the intellectual threats to Christianity that had accumulated by his time, Ramsay is forever finding the chief threat to be Spinoza: "As we must detest with horror the Spinosian blasphemy, which maintains, that nature produced is only an expansion or modification of the divine substance; so we must also reject the error of those who assert that creation is a participation or discerpation of the eternal essence, which God erects into a substance distinct from his own. This opinion attacks and destroys the immateriality of the divine nature."[563] The clear-headed Ramsay also sees that many other philosophemes of the time are tantamount to Spinozism: "the Malebranchian system is exceedingly dangerous: it seems the beginning of Spinosism; and Spinosism is Malebranchism consummated".[564]

Coleridge borrowed both volumes of Ramsay's work from the Bristol Library from 2 to 16 September 1796, and again from 12 to 16 October, and so must be presumed to have been aware of all aspects of the earlier effort.[565] Of special interest as a prefiguration of Coleridge's concerns in his own *magnum opus* is Ramsay's appendix to the first volume of his work: "Containing a Refutation of the First Book of Spinosa's Ethics; by which the Whole Structure is Undermined".

Ramsay's work, in short, is a powerful attempt to defend traditional religion in the very teeth of the Enlightenment. But it was no more successful in its halting effect than were the other *magna opera* of the eighteenth century (among which should be listed Berkeley's intriguing work of 1732—quoted, indeed, in Coleridge's own *magnum opus* below[566]—*Alciphron: or, the Minute Philosopher*, which, as its subtitle said, contained "*An Apology for the Christian Religion, against those who are called Free-Thinkers*"). The anti-Christian onslaughts, endemic in the seventeenth century and carrying the day by the eighteenth, continued.[567]

[562] Ramsay 45.
[563] Ibid. 115.
[564] Ibid. 276.
[565] Whalley 123.
[566] See below, Frag 2 f 41.
[567] For at least an introduction to the questioning and ultimately anti-Christian ferment taking place in the sixteenth and seventeenth centuries, see e.g. D. C. Allen, *Doubt's Boundless Sea: Skepticism and Faith in the Renaissance* (Baltimore 1964).

By Coleridge's time, neither Nature nor Philosophy could be counted on to confirm the truths of Christianity, and Coleridge, though he summoned a scheme of natural science that at least was not inimical to Christianity, had for the most part to rely on his own special redefinition of "reason", as opposed to "understanding", for such confirmation as he was able to supply. The redefined "reason" likewise disarmed Burnet's caveat that it is "a dangerous thing to ingage the authority of Scripture in disputes about the Natural World, in opposition to Reason." In the history of *magna opera*, Coleridge's version was very late in the day, as archaic in terms of its own surroundings as *Paradise Lost* was in the age of Dryden. There is a sense of desperation, a last-ditch quality, about Coleridge's effort; for there was by that time a near-catastrophic divergence in the directions of thought in the realms of nature and philosophy. By the advent of *On the Origin of Species* in 1859, the role of reason in assessing the natural world could no longer be claimed to reinforce the authority of scripture.

XXIV. THE CONSERVATISM OF THE *MAGNUM OPUS:* ITS MEANING WITH RESPECT TO THE PAST

The *magnum opus*, in that it attempted to hold in philosophical place the certainties of the Christian religion that had already been damagingly compromised by the anti-religious efforts of the French Enlightenment—"that atheistic philosophy, which in France transvenomed the natural thirst of truth into the hydrophobia of a wild and homeless scepticism"[568]—was a deeply conservative, indeed, a backward-looking enterprise. It was, as noted above, anachronistic in terms of its own intellectual milieu. "The purpose of the whole", said Coleridge, "is—a philosophical Defence of the Articles of the Church".[569] Yet Coleridge was fully aware that his efforts ran the risk of dismissal as, to use his language from a related theological investment, "Visionary Ravings, Obsolete Whimsies, Transcendental Trash, &c. &c.".[570]

The attempt to sustain a scheme already by-passed by the most advanced thought of the eighteenth century was not only necessary to Coleridge's consuming need for redemption; it also accorded with a temperamental tropism of his intellectual personality. Coleridge, with his reconciling and accepting attitude, felt deeply and naturally at home with the thought of the past. The "dreariest feature of Jacobinism" was for

[568] *LS (CC)* 22.
[569] *CL* III 534.
[570] *AR* (1825) 377.

him "contempt of the Institutions of our Ancestors and of past wisdom".[571]

Again, he believed that "assuredly the way to improve the present is not to despise the past; it is a great error to idolize it, but a still greater to hold it in contempt. Wordsworth has beautifully said, 'The Child is the Father of the man', and I would wish men to be taught to be, 'Bound each to each in natural' charity".[572] He said in November 1803 that "Those only who feel no originality, no consciousness of having received their Thoughts & opinions from immediate Inspiration, are anxious to be thought originals—the certainty & feeling is enough for the other, & he rejoices to find his opinions plumed & winged with the authority of venerable Forefathers".[573] "What is it", asks Coleridge passionately, "that I employ my Metaphysics on? To perplex our clearest notions, & living moral Instincts? To extinguish the Light of Love & of Conscience . . . . to make myself & others . . . *Worthless, Soul*less, *God*less?—No! To expose the Folly and the Legerdemain of those, who have thus abused the blessed Organ of Language, to support all old & venerable Truths, to support, to kindle, to project, to make the Reason spread Light over our Feelings, to make our Feelings diffuse vital Warmth thro' our Reason—these are my Objects—& these my Subjects."[574]

Coleridge's temperamental conservatism was focused by the special nature of his theological need. To be able to see Christianity as true, it was imperative that he find its message absolute, not provisional or in any way tentative or mythological. "If in this life only", said Paul in a passage Coleridge emphasised, "we have hope in Christ, we are of all men most miserable".[575] "If there be no resurrection of the dead", said Paul with the most unequivocal directness, "then is Christ not risen: And if Christ be not risen, then is our preaching vain, and your faith is also vain".[576] "I cannot conceive a supreme moral intelligence", agreed Coleridge, "unless I believe in my own immortality".[577]

That was the root of the matter. If Christianity, and the succour it promised Coleridge, were true, then it could not be conceived as changing, capable of being redefined, or subject to historical vicissitude; it must of necessity be "One clear, unchanged, and universal light". Other things might change and progress, but not Christianity; its historical circumstances could and did change, but not its fundamental message. "The True Church", as T. S. Eliot argues, "can never fail / For it is based upon

---

571 *CN* II 2150.
572 *P Lects* (1949) 284.
573 *CN* I 1695.
574 Ibid. I 1623.

575 1 Cor 15.19.
576 Ibid. 15.13–14.
577 *IS* 142.

a rock".[578] "The true simplicity of the Christian doctrine", insisted one of Coleridge's venerable forefathers, Bossuet, "consists principally and essentially forever in resolving matters, in that which regards faith, by this certain fact: Yesterday, it was believed thus; consequently, today it is necessary to believe the same."[579]

It was of supreme importance to Coleridge that the promise not be destroyed. To try to preserve it he felt himself obliged to undertake the defence known as the *magnum opus*; for by the late eighteenth and early nineteenth centuries the rock of truth was being dislodged by the onrushing stream of process and change. To protect against this destructive flood, Coleridge summoned Plato and Kant to provide girders of thought to reinforce the dam he sought to erect. That act of reinforcement, indeed, is the whole function of those two great thinkers in Coleridge's sense of his own intellectual priorities.

The extent to which Plato and Kant provided the needed girders can perhaps be gauged by considering merely a single statement by each thinker. "The argument of our Critique", says Kant near the end of the *Kritik der reinen Vernunft*, "taken as a whole, must have sufficiently convinced the reader that although metaphysics cannot be the foundation of religion, it must always continue to be a bulwark of it".[580] Consider also the implications of this passage from Plato: "We find soul to be prior to body, and body secondary and posterior . . . . And as soul thus controls and indwells in all things everywhere, must we not necessarily affirm that it controls Heaven also? Plainly we must say that it is the supremely good that takes forethought for the universe and drives it on its course."[581]

Plato and Kant further conjoined in their effect by an essential and oft-remarked similarity in their total meaning. Of greatest importance for Coleridge, both philosophies agreed with his in marking out a realm of timeless permanence, symbolised in Plato by the realm of ideas, in Kant by the thing-in-itself, and in Coleridge by the conception of God. All three thinkers opposed the powerful counter-philosophies of evolutionary change.

Plato in all his attitudes was conservative, and his thought is a citadel that repels process and change. His philosophy is not defined by conceptions of growth, transformation, and novelty, but by the conception of a timeless perfection from which all temporality is a form of lapse, and all change a mere eddying of phenomena. Indeed, his thought may

---

[578] Eliot *Poems* 57.
[579] Gaquère 133.

[580] Kant III 548–9.
[581] Plato *Laws* 896C–897C.

be described historically as a binding of the destructive flux of Heraclitus by forcing it into a reciprocal polarity with the unchanging One of Parmenides. In terms of the conceptions of historical development that were in thunderous motion during Coleridge's time, Plato, as the classical scholar Eric Havelock has emphasised,

denied that there had been any significant development at all. To understand man, you fix your gaze on what he should be. For in a sense this is what he always has been—a species apart from the brutes, rational and moral, intelligent and just. If man's practice did not fit this theory, then man was to be corrected and educated till it did. For the norms by which his behaviour is governed, while they lie within the cosmos, lie outside history and process. They are as eternal as the cosmos itself. If the cosmos had a history, well and good. But it was always a history which exhibited a complete intelligence already present at the beginning.[582]

Havelock's analysis is especially cogent in that he also calls attention to the fact that for Plato, as for Coleridge in his own day, a rival and opposing body of thought was committed precisely to conceptions of growth, development, and progress in the most fundamental human concerns. As Havelock says, this competing tradition tried "to imagine a pre-moral and pre-intellectual condition of man. They felt that what he was now could best be understood by building an historical bridge between the present and the past; and between what man had been, and still was, not-man."[583] Havelock specifically characterises the bedrock opposition of the rival traditions:

these competing conceptions rest upon competing doctrines of the origin and nature of man himself. According to the first, man ... either ... came into existence on the earth as a superior species with special prerogatives; or else he was created in the image of perfection by God. This can be called the anti-historical view of man. Civilizations may vary in their material forms, but man the human being has been a constant.

The second and non-metaphysical view of his morality and law is derived from an historical science which argues, first, that the human species emerged from non-human forms of life, by some evolutionary process, so that man's present body and brains represent the end-product of a long series of mutations; and second, that his moral and social codes have developed since he became intelligent, as a continuation of the evolutionary process.[584]

Coleridge was committed to the first of these historical positions; the dominant current of thought in his day, which was to eventuate in Dar-

[582] Havelock 26–7.
[583] Ibid. 27.
[584] Ibid. 29–30.

win's *On the Origin of Species* in 1859, was committed to the second. This second view, that of "evolutionary process", was, indeed, to gain an almost total ascendancy, leaving Coleridge as a lonely and anachronistic figure on the philosophical horizon, for he could not accept Darwin's conclusion, towards which even in his own day the evidence was pointing, that "We may thus ascend to the Lemuridae; and the interval is not very wide from these to the Simiadae. The Simiadae then branched off into two great stems, the New World and Old World monkeys; and from the latter, at a remote period, Man, the wonder and glory of the Universe, proceeded."[585]

Coleridge's *magnum opus*, among other things, was an attempt to validate the first, or Platonic, version of the origin and nature of mankind, and by doing so to dam the eroding flood of process. Undertaken, as it was, in the aftermath of such decisive and powerful argument for the evolutionary view as was set forth in Diderot's *Lettre sur les aveugles à l'usage de ceux qui voient* and his *Le Rêve de d'Alembert*, in Lessing's *Die Erziehung des Menschengeschlechts*, in Herder's *Ideen zur Philosophie der Geschichte der Menschheit*, and throughout the thought of Schelling and Hegel, the *magnum opus* from the beginning was not only conservative, but backward looking.

Though the treatises just mentioned did not display the total scientific command exhibited by Darwin's two great works of 1859 and 1871, and so had small validity as strict science, they none the less accurately encompassed the *meaning* of evolution. To take a single instance, a commentator notes of Herder: "His fashion of conceiving nature as a history of the earth, as an evolutive process, in the course of which there forms itself an individual life always more diverse and an organization ever higher, anticipates not only the *Naturphilosophie* of Schelling and Oken, but also all the theories of descent and evolution around which revolve the natural sciences of today".[586]

Sometimes the evolutionary theorists prior to Coleridge make statements almost interchangeable with those of Darwin. For a single instance, Monboddo, in 1773, said that

From savage men we are naturally led to consider the condition of the brutes; betwixt whom and the savages there is such a resemblance, that there are many who will hardly admit of any difference . . . . The mind of the brute . . . is inseparably connected his body, and bound in the chains of matter, in the same manner that we are when we first come into the world, and accordingly, in the first operations of our mind, we see the very same process: for they have the same

---

[585] Darwin *Descent* 168.   [586] Pfleiderer 43.

perceptions of sense that we have; they preserve perceptions of sense that we have; they preserve those perceptions in their memory or imagination; and they have also, as well as we, a notion of sameness, likeness, or *diversity*, in the objects of sense, and they recognize the species in the individual, as readily as our children do. Does not this plainly indicate, that there is no *natural* difference betwixt our minds and theirs, and that the superiority we have over them is *adventitious*, and from *acquired habit*?[587]

To Coleridge, who in accordance with his Platonico-Christo-Kantist commitment needed to think of the human soul as unique in nature, and who therefore placed much hope in the "wide chasm between man and the noblest animals", which no "conceivable difference of organization is sufficient to overbridge",[588] the kind of opinion represented by Monboddo's statement was anathema. It was, however, to be precisely the opinion of Darwin himself. "The difference in mind between man and the higher animals, great as it is", concluded Darwin, "certainly is one of degree and not of kind".[589] "Every one who admits the principle of evolution, must see that the mental powers of the higher animals, which are of the same kind with those of man, though so different in degree, are capable of advancement."[590] Darwin even devoted lengthy refutation, in the *Descent of Man*, to the belief that animals are without the rudiments of morality and other human virtues. As Darwin said in one of his notebooks, he would "never allow that because there is a chasm between man . . . and animals that man has a different origin".[591]

That was the wave of the future. Coleridge, gazing into the movements of both the immediate and remote past, saw it coming and did his utmost to erect a sea wall of thought to break its inundating force.

XXV. PANTHEISM AND EVOLUTIONARY MATERIALISM: THE MEANING OF THE *MAGNUM OPUS* WITH RESPECT TO COLERIDGE'S OWN TIME

The *magnum opus* was necessitated by and designed as a defence against two conceptions of reality, one formulated in the recent past, and one looming on the horizon of the near future. Together they worked synergistically against the interests dearest to Coleridge's heart. The two conceptions were, as outlined above, the pantheism of Spinoza and the evolutionary theory of Darwin.

Both conceptions rejected the Christian schematism that supplied

---

587 Monboddo I 134.
588 *TL* (1848) 33.
589 Darwin *Descent* 128.

590 Ibid. 624.
591 Quoted in Bowlby 213.

Coleridge with the possibility of redemption from the existential misery
in which he found himself. We must remind ourselves once more of how
central, in Coleridge's scheme of things, was the need for redemption.
"I am secure of my faith in the main points", he writes to Daniel Stuart
on 18 April 1826, "—a personal God, a surviving principle in Life, &
that I need & that I have a Redeemer".[592] The Trinity, the rational es-
tablishment of which was the consuming goal of Coleridge's thought,
depended entirely on the existence of redemption: "Solely in conse-
quence of our Redemption does the Trinity become a Doctrine, the *Be-
lief* of which as real is commanded by our Conscience".[593]

In neither the evolutionary materialism of Darwin nor in the panthe-
ism of Spinoza was there a place for a benevolent God, a promise of re-
demption, or a guarantee of meaning in life. Both rejected the doctrine
of final causes, that is to say, of an ultimate reason for existence. Both
were, for Coleridge, citadels of atheism. For instance, prior to the tri-
umph of Darwinism, Coleridge can with a bravado that perhaps masks
his deep anxiety, say:

And here once for all, I beg leave to remark that I attach neither belief nor re-
spect to the Theory, which supposes the human Race to have been gradually per-
fecting itself from the darkest Savagery, or still more boldly tracing us back to
the bestial as to our Larva, contemplates Man as the last metamorphosis, the gay
Image, of some lucky species of Ape or Baboon. Of the two hypotheses I should,
indeed, greatly prefer the Lucretian of the Parturiency of our Mother Earth, some
score thousand years ago, when the venerable Elder was yet in her Teens, and
her human Litter sucked the milk then oozing from countless Breasts of warm
and genial Mud.[594]

Both Spinozism and Darwinism were, for Coleridge, absolute atheisms.
Not only that, both were extraordinarily cogent and formidable explana-
tions of reality seen as without meaning or purpose, and above all with-
out succour.

After his death in 1677, Spinoza came to occupy an ever more im-
portant place in the minds of European intellectuals, until, with the ad-
vent of Romanticism, he asserted a nearly total hegemony over European
thought.[595] The matter may not be so apparent on the surface, because
Spinozism took many inexplicit and masked forms, and because almost
no one wanted to admit to Spinozism as such, which was equated with
open atheism. But Spinoza virtually inundated European thought. "Spin-

[592] *CL* VI 577.
[593] *CN* III 4005.
[594] British Library MS. Egerton 2801.

Printed in Muirhead 132.
[595] See e.g. "The Spinozistic Cres-
cendo" *CPT* 53–106.

oza", said Friedrich Schlegel in 1799, "is omnipresent in the background, like Fate in ancient tragedy".[596] Spinoza's thought not only supplied the pattern for philosophical thinking, it exerted an enormous magnetism on artists and poets as well; it seemed impeccably right in the Romantic rationale. "I cannot say", wrote the young Goethe, "that I ever read Spinoza straight through, that at any time the complete architecture of his intellectual system has stood clear in view before me . . . . But when I look into him I seem to understand him . . . I can always gather from him very salutary influences for my way of feeling and acting."[597]

In Germany, the real centre of philosophical activity in Europe, Spinoza had long been "the central point of interest". As Friedrich Schlegel had written more than a half century earlier, "Spinoza is as it were the central sun of philosophy".[598] No European thinker was unaffected by Spinoza; more startlingly, with the exceptions of Coleridge, Jacobi, and Kierkegaard, every consequent thinker of the nineteenth century became, either by open statement or by implication, a Spinozist.

Denounced as an atheist up until the advent of Romanticism—"il estoit veritablement Athée",[599] the super-intellectual Leibniz had concluded—Spinoza's pantheism, which spoke so glowingly the name of God, seemed to his enthusiastic adherents not atheism but on the contrary a higher spirituality. "Spinoza is a God-intoxicated man", exclaimed the ardent Novalis. Far from being atheism, Spinozism was "a supersaturation with divinity".[600] Less ardently, but with even more assurance, Hegel made the same defence: "bei ihm ist zu viel Gott"—with Spinoza there is too much God.[601] Indeed, even Schleiermacher, the greatest Christian theologian of the nineteenth century, in his epoch-marking *Reden über die Religion* (1799), had with glowing words invited the new century to "offer reverentially with me a lock to the manes of the holy, rejected Spinoza! He was filled with the lofty world-spirit, the infinite was his beginning and his end; the universe his only and eternal love. In holy innocence and deep humility he saw himself in the mirror of the eternal world, and saw how he too was its most lovely mirror; full of religion was he and full of holy spirit, and hence he stands there alone and unrivalled, master in his art, but exalted above the profane guild, without disciples and without civil right."[602]

Perhaps no philosopher except Plato had ever elicited such rapture ("Plato and Spinoza are the titans of philosophy" observed Schlegel).[603]

---

[596] *Friedrich Schlegel* XVIII 396.
[597] *Gedenkausgabe* XVIII 851.
[598] *Friedrich Schlegel* XVIII 401.
[599] *Leibniz* I 535.

[600] *Novalis* III 318; 317.
[601] *Hegel* XX 163.
[602] Schleiermacher I i 190.
[603] *Friedrich Schlegel* XVIII 345.

As a thinker enormously aware of what was going on the continent in his time, Coleridge was exposed to the full effect of the tidal wave of Spinozism. Indeed, Spinoza flooded his thoughts and drenched his mind for almost forty years. An awed recorder of his conversation during the Highgate years conveys this sense of Coleridge's preoccupation with what Spinoza was and what he meant:

> We heard him with the ardent glow of genius refute the impalpable pantheism of Spinoza, who gave a soul to the universe without individuality, and motion to matter without a mover. In the mazes of these metaphysical speculations, the poetical genius of Coleridge would flow on, or disport in circles like the harmonious and luminous ocean. From the refutation of Spinoza, 'who,' says he, 'withdraws God from the universe,' he proceeded in beautiful and sublime strains to illustrate the tenets and principles of religion, till, reached to the summit, where he could advance no farther or higher, he bowed himself in humility and reverence to the earth, and murmuring some sweet and mysterious verses from Dante's Paradise, he closed.[604]

Despite his rejection of Spinoza's thought, Coleridge, like Jacobi, loved Spinoza. "The ready belief which has been yielded to the slander of my 'potential infidelity'", he said wistfully at the end of the *Biographia Literaria*, "I attribute in part to the openness with which I have avowed my doubts, whether the heavy interdict, under which the name of BENEDICT SPINOZA lies, is merited on the whole or to the whole extent".[605] Like others, he could scarcely control his enthusiasm for Spinoza, but he cast his lot ultimately with Kant and with Plato, and with the Christian centralities they shored up: "Not one man in a thousand has either strength of mind or goodness of heart to be an atheist. I repeat it. Not one man in ten thousand has goodness of heart or strength of mind to be an atheist. And, were I not a Christian . . . I should be an atheist with Spinoza . . . . This it is true, is negative atheism; and this is, next to Christianity, the purest spirit of humanity!"[606] That was his lasting opinion. Very late in life, Coleridge recalled the terms of this opposition and reiterated his admiration for Spinoza: "I have ever thought . . . Atheism the next best religion to Christianity—nor does the better faith, I have learnt from Paul and John, interfere with the cordial reverence I feel for Benedict Spinoza".[607]

The opposed poles of Spinoza and Christianity, indeed, generated the electric energy of all Coleridge's speculative musings. As Henry Crabb Robinson recorded in 1812:

[604] *TT (CC)* I 556.
[605] *BL (CC)* II 245.
[606] Allsop 61.

[607] *CL* VI 850. To J. R. Reade, Dec 1830.

Coleridge walked with me to A. Robinson's for my Spinoza, which I lent him. While standing in the room he kissed Spinoza's face in the title-page, and said, "This book is a gospel to me." But in less than a minute he added, "his philosophy is nevertheless false, Spinoza's system has been demonstrated to be false, but only by that philosophy which has demonstrated the falsehood of all other philosophies. Did philosophy commence with an *it is*, instead of an *I am*, Spinoza would be altogether true." And without allowing a breathing time, Coleridge parenthetically asserted, "I, however, believe in all the doctrines of Christianity, even the Trinity".[608]

Despite Coleridge's lifelong vacillation between pantheism and Christianity, it was Christianity that at length achieved at least a formal victory. Coleridge's head became convinced by Paul and John if his heart remained with Spinoza. Yet one must not underestimate the eventual totality of his intellectual, as opposed to emotional, commitment to Christianity, and the absoluteness of his rejection of pantheism: "Now the very purpose of my system is to overthrow Pantheism, to establish the diversity of the Creator from the sum whole of his Creatures, deduce the personeity, the I Am of God, and in one and the same demonstration to demonstrate the reality and originancy of Moral Evil, and to account for the fact of a finite Nature".[609] Spinoza, indeed, notwithstanding Coleridge's reverence for him, became the absolute measure of all that Coleridge had to repudiate.

Coleridge saw clearly that Spinoza's pantheism was the ultimate opponent of the Christianity he so hungered to validate. "It was pantheism", he says of Spinoza's thought, "but in the most religious form in which it could appear . . . . On the other hand I am far from hiding the inevitable consequences of pantheism in all cases, whether the pantheism of India or the solitary cases [like that] of Spinoza."[610] Elsewhere—indeed, in the very heart of the *Opus Maximum* itself—he is less wistful about Spinoza: "The inevitable result of all consequent reasoning, in which the intellect refuses to acknowledge a higher or deeper ground than it can itself supply . . . is— and from Zeno the Eleatic to Spinosa, and from Spinosa to the Schellings of the present day, ever has been—pantheism, under one or other of its modes . . . and in all alike . . . practically atheistic".[611]

---

[608] Henry Crabb Robinson, *Diary, Reminiscences, and Correspondence of Henry Crabb Robinson* ed Thomas Sadler (London 1869) I 399–401. In her later ed of Robinson, Edith Morley changes the date of the passage from 12 Oct to 12 Nov, and introduces several inconsequential changes of wording in her transcription of it, although the larger structure remains intact.

[609] Notebook 35, f 25ᵛ. Printed in Boulger 129.

[610] *P Lects* (1949) 385.

[611] See below, Frag 2 f 38; Shedd II 470–1.

That was what Coleridge really thought.[612] The "arguments of Spinosa" were, "in more appropriate language, the *Atheistical system*".[613] "Spinozism", said Coleridge, "consists in the exclusion of intelligence and consciousness from Deity—therefore it is Atheism".[614] "Pantheism", he said still more absolutely, "= Atheism . . . there is no other Atheism actually existing or speculatively conceivable, but Pantheism".[615]

Coleridge dearly loved nature.[616] But for that very reason he took painstaking care, throughout his intellectual life, to furnish provisos that protected his delighted acceptance of nature from pantheism. Thus, for instance, he emphasised that nature must be conceived from a higher ground that is not itself nature: "And thus nature itself, as soon as we apply Reason to its contemplation, forces us back to a something higher than nature as that on which it depends".[617] He was adamant in this insistence: "even the philosophy of nature can remain philosophy only by rising above nature".[618] "There must be a spirit on the breeze, who is not the same as the breeze."[619]

It was to avoid the danger of pantheistic identification of God and nature that Coleridge instead substituted his exploration of "facts that have their sole being entirely in consciousness".[620] His endeavour was a "seeking for the first principles of all living & effective truth in the constitution and constituent faculties of the Mind itself".[621] It was the depths of the "I am", not the secrets of nature, that would ultimately provide Coleridge with what he needed and at the same time obviate the ever-looming threat of pantheism. There he would find "That very principle, of which nature knows not, which the light of the sun can never reveal, which we must either despair of finding or must seek and find within ourselves."[622] "That, which we find in ourselves", he said in an ultimate statement, is "the substance and the life of *all* our knowledge.

---

[612] For fuller discussion see "Coleridge and the Dilemmas of Pantheism" *CPT* 107–90.

[613] *CL* III 483.

[614] *Critical Annotations* 32.

[615] Brinkley 382.

[616] For a single instance, see a notebook entry of 1810–11: "The Love of Nature is ever returned double to us— not only the Delighter in our Delight, but by linking our sweetest but of themselves perishable feelings to distinct & vivid Images, which we ourselves at time & which a thousand casual associations will often recall to our memory. She is the preserver, the Treasuress of our Joys . . .—and even when all men have seemed to desert us . . . yet even then the blue Heaven spreads it out & bends over us, & the little Tree still shelters us . . . and the low creeping Gale will sigh in the Heath-plant & sooth us as by a sound of Sympathy, till the lulled Grief loses itself in fixed gaze on the purple Heath-blossom, till the present beauty becomes a Vision of Memory—" (*CN* III 4040).

[617] See below, Frag 2 f 111.

[618] See below, Frag 3 p 9.

[619] See below, Frag 2 f 62.

[620] See below, Frag 1 f 71.

[621] *CL* v 465.

[622] See below, Frag 2 f 62.

Without this latent presence of the 'I am,' all modes of existence in the external world would flit before us as colored shadows, with no greater depth, root, or fixture, than the image of a rock hath in a gliding stream."[623]

To repel pantheism and to affirm the redemptive truth of Christianity, those were the twin preoccupations, the two sides of the same coin, of Coleridge's philosophical effort. For Coleridge, contemporary religious controversies were disputes "about the neutral or interjacent ground, not about the territory itself—and . . . in this sense 9990 in every 10,000 are Ἄθεοι"; for the "territory itself" was overwhelmingly the question of whether there "be a personal God, with will, foresight, and all other attributes of personal Intelligence that distinguish the living God (the idea of) from the Spinozistic Ground of the Universe, or infinite Modificable".[624]

Spinozism as the paradigm of atheism, which at his back Coleridge always heard, conjoined with the threat on the horizon that eventuated in the evolutionary philosophy of Darwin. The issues presented by the two schemes of thought had been present to Coleridge's contemplation long before he encountered them in explicitly Spinozistic or evolutionary terms. For a single pregnant instance, all the things Coleridge ultimately ranged himself against were present, at least by implication, in the Unitarianism or Socinianism of his early theological involvement, in his early entanglement in the doctrines of Necessitarianism, and in his reading in thinkers like Joseph Priestley. Priestley, an unabashed materialist, mechanist, and Socinian, throws down the gauntlet in unequivocal terms:

Lastly, the doctrine of *necessity* . . . is the immediate result of the doctrine of the materiality of man; for mechanism is the un- doubted consequence of materialism. But whether man be wholly material or not, I apprehend that proof enough is advanced that every human volition is subject to certain fixed laws, and that the potential *self-determining power* is altogether imaginary and impossible.

In short, it is my firm persuasion, that the three doctrines of *materialism*, of that which is commonly called *Socinianism*, and of philosophical *necessity*, are equally parts of *one system* . . .[625]

Coleridge, who did not merely read but thought intensely about what he read, characteristically recast this provincial formulation into the ultimate standpoint of Spinozism. In a note on Andrew Fuller's *The Calvinistic and Socinian Systems Examined and Compared* (Priestley himself had said that "The philosophical doctrine of *Necessity*, so much

---

[623] *LS (CC)* 78.
[624] *CN* III 4341.

[625] Priestley *Disquisitions* 356.

resembles the Calvinistic doctrine of *Predestination*, in some views, that it may well be worth while to point out distinctly in what they agree, and in what they differ"),[626] he wrote: "But in both systems, as Fuller has erroneously stated his own, man is annihilated. There is neither more nor less; it is all God; all, all are but *Deus infinite modificatus*:—in brief, both systems are not Spinosism, for no other reason than that the logic and logical consequency of 10 Fullers + 10 × 10 Dr. Priestleys, piled on each other, would not reach the calf of Spinoza's leg. Both systems of necessity lead to Spinosism . . . ."[627] Coleridge was aware on all fronts of the intertwined implications of numerous modes of thought which were finally subsumed as either Spinozism or proto-Darwinism, with these two themselves finally reaching agreement as atheism. Coleridge's task, as he says in the *Opus Maximum*, was to proceed across a "narrow isthmus" with "atheism on one side or a world without God, and Pantheism or a world that is itself God" on the other.[628] In the final analysis, "it is a matter of perfect indifference, whether we assert a World without God, or make God the World. The one is as truly Atheism as the other."[629]

Those same three ultimate possibilities—a world without God, equated with the evolutionary materialism that was to be advanced by Darwin; a world that is itself God, equated with the pantheism of Spinoza; and Coleridge's own view, the world of Christian faith, presided over by the Trinity—are succinctly summoned in a note on Boehme: "there are but three possible coherent systems—I. That of Self-construction, according to which the Absolute organizes itself into the World. = Pantheism. II. That of Self-mechanism, or rather of selfless Formation, according to which aboriginal Chaos is everlastingly mechanized into Particulars, from which according to the degrees of harmony in the Multeity Life & Perception & finally Consciousness, result—= Atheism. . . . III. That of the Trinity: and this third is the only possible Escape from one or the other of the two former."[630]

The evolutionary form of materialism developed by Darwin grew out of the Romantic preoccupation with nature. Spinoza had indicated that the word God was a synonym for Nature: "Deus, sive Natura"—"God, or Nature".[631] But Spinoza's thought was not dynamic or evolutionary; the world as he presented it, as Renan said, "seems crystallized".[632] Darwin, on the other hand, presented a version of nature that was in dynamic

---

[626] Priestley *Doctrine* 149.
[627] *CM (CC)* II 803.
[628] See below, Frag 3 p 23.
[629] Brinkley 381.

[630] *CM (CC)* I 679.
[631] *Spinoza* II 213.
[632] Renan 508–9.

motion, and this version was extensively prefigured in the thought of Schelling and Hegel.

The scrutiny of nature that eventuated in the bleak understandings of Darwin originated as a vision of happiness. Wordsworth's characteristic joy in nature finds its precursor, as early as 1711, in Shaftesbury's radiant recognition of the splendour of the external world:

> O glorious nature! supremely fair and sovereignly good! all-loving and all-lovely, all-divine! whose looks are so becoming and of such infinite grace; whose study brings such wisdom, and whose contemplation such delight; whose every single work affords an ampler scene, and is a nobler spectacle than all which ever art presented! O mighty Nature! wise substitute of Providence! impowered creatress! Or thou impowering Deity, supreme creator! Thee I invoke and thee alone adore. To thee this solitude, this place, these rural meditations are sacred; whilst thus inspired with harmony of thought, though unconfined by words, and in loose numbers, I sing of Nature's order in created beings, and celebrate the beauties which resolve in thee, the source and principle of all beauty and perfection.[633]

Within this rapturous conception, however, lurked the recognition of change and process; and it was this change and process that would eventuate in the conception of Darwinian evolution:

> The vital principle is widely shared and infinitely varied, dispersed throughout, nowhere extinct. All lives, and by succession still revives. The temporary beings quit their borrowed forms and yield their elementary substance to new-comers. Called in their several turns to life, they view the light, and viewing pass, that others too may be spectators of the goodly scene, and greater numbers still enjoy the privilege of Nature. Munificent and great, she imparts herself to most and makes the subjects of her bounty infinite. Nought stays her hastening hand. No time nor substance is lost or unimproved. New forms arise, and when the old dissolve, the matter whence they were composed is not left useless, but wrought with equal management and art, even in corruption, Nature's seeming waste and vile abhorrence. The abject state appears merely as the way or passage to some better.[634]

By the 1850s this happy vision had given way, in Tennyson's phrase, to a vision of "Nature, red in tooth and claw".[635] Tennyson's words were published in 1850; *On the Origin of Species* did not appear until 1859. The antecedence is significant in that it shows that Darwin's work concluded, rather than began, the process of conceiving evolutionary reality. Indeed, Darwin always graciously acknowledged the prior and con-

---

[633] Shaftesbury II 98.
[634] Ibid. II 110–1.
[635] Tennyson *In Memoriam* § LVI, line 15. The fact that this phrase was published nine years before Darwin's book shows the foreboding that was in the air throughout the culture.

temporary efforts of others. "I am well aware", he said at one point, "that my books could never have been written, and would not have made any impression on the public mind, had not an immense amount of material been collected by a long series of admirable observers, and it is to them that honour is chiefly due".[636] Though he was here speaking of immediate predecessors and scientific contemporaries, for more than a century the outline, though not the scientific documentation, of evolutionary theory had been working in cultural history. Beginning with Maupertuis, thinkers of the French Enlightenment had fully comprehended, though they had not as yet demonstrated the articulated scientific structure of, the evolutionary hypothesis.[637] Specifically articulated versions of Darwinian natural selection were however beginning to be formulated in Coleridge's time. For a single striking example, the great geologist James Hutton (with whose work Coleridge was familiar), in a treatise on agriculture being written at his death in 1797, but not published until more than a hundred and fifty years later, took up the subject of variation among animals.

Darwin speaks of the chilling "Struggle for Existence" or "universal struggle for life" in deceptively quiet tones: "We behold the face of nature bright with gladness, we often see superabundance of food; we do not see, or we forget, that the birds which are idly singing round us mostly live on insects or seeds, and are thus constantly destroying life; or we forget how largely these songsters, or their eggs, or their nestlings, are destroyed by birds and beasts of prey; we do not always bear in mind, that though food may be now superabundant, it is not so at all seasons of each recurring year".[638] The horror of the evolutionary view, the meaninglessness it implied, especially to a culture conditioned by centuries of Christian hope, is here muted. It had been given full voice, however, by Schopenhauer some fifteen years earlier, in a passage that resounds with diapasons from the abyss:

There is nothing to show but the satisfaction of hunger and sexual passion, and in any case a little momentary gratification, such as falls to the lot of every individual animal, now and then, between its endless needs and exertions . . . . The futility and the fruitlessness of the struggle . . . are more readily grasped in the simple and easily observable life of animals . . . . We see only momentary gratification, fleeting pleasure conditioned by wants, much and long suffering, constant struggle, *bellum omnium*, everything a hunter and everything hunted, pressure, want, need, and anxiety, shrieking and howling; . . . Junghuhn relates that

---

[636] Darwin *Papers* II 204.

[637] See e.g. *Forerunners of Darwin, 1745–1859* ed Bentley Glass et al (Baltimore 1959); Émile Guyenot *Les Sciences de la vie aux XVIIe et XVIIIe siècles; l'idée d'évolution* (Paris 1941).

[638] Darwin *Origin* 116.

in Java he saw an immense field entirely covered with skeletons, and took it to be a battlefield. However, they were nothing but skeletons of large turtles five feet long, three feet broad, and of equal height. These turtles come this way from the sea, in order to lay their eggs, and are then seized by wild dogs . . . with their united strength, these dogs lay them on their backs, tear open their lower armour, the small scales of the belly, and devour them alive. But then a tiger often pounces on the dogs. Now all this misery is repeated thousands and thousands of times, year in and year out. For this, then, are these turtles born. What is the point of this whole scene of horror?[639]

Thus the gulf on the far side of Coleridge's isthmus was the evolutionary materialism of Darwin, which conceived no place for God and offered no purpose for human life. It amounted, in Coleridge's terms, to "a world without God". Hence it was that Coleridge was so concerned that Wordsworth, in the great philosophical poem that Coleridge conceived as merely a version of the *magnum opus*, should explode the "absurd notion of . . . all the countless Believers—even (strange to say) among Xtians of Man's having progressed from an Ouran Outang state—so contrary to all History, to all Religion, nay, to all Possibility".[640] And Coleridge assumed as a matter of course that his friend Green would agree with him in the "rejection of the Ouran outang Hypothesis".[641]

The Spinozan gulf on the near side of the isthmus, "a world that is itself God", though exalted in the language of its description, was capable of drowning all hope in its depths: "He, who loves God", said Spinoza, "cannot endeavor that God should love him in return".[642] "Strictly speaking, God does not love or hate anyone."[643] As to the final purpose of human life, Spinoza dismissed the question with contempt: "nature has no particular goal in view; and final causes are mere human figments"—"omnes causas finales nihil, nisi humana esse figmenta".[644]

---

[639] Schopenhauer III 404–5. See further A. O. Lovejoy "Schopenhauer as an Evolutionist" *Forerunners of Darwin: 1745–1859* 415–37.

[640] *CL* IV 574–5.

[641] Ibid. VI 723. C and Green virtually collaborated, in 1828, on "a discussion of 'the orangutan hypothesis,' the theory, stemming from Linnaeus, that man belonged to the same family of mammals as the simia. Coleridge wrote: '. . . since the world began never did there issue from the teeming Brain of Speculative Philosophy an hypothesis so utterly destitute of support'"; and Green declared his "'utter dissent from the hy-pothesis which supposes man to have been originally a congener of the orang-outang, or at least holding his superiority by no greater an interspace than that which separates the orang outang from the baboon'" (Jackson 171–2). Cf *SW & F (CC)* II 1410: "placing the Skull of the Negro beside that of the Ouran Utang, and the first glance of the Eye discovers the absolute divinity of the potter & you exclaim at once—Man and Beast—how glaring the difference—".

[642] *Spinoza* II 219.

[643] Ibid. II 291.

[644] Ibid. II 80.

The rejection of final causes was wholly unacceptable in Coleridge's orientation to the world and to experience. He even went so far as to say, in a letter of 1825: "The Hebrew Sages said—Three things were, before the World was: the Law, Messiah and the Last Judgement. With better taste & without a play on words, we may say—The World was made for the Gospel, or that Christianity is the final Cause of the World. If so, the Idea of the Redemption of the World must needs form the best central Reservoir for all our knowleges, physical or personal."[645] Thus, against Spinoza, Coleridge committed himself to think that "Christianity is the final Cause of the World". But Darwin too, no less than Spinoza, would reject final causes. What Darwin had to offer, instead of the cherished hope that life had a purpose that ultimately made sense of mankind's travails, was a kind of *ad hoc* gladness raised atop an evolutionary history of cruelty and strife.

But only if there were a final cause for existence did existence make sense to Coleridge; only if he could hope for Christian immortality and redemption were his woes bearable. "If dead, we cease to be", he cried in anguish,

> if total gloom
> Swallow up life's brief flash for aye, we fare
> As summer-gusts, of sudden birth and doom.
> . . . .
> If even a soul like Milton's can know death;
> O Man! thou vessel purposeless, unmeant,
> . . . .
> Surplus of Nature's dread activity,
> Which, as she gazed on some nigh-finished vase,
> Retreating slow, with meditative pause,
> She formed with restless hands unconsciously.
> Blank accident! nothing's anomaly!
> If rootless thus, thus substanceless they state,
> Go, weigh thy dreams . . .
> . . . .
> Why rejoices
> Thy heart with hollow joy for hollow good?
> Why cowl thy face beneath the mourner's hood?
> . . . .
> Be sad! be glad! be neither! seek, or shun!
> Thou hast no reason why! . . . [646]

[645] *CL* v 481.   [646] *PW* (EHC) I 425–6.

XXVI. A CONTINENTAL ANALOGUE:
HEGEL'S *ENZYKLOPÄDIE DER PHILOPHISCHEN WISSENSCHAFTEN*

The *magnum opus* was conceived in an historical context in which the claims of system seemed imperative. Though there had always been a tradition of opposition to system, at least from Shaftesbury (who said that the "most ingenious way of becoming foolish is by a system"),[647] through Diderot and Jacobi and Kierkegaard to the logical atomism of our own era, in the Romantic era system was in the ascendant; indeed, the French Revolution itself was from one perspective nothing other than a systematic restructuring of the conception of human society. "Everything in the human spirit", said Schelling, "strives toward system".[648] Even Kant said that the "Schulbegriff" of philosophy was that it was "das System der philosophischen Erkenntnisse oder der Vernunfterkenntnisse aus Begriffen".[649] The abandonment of philosophical system in our own day is in part a response to the overwhelming deluge of new data, which makes knowledge so chaotic as to defy even the thought of systematisation.

It was in large part to attempt to resist the chaos that loomed in the prospect of the future that the great Romantic systematists laboured. To understand one aspect of the *magnum opus*'s urgency, it will be useful to compare its structure with the chief achievement of Hegel on the continent; for Coleridge, who did not complete his system, and Hegel, who did, exhibit large similarities in matters of systematic focus and structure. As Hegel said, "philosophizing *without system* can be nothing scientific".[650]

The chief achievement of Hegel, at least in terms of system, was the *Enzyklopädie der philosophischen Wissenschaften*, which, as a commentator says, should be "accepted, as Hegel evidently intended it to be, as the work on the basis of which his philosophy is to be judged".[651]

Both the *magnum opus* and the *Enzyklopädie* found it difficult to cast their systematic nets around the Leviathan of reality. Coleridge's failure to complete the *magnum opus* owes in part to his neurotic blocks about working, but unsolved and intractable problems also militated against the interests of system. Hegel, whose awesome industry allowed no possibility of not finishing, also experienced difficulties. His great work appeared in three successively revised and augmented forms, first in 1817, then in 1827, and finally in 1830. All three editions differ, and the last

[647] Shaftesbury I 189.
[648] Schelling *SE* I 386.
[649] Kant *Logik* Einleitung III, in Kant

GS IX 23.
[650] *Hegel* VIII 59–60.
[651] Petry I 65.

one, in 1830, contained no fewer than 3,600 alterations from the 1827 edition. Moreover, the *textus receptus* of the work, prepared by Karl Ludwig Michelet in 1842, contains numerous "Additions" supplied from various manuscript sources.

Another, and structural, similarity of the systematic ventures of Coleridge and of Hegel is that they are both laid out in a trinal scheme. Coleridge said that his own great work was to be "A System of Truths, respecting Nature, Man, and Deity"; "researches and reflections concerning God, Nature, and Man"; "God, Nature, and Man: A System". Hegel, for his part, said in the preface to the second edition of his *Wissenschaft der Logik*, that "Die Philosophie überhaupt hat es noch mit konkreten Gegenständen, Gott, Natur, Geist, in ihren Gedanken zu tun"— "philosophy in general occupies itself with three concrete objects, God, Nature, and Mind".[652]

In the *Enzyklopädie*, however, Hegel alters "Gott, Natur, Geist" to "Logik, Natur, Geist". The second formula is merely a variant of the first, with God and Mind both being comprehended under the term "Geist", and "Logik" being the process by which Mind as man eventuates in Mind as God, and vice versa. The change was validated by Hegel's pantheism, which allowed the unity of all reality in the becoming of the Absolute Idea or God ("The Idea is essentially *process*").[653] Coleridge, on the other hand, committed to a separation of God and Nature and Man by the structure of his struggle against pantheism, could not collapse his terms into a reciprocal unity.

Like Hegel, Coleridge found "logic" necessary to the concept of system. Logic had been an integral part of the first projections of the task of the *magnum opus*, and it was not until about 1823 that Coleridge both somewhat completed a "logic" and began to think of it as having a separate validity from his great enterprise. The logical commitment in Coleridge's case, though different in the history of its dynamics, was similar to that of Hegel in its priority for the structure of system. Indeed, though he did not produce a closed structure of internal movement and triadic, Coleridge's larger plan of what he was doing was virtually identical with that of Hegel, as we see in an entry in the *Table Talk*:

My system, if I may venture to give it so fine a name, is the only attempt I know, ever made to reduce all knowledges into harmony. It opposes no other system, but shows what was true in each; and how that which was true in the particular, in each of them became error, *because* it was only half the truth. I have endeavoured to unite the insulated fragments of truth, and therewith to frame a perfect

---

[652] *Hegel* v 23.   [653] *Hegel* VIII 372.

mirror. I show to each system that I fully understand and rightfully appreciate what that system means; but then I lift up that system to a higher point of view, from which I enable it to see its former position, where it was, indeed, but under another light and with different relations, so that the fragment of truth is not only acknowledged but explained.[654]

Still a third major similarity between the two thinkers is that their commitment to trinal structure, though necessitated by the traditional requirements of system, was strengthened by a visceral commitment to the Christian Trinity. The subliminal effect of this commitment would be difficult to overemphasise. For an instance, in 1816 Coleridge comments, "There exists in the human being, at least in man fully developed, no mean symbol of Tri-unity, in Reason, Religion, and the Will".[655] He also said: "The mystery of the Trinity I believed to be a truth, *pointed* toward, and even negatively proveable, by *Reason*; existing in all ages, under more or less disfigurement, by *Tradition*, from the patriarch Noah; but first rendered an article of necessary *Faith* by the Incarnation and Redemption".[656] John Beer has talked of Coleridge's early involvement with trinal schemes of a Platonist kind, even in his days of Unitarian commitment;[657] and the present editor has detailed the emotional and logical process by which he came to place the Trinity at the forefront of his thinking.[658] What Coleridge committed himself to was a complementarity of philosophy and religion of which the Trinity was the keystone and joining reality. This was the final form of his thinking; on his very deathbed he was concerned that his disciple, J. H. Green, understand exactly his formula for conceiving the Trinity.[659] Hegel was equally committed.

Much the same body of reading underlay both Coleridge's and Hegel's conceivings of the relation of God and world; for instance, both thinkers were involved with the speculations of Jakob Boehme, who provides a great impetus to triplistic thinking. As Coleridge commented, "Not only the theosophical Truth, but the formal logical and theological accuracy and discriminateness of Jac. Behmen's Explication of the mysterious Tri-unity is worthy of reverential Wonder!"[660]

Hegel was profoundly influenced by Boehme; Boehme's threeness in everything is precisely Hegel's own triadic structure of the unfolding of

---

[654] *TT (CC)* II 147–8, 12 Sept 1831. See also the revised version printed at *TT (CC)* I 248–9 and dated 11 Sept.

[655] *LS (CC)* 62.

[656] *CL* IV 894–5.

[657] Beer 78–83. "There is some evidence that Trinitarian speculations had occupied him while he was still at Christ's Hospital." "From all this it appears that beneath the innocent Platonic Trinitarianism of Coleridge's early days there lay a wealth of speculation" (78, 80).

[658] *CPT* 191–255.

[659] *CL* VI 992.

[660] *CM (CC)* I 588.

the Idea. Coleridge, though perhaps not quite so profoundly obligated is equally impressed:

Böem's (or as we say, Behmen's) account of the Trinity is masterly and ortho-dox. Waterland and Sherlock might each have condescended to have been in-structed by the humble Shoe-maker of Gorlitz, with great advantage to them-selves, and to the avoidal of the perilous Errors, of which they were at least in jeopardy. Let me add to this Note, that there are three analogous Acts in the human Consciousness, or rather three dim imperfect Similitudes; and if we ever have a truly scientific Psychology, it will consist of the distinct Enunciation, and Developement of the three primary Energies of Consciousness, and a History of their Application and Results.[661]

Immediately following this curious anticipation of Freud's ego, super-ego, and id, Coleridge relates Boehme's trinitarian thinking to his own defence against Spinoza:

Even while my faith was confined in the trammels of Unitarianism (so called) with respect to all the doctrines of Sin and Grace, I saw clearly, as a truth in philoso-phy, that the Trinitarian was the only consequent Medium between the Atheist and the Anthropomorph. Spinoza, the Hercules' Pillar of human Reason, dismissed In-tellect from his System . . . . He was too profound a Thinker not to perceive, that there can be no Intellectus without a simultaneous Intelligibile and Intellectio/ the best possible logical Exponent of the Father, the Word, & the Spirit.[662]

Daniel Waterland, mentioned in the first quotation, was an eighteenth-century Anglican theologian and an important figure in Coleridge's intellectual background. As Henry Nelson Coleridge said, "Mr. Cole-ridge's admiration of Bull and Waterland as high theologians was very great."[663] Hegel too was helped in his triplistic thought by Waterland.

For both Coleridge and Hegel, the analysis of nature proved the great-est weakness in the system. The sections on the science of nature in the *Opus Maximum* are clearly the weakest and most time-bound aspect of Coleridge's endeavour, but they are, as argued above, absolutely essen-tial if system is undertaken. While Hegel's presentation of the science of nature is much fuller and more coherent than that of Coleridge, it is sim-ilarly time-bound. Both men had read hugely in the embryonic scientific literature of the time. But neither Hegel nor Coleridge was a scientist with true experimental grounding, and both, in the fashion of the time, mixed speculation with knowledge in a way that would now be regarded as scientifically impermissible.

A final large similarity between Coleridge's and Hegel's great works

[661] *CM (CC)* I 565–6. [663] *TT (CC)* II 65n.
[662] Ibid. 566–7.

was that they both originated as pedagogic ventures. The earliest plan for the *magnum opus* was contained in a scheme for educating young men (see above, Section x) while Hegel's encyclopaedic system was specifically developed as a handbook for his students.

XXVII. A CONTINENTAL ANTITHESIS: SCHOPENHAUER'S *DIE WELT ALS WILLE UND VORSTELLUNG*

Just as Coleridge's *magnum opus* is in large matters of origin, structure, and goal an analogue of Hegel's endeavour in the *Enzyklopädie der philosophischen Wissenschaften*, so Hegel's most ferocious denigrator, Schopenhauer—he never tired of such epithets as "charlatan" when speaking of his older contemporary[664]—provides a striking antithesis for Coleridge's effort. The antithesis is relevant, however, only because there is at the same time a fundamental similarity in their intent.

Both men were trying to present a systematic accounting of reality. But where Coleridge tried to guarantee meaning in human life by providing a philosophical underpinning for the Christian idea of God, with its ancillary guarantee of redemption, Schopenhauer abandoned the idea of God. In so doing he had ultimately to abandon any conception of meaning in human life. As Nietzsche observed, "Schopenhauer as a philosopher was the first declared and uncompromising atheist that we Germans have had";[665] he identified the "Schopenhauerian question" as "does existence have any meaning at all?"[666] Coleridge's message was finally one of hope; Schopenhauer's message one of despair.[667]

The absolute antithesis of Coleridge and Schopenhauer subtends an urgent similarity that extends throughout the entire philosophical spectrum of their thought. As I have said elsewhere: "Schopenhauer's great work, like Coleridge's, is deeply involved with final questions of religion and the structure of reality; like Coleridge's, it brings to the fore the question of the meaning of human existence; like Coleridge's, it sees will as philosophically central; like Coleridge's, it is based on extensive erudition, especially with regard to the legacy of Kant; like Coleridge's, it is profoundly responsive to the tidal wave of Spinozistic influence; like Coleridge's, finally, it is ambitiously and definitively systematic".[668]

---

[664] For instance he snarls that "In Germany it was possible to proclaim Hegel, a repulsive and dull charlatan and an unparalleled scribbler of nonsense, the greatest philosopher of all time" (Schopenhauer III 75).

[665] *Nietzsche* II 227.

[666] Ibid. 228.

[667] Nietzsche speaks chillingly of Schopenhauer's "terrible look into a world that has become de-Godded, dumb, blind, and questionable" (ibid. 229).

[668] *RFR* 376.

As the incompleteness of the *magnum opus* finds a counterpart in the successive and restless revisions of Hegel's great work, so too does it find a counterpart in the unique publishing history of Schopenhauer's masterpiece. *Die Welt als Wille und Vorstellung* appeared in a first edition dated 1819. Instead of moving on to other work, however, Schopenhauer continued to augment his system until, in 1844, he published a second edition, which "to an extent possibly unique in the annals of authorial afterthoughts, more than doubled the size of the treatise."[669] Even then, however, he had not completely presented his system.

The most urgent of the antitheses-within-similarity that inform the work of Coleridge and Schopenhauer are, first, the treatment of will, and, second, the attitude towards the emerging spectre of Darwinian reality. Will, of vital importance to Coleridge, is of possibly even more important to Schopenhauer. But the ways in which the two thinkers utilise will are absolutely opposed. Coleridge uses it as a chief bulwark for the immense importance of personality; Schopenhauer uses it as the explanation of a reality without God. Indeed, for Schopenhauer, will is the underlying reality of everything, both natural and human: "the will proclaims itself just as directly in the fall of a stone as in the action of man".[670] "The will, which constitutes the basis of our own inner being, is the same will that manifests itself in the lowest, inorganic phenomena."[671]

For Schopenhauer, will is not only the substrate of nature but the essence of person as well: "it is the *prius* of knowledge, the kernel of our true being. The will is the primary and original force itself, which forms and maintains the animal body, in that it carries out that body's unconscious as well as conscious functions."[672] Whereas for Coleridge will—which he, like Schopenhauer, takes as irreducible and incommensurable—coordinates itself with reason to support a defence of deity, Schopenhauer argues for the blindness of the will. The blind will is the Kantian thing-in-itself, and reason and all other structures are representations secondary to that essence.[673]

Coleridge sought to establish, or rather to defend, the Christian conception of meaning and benevolent purpose in the world. Schopenhauer, on the contrary, by substituting will for personality as the absolute essence, committed himself to the conception of a blind and meaningless activity as the ultimate nature of the world: "I have rightly declared the will-to-live to be that which is incapable of further explanation, but is the basis of every explanation; and that, far from being an empty-

[669] *RFR* 376.
[670] Schopenhauer III 339.
[671] Ibid. III 336–7.
[672] Ibid. III 331–2.
[673] Ibid. III 224–5.

sounding word, like the Absolute, the infinite, the idea, and other simi-
lar expressions, it is the most real thing we know, in fact the kernel of
reality itself".[674] Will is blind and purposeless: "absence of all aim, of
all limits, belongs to the essential nature of the will in itself, which is an
endless striving. . . . Eternal becoming, endless flux, belong to the reve-
lation of the essential nature of the will."[675] Coleridge, in uncompro-
mising opposition, urges against this "the identity and coinherence of the
Will and the Reason";[676] and insists that "In man the Will, as Will, first
appears".[677]

In his acceptance of an endless and purposeless activity as the ultimate
nature of reality, Schopenhauer accepted the Darwinian implications that
Coleridge was so concerned to ward off. He found them no less terrify-
ing than Coleridge did, but inasmuch as he was committed to a total pes-
simism as his philosophical standpoint (he argues, against Leibniz, that
far from being the best of all possible worlds, this is in fact the worst!),
he was able, unlike Coleridge, to accept them: "life swings like a pen-
dulum to and fro between pain and boredom, and these are in fact its ul-
timate constituents . . . . With cautious step and anxious glance around
man pursues his path, for a thousand accidents and a thousand enemies
lie in wait for him. Thus he went in the savage state, and thus he goes in
civilized life; there is no security for him . . . . The life of the great ma-
jority is only a constant struggle for this same existence, with the cer-
tainty of ultimately losing it."[678] With that ready acceptance of Godless
reality, Schopenhauer does not flinch before Darwinian examples:

Everywhere in nature we see contest, struggle, and the fluctuation of victory
. . . . Yet this strife itself is only the revelation of that variance with itself that is
essential to the will. This universal conflict is to be seen most clearly in the an-
imal kingdom. Animals have the vegetable kingdom for their nourishment, and
within the animal kingdom again every animal is the prey and food of some other
. . . . [A] most glaring example of this kind is afforded by the bulldog ant of Aus-
tralia, for when it is cut in two, a battle begins between the head and the tail. The
head attacks the tail with its teeth, and the tail defends itself bravely by stinging
the head.[679]

A further antithesis within similarity, or similarity within antithesis,
between Coleridge and Schopenhauer exists in the characters of the two
authors. Few figures of the first rank in all the history of culture have
been as neurotically burdened and disfigured as was Coleridge. Schopen-

---

[674] Schopenhauer III 400.
[675] Ibid. II 195–6.
[676] See below, Frag 2 f 1.

[677] Ibid. f 119.
[678] Schopenhauer II 368–9.
[679] Ibid. II 174–6.

hauer was probably one of those few. Yet the two were entirely unlike in their personalities. Coleridge was a veritable genius in social relations, able to charm people at will, always able to form new and supportive friendships. Indeed, it is probably not excessive to say that the fragmentary and incomplete aspect of Coleridge's intellectual labour was on some level a plea for the help, forgiveness, and love of others.

Schopenhauer's reaction to his sense of isolated inadequacy, on the other hand, was combative. His work is characterised by extreme haughtiness towards other thinkers, as was his life; the psychoanalyst Frieda Fromm-Reichmann speaks revealingly on the psychological dynamics obtaining in the interactions of his tormented life and towering achievement: "this schizoid, paranoid philosopher succeeded in converting his unfulfilled longing for the unattainable into the eternal spiritual monument which is his philosophical writings".[680]

XXVIII. THE RELATION OF THE *MAGNUM OPUS* TO COLERIDGE'S *PHILOSOPHICAL LECTURES*

From 14 December 1818 to 29 March 1819, Coleridge delivered each Monday night a series of public philosophical lectures at the Crown and Anchor Tavern in the Strand. As revelations of his own philosophical tropisms and opinions, especially at roughly the same period the *Opus Maximum* was being dictated, they are intimately intertwined with the reality of the *magnum opus*; more precisely, they form part of that reality.

The lectures were edited and published, with extensive notes, by Kathleen Coburn, as almost an incidental part of her titanic contribution to Coleridge scholarship. They appeared in London at a small press called The Pilot Press Limited in 1949 as *The Philosophical Lectures of Samuel Taylor Coleridge; Hitherto Unpublished*. As with so much of the difficult material Professor Coburn put before the public, the lectures were, before she came on the scene, virtually unpublishable. As she says:

Coleridge himself intended to publish them. He wrote to Southey,

"Mr. Frere at a heavy expence (I was astonished to learn thro' Mrs. Gillman from the scribe himself, at how heavy an expence!) has had my Lectures taken down in shorthand.

"It will be of service to me: tho' the Publication must of course contain much that could not be delivered to a public audience who, respectable as they have been (scanty, I am sorry to add) expect to be kept awake—I shall however God

---

[680] *Fromm-Reichmann* 12.

granting me the continuance of the power, and the strength, bring them out— first because a history of *Philosophy* as the gradual Evolution of the instincts of Man to enquire into *the Origin*, by the efforts, of his own reason, is a desideratum in Literature and secondly, because it is almost a necessary Introduction to my *Magnum opus* in which I had been making regular and considerable progress till my Lectures, and shall resume, immediately after."[681]

The reporter's manuscript of the lectures was not corrected by Coleridge himself. It eventually came into the hands of Coleridge's literary executor, J. H. Green, where it suffered much the same non-publishing fate as the *Opus Maximum* itself. In response to Ingleby's queries, discussed above (Section XVIII), as to what he was doing with the Coleridge manuscripts, Green answered with respect to *The Philosophical Lectures*:

The work to which I suppose the writer alludes as the *History of Philosophy*, is in my possession. It was presented to me by the late J. Hookham Frere, and consists of notes, taken for him by an eminent shorthand writer, of the course of lectures delivered by Coleridge on that subject. Unfortunately, however, these notes are wholly unfit for publication, as indeed may be inferred from the fact, communicated to me by Coleridge, that the person employed confessed after the first lecture that he was unable to follow the lecturer in consequence of becoming perplexed and delayed by the novelty of thought and language, for which he was wholly unprepared by the ordinary exercise of his art. If this *History of Philosophy* is to be published in an intelligible form it will require to be rewritten; and I would willingly undertake the task, had I not, in connexion with Coleridge's views, other and more pressing objects to accomplish.[682]

After Green's death the manuscript of the lectures passed to Coleridge's son Derwent, and from there to Derwent's son, the eminent Coleridgean editor Ernest Hartley Coleridge. As Professor Coburn says: "In the 1930's the first attempts to find it were unsuccessful, and it was tentatively suggested by the late Rev. G. H. B. Coleridge that the Frere manuscript might have disappeared in the ill-fated trunk that in 1895 left London and never reached Torquay. However, lurking at the back of a cupboard in his library, it eventually came to light."[683]

In preparing his lectures, Coleridge used Tennemann's *Geschichte der Philosophie* as a framework for organising the historical sequence of presentation. (Hegel made use of Tennemann in the same way when writing his own lectures on the history of philosophy.)[684] Despite his organisational reliance on Tennemann, Coleridge in *The Philosophical*

---

[681] *P Lects* (1949) 7–8.
[682] Ibid. 14.

[683] Ibid. 15.
[684] Ibid. 18.

Lectures produced an unmatched presentation of his own philosophical views. It is the richest lode for his opinions on a number of figures important in his thought, especially Pythagoras, Socrates, and Plato. The lectures are also replete with striking formulations, which emanate from his own deep reflection and profound knowledge. To adduce only a few: "Luther was one of the greatest poets that ever lived, but he was so possessed by his own genius that he acted poems not wrote them. His whole life in truth was one grand poem."[685] "Scarcely anyone has a larger share of my aversion than Voltaire; and even of the better-hearted Rousseau I was never more than a very lukewarm admirer."[686] Schelling is described as a "Roman Catholic pantheist . . . with a rosary in one hand and the Bible of Spinoza in the other".[687]

There are brilliantly sympathetic discussions of such lesser known figures as Boehme and Bruno:

Such was the character of Giordano Bruno, a man who possessed a genius perhaps fully equal to that of any philosopher of more known name . . . . This man, though a pantheist, was religious; he provoked the priests, he was seized in Rome, and in the year 1601 was burnt for an atheist. Before his death he wrote a Latin poem which I think in grandeur of moral has been rarely surpassed . . . .

In this mode the brave man passed to his death as an atheist, and it would be well if all the priests of Rome could have acquired his genuine piety according to his own apprehensions.[688]

Boehme receives an even more sympathetic testimonial: "He was indeed a stupendous human being. Had he received the discipline of education, above all had he possessed the knowledge which would have guarded him against his own delusions, I scarcely know whether we should have had reason to attribute greater genius even to Plato himself."[689]

The Philosophical Lectures are in truth a wonderful work. Where the *Opus Maximum* is, as it were, merely the torso of a work, a trunk with some of the finest leaves pulled off to be interwoven into other works, *The Philosophical Lectures* convey the true tone and subtlety of Coleridge's thought, a tone and subtlety that, had things gone well, would have informed the *magnum opus* itself. A history of philosophy—and this is the only history of philosophy he produced—had been the first of the "six Treatises" that Coleridge in 1815 had projected as comprising the *magnum opus* itself: "The first, a philosophic Compendium of the History of Philosophy from Pythagoras to the present Day, with miscel-

[685] *P Lects* (1949) 309.
[686] Ibid. 306.
[687] Ibid. 390.
[688] Ibid. 324–6.
[689] Ibid. 329.

laneous Investigations on Toleration, & the obstacles to just reasoning. (No such work exists, at least in our language—for Brucker's is a Wilderness in six huge Quartos, & he was no Philosopher—& Enfield's [Abridg]ement is below criticism)— ".[690]

That *The Philosophical Lectures* must be accepted as the desiderated first treatise of the *magnum opus* is further confirmed by considering the passage quoted above alongside Coleridge's statement in the "Prospectus" to the lectures:

Nor can these Lectures be justly deemed superfluous even as a literary work. We have, indeed, a History of Philosophy, or rather a folio volume so called, by STANLEY, and ENFIELD's Abridgement of the massive and voluminous BRUCKER. But what are they? Little more, in fact, than collections of sentences and extracts, formed into separate groups under the several names, and taken (at first or second hand) from the several writings, of individual philosophers, with no *principle* of arrangement, with no *method*, and therefore without unity and without progress or completion. Hard to be understood as detached passages, and impossible to be remembered as a whole, they leave at last on the mind of the most sedulous student but a dizzy recollection of jarring opinions and wild fancies.[691]

Coleridge goes on to specify the opposed nature of his own lectures. What he posits as his method and purpose is amply realised by the text of the lectures themselves:

Whatever value those works may have as books of reference, so far from *superseding*, they might seem rather to *require*, a work like the present, in which the accidental influences of particular periods and individual genius are by no means overlooked, but which yet does in the main consider Philosophy historically, as an essential part of the history of man, and as if it were the striving of a single mind, under very different circumstances indeed, and at different periods of its own growth and developement; but so that each change and every new direction should have its cause and its explanation in the errors, insufficiency, or prematurity of the preceding, while all by reference to a common object is reduced to harmony of impression and total result. Now this object, which is one and the same in all the forms of Philosophy, and which alone constitutes a work *philosophic*, is—the origin and primary laws (or efficient causes) either of the WORLD, man included (which is *Natural* Philosophy)—or of Human Nature exclusively, and as far only as it is *human* (which is *Moral* Philosophy). If to these we subjoin, as a third problem, the question concerning the sufficiency of the human reason to the solution of both or either of the two former, we shall have a full conception of the sense in which the term, Philosophy, is used in this Prospectus and the Lectures corresponding to it.[692]

[690] *CL* IV 591–2.
[691] *P Lects* (1949) 67.

[692] Ibid. 67–8.

Significantly, the tripartite conception of "Natural Philosophy", "Human Nature exclusively", and "the question concerning the sufficiency of the human" are tantamount to Coleridge's larger endeavour in the whole of the _magnum opus_, which was to be "A system of Truths, respecting Nature, Man, and Deity" or "God, Nature, and Man: A System".

Indeed, in one important structural respect, _The Philosophical Lectures_ are even closer to what Coleridge ultimately wanted to achieve than is _The Opus Maximum_. In describing, in 1831, what his "system" was to be, Coleridge explicitly designated an historical dimension, to be developed in the very way that characterises _The Philosophical Lectures_:

> It opposes no other system, but shows what was true in each; and how that which was true in the particular, in each of them became error, _because_ it was only half the truth. I have endeavoured to unite the insulated fragments of truth, and therewith to frame a perfect mirror. I show to each system that I fully understand and rightfully appreciate what that system means; but then I lift up that system, to a higher point of view, from which I enable it to see its former position, where it was, indeed, but under another light and with and with different relations;—so that the fragment of truth is not only acknowledged, but explained.[693]

The statement precisely correlates with the aim declared in the "Prospectus" to _The Philosophical Lectures_: "a work like the present . . . does in the main consider Philosophy historically, as an essential part of the history of man, and as if it were the striving of a single mind, under very different circumstances indeed, and at different periods of its own growth and developement; but so that each change and every new direction should have its cause and its explanation in the errors, insufficiency, or prematurity of the preceding, while all by reference to a common object is reduced to harmony . . . ."[694]

Thus the largest aims of Coleridge's "system", as well as the specific character of _The Philosophical Lectures_, form another analogue for Coleridge's endeavour and that of Hegel. Hegel also produced a series of philosophical lectures, _Vorlesungen über die Geschichte der Philosophie_, which exhibit to great advantage his immense command of the thought of all earlier thinkers. The lectures were delivered in two academic years at Heidelberg and six academic years at Berlin, encompassing the period 1816–30; they were first published in three volumes from 1833 to 1836. Like Coleridge, Hegel, considers prior philosophies not as something to be merely described, nor again to be discussed as nugatory; rather each is a stage, in Coleridge's phrase, "as if it were the striving of an individual mind . . . at different periods of its own growth". Coleridge

---

[693] _TT_ (_CC_) II 147–8, 12 Sept 1831.   [694] _P Lects_ (1949) 67.

rebukes earlier histories of philosophy as "Little more, in fact, than collections of sentences and extracts . . . with no *principle* of arrangement";[695] while Hegel observes that "eine Sammlung von Kenntnissen macht keine Wissenschaft aus"—"a collection of information does not constitute a science".[696]

Like Coleridge, Hegel conceives of earlier thought as conditioned by time and circumstance; but as the development of the Idea, the history of philosophy is philosophy itself. Thus, for Hegel, the study of the history of philosophy is really the same thing as the study of philosophy. One of the consequences of this view, for both Coleridge and Hegel, is an irenic acceptance, so wholly unlike the attitudes of the Vienna positivists and the Oxford analysts of our own century, of all prior thought. As Hegel beautifully says: "Every philosophy has been, and still is necessary. None has passed away, but all are affirmatively contained as elements in a whole . . . . No philosophy has ever been refuted. What has been refuted is not the principle of this philosophy, but merely the fact that this principle should be considered final and absolute in character."[697]

Despite the striking similarity between the philosophical lectures of Coleridge and those of Hegel, on one important point they were absolutely opposed. Hegel's system constituted a form of pantheism. Coleridge, on the contrary, saw a God presiding over both a human and an external nature, but not located within those realms, however much his effulgence shown over them. "And then too", Coleridge says in his twelfth lecture, "we shall be in that state to which science in all its form is gradually leading us. Then will the other great Bible of God, the Book of Nature, become transparent to us, when we regard the forms of matter as words, as symbols, valuable only as being the expression, an unrolled but yet a glorious fragment, of the wisdom of the Supreme Being."[698]

The Philosophical Lectures are an especially rich lode for Coleridge's awareness of, and opposition to, pantheism. For a single instance, after his enormously positive testimony about the quality of Boehme's mind, Coleridge warns against his pantheism: "I again and again wish that some more enlightened friend had been present and had rescued this man from evils. I mean the error and the delusion which, fortunately, however, his own sense of right held from him; for with all this, though he himself prized his system mainly as explaining and inferring all the mys-

[695] *P Lects* (1949) 67.
[696] *Hegel* xviii 50.
[697] Ibid. xviii 56.
[698] *P Lects* (1949) 366.

teries of religion, there is, as there was throughout in the philosophy of that time, a tendency to pantheism; or rather it was itself a disguised pantheism."[699]

Almost every aspect of Coleridge's concern is addressed in *The Philosophical Lectures*, sometimes in passages of special cogency. As we have seen, the two leading terms in Coleridge's thinking are without question "reason" and "will", and his highest aim was to validate the conception of the Christian Redeemer. All three emphases inform a quintessentially Coleridgean statement at the end of the second lecture:

Till at length the two great component parts of our nature, in the unity of which all its excellency and all its hopes depend, namely that of the will in the one, as the higher and more especially godlike, and the reason in the other, as the compeer but yet second to that will, were to unite and to prepare the world for the reception of its Redeemer; which took place just at the time when the traditions of history and the oracles of the Jews had combined with the philosophy of the Grecians, and prepared the Jews themselves for understanding their own scriptures in a more spiritual light, and the Greeks to give to their speculations, that were but the shadows of thought before, a reality, in that which alone is properly real.[700]

Likewise, Coleridge's opposition to "mechanical philosophy" and his abhorrence of French thought of the Enlightenment are well represented. He speaks of "the new French writings, which aimed at destroying all the connexions of thought, as the same philosophy strove to destroy all the connexions of society and domestic life".[701] In a report of the fourteenth lecture, Coleridge is said to speak again of "the late systems of French, and perhaps more general, philosophy—with the loss of the life and the spirit of Nature. This philosophy has, maybe, produced a few new mechanical inventions—certainly even those are not discoveries— and instead of human nature we have a French nature, which we may sum up as the *caput mortuum* of a French ferocity, audacity, frivolity, immorality and corruption."[702] He is eloquent on the subject in the following passage from the fifth lecture, which presents, as it were, a conspectus of the larger social task of the *magnum opus*:

And now I am happy to see and feel that men are craving for a better diet than the wretched trash they have been fed with for the last century; that they will be taught that what is sound must come out of themselves, and that they cannot find good with their eyes or with their ears or with their hands, that they will not discover them in the crucible or bring them out of a machine, but must look into the

[699] *P Lects* (1949) 330.
[700] Ibid. 112.
[701] Ibid. 190.
[702] Ibid. 394.

living soul which God has made His image, in order to learn, even in fragments, what that power is by which we are to execute the delegated power entrusted to us by Him. And I feel more ⟨strongly⟩ when I think that in the country where this mechanic philosophy was predominant, and most idolized, it presented a most fearful but a most instructive lesson of its consequences. We have only to put one word for the other, and in the mechanical philosophy to give the whole system of the French Revolution.[703]

The remaining adversarial philosophemes of the *magnum opus*, the pantheism of Spinoza and the proleptic schematisms of evolutionary materialism are likewise represented in *The Philosophical Lectures*. Curiously enough, though the lectures throughout counterpoint pantheism against the overriding Christianity of Coleridge's commitment, Spinoza himself receives notably gentle treatment. The cause, one suspects, along with Coleridge's unfailing reverence for Spinoza as man and thinker,[704] is the irenic tone, remarked above, of Coleridge's survey of prior philosophy. He is notably in these lectures trying to reconcile, understand, and if possible include, rather than to stigmatise and reject:

I have not felt myself allowed, from the limits which my lectures have placed round me, to enter particularly on Spinoza, because the "substance" of his life, I could have said, I have been obliged to anticipate first in the account of the Eleatic school,[705] the idealists of old, and secondly in the account of the new Platonists. But great impressions has Spinoza made on the minds of the learned and an impression on the theologians. And the theologic hatred of his name is one of the most incomprehensible parts of philosophic researches. For Spinoza was originally a Jew, and he held the opinions of the most learned Jews, particularly the Cabbalistic philosophers. Next he was of the most pure and exemplary life and it has been said of him, if he did not think as a Christian, he felt and acted like one.[706]

Yet after this loving representation, Coleridge feels it necessary to append a warning: "On the other hand I am far from hiding the inevitable consequences of pantheism in all cases, whether the pantheism of India, or the solitary cases ⟨like that⟩ of Spinoza".[707]

The Darwinism looming on the horizon is also invoked and opposed:

I could say more on this subject with reference to an opinion which has, strange to say, become quite common even among Christian people, that the human race

[703] *P Lects* (1949) 194–5.
[704] Cf e.g. a marginal note: "if ever Human Being was in earnest, totus et integer in his Conviction of the Truth of his System, it was Spinoza—" (*CM*—*CC*—III 80).

[705] Cf a marginal notation: "Spinoza re-edified the Pantheism of the old Greek Philosophy. S.T.C." (*CM*—*CC*—III 901).
[706] *P Lects* (1949) 384–5.
[707] Ibid. 385.

arose from a state of savagery and then gradually from a monkey came up
through various states to be man, and being man to form a state, and being states
to improve upon them, and so by a certain train of regular experience to explain
all things as they now exist. Which reminds one of the French lady who hearing
a story that a dead man had walked a league with his head under his arm, some-
body exclaimed, "What! a league!" with surprise. "Aye!" said the lady, "the first
step was the thing".[708]

At one point Coleridge sketches a partial model of evolution, which, as
in *Theory of Life* and elsewhere, he offers in an attempt to allay the vir-
ulence of the gathering Darwinism. Nature, he says, "does not proceed
in created beings" as she does in natural ascents, but "still in created be-
ings one thing comes forward with mighty force":

Each insect has its shop of tools about it, but with those it has instincts that act
outwardly. It constructs its nests—makes its hive . . . . Nature takes a higher step
and passes into the fishes and there the nervous ⟨*system*⟩ . . . begins . . . . She
takes another step and combines both in the birds . . . . She takes another step in
the animals—the four-footed animals. But this is so great a step before she can
come to her last [consummation] that here again we miss all, not only the acts
of the insects, but we miss all the lovely analogies to moral feelings which are
found in the birds—[709]

Coleridge's own philosophical standpoint and the standpoint of all
that he opposes are set forth in a contrast of the Platonic and Aristotelian
perspectives:

two opposite systems were placed before the mind of the world. One, whether
or not, in order to arrive at the truth, we are in the *first* place (for there is no doubt
among thinking men that both must be consulted—the question of priority is the
point) whether or not in the *first* place, and in order to gain the principles of truth,
we are to go into ourselves and in our own spirits to discover the law by which
the whole universe is acting, and then modestly to go forth and question this, that
and the other, how far it will give a favorable response to our own individual
conception of that truth; or whether on the contrary we are to regard, with Aris-
totle, the mind as being a blank or empty receiver, distinguished from it indeed
by a strange and mysterious propensity of being filled . . . .[710]

Finally, throughout the lectures, which continually refer manifesta-
tions of thought either to pantheism or to Christianity, Coleridge insists
on the necessity of philosophy as a complement to Christianity: "In truth
philosophy itself is nothing but mockery unless it is considered the tran-
sit from paganism to religion".[711]

[708] *P Lects* (1949) 239.
[709] Ibid. 274.

[710] Ibid. 188–9.
[711] Ibid. 224.

Therefore I call this the supplement of all philosophy. It is to feel that philosophy itself can only point out a good which by philosophy is unattainable; to feel that we have a disease, to believe that we have a physician, and in the conjoint action of these to exert that total energy of soul from which it is as impossible that evil or aught but good can flow . . . as that a fountain should send forth sands or a fire produce freezing around it. No, not from any external impulses, not from any agencies that can be sought for; . . . But man comes from within, and all that is truly human must proceed from within . . . . Then only will true philosophy be existing when from philosophy it is passed into that wisdom which no man has but by the earnest aspirations to be united with the Only Wise, in that moment when the Father shall be all in all.[712]

XXIX. THE RELATION OF THE *MAGNUM OPUS* TO COLERIDGE'S *AIDS TO REFLECTION*

Where *The Philosophical Lectures* establishes much the same position in reflecting upon philosophical history that the *Opus Maximum* attempts to do by formal argument, Coleridge's *Aids to Reflection* does much the same in terms of reflections upon theology. Indeed, *The Aids to Reflection*, taken with *The Philosophical Lectures* and the *Theory of Life*, make up a kind of tripod that supports Coleridge's chief aspirations in the systematic outline of natural, philosophical, and theological understandings he wished to set forth; the three works, taken together, serve as an alternative statement of the *magnum opus*.

It is important to reiterate the truth signalled throughout these prolegomena, and most especially in Section VII: The *Magnum Opus as* System: every aspect of Coleridge's thought is interconnected, tied together, and mutually interdependent. Thus *Aids to Reflections* contains a central Coleridgean emphasis that might easily have appeared in *Theory of Life*, or again in the *Opus Maximum* itself: "there is more in man than can be rationally referred to the life of Nature and the mechanism of Organization; that he has a Will not included in this mechanism; and that the Will is in an especial and pre-eminent sense the spiritual part of our Humanity".[713] That statement occurs near the beginning of *Aids to Reflection*. Near the end the treatise again takes up ontological/scientific concerns that fit exactly into the argument of *Theory of Life* and of the *Opus Maximum* as such: "I am persuaded, however, that the dogmatism of the Corpuscular School, though it still exerts an influence on men's notions and phrases, has received a mortal blow from the increasingly *dynamic* spirit of the physical Sciences now highest in public estimation. And it may

---

[712] *P Lects* (1949) 226.   [713] *AR* (1825) 132.

safely be predicted, that the results will extend beyond the intention of those, who are gradually effecting this revolution. It is not Chemistry alone that will be indebted to the Genius of Davy, Oersted, and their compeers; and not as the Founder of Physiology and philosophic Anatomy alone, will Mankind love and revere the name of John Hunter."[714] John Hunter was as it were the patron saint of the argument of *Theory of Life*, and what Coleridge calls the "dynamic" philosophy is everywhere his chief hope against the "mechanico-corpuscular philosophy" that threatened the validity of the Christian assurances that were the goal and focal point of Coleridge's life-effort.

But intertwined though it was with the whole spectrum of Coleridge's thought, *Aids to Reflection*, his most warmly received and most influential prose work, was first and foremost an essay in theology. It has always been widely regarded as the seminal text for the whole movement of American Transcendentalism, and it was broadly influential in the course of English theology in the nineteenth century. Yet *Aids to Reflection* was in a sense the death knell of the *magnum opus*, for after it was published in 1825, following the dictation of the *Opus Maximum* as we have it, Coleridge was left without full incentive to proceed with the *magnum opus* as such (although it is possible that he composed the section on "the Divine Ideas" after 1825). He indulged instead in the inflated and fanciful projection of 1828 discussed above (Section XII) and otherwise contented himself with hoping that he and his disciples together might someday finish the work.

Though the *Aids to Reflection* pre-empted the interests of the *magnum opus*, that was not its initial intention. It started as a very modest venture indeed. What seems to have happened is that Coleridge's theological formulations, brought to a boil, as it were, by the pressure of passing years and the intense prior attention to the long-delayed *Opus Maximum*, simply assumed such urgency that they began to be discharged into the modest work-in-progress. Actually, the fact that the *Aids to Reflection* was conceived in a low key paradoxically allowed the book to assume such a formidable burden, for Coleridge was never able to work when great commitments were placed before him. Only desultory or localised plans seemed to be able to evade the negating effect of his crippling neurosis.

Indeed, the dynamics of the relationship of the *Aids to Reflection* to the *magnum opus* are wholly different from those of *The Philosophical Lectures*. The latter was considered as a necessary introduction to, even

[714] *AR* (1825) 387–8.

as a first section within, the *magnum opus*; the *Aids*, on the contrary, was viewed as an interruption in Coleridge's commitment. After reading the proofs of the *Aids*, he writes to Wordsworth, "I must now set to work with *all* my powers and thoughts to my Leighton, and then to my logic, and then to my *opus maximum*! if indeed it shall please God to spare me so long, which I have had too many warnings of late (more than my nearest friends know of) not to doubt".[715] Interspersed with his letters about the plans for the *Aids* are continuously anxious assurances that it should not upset his plans for the *magnum opus*. For instance, Coleridge writes on 7 July 1823, "If I could but once get off the two Works, on which I rely for the Proof that I have not lived in vain, and had these off my mind, I could then maintain myself well enough by writing for the purpose of what I got by it".[716]

The two works mentioned are apparently the same works—the *Elements of Discourse* (which was nothing less than the organum verè organum projected as a necessity in the 1803 schematism of the *magnum opus*) and the *Assertion of Religion* (which, as we have seen, was one of the later names for the *magnum opus* itself)—that he refers to in a letter to his publishers Taylor and Hessey on 16 August 1823: "There are two or three other things of more Moment to me at least, on which I should be glad to consult you—particularly, on two Works, one of which is finished and perfectly ready for the Press, and the other nearly so—works that have occupied the best hours of the last twenty years of my Life".[717]

The earliest plans for the *Aids*, in curious fact, were not supposed to include Coleridge's theology at all. The work was initially planned as a selection of passages from the eighteenth-century Scottish Archbishop, Robert Leighton. As Coleridge wrote to the publisher, John Murray, on 18 January 1822: "I feel strongly persuaded—perhaps because I strongly wish it—that the Beauties of Archbishop Leighton selected and methodized, with a (*better*) Life of the Author, i.e. a biographical and critical Introduction or Preface, and Notes—would make not only a useful but an interesting POCKET VOLUME—".[718] The proposal was so ungrandiose that Coleridge actually deprecated it by going on to remark that "'Beauties' in general are objectionable works—injurious to the original Author, as disorganizing his productions—pulling to pieces the well-wrought *Crown* of his glory to pick out the shining stones—and injurious to the Reader, by indulging the taste for unconnected & for that reason unretained single Thought—".[719] The work thus inauspiciously

[715] *CL* v 354, 12 Apr 1824.
[716] Ibid. v 280.
[717] Ibid. v 294.

[718] Ibid. v 200.
[719] Ibid.

promulgated became, as Coleridge said in May 1825, "the long-lingering 'Aids to Reflection' which was to have been a small volume of Selections from Archbishop Leighton with a few notes by S. T. C. and which has ended in a few pages of Leighton and a large Volume by S. T. C.—".[720]

By elevating Leighton to co-author, or, if one wishes, by elevating S. T. C. to co-author, Coleridge seems to have alleviated certain psychological problems. He always worked best in collaboration, which seems to have allayed some of the anxieties connected with his feeling of rejection by his brothers.[721] Thus not only the collaboration with Wordsworth on *Lyrical Ballads* but his later habit of dictating to an amanuensis ("the slowness, with which I get on with the pen in my own hand contrasts most strangely with the rapidity with which I dictate"),[722] as indeed his compulsive plagiarisms, testify to his need to feel himself working with someone else. The at least nominal co-authorship with Leighton paradoxically allowed Coleridge to make his most comprehensive theological statement.

Why Leighton? Lamb commented to Barton on 26 January 1824 that "Coleridge's book is good part printed, but sticks a little for *more copy*. It bears an unsaleable Title, Extracts from Bishop Leighton, but I am confident there will be plenty of good notes in it, more of Bishop Coleridge than Leighton, I hope, for what is Leighton?"[723] But Coleridge did not share Lamb's good-natured contempt. He had long revered Leighton as one of the three Anglican theologians—the others were George Bull and Daniel Waterland—who seemed to him to have the best grasp of the theological essentials of the Christian church. In a note of April 1814, for instance, he says, "bless the hour that introduced me to the knowledge of the evangelical, apostolical Archbishop Leighton".[724] Leighton especially helped him with the crucial process of Trinitarian meditation; "The Trinity, as Bishop Leighton has well remarked, is 'a doctrine of faith, not of demonstration,' except in a *moral* sense".[725]

In the letter to John Murray in which Coleridge broached the plan for a book of extracts from Leighton, he speaks of the archbishop in glowing terms:

Perspicuous, I had almost said transparent, his style is *elegant* by the mere compulsion of the Thoughts and Feelings, and in despite, as it were, of the writer's wish to the contrary. Profound as his Conceptions often are, and numerous as the

[720] *CL* v 431.
[721] See e.g. "Coleridge's Anxiety" *RFR* 104–36.
[722] *CL* v 426.
[723] *LL (L)* ii 416.
[724] *CL* v 197 n 2.
[725] Ibid. iii 481.

passages are, where the most *athletic* Thinker will find himself tracing a rich vein from the surface downward, and leave off with an unknown depth for to morrow's delving—yet there is this quality peculiar to Leighton—unless we add Shakespear—that there is always a sense on the very surface, which the simplest may understand, if they have head and heart to understand any thing. The same or nearly the same, excellence characterizes his Eloquence. Leighton had by nature a quick and pregnant Fancy: and the august Objects of his habitual Contemplation, and their remoteness from the outward senses; his constant endeavour to see or to bring all things under some point of Unity; but above all, the rare and vital Union of Head and Heart, of Light and Love, in his own character;—all these working conjointly could not fail to form and nourish in him the higher power, and more akin to Reason—the power, I mean, of Imagination.[726]

Despite this encomium, Coleridge was unable to persuade Murray to print the proposed volume. Murray was interested in Coleridge's poetry, but "would have nothing to do with what he called *my Metaphysics*—which were in truth my all".[727] As Coleridge wrote about his dealings with Murray: "At the same time thro' Mr Tulk he proposed to me the Publication of my poetic Works—I waited on him—and found him all courtesy—but again and again I waited—came in on purpose from Highgate—at length ... it was evident, he wished to avoid an interview—and I received a note, declining the publication of the proposed Life [& Be]auties of Arch-bishop Leighton, in a very dry way ...."[728]

The publishers Taylor and Hessey, however, were willing to publish Coleridge's work, and on 8 August 1823 he described it to them in this way:

Now the Volume, I have prepared, will be best described to you by the proposed Title—

Aids to Reflection: or Beauties and Characteristics of Archbishop Leighton, extracted from his various Writings, and arranged on a principle of connection under the three Heads, of 1. Philosophical and Miscellaneous. 2. Moral and Prudential. 3. Spiritual—with a Life of Leighton & a critique on his writings and opinions—with Notes throughout by the Editor.[729]

Coleridge's correspondence allows glimpses of the work in progress, both with regard to its changing content and to its uneasy relationship to the *magnum opus*. On 6 November 1823 he wrote to J. A. Hessey: "You will see by the accompanying that I have been busily and anxiously employed since I last saw you—. As soon as I saw the Proof, I was struck with the apprehension of the disorderly and heterogeneous appearance

---

[726] *CL* v 198–9.
[727] Ibid. v 487.
[728] Ibid. v 488.
[729] Ibid. v 290.

which the Selections intermixed with my own comments &c would have—I had not calculated aright on the relative quantity of the one and the other—and the more I reflected, the more desirable it appeared to me to carry on the promise of the Title Page (*Aids* to reflection) systematically throughout the work—But little did I anticipate the time and trouble, that this *rifacciamento* would cost me."[730] On 18 February 1824 Coleridge writes to John Anster and reveals the emphasis of the new work along with his concern about its role with regard to the *magnum opus*:

> As to my own works, a little volume will soon appear under the title of *Aids to Reflection*, which was at first intended only for a Selection of Passages from Leighton's Work but in the course of printing has become an original work almost . . . . Tho' it is written for minds of a lower class than your's, being intended for serious young men of ordinary education who are sincerely searching after moral and religious Truth but are perplexed by the common prejudice, that Faith in the peculiar Tenets of Christianity demands a Sacrifice of the Reason and is at enmity with Common-Sense—yet you will, I flatter myself, read some parts with interest, particularly the establishment of the distinct nature of Prudence, as referable to the Sensations, Senses & Understanding; Morality, as [referable] to the Conscience and the Affections; and Spiritual Religion, as grounded in the Reason and Will, (the Supernatural in Man) and comprehending Morality.[731]

Clearly, the work took up central conceptions in the overarching concern of the *magnum opus*. But still, Coleridge was anxiously denying that it pre-empted that vast plan, for he immediately goes on to say: "—As soon as this little Pioneer is out of Hand, I go to the Press with the Elements of Discourse, or the Criteria of true & false Reasoning—and meantime shall devote myself to the completion of my great work, on the Philosophy of Religion—and in which my whole mind will be systematically unfolded".[732]

The contrasting descriptions of the *Aids to Reflection* and the *magnum opus* say much about the dynamics of what Coleridge was and was not able to do to evade the constricting force of his neurotic inability to work. Though he scorned the idea of selections or "Beauties" that underlay the *Aids*, he was nevertheless able, with that as starting point, to finish the work (just as he had been able to finish the *Biographia Literaria* by conceiving of it as merely a series of "sketches"). When contracting for a "systematic unfolding", however, he was unable to proceed to a successful conclusion. It was necessary, in short, for Coleridge to trick his

---

[730] *CL* v 306.
[731] Ibid. v 336–7.
[732] Ibid. 337.

neurotic unconscious. A "little Pioneer" could be allowed to pass, but a "systematic unfolding" could not. Hegel, who had no inhibitions whatever about working, ground away remorselessly at a systematic unfolding, and achieved such a form. Coleridge could not do so.

Coleridge is so fragmentary and incomplete that there is always a danger of dismissing parts of his utterance as inconsequential rather than inadequately developed. So it is necessary to insist on his brilliance, which many of his most gifted contemporaries recognised. Possibly no more effective way of suggesting this in a Hegelian context is to reproduce Coleridge's comment on the most important single locus in all the German philosopher's work. Commenting on the first triad of Hegel's larger logic, in which Hegel advances the foundation-thought that being is identical to nothing, the realisation of which results in becoming, Coleridge provides a logical refinement. In a marginal comment on the assertion that dialectic rests "on the establishment of the opposition of being and nothingness", Coleridge says:

I seem to perceive a logical informality in this reasoning—viz. that the "*To be*" (Seyn, εἰναι) is opposed to the "Nothing" (Nichts) whereas the true Opposite of "To be" is "Not to be." Thing, is the opposite of Nothing: for even Some thing or Somewhat (Etwas) implies more than Being and belongs to predicable Existence, having as it's proper opposite no what or not-any-thing. . . . it is an equivocation to affirm, simply, Nichts ist das Seyn in werden, whence doubtless it might be inferred, that das Werden die Einheit des Nichts und des Seyn ist—and so, again; that Nichts dem Seyn gleich sey. The true position is: das Nichts ist das Seyn im werden zur Existenz.[733]

In defence of Hegel it might be argued that he proceeds from the contemplation of a thing or *Etwas* to its being, and that movement he finds to be a progression from being to nothing. But Coleridge's refinement is none the less elegant.

As Coleridge proceeded with the Leighton volume, his own thought began to occupy an ever larger role, and accordingly the title began to change. The idea of a volume of "Beauties" from Leighton, in a letter of March 1824 to his publisher Hessey, became: "Aids to Reflection in the formation of fixed Principles, prudential, Moral and religious, illustrated by extracts from Leighton—& other eminent Divines".[734] In a letter to George Skinner later that month Coleridge said, "from the great overbalance of the original writing I have changed the Title to Aids to Reflection &c, illustrated by Aphorisms & select passages extracted from our Elder Divines, and chiefly from Archbishop Leighton".[735]

[733] *CM (CC)* II 989–90.   [735] Ibid. V 345.
[734] *CL* V 344.

Although Coleridge tried scrupulously to separate the *Aids* from the larger task of the *magnum opus*, he was not entirely successful. On 26 April 1826 he speaks of "three Works": "The first of the three, entitled 'Aids to Reflection in the formation of a manly character', is printed and on the eve of publication. The second, or the Elements of Discourse, is finished: and in preparation for the Press. Of the third and far larger and more laborious Work, on Religion in it's two- fold character of Philosophy and History, under the title of 'Religion considered as *implying* Revelation, and Christianity as the only Revelation of universal and perpetual Validity', the former Half only is completed."[736] Despite these attempts to keep things separate, the *Aids* severely compromised Coleridge's efforts on the *magnum opus* as such.

In the first place, during the two years, 1823 to 1825, that Coleridge was most involved with the *Aids*, there are no indications that he was able to work on the *magnum opus* at all. Secondly, after the volume was published in 1825, a significant part of Coleridge's hope and attention thenceforth was devoted to the prospect of a second edition, which appeared in 1831. Thirdly, not only did the *Aids* pre-empt Coleridge's time and energy before its appearance, but it also drained off the urgency of putting forth his central theological views afterwards. It contains full and explicit discussions of Coleridge's central emphases, particularly will and reason, as well as the Trinity and other theological essentials. Finally, it was warmly accepted by the public almost from the first, and this seems, rather than spurring Coleridge on to complete the *magnum opus*, actually to have relaxed him from the effort. One may gauge of how much he basked in the public approbation for the book by his comment to his brother (in a letter that excitedly announces: "My Book will be *out*, on Monday next; and Mr Hessey hopes, that he shall be able to have a Copy ready for me by tomorrow afternoon, so that I may present it to the Bishop of London")[737] about his nephew's attitude: "It was . . . an indescribable comfort to me to hear from him, that the first Third of my 'Aids to Reflection'—i.e. all he has yet seen—had 'delighted him BEYOND MEASURE'. I can with severest truth declare, that half a score flaming panegyrical Reviews in as many Works of periodical Criticism would not have given me half the pleasure, nor one quarter the satisfaction".[738]

Coleridge never thought of the *Aids to Reflection* as a substitution for the *Opus Maximum*. But in a letter that attempts to separate what the *Aids*

[736] *CL* v 427–8.
[737] Ibid. v 462.
[738] Ibid.

does theologically from what the *Opus Maximum* is to do theologically, he none the less reveals just how much of his formidable store of theological knowledge and thinking has in fact been harvested in the former volume:

> In the 'Aids to Reflection' I have touched on the Mystery of the Trinity only in a *negative* way. That is, I have shewn the hollowness of the arguments by which it has been assailed—have demonstrated that the doctrine involves nothing contrary to Reason, and the nothingness & even absurdity of a Christianity without it. In short, I have contented myself with exposing the causes of it's rejection and in removing (what by experience I know to be) the ordinary obstacles to it's belief.—But the positive establishment of the Doctrine as involved in the Idea, God—together with the *Origin* of EVIL, as distinguished from Original Sin (on which I have treated at large) and the Creation of the visible World—THESE as absolutely requiring the habit of abstraction, and *severe Thinking*, I have reserved for my larger Work—of which I have finished the first Division, namely, the *Philosophy* of the Christian Creed, or Christianity true in *Idea*. The 2nd. Division will be—Xty true in *fact*—i.e. historically. The third & last will be—Xty true in *act*—i.e. morally & spiritually.—
>
> But with the exception of the Trinity (the *positive* proof of)—the Origin of Evil, metaphysically examined—and the Creation—I may venture to say, that the Aids to Reflection (the latter 2/3rds, I mean) with the six supplementary Disquisitions contains a compleat *System* of internal evidences. At least I can think of no essential Article of Faith omitted.—At all events, no one hereafter can with justice complain that I have disclosed my sentiments only in flashes and fragments—and that no one can tell what the Opinions & Belief are.[739]

What Coleridge asserts in this letter is justified by the actual text of *Aids to Reflection*, where, under the title "Assertion of Religion", he specifically invokes the superseding authority of the projected *magnum opus*:

> To obviate a possible disappointment in any of my Readers, who may chance to be engaged in theological studies, it may be well to notice, that in vindicating the peculiar tenets of our Faith, I have not entered on the Doctrine of the Trinity, or the still profounder Mystery of the Origin of Moral Evil—and this for the reasons following: 1. These Doctrines are not (strictly speaking) subjects of *Reflection*, in the proper sense of the word: and both of them demand a power and persistency of Abstraction, and a previous discipline in their highest forms of human thought, which it would be unwise, if not presumptuous, to expect from any, who require "*Aids* to Reflection," . . . . But lastly, the whole Scheme of the Christian Faith, including *all* the Articles of Belief common to the Greek and Latin, the Roman and the Protestant Church, with the threefold proof, that it is

[739] *CL* v 444–5.

ideally, *morally*, and *historically* true, will be found exhibited and vindicated in a proportionally larger Work, the principal Labour of my Life since Manhood, and which I am now preparing for the Press under the title, Assertion of Religion, as necessarily *involving* Revelation; and of Christianity, as the only Revelation of permanent and universal validity.[740]

Elsewhere in the volume Coleridge reiterates his avoidance of the Trinity: "In right order I must have commenced with the Articles of the Trinity and the Apostacy, including the question respecting the Origin of Evil, and the Incarnation of the WORD. And could I have followed this order, some difficulties that now press on me would have been obviated. But (as has already been explained) limits of the present Volume rendered it alike impracticable and inexpedient . . . ."[741]

In light of those significant disclaimers, it becomes a fact worthy of note that the *Opus Maximum*, where the positive discussion of the Trinity is supposed to occur, does not really institute such a discussion until the treatise has moved deep into its argumentation. Indeed, part of the difficulty that readers will experience in attempting to penetrate the complex texture of the texts that constitute the *Opus Maximum* is that while the whole mass of Coleridge's argument is moving inexorably toward the vindication of the Trinity, such a progression is not made adequately clear, or at least is not signalled early on, by the texts that actually exist. Nevertheless, Coleridge himself was entirely serious about the discrepant forms of Trinitarian approach in the two works. As he says in a notebook entry of 1825:

A more positive *insight* into the true character of Reason, and a greater evidentness of its diversity from the Understanding, might be given—but then it must be *synthetically* and *genetically*. And this I have done in my larger work, in which I commence with Absolute, and from thence deduce the Tri-unity, and therein the substantial Reason (Λόγος) as the Ὁ ὤν-ὁ πρωτογενής.

But in Aids to Reflection I was obliged to proceed analytically and a posteriori—in which way it is not, I believe, possible to give a clearer proof than is given on the pages referred to.[742]

But the *Aids to Reflection* actually presents the living whole of Coleridge's passionately held theological position; it contains "a compleat *System* of internal evidences"[743] of Christianity, with "no essential Ar-

---

[740] *AR* (1825) 151–2.
[741] Ibid. 247.
[742] *CN* IV 5210.
[743] The adjective "internal" is the operative factor in the phrase, for it was against the "external" evidences of Paley and Grotius that C so totally opposed himself. In his view, Christianity could only be maintained, and had to be maintained, as a necessary consequence of the structure of the human mind itself.

ticle of Faith omitted". There are other places where one can gain know-
ledge of Coleridge's central emphasis on "will", but this treatise presents
that emphasis fully. There are other places where one can learn of Cole-
ridge's crucial distinction between "reason" and "understanding", but
this treatise presents that distinction in subtle ramification. There are
other places where one can hear of Coleridge's conception of "con-
science", but nowhere is it more fully weighted than in the *Aids to Re-
flection*.

XXX. THE RELATION OF THE *MAGNUM OPUS* TO COLERIDGE'S *THEORY OF LIFE*

The *Aids to Reflection*, like *The Philosophical Lectures*, was intimately
involved with the *magnum opus*, though, as noted above, the dynamics
of relation were different for the two works: the *Aids to Reflection* was,
as it were, a competitor for the Great Work, *The Philosophical Lectures*
a foundation element. A third work, *Theory of Life*, constitutes with
those two a kind of tripod that supports all of Coleridge's philosophical
and theological interests. Indeed, as suggested above, the three works,
taken together, virtually present an alternate version of the *magnum opus*
itself.

Theory of Life is more problematical than the other two productions.
It is not known just when it was written; it is not known just how much
of it Coleridge wrote; and it has been shown to be significantly depen-
dent on the writings of the Norwegian *Naturphilosoph* Henrik Stef-
fens.[744] The work was not published during Coleridge's lifetime. *Hints
Toward the Formation of a More Comprehensive Theory of Life*, by S. T.
Coleridge, was published in 1848 by John Churchill, Princes Street,
Soho. It was edited by Seth B. Watson, M.D., of St John's College, and
formerly one of the physicians to the hospital at Oxford. Later copies in
the run contained a postscript that read: "The Editor deems it right to
state that the contents of the foregoing pages were, amongst other Pa-
pers, placed at his disposal by an intimate friend of the late S. T. COLE-
RIDGE; and from internal evidence he was induced to attribute to that
gentleman the entire authorship. After, however, the present edition had

---

[744] It is not always easy to trace C's
use of *naturphilosophischen* writings,
which frequently employ a common fund
of observations and speculations. In *The-
ory of Life*, in addition to his large com-
mand of such knowledge, he relied es-
pecially on two works of Steffens, the
*Beyträge zur innern Naturgeschichte der
Erde* (1801) and the *Grundzüge der phil-
osophischen Naturwissenschaft* (1806),
both of which he owned and annotated.

passed through the press, and was on the eve of publication, circumstances arose which led to the belief that the work might with more propriety be considered as the joint production of Mr. COLERIDGE and the late Mr. JAMES GILLMAN, of Highgate."[745]

The present editor does not believe that Gillman had any significant hand in the essay. Coleridge loved to enter collaborative relationships, and even tried to present J. H. Green, as noted above, as part author of the *magnum opus*; certainly, much of the intense loyalty he inspired was an effect of the generosity with which he played up the abilities of his nominal partners, and Gillman may well have had the heady feeling that he had much to contribute. But the essay is so rife with *Naturphilosophie* that Gillman seems most unlikely to have written much if any of it. Sara Coleridge agreed; in a note written in a copy of the treatise, she said:

> The "intimate friend" [i.e. James Gillman, Jr] was a young schoolboy when this essay was composed . . . . He was not in his teens even when the contents of this vol. and the Treatise on Scrofula, of which it is an offset, were written . . . . The only circumstances tending to show Mr. Gillman's authorship was its being written in his name. On the wrapper was written "a Lecture by Mr. James Gillman to be read at the Royal College of Surgeons by Mr. Stanley." I repeat this from memory and a note in the work speaks of "my profession." But this—when all the circumstances of the case are considered, does not prove Mr. G.'s authorship.[746]

A manuscript of the *Theory of Life*, not in Coleridge's handwriting (which is standard for his prose writings) but containing corrections by him, was in Gillman's papers. It came into the possession of James Gillman, Jr., who made it available to his school friend Seth Watson (could Watson have been a brother of that John Watson who was Coleridge's amanuensis and "dear and particular Friend",[747] and who died in 1827 at the untimely age of twenty-eight?).[748] In a note dated 1890, the eminent Coleridge scholar, Ernest Hartley Coleridge, wrote, "The MS of the Theory of Life was written at Coleridge's dictation and in part revised and corrected by him. It was intended to form part of an Essay on Scrofula which was begun by James Gillman Senior."[749]

The date at which *Theory of Life* was composed is not certain either. The biologist and distinguished Sinologist Joseph Needham thought it

[745] *SW & F (CC)* I 557 n 3.
[746] *L&L* 16–7.
[747] *CL* v 304.
[748] Seth Watson had been "one of Coleridge's younger disciples, a member, in 1822–23, of the Thursday evening group at Highgate"; and he was, as a book dedication to him records, the uncle of "Lucy Elinor Watson (née Gillman)" (Lowes 525).
[749] *L&L* 17.

was written in 1831: "Coleridge wrote *The Theory of Life* in all probability in 1831, but this is only known from internal evidence, since it was not published till long after his death, in 1848 . . . . The date assigned to the essay rests upon a reference which Coleridge makes in the Introduction to the work of the celebrated Dr. Abernethy, who died late in 1831, and from which the conclusion follows that it must have been written early in that year."[750]

But Needham was almost certainly wrong. Kathleen Coburn notes that for the philosophical lecture delivered by Coleridge on 15 March 1819, "the manuscript edited by Seth Watson—after Coleridge's death—and entitled *Theory of Life*, was used in part for Lecture XII, a fact which throws some light on the controversy as to how much of that work was Coleridge's".[751] In his note of 1890, E. H. Coleridge said that a manuscript of *Theory of Life* bore a watermark of 1815 and conjectured that the date of composition was probably the autumn of 1816.[752] The present editor defers to the opinion of J. H. Haeger, who has carefully investigated the contexts of the treatise; Haeger concludes that while the piece was probably stirring into shape in 1816, it was unlikely to have been completed until 1819: "What evidence we have certainly points to 1819 as the logical date".[753]

Whatever its date of composition, *Theory of Life* took up a most urgent question in Coleridge's interconnected concerns: was life merely a result of organisation, or was it a principle that allowed the conception of soul? Plato had said that soul was the oldest of all things and prior to body. The countervailing view that life arose out of interactions among inorganic forms was beginning to be more and more heard in the intellectual conversations of Europe. Diderot's *Lettre sur les aveugles*, as a central mid-eighteenth-century text of the latter view, prefigured an increasing intensity of attacks on the idea that soul was somehow separate from organisational concerns.

But soul had to be separate from those concerns if Coleridge's Christian view of the world and his own peculiarly poignant need for redemption were to be validated. As he says in a letter of 25 May 1820: "A System of Materialism, in which Organization stands first, whether composed by Nature or God, & Life &c as it's results; (even as the Sound is the result of a Bell)—such a system would, doubtless, remove great part of the terrors which the Soul makes out of itself; but then it removes the Soul too, or rather precludes it".[754] Against such a system of mater-

---

[750] Needham 693.
[751] *P Lects* (1949) Introduction 20.
[752] *CL* v 50 n.

[753] Haeger 38.
[754] Ibid. 47.

ialism, in which organisation stands first, Coleridge in the same letter asserts his own over-riding concerns:

... a redemptive power must be necessary if immortality be true & Man be a disordered Being? And that no power can be redemptive which does not at the same time act in the ground of the Life as one with the ground, i.e. must act *in* my Will and not merely *on* my will; and yet extrinsically, as an outward Power, i.e. as that which *outward* Nature is to the Organization, viz. the causa correspondens et conditio perpetua ab extra?—Under these views I cannot read the VIth Chapter of St John without great emotion. The redeemer cannot be *merely* God—unless we adopt Pantheism, i.e. deny the existence of a God; & yet God he must be, for whatever is less than God, may act *on*, but cannot act in, the Will of another—Christ must become Man—but he cannot become us, except so far as we become *him*—[755]

We must remind ourselves again of the personal circumstances that made Coleridge so concerned—obsessed, really—with the Christian idea of redemption, and the ontological views that devolved from that emphasis. Strange as it may seem, aside from his need for redemption Coleridge might not even have committed himself to Christianity; certainly he was as aware of the objections to it as Diderot himself: "without it, the Redemption, what is Xtnity?" he asks bluntly.[756] And he was vividly aware of the possibility of an unmeaning universe: "We all look up to the blue Sky for comfort, but nothing appears there—nothing comforts nothing answers us—& so we die—".[757] He even recites the formula: "I believe! Lord help my unbelief!"[758] Indeed, had he lived in the later twentieth century, Coleridge—one harbours the suspicion—might have entered psychoanalysis to assuage his anxieties, and then directed his luminous and wide-ranging intelligence in entirely different directions.

But there was no therapy available to Coleridge; thus he undertook a defence of Christian theory along a vast intellectual front, for only in the Christian promise did there seem to be hope for him. He was, to put it shortly, a hurt man. A man in pain. A man sodden with laudanum and impotently hating himself. A man without hope, unless redemption were possible:

My Prayers have been fervent, in agony of Spirit, and for hours together, incessant! still ending, O! only for the merits, for the agonies, for the cross of my blessed Redeemer! For I am nothing, but evil—I can do nothing, but evil! Help, Help!—I believe! help thou my unbelief!—[759]

---

[755] Ibid. 48.
[756] *CL* IV 851.
[757] *CN* III 4294.

[758] Ibid. III 3353.
[759] *CL* III 491.

Again:

> . . . influences of incipient bodily derangement from the use of Opium, at the time that I yet remained ignorant of the cause, & still *mighty proud* of my supposed grand discovery of Laudanum, as the Remedy or Palliative of Evils, which itself had mainly produced . . . a Slavery more dreadful, than any man, who has not felt it's iron fetters eating into his very soul, can possibly imagine.[760]

And yet again:

> I feel, with an intensity unfathomable by words, my utter nothingness, impotence, & worthlessness, in and for myself . . . . But the consolations, at least the *sensible* sweetness, of Hope, I do not possess. On the contrary, the Temptation, which I have constantly to fight up against, is a fear that if Annihilation & the *possibility* of Heaven were offered to my choice, I should choose the former.[761]

So the controversies over which came first, matter or spirit, whether there was a God who created and cared for man, or whether man was simply the highest point of organisation reached by matter and then by organic life, were for Coleridge not merely intellectual problems but problems felt in the innermost fibres of his being.

What *Theory of Life* did was to enter these questions in terms of the last named controversy, but with implications extending to the whole spectrum of related concerns. In this treatise Coleridge attempts to accept what must be accepted in the gathering body of evolutionary theory and at the same time to deflect its conclusions into something acceptable to his Christian commitments. He was willing to concede, as he admitted in his letters, that "Evolution as contra-distinguished from apposition, or superinduction *ab aliunde*, is implied in the conception of *Life*".[762]

The treatise takes its immediate occasion from a continuing medico-philosophical argument between two followers of Dr. John Hunter, who interpreted that revered physician's views in opposing ways.[763] Dr. John Abernethy had given a lecture on the Theory of Life (hence Coleridge's title), but his junior colleague in the College of Surgeons, Sir William Lawrence, charged that he misinterpreted Hunter. Lawrence's own view, to quote from a lecture of 1822, was "That life then, or the assemblage of all the functions, is immediately dependent on organization, appears to me, physiologically speaking, as clear as that the presence of the sun above the horizon causes the light of day."[764] Brushing aside the notion of the soul as something for theologians to discuss, Lawrence says, "An

[760] *CL* III 495.
[761] Ibid. III 498.
[762] Ibid. VI 509.

[763] For a fuller discussion see Levere 42–54.
[764] Quoted in *L&L* 19.

immaterial and spiritual being could not have been discovered amid the blood and filth of the dissecting-room".[765]

Abernethy, on the other hand, a physician of equal eminence and a pioneer of twentieth-century theories of holistic medicine, spoke in ways that protected those interests dear to Coleridge's heart. By his somewhat circumspect references to Abernethy, Coleridge seems aware of the flaws in Abernethy's position,[766] but he nevertheless says in *Theory of Life*:

> In Mr. Abernethy's Lectures on the Theory of Life, it is impossible not to see a presentiment of a great truth. He has, if I may so express myself, caught it in the breeze: and we seem to hear the first glad opening and shout with which he springs forward to the pursuit. But it is equally evident that the prey has not been followed through its doublings and windings, or driven out from its brakes and covers into full and open view. Many of the least tenable phrases may be fairly interpreted as illustrations, rather than precise exponents of the author's meaning; at least, while they remain as a mere suggestion or annunciation of his ideas, and till he has expanded them over a larger sphere, it would be unjust to infer the contrary. But it is not with men, however strongly their professional merits may entitle them to reverence, that my concern is at present. If the opinions here supported are the same with those of Mr. Abernethy, I rejoice in his authority. If they are different, I shall wait with an anxious interest for an exposition of that difference.[767]

In *Theory of Life*, therefore, Coleridge attempts a restatement of Abernethy's position. He perhaps obliquely concedes some of its limitations: "I may, without incurring the charge of arrogance or detraction, venture to assert that, in his writings the light which occasionally flashes upon us seems at other times, and more frequently, to struggle through an unfriendly medium, and even sometimes to suffer a temporary occultation".[768] He also regrets that Abernethy had not "developed his opinions systematically, and carried them yet further back, even to their ultimate principle!"[769] Coleridge intends "as it were, to climb up on his shoulders, and look at the same objects in a distincter form, because seen from the more commanding point of view furnished by himself".[770] He then says, "Without further preface or apology, therefore, I shall state at once my objections to all the definitions that have hither been given of Life, as meaning too much or too little".[771] In this venture, however, his main opponent is not Lawrence. Though Coleridge quotes seven passages

[765] *L&L* 19.
[766] Cf e.g. Levere 51–2.
[767] *SW & F (CC)* I 531–2.
[768] Ibid. 18.

[769] Ibid. 19.
[770] Ibid. 18.
[771] Ibid.

from Lawrence and attempts to rebut them,[772] the initial thrust of his op-
position is focused, fittingly in terms of his longstanding preoccupation
in the *magnum opus*, on a representative of the hated and despised
French, "the eminent French physiologist, Bichat".[773]

Marie-François-Xavier Bichat (1771–1802), an anatomist and pio-
neering histologist, had published in 1800 a work called *Récherches
physiologiques sur la vie et la mort*, which created a sensation and had
gone into three editions by the time Coleridge opposed him. How for-
midable a threat Bichat was to all Coleridge wished to preserve may be
gauged from the ecstatic way in which Schopenhauer, Coleridge's philo-
sophical antithesis, accepted him: "Bichat cast a deep glance into human
nature, and, in consequence, gave an exceedingly admirable explanation
that is one of the most profoundly conceived works in the whole of
French literature".[774] "Nothing"' wrote Schopenhauer, "is better calcu-
lated than this admirable and thorough book to confirm and bring out
clearly that the body is only the *will* itself embodied (i.e. perceived by
means of the brain-functions, time, space, and causality). From this it fol-
lows the will is primary and original, but that the intellect, on the other
hand, as mere brain-function, is secondary and derived."[775] If the intel-
lect is secondary and derived, then soul must be secondary and derived,
which means that it is not soul. As Schopenhauer says, Bichat "knows
neither soul nor body, but merely an animal and organic life".[776]

Theory of Life thus begins by engaging this formidable antagonist as
the leading definer of what Coleridge thinks life cannot be allowed to be:
"I will begin with that given by Bichat. 'Life is the sum of all the func-
tions by which death is resisted,' in which I have in vain endeavoured to
discover any other meaning than that life consists in being able to live.
This author, with a whimsical gravity, prefaces his definition with the re-
mark, that the nature of life has hitherto been sought for in *abstract* con-
siderations; as if it were possible that four more invertebrate abstractions
could be brought together in one sentence than are here assembled in the
words, life, death, function, and resistance."[777] Bichat, however, is both
a scientist and a Frenchman, and against his formidable modernity Cole-
ridge summons the competing modernity of the German *Naturphilo-
sophen*. He counters the definition of "the sum of all the functions by
which death is resisted" with the conception of "*principium individua-
tionis*", repeatedly met with in German thought from Goethe through
Nietzsche: "I define life as the principle of individuation, or the power

---

[772] *S W & F (CC)* 60–5.
[773] *P Lects* (1949) 355.
[774] Schopenhauer III 300.

[775] Ibid. III 296–7, 298.
[776] Ibid. III 301.
[777] *S W & F (CC)* I 489.

which unites a given all into a whole that is presupposed by all its parts. The link that combines the two, and acts throughout both, will, of course, be defined by the tendency to individuation."[778] The conception was advanced against the dread thought that life consisted merely in organisation of matter: "I repel with still greater earnestness the assertion and even the supposition that the functions are the offspring of the structure, and 'Life the result of organization,' connected with it as effect with cause".[779]

Both emphases, the opposition to Bichat's definition, and the opposition to Lawrence's assertion that life was the result of organisation, are repeated in *The Philosophical Lectures*, and the repetition is an index of the importance Coleridge attached to these threats. Both Bichat and Lawrence are treated as heirs of "the earliest materialists":

> The moderns were ashamed of these angular and these round atoms, and they had substituted therefore for it, organization, some, and others life or a vital principle. We will examine both. First then what is this organization? . . . . Not the mere arrangement of parts as means to an end, for in that sense I should call my watch organization, or a steam engine organization. But we agree that these are machines, not organizations. It appears then, that if I am to attach any meaning at all to the word organization, it must be distinct from mechanism in this, that in all machines I suppose the power to be from without, that if I take my watch there is nothing in the component parts of this watch that constitutes it peculiarly fit for a watch, or produce[s] it . . . . Organization therefore must not only be an arrangement of parts together, as means to an end, but it must be such an interdependence of parts, each of which in its turn being means to an end, as arises from within. The moment a man dies, we can scarcely say he remains organized in the proper sense . . . . To say therefore that life is the result of organization, and yet at the same time to admit that organization is distinguished from mechanism only by life, is assuredly what I before said, to affirm a thing to be its own parent or to determine the parent to be the child of his own child . . . . At all events in order to justify materialism, and in materialism the assertion that life, and much more, that thought or will, are the results of organization, it would be necessary to call for a fact of organization subsisting prior to life . . . . But if you can shew an arrangement of means to an end without life and declare it not to be mechanism, and if by the superadding the idea of life, that is, a power from within, it follows self-evidently not that life is the result of organization but that organization is in some way or other dependent on life as its cause.[780]

Following this closely reasoned attack on the idea of a human as mere organisation, Coleridge attacks Bichat in the same terms as he did in *Theory of Life*:

[778] *SW & F (CC)* 510.
[779] Ibid. 561–2.

[780] *P Lects* (1949) 353–5.

We come then to what is life . . . . I turn to a work by the eminent French phys-
iologist, Bichat, where I find this definition: Life is the sum of all the functions
by which death is resisted. I could not after a long pause but ask myself, what is
the meaning of this? Life is the sum of all the functions by which death is re-
sisted, that is, that life consists in being able to live! And more was I surprised
when I observed the whimsical gravity with which the author has informed us
that hitherto life has been sought for in abstract considerations; as if four more
inveterate abstractions could be brought together than the words, life, death,
function, and resistance.[781]

At the end of his discussion in *The Philosophical Lectures*, Coleridge
focuses his reasons for opposition to the materialists: they preclude the
soul, God, and the related concerns he found so necessary for his hope:
"For a man who affirms boldly that what the senses have not given to
his mind (which mind itself is but, like the senses, an organization of his
body) . . . Such a man cannot pretend to believe in a God".[782]

But for Coleridge, the belief in a personal, as opposed to a pantheis-
tic, Deity, or no Deity at all, was the linchpin of his entire orientation in
life. Destroying the "belief in God" destroys "the basis of all truth":

That is, it destroys the possibility of free agency, it destroys the great distinction
between the mere human and the mere animals of nature, namely the powers of
originating an act. All things are brought, even the powers of life are brought,
into a common link of causes and effect that we observe in a machine, and all
the powers of thought into those of life, being all reasoned away into modes of
sensation, and the will itself into nothing but a current, a fancy determined by
the accidental copulations of certain internal stimuli. With such a being, to talk
of a difference between good and evil would be to blame a stone for being round
or angular. The thought itself is repulsive.[783]

This, then, was why *Theory of Life* was written. Not out of an interest
in science as such, though Coleridge had such an interest, but for the de-
fence of the conception of a personal God who would redeem the
foundering Samuel Taylor Coleridge. As a venture in science, *Theory of
Life* has no more (and no less) validity than any other of the phantasms
of *Naturphilosophie*; as a schematic placing of the scientific concern
within the framework of Coleridge's moral desiderata it contains bril-
liant formulations.

The utilisation of *Naturphilosophie* is the chief difference between
Coleridge's address to the idea of life in *Theory of Life* and his address
to it in *The Philosophical Lectures*. To utilise *Naturphilosophie*, how-

[781] *P Lects* (1949) 355.
[782] Ibid. 361.
[783] Ibid. 362.

ever, involved dangers, not because of its scientific flimsiness, which Coleridge no less than its originators tended not to see, but because of its pantheism ("The cause of this, as of almost every other, mistake of the Natur-philosophen", he says at one point, "is to be found in their Pantheism").[784] Why then did he use it? Probably for one overarching reason that subsumed all others: *Naturphilosophie* was opposed to the "mechanic corpuscular system" represented by Bichat. As Coleridge wrote Green in 1817, "Of the Natur-philosophen, as far as physical Dynamics are concerned and as opposed to the mechanic corpuscular system, I think very highly".[785] There are probably three subsidiary reasons. First, as has already been suggested, *Naturphilosophie* countered modernity with modernity, checked the pernicious French by the prestige of the Germans. Second, it allowed Coleridge to pre-empt, as it were, the gathering pertinence of evolutionary speculation for his own concerns. Third, and perhaps most important, it allowed him to introduce a complex rather than a simple argument; for here, to perhaps the most sustained extent in his writing, Coleridge was able to call upon the principle of polarity that loomed so important in all his attitudes (see above, Section x). For *Naturphilosophie*, as indicated above (see Section IX), was before all else the play of polarities.

Coleridge, in utilising *Naturphilosophie*, protected himself by early on declaring his theism and thereby obviating pantheism: *"To account* for Life is one thing; to explain Life another. In the first we are supposed to state something prior (if not in time, yet in the order of Nature) to the thing accounted for, as the ground or cause of that thing, or (which comprises the meaning and force of both words) as its *sufficient cause, quae et facit, et subest.* And to this, in the question of Life, I know no possible answer, but God."[786]

Having established this shield, Coleridge is able to adopt the evolutionary conception of ascent (*Steigerung*) so beloved by Goethe and by Schelling: "this is one proof of the essential vitality of nature, that she does not ascend as links in a suspended chain, but as the steps in a ladder. . . ."[787] Under this conception, he can observe "The arborescent forms on a frosty morning, to be seen on the window and pavement, must have *some* relation to the more perfect forms developed in the vegetable world".[788] He says that "In the lowest forms of the vegetable and animal world we perceive totality dawning into individuation, while in man,

[784] Henri Nidecker, "Notes marginales de S. T. Coleridge III. En marge de Schubert" *Revue de littérature comparée* 8 (1928) 715.

[785] *CL* IV 792.
[786] *SW & F (CC)* I 503.
[787] Ibid. 41.
[788] *SW & F (CC)* I 508*.

as the highest of the class, the individuality is not only perfected in its corporeal sense, but begins a new series beyond the appropriate limits of physiology. The tendency to individuation, more or less obscure, more or less obvious, constitutes the common character of all classes . . . ."[789]

Coleridge's idea of "a new series" allows him to adopt the attractive features of evolutionary ascent and at the same time to reserve a special place for man and God, one exempt from the implications that Darwin would develop. As he says in a many-coloured passage in *The Statesman's Manual* in 1816:

I have at this moment before me, in the flowery meadow, on which my eye is now reposing, one of its most soothing chapters . . . . For never can I look and meditate on the vegetable creation without a feeling similar to that with which we gaze at a beautiful infant that has fed itself asleep at its mother's bosom . . . . I seem to myself to behold in the quiet objects, on which I am gazing, more than . . . a mere *simile* . . . . I feel an awe, as if there were before my eyes the same Power, as that of the REASON—the same Power in a lower dignity. . . . I feel it alike, whether I contemplate a single tree or flower, or meditate on vegetation through out the world, as one of the great organs of life and nature. Lo!— with the rising sun it commences its outward life and enters into open communion with all the elements, at once assimilating them to itself and to each other. At the same moment it strikes its roots and unfolds its leaves, absorbs and respires, steams forth its cooling vapour and finer fragrance, and breathes a repairing spirit, at once the food and tone of the atmosphere, into the atmosphere that feeds *it* . . . . Lo!—how upholding the ceaseless plastic motion of the parts in the profoundest rest of the whole it becomes the visible organismus of the whole *silent* or *elementary* life of nature and, therefore, in incorporating the one extreme becomes the symbol of the other; the natural symbol of that higher life of reason, in which the whole series (known to us in our present state of being) is perfected, in which, therefore, all the subordinate gradations recur, and are reordained *"in more abundant honor."* We had seen each in its own cast, and we now recognize them all as co-existing in the unity of a higher form, the Crown and Completion of the Earthly, and the Mediator of a new and heavenly series.[790]

But how does nature ascend and manifest the tendency to individuation? "I restate the question", says Coleridge: "The tendency having been ascertained, what is its most general law? I answer—*polarity*, or the essential dualism of Nature, arising out of its productive unity, and still tending to reaffirm it, either as equilibrium, indifference, or identity."[791] The conception of polarity is of greatest importance in the complexity of the answers Coleridge wants to give, as it is throughout his intellectual attitudes:

[789] *SW & F (CC)* 516.   [791] *SW & F (CC)* I 518.
[790] *LS (CC)* 71–3.

Life, then, we consider as the copula, or the unity of thesis and antithesis, position and counterposition,—Life itself being the positive of both; as, on the other hand, the two counterpoints are the necessary conditions of the *manifestations* of Life. These, by the same necessity, unite in a synthesis; which again, by the law of dualism, essential to all actual existence, expands, or *produces* itself, from the point into the *line*, in order again to converge, as the initiation of the same productive process in some intenser form of reality. Thus, in the identity of the two counter-powers, Life *sub*sists; in their strife it *con*sists; and in their reconciliation it at once dies and is born again into a new form, either falling back into the life of the whole, or starting anew in the process of individuation.[792]

Playing with such attractive dynamisms of opposition and ascent, Coleridge continually reassures himself by theistic provisos that forestall any possibility of Darwinian conclusion:

Convinced—by revelation, by the consenting authority of all countries, and of all ages, by the imperative voice of my own conscience, and by that wide chasm between man and the noblest animals of the brute creation, which no perceivable or conceivable difference of organization is sufficient to overbridge—that I have a rational and responsible soul, I think far too reverentially of the same to degrade it into an hypothesis, and cannot be blind to the contradiction I must incur, if I assign that soul which I believe to constitute the peculiar nature of man as the cause of functions and properties, which man possesses in common with the oyster and the mushroom.[793]

Feeling himself sufficiently protected, Coleridge embarks on his *naturphilosophische* exposition of polarity and ascent. He refers to "potentiated length in the power of magnetism; to surface in the power of electricity; and to the synthesis of both, or potentiated depth, in the constructive, that is, chemical affinity";[794] and at length he says:

It is not improbable that there may exist, and even be discovered, higher forms and more akin to Life than those of magnetism, electricity, and constructive (or chemical) affinity appear to be, even in their finest known influences . . . . But in the present state of science, the magnetic, electric, and chemical powers are the last and highest of inorganic nature. These, therefore, we assume as presenting themselves again to us, in their next metamorphosis, as reproduction (i.e. growth and identity of the whole, amid the change or flux of all the parts), irritability and sensibility; reproduction corresponding to magnetism, irritability to electricity, and sensibility to constructive chemical affinity.[795]

The largest framework in which this all coheres, the tendency to "individuation" as well as the polar ascent of magnetism, electricity, and

[792] *SW & F (CC)* 518–20.
[793] Ibid. 501.
[794] Ibid. 523.

[795] Ibid. 526. See above, Section IX: The *Magnum opus* and *Naturphilosophie.*

chemical affinity, is sketched by Coleridge in a letter to Gillman of 10 November 1816 (which no doubt has some bearing on whether the treatise was written in 1831, as Needham posited, in 1823, which was the opinion of Nidecker, or in 1816, as E. H. Coleridge thought):

> Leaving therefore all of more universal consideration for a future Time, I propose to begin at once with Life; but with Life in it's very first manifestations—demonstrating that there is no other possible definition of Life but *Individuality*—that *this*, again is impossible without the assumption of a *universal Life*, you will see; but there is no necessity of mentioning. But in the fluxions or nascent forms of Individuality it will be absolutely necessary to shew the analogy between organic growth, and self-repetition, and a more universal form whether it be called Magnetism or Polarity—All the previous steps I shall have for *your own* Overlooking.[796]

Coleridge quotes Lawrence as saying that "there is no resemblance, no analogy, between Electricity and Life; the two orders of phenomena are completely distinct; they are incommensurable. Electricity illustrates life no more than life illustrates electricity."[797] But Coleridge counters: "I do not make Life *like* magnetism, or *like* electricity . . . the difference between magnetism and electricity, and the powers illustrated by them, is an essential part of my system, but . . . the animal Life of man is the identity of all three".[798] He attempts to press home his argument against analogy:

> Analogy implies a difference in sort, and not merely in degree; and it is the sameness of the end, with the difference of the means, which constitutes analogy. No one would say the lungs of a man were analogous to the lungs of a monkey, but any one might say that the gills of fish and the spiracula of insects are analogous to lungs. Now if there be any philosophers who have asserted that electricity as electricity is the *same* as Life, for that reason they cannot be *analogous* to one another; and as no man in his senses, philosopher or not, is capable of imagining that the lightning which destroys a sheep, was a means to the same end with the principle of its organization; for this reason, too, the two powers cannot be represented as analogous. Indeed I know of no system in which the word, as thus applied, would admit of an endurable meaning, but that which teaches us, that a mass of marrow in the skull is analogous to the rational soul, which Plato and Bacon, equally with the "poor Indian," believe themselves to have received from the Supreme Reason.[799]

However suspect Coleridge's reasoning may be in the foregoing argument, his ever-vigilant protection of Deity, and of man's uniqueness as the special creation of God, is quite apparent. This unique place for

[796] *CL* IV 690.
[797] *SW & F (CC)* I 528.
[798] Ibid. 530.
[799] Ibid. 531.

man follows nicely from Coleridge's version of ascent and opposition: ". . . my opinions will be best explained by a rapid exemplification in the processes of Nature, from the first rudiments of individualized life in the lowest classes of its two great poles, the vegetable and animal creation, to its crown and consummation in the human body; thus illustrating at once the unceasing *polarity of life, as the form of its process, and its tendency to progressive individuation as the law of its direction*".[800] The emphases of that passage are reiterated throughout the treatise. "The vegetable and animal world are the thesis and antithesis, or the opposite poles of organic life."[801] "The whole *actual* life of Nature originates in the existence, and consists in the perpetual reconciliation, and as perpetual resurgency of the primary contradiction, of which universal polarity is the result and the exponent."[802] He speaks of "the great fundamental truth that all things spring from, and subsist in, the endless strife between difference and indifference. The whole history of Nature is comprised in the specification of the transitional states from one to the other."[803]

As do all the *Naturphilosophen*, Coleridge attempts to link together the inorganic and the organic, as well as the animal and vegetable:

> But no sooner have we passed the borders, than endless variety of form and the bold display of instincts announce, that Nature has succeeded. She has created the intermediate link between the vegetable world, as the product of the reproductive or magnetic power, and the animal as the exponent of sensibility . . . . The insect world, taken at large, appears as an intenser life, that has struggled itself loose and become emancipated from vegetation . . . . Beyond and above this step, Nature seems to act with a sort of free agency. . . . Had she proceeded no further, yet the whole vegetable, together with the whole insect creation, would have formed within themselves an entire and independent system of Life. All plants have insects . . . . THE INSECT WORLD IS THE EXPONENT OF IRRITABILITY, AS THE VEGETABLE IS OF REPRODUCTION.[804]

Again:

> The intropulsive force, that sends the ossification inward as to the centre, is reserved for a yet higher step, and this we find embodied in the class of *fishes* . . . . [C]ompare the most perfect bone of a fish with the thigh-bones of the mammalia, and the distinctness with which the latter manifest the co-presence of the *magnetic* of the *electrical* in its branching arteries, and of the third greatest power, viz., the *qualitative* and interior, in its marrow.[805]

Such passages illustrate why *Naturphilosophie* was so rapidly and decisively discredited. Its easy and attractive arrangements of polar oppo-

[800] *SW & F (CC)* 533.
[801] Ibid. 538.
[802] Ibid. 537.
[803] Ibid. 534.
[804] Ibid. 542.
[805] Ibid. 546.

sitions and ascending stages constituted far too coarse a schematism for addressing the complexities of nature. Coleridge devoted a rather dismaying amount of his time (see, for instance, his marginal comments on *Naturphilosophen* and on Boehme) to conceiving the *naturphilosophischen* network of oppositions and adhesions.[806] As I have argued elsewhere, "Not only does Coleridge seem to think that drawing a circle quartered by axes, or making thesis-antithesis-synthesis play with the conceptions of galvanism, light, gravity, and so forth, constitutes permissible scientific method, but, led on by the fancies of Schelling and his school, he renders opinions on subjects where he has no right to speak at all".[807]

Even at the time of *Theory of Life*, Coleridge had reservations about the *Naturphilosophen*. Their opposition to "mechanic" philosophy, however, seems to have made them too attractive to pass by. As Coleridge wrote his Swedenborgian friend C. A. Tulk in November 1818, correctly identifying *Naturphilosophie* as a "new Hylozoism", that is, the view that holds that matter is alive:

> Schelling is the Head and Founder of a philosophic Sect, entitled Naturphilosophen, or philosophers of Nature. He is beyond doubt a Man of Genius, and by the revival and more extensive application of the Law of Polarity (i.e. that every Power manifests itself by opposite Forces) and by the reduction of all Phaenomena to the three forms of Magnetism, Electricity, and constructive Galvanism, or the Powers of Length, Breadth, and Depth, his System is extremely plausible and alluring at a first acquaintance. And as far as the attack on the mechanic or corpuscular Philosophy extends, his works possess a permanent value. But as a *System*, it is little more than Behmenism, . . . and like Behmen's it is reduced at last to a mere Pantheism . . . . Schelling is a zealous Roman-Catholic, and not the first Philosopher who has adopted this sort of Plotinised Spinozism for the defence of the Polytheism and Charms of the Church of Rome.[808]

But though Coleridge's efforts, as those of his German compeers, are nugatory as science, they do maintain a real relationship to the larger purpose of his systematic effort. That larger purpose was to protect the Christian idea of God and man. And the *Theory of Life* attempts to do just that:

> . . . the advance of Nature, under the predominance of the third synthetic power, both in the intensity of life and in the intenseness and extension of individuality, is so undeniable, that we may leap forward at once to the highest realization and reconciliation of both her tendencies, that of the most perfect detachment with

---

[806] For perhaps the most determined attempt to follow him into the specifics of his *naturphilophischen* lucubrations, see Miller.

[807] "Coleridge and Scientific Thought" *CPT* 323.

[808] *CL* IV 883.

the greatest possible union, to that last work, in which Nature did not assist as handmaid under the eye of her sovereign Master, who made Man in his own image, by superadding self-consciousness with self-government, and breathed into him a living soul.[809]

A commentator once posed the question "Was *Theory of Life* Coleridge's *Opus Maximum?*"[810] The answer (as the commentator realises) is of course no, but one can certainly say that *Theory of Life* is profoundly entwined with the aims and texture of the *Opus Maximum*. And its concluding passage takes up all the perplexities of Coleridge's system:

My hypothesis will, therefore, be thus expressed, that the constituent forces of life in the human living body are—first, the power of length, or REPRODUCTION; second, the power of surface (that is, length and breadth), or IRRITABILITY; third the power of depth, or SENSIBILITY. With this observation I may conclude these remarks, only reminding the reader that Life itself is neither of these separately, but the copula of all three—that Life, *as* Life, supposes a positive or universal principle in Nature, with a negative principle in every particular animal, the latter, or limitative power, constantly seeking to individualize, and, as it were, *figure* the former. *Thus*, then, Life itself is not a *thing*—a self- subsistent *hypostasis*—but an *act* and *process*; which, pitiable as the prejudice will appear to the *forts esprits*, is a great deal more than either my reason would authorise or my conscience allow me to assert—concerning the Soul, as the principle both of Reason and Conscience.[811]

XXXI. THE RELATION OF THE *MAGNUM OPUS* TO COLERIDGE'S *LOGIC*

The *Opus Maximum* as we have it contains no extensive separate section on logic (though it is concerned with logic throughout). A logic, nevertheless, was from the earliest inception of the *magnum opus* an integral part of the conception of the Great Work. What happened—and while the manoeuvre seems particularly striking here, it is actually in less noticeable ways something that Coleridge, in the last years of his life, repeatedly did—was that the logical treatise was separated from the plan for the Great Work and became an entity of its own. It was not published during Coleridge's lifetime, nor was it published after his death by Green. With the advent of Kathleen Coburn's vast *Collected Coleridge* in the middle years of the twentieth century, however, it became necessary to publish even the seemingly unpublishable, and as consequence the *Logic* was edited by J. R. de J. Jackson and is now in print.

---

[809] *SW & F (CC)* I 550.
[810] Barnes 494–515.

[811] *SW & F (CC)* I 557.

Why the *Logic* appeared unpublishable was well described by Alice D. Snyder: ". . . it would not redound either to the enlightenment of a twentieth-century public or to the credit of Coleridge to foist on the world in their entirety the masses of unorganized, unfocused material, much of it professing to be little more than an exposition—often a translation—of the *Critique of Pure Reason*, that make up the manuscript "Logic," Egerton 2825 and 2826".[812]

It is bemusing to note, however, what actual publication can do for the status of a manuscript. A more recent commentator has this to say of the edited version of the *Logic*:

Coleridge's *Logic* is undoubtedly his most coherent, systematic, and intellectually sophisticated work. As Orsini points out, "it is more detailed and orderly than any of his published works that deal with philosophy and theology. It is not a miscellany like *The Friend*; it does not break down in the middle, like the *Biographia Literaria*, and then turn in another direction; it does not lose itself in a mass of quotations from another author, like the *Aids to Reflection*; nor does it allow itself any excursions into autobiography, like most of those works; but it proceeds continuously with the main topic from beginning to end." The *Logic* has remained unknown to anyone outside a small circle of Coleridge scholars for reasons that have little to do with its inherent qualities. It languished in manuscript until 1981, when it was published as a volume of Coleridge's collected works. It has not yet received anything like the attention it deserves.[813]

That is a reversal indeed! Moreover, however idiosyncratic the *Logic* might seem when compared, say, with Bolzano's roughly contemporary contribution or that of John Stuart Mill, it was an integral part of the earliest scheme of the Great Work. Only those who know Coleridge superficially through his exotic poems or through a half-understanding of his Christian commitment can think that he was in any way mystical in his approach. On the contrary, as De Quincey says, "logic the most severe was as inalienable from his modes of thinking as grammar from his language".[814] Coleridge's contest with the French Enlightenment, "the Age of Reason", was thus to be neither more nor less than a battle conducted on logical grounds. The Enlightenment was reason gone astray, a "perversion" of reason, and to set it right would require an appeal to exact logic.

In the first comprehensive projection of the scope of the *magnum opus* in 1803, just underneath his statement that it was to be "My *last & great work*—always in mind", Coleridge proposes "The History of Logic with a Compendium of Aristotelean Logic prefixed". As with virtually all

---

[812] *L&L* vii.
[813] McKusick 119.
[814] *De Q Works* II 153.

other emphases of Coleridge's thought, the necessity for a logical foun-
dation never changed. In the plan of the *magnum opus* communicated to
John May on 27 September 1815, Coleridge referred to his "most im-
portant work" as consisting of "six Treatises", the second of which was

> on the science of connected reasoning, containing a system of Logic purified from
> all pedantry & sophistication, & applied practically to the purposes of ordinary
> life, the Senate, Pulpit, Bar, &c—I flatter myself that I have not only brought to-
> gether all the possible Forms of Deception and Delusion in Reasoning, from the
> grossest Bull which raises the laughter of a Taproom to the subtlest Sophism
> which set nation against nation, illustrated by instances from writers of the high-
> est name; but have likewise given some rules for the easy detection of false rea-
> soning. I have labored to make it not so much a Novum Organum, as an Organum
> verè Organum.[815]

On 7 October 1815 he wrote Daniel Stuart about the work on which he
would wish to ground his "reputation with Posterity". Its title was to be
"Logosophia, or on the Logos human & Divine, in six Treatises". The
second treatise was to be "The science of connected [reasoning] (with the
History of Logic from Aristotle to Condillac) freed from [sophistication
&] pedantry, and applied to the purposes of real Life—the Bar, the
[Pul]pit, the Senate, & rational Conversation". The third was to be "the
Science of Premises, or transcendental Philosophy—i.e. the examination
of the Premises, which in ordinary & practical reasoning are taken for
granted. (As the whole proceeds on actual Constructions in the mind, I
might call it, *intellectual Geometry*.) The fourth, a detailed Commentary
on the Gospel of St John:—to which the former is introductory." That the
logical enterprise was always specifically conceived as a propaedeutic for
the central mission of the *magnum opus* is explicitly guaranteed by the
words that follow: "The object of both [is] to prove, that Christianity is
true Philosophy, & of course that all true Philosophy is Christianity".[816]
  But as time moved on the treatise on logic became separated from the
original projection. The *Logic* as now published is a separate work, not a
part of the *Opus Maximum*. What happened here is what happened re-
peatedly with Coleridge's aspiration towards the Great Work. The *Opus
Maximum* is a torso, or better still, a plant, some of whose flowerings
tended to be picked as soon as they bloomed. The *Aids to Reflection* is
perhaps the most beautiful of these blooms separated for another purpose;
the *Logic*, though possibly less striking, is simply another example of the
same procedure.
  It was apparently in 1817 that Coleridge began to think of the logical

---

[815] *CL* IV 589.   [816] Ibid. IV 591–2.

groundwork as a separate venture from the *Opus Maximum*, for early in that year in a letter to Gutch he listed some items whose copyrights he had consigned to the publishers Gale and Fenner in return for a hundred pounds; one was "a volume, on the method of forming first and detecting fallacious Arguments, or on practical Logic for the use of the Student, for the Pulpit, the Bar, &C".[817] The specification of "the Pulpit, the Bar" takes up the language of Coleridge's projection to Stuart of October 1815, and proves beyond doubt that the separate work now spoken of was actually the projected second treatise of the *magnum opus* itself.

Jackson conjectures that "Coleridge had completed a rough draft of the *Logic* by June 1823".[818] In the six years since he had first allowed himself to think of the work as separate from its original matrix, the apparently precipitating factor in its actual emergence was Coleridge's commitment to teaching a class of "young men of ingenuous birth and education from 18 or 19 to six or seven and twenty years old, to go thro' a steady course of Philosophy on a plan which I am now trying with two medical friends".[819] There were other factors. Discovering in March 1819 that his publishers Rest Fenner had gone bankrupt, he was "forced", as Jackson says, "to look about him for those parts of his literary and philosophical plans which it seemed most practical to turn into book; the Logic and, later, Aids to Reflection, both designed for young men about to enter the professions, were the most appropriate". Jackson concludes, "Although it has been claimed that the *Logic* was a result of Coleridge's philosophical class of 1822–3, it seems . . . more likely that the sequence was the other way round. We know that Coleridge had already "conceived the outlines of his *Logic* before he announced the class; he claimed in quite specific terms that he was already dictating a manuscript that sounds like the Logic; and the only account we have of the class does not correspond with the *Logic*. Perhaps the most that we can conclude is that the momentum that produced the *Logic* was shared with the philosophical class and that the class provided him with samples of the kind of audience he was aiming at in the Logic, of young men preparing for the professions".[820]

Be that as it may, it is clear that by the early 1820s the *Logic* and the *magnum opus* were as firmly separated in Coleridge's plans as they had once been firmly intertwined. As he wrote to Lockhart in December 1820, Coleridge was engaged in forwarding his "'Logic' and 'Assertion of Religion as implying Revelation, & of Christianity as the only Revelation

---

[817] *CL* IV 701.
[818] *Logic (CC)* xlvii.

[819] *CL* IV 862–3.
[820] *Logic (CC)* xlv.

of universal Validity'".[821] The "Assertion of Religion", as has been shown, was one of the names Coleridge assigned to the *magnum opus*, and here it clearly does not include the *Logic*.

By January 1821 Coleridge was saying, "I am, however, getting regularly on with my LOGIC"; he then specified that it was "—in 3 parts— 1. The Canons (Syllogy) 2. the Criterions (Dialectic) 3. Organic or Heuristic (εὑριστικόν) with a sketch of the History of the science from Aristotle to Bacon, & a disciplinary Analysis of Condillac's Ψευδο-Logic prefixed, & concluding with a Glossary of philosophical Terms arranged *methodically* in the order & connection of the Thoughts; but with an Alphabetical Index—".[822] Immediately following that dash, Coleridge insisted on the absolute distinction between the *Logic* and the *magnum opus* "and every Sunday I devote with Mr Green, my Fellow-student & Amanuensis, to my (Anti-Paleyo-grotian) Assertion of Religion as necessarily implying Revelation, and of Xtianity as the only Revelation of universal validity.—Of the latter something more than a Volume is written".[823]

Though Coleridge continued to mention the *Logic* in tandem with the *magnum opus*, he always discriminated between the two. For instance, on 9 February 1822 he wrote to Allsop, "The Logic goes on briskly— and my greater work is at least *accelerating* it's pace".[824]

In the course of conducting the seminar mentioned above, Coleridge began more explicitly to meld strict logic with the logic of linguistic and grammatical forms. As he told Stuart on 16 March 1822, the teaching of his five or six young gentlemen involved "the principles and laws of Language, as the Organ of Thinking, of appropriate Language, and the inherent forms of the Understanding, 1. as the Canon or formal Outline of all conclusive reasoning—2. as the Criterion for the detection of error in all the possible species of conscious or unconscious Sophistry—and lastly, the principles of Reason as the Organ of Discovery, whether in Man or in the science of Nature—with sufficient Psychology, to apply the whole to the Art of Persuasion—".[825]

Coleridge specifically aligned the linguistic emphasis with the logical emphasis. On 16 May 1822 he wrote to Southey and spoke of his young friend John Watson's "weekly attendance" on Coleridge's "Lectures on the principles of Reasoning, or Logic as a Canon, a Criterion, and lastly an Organ of the mind".[826] He then said, "I expect to have my introductory Work, on the art and Science of Conclusive Discourse, or the Laws

[821] *CL* v 127.
[822] Ibid. 133–4.
[823] Ibid. 134.
[824] Ibid. 210.
[825] Ibid. 220.
[826] Ibid. 227.

of Thinking & Inquiring, with the rules of Acquiring, testing, arranging and applying Knowlege, ready for the Press by August, with the History of Logic prefixed and a Glossary of Philosophical Terms in the order of the Thoughts but with an alphabetical Index, as the Appendix.—This done, I shall attempt the publication of my (Anti-Grotian) Assertion of the Christian Religion on the principle stated in a Note to my first Lay-Sermon".[827]

On 26 December 1822 Coleridge wrote to Allsop that there were two ways of giving Allsop pleasure and comfort: "the first, the having finished the Logic, in all it's three main Divisions, as the Canon, or that which prescribes the rule and form of all *conclusion* or conclusive reasoning: 2. as the Criterion, or that which teaches to distinguish Truth from Falsehood—containing all the possible sorts, forms, and sources of Error, and means of deceiving or being deceived—3. as the Organ or positive instrument for discovering Truth—together with the general Introduction to the whole—".[828] The second way of giving Allsop pleasure, said Coleridge, "was, to come to Town & pass a week with you & Mrs A."[829]

In the same letter Coleridge spoke about dictating to his amanuenses "Mr Stutfield & Mr Watson", and said that the whole work would be ready for the press by the "end of January": "I shall have the Logical Exercises—or the Logic exemplified and applied in a Critique on 1. Condillac, 2. Paley. 3. the French chemistry & Philosophy—with other miscellaneous matters, from the present Fashions of the age, moral & political, ready to go to the Press with, by the time the other is printed off—& this without interrupting the greater Work on Religion, of which the first Half, containing the Philosophy *ideal* Truth, Possibility and a prior Probability of the Articles of Christian Faith, was completed Sunday last.—"[830]

On 5 June 1823, to John Taylor Coleridge, Coleridge referred to the *Logic* as *The Elements of Discourse* (Snyder points out that the title of Coleridge's work on logic "vacillated between the 'Organum verè Organum,' 'The Power and Use of Words,' 'Elements of Discourse,' and plain 'Logic'"):[831]

'The Elements of Discourse, with the Criteria of true and false Reasoning, as the ground-work and preparation for Public Speaking and Debate—addressed to the Students and Candidates for the Pulpit, the Bar, or Senate'—this Product of how many Years' Labor is now in such a state that I am most anxious that it should be, not indeed read but, sufficiently looked over and into by some man of good sense and academic education, as to enable him to form a satisfactory

---

[827] *CL* v 227.
[828] Ibid. 263–4.
[829] Ibid. 264.

[830] Ibid. 264–5.
[831] *L&L* 69.

general notion of the Plan, principal Contents, and Style of Execution . . . . It is (tho' I avoid the name in the Title-page) a Work of Logic—namely, *forensic* purposes, denying its applicability, as a positive Organ, to all subjects, whether in natural, moral or religious Philosophy, in which the absolute Truth is sought for—while he admits not only it's great utility but asserts it's indispensability (as far as any discipline or —ἄσκησις can be called indispensable) in all subjects of discussion or inquiry, in which the Truth relatively to the Sense and Understanding of *man* in all his social and civil Concerns and Functions is alone required or of pertinence."[832]

On 26 April 1825, Coleridge speaks of "three Works, the preparations for, and composition of, which have employed every hour during the last 20 years of my Life, that Ill-health and the exactions of that imperious Taskmaster, the ever-recurring TO-DAY, have allowed me to call *my own*".[833] Of the three works, "The second, or the Elements of Discourse is finished and in preparation for the Press".[834] (The first was the *Aids to Reflection*, and of the "third and far larger and more laborious Work, on Religion in it's twofold character of Philosophy and History, under the title of 'Religion considered as *implying* Revelation, and Christianity as the only Revelation of universal and perpetual Validity', the former Half only is completed").[835]

The use in the *Logic* of appropriations from continental logicians, mainly Kant, which had so dismayed Snyder and led to her acquiescence in Green's decision not to publish the work, is, for the later scholar James McKusick, scarcely a problem at all:

Coleridge's carefully qualified attitude toward Kant should be borne in mind when considering the fact that part 2 of the *Logic*, in the structure and details of its argument, follows very closely Kant's Critique of Pure Reason. Large portions of its text are translated or paraphrased directly from the *Critique*. The question of plagiarism is not really relevant here, since the *Logic* is avowedly an exposition of Kant; but the question of Coleridge's philosophical originality certainly does arise. Is the *Logic* merely a derivative and somewhat unreliable account of Kant's *Critique*? Or does it significantly revise Kant's argument in the light of Coleridge's own philosophy?[836]

McKusick emphatically urges acceptance of the second viewpoint. He argues that "Coleridge's concept of the understanding differs from that of Kant in that he regards it as identical with the faculty of discourse", and that the "*Logic* seeks to revise Kant's *Critique of Pure Reason* in the light of linguistic theory":

832 *CL* v 275.
833 Ibid. 427.
834 Ibid. 428.

835 Ibid.
836 McKusick 120.

A careful reading of the text should enable us to establish the philosophical originality of the *Logic*. Coleridge's exposition of Kant's philosophy is neither "slavish," as Wellek has asserted, nor merely "faithful," as Orsini claims, but radically revisionary. Coleridge goes so far as to criticize Kant's choice of a title for his *Critique of Pure Reason*. This work, says Coleridge, "would have been open to fewer objections, had it been proposed by the author under the more appropriate name of 'Transcendental Logic.'" Kant's title is misleading, in Coleridge's view, because the *Critique of Pure Reason* consists mainly in a transcendental analysis of "logic itself (that is, the forms of the understanding and the rules grounded on the same)." It is, in short, a critique of the pure understanding, not of pure reason.[837]

McKusick goes on to insist that "Coleridge's concept of the understanding differs from that of Kant in that he regards it as identical with the faculty of discourse": "Kant does, to be sure, refer to the understanding as 'discursive,' but he does not give much attention to the role of language in its actual functioning. Much more clearly than Kant, Coleridge sees that epistemological questions cannot be resolved without recourse to a prior analysis of the linguistic structures that constitute the means of intellectual inquiry. The *Logic* seeks to revise Kant's *Critique of Pure Reason* in the light of linguistic theory, and in this sense it enacts a "linguistic turn" on Kant's philosophy."[838]

XXXII. THE RELATION OF THE *MAGNUM OPUS* TO WORDSWORTH'S *RECLUSE*

In view of Coleridge's intense psychological need for collaborative support in almost anything he did,[839] it is on balance not really surprising that the *magnum opus* took shape under the demands of this need. The fragments of the work that exist were all dictated to an amanuensis, who by the fact of that relation served as a kind of collaborator for the monumental enterprise. Another part of the reaching for mutuality is evident in its relation to Wordsworth's vast philosophical poem, "The Recluse".

For "The Recluse", unfinished exactly as the *magnum opus* is unfinished, was projected as an alternate version of Coleridge's own system of philosophy. As Coleridge recalled, speaking in 1832 of the projected reality of "The Recluse":

. . . the plan laid out, and, I believe, partly suggested by me, was, that Wordsworth should assume the station of a man in mental repose, one whose principles were made up, and so prepared to deliver upon authority a system of philosophy. He

---

[837] McKusick 120.
[838] Ibid.

[839] See above, Section XXX; see also "Coleridge's Anxiety" *RFR* 104–36.

was to treat man as man . . . in contact with external nature, and informing the senses from the mind, and not compounding a mind out of the senses; then he was to describe the pastoral and other states of society, assuming something of the Juvenalian spirit as he approached the high civilization of cities and towns, and opening a melancholy picture of the present state of degeneracy and vice; thence he was to infer . . . a redemptive process in operation, showing how this idea reconciled all anomalies, and promised future glory and restoration. Something of the sort was, I think, agreed on. It is, in substance, what I have been all my life doing in my system of philosophy.[840]

Though "The Recluse" was never completed, its planned completion not only drained much of Wordsworth's poetic energy but undoubtedly was a factor—not perhaps the most important factor, but one that was operative nevertheless—in Coleridge's inability to proceed vigorously with his own *magnum opus*. For "The Recluse" soaked up much of the hope and anticipation Coleridge devoted to the prospect of great philosophical statement.

Thus when Wordsworth in 1814 published "The Excursion", which was to have been the second part of "The Recluse", he spoke of the entwinement of his poetic endeavour with the hopes of another figure:

Several years ago, when Author retired to his native mountains, with the hope of being enabled to construct a literary Work that might live, it was a reasonable thing that he should take a review of his own mind, and examine how far Nature and Education had qualified him for such employment. As subsidiary to this preparation, he undertook to record, in verse, the origin and progress of his own powers, as far as he was acquainted with them. That Work, addressed to a dear Friend, most distinguished for his knowledge and genius, and to whom the Author's Intellect is deeply indebted, has been long finished, and the result of the investigation which gave rise to it was a determination to compose a philosophical poem, containing views of Man, Nature and Society; and to be entitled, The Recluse.[841]

The "dear Friend" was Coleridge, who had occupied himself deeply in Wordsworth's aspiration towards great poetry. When Coleridge as early as 13 May 1796 referred to Wordsworth as a friend who was in his opinion, "the best poet of the age,"[842] he gained an enormous and on the whole salubrious purchase on Wordsworth's subsequent career. But this influence, so benign and so important, became alien when it led him to demand of the by then wholly acquiescent Wordsworth, "a philosophical poem, containing views of Man, Nature and Society". "[M]editative" as Wordsworth was, "his mind was radically unphilosophical".[843]

---

[840] *TT (CC)* I 307–8.
[841] *WPW* v 1–2.

[842] *CL* I 215.
[843] Robson 139.

Coleridge none the less proselytised vigorously for Wordsworth to set out on a great philosophical poem. Of a portrait of Wordsworth painted by Hazlitt, he comments to Wordsworth, "Sir G[eorge Beaumont] & his wife both say, that the Picture gives them an idea of you as a profound strong-minded Philosopher, not as a Poet—I answered (& I believe, truly—) that so it must needs do, if it were a good Portrait—for that you were a great Poet by inspirations, & in the Moments of revelation, but that you were a thinking feeling Philosopher habitually—that your Poetry was your Philosophy under the action of strong winds of Feeling—a sea rolling high".[844] In another place he says that Wordsworth is "the first & greatest philosophical Poet—the only man who has effected a compleat and constant synthesis of Thought & Feeling and combined them with Poetic Forms".[845] Since Coleridge's own endeavour, as we have seen, always looked to philosophical system, it is not surprising, however immense the burden it placed upon Wordsworth, that he "looked forward to the Recluse, as the *first* and *only* true Phil[osophical] Poem in existence . . . not doubting . . . that the Totality of a System was not only capable of being harmonized with, but even calculated to aid, the unity . . . of a *Poem*".[846] The first of these two statements was made in 1804, the second in 1815, and the comparative dates dramatise not only how unremitting was the pressure on Wordsworth, but how large a part of Coleridge's own aspiration had been projected into Wordsworth's venture.

Indeed, in 1799 Coleridge had written, "I long to see what you are doing. O let it be the tail-piece of 'The Recluse!' [that is, 'The Prelude'] for of nothing but 'The Recluse' can I hear patiently".[847] Even as late as the *Biographia Literaria* in 1817, when it should have become apparent that there was never going to be a "Recluse", Coleridge was remorselessly insisting, "what Mr. Wordsworth *will* produce, it is not for me to prophesy; but I could pronounce with the liveliest conviction what he is capable of producing. It is the FIRST GENUINE PHILOSOPHIC POEM".[848]

Along the way, Coleridge had repeatedly spoken with unbridled enthusiasm about the venture, and the more praise he bestowed on Wordsworth, the more the urgency of his own future plans was vitiated. To Cottle in 1798 Coleridge said, "The Giant Wordsworth—God love him! . . . he has written near 1200 lines of a blank verse, superior, I hesitate not to aver, to any thing in our language which any way resembles it".[849] In 1803, to Poole, he rejoiced that Wordsworth "has at length

[844] *CL* II 957.
[845] Ibid. 1034.
[846] *CL* IV 574.

[847] Ibid. I 538. See also I 527.
[848] *BL* (*CC*) II 155–6.
[849] *CL* I 391.

yielded to my urgent & repeated—almost unremitting—requests and re-
monstrances—& will go on with the Recluse exclusively.—A Great
Work, in which he will sail; on an open Ocean, & a steady wind; unfret-
ted by short tacks, reefing, & hawling & disentangling the ropes—great
work necessarily comprehending his attention & Feelings within the cir-
cle of great objects & elevated Conceptions."[850]

We may gauge the psychic force that went into Coleridge's exhorta-
tions to write "The Recluse" by Wordsworth's own complete concur-
rence in attempting the alien poem. To De Quincey in 1804 Wordsworth
referred to "The Recluse" as a work to which "I mean to devote the Prime
of my life and the chief force of my mind". He identified this work as "a
moral and Philosophical Poem"—after all, it is only fitting that a man
firmly identified as the "first & greatest philosophical Poet" should em-
bark on such a poem—"the subject whatever I find most interesting, in
Nature, Man, Society, most adapted to Poetic Illustration".[851]

The phrase about "Poetic Illustration" may suggest an anxious differ-
ence between what Wordsworth felt able to do and what Coleridge
wanted him to do, which was to present "the Totality of a System". But
Wordsworth gamely tried. "My brother", wrote Dorothy in January 1806,
"though not actually employed in his great work, is not idle, for he al-
most daily produces something and his thoughts are employed upon the
Recluse".[852] And Wordsworth always spoke of "The Recluse" as the
supreme effort of his life. To Tobin in 1798 he called it "a poem in which
I contrive to convey most of the knowledge of which I am possessed. My
object is to give pictures of Nature, Man, and Society. Indeed, I know not
any thing which will not come within the scope of my plan."[853] When-
ever he spoke of "The Prelude", it was not that poem but always "The
Recluse" that occupied the pedestal of honour. To Sir George Beaumont
in 1804 he said:

I do not know if you are exactly acquainted with the plan of my poetical labours;
it is twofold, first a Poem to be called, *"The Recluse,"* in which it will be my ob-
ject to express in verse my most interesting feelings concerning Man, Nature, and
society; and next, a Poem (in which I am at present chiefly engaged) on my ear-
lier life, or the growth of my own mind, taken up upon a large scale; this latter
work I expect to have finished before the Month of May; and then I purpose to
fall with all my might on the former, which is the chief object upon which my
thoughts have been fixed these many years.[854]

To De Quincey Wordsworth said that he intended to devote to "The
Recluse" the "Prime of my life and chief force of my mind". He said that

[850] *CL* II 1013.
[851] *WL (E)* 454.
[852] *WL (M)* I 2.
[853] *WL (E)* 212.
[854] Ibid. 518.

he was also engaged on a narrative poem ("The Excursion") and a poem on his "own earlier life"; but that the poem on his own life was "the least important of the three".[855] To Wrangham in 1804 he says, "I have great things in meditation [i.e. "The Recluse"], but as yet I have only been doing little ones. At present I am engaged in a Poem on my own earlier life."[856]

As to how much of Coleridge's own aspiration and energy were hypothecated in the plan of "The Recluse", an interesting indicator is the almost total reliance on him expressed by Wordsworth. Wordsworth sounds almost frantic as he writes to Coleridge of his need for guidance: "I am very anxious to have your notes for the Recluse. I cannot say how much importance I attach to this, if it should please God that I survive you, I should reproach myself for ever in writing the work if I had neglected to procure this help."[857] This was in March 1804. In December 1805, Dorothy wrote to Lady Beaumont about William's progress, "He is very anxious to get forward with The Recluse, and is reading for the nourishment of his mind, preparatory to beginning; but I do not think he will be able to do much till we have heard of [from] Coleridge".[858]

The anxiety expressed in these two statements pales before the virtual terror of Wordsworth's letter to Coleridge of 29 March 1804: "Your last letter but one informing us of your late attack was the severest shock to me, I think, I have ever received . . . . I will not speak of other thoughts that passed through me, but I cannot help saying that I would gladly have given 3 fourths of my possessions for your letter on The Recluse at that time. I cannot say what a load it would be to me, should I survive you and you die without this memorial left behind. Do for heaven's sake put this out of the reach of accident immediately."[859]

To call upon Coleridge for immediate action about anything was always to invite disappointment. In this instance, however, Coleridge may fairly be thought to have outdone himself in procrastination: the letter of 29 March 1804 was not answered until 30 May 1815.[860] On that date, some eleven years after Wordsworth's request, Coleridge wrote down for his friend the supposed content of "The Recluse", which proved to be intensely Coleridgean:

[855] *WL* (*E*) 454.
[856] Ibid. 436.
[857] Ibid. 452
[858] Ibid. 664.
[859] Ibid. 464.
[860] C did claim in Malta in 1805 that he had complied with Wordsworth's request but that his notes had been lost: "My Ideas respecting your Recluse were burnt as a Plague-garment, and all my long letters to you and Sir George Beaumont sunk to the bottom of the Sea!" (*CL* II 1169). However sceptical one may find oneself when confronted with this quintessentially Coleridgean excuse, the excuse does suffice to demonstrate that Wordsworth's poem was very much on C's mind.

I supposed you first to have meditated the faculties of Man in the abstract, in their correspondence with his Sphere of action, . . . to have laid a solid and immoveable foundation for the Edifice by removing the sandy Sophisms of Locke, and the Mechanic Dogmatists, and demonstrating that the Senses were living growths and developements of the Mind & Spirit in a much juster as well as higher sense, than the mind can be said to be formed by the Senses—. Next, I understood that you would take the Human Race in the concrete, have exploded the absurd notion of Pope's Essay on Man, Darwin, and all the countless Believers—even (strange to say) among Xtians of Man's having progressed from an Ouran Outang state—so contrary to all History, to all Religion, nay, to all Possibility—to have affirmed a Fall in some sense, as a fact, the possibility of which cannot be understood from the nature of the Will, but the reality of which is attested by Experience & Conscience—Fallen men contemplated in the different ages of the World, and in the different states—Savage—Barbarous—Civilized . . . and not disguising the sore evils, under which the whole Creation groans, to point out however a manifest scheme of Redemption from this Slavery, of Reconciliation from this Enmity with Nature . . . and to conclude by a grand didactic swell on the necessary identity of a true Philosophy with true Religion . . . in short, the necessity of developing & disciplining the human mind by the substitution of Life, and Intelligence . . . for the philosophy of mechanism which in every thing that is most worthy of the human Intellect strikes *Death* . . . . In short, Facts elevated into Theory—Theory into Laws—& Laws into living & intelligent Powers— true Idealism necessarily perfecting itself in Realism, & Realism refining itself into Idealism.— Such or something like this was the Plan, I had supposed you were engaged on—.[861]

It was certainly the plan, in largest outline, that Coleridge himself was engaged on in his aspiration towards the *magnum opus*. In fact, the hope of "developing & disciplining the human mind by the substitution of Life, and intelligence" for "the philosophy of mechanism" subsumes every aspect of Coleridge's hope and underlies his every systematic endeavour.

If "The Recluse" was a shadow version of Coleridge's own labours, another shadow version connected with that poem, and also unmistakably an alternate receptacle for the thoughts to be presented in the *magnum opus*, was sketched by the projection of another poem. Always symbiotic with respect to Wordsworth, Coleridge planned a huge poem called "The Brook", which was to contain "impassioned reflections on men, nature, and society"—clearly an alternate version of Wordsworth's prospects for "The Recluse",[862] though it may have been in his mind earlier. Yet if the complex dynamics of Coleridge's and Wordsworth's mutual entwinement in the plan for Wordsworth's great work, "The Recluse", allowed no completion for Wordsworth, they also drained off and otherwise ad-

---

[861] *CL* IV 574–5.   [862] *BL* (*CC*) I 196.

versely affected Coleridge's chances for a satisfactory completion of his own great work, the *magnum opus*.

XXXIII. THE RELATION OF THE *MAGNUM OPUS* TO GREEN'S *SPIRITUAL PHILOSOPHY*

In quite a different way, another work also militated against a satisfactory completion of Coleridge's *magnum opus*. Though here the dynamics were idiosyncratically different, in both instances the outcomes were an effect of Coleridge's compulsion towards symbiotic intellectual functioning. For if Wordsworth's unrealised "Recluse" stood as a shadow alternate for the *magnum opus*, that was also precisely the role of Green's *Spiritual Philosophy*. As argued above,[863] those existing fragments of the *magnum opus* known as the *Opus Maximum* were not published by Green largely because the intellectual energy and urgency needed for their presentation were diverted into his own published work, the two volumes of which appeared in 1865. The exact title was: "*Spiritual Philosophy: Founded on the Teaching of the Late Samuel Taylor Coleridge*: by the Late Joseph Henry Green, F.R.S. D.C.L., edited, with a memoir of the author's life by John Simon, F.R.S., Medical Officer of Her Majesty's Privy Council, and Surgeon to St. Thomas's Hospital. Volume I. London and Cambridge: Macmillan and Co. 1865."

Though Green's work is extraordinarily faithful to Coleridge's distinctions and even almost to his tone of voice, it possesses almost none of the characteristic Coleridgean vitality that caused "glorious islets" to emerge from even the most meandering and unintelligible flow of his discourse. *Spiritual Philosophy* is clear in prose and reverent in tone, but it is not Coleridge. As the anti-Coleridgean gadfly C. M. Ingleby said, "I dare not speak of Green as well as I could wish, because I can do so only by speaking of Coleridge worse than he deserves. In short, they who would master the philosophy of Coleridge will do wisely to study it in Coleridge's works, and not in the digest of his disciple. . . . Green's 'Spiritual Philosophy' was in every sense still-born. It was a still-birth of his brain, and it was a still-birth of Messrs. Macmillan's press."[864]

Mean-spirited though he is, one must concede that Ingleby puts his finger on the curious unsatisfactory character of Green's devoted offering to his master's thought:

De Quincey proposed to supersede the proverb, "as dead as a door nail," by another, "as dead as Gillman's Coleridge". . . . But dead as Gillman's book is,

[863] See above, Section XXI: Why the Existing Fragments of the *Magnum* *Opus* were not Published.
[864] Ingleby 110.

Green's 'Spiritual Philosophy,' 2 vols., 1866, is, in De Quincey's phrase, *deader*; that is, dead in a far profounder sense. As Coleridge used to say of other works, the parts cohere by *synartesis*, not by *synthesis*—in fact, Green's book mainly consists of extracts from other men's writings, tacked together by a few flimsy notes. It is no more a Spiritual Philosophy than the fragments of an Ichthyosaurus cemented together is an animal, nay it is less so, for Green's book has not even the evidences of a past vitality.[865]

Ingleby rehearses the history of his past dealings with Green and says:

I dare say it has seemed to you that I have dwelt with unnecessary length on this posthumous work of Coleridge's loving friend and disciple, but the sequel will show you that I have not said a word too much. It was for the sake of writing this work, that Mr. Green, by his own confession ('Notes and Queries,' May 27, 1854), excused himself from undertaking the editorial labour of preparing any of Coleridge's unpublished manuscripts for the press. He writes, in answer to one of my applications, "I have devoted more than the leisure of a life to a work in which I hope to present the philosophic views of my 'great master' in a systematic form of unity—in a form which may best concentrate to a focus and principle of unity the light diffused in all his writings, and which may again reflect it in all departments of human knowledge, so that truths may become intelligible in the one light of divine truth." To this I replied that— "I, for one, must enter my protest against the publication of Mr. Green's book being made the pretext of depriving the public of their right (may I say?) to the perusal of such works as do exist in manuscript, finished or unfinished."

The protest, of course, was unheeded. Mr. Green pursued his labours, and died, I believe before his own work had received its final touches. We now know how stupendous was the mistake he committed; and in comparison with the veriest fragment of Coleridge's how barren is that creation for which he allowed some of his great master's manuscripts to remain unedited.[866]

Several reasons for the peculiar deadness of the *Spiritual Philosophy* may be identified. First of all, Coleridge's own defence of Christianity was always vitally suffused by the dynamism generated by contradictory realisations: "I believe, help thou my unbelief". His Christian faith was profoundly responsive to the arguments opposed to Christian faith: "For a very long time I could not reconcile personality with infinity; and my head was with Spinoza, though my whole heart remained with Paul and John".[867] Again, "Not one man in a thousand has either strength of mind or goodness of heart to be an atheist. I repeat it. Not one man in ten thousand has goodness of heart or strength of mind to be an atheist. And, were I not a Christian . . . I should be an atheist with Spinoza . . . . This, it is

---

[865] Ingleby 109–10.
[866] Ibid. 111–12.

[867] *BL (CC)* I 201.

true, is negative atheism; and this is, next to Christianity, the purest spirit of humanity!"[868] Green's thought, on the other hand, has no sense of having been won through intense thinking through of philosophical *aporiae*; it is rather a reverential setting forth of a pre-established system, that of Coleridge himself. For a characteristic instance, in his Hunterian Oration of 1840, Green says that he has "an ulterior object" in the address, which is that of "vindicating the original merit of John Hunter as a philosophical physiologist" and "of connecting science . . . with the philosophy of Coleridge; which, as far as my knowledge extends, pre-eminently, if not alone, gives life and reality to metaphysical pursuits, by showing their birth, growth, and requisite foundation in the whole man, head and heart".[869]

Second, where Green's Hunterian Oration attempts to connect Coleridge's thought with science, the *Spiritual Philosophy* leaves science out of its concern, thereby radically distorting Coleridge's position. Green was obviously unhappy with the specious nature of Coleridge's scientific ventures, but science—even though the *naturphilosphischen* analyses he espoused (and which Green had at one time espoused) were eventually to have no scientific validity[870]—was schematically necessary to Coleridge's position. Thus in the *Opus Maximum* as here presented, the scientific section comprises approximately a third or a quarter of the entire treatise.

The third of the reasons is a matter of tone. Green, though clearheaded, does not really argue a position. He simply repeats, over and over, the points he wishes the reader to accept (both volumes, though straightforwardly written, are astonishingly repetitive). Coleridge, on the other hand, although he does not customarily argue a position, presents his conclusions in the intense context of his own living concerns. As Richard Holmes has said, "Coleridge's best work, 'both poetry and prose, has the inescapable glow of the authentic visionary'".[871] Green's work, sadly, has no glow at all, for it lacks the vitalising contexts of Coleridge's lived-through intellectual experience. Coleridge's thought is always the expression of what Dilthey calls *Erlebnis*; *Erlebnis* is entirely absent as the foundation of Green's *Spiritual Philosophy*.

Despite its deadness, however, the *Spiritual Philosophy* repeatedly provides cogent formulations of Coleridge's most central contentions; it sets forth the distinction between reason and understanding and urges the centrality of will, the omnipresence of polar dialectic, and the controlling

[868] Allsop 61.
[869] Green *Dynamics* xix–xx.
[870] See further "Excursus Note

XVIII: Coleridge and Scientific Thought" *CPT* 323–5.
[871] Holmes xv.

importance of idea. Other key Coleridgean emphases are advanced, among them the conception of God as *Deus alter et idem*, the necessity of avoiding pantheism, and the centrality of the *logos* of the fourth gospel. These emphases are intertwined in a true Coleridgean manner.

Green often refers to Coleridge, and sometimes quotes him; he also quotes lengthy excerpts from his two Hunterian Orations of 1840 and 1847. Equally cogent and equally Coleridgean are Green's presentation of a fourth and fifth defect in current schemes of philosophy. The fourth involves an appeal to the distinction between reason and understanding. If it seems to repeat once again what Green has on numerous occasions maintained in his book, that is a notable characteristic of his mode of presentation. Green continually circles around his theme; indeed, he seems constantly to be, as it were, treading water:

> But the fourth grievous impediment to philosophy is the want of an adequate notion, and in too many instances the utter ignorance, of Reason, as contradistinguished in kind from the Understanding and merely logical faculties, as the peculiar gift to man constituting his rationality, as the Light or influx common to all men, manifesting itself in Ideas, or those principles in which the proper humanity essentially consists. Reason is the potentiating force, of which the spiritual or real man is the result. It is the idealizing power;—the power, instinct, and inherent tendency of man to contemplate all his thoughts, feelings and strivings, in their perfection, integrity, unity, universality, totality, absoluteness. It is the immediate revelation to him of the spiritual image in which he was created, and towards which he cannot but acknowledge himself bound to strive:—[872]

The fifth impediment, faithful as always to Coleridge's own emphases, involves the Coleridgean distinction between θεός and θεῖον, and invokes the quintessential Coleridgean attraction/repulsion attitude towards pantheism:

> "Fifthly and lastly, we have to deplore amongst the defects of philosophy, the sad forgetfulness of the θεῖον, of the divine Spirit in and through all. That this arises from too exclusive attention to the senses and to the faculty judging according to sense, can scarcely be doubted; and this defection from his spiritual nature can scarcely be otherwise than expected, so long as man remains the ἄνθρωπος ψυκικός.
>
> Something may likewise be attributed to the erroneous schemes of theology, which on the one hand confound God with the world, and end in pantheistic atheism, and which on the other separate God from the world, and by aiming at a pseudo-monotheism resolve themselves into a negative and lifeless abstract of spirituality, to which there is no human correspondency."[873]

[872] *SP* I 174–5.   [873] Ibid. 175.

Green's second volume is as faithful to central Coleridgean emphases as the first. Chapter III is entitled "The Blessed Trinity"; Chapter IV, "The Fall and Redemption" (though here, instead of a text, one finds an apologetic note from the editor: the "intended chapter on the doctrine of the Fall and Redemption had not been written out in readiness for publication . . . . Not feeling confident that, if I attempted to make the intended combination of these materials, I could do full justice to the Author's intention, I have thought it best to print the materials themselves in extenso, and to subjoin them at the end of this volume, as Appendices").[874] Chapter II in the Part Fourth is called "The Fall of Man, the Origin of Evil, and Original Sin". In Chapter II, "The Idea of God", Green asserts the Coleridgean fundamental of the unacceptability of pantheism:

> On the *Pantheistic Views of the Idea of God* and the nature of Deity it is not necessary for our purpose to enlarge. The fundamental error of this philosophy, which has exerted a seductive attraction on many of the highest intellects, consists in confounding God and the world. Or, if we contrast it with the christian doctrine according to a dry formula which we have already adopted after Coleridge, the pantheistic scheme be represented by "God *minus* World = 0," the christian doctrine by "God *minus* World = absolute perfection and reality." In the school of Hegel (who contemplates God as the absolute process of thought, which first attains its consciousness in the human mind) the antagonism to the position, that God is a self-dependent reality, distinct and above, nature, is prominently maintained in the often-repeated assertion, that God is *immanent* but not *transcendent*, indwelling throughout the whole ascent of nature, but inconceivable without it.[875]

Green correctly identifies Coleridge's central conception of will as essential to personality (and opposed to the blind will of Schopenhauer and Nietzsche, though the point is not made with overt reference to Schopenhauer). He asserts its efficacy as a chief bulwark against pantheism:

> In order to be a Will, in any proper sense of the word, the Will must will, what it cannot otherwise than will, its own Being as one undivided Will;—it must will itself continuously, permanently, invariably, self-consistently;—and this is what we mean by an *individual Will* or a *Person*. . . .
> The very term "Will" loses all force and significance, when divided from conscious predetermination, intention, deliberation, judgement, and the like attributes of conscious mind and personality; . . . The Absolute Will causative of all reality, and therefore of its own, is the eternal act of self-affirmation or self-potency; and this act, which we dare not divide (as any stage in a process) from the Absolute Will causative of reality, is in this relation, the essential act of Personeity, and may be designated *Deus Subjectivus*, Ipseity, the Absolute Subject, "I

---

[874] *SP* II 73.   [875] Ibid. II 43.

am." And we entreat the reader's attention to this all-important relation, as the very ground and foundation of all morals, and as the only effectual antidote to the demoralizing influence of Pantheism with its necessary consequence of confounding God with the world. The school of Hegel—following the systems, which from the most ancient times have propounded the doctrines of Pantheism, and all based on the misconception of the position expressed by the ἕν καὶ πάν (Compare Jacobi on Spinoza)—rejects the Personality of God . . . [876]

To this correct understanding and emphasis on Coleridge's conception of Will, Green subjoins an equally accurate presentation of the other chief term in Coleridge's philosophical defence of person, Reason:

the Principles of Christianity are essentially part of the original constitution of the human mind, and are implied in the gift of Reason, considered, as has throughout been inculcated, as the divine Logos . . . [877]

I affirm that the Reason, considered as the light and spiritual presence of the Word of God in His creatures, is in and for them the idealizing power—the power, instinct and inherent tendency, to contemplate all their thoughts, feelings, and strivings in their integrity and perfection. I repeat that the Reason, so conceived, and so accepted by the Conscience, as the transcendent Idea of Spiritual Integrity, and as the universal and absolute power of integration, is and can be no other than the "Idea of God." [878]

Despite the honourable accuracy of its formulations, however, the *Spiritual Philosophy* is inert. It is wholly without the unique intensity that raised Coleridge's systematic network of abstractions to an insistent pertinence; and that made his intellectual existence, despite the fragmentation and pathos of his physical existence, so cohesive and vital. Coleridge's mind churned throughout his life with the urgency of the truths he wished to extricate and impart. His almost inconceivable range and depth of reading, his amazing tenacity, his relentlessly dialectical procedure, his flashing insight, his constant and incessant thinking, lent his cultural utterance a unique and compelling voice. That voice can be heard everywhere in the ensuing edition; it cannot, sadly, be heard in Green at all.

[876] *SP* II 45–6. [878] Ibid. II 50.
[877] Ibid. II 205.

OPUS MAXIMUM

PROPOSED PREFACE

MS NYPL (Berg Collection); in a copybook containing a transcript of C's letters "To Mr. Justice Fletcher". The "Proposed Preface to the first Volume" of *Op Max* is written and signed by C in ink on the pastedown inside the back cover of the copybook. See the frontispiece for an illustration.

DATE. After 1828, probably 1832. It is not known when the transcript of C's eight letters to William Fletcher (published in *The Courier* 20 Sept–10 Dec 1814) was made, but C's annotations of the transcript are dated 1832 and other entries in the copybook date from early in the same year: see *EOT* (*CC*) II 373–4 and nn, and *SW & F* (*CC*) 1500, 1502–4. Some of the leaves in the copybook bear the wm date 1828, others 1829.

Proposed Preface to ~~my~~ ⟨the first⟩ Volume of my Work,[1]
the "Magnum Opus
et labor [a](mea vitae)"[b]

In my judgement, there are but two schemes worthy the name of Religion: and I believe that the first is to the Second, as the Acorn to the same Acorn expanded into ~~the~~ ⟨an⟩ Oak. The first is that of Lieutenant Bowling—in his reply to ⟨the⟩ Zealous Romish Priest—"As for me, friend! d'ye see, I have no objection to what you say. It may be either true or false for what I know. I meddle with nobody's affairs but my own—the Gunner to his Linstock,[2] and the Steersman to the helm, as the saying is. I trust to no creed but the compass, and do unto every man as I would be done by: so that I defy the Devil, the Pope and the [c]Pretender, and hope

---

[a] The parentheses are written in pencil
[b] Closing quotation mark inserted
[c] Just above the above the first letter of this word is the apex of a triangle, the sides of which extend just below the "e" in "the" and the "n" in "second" of the next sentence. The diagram is in ink and appears to have been made before the preface was written. The top and bottom of the triangle are labelled thus:

[1] For the significance of Coleridge's word here see Prolegomena VII: The *Magnum Opus* as System. Note that immediately below Coleridge changes the word "Work" to "System".
[2] A long stick used to hold a lighted match for firing a cannon.

3

to be saved as well as another."—The second Scheme the Reader will find in the following System of Faith and Philosophy: or ~~Chain of Truth~~ ⟨Catena Veritatum⟩ de Deo, Homine et Naturâ.[3]

S. T. Coleridge.

The ~~Work~~ ⟨System⟩ is divided into three unequal parts, each of which forms an independent Work—the whole comprized in five Volumes. Two of these, and the larger part of the third,[4] are prepared for the press—and ⟨of⟩ the remainder the materials & principal contents exist [d]in Sybilline MSS—⟍

God

—th——

[d] There is a stray quotation mark here in the ms

[3] Tr: "Chain of Truths Concerning God, Man and Nature". *Catena* (chain) is a favorite Coleridgean conception, and indicates the progression of necessary implications that made system such an important commitment for him. "The Christian Preacher should abjure every argument, that is not a link in the chain of which Christ is the Staple & Staple Ring" (*CM—CC*—II 291). Again: "Ah! poor Hobbes, he possessed fine talents: in forming his theories, however, he fancied the first link of his chain was fastened to a rock of *adamant*; but it proved to be a rock of *ice*." (Brinkley 63). Yet again: "But in the human mind, the succession of whose thoughts constitutes *Time* for us, and of course therefore in Grammar and in Logic we assume one

circle, like the staple of a Chain, as the only means of letting all other Links follow each other in one Line of Dependency" (*CN* IV 4644). For a single example—among several—in the work at hand, see below, Frag 4 f 76: ". . . the chain of our disquisition in the last link". Cf another Latin rubric that constitutes an alternate formulation to the one that follows. The alternate reads "Coleridgii Fides et Doctrina de Deo, Mundo, et Homine."—"The Faith of Coleridge and the Doctrine concerning God, World, and Man" (*CN* IV 4645).

[4] For variations in the number of treatises projected see the discussions in Prolegomena XII: The Content of the *Magnum Opus* and XIII: The Transformations of the *Magnum Opus*.

FRAGMENT 1

VCL S MS 29, "Say Vol. III" (*L&L* B2); wm "JOHN HALL | 1819". This, the thinnest of the three clasped vellum notebooks of S SM 29, was mistakenly identified as Vol III by C. A. Ward in pencil on the verso of the second unfoliated flyleaf at the beginning of the notebook. The text is written in ink in the hands of JHG (ff 1–28, 38–122) and a second amanuensis (ff 28–37), almost certainly John Watson, with occasional corrections and insertions in C's hand. A number of corrections and comments have been made in pencil, probably by Ward; these are recorded in the textual notes.

DATE. 1820–3. On 16 May 1822 C reported to RS that John Watson (1799–1827), a "temporary Partner" of JG's, had been living with him in the Gillman household for "the last 18 months", i.e. since Dec 1820 (*CL* v 226–7). By Jan 1822 he had become one of C's amanuenses for the *Logic* (see *Logic—CC—* xliv–xlv), and on 11 Oct 1823 he left for Germany with letters of introduction from C (*CL* v 287–8, 303–4, 335). Ff 1–28 could have been written no earlier than 1819, the wm date; ff106–22 derive from C's "Essay on Faith" of c Jul 1820 (*SW & F—CC—*836–44).

[*f 1*]   Chapter III[1]

In every science something is assumed, the proof of which is prior to the science itself, whether supplied by some other science or consisting of some fact, the certainty or validity of ~~the maxims derived from~~ which is of common acknowledgement, or lastly of some idea or conception without which the science itself would be impossible and the denial of which implies the logical falsity of the whole, and consequently stamps the very act of commencing it in detail with the character of absurdity. We have spoken of *Science*, of *Sciences*, in the severest sense of the word, viz. those superstructures of the pure intellect in which the speculative necessity reigns throughout and exclusively, the act itself of reasoning and imagining being the only practical ingredient, or that alone in which any reference is made to the Will, and even in this to the Will in that sense only in which it remains utterly undetermined, whether it be a simple

---

[1] Chapters I and II, which presumably set the scope and goal of the *magnum opus* (if this is the beginning, which is not certain, and perhaps not even probable), are not contained in this fragment, and are not known to exist.

spontaneity, [*f2*] which as in the growth of plants or the unconscious functions of ⟨the lower⟩ animal life no more excludes the predicate of necessity than a motion proceeding from an outward impact, to which alone, namely causation ab extra,[2] spontaneity as an act, actio ab intra,[3] doth in philosophical language stand in antithesis.[4] For example, the Practical or the postulate is merely the power of imagining the shortest possible line between two points, or a line deviating at each point from the former, and in these the figures composed of one or other or both of these two classes of lines. When, in asserting the existence of such a power as the universal predicate of intelligence, we assert at the same time the impossibility of either withholding our assent and of imagining anything contrary to the former acts, and thus attach a necessity to them which has no opposite, and the contrary of which is an absurdity, we have the whole foundation of *Geometry*, as far as the Practical is concerned.[5]

It has likewise been shown [*f3*] that the power of withholding and, indirectly at least, of refusing our assent to the necessary foundation of an intellectual superstructure forms the essential difference between the moral and sciential systems. The assent having been given, this difference ceases, and moral positions both may and ought to be treated as sciences subject to the same universal logic as those ~~weight~~ of number and measure.[6] Still, however, a weighty difference would remain as the result if there be no other distinction. A fact, for instance, having been taken for granted, whatever is legitimately deduced and concluded [from it] becomes a logical truth, for in reality in all such reasoning nothing more is affirmed than the legitimacy of a given connexion according to the necessary and inherent forms of thinking. ~~The~~ ⟨As⟩ proof of this it need only be noticed that in all syllogisms, the major of which consists

---

[2] Tr: "from without".

[3] Tr: "action from within".

[4] The phrases *ab extra* and *ab intra* occur frequently in C, and are the basic distinction from which flows his characteristic emphasis on organic form. They occur as early as Feb 1805, where he speaks of the "difference" between "Fabrication and Generation": the "Form" of the latter is "ab intra, *evolved*, the other ab extra, *impressed*" (*CN* II 2444).

[5] Both from his commitment to logic, and from his instinctive identification with Pythagoras and Plato, C frequently takes examples from the realm of mathematics. It is to be regretted—and he

himself regretted it bitterly (see *CN* IV 4542)—that he had had no formal training in mathematics. Again, see *TT* (*CC*) I 8 and n 17. See also *CM* (*CC*) III 349: "O my most unhappy unwise neglect of Mathematics at Jesus College, Cambridge! No week passes, in which I do not groan for it!"

[6] Underlying C's insistence on the parallelism of moral and sciential logic is Spinoza's insistence, in his *Ethica*, that "I shall consider human actions and desires in exactly the same manner, as though I were concerned with lines, planes, and solids" (*Spinoza* II 138).

of a fact, i.e. by which, both here and elsewhere, we mean nothing more than an assertion respecting particulars or individuals ^a((in antithesis to universal truths) or positions [ƒ4] affirmed as such, that this often is the sense of the word *Fact*, and that at the same time it is an unfortunate word in consequence of its etymology may be seen from the frequency with which we speak of a false or mistaken fact and yet the feeling of embarrassment, as if dissatisfied with the term and yet unable to find a substitute except by a periphrasis—so too, "I deny the fact", which from the evideneetness of our meaning we use without hesitation, tho' relatively to the etymon it involves the same contradiction as a false or mistaken fact. I apprehend that the negative use will likewise bear out the definition of "fact" given out in the text. If I am not greatly mistaken, no one in the habit of correct speaking would say, "it is a fact that two straight lines cannot enclose a space", or that "two and two make four", though he would not hesitate to call his position⟨say⟩, "it is a fact that this position is to be found in Euclid's axioms")^b.

We may always prefix, and indeed most commonly understand, an "if".[7] Thus all stones think; but a flint is a stone; therefore a flint thinks. No less to the minor, [ƒ5] where the fact of inclusion is not of universal knowledge: thus all stones think; but men are stones; therefore men think. It may be worth remarking that this ridiculous syllogism has been adduced in a recent work on logic to prove that a truth may be syllogistically deduced from a falsehood and vice versâ.[8] But the whole purpose ⟨amount⟩ of the assertion is merely that "*if*" was a predicate common to all stones; and if men were a particular sort of stones, then it would necessarily follow that men must think. The proper answer to this syllogism, and all of the same kind—if such nonsense deserved an answer—would

---

^{a–b} Square brackets are placed around this passage in the ms, the opening bracket being written over the parenthesis

[7] That is to say, logical formations can always be rendered as if/then sequences.

[8] The "recent work on logic" should seemingly be that of Richard Whately, but the editor has not found the instance. Other popular works on logic, such as that of Watts and that of Aldrich, could hardly be called "recent". Whately wrote the section on logic for the *Encyclopaedia Metropolitana*, and the work in revised form was pubished in 1826 as *Elements of Logic*, which eventually went into nine editions. Whately incurred C's animosity because as Dean of Oriel College at Oxford he had presided over Hartley Coleridge's expulsion in 1820. Not least perhaps for that reason C rejected Whately's logic with contempt. As he said in 1830: "I never read such wretched stuff as those two books of Whately's on Logic and Rhetoric. There are two kinds of Logic. 1. Syllogistic 2. Criterional. How any one can by any spinning make more than ten or a dozen pages about the first is inconceivable to me; all those absurd forms of syllogisms are one half pure sophisms and the other mere forms of Rhetoric" (*TT—CC—* I 201).

be, "Men^c think, I own, but not 'therefore', unless except on the condition of conceding a notorious absurdity." It follows, then, that if the ~~moral~~ truths of the moral world are to maintain an equality of rank with those of science—not to speak of a superior dignity, which indeed would supersede the equality in the very moment in which the latter is admitted—we^d must discover an opposite to hypothetical positions no less than to the unconditionally necessary, [$f6$] i.e. the positions of pure ^{e}science. And^f in order to this we must find [that] which agrees with the positions of pure science in as far as its affirmations are universal and not of particulars or individuals, the contingency of which ~~the~~ still remains for the mind even when it is removed by the ~~fact~~ knowledge of the fact, and yet agreeing with the latter in its distinction from the former by the possibility of affirming the contrary. It must in some sense, therefore, be necessary, or it could have no point of connexion with the sciences; and yet it must not be unconditionally so, or it would be one and the same with science. Again, in its relation to hypothetical positions or those grounded on facts, it must be contingent and yet contingent in a different manner, which can only be that as in the hypothetical affirmations the contingency remains for the mind when it is removed by the ~~fact~~ establishment of the fact, so here the necessity must remain in the mind while the contingency is retained in the fact.

Such, indeed, is the usage in all languages. When, [$f7$] speaking of some duty or its contrary, we say of ourselves or to another, "I, or you, must do this or that," we well know that the necessity is not absolute but ^{g}conditional. But^h still a necessity is acknowledged, and the "if" or condition is ~~of a divers~~ diverse in kind from the contingency expressed in all affirmations of mere facts. ~~w~~ We content ourselves in resolutely asserting—and if our word be doubted, in calling others to witness—that such and such sheep *are* always white, but never think of seriously asserting that they must be so, though we have not the slightest doubt on our minds respecting the accuracy of the observation. Whereas we tell another that he must abstain from any given act of baseness or ingratitude with the same fullness of conviction when we anticipate that he will do the contrary as when we are most confident that he will act in consonance to the obligation. In the position itself we admit no more contingency than is found in the mathematics; and yet the position must be itself more or other than the positions of the mathematicians, or the difference between the two [$f8$] would vanish and the contingency be wholly divided from the position itself, just as in the case of sciences em-

---

^{c} ms: men ^{d} ms: We $^{e-f}$ ms: science and $^{g-h}$ ms: conditional but

pirically applied, where the position respecting the properties of a mathematical arch remains altogether unaffected by the contingency of the materials employed in the construction of a bridge or the probability of their greater or lesser approximation.

The moral position, therefore, must have a reality of its own, even independently of its application, and its necessity must not only remain ~~even~~ where the application is refused or subverted, but the denial of the position must be itself a reality and a realizing act in addition to and even independent of the contingency of the accordance or discordance of the fact connected therewith.[9] You must do your best to relieve a deserving and afflicted parent; if you do not, the import contained in the term "must" remains, and still you ought to have done so—you *ought* still to make compensation for that neglect, and [even] if you reply, [*f*9] "There[i] is no 'must' in the matter, for who shall make me?[j] If you threw me out of the window, I must go; but while you are no stronger than I believe you to be, I know and feel that I can and shall stay where I am. And as to your 'ought', so you and the parson say, but I deny it and believe what nature tells me more than all the priests in the creation and all the herd of ninnies that are duped by them. Does the young lion ~~deny himself a m~~ lessen his meal to feed his old dam, or waste and fret his season of power and enjoyment to lengthen out the misery of his toothless sire's old age?" If such were the reply, the retort, I presume, would be to this purpose: "Hateful as your conduct is, it is in and of itself less affrightful, because less certainly of inmost wickedness and a series of past guilty acts within or without than ~~the ve~~[k] this very act of mind by which you reject the [l]obligation. Nay,[m] that you are capable of so doing, and consequently that the principle partakes of contingency as far as you [*f 10*] are included in it, of which yet it must not partake inasmuch as it is essentially of the highest necessity, excludes you from the name and rank of manhood. You appeal to the beasts: well for you if this appeal could lawfully have been made for you as being one of the[ir] [n]number. But[o] you are not a beast, for beasts are not capable of reasoning; and you are not a man, for you disown the principles of reason.[10] To transgress

---

[i] ms: there   [j] ms: me.   [k] ms: the ~~ve~~
[l-m] ms: obligation nay   [n-o] ms: number but

[9] The great stress on this point is necessitated by C's dealing so exclusively here in purely mental functions, or "facts that have their sole being entirely in consciousness" (f 75). The possibility that the moral is the figmental must be rejected; since so much is to be built on it, the moral must have an impregnable foundation.

[10] Not only in the *Op Max*, but repeatedly throughout his theological and philosophical argument on other occasions, C is concerned with the essential distinction between man and beast, on

but still to acknowledge is that which, dividing us in our conception at least from angels or in whatever other form we represent to ourselves the idea of human nature in all its possible perfection, forms the riddle of humanity, the problem which all ages labour to solve and is the mystery of the world. But at once to transgress and disown, or rather to include, the guilt of all transgressions in the deliberate act of disowning is proper neither to man nor beast, and constitutes the idea of a fiend, the real existence of which you are employing your endeavour to make manifest."

[*f 11*] In this imagined conversation we have insensibly developed the first and most general forms of morality and of religion.[11] While the nature of the actions, which here take the same place as facts, holds*p* in hypothetical affirmations, gives*q* the contents ~~and form the conception of~~ morality, ~~in as much~~ and are so far akin to that class as that there is a contingency inherent in the same and yet still more nearly to the affirmations of science, inasmuch as this contingency, so far from removing all necessity, inheres in its first specific conception in like manner to the principles or universal positions, which have the same place as the definitions, postulates, and axioms in the propositions and demonstrations of pure science, and yet preserve a point of connexion or kindred with the class of empirical positions, [which] by their reality and realizing power contain the substance and form the first general conception of religion. If, therefore, [*f 12*] we recapitulate the code and creed given in the first chapter ⟨we shall see at once⟩ both ⟨what⟩ the assumptions and the postulates are, without which there would be an absurdity in the commencement of any investigation of the truth or falsehood of the particular positions contained in that code, and that their necessity does not consist merely or chiefly in their indispensableness to this investigation, or as the condition of our assent to the truth of the particulars. In other words, that the conclusion does not rest on an understood "if" prefixed as in the syllogism above-stated—that the truths are not hypothetically

---

p ms: hold   *q* ms: give

---

which man's hope of immortality depends. He speaks, for instance, of "the chasm, the *diversity* in *kind*, between man & beast" (*CL* IV 856). The establishment of that distinction was one of the most welcome services rendered by the differentiation between "reason" and "understanding". Cf *The Friend*: "But Reason is wholly denied, equally to the highest as to the lowest of the brutes;

otherwise it must be wholly attributed to them, and with it therefore Self-consciousness, and *personality*, or Moral Being" (*Friend—CC—*I 155).

[11] Cf the overarching definition in *The Friend*: "Religion, in its widest sense, signifies the act and habit of reverencing THE INVISIBLE, as the highest both in ourselves and nature" (*Friend—CC—*I 440).

true, but that the necessity arises out of and is commensurate with human nature itself, the sole condition being the retention of humanity, while that this is contingent, i.e. that a human being may be dishumanized,[12] which it cannot be but by his own act, all calamities from without having at the utmost only the power of suspending it instead of subordinating it to science, or in any way constituting an inferiority, [*f 13*] is the very ground and efficient cause of its supremacy, differencing it from science by addition, not subtraction, by addition, too, not of an alien ~~prop~~ quality but of the same power in a higher dignity, namely by adding goodness to truth while it realizes truth by goodness, enlightens goodness by truth and transubstantiates, as it were, truth and goodness each into the nature of the other. In one concluding sentence: there are several positions, each of which might be legitimately assumed and each of which might stand on its own grounds as a postulate of humanity, and à fortiori, therefore, of every code of religion and morality. But the one assumption, the one postulate, in which all the rest may assume a scientific form, and which granted we may ~~give~~ coercively deduce even those which we might allowably have assumed, is the Existence of the *Will*,[13] which a moment's reflexion will convince us is the same as *Moral Responsibility*, and that again with the reality and essential diffe[*f 14*]rence of ⟨moral⟩ *Good* and *Evil*. ~~Morally both.~~[14] [15]

---

[12] What is entailed in being human, and what is the distinction between person and thing, are at the very centre of C's thinking throughout his life. "Every Man is born with the faculty of Reason; and whatever is without it, be the Shape what it may, is not a Man or PERSON but a THING. Hence the sacred Principle indeed, which is the *ground*work of all Law and Justice, that a Person can never become a thing" (*Friend—CC—*II 125). Again: "morality commences with, and begins in, the sacred distinction between Thing and Person" (*AR—CC—*327). See *AR* (*CC*) 78 and nn 11, 137, 269.

[13] Will, which is the first of the great central abstractions to be encountered in the *Op Max*, is for C the very first principle both of God and man. See Prolegomena XVII: The Concept of Will, and below *passim*. Cf e.g. Frag 2 f 242: "An absolute Will, which, therefore, is essentially causative of reality and therefore *in origine* causative of its own reality, the essential causativeness, however, abiding undiminished and indiminishable, this is our first Idea."

[14] This, for C, is the foundation of everything else. Cf a notebook jotting: "The moral responsibility of man, and the truths implied in this, either as presupposed or necessarily consequent. 2. the Personeity and the *Holiness* of God?—3. The Pauline Ethics resulting from the admission of the 1. and 2.? 4. From the *fact* of moral Evil and No. 3. the reality of *Original* Sin?—5. The removal of this by the incarnation and Cross of the Son of God, as the *only possible* Redemption, thro' Faith as the only possible means of appropriating the boon in each Individual redeemed?—I affirm that each of these five, and each in the full and literal sense of the words in which it is stated, and that all five collectively, are essential to Christian Belief—" (*CN* IV 5215).

[15] This initial complex will bear the burden of the entire elaboration of the *Op Max*. The extrication of the "essential

Chapter IV

There is one point on which we are particularly anxious to prevent any misunderstanding. This respects the difference between the two ⟨possible⟩ assertions, "such a truth may be known as truth by the light of reason" and "the same truth was discovered, or might have been discovered, by men by means of their reason exclusively". We may assert the former, and in the course of this work shall find occasion to assert it without involving, nay, we altogether disbelieve and deny, the latter. The facit[16] or sum total affixed to the examples in the common elementary school books of arithmetic are all capable of being demonstrated by the science of arithmetic, and yet it is very possible that the children might never attain to that scientific insight without that and similar a̶s̶ helps and assistances. To take another instance, which may bring us still nearer to the point in question. An object may be placed at so great a distance or so dense an [*f 15*] atmosphere may intervene as to render it in the highest degree improbable that it could ever be noticed by persons placed at the given point under the supposed impediment of distance and misty air, which yet may become recognisable without much difficulty by the naked eye after it had been once pointed out and accurately described by others familiar with the object, or seen by means of a telescope. Instances in which a knowledge given to the mind quickens and invigorates the faculties by which such knowledge is attainable independently cannot have escaped the most ordinary observer, and this is equally true whether it be faculties of the mind or of the senses. Who has not experienced the help which a good county map affords to a traveller in a country where, as in Wales for instance, the names of places, villages, etc. are relicks of a language unknown to him? It is indeed wonderful both how small a likeness will suffice a full apprehension of sound or sight when the correspondent sound or object is foreknown and foreimagined, and how small a deviation or imperfection will render the whole confused and indistinguishable or mistaken where no such previous intimation has been received.[17] Hence [*f 16*] all unknown languages appear to a foreigner to

---

difference of moral good and evil" is not only of critical importance to C's own needs but is something that cannot occur if pantheism is adopted as the system of reason. In C's view, it goes hand in hand with the doctrine of the Trinity, which the progress of the *Op Max* is also moving to extricate, e.g. "the Doctrines of the Tri-une God and Eternal Life; of Sin

& originative Evil; Theanthropy; Incarnation, and Redemption by the Cross" are all linked together in a single passage (*CN* IV 4924).

16 Tr: "it makes".

17 In this observation C resumes a thread that runs through both his conception of symbol and his conception of method. The "great law of imagination",

be spoken by the natives with extreme rapidity, and to those who are but beginning to understand it, with a distressing indistinction. But nearest of all, and on a scale ~~and~~ in extent and importance commensurate which it is brought to illustrate as an instance and to prove by its strict analogy, is the education of the human race[18] at large and of each individual in all its different periods. A language may now be formed by agreement: every system of cyphers and of short hand is such a language, but how could language in reference to which these conventional languages are constructed have arisen?[19] Convention itself, nay, even the very condition and materials of all convention, a society of communicants, presupposes a language. It is not impossible, ~~indeed~~ perhaps, what we may without much hazard assume, that all the grounds and causes of language may exist in the human mind, just as all the faculties of the adult body exist potentially in the new born infant. But yet this does not in the least degree lessen the necessity of ~~an adult~~ the pre-existence of an adult or of some cause equivalent in order to explain the infant's [*f 17*] own existence, nor the coexistence of an adult in order that the infant should become a full-grown man. In short, it is as inconceivable that language should have been given to a mind that did not contain in itself the grounds and principles of language, as that these grounds and principles should ever emerge from latency, had not a language in its rudiments at least have been previously given. What the impregning power is to the egg or germen, what soil, heat, and moisture are to the seed or egg so fecundated—that is [the] example, the presentation, of a something to be

---

as he said, is "that a likeness in part tends to become a likeness of the whole" (*Friend—CC*—I 146). That law empowers the functioning of symbol, which "always partakes of the Reality which it renders intelligible, and while it enunciates the whole, abides itself as a living part in that Unity, of which it is the representative" (*LS—CC*—30). The same movement from part to whole characterizes Coleridge's theory of method. He asserts that the principles of method he presents should be regarded "as the basis of my future philosophical and theological writings, and as the necessary introduction to the same" (*Friend—CC*—I 446). A chief characteristic of method is that it must employ a "mental antecedent" (513): "We have seen that a previous act and conception of the mind is indispensable even to the mere semblances

of Method: that neither fashion, mode, nor orderly arrangement can be produced with a prior purpose, and 'a pre-cogitation *ad intentionem ejus quod quaeritur*'" (475).

[18] The education of the human race was a famous rubric of Lessing (*Die Erziehung des Menschengeschlechts*), of whom C in his early years planned to write, and read widely to gather materials for, a biography (see e.g. *CL* I 518–19).

[19] C often addresses problems of language and grammar, both in the *Op Max* and elsewhere, on the ground that grammar is connected with the fundamental processes of reason: e.g. "the science of grammar is logic in its first exemplification" (Frag 2 f 273). See below, in addition to the notes to that citation, Frag 4 f 38.

imitated and repeated for the human faculties. As the reason is compelled to the alternative of assuming either an infinite series or a creation, even so when it has assumed the latter it still finds the problem imperfectly solved, unless in some way or other it combines both by some equivalent for that which it has excluded. The creation, as the simple production of ~~seed~~ the individual, would still leave us in the same[r] inconclusive state of mind as the new-born infant without the idea of the parent,[20] and even at the risk of the contradiction involved [*f 18*] in the hypothesis, we should feel ourselves compelled to presume an Adam before Adam, were it not that in creation we imply a creator and thus prepare ourselves for the equivalent to the advantage which the infinite series forever gives and snatches away, according as we contemplate each part severally or attempt to account for the All: the Creator, I say, is again ~~prequired~~ by and presented by the reason and by the imagination in the service of the reason as the fosterer, the teacher, the Providence.[21] In what particular mode this may be effected, whether by a sudden infusion of habits, or by an accommodation of the divine guide through the medium of forms correspondent in kind to the creature who is to be educated, or by a providential arrangement of all external forms under peculiar directive stimulants acting on an extraordinary and prepared susceptibility, no sane man will expect, no wise man be solicitous, to determine. Rather, perhaps, he will ~~deem it~~ rest in the probability that all these means may have acted in providential [s]concert, and[t] deem [*f 19*] himself amply remunerated for this enquiry that he has acquired an insight into one most important truth alike for the purposes of practice and speculation, namely that this is one distinctive mark of the human being, arising out of its double nature, namely the *animal* and the [u]*rational*[22]— that,[v] if we may use so humble an illustration, as certain pumps will flow

---

[r] ms: same state   [s-t] ms: concert. And   [u-v] ms: *rational*. That,

[20] Here C first broaches that concern with the relation of mother and child that assumes such enormous importance as the *Op Max* progresses. Also, the unconditioned Idea of the parent, as it antecedes the conditioned reality of the child, is a happy example of a fundamental of C's position throughout all his argumentation: that is, to cite merely one form of his expression of the contention, that "From the indemonstrable flows the sap which circulates through every branch and spray of the demonstration" (Frag 2 f 36). Again: "The grand problem . . . is this: *for all that exists conditionally . . .*

to *find a ground that is unconditional and absolute . . .*" (*Friend—CC—*I 461).

[21] Cf C's story about the childhood of Epicurus: "he received his first impulse from Hesiod when he was twelve years old in a line beginning 'First of all things arose Chaos', 'And out of what', said the boy, 'did Chaos arise?'" (*P Lects—*1949—213). The source of the story is Apollodorus the Epicurean as reported by Diogenes Laertius (*DL* II 529–31).

[22] It must be reiterated that the absolute distinction of the claims of the animal and of the rational, along with the conceding that both are necessary to the

only when a portion of water has been previously thrown in, so in order to all the products of the mind a similar product must be presented as the inceptive or fermenting principle of the process by which the product may be after knowingly and regularly obtained. When Euclid, or Pythagoras, ~~asserted~~ promised his pupils or followers[w] ~~const~~ to teach them to construct the circle and to deduce its astonishing properties independently of all outward experience, he neither denied nor meant to deny that the very words in which he expressed his promise might have conveyed neither meaning nor inducement but for the empirical necessities, discoveries, and technical inventions occasioned by the overflowing of the Nile.[23] In like manner, [*f 20*] when we affirm of any moral or religious truth [that] it is susceptible of rational or philosophical demonstration, we are so far from implying that the knowledge of its truth had its primary origin in the ⟨unaided⟩ efforts of human reason that we regard the ~~actual~~ ⟨present⟩ existence ⟨and actual exercise⟩ of such a power as the result of a revelation which had, by enlightening the mind, roused, disciplined,[x] and invigorated all its faculties and appealed to experience and history for the confirmation of the fact. Whether we direct our historical researches to Egypt, to India, or to the earliest scientific schools of Greece, there, where the sciences are, we find either claims to a revealed religion or traditions of the same. And in the religions themselves for which the claims are made, the farther back we are enabled to trace ~~the~~ ⟨its⟩ existence, the more simple do its creed and forms become, the more clearly do they discover themselves to be the reliques of a religion, having every claim to the character of revelation that internal evidence and congruity with the philosophic idea of God and the nature and needs

---

[w] ms: followers to   [x] ms: discipline [*correction supplied in pencil on f 19ᵛ*]

---

composition of the human being, are essential to C's edifice of thought. "Either we have an immortal soul or we have not; if we have not, we are beasts; the first and wisest beasts, but still beasts; we only differ in degree, and not in kind; but we are not beasts by the concession of materialists, and by our own consciousness; therefore it must be the possession of a soul within us that makes the difference" (*TT—CC*—ɪ 31).

[23] Cf *Philosophical Lectures*: "What the state of information must have been when Pythagoras, after having travelled through Egypt, Persia, and India, came back and was transported and offered

a hecatomb on having discovered the thirty-seventh [forty-seventh] proposition of Euclid, is a pretty good answer to those men who would suppose a high state of knowledge in scientific men who were nobody knows who. But such an idea has been carried to a most extravagant height by some of our modern contenders for Indian wisdom. Was it to be supposed that Pythagoras, who had passed his life in seeking knowledge wherever he went, should when he came back express a delight amounting to rapture at the very elements of geometry if geometry had been already carried to a system?" (*P Lects*—1949—110).

of man can supply. [*f 21*] The main purpose of this digressive chapter has been to preclude offence in one class of readers, and the opportunity of flattering their unbelief in another, and misunderstanding in all. But the reflecting mind will, we trust, hereafter recur to ~~the facts and truths~~ the contents of this chapter with another and higher end—will trace in it a cycle of action and re-action in which the facts that constitute the history of revelation awake[y] the reason to the knowledge and possession of its powers. The fruits and attainments of the reason are at hand to compensate and make indemnification for whatever diminution, either of the proofs or their influence on the mind, may be inherent in the nature of all historical testimony by the ravages or even the mere lapse of time.[24] Thus will the one main object of the present work be justified and the true spirit of the following chapters be recognised, that, namely, of invalidating the most plausible objections of infidels, those which are built on the uncertainties and chasms occasioned by the loss or corruption of documents and outward testimony, by a proportional diminution [*f 22*] of their necessity, which can alone be effected by ~~ine~~ establishing and increasing the anterior probability.[25] For the probability of an event is part of its historic evidence and constitutes its proof presumptive or evidence à priori, and the degree of the evidence à posteriori requisite to the satisfactory conviction of the actual occurrence of an event stands in an inverse ratio to the strength or weakness of the evidence à priori. Nay, there are conceivable cases in which the proof presumptive or the anterior probability may be so strong as that the mere circumstance of its having been asserted by any respectable man or believed by any number of men shall suffice for the proof of its actual occurrence.

[*f 23*]   Chapter V

At the close of the last chapter but one, we had agreed to reduce the postulates and assumptions, the denial of which would stamp the very act of

---

[y] ms: awaking

[24] This was an essential of C's theological position, and allowed him to withstand the ravages of the Higher Criticism. See Prolegomena VI: The Higher Criticism. See also the whole of the posthumous tract, *Confessions of an Inquiring Spirit*.

[25] For the necessity of this statement, for C's assumption of the task of defending against "plausible objections" arising from "the uncertainties and chasms occasioned by the loss or corruption of documents and outward testimony", and for the added urgency thereby imparted to the conception of the *magnum opus* by the rise of the Higher Criticism of the Bible, see above, Prolegomena VI: The Higher Criticism. C spoke of himself as "I, who hold that the Bible contains the religion of Christians, but who dare not say that whatever is contained in the Bible is the Christian Religion" (*CIS* 61).

commencing the investigation with the character of absurdity, to the one great and inclusive postulate and moral axiom—the actual being of a *responsible Will*. À fortiori, therefore, the actual being of WILL in genere. We suppose, too, that in conceding this, it is at the same time admitted that a something is meant by the Will distinct from all other conceptions, and which, therefore, no other term[26] expresses with the exception of perfect and therefore superfluous synonyms, if any such should exist in one and the same language. We do not apply the term to the current of a stream, whether necessitated by the inclination of its channel or as the varying effect of wind or tide or gusts from the openings of mountains on either bank. Nor do we apply it to any necessitated motion combined with life, as the circu[*f 24*]lation of the blood. Nor when identified with action, as when we attribute instinct, not Will, to bees and other insects. The very term[27] implies a necessitation, "Instinctus", a goading or pricking, the essential power of which is not affected by the accessory circumstance of its being inward and invisible. Again, even though this moving or goading should be accompanied with sensation and consciousness, still we do not designate it as a will as long as it is contemplated as an effect, the ⟨sufficient⟩ cause of which pre-existed in an antecedent. No man ~~attributes~~ calls hunger ~~to h~~ a will, but an appetite—or the migration and peculiar habits characteristic of whole kinds or classes in the animal world, or (to give particular instances)[z] the flight of the wild duck while the fellow-nestling remains content in the farm yard, where both eggs had been hatched under the same bird. These and whatever resembles them we call natural or acquired Tendencies, Propensities, etc., but we need not the term "Will" to express them; and if [*f 25*] in such cases we ever employ that term, it is done either ignorantly or wantonly or metaphorically for the purposes of elevation and poetic passion. But even though no antecedent be known, and though the ~~thing~~ ⟨predicate⟩ be one with the subject and implied in the idea of the subject, we cannot always designate it as the *Will*. The various acts, products, and educts which accompany or follow the growth of plants—the irregular oscillatory motions, for instance, of the hedynrum gyrans[28]—and with these the organisation and the correspondent circumstances, as the joint result of which we explain these several peculiar acts, we infer *Spontaneity*, indeed, but do not recur to the Will unless it be as to the principal or causa causarum[29] of the compages[30] or organismus itself, and

---

[z] Parentheses inserted

[26] That is, Will.
[27] That is, instinct.
[28] A genus of tropical Asiatic herbs, having showy labiate flowers.

[29] Tr: "cause of the causes".
[30] A whole formed by the compaction or juncture of parts; a system of conjoined parts.

therefore pre-existent to the plant or animal of which the spontaneity is predicated. If we carefully collate these negatives, the only positive which will present itself as the result we shall find to be the *power* of *originating* a *state*.[31] This, however, though an accurate is still [*f* 26] but a verbal definition of the *a*Will. It*b* informs us sufficiently what we cannot attribute to a Will, but not what that is—which is a power to begin or originate a state—much less whether such a power exists. This is true, but yet we gather so much from the definition that we see clearly, or at least cannot reflect on the force of, the defining words without seeing that the question must be confined to its reality, namely whether a ~~w~~ Will *is*, and cannot be extended to its conceivability, namely whether a Will be conceivable or—which in the present case is fully equivalent—can be explained or accounted for. For if it be that which can absolutely begin a state or mode of being, it is evidently not the result or aggregate of a composition. It must be ens simplicissimum,[32] and therefore incapable of explication or explanation. As little can it be accounted for, for we account for a thing when we ~~place something~~ name its antecedent or that which contained potentially what appeared really in the thing ~~expli~~ to be accounted for as the consequent: thus we account for the motion of the billiard ball from the [*f* 27] impact given by the cue as the antecedent.[33] But again, for this very reason and inasmuch as it is an origin and not originated, and simple, not composite, it is likewise unique—that which it is, it alone is; consequently, there can be nothing like it or analogous to it. Now if we consider what we mean by the term "conceive" (concipio, i.e. capio hoc comparativè cum alio),[34] or I take two or more things under some common predicate), we shall see at once that the Will cannot be an object of conception. This indeed applies to all unique ideas; and in the strict and purest sense of the term, all ideas are unique, and by their very unicity are contradistinguished from all images, conceptions, theorems, and notional forms. Thus life is in its idea inconceivable, and falls under that class of which the Schoolmen say, "dantur non intelliguntur",[35] they may be known but cannot be understood.

a–b ms: Will it

[31] Cf a note of Sept 1825: "Will is that which originates . . . Will is the Subject, the sole predicate of which is to be essentially causative of Reality. COROLLARY: Therefore and in origine causative of its own reality, the essential might abiding unexhausted, indiminishable" (*CN* iv 5256).

[32] Tr: "most simple thing".

[33] The philosophical use of billiard balls and cues in discussions of events and their antecedents was inaugurated by Hume, *An Enquiry concerning Human Understanding* iv i 24–5.

[34] *concipio* means "to take hold of", as does *capio*; the emphasis is on the *con*: "to take hold of this in comparison with another".

[35] Tr: "they are given, not understood".

In a more advanced stage of this investigation, when it will be required of us to speak of the Will in its absolute sense and not as now, under the predicate of respon[*f 28*]sibility, or the Will in the finite and creaturely—this consideration of absolute antecedency in the necessity of thought and without any relation to time[36]—we shall be compelled to fix our attentions longer and more steadfastly on the necessities involved in this definition, the most abstruse of all metaphysical speculations and the one great mystery of the mind.[37] As how, indeed, should that, which is to contain in itself the explication and conceivability of all things, be otherwise than the abysmal mystery into which all causes must at last resolve themselves?[38] *c*Had we purposed in this Place to have treated of the absolute Will, we have*d* must have propounded it under the above verbal definition th̶a̶s̶ an idea, the acknowledgment or acceptance of which would have been recommended by a scientific interest only, namely by a demonstration that without such an idea as the ground or inceptive position, a system of Philosophy and therefore a ⟨consistent⟩ Philosophy of any kind, [*f 29*] as distinct from mere history and empirical classification, would be impossible, A̶and the very attempt absurd.[39] This we mean on the supposition that the enquirer has not mastered the idea so as to know its truth by its own evidence.[40] While this evidence is not present to the mind, the position is not indeed an idea at all but a notion, or like the letters expressing unknown quantities in algebra, a something conceded in expectation of a distinct significance which is to

c At this point the transcription continues in the second transcriber's hand
d Cancelled in pencil

[36] For the absolute Will's "absolute antecedency in the necessity of thought" cf a formula contained in a notebook entry of 1825: "As the Absolute Will, essentially causative of all Reality + 0. The Will, causative of its own Reality I = The Father, Contemplative of all Reality in itself and in the contemplative generative II = the adequate Idea, the eternal Alterity, the Son" (*CN* IV 5249).

[37] "What is A Mystery! that which we apprehend but can neither comprehend or communicate—a truth of Reason which the Understanding can represent only by Negatives, or contradictory Positives" (*CN* IV 5170).

[38] The "absolute Will" is "the universal *Ground* of *all* Being" (*AR*—1825—328).

[39] Cf C's statement in the *Biographia Literaria*: "After I had successively stud-

ied in the schools of Locke, Berkeley, Leibnitz, and Hartley, and could find in neither of them an abiding place for my reason, I began to ask myself; is a system of philosophy, as different from mere history and historic classification, possible? If possible, what are its necessary conditions? I was for a while disposed to answer the first question in the negative, and to admit that the sole practicable employment for the human mind was to observe, to collect, and to classify. But I soon felt, that human nature itself fought up against this wilful resignation of intellect" (*BL*—*CC*—I 140–1). And see above, Prolegomena VII: The *Magnum Opus* as System.

[40] C at one point speaks of the "Pleroma in the Idea—and the Birth of the Distinctities, the Forms, the Infinite in the Finite" (*CN* IV 5233).

be hereafter procured.[41] With him, however, who possesses the idea we
have only to proceed with the involved and consequent truths in order to
determine by the fact itself whether a Philosophy can be constructed
thereon.[42] That it has not been hitherto, or that the renewed attempt
should have again fail'd, is no proof that it is impossible. But ~~that~~ the
success, i.e. the existence of such a Philosophy, is the sufficient [*f 30*]
and only proof of its possibility. Here, however, we begin not with an
idea in this high and pure sense of the term[43] but with the postulate of a
fact and the assumption of a truth as a necessary consequence of the
*e*fact—the*f* logical principle on which the reason proceeds being this:
whatever is real must be possible and therefore whatever is necessary to*g*
the possibility of a reality must be itself both possible and real. The
reader will not, we trust, so far misunderstand us as to confound the
~~p~~term "⟨im⟩possibility" with "incomprehensibility";*h* or that in affirming
that A is necessary to the possibility of B we mean no more than with-
out A, we should not be able to account for B;*i* or if A be supposed, B
may be theoretically solved. Far other is our meaning. That without
which the conception of B [*f 31*] would involve a contradiction equal to
that, perhaps, of declaring the same thing in the same sense to be second
and first a dependent on another without any other to depend from—that
alone is here said to contain or to be necessary to the possibility of B
when we affirm that B having been granted as real and ⟨the position of⟩

---

e–f ms: fact—The   *g* ms: in order to
h No punctuation in ms   *i* No punctuation in ms

[41] Here C approximates Hegel's dis-
tinction between "Idea" (*Idee*) and "No-
tion" (*Begriff*). But the "notion" that C
specifies above, when referred to the
conscious subject, may in another per-
spective be the unconscious Idea: "You
may see an *Idea* working in a man by
watching his tastes & enjoyments: tho'
the man's understanding may have been
enslaved to the modern Metaphysics, or
rather tho' he may hitherto have no con-
sciousness of any other reasoning but
that by conceptions & facts—On such a
man you may hope to produce an effect
by referring him to his own experience &
by inducing him to institute an analysis
of his own acts of mind and states of
being, that will prove the *negative* at last
. . . . But to talk of Ideas to men who nei-
ther have them or or *had* by them, is pro-
fanation & folly to boot" (*CN* iv 5409).

[42] "*The first man, on whom the Light
of an IDEA dawned, did in that same mo-
ment receive the spirit and the creden-
tials of a Law-giver*: and as long as man
shall exist, so long will the possession of
that antecedent knowledge (the maker
and master of all profitable Experience)
which exists only in the power of an
Idea, be the one lawful qualification of
all Dominion in the world of the senses"
(*LS—CC*—42–3).

[43] In the high and pure sense of the
term, "no Idea can be rendered by a con-
ception. An Idea is essentially incon-
ceivable" (*CM—CC*—ii 1145). Again:
"one Diagnostic, or contra-distinguish-
ing Mark, appertaining to all *Ideas*, is—
that they are inexpressible by adequate
words—an Idea can only be expressed
(more correctly *suggested*) by two con-
tradictory Positions" (Brinkley 291).

that reality involving a contradiction except under the condition of A, A̶ i̶t̶s̶e̶l̶f̶ the reality of A likewise is co-assumed. On this rests another canon of logic, v̶i̶z̶ namely an argument which, if valid, would disprove a certain truth is ex absurdo[44] invalid. The fact, then, with the demand of which we commence our investigation, is the existence of conscious responsibility;[45] and of its existence every conscious and rational ᵇBeing must himself be the judge, the consciousness being the only organ by which it can be directly known. But the [*f 32*] consciousness of a conscience is itself conscience. All that words and outward reasoning can effect is t̶h̶a̶ first to state an instance which is supposed to exemplify and thus expected to convey the direct, proper, and exclusive meaning, which as in the case of all terms representing simple truths[46] or acts of knowlege[*j*] is insusceptible of any definition or periphrasis. We can only explain the sense of the word "red" by referring to the phenomenon itself. If the r̶e̶s̶p̶o̶n̶d̶a̶n̶t̶ ⟨Individual to whom we address the discourse⟩ hardly denies that the example has any correspondent in himself; or if he professes to have a correspondent indeed, but ⟨a something⟩ which instead of being unique in its nature and therefore incapable of being expressed by any other appropriate ⟨word⟩,[*k*] not a mere superfluous synonime of the former; or lastly if he make t̶ ⟨the term⟩ "conscience" itself properly synonimous with any other term [*f 33*] having an appropriate sense, a̶n̶d̶ [. . .] c̶o̶r̶r̶e̶s̶p̶o̶n̶d̶e̶n̶t̶ or [? i̶n̶] ⟨uses it⟩ to express̶i̶n̶g̶ a *result* from t̶w̶o̶-o̶r̶ m̶o̶r̶e̶ [? a̶c̶t̶s̶] o̶r̶ t̶h̶i̶n̶g̶s̶ t̶a̶k̶e̶n̶ the[*l*] combination of two or more distinct predicates or predicabilia[47] of the human Being—in this case the respondent can do no more than restore the terms to their proper meaning, thus showing what that conscience, w̶h̶i̶c̶h̶ the existence of which he asserts, is ᵐnot.[48] Andⁿ if in addition to this he proves by induction that all known languages of the civilized World a̶r̶e̶ manifestly suppose an appropriate sense in the term "ᵉConscience" distinct to each and all of those

---

[*j*] This is C's habitual spelling, though the hand is not his
[*k*] No punctuation in ms   [*l*] Mistakenly cancelled in ms   ᵐ⁻ⁿ ms: not and

44 Tr: "by reason of its absurdity".
45 Cf *Aids to Reflection*: "if I asked, How do you define the *human mind*? the answer must at least *contain*, if not consist of, the words, 'a mind capable of *Conscience*.' For Conscience is no synonime of Consciousness, nor any mere expression of the same as modified by the particular Object" (*AR*—1825—19).
46 That is, as distinguished from complex truths, which by that fact can be analysed into their components.

47 Tr: "things that may be predicated".
48 "Above all things it is incumbent on me who lay such a stress on Conscience, & attach such a sacredness to it, to shew that it is no Socratic Daimon which I mean, but the dictate of universal Reason, accompanied with a feeling of free Agency—that it is *Light*—that an Erring Conscience is no Conscience, and as absurd as an erring Reason—i.e. not Reason/—" (*CN* III 3591).

into which the opponent would reduce it, and that the presumption there-
fore is strong against a position thus contradicting the general accordant
sense of mankind as best revealed in the common form and structure of
all known languages, he has done all that it is either [*f 34*] possible or
desirable to effect. To a Reason higher than that of Man and a tribunal
incomparably more awful must both ⟨the⟩ denial ~~he that makes it~~ [? regu]
and the recreant who dares hazard it be remitted. It has been said [that]
all would have been attempted that is either practicable or desirable, but
in effecting this much will have been done that is indeed most desirable
and not only of high importance in its own worth but, we apprehend, of
strong moral necessity in the present ~~a~~Age. The following chapter will
therefore be devoted to the attempt in which we propose these several
objects—[49]

*o*First, to convey as far as the nature of the subject in connection with
the nature of language will permit the proper and only proper sense of
"Conscience", or if this be too bold a phrase for a professed enquirer to
adopt, the one sense in which we [*f 35*] ourselves understand the term.[50]

2^{ndly}, to enumerate the several meanings in which the term is *not* to
be understood ~~and~~.

*p*Thirdly,*q* to confute the reasons or grounds which have been assigned
in justification of such misappropriation as far as this can be done by out-
ward facts and arguments of Philology, ~~the~~ our opponent persevering in
denying or otherwise explaining of the facts of which we affirm our-
selves assured by inward evidence.

---

o Paragraph break inserted　　*p* Paragraph break inserted
q Written over another word, possibly "lastly"

---

[49] This prospectus for the chapter,
coming as it does as late as f 34, shows
with what a deliberate pace C has been
occupied in laying the foundation stones
for his system. From early in his career
C had stressed the need for such careful
procedure: "With the Metaphysical Rea-
soner every fact must be brought forward
and the ground must be well & carefully
examined where the system is to be
erected" (*Lects 1795—CC—*95). As
John Taylor Coleridge recorded of his
uncle's conversation: "It is impossible to
carry off or commit to paper his long
trains of argument, indeed it is not al-
ways possible to understand them, he
lays the foundation so deep and views
every question in so original a manner"
(*TT—CC—*I 16). Again, in 1809: "I
should first lay the *foundation* well, but

the merit of a foundation is it's depth
and solidity—the ornaments and conve-
niences, the pictures, and gilding, and
stucco-work, the Sunshine and sunshiny
Prospects will come with the superstruc-
ture" (*CL* III 237).

[50] Cf *The Statesman's Manual*: "The
conscience is neither reason, religion, or
will, but an *experience* (sui generis) of
the coincidence of the human will with
reason and religion. It might, perhaps, be
called a *spiritual sensation*; but that there
lurks a contradiction in the terms, and
that it is often deceptive to give a com-
mon or generic name to that, which
being unique, can have no fair analogy.
Strictly speaking, therefore, the con-
science is neither a sensation or a sense,
but a testifying state …" (*LS—CC—*
66–7).

Fourthly, to compare the experience of mankind individual or collective as effects with our opponent's statements on the one hand and with our own on the other as the adequate ʳcauses. ~~and~~

Lastly,ˢ leaving to the reason of mankind to determine on the comparative sufficiency of the two hypotheses as causes, and to the hearts and ⟨the⟩ conscienceness ͭ of the reader, which is the more correspondent to his own ~~in~~ ͧ inward experience as ͮ asserted facts [*f 36*] and which of the two may ʷ safeliest be preferred, which of the two he knows and feels he ought to prefer as maxims of life and principles of morality. ˣ⟨We⟩ will ~~be~~ add one other remark ʸ which, as containing a preliminary of our next chapter, will aptly ~~the~~ form the conclusion of the present. It is this, that as the affirmant or postulant of the fact in question we adhere strictly to the forms of science and refer to no other positions or propositions as Truths, aware that we have undertaken to deduce these from the postulates and the assumption built on the conception of the postulate; and if the arguments of the opponent refer to positions susceptible of an evidence not in themselves or dependent on other positions without arriving at any [*f 37*] one self-evident (like the world of the Brahmains⁵¹ resting on the Elephant which is supported by the Tortoise,⁵² or in a giddy circle in which the motion of the horse is explained by that of the cart, the motion of the cart solved by that of the horse),ᶻ it will be but a further proof of the ~~Philosophical qualifi~~ fitness of our postulate considered as the possible commencing principle of a Philosophy and ~~consequently as long~~ therefore for as many men as have a strivingᵃ after connected insight,⁵³ a presumption of its Truth.

It is enough, if the replies rendered necessary by the desultory argu-

---

ʳ⁻ˢ ms: causes; ~~and~~ lastly [*A vertical stroke has been made here in pencil in the ms*]
ͭ A slip for "conscience" or "consciousness"?
ͧ Cancelled in pencil
ͮ The suggested interpolation "to the" is written in pencil on f 34ͮ and marked for insertion here
ʷ ms: may be
ˣ⁻ʸ Written "One other remark ⟨we⟩ will ~~be~~ add" and marked for transposition
ᶻ Parentheses inserted
ᵃ Written over another word, now illegible

---

⁵¹ C customarily refers to Hindu philosophy as that of the Brahmins, who were the highest Hindu caste, therefore the priestly caste in charge of all religious and philosophical conceiving.

⁵² Cf *Biographia Literaria*: "We might as rationally chant the Brahmin creed of the tortoise that supported the bear, that supported the elephant, that supported the world, to the tune of 'This is the house tht Jack built'" (*BL—CC—* I 137–8).

⁵³ "Connected insight" is the very essence of C's mentation throughout his life, hence the title of the *magnum opus* as a "chain of truths" (*Catena Veritatum*). As L. C. Knights cogently observed: "In the Coleridgean world everything is connected with everything else" (Knights 26).

ments of our antagonist be not charged on us as our own anticipations or as regular parts of the System we are labouring to construct—

[*f 38*]   *b*Chapter VI

When an adherent of the scheme[54] which considers virtue as a species of prudence,[55] giving the name of the latter to those prudential actions, which originate in motives supplied by the present state of existence, while it appropriates the name of Virtue to a prudence determined likewise, and in case of competition, predominantly by ~~motives~~ ⟨self-interest⟩ of a supposed futurity[56]—when such an adherent is pressed with facts of immediate impulses "to do as we should be done by", which, as far as we can know or discover, have reference to neither class of motives, those of this life or those of the life to come, ~~the answer~~ ⟨it⟩ depends on the moral character of the respondent[57] which of the two following assertions will constitute his reply to the objection. The inveterate

b At this point the transcription resumes in JHG's hand

[54] I.e. the scheme espoused, among C's nominated opponents of Christianity, most prominently by Paley. C elsewhere says that "the late Dr. Paley, by a use of terms altogether arbitrary" urged a "distinction between Prudence and Virtue, the former being Self-love in its application to the sum of pain and pleasure" *LS—CC*—186). "The spirit of prudential motive . . . is not, even in respect of *morality* itself, that abiding and continuous principle of action, which is . . . *one* with the faith spoken of by St. Paul" (*LS—CC*—186-7). See further *Friend (CC)* I 108, 313–25 for strictures on Paley and "selfish prudence eked out by superstition".
[55] As C says in *The Friend*, "there is a Wisdom higher than Prudence, to which Prudence stands in the same relation as the Mason and Carpenter to the genial and scientific Architect" (*Friend—CC*—I 118). Again: "The widest maxims of *prudence* are like arms without hearts, disjoined from those feelings which flow forth from *principle* as from a fountain" (*Friend—CC*—I 123).
[56] The fact that C does not name Paley (who did not die until 1805) in this

attack is consistent with his practice on other occasions. For instance, in the *Statesman's Manual* he says "I am most fully persuaded, that the principles both of taste, morals, and religion taught in our most popular compendia of moral and political philosophy, natural theology, evidences of Christianity, &c. are false, injurious, and debasing" (*LS—CC*—110). But in that statement, "the principles . . . taught in our most popular compendia of moral and political philosophy" refers to Paley's *The Principles of Moral and Political Philosophy* of 1785, which was immediately adopted at Cambridge as a standard textbook; the phrase "natural theology" refers to Paley's last book, *Natural Theology* (1802); and the phrase "evidences of Christianity" refers to Paley's famous *View of the Evidences of Christianity* (1794).
[57] Cf C in 1805: "almost all men nowadays act and feel more nobly than they think / yet still the vile cowardly selfish calculating Ethics of Paley, Priestley, Lock, & other *Erastians*, do woefully influence & determine our course of action/" (*CN* II 2627).

worldling^c will boldly deny the fact and, if his understanding be better than his heart, will attempt to explain the appearance by distinguishing between Selfishness, or the unconsidered obedience to [*f* 39] an immediate appetite or restlessness, and a Self-interest, i.e. the extension and modification of the same selfishness by Fore-thought, i.e. by an imagination of the future and the present. Then what he cannot derive from motives of Self-interest he will attribute to impulses of selfishness. Now this argument supposes the plenary causative or determining power in these motives or impulses, so that both the one and the other do not at all differ from physical impact as far as the relation of cause and effect is concerned. For if it were otherwise, we should still have to ask what determined the mind to permit this determining power to these motives and impulses.^{d} Or why did the mind or Will sink from its proper superiority to the physical laws of cause and effect, and place itself in the same class with the bullet or the billiard-ball? It would be most easy to trace this whole mechanical doctrine of causative impulses and determining motives to a mere impersonation of general terms. For what is a Motive?[58] Not^e a thing, but the thought of a thing. But as all thoughts are not motives, [*f* 40] in order to specify the class of thoughts we must add the predicate a "determining" ~~thought~~, and a motive must be defined [as] a determining thought.[59] But again, what is a Thought? Is this a thing or an individual? What are its circumscriptions, what the interspaces between it and another? Where does it begin? Where does it end? Far more readily could we apply these questions to a notion below, or the drops of water which we may imagine as the component integers of the ocean; or [as] by "a billion" we mean no more than a particular movement of the sea, so neither by "a thought" can we mean more than the mind thinking in some one direction. Consequently, a motive is neither more nor less than the act of an intelligent being determining itself, and the very watchword of the necessitarian is found to be, in fact, at once an assertion and

---

^{c} ms: wordling ^{d} ms: impulses? ^{e} ms: not

[58] Cf *Aids to Reflection*: "the Man makes the motive, and not the motive the Man. What is a strong motive to one man, is no motive at all to another. If, then, the man determines the motive, what determines the Man—to a good and worthy act, we will say, or a virtuous Course of Conduct? The intelligent Will, or the self-determining Power?" (*AR*—1825—67)

[59] This continuing discussion of "motive" is a necessary corollary to the ex-

trication of "responsible Will". For a pertinent parallel discussion, not only of "motive", but of "cause" and "ground" as well, see *SW & F* (*CC*) I 399–401. The necessitarianism in which C had steeped himself in youth was tantamount to the views of Spinoza against which C directed his whole force of opposition. See "Excursus Note XIV: The Religious Heterodoxy of Hartley, Priestley, and Godwin" *CPT* 311–14.

a definition of frequency, i.e. the power of an intelligent being to determine its own agency. But even this is for us superfluous; it is enough that ~~the upholder of this~~ he who upholds this scheme of universal selfishness [*f 41*] or self-interest, not from any corruption but from the original necessity of our nature, implies the denial of a responsible Will. He refuses our postulate: he considers our foundation as emptiness, and it would be equally absurd on both sides to enter into any examination of the intended superstructure. The other answer differs from the preceding not perhaps in substantial value, for by fair consequence it would lead to the same result—yet still it differs as symptomatic of a different character in the respondent himself. If we object to such a man, "Will*f* you be faithful to a confiding friend, or grateful to a benefactor in the hour of his distress, only as far as you calculate on a renewal of his power and will to benefit you?", *g*or, "Would*h* you ~~do other~~ have done otherwise, though at the moment you had not been reflecting on the consequences after death?", "Nay!", would be the reply, "I should, I must have done my duty without the immediate anticipation of any consequences from without, present or future, and yet my actions originate in Self-love, though I did my duty solely [*f 42*] for the pleasures of a good Conscience." Various are the ways in which the hollowness of this position, every word of which it is composed, ~~pl~~ the very terms, "Pleasure", "Self", "Love", "Conscience", nay, the very preposition "For"*i* would, if strictly defined and appropriated, lead to its ~~confrontation~~ exposure by a detection of the equivocation contained in each. We will confine ourselves for the present to the term "Pleasure".[60] Not without some attention to a kindred sentiment expressed in the thousand times quoted line, "O Happiness, our being's end and aim",[61] not ignorant how innocently thousands have used both the one and the other as expressing their own thoughts, but at the same time fully aware of the exceeding importance of Hobbes'*j* remark, "animadverte quiam sit ab improprietate verborum pronam hominibus prolabi in errores circa res",[62] in accurate language is ~~both~~ the

---

f ms: will   *g–h* ms: Or would

i An unnecessary "it" is written on f 41ᵛ and marked for insertion here, evidently because "For" was interpreted as the first word of a new sentence rather than as the preposition to which C refers

j ms: Hobbe's

[60] That is, to the word that indicates the central core of Epicureanism, which C saw as infecting the whole spiritual climate of the Europe of his time. See Prolegomena III: The Epicurean and Stoic Background.

[61] Alexander Pope *An Essay on Man* Epistle IV line 1.

[62] Hobbes *Examinatio et emendatio mathematicae hodiernae*, in *Opera Philosophica* ed Molesworth IV 83. Cf *CN* I 911 and tr in 911n.

effect ~~and cause~~ of confused, and the cause of erroneous, conception.[63] Under the vague term "Happiness" there are three ~~kinds of~~ states of being confounded, and as the term can by no means be taken as a [*f 43*] summum genus having the other as its subgenera, it would be most desirable to confine it to the sense included in its etymon.[64] "*Hap*" originally designated not mere chance but a fortunate chance, as is the case with the word "Fortune" itself and our own anglo-saxon "*Luck*". "Fortunate", "lucky" imply good luck, good fortune; to express the contrary, we must add the epithet by which the contrary is *ᵏ*expressed. And*ˡ* in like manner "hap", "happy"; the simple negation "hapless" expresses mishap, and "unhappy" [. . .] has the like force. Happiness, therefore, is the aggregate of fortunate chances; but our birth, wealth, person, natural talents, opportunities of cultivating them, health, country—~~and~~with the other *circumstances* ⟨of man,⟩ quicquid homines cicumstat,[65] are all prizes in the lottery of life. These, therefore, are all so far "haps"; and the aggregate, and the state that results therefrom, are ~~in~~ [. . .] "*Happiness*" in the only proper sense of that word. The more reflecting who reject alike the notions of chance and of fate are accustomed [*f 44*] to express the same meaning by the words "favorable providence". And even so in the greek, the epicurean would express our "happiness" by "ευτυχια", the Stoic or Platonist[66] by "ευδαιμονια". Those, therefore, who have not so far entangled their better mind as to have rejected the belief that man is a responsible agent, and who consequently must adopt the division of Epictetus[67] of the τα εφημεν, or that which appertains to our Will as our

---

ᵏ⁻ˡ ms: expressed: &

[63] "'Notice how easily men slip from improper use of words into errors about things themselves' . . . . This was a favourite maxim of Coleridge's; he copied it into a notebook early in 1801, used it as a 'text' for 'a sort of sermon' in the third of the four philosophical letters he wrote to Josiah Wedgwood (Feb 1801), and had more recently resurrected it as one of the mottoes for Essay III in *PGC* (1814). *CN* I 911 and n; *CL* II 961; *BL* (1907) II 228" (W. Jackson Bate).

[64] In the *Philosophical Lectures* C, in speaking of Greek philosophy, says "Happiness is everywhere stated as the aim of man" (*P Lects*—1949—140) and complains about the confusion induced by lack of distinction in usages: "I know not a more impressive instance than this of the word 'happiness'. There are four perfectly distinct states" (*P Lects*—1949—141).

[65] Tr: "whatever surrounds men".

[66] "It is one of my Objects to prove the difference of the Christian Faith from Platonism even in its purest form—but so is the Xtn Moral System different from the Stoic—but as no one on this account denies the resemblances & coincidences in the latter, so neither ought we to do so in the former" (*CN* III 4316).

[67] Greek Stoic philosopher (*c* 55–135 A.D.). Originally a slave, was freed and taught philosophy in Rome, from which he was expelled by Domitian in 90 A.D. Epictetus left no writings, but his philosophy is contained in the *Discourses* and *Enchiridion* of his pupil Flavius Arrian.

proper self, and the τα εφ ουκ 'ημεν, ought to accept the former, τα εφ ημεν, and find some more appropriate term for them, which belongs exclusively to the latter, τα ουκ εφ ημεν. The things to be thus excepted, and for which "happiness" is an inappropriate term, are all those which we have produced in the first instance from within by the exertion of the Will in obedience to our sense of duty. I should not hesitate to say, "I am happy in a father or mother"; but had I successfully devoted my best efforts to the virtuous education of a child, or had I sought out a man from having received proof of his virtues, and if [*f 45*] by the likeness of my own character, a likeness produced in me by many struggles, many defeats earnestly bewailed, and some ~~consequences~~ conquests achieved by my own efforts, and lastly by giving and receiving moral support and comfort, I had become this man's friend, ~~I sh~~ in these cases I should prefer saying, "I am blessed in a virtuous son, I am blessed in a noble friend". And yet tempering stoic dignity, I should gratefully acknowledge my "happiness" too in these blessings, i.e. I should acknowledge how much even of these things I owed to the favour of providence, ευ-δαιμονια. To contemplate the state in which the offspring of ignorant and vicious men are commonly found, to walk through the purlieus of S! Giles's, and to deduce from the facts there seen grounds of thankfulness for mine own happier lot, and at the same time of pity and allowance for the unhappy, without losing our faith in the amenability of all men to moral judgement—this*ᵐ* is indeed a giant difficulty, a difficulty the single fact of thousands [*f 46*] of these ignorant, vicious, and most unhappy men suddenly awakened as they have been to compunction and repentance by a single discourse, a single well-timed appeal to their conscience—this,*ⁿ* I say, this strong testimony, which the heart gives concerning its own state when the unhappy man loses the sense of regret, which alone is the appropriate feeling for unhappy or calamitous circumstances, in remorse and self-reproach—nay, the struggles of the guilty criminal to find a refuge from the anguish of guilt in the ~~assumption~~ doctrines of necessity or fatal influence, and the vanity of these efforts, will more avail to overcome than all the mere reasonings which the logician can draw from all the premises which outward experience can supply—and the intellectual solution of this awful enigma does not be-

---

ᵐ ms: This   *ⁿ* ms: This

For C's longstanding knowledge of and interest in Epictetus see e.g. *CN* ii 2236.

See in general Prolegomena iii: The Epicurean and Stoic Background.

long to the present place and subject. Enough has been done if we have shown and elucidated the proper force and extent of the term "happiness".[68]

To express ourselves accurately and thereby to prevent that confusion [*f 47*] of thought which the use of equivocal terms cannot fail to engender, we must reduce the aggregate of desideranda[69]—whatever, I mean, a man is bound or permitted to pursue—to four heads, ~~the several relations of which will appear without any further analysis than that which has been given above; Of the~~ of which we take "happiness" as the third. Of the remaining three, the second only presents any difficulty as to the name fittest to express it. The first, or "Pleasure," comprises all the modes of being which arise from the correspondence of the external stimuli in kind and degree to our sensible life, as variously stimulable and vice versa under the universal law of reciprocity or action and reaction. It is peculiar to this ~~term~~ that considered irrelatively for itself alone, it offers no other criterion of preference but that of quantity in degree or in duration. ~~w~~Where pleasure alone is the object, the choice between different pleasures depends on the question, how much! and how long will it continue? and with what effects on other [*f 48*] pleasures? But even in this we admit too much, for in extending ~~judgement concerning~~ ⟨the notion⟩ of pleasure from quantity or present amount to comparative duration and causative influence, we already suppose the intervention and union both of power and motives which do not result from the relations between the animal life and the stimulants, organic or external, that call it into sensibility. The doctors of Self-love[70] are misled by the wrong ~~ap-~~

---

[68] Of the four distinctions of happiness described by C in *Philosophical Lectures*, "The third is a speculative point which arises from the consideration of our extreme dependence on external things. That a man has reason to congratulate himself on having been born in such an hour and climate under such and such circumstances, this the ancients called Εὐυχτια, Εὐδαιμονία". That is when the Gods were favorable to them, and we call it 'happiness' when things happen well" (*P Lects*—1949—141).

[69] Tr: "things to be desired".

[70] Paley's "prudence" was "Self-love in its application to the sum of pain and pleasure" (*LS—CC—*89). Kant frequently uses the term "self-love" (*Selbst-*

liebe) in his discussions of moral desirability. See e.g. *Kant* IV 406. Elsewhere C attributes the first explicit philosophy of "self-love" to Aristippus, "who took the principle of self-love to himself, and (as a man who felt in himself, in the enjoyment of good health, good fortune, and high connexions, that he was doing no great harm in the world, and thought, as many men of the kind have, that to live well and comfortably was the great end of life) he founded a system" (*P Lects*—1949—154). For C the doctors of self-love were pre-eminently the representatives of modern Epicureanism. See below f 126ᵛ. See the equation of Paley and Epicurean doctrine at f 62ᵛ. See further Prolegomena III–IV.

plication or equivocal use of words. "We love ourselves", they ^osay. Now^p this is impossible for a finite being in the absolute meaning of the term "Self". For if [. . .] by the "Self" we mean the principle of individuation—the band or copula which gives a real unity to all the complex products, functions, and faculties of an animal—a real unity, I say, in contradistinction from the mere semblance or total impression produced by an aggregate on the mind of the beholder, and even from that combination of parts which originates and has its whole end and object [*f* 49] in an external ageneyt—a unity different, in short, from a steam engine or other machine, it is manifest that the self in this sense must be anterior to all our sensations, etc., and to all the objects toward which they may be directed. Befor Nothing can become an ⟨the⟩ object of consciousness but by reflection, not even the things of perception. Now the Self is ever pre-supposed, and like all other supersensual subjects can be presented ⟨made known⟩ to the mind only by a ^qrepresentative. And^r again, what that representative shall be is by no means unalterably fixed in human nature by nature itself, but on the contrary varies with the growth, bodily, moral, and intellectual, of each individual. Even the combination of the sense of Touch, and more strictly of Double-touch,[71] with the visual image of such parts of our body as we are able or accustomed to behold is so far from being the only possible representative of self that it is not even the first in the earlier periods of infancy: the mother or the nurse is the self of the child. And who has not experienced in dreams the attachment [*f* 50] of our personal identity to forms the most remote from our own?[72] All actions, therefore, which proceed directly from the individual without reflection, as those of a hungry beast rushing to its food, all those in which the volition acts singly and immediately towards the object to be appropriated, may be classed as selfish,

^{o-p} ms: say: now   ^{q-r} ms: representative: and

[71] Keats, in his recountal of the variegated contents of Coleridge's conversation, lists one of the topics as "single and double touch" (Keats *Letters* II 89). Double touch—a phrase used by Euler before C (Beer *Intelligence* 84)—was a complex and recurring Coleridgean emphasis. It was "the generation of the Sense of Reality and Life out of us, from the Impersonation of double Touch" (*CN* I 1827); and C had a "theory of Volition as a mode of double Touch" (*P Lects*—1949—423–4). At the centre of the elusive complex seems to be a conception of double touch as an orientating phenome-non: "Babies touch by taste at first—then about 5 months old they go from the Palate to the hand—& are fond of feeling what they have taste—/Association of the Hand with the Taste" (*CN* I 924).

[72] The focus on the importance of dreams is a characteristic both of C and of Romanticism as such. See Albert Béguin *L'Ame romantique et le rêve* (Paris 1939). As Henry Nelson Coleridge noted in 1823: "My uncle in great force at John's. He treated the subject of ghosts and dreams at great length." And see Woodring's long note (*TT—CC—*I 52, 52–3 n 2).

perhaps, but have no pretence to the name of ^sSelf-love. Or^t as far as any reflection is supposed, or as far as the simple perception of the object is taken as a substitute for reflection, we ought to say that the food in the trough is the temporary *self* of the hog,[73] i.e. it is that form with which the volition, the thoughts, and the sensations of the animal are ~~con~~ united without any intermediate. In the absolute meaning of "Self" as the perpetual antecedent within us, Self-love, we repeat, is inconceivable; and in its secondary, representative or symbolical meaning "Self" signifies only a less degree of distance, a determination of value by distance, and the comparative narrowness of our moral view. Hence the body becomes our *self* when the reflections [*f 51*] on our sensations, ~~obj~~ desires, and objects have been habitually appropriated to it in too great a proportion. But this is not a necessity of our nature. Even in this life of imperfection there is a state possible in which a man might truly say "my Self loves A or B",^u freely constituting the object, i.e. the representative or objective ~~love~~ ⟨Self⟩ (~~as~~ distinguished from the primary originative and subjective self) in whatever it wills to love, commands what it wills, and wills what it commands. ^wWithout this power, indeed, the commandment "that we should love our neighbour as our self and God more than either" would be a mockery.[74] The difference between Self-love and a Self that loves consists in this: that the objects of the former are *given* to it according to the law of the senses and organization, while the latter (a Self that loves freely) determines the objects according to a higher law. The first loves, if we may dare use that term to express so unworthy a relation, because in its abandonment to its animal life it must; the second, because [*f 52*] it ^vshould. And^w we trust that we shall hereafter make it appear that the guilt of the first, in any particular ~~objective~~ thought or ~~deed~~ single deed or series of deeds but pre-existent, by which the Self of the individual, which in this sense is equivalent to the Will, abandoned its power of true agency in that action in and by which the Self willed its own form, or in and by which the Will engendered a false and phantom self. This is indeed a ^xmystery! How^y can it be otherwise?

---

^{s−t} ms: Self-love or   ^u Quotation marks inserted
^{v−w} ms: should and   ^{x−y} ms: mystery!—how

[73] The subtext here is the identification, stemming from antiquity, of the Epicurean as a hog. For the famous phrase, "a hog from Epicurus's herd" (*Epicuri de grege porcum*) see Horace *Epistles* I iv 16.
[74] Cf Mark 12.30−1: "And thou shalt love the Lord thy God with all thy heart, and with all thy soul, and with all thy mind, and with all thy strength. This *is* the first commandment. And the second *is* like, *namely* this, Thou shalt love thy neighbour as thyself. There is none other commandment greater than these." See also Matt 22.39, Luke 10.29, Rom 13.9, Gal 5.14, James 2.8.

For if the Will be unconditional, if it either be not at all (except as a su-
perfluous word)[z] or properly originative, it must of necessity be inex-
plicable and incomprehensible.[75] For to understand and comprehend a
thing is to see what the conditions and causes of it are.[76] mMore [a]we
cannot say[b] in the present state of our investigation; nor indeed, accord-
ing to the announced plan of our procedure, is there any need that more
be said, for we have begun by proving that ~~the~~ a responsible Will is not
only the postulate of all [*f 53*] religion but the necessary datum inca-
pable from its very nature of any direct proof—the datum,[77] we say, and
ground of all the reasonings and conclusions, which in the particular re-
ligion are assumed as already granted. We will merely suggest, as a sort
of corollary to the above definition of the objective Self and its depen-
dence on proximity, that the grossness of Self-love is no less diminished
by distance in time than by distance in space, and that an individual who
is capable of deliberately sacrificing an immediate and certain gratifica-
tion of the Self to a greater good, of that which his reason enables him
to look forward to as a Self fifty years[c] hence, perhaps even under the
supposition of such relations as imply the cessation of all animal sensa-
tions and the gratifications resulting therefrom, exhibits as unselfish a
love, as complete a transfer of the idea "Self" from his visual form and
the feelings and impulses connected ~~the~~ with it as if the distance had been
in space, [*f 54*] and the transfer had been made towards a contemporary.
In both instances the term "*Self*" is generalized, in both instances the self
and the neighbour are rendered visual synonymes, inasmuch as both are
taken up into and become One in a higher Love which comprehends both
not as the result but as the cause and principle of their union. Not the sin-
gle soul, as One of a class, is it that contributes to the idea of that which

---

[z] Parentheses inserted   [a–b] This phrase is written twice in the ms
[c] ms: hears [*correction supplied in pencil on f 52ᵛ*]

[75] This insistence is a crucial source
of will's value for C. Cf a marginal note:
". . . the Will, the ineffable Causa Sui, et
Fons Unitatis in tota infinita entis sui
plenitudine, is evermore and eternally
impassible" (*CN* IV 5413). See Prole-
gomena XVII: The Concept of Will.

[76] C attached importance to the dis-
tinguishing of "comprehend" and "ap-
prehend". Thus, "how can any Spiritual
Truth be comprehended? Who can *com*-
prehend his own Will or his own Per-
sonëty? (i.e. his 'I') or his own Mind, i.e.
his Person, or his own *Life*? But we can

distinctly *ap*prehend them" (Brinkley
385). Again: "Well may I *believe* what I
do not *comprehend*, when there are so
many things which I *know* yet do not
comprehend—my Life, for instance, my
Will, my rationality, &c. But let us be on
our guard not to confound *com*prehend-
ing with *ap*prehending. I do not, even
because I can not, believe what I do not
*ap*prehend—i.e. I cannot assent to the
meaning of words, to which I attach no
meaning, tho' I may believe in the wis-
dom of the Utterer" (Ibid. 17–18).

[77] Tr: "given".

we call the soul, as the subject of woe or weal in a permanent state; but it is the idea alien from all insulated forms, and which can be as little appropriated by an individual consciousness as the light of the sun by an individual eye—it is the idea which gives the meaning to the soul, a meaning unattainable by those who have not learnt the possibility of finding now a Self in another and now another, yea! even an alien and an enemy in the self.

[*f 55*] We may now see the nature and origin of that position, which is commonly the last resort to which the better-minded advocates of Self-love betake themselves when all other pretexts have been evacuated. To wit: "They do their duty in expectation of the pleasures of a good conscience. Their Will, still as before derivative and dependent, originates in a motive, and their motive is the expected pleasure of a good conscience." Where the whole proposition consists of sophisms and equivocations, it is indifferent at what point we commence the series of detections. If the Will originate in motives, in what do the motives originate? If we consider the Will (and in this place it must be so considered) as an abiding faculty, a habit or fixed ~~pre~~ and systematic predisposition, the reverse of the position is evident to the most superficial observation. ⟨It is⟩ not*d* the motives [that] govern the man, but it is the man that makes the [*f 56*] motives—and these, indeed, are so various, mutable, and chameleon-like that it is ~~a matter~~ often as difficult as fortunately it is a matter of comparative indifference to determine what a man's motive is for this or that particular action. A wise man will rather enquire what the person's *e*general objects*f* are—"What does he habitually wish?"[78]— thence*g* deducing the state of the Will and the impulses in which that state reveals itself, and which are commonly the true efficient causes of human actions, inasmuch as without these the motive itself could not have become *a motive*. Let a haunch of venison represent the motive, and let a keen appetite, the consequence of exercise and the symptom or manifestation of health, represent the impulse: then place the same or some more favorite dish before the same man, sick, dyspeptic, and stomach-worn, and we may then ~~weigh~~ estimate the comparative weight of motives and impulses. If in the present work we may without impropriety

---

d ms: Not

e–f In the ms these words are reversed, but their intended order is indicated by the numbers "1" and "2" written above them

g ms: Thence

[78] "It is a matter of comparative indifference & infinite difficulty to determine what a man's *motives* are for this or that particular action. Know his *objects*—what does he habitually wish? habitually pursue?" (*CN* I 947).

refer [*f 57*] to the work of an author, next to Holy Writ, the most in-
structive, we would add that without the perception of this truth it is
impossible to understand (I might say Shakespeare generally, but more
particularly) the character of Iago,[79] who is represented as now as-
signing one and now another and again a third motive for his conduct,
each a different motive and all alike the mere fictions of his own rest-
less nature, distempered by a keen sense of his own intellectual supe-
riority and a vicious habit of assigning the precedence or primacy to the
intellectual instead of the moral, and haunted by the love of exerting
power on those especially who are his superiors in moral and practical
estimation. Yet how many among our modern critics have attributed to
the profound author this, the appropriate inconsistency of the character
itself. A second illustration: did[h] Curio,[80] the quondam patriot, re-
former, and semi-revolutionist,[81] abjure his opinions [*f 58*] and yell
the foremost in the hunt of persecution against his old friends and fel-
low-philosophists with a cold, clear pre-determination, formed at one
moment, of making £5,000 a year by his apostasy?[82] I neither know or

[h] ms: Did

[79] Cf *Omniana*: ". . . the character of Iago, who is represented as now assigning one, and then another, and again a third, motive for his conduct, all alike the mere fictions of his restless nature, distempered by a keen sense of his intellectual superiority, and haunted by the love of exerting power, on those especially who are his superiors in practical and moral excellence" (*SW & F—CC—*I 310).

[80] Caius Scribonius Curio (84–49 B.C.) was a turncoat in the struggle between Pompey and Caesar, defecting from the former to curry favour with the latter.

[81] Cf *Omniana*: "A second illustration,—Did *Curio*, the quondam patriot, reformer and semi-revolutionist, abjure his opinions, and yell the foremost in the hunt of persecution against his old friends and fellow-philosophists, with a cold clear pre-determination, formed at one moment of making 5000l. a-year by his apostasy?—I neither know nor care. Probably not" (*SW & F—CC—*I 311).

[82] Curio is James Mackintosh (later Sir James Mackintosh). Cf C in 1801: "Did Mackintosh change his opinions, with a cold clear predetermination, formed at one moment, to make 5000£ a year by that change?" (*CN* I 947). Mackintosh, like C, had been an early enthusiast for the French Revolution, and had in 1791 written a much-noticed rebuttal to Burke's *Reflections on the Revolution in France* called *Vindiciae Gallicae*. Later in the decade, however, Mackintosh became a friend and disciple of Burke, and in 1800 totally abjured his earlier support for Jacobinism and the French Revolution. He went on to have a varied and successful career as lawyer, academic, and doctor. He was related by different marriages both to C's newspaper editor-friend, Daniel Stuart, and to C's benefactors, the Wedgwoods; and C seems to have felt himself in direct competition with Mackintosh's intellectual versatility. He frequently spoke of Mackintosh dismissively ("Never yet did any human Being gain any thing by self-desertion. I shall never forget the *disgust*, with which Mackintosh's 'bear witness, I *recant, abjure* and *abhor* the principles'—i.e. of his own Vindiciae Gallicae, struck his Auditors in Lincoln's Inn—" (*CL* IV 713). Hazlitt records that in reference to *Vindiciae Gallicae* C stigmatized Mackintosh as "a clever scholastic man—a

care. Probably not.[83] But this I know, that to be thought a man of conse-
quence by his contemporaries, to be admitted into the society of his su-
periors in artificial rank, to excite the admiration of Lords, to live in splen-
dor and sensual luxury, have been the objects of his habitual wishes.[84] A
flash of lightning has turned at once the polarity of the compass needle,
and so, perhaps, now and then but as rarely, a violent motive may revo-
lutionize a man's opinions and professions.[85] But more frequently his
honesty dies away imperceptibly from evening into twilight, and from
twilight to utter darkness. He now turns hypocrite so gradually and by
such tiny atoms of motion that by the time he has arrived at a given point
he forgets his own hypocrisy in the imperceptible [*f 59*] degrees of his
own conversion.[86] The difference between such a man and a bolder liar
is merely that between the hour hand and that which tells the seconds on
a watch. Of the former you can see only the motion, of the latter both the
past motion and the present moving. Yet there is perhaps more hope of
the latter rogue, for he has lied to mankind only and not to himself[87]—
the former lies to his own heart, as well as to the public.[88]

---

master of the topics,—or as the ready
warehouseman of letters, who knew ex-
actly where to lay his hand on what he
wanted, though the goods were not his
own. He thought him no match for
Burke, either in style or matter. Burke
was a metaphysician, Mackintosh a mere
logician. Burke was an orator (almost a
poet) who reasoned in figures, because
he had an eye for nature; Mackintosh, on
the other hand, was a rhetorician, who
had only an eye to common-places" (*H
Works* XVII 111).

[83] Cf C in 1801: "I neither know nor
care. Probably not" (*CN* I 947).

[84] Cf C in 1801: "But this I know,
that to be thought a man of consequence
by his contemporaries, to exercise power,
to excite admiration, & to make a fortune
are his habitual objects of wish & pur-
suit—" (*CN* I 947). For further adverse
comment: "Sir James Mackintosh was
the King of the Men of Talent. He was
an elegant converser . . . . The mind of
Mackintosh was a hortus siccus, full of
specimens of every kind of plant, but
dwarfed, ready cut and dried . . . . what-
ever was the subject, Mackintosh had a
prearranged discourse on it. . . . but he
possessed not a ray of Genius" (*TT—
CC—*I 40–2; and see Woodring's long

note, 40–1 n 4).

[85] Cf C in 1801: "A flash of Lightning
has turned at once the polarity of the
Compass Needle—& so perhaps now &
then but as rarely, a violent motive may
revolutionize a man's professions—"
(*CN* I 947).

[86] Cf C in 1801: "but more frequently
his honesty dies away from evening into
twilight & from twilight to night—he
turns hypocrite so gradually, by such lit-
tle tiny atoms, that by the time he has ar-
rived at a given ⟨point⟩ he forgets his
own hypocrisy in his *conversion*"(*CN* I
947). The historian E. P. Thompson has
stigmatized C himself as exactly con-
forming to such a description, as did
some critics in his own day. See Thomp-
son's review of David Erdman in *The
Wordsworth Circle* (1979).

[87] Cf C in 1801: "The difference be-
tween such a man, & a bolder Liar, is
merely that between the Hour Hand, &
the Hand that tells seconds, on a Watch.
Of the one you can see only the Motion,
of the other both the motion & the mov-
ing.—yet there is more hope of the latter
Rogue—he has only lied to mankind, &
not to himself—" (*CN* I 947).

[88] Cf *Omniana*: "But this I know, that
to be thought a man of consequence by

Having thus dispatched the term "Motive", we may now proceed to the term "Pleasure" for the purpose of comprizing in a few words what has been unfolded more at large on the preceding pages. And here it may be permitted us to observe in general that words truly synonymous, i.e. having precisely the same definition, as they cannot exist in an original and homogeneous language, except as a through the degeneracy of the nation whose language it is (ex.gr., κρασις[89] and οινος[90] in the modern greek, both [*f60*] synonymes for wine), so are they defects in the languages of mixed origin.

Defects, we say, as long as they words remain synonymous,[91] though as ready-made materials of future appropriation, when in the progress of intellectual development new distinctions are brought into consciousness, they may be regarded as the reversionary wealth of a language. But while they remain they are not merely excrescences but those in which all the bad humours lurk and obtain a semblance of organization. The use which Hobbes and his disciples made of the terms "Compulsion"and "Obligation", till his antagonist,[92] Bishop

his contemporaries, to be admitted into the society of his superiors in artificial rank, to excite the admiration of Lords, to live in splendor and sensual luxury, have been the objects of his habitual wishes. A flash of lightning has turned at once the polarity of the compass needle; and so, perhaps, now and then, but as rarely, a violent motive may revolutionize a man's opinions and professions. But more frequently his honesty dies away imperceptibly from evening into twilight,—and from twilight to utter darkness.—He turns hypocrite so gradually, and by such tiny atoms of motion, that by the time he has arrived at a given point, he forgets his own hypocrisy in the imperceptible degrees of his own conversion. The difference between such a man and a bolder liar, is merely that between the hour-hand, and that which tells the seconds, on a watch. Of the former you see only the motion, of the latter both the past motion and the present moving. Yet there is, perhaps, more hope of the latter rogue, for he has lied to mankind only and not to himself—the former lies to his own heart, as well as to the public" (*SW & F—CC*—I 311).

[89] Tr: "a mixture of wine and water".
[90] Tr: "wine". Actually *krasis* and

oinos are not perfect synonyms, for the former refers to a mixture of wine and water.

[91] C placed great philosophical emphasis on the necessity of desynonymizing terms. For him that was always the true path to intellectual cogency, as can be seen in his desynonymization of imagination and fancy, reason and understanding, and a multitude of other dialectical terms. He insists that "all Languages perfect themselves by a gradual process of desynonymizing words originally equivalent" (*CN* III 4397). Again, "The whole process of human intellect is gradually to desynonymize terms" (*P Lects*—1949—173); "in all societies there exists an instinct of growth, a certain collective, unconscious good sense working progressively to desynonymize those words originally of the same meaning" (*BL—CC*—I 82).

[92] See in Vol IV of Molesworth's ed of the English Works of Hobbes, *The Questions concerning Liberty, Necessity, Chance Clearly Stated and Debated between Dr. Bramhall Bishop of Derry, and Thomas Hobbes, of Malmesbury* (1656). In the same volume see pp 279–384: "An Answer to a Book Published by Dr. Bramhall, late Bishop of Derry,

Bramhall,[93] had de-synonymized[94] them and thus enabled his readers to call into distinct consciousness the proper contradistinguishing character already implied in the words "*Should*" and the conditional "*Must*", i.e. "I *must* do this, though I *can*, perhaps, far more easily and pleasurably—yet still I *must* if I will not forfeit my sole proper claim to the name of *i*man." These,*j* I say, and the confusion still existing [*f 61*] among the followers of Hartley[95] and Priestley[96] between necessity,

i–j ms: man—Thus

called the 'Catching of the Leviathan'". This tract consists of Bramhall's attack on Hobbes's *Leviathan*, which attack Hobbes says was written ten years ealier, interspersed with Hobbes's answers, the whole in the form of a dialogue.

[93] John Bramhall (1594–1663), Anglican Bp of Derry, then Abp of Armagh (1661); speaker, Irish House of Lords (1661). Argued against Hobbes on free will.

[94] Cf C in 1821: "It is sufficient that no heterogeneous senses are confounded under the same term, as was the case prior to Bishop Bramhall's controversy with Hobbes, who had availed himself of the (at that time, and in the common usage) equivalent words compel and oblige to compound the thought of moral obligation, with that of compulsion and physical necessity" (*SW & F—CC*—II 933). See *Philosophical Lectures*: "Even so late as the time of Charles the First and the Republic of England, the words 'compelled' and 'obliged' were perfectly synonymous. Hobbes and other men of his mind took advantage of this one term and contended therefore that as everybody acknowledged that men were obliged to do such and such things, and that if a man were obliged it was synonymous to say he was compelled, there could never arise anything like guilt.... In this instance they are two perfectly different things and every man feels them to be different, and the best way is to use 'obliged' when we mean what a man ought to do, and the word 'compelled' when we mean what a man must do whether he likes it or not. And with this single clearing up of the terms the whole basis fell at once, as far at least as that argument was convincing" (*P*

Lects—1949—174). See further *Logic* (*CC*) 123: "Hobbes repeatedly speaks of the will as compelled by certain causes where an accurate speaker would say impelled." See also *BL* (*CC*) I 87. For Bramhall's point C drew on its citation in Mendelssohn's *Jerusalem* (1791) 12.

[95] David Hartley (1705–1757), English psychologist and philosopher. His *Observations on Man, his Frame, his Duty, and his Expectations* (1749) was built on the philosophy of Newton and Locke, and espoused association psychology, mechanism, necessitarianism, and Christianity. C's early enthusiasm for it is attested by his naming his eldest son after Hartley; but later on Hartleyan associationism became one of his most strenuously opposed antagonists. In 1794, in his early poem, *Religious Musings*, C rendered the opinion that Hartley was "he of mortal kind / Wisest, he first who marked the ideal tribes / Up the fine fibres through the sentient brain" (*PW—EHC*—I 123 lines 268–70). Also in 1794 C said "I am a compleat Necessitarian and understand the subject as well almost as Hartley himself" (*CL* I 137).

[96] Joseph Priestley (1733–1804), English anti-Trinitarian clergyman, controversialist, scholar, and scientist. Discovered oxygen, was a founder of Unitarianism ("Priestley was the author of the modern Unitarianism", said C in 1834 (*TT—CC*—I 488)). He moved to America after his house in Birmingham was burnt by a mob because of his sympathy for the French Revolution. Among his many works were *The History and Present State of Electricity* (1767), *Essay on the First Principles of Government* (1768), and *General History of the Christian Church* (1790–92). Priestley,

which in its absoluteness is one with, or rather implied in, perfect liberty, and necessitation per alium[97] sive ab extra,[98] or compulsion proper, are striking instances and illustrations.*

Now apply this to the word *"Pleasure"*—will you contend that it is a nomen genericum[99] including all things that are to be pursued, "our being's end and aim", and of course as its correspondent antithet, ⟨that⟩ *pain* comprizes all things that are to be eschewed? But if this were so, both pleasure and pain must be mere superfluities, ⟨both⟩ in our ~~and all other~~ languages and in the languages of all civilized nations—which yet no man in his senses would assert, for we have already two words expressing their generalisation, viz., *"good"* and *"evil"*.[100] If I say pleasure is a good and pain an evil, will it be pretended that I convey the same impression, and am talking as childishly, as if I had said black is black and white is white?[k] [*f 62*] Shall I not be as intelligible to all men ⟨as when I say that⟩ green is a colour and an octave a sound? Even so: when I say pleasure is a good, I imply that it is one of a *class* and, of course, needing some additional definition ⟨to distinguish it⟩ from others co-ordinated with it. If a sensualist[101] should say, "I know no good but pleasure and no evil but pain", the best personal answer might be, "the more beast you!"[102] But logically it might be replied, "Your[l] own

---

* [*Written on f 61ᵛ:*] For a list of those equivocal terms connected with ethics and intellectual analysis, I refer [to] the logical prolegomena and glossary which is intended as an introduction to this work.

---

[k] ms: white.   [l] ms: your

---

like Hartley, espoused the doctrine of necessitarianism, and he produced a shortened version of Hartley's *Observations on Man* in 1775. C called him "patriot, and saint, and sage" in his poem *Religious Musings* (*PW*—EHC—I 123 line 371).

[97] Tr: "by means of another".

[98] Tr: "or from without".

[99] Tr: "generic name".

[100] The argument continues to press towards the question of the existence of good and evil, for this whole chapter is devoted to the illumination of "three ultimate *Facts*; namely, the Reality of the LAW OF CONSCIENCE; the existence of a RESPONSIBLE WILL, as the subject of that law; and lastly, the existence of EVIL—of Evil essentially such, not by accident of outward circumstances, not derived from its physical consequences,

or from any cause, out of itself" (*AR*—1825—135).

[101] That is, the heir to the Epicurean tradition, as that tradition was generally understood (though not as it actually was taught by Epicurus himself). Cf C: "It appears that at least ninety-nine out of a hundred of Epicurus's adherents were Cyrenaics or voluptuaries in the grossest sense" (*P Lects*—1949—217). See in general Prolegomena III: The Epicurean and Stoic Background.

[102] The answer incorporates both Horace's famous equation of Epicureans and hogs, and the still older tradition associated with Homer's Circe. Cf further Shakespeare: "What is a man, / If his chief good and market of his time / Be but to sleep and feed? A beast, no more" (*Hamlet* IV iv 33–5).

words ⟨imply⟩ that you know the possibility of other goods, for you would not yourself have been guilty of the truism 'I know no pleasure but pleasure and no pain but pain', which yet must be your meaning if you assert 'pleasure' to be the ~~pure~~ ⟨mere⟩ and adequate synonyme of 'good'.[103] ~~which~~ ⟨This⟩ latter word ⟨indeed⟩ you would act consistently in striking out of your dictionary, even as the philosophy on which our definition is grounded will have no small influence in striking the thing meant out of your heart."

But if *good* and [*f 63*] *evil* be what the logicians call genera generalissima,[104] under which many sorts are subordinated, it follows ~~it~~ ⟨that each of these sorts⟩[m] must be good or evil in different senses, that each must have its ⟨characterising⟩ mark ~~of distincion~~ by which it is distinguished from others of the same class. Thus, for instance, a thing may be relatively ~~good~~ or conditionally ~~and~~ ⟨or⟩[n] contingently or comparatively ⟨good. Or,⟩[o] on the other hand, ⟨a thing may be⟩[p] *positively* good, ⟨i.e. good⟩[q] in itself. Or lastly, it may ~~be good absolutely~~ be itself THE GOOD. ~~by participation of which the one immediately preceeding, and~~ ⟨is good⟩ ~~is a means to.~~ [r]"Why callest thou me good? There is none good save only one, the Father."[t] [105]—That which is good in itself, is such by participation of the absolute Good: and only as means to *this*, ⟨viz.⟩ the good in itself, do other things *become* good.[s] There is, observes the great restorer* of the Stoic Moral Phi-

---

* [*Written on f 62ᵛ:*] Immanuel Kant, Grundlegung zur Metaphysik der Sitten, with whom I accord only as far as it is opposed to the modern Epicurean, whether under its grossest form in the philosophy of Helvetius[106] and its scholars, or in its more plausible religious dress as it presents itself in the writings of Paley, Priestley and the other masters of the school which began, or rather obtained the predominance, from the ascension of Charles 1ˢᵗ to the death of his son and successor.[107] The points in which I disagree with the illustrious sage of

---

[m] Insertion in C's hand   [n] Insertion in C's hand   [o] Insertion in C's hand
[p] Insertion in C's hand   [q] Insertion in C's hand   [r-s] In C's hand
[t] Quotation marks inserted

[103] Running throughout this argumentation is the submerged presence of C's preoccupation with the prevalence of Epicureanism: "Romanism and Despotic Government in the larger part of Xtendom; and the prevalence of Epicurean Principles in the remainder—these do indeed lie heavy on my heart!" (*CM—CC*—I 305).

[104] Tr: "most general kinds".

[105] "And he said unto him, Why callest thou me good" there *is none* good but one, *that is*, God" (Matt 19.17).

[106] Claude-Adrien Helvétius (1715–1771), French Enlightenment philosopher. Author of *De l'esprit* (1758). See Prolegomena III: The Epicurean and Stoic Background for C's insistence that the emphases of the French Enlightenment were virtually the same as those of the Epicurean tradition.

[107] Cf C's unequivocal opposition to

losophy,[109] nothing in the world, yea! nothing out of the world within the power of human conception that can without qualification or limit be regarded as good save the Good Will alone.[110] Understanding, Wit, Judgement, [*f 64*] and by whatever other name the talents of the mind or intellectual faculties, and again Courage, Resolution, Perseverance in resolve, as properties of the temperament, are doubtless in many respects good and desirable; but that may become likewise extremely evil and pernicious if the Will which is to make use of these gifts of nature, the peculiar constitution of which is on this account named "Character", is not good. Even so is it with the gifts of fortune, Power, Wealth, Honour, even Health, and all that which is implied in complacency with a man's state and circumstances, all that ~~we~~ ⟨a man⟩ means when he says that he *finds* himself well and well off, and which we generalize under the term

Königsberg[108]—those, namely, in which he differs from the Christian code—and the philosophical grounds of my disagreement will appear in its own place in another part of this work.

modern Epicureanism: "During five and twenty, I might say thirty years", he says, "I have been resolutely opposing the whole system of modern illumination, Epicurean (in our country Pelagian) Christianity, Pelagian morals, Pelagian politics" (*CL* v 453). In 1796–7 the radical political Jacobin and classical scholar Gilbert Wakefield published an influential ed of Lucretius, who was the chief proponent of Epicurus's thought in the Roman world, and thereby made even more explicit the connection of Epicureanism and the currents of "modern illumination" that Coleridge despised. See further Prolegomena III: The Epicurean and Stoic Background.

[108] Kant.

[109] I.e. Kant. But in a letter of 1817 C says "I reject Kant's *stoic* principle, as false, unnatural, and even immoral, where in his Critik der Practischen Vernun[f]t he treats the affections as indifferent αδιαφωρα" in ethics, and would persuade us that a man who disliking, and without any feeling of Love for, Virtue yet *acted* virtuously, because and only because it was his *Duty*, is more worthy of our esteem, than the man whose *affections* were aidant to, and

congruous with, his Conscience. For it would imply little less than that things not the Objects of the moral Will or under it's controul were yet indispensable to it's due practical direction. In other words, it would subvert his own System—" (*CL* IV 791–2). It is notable that C taxes Kant only with Stoic "moral" philosophy; for he clearly understood that Stoic natural philosophy was pantheism, and that Kant was anything but a pantheist. C at one point equates "the *una et unica substantia* of Spinosa" with "the World-God of the Stoics" (Brinkley 367). And elsewhere he said that "throughout they confounded God and Nature" (*P Lects*—1949—219). See further Wilhelm Dilthey "Spinoza und die stoische Tradition" *Gesammelte Schriften* II (Leipzig and Berlin 1914) 283–9; Max Pohlenz *Die Stoa; Geschichte einer geistigen Bewegung* (Göttingen 1959) I 470. See Prolegomena III: The Epicurean and Stoic Background.

[110] "Es ist überall nichts in der Welt, ja überhaupt auch ausser derselben zu denken möglich, was ohne Einschränkung für gut könnte gehalten werden, als allein ein *guter Wille*" (*Kant* IV 393).

"*Hap*piness",* produce Boldness, Courage, Confidence, Assurance, but too often Insolence, ~~or~~ Temerity, ~~in short~~ or the Disposition to oppress, unless a Good Will be present to direct and rectify the influence[112] of the former qualities on the heart (or moral being), and through this on the whole principalle of action, subordinating it to aims of universal validity—not to mention that no [*f* 65] rational, impartial spectator can view with complacency the uninterrupted prosperity of a being without ~~a single~~ ⟨any⟩ trait of a pure Good Will.[113] Thus the Good Will seems to contribute the indispensable condition even of the being worthy to be happy.[114]†

* [*Written on f 63ᵛ:*] *Glück*seligkeit, i.e. ea beatitudo vel rectius istud beatitudinis analogon quod à fortunâ et quasi ab extra datum est et dependet.[111]

† [*Written on f 64ᵛ:*] This may be aptly illustrated by the poignant disapprobation expressed in old times, while yet the doctrine of a probationary state and a moral world to succeed it had spread no steady light; and by the sharp complaints which not only the poets and philosophers of early Greece, but the Patriarchs and Prophets poured forth: "⟨cum⟩ res hominum tanta caligine volvi Adspicerent, laetorsque diû florere nocentes."[115] In the language of scripture, "When they beheld the unrighteous man and how all things went well with him"—instances which by the providential disposition of things must have been at all times exceptions, and therefore make these keen remonstrances, and the

[111] Tr: "beatitude, or more properly, with an analogue of beatitude, which is given by fortune and as though from without, and depends on it".

[112] For C's passage, beginning with "Understanding, wit, judgement" cf Kant: "Verstand, Witz, Urtheilskraft und wie die Talente des Geistes sonst heißen mögen, oder Muth, Entschlossenheit, Beharrlichkeit im Vorsatze als Eigenschaften des Temperaments sind ohne Zweifel in mancher Absicht gut und wünschenswerth; aber sie können auch äusserst böse und schädlich werden, wenn der Wille, der von diesen Naturgaben Gebrauch machen soll und dessen eigenthümliche Beschaffenheit darum *Charakter* heißt, nicht gut ist. Mit den Glücksgaben ist es eben so bewandt. Macht, Reichtum, Ehre, selbst Gesundheit und das ganze Wohlbefinden und Zufriedenheit mit seinem Zustande unter dem Name der *Glückseligkeit* machen Muth und hiedurch öfters auch Übermuth, wo nicht ein guter Wille da ist, der den Einfluß derselben aufs Gemüth und

hiemit auch das ganze Princip zu handeln berichtige und allgemeihn-zweckmäßig mache" (*Kant* iv 393).

[113] Beginning with "Not to mention", cf Kant: "ohne zu erwähnen, daß ein vernünftiger unparteiischer Zuschauer sogar am Anblicke eines ununterbrochenen Wohlergebens eines Wesens, das kein Zug eines reinen und guten Willens ziert, nimmermehr ein Wohlgefallen haben kann" (*Kant* iv 393).

[114] Cf Kant: "und so der gute Wille die unerlässliche Bedingung selbst der Würdigkeit glücklich zu sein auszumachen scheint" (*Kant* iv 393). Cf C in 1812: "To be happy and deserve to be happy is WELL-BEING" (*SW & F—CC*—i 290).

[115] "But when I saw the impenetrable mist that surrounds human affairs, the wicked happy and long prosperous" (Claudian *In Rufinum* i 12–14). Claudian was a favourite with C; for comments on a variety of his works see *SW & F (CC)* ii 1224–50.

Certain properties are even conducive and serviceable to this Good Will, and capable of greatly lightening its task, but yet possess no inward unconditional worth; but on the contrary must always presume a Good Will which limits the estimation in which we may otherwise hold it with good right and forbids us to regard it as positively good on its own account. Moderation in affections and passions, Self control, and ~~cool~~ sober ᵣReflexion are not alone good for many purposes, but appear to constitute a part even of the inner worth of the person possessing the same ~~but in order~~. There wants, however, a great deal before we can declare it without limit, however unconditionally they were extolled by the ancients. For without the principles of a Good Will, [*f 66*] they are capable of becoming in the highest degree evil; and the cold blood of a villain makes him not only far more dangerous in our eyes, but likewise, immediately, without relation to consequences, yet more detestable, an object of yet greater abhorrence, than we should have considered him,[116] had he not been master of this valuable quality of calm temperament and self-possession.

"The good Will, ~~and that alone is good~~ not in account of that which it effectuates or brings to pass, not through its instrumentality to the realization of a⟨ny⟩ proposed end of whatever nature it may be, but wholly and exclusively ~~for~~ ⟨on account of⟩ *the act* ~~itself is willing~~ ~~good in itself~~ ⟨itself, namely ⟨of⟩ that [of] willing rightly⟩ in and for itself considered, is beyond comparison to be prized far higher than all which ~~can be thereby~~ by any act of the Will could be brought to pass in favor of any inclination, or of all our inclinations collectively."[117]

---

too general form ~~in which they are conveyed~~ by which the exceptions are represented as all but the rule, more striking proofs, how strong and deep in the human ⟨is⟩ the feeling here spoken of.

[116] Beginning with "Certain properties", cf Kant: "Einige Eigenschaften sind sogar diesem guten Willen selbst beförderlich und können sein Werk sehr erleichten, haben aber dem ungeachtet keinen innern unbedingten Werth, sondern setzen immer noch einen guten Willen voraus, der die Hochschätzung, die man übrigens mit Recht für sie trägt, einschränkt und es nicht erlaubt, sie für schlechthin gut zu halten. Mäßigung in Affecten und Leidenschaften, Selbstbeherrschung und nüchterne Überlegung sind nicht allein in vielerlei Absicht gut, sondern scheinen sogar einen Theil vom innern Werthe der Person auszumachen; allein es fehlt viel daran, um sie ohne Einschränkung für gut zu erklären (so unbedingt sie auch von den Alten gepriesen worden). Denn ohne Grundsätze eines guten Willens können sie höchst böse werden, und das kalte Blut eines Bösewichts macht ihn nicht allein weit gefährlicher, sondern auch unmittelbar in unsern Augen noch verabscheuungswürdiger, als er ohne dieses dafür würde gehalten werden" (*Kant* IV 393–4).

[117] "Der gute Wille ist nicht durch das, was er bewirkt oder ausrichtet, nicht durch seine Tauglichkeit zu Erreichung irgend eines vorgesetzten Zweckes, sondern allein durch das Wollen, d.i. an sich,

So far Kant, to which let me be permitted to add an extract from [*f 67*] a work of my own, The Friend, Vol. 2, p. 220:[a] "Our fellow creatures can only judge what we *are* by what we *do*; but in the eye of our Maker what we *do* is of no worth, except as it flows from what we *are*. Though the fig tree should produce no visible fruit, yet if the living sap is in it, and if it has struggled to put forth buds and blossoms which have been prevented from maturing by inevitable contingencies of tempests or untimely frosts, the virtuous sap will be accounted as fruit: and the curse of barrenness will light on many a tree, from the boughs of which many hundreds have been satisfied, because the omniscient judge knows that the fruits were threaded to the boughs artificially[118] by the outward working of base fear and selfish hopes, and were neither nourished by the love of God or ⟨of⟩ man, nor grew out of the graces engrafted on the stock by religion."[119]

"Just and generous actions may proceed from bad motives. But this is not all, they both may, and often do, originate in *parts*, and as it were *fragments* of our nature. A lasci[*f 68*]vious man may sacrifice half his estate to rescue his friend from prison, for he is constitutionally sympathetic, and the better part of his nature happened to be uppermost. The same man shall afterwards exert the same disregard of money in an attempt to seduce that friend's wife and daughter. But faith (faith, which is used here in the same sense as Kant uses the Will, as the ground of all particular acts of willing)[120] is a *total* act of the soul: it is the *whole* state of the mind, or it is not at all! and in this consists its power, as well as its exclusive worth."*[121]

* [*Written on f 67ᵛ:*] As this work may fall under the perusal of many who have not seen ~~the Friend~~ the volumes entitled the Friend, I am tempted by the

---

---

gut und, für sich selbst betrachtet, ohne Vergleich weit höher zu schätzen als alles, was durch ihn zu Gunsten irgend einer Neigung, ja wenn man will, der Summe aller Neigungen nur immer zu Stande gebracht werden könnte" (*Kant* IV 394).

[118] For the metaphor of the tree in moral concerns see again C in a letter of 1809: "I . . . shall deem myself amply remunerated if in consequence of my exertions a Few only of those, who had formed their moral creed on Hume, Paley, and their Imitators . . . shall consider what they *are* instead of *merely* what they *do*; so that the fig-tree may bring forth it's own fruit from it's own living principle, and not have the figs tied on to it's barren sprays by the hand of outward Prudence & Respect of Character" (*CL* III 216).

[119] *Friend* (*CC*) I 314–15.

[120] "The *root* of Faith is in the Will" (*CM—CC*—I 287).

[121] *Friend* (*CC*) I 315. The parentheses enclose words interpolated into the passage here, and not in the passage as it appears in *The Friend*.

But as there lies a something so strange in this idea of the absolute worth of the mere gGood Will in itself without bringing its consequences into the calculation, that notwithstanding its coincidence with the common reason and moral sense of mankind, it may yet excite a suspicion of its being grounded in enthusiasm and high-flying Fancy,[122] we will content ourselves for the present with the mere statements, [*f* 69] the confirmation or rejection of which we leave for a while to the inward experience of our *w*readers. For*x* our immediate purpose, we need only remind the enquirer of the decisive differences, the distinction in kind between those things which are good because they are desired, and those things which are or ought to be desired because they are *good*. Such a form of food, for instance, ("the savoury meat", said Isaac, "such as I love")[123] is better to that individual simply because he desires it; but we need only suppose what may so easily be the case, that a less savoury food would be better for him, to exemplify a higher good which would and should be desirable because it was good, and good because self-preservation, with every other form of utility not overbalanced by a weightier utility or by that in which utility itself finds at once its ultimate solution, becomes his duty, and is thus ennobled and taken up into that unconditional good inasmuch as means in themselves innocent acquire a character from the fore-intended [*f* 70] end. In short, the mere difference between the particles "*to*" and "*for*" are sufficient to destroy the sophism, which is in fact of the same kind with that of a contemporary annalist[124] who has confounded the taste *of* mutton with a taste *for* Milton, and gravely sought for the origin of the latter in the same place with that of the former, viz. the papilla of the tongue and palate.[125] I have said

---

deep interest to reprint, in the form of a note, the paragraph follows, fr[om] p. 221, last line but two, to p. 225,*4v* ending with the word "sake of the love".

---

v ms: 225 p   *w–x* ms: readers: for

[122] From "there lies" cf Kant: "Es liegt gleichwohl in dieser Idee von dem absoluten Werthe des bloßen Willens, ohne einigen Nutzen bei Schätzung desselben in Anschlag zu bringen, etwas so Befremdliches, daß unerachtet aller Einstimmung selbst der gemeinen Vernunft mit derselben dennoch ein Verdacht entspringen muß, daß vielleicht bloß hochfliegende Phantasterei ingeheim zum Grunde liege, und die Natur in ihrer Absicht, warum sie unserm Willen Vernunft zur Regiererin beigelegt habe, falsch verstanden sein möge" (*Kant* IV 394–5).

[123] "And make the savoury meat, such as I love, and bring it to me, that I may eat; that my soul may bless thee before I die" (Gen 27.4).

[124] A slip for "analyst". Richard Payne Knight, whose *Analytical Inquiry Into the Principles of Taste* (3rd ed 1806) was annotated by C, is meant. See *SW & F* (*CC*) I 363 n3.

[125] Cf *The Principles of Genial Criticism*, where C says "If a man upon ques-

"sufficient", for the same distinctions exist^y in all the languages of the civilized world, and they refer to facts that have their sole and entire being in the consciousness. Now whatever ~~in all~~ is common to all languages of the civilized world, in all climates and at all times, must be the exponent, because it must be a consequent of the common consciousness of man as man. Whatever, ⟨therefore,⟩ contradicts this universal language, contradicts the universal consciousness, and the facts in question subsisting wholly in consciousness.*

[*f 71*] But what shall we say of the pleasures of a *good conscience*? Only this, that it is a gross instance of the ʜHysteron ᴩProteron[127] or, in our homely English, "the cart before the horse". At all events it is a mere petitio principii.[128] For the conscience must be good in order to this plea-

* [*Written on f 69ᵛ:*] Mem: to transcribe as a note, pg. 10 and 11, ending at the word "record", last line but one of p. 11, of the Omniana, Vol. ii.[126]

^y ms: exist~~s~~ [*the last letter cancelled in pencil*]

---

tioning his own experience can detect no difference in *kind* between the enjoyment derived from the eating of turtle, and that from the perception of a new truth; if in his feelings a taste *for* Milton is essentially the same as the taste *of* mutton, he may still be a sensible and a valuable member of society; but it would be a desecration to argue with him on the Fine Arts" (*SW & F—CC—*ɪ 363). Cf *Philosophical Lectures*: "One may say, 'I delight in Milton or Shakspeare more than turtle and venison.' Another man, 'That is not my case. For myself, I think a good dish of turtle and a good bottle of port afterwards give me much more delight than I receive from Milton and Shakspeare.' You must not dispute about tastes. And if a taste for Milton is the same as a taste for venison there is no objection to be found in the argument" (*P Lects—*1949—142).

[126] The indicated passage is from C's longest entry in Southey's compendium, No. 174, "The Soul and its organ of sense", and is itself so leisurely that it will be truncated here: "It is a strong presumptive proof against materialism, that there does not exist a language on earth, from the rudest to the most refined, in which a materialist can talk for five minutes together, without involving some contradiction in *terms* to his own sys-

tem. . . . Thus, the language of the scriptures on natural objects is as strictly philosophical as that of the Newtonian system. Perhaps, more so. For it is not only equally true, but it is universal among mankind, and unchangeable. It describes facts of *appearance*. And what other language would have been consistent with the divine wisdom? The inspired writers must have borrowed their terminology, either from the crude and mistaken philosophy of their own times, and so have sanctified and perpetuated falsehood, unintelligible meantime to all but one in ten thousand, or they must have anticipated the terminology of the true system, without any revelation of the system itself, and so have become unintelligible to all men; or lastly, they must have revealed the system itself, and thus have left nothing for the exercise, development, or reward of the human understanding, instead of teaching that moral knowledge, and enforcing those social and civic virtues, out of which the arts and sciences will spring up in due time, and of their own accord" (*SW & F—CC—*ɪ 332–3).

[127] Tr: "the last first", a term in logic.

[128] Tr: "begging the question", a term in logic indicting the fallacy of assuming in the premise of an argument the conclusion that is to be proved.

sure, but a good conscience can only result from or subsist in the consciousness of having done our duty because it is our duty. But if instead of this we did our duty, i.e. certain acts dictated as such by our reason, only with a view to some supposed pleasure that was to follow it, we should not obey our reason but our sensuality—we should not have done our duty, therefore not have a good conscience but a conscience ~~either~~ suspended by an usurping counterfeit, and which, as soon as it has become awakened from its torpor, will express much the same satisfaction as if ~~we~~ ⟨a son⟩ had performed the offices of filial^z [*f 72*] piety to ⟨a father with a view solely to⟩ a larger portion of his fortune, which the father might be thus induced to leave him in his last will and testament. "But if it be not a sensation, why do you call it 'pleasure'?" "Aye, but this is a spiritual sensation, i.e. a sensation which is no sensation at all." "But if you tell me that you understand nothing beyond this, I should perhaps answer, neither do I, for ~~I refer to⟨that which I have spoken⟩~~ ⟨that which I have spoken of as both beyond pleasure and beyond states of being that I deem worthy of a nobler designation is⟩^a 'the peace of God, which passeth all understanding'!"¹²⁹ But if you rejoin that you know of nothing beyond that the words last used have no meaning for you, there is but one answer: "So much the worse, if it be so, but I am bound to hope that in the fervor you have calumniated your own moral state."

We will conclude this chapter with a re-enumeration of the three distinctions which, though in our present state united in one person, it is yet of vital importance that we should not confound. [*f 73*] The first is that testifying state of the Good Will best described in the preceding words of our liturgy, to which the ~~Greeks~~ later Greek philosophers appropriated the term "μακαριοτης", "μακαριος"¹³⁰ (thus "θεοι μακαιοι"),¹³¹ and the correspondent to which in our language is "Bliss", "Blessedness", "Blessed". Independent of this investigation, we dared almost appeal to the *moral taste* of an uncorrupted mind, which it would prefer as the more appropriate phrase "the pleasures or the blessedness of a calm approving conscience". This, however, is the Spiritual in our nature. The

---

^z ms: fial [*correction supplied in pencil below this word*]
^a ms: is "the peace &c [*inserted passage written on f 71ᵛ and marked for insertion here*]

¹²⁹ Phil 4.7. Cf *The Statesman's Manual*: "the CONSCIENCE . . . . might, perhaps, be called a *spiritual sensation*; but that there lurks a contradiction in the terms, and that it is often deceptive to give a common or generic name to that, which being unique, can have no fair analogy. Strictly speaking, therefore, the conscience is neither a sensation or a sense; but a testifying state, best described in the words of our liturgy [Phil 4.7 (var)], as THE PEACE OF GOD THAT PASSETH ALL UNDERSTANDING" (*LS—CC*—66–7).
¹³⁰ Tr: "blessedness, blest".
¹³¹ Tr: "the blessed gods".

second belongs in like manner to the intellectual, and the term appropriated to it would designate the immediate consequent or accompaniment of the intellectual energies exerted in conformity with the ~~inherent~~ laws of the intellect and its inherent forms. So vague and general has the use of words not immediately referring to [*f 74*] the forum or the market, and neither subserving the purposes of gain or destruction or vanity or appetite, that I confess myself unable to fix on any one of the numerous so-called synonymes in our language for the purpose of setting it apart for this one sense, and therefore merely as a symbolical mark, like those used in algebra as an instrument of thought and recollection, have ventured to propose the term "eunoya" or "eunöy".* The third is "Pleasure", the "ηδονη" of the Greeks, i.e. the aggregate of the sensations arising from the co-incidence, conformed in kind and degree with the stimulability of the sentient individual. The first is alone unconditionally good; the second good when employed in the service of the first, and innocent except when employed to its difference; the third (i.e. considered in relation to a moral and rational being [*f 75*] in a probationary state)† innocent only when made assistant to the second and first. The first would be produced; the second should be employed; the last can be used. The first is commanded, the second recommended, the third conditionally

---

* [*Written on f 73ᵛ:*] Those readers, who think an excuse for this liberty requisite, I refer to my remarks on this subject in my Treatise on Logic, which was in fact written as the Prolegomena, προπαιδευτικα, of the present work.

† [*Written on f 74ᵛ:*] Still[5b] more forcible must this appear to a Christian, who believes with S! Paul that the ground and conditions of this corporeal stimulability or sensuality, in the universal and indifferent use of the word, as expressing the kind and not the excess—in the language of scripture, "the flesh and the world"—constitute the probationary state. "Now this I say, Brethren, that flesh and blood ~~that~~ ⟨can⟩ not inherit the kingdom of God; but we shall all be changed." I think, therefore, that both ~~Kant~~ the philosopher of Königsberg and his first disciple and rival, Fichte, have erred and verged towards enthusiasm in their confusion of the second with the third, the eunöya with the Hedone, the desirable of the intellect with the desirable of the body, and the exclusion of both indifferently from the permanent objects of the rational Will. The former is not indeed spiritual in the highest and most proper sense of that term, but [*f 75ᵛ*] still it may be to the spirit as the body to the soul. There is a body terrestrial, and this we leave behind when it is worn out or its purposes fulfilled; but there is a body celestial, which is imperishable and reproduced by the spirit for ever, abides as its Logos, its Word and express image (εικιον), through which and with which it energizes.

[. . .]ᶜ

---

permitted. The first is the master working at the head of his labourers;
the second is the free servant, the unhired tenant, who offers the first
fruits to his Lord, and on what remains receives a blessing of increase;
the third is the harnessed buffalo that is unmuzzled only while it treads
out the corn, and is fed when it must be and because it must be and as
little as it can be, and is tolerated only as far as it is serviceable to the
second and compatible with the first.

[*f 76*]   Chapter VII

Before we proceed, let us devote a few sentences to the review of our
⟨course⟩ passed^d ~~progress~~ ⟨over⟩, that in the very act of drawing up our
train we may secure at once fulcrum and impulse for ~~our next progres-
sive movement~~ the recommencement of our progress.[132] The object ~~and
distinctive~~ character of this work consists in the assertion[133]—first, of
religion as implying revelation, or that the words "*revealed religion*" is
a pleonasm[134] or definitio per idem;[135] secondly, that christianity is the
only revelation of universal validity. But its distinctive character ~~consi~~
depends on the preference given by the author to an order of proof, the
reverse of that which from Grotius inclusively has been adopted only not
universally by all the defenders and demonstrators of christianity, of all
sects and churches, but which the author nevertheless believes to be in
the [*f 77*] spirit of Luther and his great fellow-labourers in the work of the
reformation. Conscious of his own weakness, he would have wanted the
confidence requisite for an undertaking so comprehensive and momen-
tous had he not been supported by a conviction, founded on a long and
careful study of the elder theologians and especially of the great founders
and fathers of our own church prior to the ascendancy of Arminianism

---

^d ms: past [*When "over" was substituted for "progress", the past participle "passed"
should have been substituted for the adjective "past"*]

[132] C was fond of this image. For in-
stance, in arguing that "the interest of
permanence is opposed to that of pro-
gressiveness; but so far from being con-
trary interests, they, like the magnetic
forces, suppose and require each other",
he says that "Even the most mobile of
creatures, the serpent makes a *rest* of its
own body, and drawing up its volumi-
nous train from behind on this fulcrum,
propels itself onward" (*C&S—CC—
24n*).
[133] By saying that the "object of this
work consists in the assertion of religion

as . . ." C takes up one of the changing ti-
tles of the *magnum opus* called *Assertion
of Religion* (see Prolegomena xiii: The
Transformations of the *Magnum Opus*).
Cf below, Frag 2, where C speaks of
"The religion, the cause of which I have
proposed to assert . . . ." (f 31).
[134] Cf *Aids to Reflection*: "I regard
the very phrase '*Revealed* Religion' as a
pleonasm, inasmuch as a religion not re-
vealed is, in my judgment, no religion at
all" (*AR*—1825—176).
[135] Tr: "definition by the same", a
term in logic.

at the close of the reign of James 1ˢᵗ, that he had not diverged from the
tenets and example of one ~~party~~ ⟨class⟩ of divines, brilliant as that must
needs be which contains such names as Grotius,[136] Baxter,[137] Bishops
Taylor,[138] Stillingfleet,[139] and Watson,[140] Lessius,[141] Lardner,[142] and

[136] Hugo Grotius (Huig van Groot) (1583–1645), Dutch jurist, theologian, and polymath. An adherent of Arminius, his principal religious work was *De Veritate religionis Christianae* (1622). Of his other theological writings, his *Annotationes in vetus et novum testamentum* (1642) supplanted the assumption of Biblical inspiration by the method of philological criticism, and was thus an early document in the tradition of the Higher Criticism. Despite his stupendous learning, Grotius was for Coleridge a chief opponent of his own theological position e.g.: "Before the time of Grotius's de Veritate Christianâ no *stress* was lay'd on the judicial, law-cant kind of evidence for Christianity which has been since so much in Fashion/ & Lessing very sensibly considers Grotius as the greatest Enemy that Xtianity ever had" (*CL* II 861, 9 Sept 1802).

[137] Richard Baxter (1615–1691), Puritan divine, praised by Coleridge as the first formulator of the principle of trichotomy in intellectual procedure. "It is impossible to read Baxter without hesitating which to admire most, the uncommon clearness (perspicuity and perspicacity) of his understanding, or the candour and clarity of his spirit" (*CM—CC*—I 273).

[138] Jeremy Taylor (1613–1667), Anglican Bp of Connor and Down, called "the Shakespeare of Divines" by Emerson. Taylor was an especial favourite of C ("Taylor's was a great and lovely mind" (*TT—CC*—I 154); "The writings of Bishop Jeremy Taylor are a perpetual feast to me" (*SW & F—CC*—I 300)), but C had strong reservations about his theological position. "Taylor never speaks with the slightest symptom of affection or respect of Luther, Calvin, or any other of the great reformers—at least, not in any of his learned works; but he *saints* every trumpery monk or friar; down to the very latest canonizations by the modern Popes. I fear you will think me harsh,

when I say that I believe Taylor was, perhaps unconsciously, half a Socinian at heart" (Brinkley 268). Again: "He was the Origen of our Church. There was much in him to be forgiven; but a thousand excellencies demand our forgiveness of the former, as the best form in which we can shew our gratitude for the latter. His faith in the article of the Trinity was, I doubt not, far more sound than many of his expressions and concessions were cautious, or strictly defensible" (Brinkley 266–7). Again: "I think Taylor was in heart very near to Socinianism" (*TT—CC*—I 155). For C's extensive annotations, always admiring but frequently criticising, to Taylor's work, see Brinkley 258–316. In the *Aids to Reflection*, C quotes Taylor on original sin and then opposes him (*AR*—1825—251ff).

[139] Edward Stillingfleet (1635–1699), Bp of Worcester and latitudinarian divine. He was famous for a controversy with Locke about substance, faith, and knowledge, and the Trinity, which lasted between 1696 and 1699 with several publications on each side. Stillingfleet died before he could compose his last reply. Most people, but perhaps not C, thought that Stillingfleet had been worsted. For an account of the controversy see Cranston 412–15. Cf *The Stateman's Manual*: ". . . the asserted and generally believed defeat of the Bishop of Worcester (the excellent Stillingfleet) in his famous controversy with Mr Locke" (*LS—CC*—105). See also *P Lects* (1949) 379–81 and 462 n 18.

[140] Richard Watson (1737–1816), Bp of Llandaff, personally known to C and the man addressed in Wordsworth's famous letter.

[141] Leonhard Lessius (1554–1623), Jesuit theologian and friend of Lipsius, censured by the theological faculty at Louvain.

[142] Nathaniel Lardner (1684–1768), author of *The Credibility of the Christian*

Paley;[143] but that in the same proportion he was moving under the auspices of authorities still more venerable, and whether mistaken or not, he was at least secure from [the] charge of heretical pravity in deriving his opinions from the framers of [ƒ78] those Articles[144] which still remain the lawful criterion of orthodoxy. The difference between the Grotian ~~pr~~ scheme[145] and its opposite, which I would designate as the Lutheran, is briefly this: the[e] Grotian essays to prove the truth of the christian revelation and our obligation to believe the same by the miracles recorded in the biography of Christ,[146] while the Lutheran would place the credibility of the miracles mainly on their strong previous probability, and this again on the truth and necessity of the revelation. Our problem, therefore, may be thus stated. From the necessity[ƒ] of the objects of the christian religion ⟨and from its⟩ correspondency, ~~the~~ adequateness, [ƒ79] and divine character, ~~of the gospel revelation as A FACT professing its evidence in itself~~ to establish the perfect à priori probability of the miracles ~~retailed in that gospel~~ attributed to Christ—which being satisfactorily

[e] ms: The
[ƒ] ms: (the necessity of in order to regeneration, or the capability of being redeemed; the necessity of faith in the subjects or persons to be redeemed, in order that they may be capable of appropriating ~~these objects~~ ⟨such redemption⟩ to themselves; the necessity of a revelation in order to this faith, ~~adding thereto~~ [*cancelled in ink with vertical lines*]

Gospels (14 vols) and disciple of Grotius. C was aware of his work as early as 1796: *CL* I 197; see also 171, 554, II 821–3, and *CN* I 851. For C's continuing admiration of Lardner, see *IS* 50.
[143] William Paley (1743–1805), Archdeacon of Carlisle, latitudinarian divine and author of *Evidences of Christianity* (1794); the most popular theologian of C's day. Paley, though not unequivocally important as a strict theologian, was for C a constant symbol of all the modern tendencies he opposed. E.g. he proposes "a Critique on 1. Condillac, 2. Paley. 3, the French Chemistry & Philosophy—with other miscellaneous matters, from the present Fashions of the age, moral and political" (*CL* V 265). See Prolegomena IV: Paley and Morality.
[144] That is, the Thirty-nine Articles, a series of theological propositions that represent the core of Anglican teaching; they were adopted in 1563, largely under the influence of John Jewel (1522–1571), Bp of Salisbury and author of

Apologia Ecclesiae Anglicanae.
[145] In 1805 C commented that "The Grotian Paleian Defence of X[tianity] how injurious to X" (*CN* II 2640).
[146] Of Richard Field's *Of the Church*, C says: "See Book IV. Chap. 7, p. 353, both for a masterly confutation of the Paleyo-Grotian Evidences of the Gospel & a decisive proof in what light it was regarded by the Church of England in its best age—like Grotius himself, it is halfway between Popery and Socinianism" (*CM—CC*—II 651–2). "One among the countless internal evidences & features of truth, that I find in the Gospel—& this strangely at variance with the fashionable 'Evidences,' which Grotius first brought into fashion (followed in England first, I believe, by Richard Baxter and Bishop Jeremy Taylor) is the justly subordinate and accessory character assigned to his miracles by our Lord" (Brinkley 359). "This passion for Law Court Evidence began with Grotius" (*CM—CC*—I 317).

done, the very fact of their having been recorded by contemporaries becomes a *sufficient proof** *g* of the facts themselves.

* [*Written on ff 78ᵛ–84ᵛ:*] If a man ~~against~~ whose ⟨general⟩ veracity had not been previously known or suspected—if any one, in short, not known beforehand for an habitual liar or trifler—informs me that he met the parson and the clerk passing through the churchyard together at a day and hour when I knew that the church service was commonly finished, I believe ~~him~~ the fact at once, and without a question—simply because there is no reason why I should not believe it, and because to believe is the rule and to disbelieve an exception—a frequent exception, perhaps, still, however, but an *ʰ*exception. But*ⁱ* if a man, even of hitherto unsuspected veracity, should tell me that the parson and the clerk [were] both in the pulpit, and the ~~former~~ ⟨latter⟩ astride on the ~~latter's~~ ⟨former's⟩ shoulders, notwithstanding the credibility of the narrator I should expect ulterior and very strong proof before I gave credit to the narration. If I had no opportunity of further questioning him, I should bethink myself whether he might not have [*f 79ᵛ*] used the words with a sportive equivocation, meaning only that he had seen a picture or caricature representing ~~such figures~~ the same; or whether he might not have meant the words metaphorically or figuratively, signifying some gross instance of insubordination as, ex.gr. the usurpation of the pulpit by men not educated or set apart for the duties of public instruction, but who repeated what they had at different times caught up or learnt from the established ministry with pretence to an higher exaltation; or if neither these nor other possibility of a similar sort would apply, I should begin in good earnest to make enquiries after my friend's state of health and whether he might not have been seized with a delirium or those unusually vivid ocular spectra, which in some instances have been the precursors or symptoms of an approaching or commencing disease. Not till I had satisfied myself as to the non-existence or [*f 80ᵛ*] utter comparative improbability and inappropriateness of all these solutions, should I think myself bound to enquire whether there were other testimony who were in the church at the same time with the narrator, whether they had been and were willing to attest the same—nay, supposing even this and that my friend's narration should be confirmed by other respectable eyewitnesses, still I can conceive an ⟨im⟩probability so great as to justify one in suspecting, so far at least as to enquire whether or not it might have been one of those rare, indeed, but yet [not] unprecedented instances of nervous derangements, not more sudden in its origin than rapid and extensive in contagion. Speaking in my own person, I should remember that I had received the most convincing proof that a multitude of not less than ten thousand persons [. . .] before the church Della Sacra Lettera at Messina,[147] there waiting in hope of some miracle which a crazy [*f 81ᵛ*] man

g The note indicator was originally placed at the end of the sentence, then cancelled and relocated here
ʰ⁻ⁱ ms: exception, but

[147] On his way back from Malta C records that he "arrived at Messina on Thursday Night, 4 Oct. 1805—" (*CN* II 2695) and shortly afterward that "The

What the objects or component articles of this religion are, we have at first no other way of discovering but by collecting from all the churches and communities of christendom the points of faith common to all, with the additional confirmation that in all ages of which we possess any credible documents the same points have had the same catholic character or

had dreamed, that the Virgin of the Sacred Letter would on that day gratify her favorite Messinese, and actually believed themselves to have seen the steeple nod repeatedly to them, and hastened to deliver in their affidavits an oath to be forthwith presented to the bishop in order to a day of public thanksgiving for this stupendous act of celestial courtesy! That I had conversed myself not only with several ⟨of these eyewitnesses⟩ and sworn attestors—for the event took place just fifteen years before—but likewise with the priest, an honest and truly intelligent man whom the mob had compelled to swear them, and with a relation of the notary, whom they had in like manner obliged to take down their names. Though I have prolonged this note already far beyond its intended limits, I must not withhold from the curiosity of my readers what this honest and intelligent priest's own experience had been. He was in fact secretly sent for by the bishop [*f 82ᵛ*] as soon as his lordship had by fair words and a sort of conditional promise succeeded in dispersing the multitude. The dialogue is worthy of record. Bishop: "Well! an astonishing event this?" Priest: "Very much so, indeed, my Lord". B.: "Perfectly calm day, too, and the church in excellent repair". P.: "Not a breath stirring, scorching hot, my Lord". B. (fixing his eyes steadfastly on the priest): "Quite miraculous!" (P. bows assent.) B.: "You are a man of sense, and you saw all this, you informed me, in the presence of the people." P.: "Yes, my Lord, in the presence of the people". B.: "Come my ~~friend~~ son, we will be candid with each ʲ⁻ᵏother. I⁵ᵏ have received a hint from Rome that the fervor of our good fellow citizens had in some too well known instances exposed our holy church to the scoff of the ⁵ˡheretics. Speakⁿ to me, I pray you, in perfect confidence, did you, yourself, see the steeple nod?" P.: "Yes, my Lord, and if your Lordship had been where I was and dared not, your eyes might [*f 83ᵛ*] perhaps have remained in your head, but whether the head would have remained on the shoulders or the brains within the skull, that is the question." B. (smiling): "We understand each other, my son! I foresee that the opprobrium must fall on me for an unbelieving bishop, abi in pace!"[148]

Now to recur to our former case and to make an end of this disproportionate

ʲ⁻ᵏ ms: other I   ˡ⁻ᵐ ms: heretics, speak

view of Messina, rising up upon the Mountain in almost the form of the *altar-screen* = like two or three churches in Messina, from the Terra Nuova returning from the Lazarette, the most impressive I ever beheld" (*CN* ɪɪ 2696). On 20 Oct C produced a lengthy and vivid description of the city seen in panoramic view from its hills (*CN* ɪɪ 2705).

[148] Tr: "go in peace".

universality, the exceptions being either too transitory or too doubtful, or the number of adherents too insignificant, to have any perceptible weight in the counterbalance. These articles [*f 80*] constituting the common creed of christendom have been stated in our first chapter, and may be thus compressed: the[n] necessity and actual existence of a *spiritual redemption* for man,[152] the necessity of a *regeneration* in order to the susceptibility of being redeemed, and lastly the necessity of *Faith* in each individual in order to his appropriation of this redemption.[153] To which we may add the ~~attesting~~ *fruits of their faith* as ~~the~~ tests and criterion of its existence, and which are at the same time a necessary part of the appointed means of its growth and progress. Now as in all reasoning, even in the simplest ⟨physical⟩ sciences, the argument must commence with some assumption which is supposed and may be demanded but cannot be proved, so in the present subject. But as it belongs to the moral world, its ⟨postulates are⟩ of necessity different from those of geometry in this one respect: that though both may with equal right be demanded, the lat-

---

note, we will only suppose that the case which we ⟨have⟩ imagined had been related as having occurred in ~~Fran~~ Paris or somewhere in France about the time the Archbishop of Paris[149] had made his open profession of [. . .] atheism, and under the influence of Danton[150] and the Septembrizers[151] had been related as one among the many insults which the madness of ~~superstition~~ ⟨the people⟩, in the first dreadful recoil from superstition to its opposite extreme—or rather, which superstition seized with a mad hatred of its former externals, had offered to religion—the whole argument would have [*f 84*[v]] taken a different position and, as in the first instance, I should have believed my friend at once and without a question. The knowledge of the circumstances had established the previous probability ⟨of the event⟩, and that being done, the mere fact of its having been related by a contemporary against whose veracity and common sense there were no known presumptions becomes a sufficient proof that the event had actually taken place. (End of the Note).

[n] ms: The

---

[149] Jean-Baptiste-Joseph Gobel (1727–1794). He became the first prominent clergyman to take the oath for the civil constitution of the clergy, which led to his election as Abp of Paris. He was later executed. See Michelet II 1423–4.

[150] Georges-Jacques Danton (1759–1794), French Jacobin and chief leader, along with Marat and Robespierre, of the French Revolution. He was sent to the guillotine by the more radical Robespierre.

[151] Referring to the bloody massacres of Sept 1792.

[152] Note the priority of redemption in this enumeration. "For Redemption is the sine qua non" of the "Christian Religion" (*CN* IV 4797).

[153] Cf C in 1826: "I am secure of my faith in the main points—a personal God, a surviving principle of Life, & that I need & that I have a Redeemer" (*CL* VI 577).

ter can [*f 81*] not be extorted. In geometry, ~~the man~~ a negative answer
to the postulate would prove only either the conscious falsehood or jest
of the denier, or the suspension of his humanity by madness or idiotcy.
But ~~in morals~~ the assumptions of morality [are that] it is in a man's power
to reject believingly without the absolute forfeiture of his human under-
standing, though not without forfeiting that which, even more than the
understanding, forms the contradistinction of the human from the bestial
nature. These assumptions we have found comprized in one position:
man is a responsible agent, and in consequence *hath a Will*. Have I a re-
sponsible Will? eConcerning this each individual must be ⟨himself⟩ ex-
clusively ⟨both⟩ querist and respondent. It is self-evident, however, that
the affirmative to this question, being not so properly supposed as the
foundation of the whole fabric, as it is itself repeated in each of the com-
ponent parts, constituting, in fact, the major [*f 82*] ~~in~~ of each particular
~~p~~conclusion; and this again being ⟨not only⟩ per hypothesin[154] but in its
own nature insusceptible, nay, preclusive of all direct proof, the rejec-
tion of the same would stamp all further enquiry of the system founded
thereon with no less absurdity than would mark the individual who, hav-
ing denied the solidity (in the common sense of the word)*o* which some
visionary had assumed as a property of the atmosphere, should then se-
riously employ himself in discussing the degrees and modifications of
the same asserted concerning a castle of air, and fabled to exist in the air.
~~In like manner~~ ⟨As little can⟩ the truth or falsehood of Christianity even
commence its pleadings before a judge who had refused to acknowledge
the existence of a responsible Will in man. ~~f~~For the Judge himself the
conclusion pre-exists in his premise, and to the other party nothing re-
mains but ~~to disclaim the right authority~~ remove his*p* cause to some other
court [*f 83*] where at least a trial was possible, by virtue of some prin-
ciple admitted ~~in common~~ on ~~all~~ both sides. But though more than this
would not be necessary for the assertor of religion, and though this alone
would be practicable as a mere question of facts, yet something more
may be attempted in moral questions. ~~d~~Direct proof, indeed, is impossi-
ble, but indirect proofs, arguments from extreme improbability, and mo-
tives of strongest inducement to the re-consideration of the point denied
may be brought forward. It is possible that the denegant may not be
aware of all that is implied, or of necessity to be deduced, from the po-
sition contained in his denial; and it is likewise probable, and a proba-
bility of much greater practical interest, that the generality of those who

---

o Parentheses inserted   *p* ms: to his

[154] Tr: "hypothetically".

at once and without all the confidence of habit had granted the postulate
and acknowledged the assumption may ~~yet partake with the denier~~
labour under the same imperfection, the same lack of [*f 84*] distinct in-
sight into the contents and full meaning of their own concession. To ~~af-
fect~~ correct this defect, to mature this general assent into distinct ~~compr~~
conceptions, and by means of these to bring a consistency of thought and
language in all other ~~prin~~ important conceptions included in the same
class, truly or falsely, and in the latter instance for the purpose of trans-
ferring them to their ~~own and~~ proper department or birthplace—this
[. . .] was the object, and this forms the contents of the following chap-
ters under the several terms ~~of~~ "GOOD", "EVIL", ⟨"SELF",⟩ "PLEA-
SURE", "PAIN", "INTELLECTUAL SATISFACTION", and *q*"BLESSED-
NESS". And*r* in the course of this analysis we have necessarily touched
upon the ~~o~~two only remaining subjects, the distinct comprehension of
which is indispensable to a full and distinct insight into the fundamental
truth, [? and] primary assumption and postulate, of the whole system,
viz. [*f 85*] the subjects contained in the terms *"Conscience"* and *"Faith"*.
Hitherto, however, we have only touched upon them. ~~in~~ The ensuing
chapters, therefore, we devote to a more exact analysis, and a fuller and
more orderly display of their import. And thus we shall have concluded
the first main section of this work,[155] namely the preparations for the
proof—the tools, as it were, and the instruments, and at the same time
the cement by and with which the various truths of philosophy and facts
of history are to be shaped and adapted each to the other and made into
the ~~diffe~~ several ~~component~~ integral parts of the edifice—even as these
again, by a right adjustment of weight and order, ~~or~~ to cohere and ~~har-
monize~~ ⟨unite⟩ into ~~ample~~ one ⟨~~uniform~~ harmonious⟩ and enduring
temple.

In the next section, we proceed at once to the Evidences[156] and An-
ticipations of the Reason concerning the articles of the Religion,[157] each
[*f 86*] in the order in which they are capitulated in our introductory chap-
ter as far as they can be separated from the ~~facts~~ ⟨~~of the~~ Revelation⟩ his-
tory ~~re~~ ⟨of the religion, i. e.⟩ from the facts, circumstances ⟨and vehicles⟩

---

[155] The statement about concluding
"the first main section of this work" may
lend some countenance to the decision to
nominate "Say Vol. III" as the beginning
of this ed.
[156] By the use of the word "evi-
dences" as restricted solely to reason, C
rejects the Christian "evidences" of
Grotius and Paley. See above f 87. See
Prolegomena IV: Paley and Morality.
[157] Perhaps this statement tends to
justify this ed's placing of "Say Vol II"
as Frag 2 below.

of its communication, promulgation, and ~~dispersion~~ successive diffusion.

Whatsoever (says our eloquent Bishop Jeremy Taylor)[158] is against right reason, that no faith can oblige us to believe. For although reason is not the positive and affirmative measure of our faith, and God can do no more than we can understand, and our faith ought to be larger than our reason, and take something into her heart that reason can never take into her eye; yet in all our creed there can be nothing against reason. If true reason justly contradicts an article, it is not of the *household* of *faith*. In this there is no difficulty, but that in practice we take care that we do not call that reason which is not so: for although a man's reason is a right judge, yet it ought not to pass sentence in an [*f* 87] enquiry of faith until all the information be brought in; all that is within, and all that is without; all that is above, and all that is below; all that concerns it in experience, and all that concerns it in act; whatsoever is of pertinent observation, and whatsoever is revealed: for else reason may argue very well, and yet conclude falsely; it may conclude well in logick, and yet infer a false proposition in theology. But when our judge is truly and fully[159] informed in all that where she is to make her judgement, we may safely follow it, whithersoever she invites us.[160] If,

---

[158] Jeremy Taylor *Worthy Communicant* ch 3 §5 para 2 (1674) 176. See also *AR* (*CC*) 339.

[159] The phrase "truly and fully" here is "fully and truly" in Taylor.

[160] Cf *Aids to Reflection*: "APHORISM XX. Jer. Taylor. Whatever is against right reason, that no faith can oblige us to believe. For though Reason is not the positive and affirmative measure of our faith, and our faith ought to be larger than our (*speculative*) Reason (*see p.* 179) and *take* something into her heart, that Reason can never take into her eye; yet in all our creed there can be nothing *against* reason. If Reason justly contradicts an article it is not *of the household of Faith*. In this there is no difficulty, but that in practice we take care that we do not call *that* Reason which is not so (see *p.* 161, 162; *p.* 216). For although Reason is a right Judge, yet it ought not to pass sentence in an inquiry of faith, until all the information be brought in; all that is within, and all that is without, all that is above, and all that is below; all that concerns it in experience and all that concerns it in act; whatsoever is of pertinent observation and whatsoever is revealed. For else Reason may argue very well and yet conclude falsely. It may conclude well in Logic, and yet infer a false proposition in Theology (*p.* 161, *lines* 16–28). But when our Judge is fully and truly informed in all that, whence she is to make her Judgement, we may safely follow her whithersoever she invites us" (*AR*—1825—334–5). The lifting of this passage out of the *Op Max* to make an Aphorism in *Aids to Reflection* provides a revealing example of the tendency, noted in the Prolegomena, for C to drain off the *magnum opus* in the interests of works that did see publication. On the other hand, he frequently quoted or paraphrased his own works in the *Op Max*, e.g. the *Essay on Faith*.

therefore, any society of men calls upon us to believe in our religion what is false in our experience, to affirm that to be done, which we know is impossible it ever can be done, to wink hard that we may see the better, to be unreasonable men, that we may offer to God a reasonable sacrifice, [*f 88*] they make religion so to be sealed in the Will, that our understanding will be useless, and can never minister to it. But as he that shuts the eye hard, and with violence curls the eyelid, forces a phantastick fire from the crystalline humour, and espies a light that never shines, and sees thousands of little fires that never burn; So is he that blinds the eye of his reason, and pretends to see by an eye of faith, he makes little images of motion, and some atoms dance before him; but he is not guided by the light, nor instructed by the proposition, but sees like a man his sleep, and grows as much the wiser as the man that dreamt of a Lycanthropy, and was for ever after wisely wary not to come near a river.[161] He that speaks against his own reason, speaks against his own conscience, and therefore it is certain, no man serves God with a good conscience [*f 89*] that serves him against his reason.[162] For though in many cases reason must submit to faith, that is, natural reason must submit to supernatural, and the imperfect informations of art to the perfect revelations of God; yet in no case can true reason and a right faith oppose each other.[163]

[*f 90*]   CHAPTER VIII

                         FAITH and CONSCIENCE

The title of the present chapter, particularly the term *"Faith"*, makes it expedient to remind the reader that we are hitherto within the bounds of the unaided *reason* and *understanding*: in that sense, namely of unaided, which has been fully explained in the Chapt.[s]. That is, we use no arguments and refer to no authorities borrowed from or grounded upon any particular supposed revelation, though meantime we may be abundantly convinced that but for a particular revelation this sufficiency of the rea-

---

[s] A space was left in the ms for the chapter number, but none was written in

[161] Taylor *Worthy Communicant* (1674) 176–7.

[162] Cf *Aids to Reflection*: "APHORISM XXI. Jer. Taylor. He that speaks against his own Reason, speaks against his own Conscience: and therefore it is certain, no man serves God with a good conscience, who serves him against his reason" (*AR*—1825—335).

[163] Taylor *Worthy Communicant* (1674) 177.

son for itself would not have existed. The Boy walks unaided, though without aid he never might have learnt to walk.

Having thus, perhaps with superfluous anxiety, guarded against ~~per~~ ⟨miscon⟩ception, we may pro[*f 92*]ceed[*r*] to consider the *Faith* of *Reason*, or *Faith* in its general import.[164]

Faith [. . .] is to be defined [as] "fidelity to our own being as far as such being is not and cannot be an[*u*] object of the sense": hence by clear inference it supposes fidelity to being universally as far as the same is not the object of the senses, and herewith to whatever is necessarily affirmed or understood as the condition, concomitant, or consequence of the same. This will be best explained by an ~~instance~~ ⟨example⟩. [*v*]⟨We will take, for instance, the moral precept, "Do to others as ye would that others should do unto you." Let us translate this from the practical language of the heart into the more precise though less generally intelligible terms of the schools—the maxim⟩[*w*] [*x*](regula maxima) or paramount [*f 93*] rule of my action, both inward and outward, should be such as I could, without any contradiction ~~will to be the lawof all moral rational beings~~ therefrom arising, will to be the law of all moral and rational beings.[165] Now that I am conscious of a somewhat within me which peremptorily commands the above, that it is a primary and unconditional injunction (hence termed the *categorical imperative*)[166] which neither derives its authority nor

[*r*] The text jumps from f 90 to f 92, f 91 being left blank

[*u*] ms: an an

[*v-w*] This passage, written on f 91[*v*] with the instruction "Insert", replaces the following passage, which is cancelled in ink: "That I am conscious of a somewhat within me peremptorily commanding me to do to others as I would that others should do unto me, or to speak less popularly and in the scholastic form, that I am conscious of an unconditioned ~~imperative~~ injunction, a command which derives its authority from no anterior reason but categorically requiring obedience to itself for its own sake"

[*x*] The following words, written on f 92 before the parenthesis, were made redundant by the insertion but not cancelled: "that the maxim"

[164] "Faith is the marriage of the Will and the Reason: or shall I call it the off-spring of that Union? Where the Reason is the Eye, and the Light of the Will, and the Will is the Substance and the Life of the Reason—there Faith is" (*CN* IV 5048).

[165] Cf Kant: "so könnte der allgemeine Imperativ der Pflicht auch so lauten: *handle so, als ob die Maxime deiner Handlung durch deinen Willen zum allgemeinen Naturgesetze werden sollte*" (*Kant* IV 421).

[166] The phrase categorical imperative (*kategorischer Imperativ*) is of course taken from Kant. It functions in his *Grundlegung zur Metaphysik der Sitten* of 1785 where it is defined: "There is, therefore, only one categorical imperative. It is: Act only according to that maxim by which you can at the same time will that it should become a universal law" (*Kant* IV 421). The categorical imperative also may be defined as the injunction to treat people only as ends, and never as means: "Man, however, is not a thing, and thus not something to be used merely as a means; he must always be regarded in all his actions as an end in himself" (429).

permits it to be derived from any reason or source extrinsic to itself,[167] nor anterior except where it is implied in itself—this, I say, is *a fact* of which I am no less conscious and (though in a different way) no less assured than I am of any appearance presented to my mind by my outward senses. Nor is this all—this very consciousness possesses a character peculiar to itself, for I cannot be conscious of this as a fact in my own nature without at the same time knowing, with the same clearness, that it is a [*f 94*] fact of which all men either are or ought to be conscious— that it is a fact, the ignorance of which establishes the non-personality of the *ignorant*, or the guilt, and that in the latter case the ignorance is distinguished from that of the former as negative from privative—in other words, that it is equivalent to knowledge wilfully darkened. I know that I possess this consciousness as a man and not as the individual John or James. Now this consciousness being thus distinguished from all other acts of consciousness by its universality, and further by the circumstance that it at the same time constitutes the only practical contradistinction (i.e. diversity or difference in kind as opposed to mere difference in degree), of good right have mankind designated it by a particular term and named it the *Conscience*, as that by the natural absence or presumeable presence of which the law, both human and divine, determines [*f 95*] whether any given subject be a thing or a person;[168] or as that which never to have professed places the subject in the same order of things, e.g. in cases of idiocy, while to have lost the same implies either insanity or apostasy from man's original nature. Still more satisfactory will ⟨be⟩ our insight into the propriety [of giving] a particular rank and name to this particular act or sort of consciousness, should we be made to see that the consciousness in question is not only distinguished from all others by its universality and transcendent dignity, but that it is likewise the root and precondition of all other consciousness. Paradoxical as it may sound to describe the conscience as the ground of all proper conscious-

---

[167] Cf Kant: "alle sittliche Begriffe völlig *a priori* in der Vernunft ihren Sitz und Ursprung haben . . . . Der kategorische Imperativ würde der sein, welcher eine Handlung als für sich selbst, ohne Beziehung auf einen andern Zweck, als objectiv-nothwendig vorstellte" (*Kant* IV 411, 414).

[168] "Morality commences with, and begins in, the sacred distinction between Thing and Person: on this distinction all Law human and divine is grounded: consequently, the Law of Justice" (*AR*—

1825—321). Again: "all morality is grounded in reason. Every man is born with the faculty of Reason: and whatever is without it, be the shape what it may, is not a man or PERSON, but a THING. Hence the sacred principle recognized by all Laws, human and divine, the principle indeed, which is the *ground-work* of all law and justice, that a PERSON can never become a THING, nor be treated as such without wrong" (*Friend*—*CC*—I 189–90).

ness—anterior, therefore, to it in the order of thought,i.e. without reference to time—we yet doubt not of establishing the truth of the position, and of displaying the importance and fruitfulness. But before [*f 96*] we proceed to this attempt, it will be of the highest utility, with a view to the following ~~subj~~ points of enquiry, if we can assist the student in ~~making~~ ⟨acquiring for⟩ himself a compleat mastery of the former position—I mean that of the underived, unconditional authority of the Conscience as manifesting itself in giving to the above dictum of reason a legislative force and anchor which admits of no why or wherefore, inasmuch as it assumes to itself the ~~determination~~ solution, determination, and principle, the final judge and criterion, that is, the true ultimate why and wherefore of all other things within the sphere of morals and the practical reason. Nor will the student to whose service the present work is intended attribute any unworthy motive to the author when he eventually recommends the previous study of the *Friend*, from the 65th page with the 11th Essay, p. 217 to 240, Vol. 2d; and the Appendix to the Author's First Lay Sermon.[169] I will here [*f 97*] transcribe from the Friend, Vol. 3d, one short paragraph, or rather I will express the substance ~~with such correction~~ in the form in which the passage would stand should the work ever be reprinted under my own inspection:

"Amour de moi meme mais bien calculé"[170] was the motto and maxim of a French philosopher.[171] The powers or passions of hope and fear prompt us, and fancy enables us, to ~~present~~ ⟨bring⟩ the future ~~to~~ ⟨before⟩ our minds as present. Hence it is in our power to form a scheme of self-love,[172] and to adopt it for a system of morality. Now we will not deny, at least we will not dispute, the assertion that an enlightened self-inter-

---

[169] Of the five sections to this App, the one nominated by the letter C constitutes one of the most pregnant concentrations of important statements in all of C. There he says "neither can reason or religion exist or co-exist as reason and religion, except as far as they are actuated by the WILL" (*LS—CC*—65), but that "The conscience is neither reason, religion, or will, but an *experience* (sui generis) of the coincidence of the human will with reason and religion. It might, perhaps, be called a *spiritual sensation*; but that there lurks a contradiction in the terms, and that it is often deceptive to give a common or generic name to that, which being unique, can have no fair analogy. Strictly speaking, therefore, the conscience is neither a sensation or a sense; but a testifying state, best described in the words of our liturgy, as THE PEACE OF GOD THAT PASSETH ALL UNDERSTANDING" (*LS—CC*—67).

[170] Tr: "love of myself but well calculated". The statement has not been traced.

[171] The "French philosopher" was repeating the doctrine of Aristippus, "who took the principle of self-love, and . . . founded a system, since repeated by a French philosopher, that the ground of all morality was self-love, but that well calculated" (*P Lects*—1949—154).

[172] See above f 48.

est would recommend the same course of outward conduct as the sense of duty would prescribe, even though the motives in the former case had respect to^y this life exclusively and without aiding the scale of hope or fear by images of pain or enjoyment anticipated in a life to come. But to show the desirableness of an object or the contrary is one thing; to ex[*f 98*]cite the desire ⟨to constitute the aversion is another⟩. Compared with each other, they stand in the same relation as a common guide post would have to A̶ "a chariot instinct with spirit"^{173} which at once directs and conveys. To use a more familiar image, the maxim deduced from the calculations of self-love, compared with the law of^z ~~reason and~~ conscience as made known by the universal reason, would be as a watch with an excellent hand, hour plate, and regulator, but without spring or wheel work. Nay, where the sufficiency and exclusive validity of ⟨a calculating⟩ self-love are adopted as the maxim (regula maxima) of the moral sense, it would be a fuller and fairer comparison to say that it [is] in compare̶d̶⟨ison⟩ t̶o̶ ⟨with⟩ the conscience as the dial to the sun, indicating its path by intercepting its radiance.^{174} (Friend, Vol. 3)

The difference may be made obvious by two syllogisms, having apparently the same or equivalent conclusions. First

[*f 99*]   It is my duty to love all men.
               But I am myself a man.
               Therefore it is my duty to love myself.

^{a}⟨Or perhaps

               It is my duty to love all ~~men~~ persons.

---

^{y} ms: to to ^{z} This word mistakenly cancelled in ms
^{a} The following inserted passage is written on the verso leaves from ff 98^v–111^v

^{173} Milton *Paradise Lost* VI 750–2.
^{174} But compare this version to the version as actually printed in *The Friend* of 1818: "Amour de moi même; mais bien calculé: was the motto and maxim of a French philosopher. Our fancy inspirited by the more imaginative powers of hope and fear enbles us to present to ourselves the future as the present: and thence to accept a scheme of self-love for a system of morality. And doubtless, an enlightened self-interest would recommend the same course of outward conduct, as the sene of duty would do; even though the motives in the former case had respect to this life exclusively. But to show the desirableness of an object, or the contrary, is one thing: to excite the desire, to constitute the aversion, is another; the one being to the other as a common guide-post to the 'chariot instinct with spirit,' which at once directs and conveys, or (to use a more trivial image) as the hand, and hour-plate, or at the utmost the regulator, of a watch to the spring and wheel-work, or rather to the whole watch. Nay, where the sufficiency and exclusive validity of the former are adopted as the *maxim* (regula *maxima*) of the moral sense, it would be a fairer and fuller comparison to say, that it is to the latter as the dial to the sun, indicating its path by intercepting its radiance" (*Friend—CC*—I 424–5).

I am myself a ~~man~~ person.
Therefore it is my duty to love myself.

It is my duty to love all persons.
My neighbour is a person.
Therefore it is my duty to love my neighbour.

And as two conclusions standing in equal relation to the same major and minor are necessarily erqual to each other: "It is my duty to love myself as my neighbour, and my neighbour as myself."

Now I challenge the supporters of any scheme in which SELF is made the first principle to express the connexion between his major, or premise, and any moral conclusion in a legitimate syllogism, or in any formula which shall not transgress or be deficient in some one or more of those logical canons within which alone truth is possible. For instance, that a syllogism is necessarily vicious which contains [$f\,99^v$] more than three terms, etc. We will suppose such an attempt to be made in the following, the sense of which may indeed be better disguised and thus rendered more plausible, but by no change either in words or their arrangement will it be found really excluded:

It is my nature to love myself.
But my nature is the same as myself.
Therefore it is ⟨my⟩ nature to love my neighbour.

Now passing by the notorious falsehood, inasmuch as ~~reason~~ "nature" is either here instead of "reason", and the major is a falsehood in terms; or the word is used in its ordinary and accepted sense, as when we say it is the nature of the human female to nurse her young at the breast, and then it is a falsehood in *b*fact. For*c* nature simply impells the man to gratify himself, and even this not directly or immediately; for in fact it impels us only to remove the pain inflicted by positive want, or the restlessness and uneasiness [$f\,100^v$] produced by the fancy from the remembrance of prior gratification. Nature in this respect does not difference man from other animals but the animal, including man, from the vegetable, inasmuch as the latter is forced into motion by the presence of stimulants, soil, heat, moisture—in short, by growth—while the former is impelled to motion by the absence of the requisite stimulants, of which locomotion and action are the consequences. But passing over this and likewise the other consideration that self and its supposed instincts ([such] as the desire of gratification or the generalizing of this desire by means of the

---

b–c ms: fact; for

reflecting understanding,[175] viz. the desire of happiness or consistent, continuous, and enduring gratification)*d* are the material, the subject matter, of the moral law, the thing to be regulated, consequently not itself the rule or maxim (regula maxima). And if it be the fact that we are naturally compelled [*f 101ᵛ*] to desire our own happiness, what can be more absurd, the subject of a command, as if I should force a man's hand into the fire and command him to feel pain?*e* Passing by, I say, with this slight notice these and other defects of my opponent's major, I ask for the nexus,[176] or logical copula,[177] between this and the minor.*f* The term "neighbour" is assuredly not subsumed in the term "Self", as a species in its genus or as the term "I" in the term "person", in the first syllogism; and if not, if it be merely two distinct facts, both indeed may be true, and it may happen that you may add some third position which ~~includes~~ asserts the truth of both: each may be true, but where is the proof of either? and in what respect does the one imply the other? [and] where is the including which characterizes the minor?*g* and if nothing be included, how can the major and minor be concluded? In short, what be[*f 102ᵛ*]comes of the syllogism? ~~Lewis 15ᵗʰ is King of France~~

Lewis 15ᵗʰ was king of France, and Louis 16ᵗʰ was king of France— therefore it is indifferent which of them we place before or after the other. ~~Who would not~~ What child would not reply, "But Louis 16ᵗʰ could not have been king but for the death of Louis 15ᵗʰ", and the usurper Napoleon could not have possessed the same throne but by the suspension of his rights and those of his successor. Even so, it might very well happen that nature might prompt me to love my neighbour when I did not feel or had suspended the love of myself, and vice versa, even as she prompts me to drink instead of eating, now to exercise my senses and voluntary muscles, and now to resign them in sleep.

But we will suppose our opponent's minor to stand thus: "But reason, or reflexion, foresight, or experience inform me that my neighbour's happiness is a [*f 103ᵛ*] necessary condition of my *h*own." Still*i* it will be found to succeed no better, for in the first place either the assertion is false or a meaning is given to "happiness" which supposes the very truth

---

d Parentheses inserted   *e* Full stop in ms
f Question mark in ms   *g* Comma in ms
h–i ms: own:—Still

[175] For C's belief that "the products of the mere *reflective* faculty partook of DEATH, and were as the rattling twigs and sprays in winter" see *BL* (*CC*) I 152; for Schelling's similar animadversion against "*bloße* Reflexion" see Engell's note (*BL—CC*—I 152 n 1).
[176] Tr: "joining".
[177] Tr: "connection".

which the opponent denies, and a truth utterly incompatible with his system, namely the consciousness of having been actuated by the principle of duty, i.e. that duty was the principium.[178] And secondly, if this were otherwise, yet this formula would present the worst of all *Logisms*, a syllogism of four terms. Finally, if an inconsistency yet grosser than the preceding were possible, it would be found that each of the three integral parts of the syllogism are merely assertory, as in knowledges purely theoretical; but the argument here belongs to the practical, and the problem to be proposed respects the sources of moral obligation—and concerning this, not a word appears. Add the [*f 104ᵛ*] the words "I sh ought" to the "ergo"[179] of the syllogism, and the non sequitur, the chasm, becomes obvious, and the logical salto[180] of more than Rhodian temerity.[181]

But still further, as I have challenged the advocates of Self-love to supply a substitute for the syllogisms announced by me, so I now challenge them to place any syllogism before mine, so that mine shall be derived from the former, as a consequent from its antecedent. We will soon find The attempt will convince that they have ei must either alter the kind, μεταβασις εις αλλον γενος,[182] substituting the theoretical from ⟨or⟩ the practical, or have made the predicate a mere synonyme of the subject, or have actually presupposed what they are atempting to derive. In The two former the will be known by the subject and predicate being convertible terms: "As it is my duty to obey my conscience", i. e. my duty is my duty, while "God has commanded me to love my [*f 105ᵛ*] neighbour as my self" presupposes the position, "It is my duty to obey God"—which is indeed implied in the word "command", as distinguished from "compulsion", not to say mention the impossibility of determining whether or no it was a command of God, or, indeed, of attaching any sense containing a moral obligation to the term "God" otherwise than as the idea is manifested to us through the medium of the moral sense or idea of duty.[183] If, then, nothing diverse from the position ("it is my duty") can

---

178 Tr: "beginning".
179 Tr: "therefore".
180 Tr: "leap".
181 C more than once alludes to the "Rhodian leap". What he may have been referring to was that the two feet of the Colossus of Rhodes were planted on opposite sides of the harbour at Rhodes: "It gave us the hint of a small legion of honour . . . and one *lengthy* gentleman (excuse an Americanism on so motley a subject), who with an enormity of stride, which reduces the Rhodian Colossus to a mere idol of Lilliput, places one foot on this, and the other on the opposite, shore

of the Irish channel, and entitles himself Hibern-Anglus" (*EOT—CC*—ii 289).
182 Tr: "transfer to another kind". Cf C's own translation: "Transition into a new kind" (*AR*—1825—215). The Greek is from Aristotle *Posterior Analytics* i 7.
183 C's emphasis on duty in this paragraph and the ensuing ones is sadly ironic in view of his striking inability to heed duty's call in his own life. Cf a despondent statement from Wordsworth to Thomas Poole, in May 1809, about their mutual friend's disability. Wordsworth emphasises that he is speaking "as one of Coleridge's nearest and dearest

be true, and nothing different can be placed before it, it follows that the moral imperative or obligation of duty is, and gives to all its predicates the character of, underived, self-grounded, therefore unconditional, and of course subject to no other question than that of the fact: whether the case in point be my ^{j}duty—i.e.^{k} whether the term in question be or be not ^{l}a ⟨rightful⟩^{m} predicate of its subject. [$f 106^v$] Might I dare hope that my reader would attribute it neither to arrogance nor presumption?^{n} I would pause a moment, and indulge the fond yet earnest wish that I had the patent and the power to communicate to his mind the clear insight which I seem to myself to possess concerning the matchless importance of this familiar, alas! too familiar, and almost trivial principle, and that I could rescue it from the inertness caused by the very circumstantia of its universal admission: "Truths of all others the most awful and mysterious, and at the same time of universal interest, are too often considered as so true that they lose all the powers of truth, and lie bedridden in the dormitory of the soul, side by side with the most despised and neglected errors."^{o} It is not the avowed disciples of Hume and Helvetius; it is not the direct and unqualified denial of the position contained in the words "*I ought*"^{184} [$f 107^v$] because I ought, i.e. because I see the act in question inclusively in that law of conscience by which this "*ought*" is the contradistinguishing ground and predicate of all humanity; it is not the denial of this principle which I contemplate with alarm, but its sophistication, but its adulteration with ingredients which are meant or pretended to strengthen or quicken the operation of the ~~basis~~ ⟨principal substance⟩, or perhaps to render it more palatable, but which are destructive of the basis and like an attempt to unite acids with alkalies, neutralize both, and leave the compound at best an inert drug, and not seldom a deadly poison. Or shall we compare th~~e~~is process of moral compromise to the jarring prescriptions of the elder pharmacy^{185} in which the main ingredi-

---

$^{j-k}$ ms: duty?—i.e. $^{l-m}$ ms: ⟨rightful⟩ a
^{n} No punctuation in ms ^{o} Closing quotation mark inserted

---

Friends": "I give it to you as my deliberate opinion, formed upon proofs which have been strengthening for years, that he neither will nor can execute any thing of important benefit either to himself his family or mankind. Neither his talents nor his genius mighty as they are nor nor his vast information will avail him anything; they are all frustrated by a derangement in his intellectual and moral constitution—In fact he has no voluntary power of mind whatsoever, nor is he capable of acting under any *constraint* of duty or moral obligation" (*WL—M—*i 352).

^{184} Cf Kant: "All imperatives are expressed by an 'ought' and thereby indicate the relation of an objective law of reason to a will which is not in its subjective constitution necessarily determined by the law" (*Kant* iv 412).

^{185} The Greek word for medicine, *pharmakon*, signified both a remedy and a poison.

ent, ~~unknown~~ unnoticed by the compounder, was sure after a time to be precipitated by the several combinations of its pretended allies, and [p]the too frequent mixt[ures] [*f 108*^{v}]—I had almost said, amphibious thought, that honesty is the best policy—are so assimilated,[q] have its two heterogeneous ingredients so assimilated by close intimacy and constant juxtaposition as first to be taken as convertible, and that once effected, to permit undisputed continuance in the place of honor, and priority, to the party of which the world is the best remembrancer, and "honesty is the best policy" end in policy being the best honesty. Hence I repeat my aspiration: would that I could in this early period of our investigation[186] bring before the eye of the reader, as vividly as it is present to myself, the beautiful series of truths, philosophical, religious, yea, and fundamental likewise, which proceed from the one, for us, primary principle, groundless, indeed, because it is itself the ground of all, and indemonstrable because it is the postulate presumed in all demonstration: "That it is obli[*f 109*^{v}]gatory upon us to do our duty only because it is our duty, that in questions of duty their practicality is a second consideration which cannot even rationally be entered on [? ~~but~~] ⟨but⟩ ~~that~~ after the determination of the first, that ~~whether~~ ⟨what⟩ we can do ~~this~~ is a question without meaning or measure except in relation to the prior light what should be done, even as the mathematical ~~theorem of a~~ circle is necessary as the measure and criterion of all degrees of approximation in the material or realized figures"[r], ~~w~~While the objection, derived from religious scruples, to the doctrine of the absolute primacy, the underived nature, of the obligation contained in the moral law rests wholly on a misconception which may be elucidated by a case strictly analogous in speculative science. If I am asked how I know that I am, I can only reply, "because I am":[187] this is the absolute ground of my [*f 110*^{v}] [s]knowledge. But[t] if I were asked for the ~~ground~~ cause not of my knowledge but

[p–q] The incoherent syntax and C's use of the phrase "honesty is the best policy" later in the sentence suggest that this passage was supposed to be cancelled

[r] Closing quotation mark inserted

[s–t] ms: knowledge: but

[186] Possibly another indication that this fragment should be placed at the beginning of the *Op Max.*

[187] Cf *Biographia Literaria*: "the ground of existence, and the ground of knowledge of existence, are absolutely identical, Sum quia sum; I am, because I affirm myself to be; I affirm myself to be, because I am" (*BL—CC—*I 275). C is here modifying Descartes's "*Cogito ergo sum*" by Fichte's "*Ich bin schlechtin, weil ich bin*" (*Fichte* I 292). C's Latin—sum quia sum—looks to Descartes's formula while precisely translating Fichte's German. Cf *Logic* (*CC*) 84: "If a man be asked, 'How do you know that you are?', he can only reply, 'Sum quia sum', 'I am because I am', that is, 'I know myself to be, because I know myself to be'". Again: "If then we elevate our conception to the absolute Self, Spirit, or Mind, the under-

of the thing known, and in this sense the question were put, ~~"whence are~~ "How came you to be?", the answer must be, "Because God is." And vice "versâ. The^v knowledge is derived from the former knowledge as the cause is known in and through its effect: "quod prius est in ordine essendi, ~~terum~~ posterius in ordine sciendi".[188]

Man, with all finite self-conscious beings, knows himself to be because he is a man, but he is a man because God is and hath so willed it.[189] It is the great "I am" only, who is because he affirmeth himself to be, because, or rather in that, He is. Thus in like manner, because we have a conscience, we know that there is a God, i.e. that God is the reality of the Conscience, on the principle that the necessary condition of a certain truth must itself be true. Thus in the order [*f 111ᵛ*] of dignity and objective dependency, the principle of religion is before the moral principle, but in the order of knowledge; the moral principle is the antecedent of *our* Faith in the principle of religion.)^w

[*f 99*] ^{x}Nature prompts me to benefit myself
But in benefiting others I benefit myself
Therefore nature prompts me to benefit others as my self.

Now it is evident that the latter syllogism is defective logically in all points. It is not true that nature prompts a man to benefit himself. Nature only prompts him to gratify himself, and that, too, often even [*f 100*] to his foreknown injury. ~~And secondly~~ ⟨Again the minor⟩ is^y, as far as appears, a mere gratis dictum:[190] most assuredly it is a truth [of] which nei-

---

$^{u-v}$ ms: versâ the
^{w} At this point the insertion ends and the text resumes on f 99
^{x} At this point the following passage is cancelled in ink with an "X":
Second: Nature prompts me to love myself.
But I cannot realize this instinct without including my fellow-men in the scheme by which I realize the same.
Therefore my nature prompts me to comprehend myself and others in the same scheme of action.
Or
^{y} ms: it is

---

ived and eternal 'I Am', then and herein we find the principle of being, and of knowledge, of idea, and of reality: the ground of existence, absolutely one and identical; both are alike adequately expressed in the term 'sum quia sum', 'I am because I affirm myself to be'" (*Logic—CC*—85).

[188] Tr: "what is first in the order of being is last in the order of knowing".

[189] "The first great Truth which all men hold implicitè and the knowlege of which it is the highest business of education to make *explicit*, ut sciamus nos scire [so that we may know ourselves to know]—in other words, to lead the mind to reflect on its knowledge and by reflection to bring it forward into distinct consciousness—the first great Truth is—GOD" (*CN* IV 4644).

[190] Tr: "gratuitous saying".

ther his senses nor his appetites can have informed him, and the utmost that his understanding could do would be to render it probable that in certain instances it would be so. "Universal" and "necessary" are terms which do not belong to the decision of the understanding: and were it otherwise, yet the position, "I cannot benefit myself without benefiting other men", nor vice versâ, can never be made out but by the assumption of a species both of benefit and of principle wholly subversive of the hypothesis. But most false of all, it is not a fact that "nature prompts etc." "Nature" in this sense draws no logical conclusions; and were we abandoning the strict form of syllogism to substitute, for "nature", "reason" or "the understanding", the latter is incommensurate to the [*f 101*] task, and but by the superior light of reason could not even propose it to herself as a problem, while the reason, essentially self-less, would reject the scheme in toto. And, after all, "that is wanting without which"[z] is as lifeless as the assertion that there are trees in China, or that Mary reigned before Elizabeth. Where is the obligation? If, as will be too frequently the case, the sensualist should say to the philosophic Epicurean,[191] "The gratification of your pity, or of a fine taste in the order or proportion of things, or a mere absence of pain with a long continuance of an indifferent state, may be the prompting of your nature, and you may gratify yourself—but my nature prompts me to a merry life though short one, and instead of the sweet pleasures of weeping and sighing over disgusting objects in sympathy with doleful faces, I find my pleasure, and as [*f 102*] I think, more naturally, in laughing with those that laugh and in receiving pleasure from that which gives it, whether it receives it in return as my boon companion or [a]not. Like[b] my mantling bowl,[192] I trouble not myself about the difference!" How, I say, is this man to be confuted? What sense can the refined Epicurean place under the words, "But *you ought* to do otherwise"? So true is it that the forms of science are not tenable without assuming a truth higher than science can supply.

---

[z] Quotation marks inserted   [a-b] ms: not, like

[191] Note once more the constant undercurrent of argument against Epicurean doctrine. The "philosophic" Epicurean, that is, the adherents of what Epicurus actually said, is here distinguished from the unthinking hedonist. In general cf *The Friend*: "If we would drive out the demons of fanaticism from the people, we must begin by exorcising the spirit of Epicureanism in the higher ranks and restore to their teachers the true Christian enthusiasm" (*Friend—CC*—I 432). C would have been aware of the ed of Lucretius published by Gilbert Wakefield in 1796–97, and he was explicitly aware that Lucretius presented a "complete view" of Epicurean doctrine (*TT—CC*—I 202). See Prolegomena III: The Epicurean and Stoic Background.

[192] A sparkling "head" or froth.

Well then! That all actions and the impulses thereof, as distinguished from the motives,[193] proceed from self (in one sense of th~~ate~~ term "Self") is a point which we readily concede, or rather, it is but a disguised way [of saying] that the agent is the agent, or that every action supposes its own agent. But on the other hand we affirm with no less consequence that every action does not ne[*f 103*]cessarily proceed to~~ward~~ Self, ~~but~~ and that in many cases it both ought to and may proceed directly toward another person—that if we conceive the Self at the apex of ⟨an isosceles tri⟩angle ~~formed~~ inverted, abstracting the base, we have it in our power to contemplate our objective S~~s~~elf and our neighbour as morally equidistant from S, and of proceeding in the line SN or Ss, according as the moral law shall have predetermined to be our duty. This, I contend, is a fact of which every honest man is as fully assured as he is of his ~~seeing~~ ⟨touching⟩, ~~hearing~~ ⟨tasting⟩, or smelling, though I will not deny that in all mere acts not accompanied by an appropriate image, whether of the Will, as ⟨in⟩ the first case, or of the senses, as in the second, it is difficult to say to what extent a man in the ardour of disputation may not produce a sort of wilful forgetfulness, or substitution of one class of facts for another by dex[*f 104*]terous management of imperfect synonymes or equivocal terms. But though the former assurance does not differ from the latter in the degree, it is altogether diverse in the kind, the senses being morally passive while the conscience is essentially connected with the Will, though not always; nor indeed, in any case, except after repeated attempts and aversions of the Will itself, can the ~~e~~Conscience become dependent on our choice. Observe, too, that whenever such a case occurs, the immediate dictate of the Conscience is no longer gratificatory on its own account, but must be contemplated as ~~any other mechanic~~ ⟨a mere⟩ product of the Will mechanized wilfully into a habit which becomes the destructive, ~~subs~~ or at least suspensive, substitute of the will, and must therefore derive from the ~~inchoative~~[c] ⟨initial⟩ principle of the process.

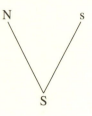

[c] An uncertain reading: a line is drawn above the words "inchoative principle" and may

[193] Note the desynonymization of "impulse" and "motive". For "motive" see ff 55–6. Cf *Omniana*: "It is a matter of infinite difficulty, but fortunately of comparative indifference, to determine what a man's *motive* may have been for this or that particular action. Rather seek to learn what the *objects* in general are!—What does he habitually wish? habitually pursue?—and thence deduce his impulses, which are commonly the true efficient causes of men's conduct; and without which the motive itself would not have become a *motive*" (*SW & F— CC*—I 310).

=cessarily proceed ~~toward~~ Self ~~but~~ and that in many cases it both ought to, and may, proceed directly toward another person— that if we conceive the Self at the apex of an isosceles tri= angle ~~formed~~ inverted abstracting the base we have it in our power to contemplate our ob: =jective Self and our neighbour as morally equidistant from S and of proceeding in the line SN or SS, according as the moral law shall have predeter: =mined to be our duty. This I contend is a fact of which every honest man is as fully assured as he is of his ~~seeing~~ touching ~~tasting~~ or smelling: though I will not deny that in all mere acts not accompanied by an appropriate image, whether of the Will as the first case, or of the senses as in the second it is difficult to say to what extent a man in the widow of disputation may not produce a sort of wilful forget =fulness or substitution of one class of facts for another by dex.

2. Diagram from Fragment 1 in Joseph Henry Green's hand. VCL S MS 29 Vol II f 103. Victoria College Library; reproduced by kind permission

In other words, not *what* the conscience of an inquisition may have dictated, [*f 105*] but *how* any man with a conscience could allow himself to become an inquisitor in the first instance is the first instance which the man of single heart would alone consider to determine the moral nature of the act dictated, and inclusively of the agent. ~~We~~ In affirming the equality of the assurance derived from the conscience and from the senses in degree of conviction, we have admitted a difference in kind, and ~~this in strict correspondence with language~~ this same difference is expressed in our ordinary language. The presentations of our senses we call impressions; those of the conscience, commands or dictates. In the senses, as far as our *personal* being is concerned, we are passive: in the language of the schools, in the senses and sensations we *find* our receptivity, but in the facts of the conscience we are not only agents; but it is by these alone that we know ourselves to be such. Nay! we are aware [*f 106*] that our very passiveness herein is *an act* of passiveness, that we are patient, not simply, as in the other case, passive. The result is a consciousness of responsibility, and the proof is afforded by the inward experience of the positive diversity (i.e. difference in kind, not merely in degree, between regret and remorse).[194] While I retain sound ears, my companion speaks to me with a due proportion of voice; ⟨tho'⟩ I may persuade him that I did not hear,[195] I cannot deceive ^{d}myself. But^e when my conscience speaks to me, I can by repeated efforts render myself finally insensate, to which add this other difference, that to make myself deaf relatively to the voice of my conscience is one and the same thing with making my conscience dumb. Frequent are the instances in which the conscience is suspended, or, as it were, drowned in the inun-

---

be intended to cancel both words or neither word, while "initial" is written above both the word "inchoative" and the line

$^{d-e}$ ms: myself; but

[194] Another of C's "desynonymized" pairings, which were of such moment for his dialectical procedure. This one occurs in other places than this, e.g. *SW & F (CC)* II 836, *CL* v 162. "That Regret and Remorse are feelings different in kind, and not merely as degrees and modifications [of] one and the same feeling, is a fact, which it only requires solitude & sincere self-questioning to establish in the mind—so, that no sophistry can reason it away, no fear of being deemed superstitious & unenlightened by philosophy can scare it, no ridicule scoff it, out of our consciences.

Where ever we are distinctly conscious, that our Will has had no share direct or indirect in the production of a given event or circumstance, that is painful and calamitous to ourselves or others, we feel *Regret*" (*Lects 1808–1819—CC*—I 63).

[195] Repeatedly through this and the succeeding run of argument C virtually and often exactly quotes his *Essay on Faith* of 1820. Cf the sentence above with the *Essay on Faith*: "If I have sound Ears, and my Companion speaks to me, I may persuade *him* that I did not hear, but I cannot deceive myself" (*SW & F— CC*—II 836).

[*f 107*]dations of the appetites, passions, and imaginations to which the man had, and in the beginning willingly, resigned himself, making use of his Will in order to abandon his *f* Free-will. And*g* there are not, I fear, examples wanting of the conscience being utterly destroyed, or of the passage of wickedness into madness—that species of madness, namely, which implies the loss of the reason, and a mere derangement of the understanding (v. The Friend, vol. i, p. 261–277).[196] For as long as the reason continues, so long must the conscience exist in some form, as a good conscience or as a bad. ~~It appears then~~

It appears, then, that the first step that even the iniative of this process, the becoming conscious of a conscience, partakes of the nature of an act.[197] It is an act,[198] namely, in which and by which we take upon ourselves an allegiance, and [*f 108*] consequently the obligations of fealty. And this fealty, or fidelity, implying the power of being unfaithful, is the *primary* and *fundamental meaning* of FAITH. But it is likewise, paradoxical as it may appear, the commencement of experience and the indispensable pre-condition of all experience.[199] The position ⟨is⟩, I am well aware, somewhat more than paradoxical: it is not only *praeter*[200] but *contra* opinionem ferè omnibus hujus seculi philosophi acceptam.[201] Such, however, is my conviction, and this is at once the distinctive and constitutive basis of my philosophy—~~T~~that I place my first principle, the ground and genesis of my system, not, as others [do], in a fact impressed, much less in a generalization from facts collectively, and least of all from an abstraction embodied into an hypothesis in which the pretended solution [*f 109*] is most often but a repetition of the problem in disguise, a mere abbreviation of the thing to be solved. In contradistinction from this I place my principle in an *act*. In the language of grammarians, I begin with the verb, but the act involves its reality—it is the act of being,

f–g ms: Freewill: and

[196] See *Friend* (*CC*) I 189 ff.

[197] Cf a statement of 1815: "The transcendental Philosophy first solved this problem,—by beginning not with a Thing or Theorem, as all others do, but with an *act*" (*SW & F—CC*—I 407). Coleridge's insistence upon the role of "act" in the psychic economy is conditioned at least in part by his early adherence to Necessitarianism, which emphatically makes man a passive vehicle.

[198] Cf C in 1816: "Now all Power is but Will realizing itself in Act, of which Being (as in the absolute Will, or omnipotence) or some mode of Being as in finite Wills (ex. gr. that of the Artist) is the product—" (*SW & F—CC*—I 429).

[199] Cf *Essay on Faith*: "It appears then, that even the very first step, that the initiative, of this Process, the becoming conscious of a Conscience, partakes of the nature of an *Act*. It is an Act, in and by which we take upon ourselves an allegiance & consequently, the obligation of *Fealty*. And this Fealty or Fidelity implying the power of being unfaithful is the first and fundamental sense of Faith. It is likewise the commencement of Experience" (*SW & F—CC*—II 836–7).

[200] Tr: "outside".

[201] Tr: "against the view generally held by all philosophers of this age".

a verb substantive of which, as the radix containing both as in one, the substantive and the verb are the two poles. In other words (and in a subject so remote from common apprehension, in which it is well if we can make ourselves intelligible by any means, we may be allowed to vary our metaphors, provided we offer them as no more than tentative illustrations)^h, I contemplate the line not as the result of the aggregate of the component points, as in the mechanico-corpuscular system, but as the product of the point, the production of the point into a line, [*f 110*] the evolution of the plant out of the germ which virtually had contained it previous to the evolution—according to which view, in the primary sense above given, i.e. in its simplest form, must be supposed in order to consciousness, I mean human ^{i}consciousness. The^j conscience, I say, is not a mere mode of our consciousness, but presupposed therein.[202] Brutes may be and are *scious*, but not conscious.[203] Here, however, our present language fails in affording a term sufficiently discriminative. I affirm that all proper consciousness is conditioned by self-consciousness, i.e. that the latter is the indispensable antecedent of the former;[204] but ⟨in objection⟩ to this it might be asked, "Nonne potest animal (bos vel cervus) scire truncam arboris? aeque ac se cum arbore vel arborem unà cum se!"[205] If we ~~answer~~ allow that the two consciousnesses are co-ordinate, we must of course [*f 111*] negative the position of the antecedence of the latter. But if we answer that the former (scientiam arboris cum ramis)[206] must have begun in the latter, viz. in scientia cujus libet rei cum se,[207] we must either allow self-consciousness to animals or find another term for self, as objective self, corpus sensibile seu forma corporis exterior,[208] in distinction from the subjective Self, as abstracted from all objects and considered as that which reflects on and contem-

---

^{h} Closing parenthesis inserted

$^{i–j}$ ms: consciousness;—the

[202] "The Sum of the Philosophy which I receive as the only true Philosophy may be thus exprest. 1. Con*science* is not a Result or Modification of Self-Consciousness; but its Ground and Antecedent Condition. (*Conditio sine qua non*.)" (*CN* IV 5167).

[203] C's continuing argument is an explication of the implications contained in the prefix "con"—"with". Thus consciousness is necessarily a "knowing withness". Cf *Essay on Faith*: "in other words, *Conscience* must, in this its simplest form, be supposed in order to *Consciousness*. Brutes may be and are *scious*" (*SW & F—CC*—II 837).

[204] "The Act of Self-consciousness contains in itself (ponit et imponit) the highest and most general *formula* of all real Science. A = A is the Key of Universal Nature" (*CN* IV 5167).

[205] Tr: "is an animal (ox or deer) not able to know the trunk of a tree . . . and itself with the tree or the tree along with it?" Cf a note of Sept 1820: "Might not an animal scire truncum arboris cum ramis, as well as se cum arbore, or arborem cum se?" (*CN* IV 4717).

[206] Tr: "knowledge of a tree with branches". Cf *CN* IV 4717.

[207] Tr: "knowledge of anything at all with itself".

[208] Tr: "the sensible body, or exterior form of the body".

plates all, or another term for consciousness ~~expressing~~ ⟨in order that this term may be appropriated [. . .]^k⟩ to the self-knowledge in this latter, higher sense of the term "Self". Such a term—if, as I believe, this should be the more advisable expedient—might be easily supplied without any violence to the habit of our language: "*Self-sentience*", for instance, or "*Self-percipience*", and with this additional power of conveying the strict purport of my position.[209] I should re-~~affirm~~⟨avow⟩ my conviction [*f 112*] that all proper consciousness is both conditioned by and involves, though it may not be demonstrable or even probable that all *consentiency* suppose *Self-consentience*, or, which is perhaps a less ambiguous term, that all *con-percipiency* supposes *self-conpercipience*. Exchanging the term "scire"[210] for "percipere",[211] I should agree, "animal truncum cum ramis percipere posse aeqe ac se, i.e. corpus suum cum arbore vel arborem cum se".[212] But further, I should assert, nevertheless, that those beings only who possess a proper self, ego ⟨sensu⟩ subjectivo scire posse hoc vel illud unà cum se ipsis ⟨~~hoc quidem~~⟩ ~~in sensu eodem~~.[213] Henceforward I shall presume my reader's recognition of the "conscire"[214] as equal with "scire aliquid cum me",[215] ~~to~~ i.e. to know something in its relation to myself in and with the act of knowing myself as acted on by that something,[216] and proceed to prove [*f 113*] the dependence of all consciousness on a self-consciousness,[217] thus: the^l third pronoun "*he*",

---

^{k} One or two words crowded into the margin ^{l} ms: The

[209] Compare, with the foregoing and succeeding paragraphs, a note of 1820 where C argues that "*all* Consciousness is necessarily conditioned by Self-consciousness—": "Might not an animal *scire* truncum arboris *cum* ramis, as well as *se* cum arbore, or arborem cum *se*? If it be answered, that it must have *begun* in Self-consciousness, as the first Link, we must either allow Self-consciousness to animals, or find another term either for 'Self' as objective Self, distinguished from the Subjective by abstraction, or for Consciousness, as Self-Consciousness. The latter will perhaps be more advisable;—as Self-sentience, Self-percipience, as we might then say, that all *consciousness* is conditioned by Self-consciousness, tho' it may not be demonstrable, that all Consentiency supposes Self-consentience, or all Conpercipiency Self-conpercipience—" (*CN* IV 4717).

[210] Tr: "to know".

[211] Tr: "to perceive".

[212] Tr: "the animal can perceive the trunk with branches, equally with itself, i.e., its body with the tree or the tree with itself".

[213] Tr: "the I, in the subjective sense, can know this or that as one with itself".

[214] Tr: "consciousness of".

[215] Tr: "to know something with myself".

[216] Cf *Essay on Faith*: "Brutes may be and are *scious*; but those Beings only who have an *I*, *scire* possunt hoc vel illud una *cum* se ipsis. Conscire = scire aliquid cum *me*; or to know something in its relation, and in the act of knowing myself as acted on by that something" (*SW & F—CC—*II 837).

[217] Cf a letter of Apr 1818: "Does not personality necessarily suppose a *ground* distinct from the Person, id, *per* quod sonat A, ab A sive materiâ soni? Conscire, = scio et me et salterum simul vel scio me dum scio alterum—Ergo, Sui Conscientia = scio me quasi alterum. The *Me* in the objective case is clearly distinct from the *Ego*" (*CL* IV 849).

"*it*", etc. could never have been contradistinguished from the first, ~~but~~ "I", "me", etc. but by means of the second. There could be no "*He*" without a previous "*Thou*", and I scarcely need add that without a "*Thou*" there could be no opposite,[218] and of course no distinct or conscious sense of the term "*I*", as far as the consciousness is concerned, without a "*Thou*". But whatever may be affirmed or believed respecting the soul as a substraction or hypostasis of the Self, the "I" ~~subsi~~ exists wholly in consciousness. Much less, then, could the neuter pronoun "*it*" exist for us except as it exists during the suspension of the will, as in dreams or states analagous thereto, and I may be permitted to observe in transitu[219] that the clearest conception I can form respecting [*f 114*] the nature of beasts—of course conjectural at best—is to regard them as somnambulists. If, then, there can be no "*He*" nor "*It*" without an "*I*", and no "*I*" without a "*Thou*", the solution of the problem must be sought for in the genesis or origination of the "*Thou*". But in order to this I must require from the reader an energy of attention correspondent to the subtlety of the subject, far beyond what I shall have occasion to require in any following part of the work. But if the reader will place himself so far in the same state of Self-observation as the writer, he will discover that the consciousness expressed in the term "*Thou*" is only possible by an equation in which "*I*" is taken as equal to but yet not the same as "*Thou*", and that this again is only possible by putting the "*I*" and "*Thou*" in opposition to each other[220]—in logical antithesis, I mean—as correspondent [*f 115*] opposites, as harmonies or correlatives.[221] And again he will find that in order to this a something must be affirmed in the one, which is negatived in the other[222]—without which, indeed, they would be

---

[218] Cf *Essay on Faith*: "Now the third pronoun could never have been contradistinguished from the first but by means of the Second: no He without a previous Thou—and of course, no *I* without a *Thou*" (*SW & F—CC*—II 837).

[219] Tr: "in passing".

[220] "I and my Fellow-man live, we know not how—or the viewless Air nourishes us—. We know each other's presence tho' we do not yet see each other—e contra, our communion consists in the reciprocal knowledge in the generation of an I by a Thou" (*CN* IV 5157).

[221] In various places in his notebooks, C reveals himself struggling towards this conclusion, e.g. a query in 1818: "Whether in the Dynamic Construction of Grammar the second person ought not to be advanced to the Third, and the Third retracted to the second place?—It is an evident Trichotomy, consequently, Thesis, Antithesis, and Synthesis—Now I and It are evidently the antitheses—He, She are It potenziated by the original and perpetual Thesis—but Thou seems clearly to be I + it + i = he = Thou. It must never be forgotten that I is a perpetual, i.e. ever recurring Thesis", and so on for two more paragraphs (*CN* III 4426).

[222] Cf *Essay on Faith*: "—This is a deep meditation, tho' the position is susceptible of the strongest proof—namely that there can be no *I* without a *Thou*, & that a Thou is only possible by an equation in which I is taken as ⟨equal to⟩ a

Sames and indistinguishable. Now this something can only be the Will.[223] I do not will to consider myself equal to myself, for in the very act of Self-constitution I declare that the Self or the object is one and the same with the *I*, the subject:[224] if, then, the same, not susceptible of comparison; but to compare is, in its largest sense, that part of the intellect which appertains to the Will, from the suspension of which, under the specific form of volition, the characteristic phaenomena of sleep are confessedly derived. It follows, therefore, that in the affirmation of the *I* primary as equal to the reflex *I*—in other words, that in the identification of the subject and [*f 116*] object, in which self-consciousness consists,[225] there is no application or intervention of the Will. If, then, *I* — Will be the Thesis, the antithesis must needs be + the Will, and the *Thou*, which is the admitted antithesis, becomes so, that is, doth itself become ~~by I~~ inasmuch as it is + Will. Now this equation of *Thou* with *I*, by means of a free act ⟨by⟩ which ⟨we⟩ negative the sameness in order to establish the equality—this, I say, is the true definition of Conscience.[226] But as the plural presupposes the singular, as without a *Thou* there can be no *Ye*, and without these no *They*, whether *These* or *Those*, and as all these conjointly constitute the materials and subjects of consciousness, and these again the conditions of experience, it is evident [that this] is the root of all human consciousness, and à fortiori the pre-condition of all experience; and therefore that the conscience in its first revelation cannot have been [*f 117*] deduced from experience. Q. E. D.[227] *Scholium.* In order to complete the foundation of the following argument, it will be necessary to establish the disparateness of the reason from the under-

---

Thou, & yet not the same. And this again is only possible by putting them in *opposition*, as Correspondents Opposites or Correlatives; in order to this, a something must be affirmed in the one which is negatived in the other" (*SW & F—CC*—ii 837).

[223] Cf *The Friend*: "all true reality has both its ground and its evidence in the *will*" (*Friend—CC*—i 519–20).

[224] Cf a statement in 1821: "and yet without confounding the inherent distinction between subject and object, the subject witnesses to itself that it is a mind, i.e. a subject-object, or subject that becomes an object to itself" (*SW & F—CC*—ii 928). See Prolegomena xviii: Subject and Object.

[225] Cf a note of 1825: "the human 'I Am' as known in the act of Self re-

flection, is expressed in the formula, I affirm myself— *Ipse me pono*—the *I* representing the Subject, & the *myself* the *Object*, while the Ειμι, or Sum, is the Identity of both" (*CN* iv 5280).

[226] Cf *Essay on Faith*: "the equation of *Thou* with *I* by means of a free Act, negativing the sameness in order to establish the equality is the true definition of *Conscience*—" (*SW & F—CC*—ii 837).

[227] Cf *Essay on Faith*: "it is evident, that the Conscience is the root of all Consciousness, and a fortiori the precondition of all Experience, & that the Conscience in its first revelation cannot have been deduced from Experience. Quod erat demonstrandum—" (*SW & F—CC*—ii 837–8).

standing and the distinct nature of each. For this, however, the reader is supposed to have been prepared by a preceding reference to the 1st Vol. of the Friend,[228] in which this subject is fully treated, or to the glossary[229] of philosophical terms under the words "reason" and "understanding", where the substance of the ⟨author's⟩ former lucubrations will be found with additional authorities and elucidations. For the present, or where the opportunities of making the desired references are wanting, I must content myself with the attempt to convey some general notion of the disparateness by the following definitions—UNDERSTANDING: i.e. where it is not used as a synonyme for the soul ~~itself~~ or for the man himself considered as an intelligent being, but as a [*f 118*] distinct faculty, the Understanding is the faculty ~~by which~~ of adapting means to ends according to varying circumstances; while the REASON ~~supp~~ implies an insight into the necessity and universality of ~~the~~ relations ~~of thing~~, and may be defined [as] the power of drawing universal and necessary conclusions from individual forms or facts, ex.gr. from any three-cornered ~~figur~~ object or outline we conclude that in all triangles the two sides ⟨conjointly⟩ are necessarily greater than the third.[230] We ~~p~~have as little doubt that the sun will rise tomorrow as that the two sides of ~~a~~ every possible triangle are greater than the ^{m}third. But^n before we could venture to affirm that the sun *must* rise tomorrow, that there is an absurdity in the words "the ~~sha~~ sun shall not rise", even though they were attributed to omnipotence, we must first have proved that gravitation and what are called the laws of nature are God, or one and the same [*f 119*] with the being of God, and not effects or consequents of the Will contained in his wisdom. In short, whatever in its own nature, speculatively considered, excludes contingency, and the certainty of which, incapable of all degrees, receives no increase from increase of experience, belongs to the Reason,[231] and to the Understanding only as far as the reason is co-present with the same.

Soon, however, experience comes into play. ~~w~~We learn that there are

$^{m-n}$ ms: third: but

[228] See *Friend* (CC) I 154–61.

[229] C attempted such glossaries on several occasions, e.g. "A Glossary of Terms" *SW & F (CC)* I 687–94.

[230] Though C will supply a comprehensive examination of Reason and Understanding in the fragment immediately succeeding, it is interesting to note that he seems to feel it advisable, as this fragment comes to its conclusion, to illuminate the discussion here. As impetus for the discussion, cf a note on Boehme: "Scarcely a Day in my Life passes in which I do not meet with some fresh instance of the Evils or Inconveniences arising from the misuse of the word, Reason, instead of the Understanding, or φρονημνα σαρκος—" (*CM—CC—*I 693). In general see Prolegomena v: Reason and Understanding.

[231] Cf C in a note on Boehme: "The Reason is a Participation of *Ideas*: &

other impulses besides the dictates of conscience, that there are powers within us and without us ready to usurp the throne of conscience, and busy in tempting us to transfer our allegiance. We learn that there are many things contrary to conscience, and which must on this account be repelled and utterly excluded; that there are many things that can co-exist with the conscience only by being subjugated to it, as ~~in beasts of burthen~~ [*f 120*] larger and more powerful beasts are privileged to co-exist with the human race ⟨only⟩ by becoming beasts of burden; and there are other things, such, for instance, as the social tendencies and affections, and the faculties and exercitations of the intellect, that must be at least subordinated, that are compatible with the full rights and claims of the conscience only as far as they acknowledge its supremacy, and are at least in negative obedience to its laws. Now the preservation of our loyalty and fealty against all these rivals and under all these trials constitutes the second sense of faith, ~~The first~~ if that sense can indeed be called second which is but an evolution of the former when the term is applied to man. Faith is fidelity,[232] but all human fidelity that is consistent with itself is fidelity to the conscience.[233] But this again cannot exist as fidelity to the sole supre[*f 121*]macy of the conscience, and this admitted, we have only to determine what the objects are in which it is to be manifested, and what the competitors are against which it is to be supported, in order to complete the full and final import of the term. And, again, in order to determine these points, we have only to ~~seek~~ ⟨ask of ourselves⟩, what is pre-supposed in the human conscience? The answer is ready.[o] ~~a~~As in the preceding equation of the correlatives *I* and *Thou*, ~~one of these twin constituents was to be taken as A − Y, the other as A + Y, the Y here signifying the Will~~ these twin constituents were differenced from each other as I = A − Z: Thou = A + Z (Z here meaning the Will), so must it be in the present case; and the question cannot be placed distinctly before the mind, but it ⟨must⟩ become obvious that here the reason, or the universal in each individual man, ~~by~~ ⟨without⟩ which he would not be [*f 122*] man, is the factor which we are to take as − Z, or

---

[o] Dash in ms

---

strictly speaking, it is no *Faculty*, but a Presence, an Identification of Being & Having" (*CM—CC—*I 682).

[232] Cf *Essay on Faith*: "FAITH may be defined as = *Fidelity* to our own Being as far as such Being is not and cannot become an object of the sense" (*SW & F—CC—*II 834).

[233] Cf C on the definition of faith in Hebrews: "Faith is the evidence (i.e. not a mere probable conclusion from a chain of inductions, but an evidence, or intuitive Assurance) of things that cannot be seen by the bodily Eyes" (*SW & F—CC—*II 845).

not the subject of Will, ex.gr. in the perception of mathematical truth. It would be absurd to command a man to believe, i.e. to bid him will to believe that two and two make four: he cannot help doing so if he but understands the position. But there would be no absurdity in bidding him yield a willing attention in order that he might understand the equality of some position with some axiom of the reason, the perception of ⟨the truth of⟩ which has no dependence on his Will.

FRAGMENT 2

VCL S MS 29; "Say Vol. II" (*L&L* B3); wm "JOHN HALL | 1817". This is the largest of the three clasped vellum notebooks of S MS 29, and is identified as Vol II by C. A. Ward in pencil on the verso of the second blank flyleaf, facing f 1. The ms is written in the hands of JHG (ff 1–39, 73–268) and a second amanuensis (ff 39–73), almost certainly John Watson, with occasional corrections and insertions in C's hand. Additional corrections and comments in pencil, evidently by Ward, have been made throughout the volume; these are recorded in the textual notes. Pasted inside the front cover of the notebook is an envelope containing the following items: (1) a two-leaf autograph note by Alice D. Snyder, signed and dated 27 Jan 1927, identifying the pencilled notes on the versos as Ward's, reversing his ordering of Vols II and III, and suggesting that the second amanuensis was JG; (2) five scraps of paper with notes on the text in black ink by Warren E. Gibbs (identified in pencil by Kathleen Coburn); (3) three scraps of paper with notes in blue ink by James Boulger, noting that ff 209–13 were published in *L&L* 131–3 and that the quotation from Vico on f 35 was published in Shedd I 383; (4) a scrap of paper with note in pencil by Kathleen Coburn, noting that f 8 of the ms was also published in Shedd.

DATE. 1820–3. See headnote to Frag 1 on Watson. Ff 7–25 derive from C's "Essay on Faith" of c Jul 1820 (*SW&F—CC*—838–44). On f 25 C quotes from Proclus's *In Platonis theologiam*, which JHG had given him on 22 Nov 1820 (*CN* IV 4744 and n).

[*f 1*]   Chapter

We have thus ~~substantiated~~ found the correspondent to the one factor A − Z in the reason.[1] The factor A + Z can be no other than the ~~individual~~ Will itself but as the individual Will, or the Will considered as the principle of personality and free-agency, and which, under the sanction of Milton's authority, we might venture to distinguish by the term "*Arbitrement*"—"free in thine own Arbitrement it lies" (Paradise Lost) [a].[2]

As we are still within the bounds ~~of the mind~~ prescribed by the mind, exerting its powers unaided on such factors alone as are found within its

[a] Parentheses inserted

[1] This statement clearly follows on directly from the close of the preceding fragment, and identifies the sequence of the fragments.
[2] Bk VIII, line 641.

80

own consciousness, and as we have been [enquiring]^b hitherto what these facts are and have not yet arrived at the point in which we can apply the deductions therefrom so as to c~~l~~onclude the reality of any object or article of our faith, we are permitted only to affirm that if the word have a meaning essentially different from that conveyed [f 2] by any other term, it must be conceived as asserting the identity, or co-inherence, of the Will and the Reason; and, therefore, in order ~~not~~ for the one not to be differenced as in the former equation, in which the equality and not the identity is supposed, we must take the Will as the absolute Will. We may then, without anticipation, affirm that the identity of the absolute Will and the ~~supreme~~ universal Reason is peculiar to the idea of God.^{3}

In man, therefore, we must be able to discover a substitute, or analogon, for *identity*, and likewise for *absolute*, these being peculiar to the divine idea. This we find in one instance in the conception of synthesis, and in the other, by the substitution of individual: so that what in God is the identity, or ⟨necessary⟩ co-inherence, of the absolute Will and the reason subsists in man as the possible, either realized or realizable, synthesis and the common, or universal, reason by the subordination of the former to the later. Now as "likeness", or "image", unites in itself [f 3] the notions of sameness and ~~identity~~ diversity, this possible synthesis of the individual with the given universal is the only conceivable likeness, or image, of the necessary identity^4 of the absolute and self-originating universal. In the latter both factors pre-exist, each in the other, a perfect One as Prothesis; in man the analogous factors appear ~~a~~severally as Thesis and Antithesis, and he himself is to complete the analogon by uniting them ~~by~~ ⟨in⟩ a Synthesis which, as^c is before shown, he can effect only by a continued act of subordinating the one to the other. Antecedently, therefore, to the question whether we are authorized or obliged by or with reason to ^{d}affirm ⟨attribute⟩^{e} reality to the idea of

---

^{b} Word supplied in pencil on blank verso facing f 1, probably by C. A. Ward

^{c} ms: is as

$^{d-e}$ In the ms "attribute" is written directly above "affirm" and a horizontal line, which may have been intended to cancel "affirm", separates the two words

^{3} But as those two ultimates reveal themselves in the world, certain gradations occur: "the Universe of Finite Existences began, & is not a co-eternal Effect of an Eternal Ground & Cause, a creation, not an emanation—Consequently, that Will is no less a real & essential Principle of ·Things than Reason, yea, that the Will is deeper than Reason, and is to Reason as the spring & basin water of an artificial Fountain to the Salient Column (*CN* iv 5144).

^{4} Cf a note on Donne: "Now Will is the true principle & meaning of *Identity*, of *Selfness*: even in our common Language. The Will therefore being indistinguishably one, but the possessive Powers triply distinguishable do perforce involve the notion expressed by three *Persons* and one *God*" (*CM—CC*—ii 250).

God,[5] reason itself sanctions and enforces the conclusion: 1st, that[f] there is the idea, and as will, I trust, be made still more clear hereafter, that the idea is unique and not composed by any processes of imaginary comparison,[6] or arbitrary assertion of indefinite intensity or magnitude; 2[dly], that[g] if we assume the existence [*f 4*] of the Supreme Being, it is by affirming reality of this idea exclusively[7] that we can attach any rational meaning to the term "God", or to the position [that] *God is* and *exists*; 3[dly], that this idea is both the canon and the criterion by which the character and legitimacy of whatever is offered to us as representing or proceeding from God [is to be tested][h], and, of course, that the idea is presupposed in, and in order to, every such legitimate determination[8]— suppose that an appearance of light in the human figure, or some modification of the same, as of a man of wings, or as a mere blaze of glory, should present itself to the senses of an individual, and a voice should be heard, "I am God", or "sent from God", the individual must have previously formed a conception, which he had appropriated to the word God, or the voice heard might as well have been an inarticulate sound, the glory a mere ~~aceum~~ extrication of electrical light and the sound a thunder-clap. And according to the purity or sophistication, the adequateness or inadequateness, of the [*f 5*] conception, i.e. according to its greater or lesser coincidence with the above idea, must be the faith built by him on this phaenomenon. And, in like manner, without the ideas as a criterion ⟨applied to the following command or message⟩[i], how can he ascertain whether the apparition speaks truth or falsehood?[j] [9] 4[thly] and lastly, the

---

f ms: That   *g* ms: That
h Insertion written in pencil on f 3[v] and marked for insertion here
i Insertion written in ink on f 4[v] and marked for insertion here
j Dash in ms

---

[5] Cf a note on Baxter: "A *Conception* of God, whether in or out of the flesh, is an Absurdity; but the *Idea*, God (for a temptation to error lurks in the phrase, Idea *of* God) is for Man, yea, as the form, norm, ground and condition of all other Ideas may be affirmed to constitute his Reason" (*CM—CC—*I 237).

[6] Cf C on Hooker: "the Trinity is an Idea, and no Idea can be rendered by a conception. An Idea is essentially inconceivable" (*CM—CC—*II 1145).

[7] Here, as elsewhere, C restates the hugely influential position of Anselm, that existence must be predicated of the idea of God that we find in our minds, otherwise the idea is not an idea of God.

[8] Cf a note on Waterland: "The *Idea*, God, like all other *Ideas*, rightly so called and as contra-distinguished from 'Conceptions' as not properly *above* Comprehension, as *alien* from it" (Brinkley 386).

[9] "How got the Atheist his idea of that God which he denies—I have always held Des Cartes' Proof the best & tenable" (*CN* III 4087). Descartes's proof is a variant of the *a priori* proof of Anselm, that the idea is necessitated by the structure of the human mind, and that it is an idea of a perfection that to be perfect necessarily requires the existence of its subject. Elsewhere C refers to "the famous Cartesian demonstration. He found that the idea of God was the only idea of

reality of the idea, i.e. the existence of God, having been conceded, reason itself obliges us to conclude[10] that God-likeness, or to be the image of God, must be the proper character of man;[11] that, however, as this likeness is not self-existent or necessary, but the product of the individual Will, then if it existed originally in man, it must have been given by some other Will as the inceptive momentum or condition, in order to the commencement and continuance of the act by the individual Will; that, therefore, the proper character may be lost, and that if it should be lost—which, like all other facts, i.e. results of the individual Will, is determinable only by history, that is, the fact itself—the restoration ~~of~~ to this, his proper character, [*f* 6] must be the proper duty, the moral destination, of man. Thus even before we have arrived at any outward proofs, while we are yet within the limits of pure reason, and of ideas, the reality of which is still problematic, we no sooner come to the conditions of a religion, but we verify the definition of religion with which we commenced the first chapter of our work, viz. "That religion differs from philosophy on the one hand, and from history on the other, by being both."[12] Nor is it of mean importance that we have thus learnt and ascertained, not indeed whether a true religion exists, but what it must be, and what it cannot be, if it ~~does~~ have, or ⟨at any future time⟩ should ~~actually exist~~ have, a real existence.

We may now speak determinately, and with a fuller light, concerning the nature and function of conscience. We have seen that the reason in man, as far as it is reason, i.e. on the supposition that the word [is understood] correctly, is the same [*f* 7] with the divine reason considered

---

which man was capable which involved the necessity of its existence, not only because man [was a microcosm] and therefore implied an infinite Being as its Cause, but principally from its being involved in the idea itself. For what do we mean by God but that which contains all perfection without any negation? But [essence] is the perfection, therefore it must contain, of necessity, the existence" (*P Lects*—1949—277). As illustration of how repeatedly and intensely C thought about these abstractions, contrast his praise for the Cartesian demonstration with his identification of "the sophism in Des Cartes' celebrated demonstration of the existence of the Supreme Being from the idea" (*SW & F—CC*—II 924).

[10] Cf Frag 1, f 29: "With him, however, who possesses the Idea, we have only to proceed with the involved and consequent truths in order to determine by the fact itself whether a philosophy can be constructed thereon."

[11] "So God created man in his *own* image, in the image of God created he him; male and female created he them" (Gen 1.27).

[12] Cf a notebook entry of Sept 1825: "Now my fundamental position is: Religion differs from Philosophy (= Eternarum sive ἀχρόνων Veritatum Summa) on the one hand, and from History on the other, by being both in one. (=the identity of both, or the co-inherence of Philosophy in History, of History in Philosophy.—" (*CN* IV 5241).

objectively; and subjectively it is no other than the knowledge of the divine reason, quoad hoc vel illud[13]—further, that the divine reason is one with the absolute will, consequently ⌈. . .⌉ A being = B, and B = C, A is = C, i.e. that the reason in man is the representative of the Will of God.[14] It follows, therefore, that the conscience is the specific witnessing respecting the unity, or harmony, of the will with the reason,[15] effected by the self-subordination of the individual Will as representing the self to the reason, or the representative of the Will of God.[16]

But the personal Will is a constituent or, if I may borrow a convenient and appropriate term from arithmetic, a factor in other moral syntheses: thus sensuality is the synthesis of the appetites and the personal Will; the lust of power in synthesis with the personal Will constitutes ambition, etc., etc.;[17] the personal Will is present in these, as in the synthesis described above, and the witnessing concerning these, [*f 8*] not for themselves but as not being that synthesis, is likewise Conscience.* The specific characters of the Conscience cannot, therefore, be supplied by this factor—the personal or individual Will, I *ᵏ*mean.[19] We*ˡ* must seek for

---

* [*Written in ink on f 7ᵛ:*] In this may be found the true origin of ~~the positiveness~~ positive ideas respecting negations noticed by Locke, and still more clearly established, before Locke, by Spinoza in his Principia philosophia Cartesiana more geometrico demonstrata.[18] But it would lead us too far at present to exhibit the mode of the derivation and dependency of this power from the Conscience, with a fullness worthy the importance of the truth or satisfactory to the reader.

ᵏ⁻ˡ ms: mean; we

[13] Tr: "with respect to this or that".

[14] This conception allows for the use of reason in the theological investigation of faith.

[15] As C asks in 1826, "how could the Will be ever opposed to the Reason?—yet it is *the condition*, the *sine qua non* of a *free*—i.e. of *actual*) Will—Therefore Reason and *the* Will are the *co.efficients* of *actual* personality" (*CN* IV 5377).

[16] In the discussion of reason that here ensues, C parallels, and frequently quotes, his *Essay on Faith*, e.g. "Conscience then is a witnessing respecting the unity of the Will and the Reason effected by the Self-subordination of the Will, as = Self, to the Reason, as = the Will of God" (*SW & F—CC*—II 838).

[17] Cf *Essay on Faith*: "But the personal Will is a factor equally in other moral Synthesis, ex. gr. Appetites & pers. Will = Sensuality; Lust of Power + pers. Will = Ambition; &c &c" (*SW & F—CC*—II 838–9).

[18] In *Renati Des Cartes Principiorum Philosophiae Pars I, & II, More Geometrico demonstratae* (1663), Spinoza, in his Scholium to Proposition XV of Part One (which states that "Error non est quid positivum"), concludes that "error in man is nothing but privation; but relative to God as its cause, it is not privation, but negation" (*Spinoza* I 174–5, 176).

[19] "Not this therefore, but the other Factor, must supply the specific characters of the Conscience" (*SW & F—CC*—II 839).

them, therefore, in the other, i.e. the reason.[20] We must enter into an analysis of the reason. Such as the nature and objects of the reason are, such must be the functions and objects of the conscience. But the nature and objects of the reason we shall best ascertain by capitulating those constituents of the total man, which are either contrary to or disparate from the reason.[21]

§ 1

The reason and the proper objects of reason are wholly alien from sensation. Reason is supersensual. Its antagonist, therefore, is Appetite, with the objects of appetite, generalized by the scriptures as the LUST OF THE FLESH.[22]

§ 2

The reason and its objects do not [*f*9] appertain to the world of the senses, outward or inward. They partake neither of sense nor of fancy. Reason is supersensuous, and here its antagonist is the LUST OF THE EYE.[23]

SCHOLIUM. I use this phrase, again in imitation of scripture, as a *pars pro toto*.[24] It is scarcely necessary to remind the reader that the phrase "lust of the eye" is meant to include all the forms of all the senses, real

---

[20] Cf a note on the Fourth Gospel: "What is the Door of the Sheepfold?—the practical Reason? The power of Reason in the Conscience? or Reason as the Entrance-way of Ideas?—In this sense of the term, Reason, the only sense in which the term can be used to designate a *faculty of* the Human Mind, comprehended in its *propriety*, Reason is the capability of Ideas—and thus most truly the Door of the Sheepfold" (*CN* IV 5393).

[21] Cf *Essay on Faith*: "We must enter into an Analysis of the REASON. Such as the nature and objects of THE REASON are, such must be the functions and objects of the Conscience: and the former we shall best learn by capitulating those Constituents of the total Man, which are either contrary to, or disparate from, THE REASON" (*SW & F—CC*—II 839).

[22] Cf *Essay on Faith*: "S. 1. The Reason and the proper Objects of Reason are wholly alien from *Sensation*. Reason is *supersensual*: and its Antagonist is *Appetite* with the Objects of Appetite, = THE LUST OF THE FLESH" (*SW & F—CC*—II 839).

[23] Contrast C's definition of religion in *The Friend*: "Religion, in its widest sense, signifies the act and habit of reverencing THE INVISIBLE, as the highest both in ourselves and in nature" (*Friend—CC*—I 440). Cf *Essay on Faith*: "The Reason and its Objects do not appertain to the World of Senses, outward or inward—i.e. they partake neither of Sense nor of Fancy. Reason is *supersensuous*: and here its Antagonist is the LUST OF THE EYE" (*SW & F—CC*—II 839).

[24] Tr: "part for the whole".

or imagined, objective or subjective, as far as the desire of the same and the delight therein are pre-ordinated to the reason, or even co-ordinated therewith. By the same figure of speech, St Paul describes the objects and evidences of faith as *invisible*, the noblest sense standing for all the senses.[25]

§ 3

The reason and its objects are not things of reflection, association, or *discourse*,[26] the latter word used as opposed to "intuition", a use frequent and established in our elder writers, thus Milton, "dis[*f 10*]cursive or intuitive".[27] Reason does not indeed necessarily exclude the finite, whether in time or in space, in figure or in number, because it includes them eminentèr.[28] Thus the prime mover of the material universe was affirmed in the elder philosophy to contain all motion as its cause, but not to be, or suffer, motion in itelf. The reason is not the faculty of the finite.[29] The faculty of the finite is that which, reducing the confused impressions of sense to its own essential forms—to quantity, quality, relation, and, inclusively, to the forms of action, reaction, cause and effect, etc., etc.—thus raises the materials furnished by the senses and sensations into objects of reflection, i.e. renders them capable of being reflected on, and thus makes experience possible. Without this faculty the man's representative power would be a delirium, a mere chaos and scud-

---

[25] "For the invisible things of him from the creation of the world are clearly seen, being understood by the things that are made, *even* his eternal power and Godhead" (Rom 1.20). Cf *Essay on Faith*: "I use this phrase, in imitation of Scripture, as a Pars pro Toto. It is scarcely necessary to remind the Reader, that the phrase is meant to include all the forms of all the Senses, real or imagined, objective or subjective, as far as the Desire of the same & the Delight therein are made prae- or co-ordinate with the Reason. By the same figure of speech St Paul describes the Objects of & evidences of Faith as invisible, the noblest sense standing for all the senses" (*SW & F—CC*—II 839n).

[26] "The Reason and its Objects are not things of Reflection, Association, Discursion" (*SW & F—CC*—II 839).

[27] Cf *Paradise Lost* v 486–9:

"whence the Soul/ Reason receives, and reason is her being,/ Discursive, or Intuitive; discourse/ Is oftest yours, the latter most is ours".

[28] Tr: "eminently". See *SW & F (CC)* II 840 n 1.

[29] "On the contrary, Reason is the Power of universal and necessary Convictions, the Source and Substance of Truths above Sense, and having their evidence in themselves" (Brinkley 114). Cf *Essay on Faith*: "Reason does not indeed necessarily *exclude the Finite*, whether in Time or in Space, in Figure or in Number, because it *includes* them *eminenter*—thus the Prime Mover of the Material Universe is affirmed to *contain* all Motion as its cause, but not to *be* or to *suffer* Motion in itself. ⟨R is not the Fac. of the Finite.⟩" (*SW & F—CC*—II 839–40).

ding-cordage of shapes, and it is therefore most appropriately called [*f 11*] "the understanding", or "sub⟨-⟩stantiative*ᵐ* faculty".³⁰ Our elder metaphysicians, down to Hobbes inclusively, named it "interlogical exercise", likewise "discourse", "discursus", "discursio", afrom its mode of action as not staying at any one object but running, as it were, from this to that, to abstract, generalize, classify, etc. Now when this faculty is employed in the service of the reason to bring out the necessary and universal truths contained in the infinite into distinct contemplation by means of the pure acts of the imagination, ex.gr. in the production of the forms of space and time, abstracted from all corporeity, or of the inherent forms of the understanding itself, abstractly from the consideration of particulars—processes which constitute the sciences of geometry, numeral mathematics, universal logic, and pure metaphysics—in this case the discursive faculty becomes what our Shakespeare, with equal felicity and precision, entitles "dis[*f 12*]course of reason."³¹

It is evident, then, that the reason as the irradiative power of the understanding and the representative of the infinite, i.e. the boundless,* judges the understanding as the faculty of the finite, and cannot without grievous error be judged by it.³² When this is attempted, where the understanding in its synthesis with the personal Will usurps the supremacy of the reason, or affects to supersede the reason, it is that what St. Paul

---

* [*Written on f 11ᵛ:*] *Infinite*—that is, sine finibus, not having, or essentially incapable of having, outlines; not bounded or boundable from without. The reader must be on his guard not to substitute for this, the proper and scientific sense of "infinites", the popular meaning of "infinite", viz. what is immeasurably vast.

ᵐ Hyphen inserted in the ms with a caret

³⁰ Cf *Logic*: "The understanding is the substantiative power, that by which we give and attribute substance and reality to phenomena and raise them from mere affections and appearances into objects communicable and capable of being anticipated and reasoned of" (*Logic—CC*—239).

³¹ *Hamlet* I ii 150. Cf *Essay on Faith*: "Now when this Faculty is employed in the service of the Reason to bring out the necessary and universal ~~Forms~~ Truths contained in the Infinite into *distinct* contemplation, by the *pure* Acts of the sensuous Imagination, i.e. in the production of the Forms of Space and Time abstracted from all corporëity, and likewise ⟨of⟩ the inherent Forms of the Understanding itself abstractly from the consideration of Particulars; as takes place in Geometry, numeral Mathematics, universal Logic, and *pure* Metaphysics; ~~it~~ the Discursive Faculty then becomes what our Shakespear with happy precision entitles "Discourse of Reason" (*SW & F—CC*—II 840).

³² Cf *Essay on Faith*: "It is evident, then, that the Reason, judges as the irradiative Power & the representative of the Infinite, judges the Understanding as the Faculty of the Finite: and cannot without grievous error be judged by it" (*SW & F—CC*—II 841).

calls "φρονημα σαρκος", "the mind of the flesh",[33] "σοφια του κοσμου τουτου", "the wisdom of this world",[34] etc.[35] (The reader will observe that in this part of the work, I can refer to the sacred writers for fit expressions only as I might do to any other well known books, and not for authority, or in evidence of the truth of the distinctions conveyed by those expressions). The result, then, of this our third subdivision is— the[n] reason is superfinite, and in this relation it hath for its antagonist the uns[ub]ordinated *understanding*, the φρονημα σαρκος or MIND OF THE FLESH.[36]

[*f 13*] § 4

In the idea we have found the reason one with the absolute Will (εν αρχη ὅ Λογος και ὅ Λογος ην ~~και~~ ὅ Θεος).[37] Whatever, therefore, attests the former must imply the presence of the latter. If there be that in man, which is one with the universal reason, it cannot but coincide with, ~~with~~ or be congruous with, the absolute Will:[38] the perfect time-piece, for instance, contains neither the light nor the heat of the sun, but its movements are one with, i.e. adequately represent, the sun's motions relative to the place etc. of the time-piece; but the sun's motions are inseparably connected with its relative heat and light; therefore the motions of the time-piece are scientially one with, or we may from them securely conclude, the sun's relative heat and [o]light. If[p] A = B and C = A, then C = B. Reason, then, inasmuch as it is the representative of the Will of God, is above the Will of man, as an individual Will. In the very nature of the subjects, a Will ~~is very~~ ⟨may easily be⟩ conceiv~~ably~~⟨ed⟩ ~~differing~~ ⟨as contrary⟩ [*f 14*] from ⟨to⟩ a Will, ~~an individual~~ ⟨personal⟩ Will ~~from~~ ⟨to⟩ the Will absolute, or ~~from~~ ⟨to⟩ the individual Will, or ~~from~~ ⟨to⟩ the

---

[n] ms: The   [o-p] ms: light; if

[33] Col 2.18: "vainly puffed up by his fleshly mind".

[34] 1 Cor 1.20: "hath not God made foolish the wisdom of this world?"

[35] Cf *Essay on Faith*: "When this is attempted, or when the Understanding in its synthesis with the personal Will usurps the supremacy of the Reason or affects ~~the~~ to supersede the Reason, it is then what St Paul calls Φρονημα σαρκος, the mind of the Flesh—or σοφια του κοσμου τουτου, this wisdom of this world—&c" (*SW & F—CC*—II 841).

[36] Cf *Essay on Faith*: "The Result is,

The Reason is *super*finite, and in this relation its Antagonist is the Φρονημα σαρκος or the UNSUBORDINATED UNDERSTANDING, or the MIND OF THE FLESH" (*SW & F—CC*—II 841).

[37] The opening words of John's gospel, which mean, "In the beginning was the word, and the word was with God."

[38] Cf a note on Donne: "the eternal Antecedent of Being—I that shall be in that I will to be—the absolute Will, the ground of Being—the Self-affirming Actus purissimus" (*CM—CC*—II 287).

personal Will in another individual; but a reason that differs from reason is an absurdity and contradiction in terms. We have seen in § 3 that the reason is above all particulars, that it is superfinite; but here, by virtue of its representative character as one with the absolute Will, the reason stands in opposition to all mere individual interest, as so many Selfs to the personal Will, as far as it seeks an object in the manifestation of itself, for itself, in opposition to the "sit pro ratione voluntas".[39] Whether this be realized with adjuncts, as in the lust of the flesh and in the lust of the eye already enumerated in §§ 1 and 2, or (which is the proper subject of this §) without adjuncts, as in the thirst and pride of power, despotism, egoistic ambition.* The fourth antagonist of the reason, then, is the LUST OF THE WILL.[41]

§ 5

Deducible from § 4, but well [*f 15*] deserving a separate head. Unlike a multitude of tygers, a million of men is far other and more than one man repeated a million times. Each man in a numerous society is not simply co-existent, he is virtually co-organized with, and into, the multitude of which he is an integral part.[42] And for the same cause this mul-

---

* [*Written on f 13*ᵛ:] Here quote pp. ix and x of the Appendix to the Statesman's Manual.[40]

[39] Tr: "may there be a will in accord with reason".

[40] Speaking of the fact that "neither can reason or religion exist or co-exist as reason and religion, except as far as they are actuated by the WILL (the Platonic Θυμòς)", C mentions extremes in which "the Will becomes satanic pride and rebellious self-idolatry" (*LS—CC—*65) and exhibits "the fearful resolve to find in itself alone the one absolute motive of action, under which all other motives from within and from without must be either subordinated or crushed". He observes that "whenever it has appeared, under whatever circumstances of time and country, the same ingredients have gone to its composition; and it has been identified by the same attributes. Hope in which there is no Chearfulness; Stedfastness within and immovable Resolve, with outward Restlessness and whirling Activity; Violence with Guile; Temerity

with Cunning; and, as the result of all, Interminableness of Object with perfect Indifference of Means; these are the qualities that have constituted the COMMANDING GENIUS! these are the Marks, that have characterized the Masters of Mischief, the Liberticides, and mighty Hunters of Mankind, from NIMROD to NAPOLEON" (*LS—CC—* 65–6).

[41] Cf *Essay on Faith*: "whether this be realized with adjuncts, as the ~~Lust Passions~~ Lust of the Flesh and in the Lust of the Eye, already enumerated in §. 1. and §. 2.; or without adjuncts, as in the Thirst and Pride of *Power*, Despotism, egoistic Ambition (See Appendix to the Statesman's Ma[nua]l, pages ix. and x.). The fourth Antagonist of the Reason then is the Lust of the Will" (*SW & F—CC—*ɪɪ 841).

[42] Cf *Essay on Faith*: "COROLLARY—which might perhaps have not

titude is no mere abstraction, but is capable of becoming a true and living whole, a power susceptible of personal attributes, a nation.[43] When we contemplate man as the member of a country, his *idem* is modified, and there arise impulses and objects from this synthesis of the idem and the alter[44] myself and my neighbour, which would not otherwise have existed and have a character of their own. This is strictly analogous to what finds place in the vital organism of the individual man: the cerebral system of nerves has its correspondent antithesis in the abdominal system, and hence arises a synthesis of the two in the pectoral system, as the intermediate, the drawbridge, as it were, at once conductor and boundary. And in this [*f 16*] arise the emotions, the affections, or in one word, the passions, as distinguished from the appetites on one hand and the cognitions on the other.[45] Now the reason, the Logos,[46] has been shown to be super-individual in genere et universaliter,[47] therefore not

---

improperly formed a 5th §; but is however deducible from §. 4.—Unlike a multitude of Tygers, a million of men is far other from a million times one man. Each man in a numerous society is not simply co-existent but virtually co-organized with and into the multitude, [o]f which he is an integral Part" (*SW & F—CC*—ii 841–2).

[43] In a letter to Thomas Clarkson in Oct 1806 C said: "A male & female Tyger is neither more or less whether you suppose them only existing in their appropriate wilderness, or whether you suppose a thousand Pairs. But Man is truly altered by the co-existence of other men; his faculties cannot be developed in himself alone, & only by himself. Therefore the human race not by a bold metaphor, but in a sublime reality, approach to, & might become, one body whose head is Christ (the Logos)" (*CL* ii 1197).

[44] The *idem* (same) and *alter* (other) formula, extrapolated from the consideration of the conscious self (see Frag 1) into the conception of God himself, is perhaps the most pervasive of the dialectical oppositions that C employs throughout the *Op Max*. Cf a letter of 14 Apr 1816: ". . . the essential meaning of *personality*, from the consideration of which Plato and Philo Judaeus deduced the necessity of a Deus alter et Idem"

(*CL* iv 632). It is interesting that C's sociological prescience arose from his meditations on the Trinity (see *CL* ii 1195–7). Cf *TT* (*CC*) i 77: "In the Trinity there is the 1. Ipseity. 2. Alterity. 3. Community".

[45] Cf *Essay on Faith*: "His *idem* is modified by the *alter*—and there arise impulses & objects from this synthesis of the Idem and the Alter, Myself and my Neighbor.—This again is strictly analogous to what finds place in the vital organism of the individual Man. The cerebral System of Nerves has its correspondent Antithesis in the Abdominal System; but hence arises a Synthesis of the two, in the Pectoral System, as the Intermediate, and (like a Draw-bridge) at one Conductor & Boundary.—In the Latter as objectivized in the Former arise the Emotions, Affections, & in one word the Passions as distinguished alike from the Appetites and the Cognition" (*SW & F—CC*—ii 842).

[46] Cf C in commenting on Edward Irving: "Christ has been revealed in his identity with the Logos, (i.e. as the) Substantial personal Reason in whom Life is—the universal communicative Reason 'who lighteth *every* Man', & therein constitutes the proper Humanity" (*CM—CC*—iii 23). See further Prolegomena xiv: The *Magnum Opus* and the *Logos*.

[47] Tr: "in kind and universally".

less so when the form of individuality subsists in the alter than when it is confined to the idem, not less when the emotions have their conscious or believed object in another, than when their subject is the individual's personal self. These emotions, affections, attachments, etc. are indeed the prepared ladder by which the lower nature is taken up ⟨into⟩, and made to partake of, the higher, even as we are taught to give a feeling of reality to the higher by means of associating it with the lower through this common medium.[48] It is true, likewise, that it is by this process that we are enabled gradually to see the reality of the higher—the reality of the objects of reason, I mean—in and for itself, and finally to know that these are indeed and pre-eminently real. If you love [*f 17*] not your earthly parents whom you see, by what means will you love your heavenly father who is invisible?[49] This is true, but it holds true so far only as the reason maintains its ~~preeesidency~~, and as the objects of reason form the ultimate aim. And cases may arise in which the reason may declare—the reason, I say, as the representative of the supreme Will—"He that loveth father or mother better than me is not worthy of me."[50] Nay, the person who permits his emotions towards individuals to stand on an equality or rivalry with the universal reason is in enmity to that reason. Here, then, reason appears as the LOVE OF GOD, and its antagonist is earthly love, or attachment to individuals, whenever it exists in diminution of, or in competition with, the love which is one with reason.[51]

In the five §§ preceding we have enumerated and explained the sev-

---

[48] Cf *Essay on Faith*: "Now the Reason ⟨= Logos⟩ has been shown to be superindividual, *generally*; & therefore not less so, when the *form* of Individuality subsists in the Alter, than when it is confined to the *Idem*; not less, ~~in~~ when the Emotions have their conscious or believed Object in *Another*, than when their subject is the Individual's personal Self.—For tho' these Emotions, Affections, Attachments &c are the prepared Ladder by which the lower nature is taken up into and made to partake of the higher; even as we are taught to give a feeling of *reality* to the higher by this association, per medium commune, with the Lower" (*SW & F—CC*—II 842).

[49] The Bible insists on the invisibility of God, e g., Christ "is the image of the invisible God" (Col 1.15).

[50] Matt 10.37.

[51] Cf *Essay on Faith*: "and thus gradually to *see* the reality of the higher (viz. the objects of Reason) in ~~themselves~~ itself, and finally to know, that the latter is indeed and pre-eminently *real*; and if you love not your earthly Parents whom you see, by what means will you learn to love your heavenly Father who is invisible?—Yet this holds true so far only as the Reason is the President and its Objects the ultimate Aim—and cases may arise in which the Christ, as the *Logos* or redemptive Reason, declares—He that loveth Father or Mother better than me, is not worthy of me!—Nay, he who even permits his emotions towards individuals to an equality with the universal Reason, is in enmity to that reason. Here then Reason appears as the LOVE OF GOD: and its Antagonist is Attachment to Individuals, whenever it exists in diminution of or in competition with the Love which is Reason.—" (*SW & F—CC*—II 843).

eral powers and forces belonging or incident to human nature which, in all matters cognizable by reason, the man is bound either to [*f 18*] subjugate or to subordinate to reason. The application of these §§ to Faith follows as of its own accord.[52] The first, or most ~~indefinite~~ universal, sense of faith is FIDELITY;[53] then, fidelity under previous contract, or under particular moral obligation. In this sense faith is FEALTY.[54] Then, as fealty to a rightful superior, faith is ALLEGIANCE—the duty[55] of a faithful subject to a legitimate governor. But, fourthly, it is allegiance in active service, fidelity to the liege lord under the circumstances and amid the temptations of usurpation, rebellion, and intestine discord. Fifthly, we seek for that superior, on our duties to whom all duties to all other superiors, on our faithfulness to whom our bounden relations to all other objects of fidelity are *q*founded.[56] We*r* must enquire after that duty in which all other duties find their several degrees and dignities, and from which they derive their obligative force or moral necessity. We are to find a superior in no comparative sense of the word, but in a sense which precludes comparison, a superior who is absolutely [*f 19*] supreme, and whose rights, involving our duties, are presented to the mind in the very idea of that supreme one, [and] lastly, a superior whose sovereign prerogatives are predicates implied in the subject, even as the essential properties of a circle are co-assumed in the very act of assuming a circle—consequently underived, unconditional, and as rationally insusceptible, so morally prohibitive of all further question.[57] In this sense, then, faith

q–r ms: founded; we

[52] "I consider it as the contra-distinguishing principle of Christianity that in it alone πᾶς πλοῦτος τῆς πληροφορίας τῆς Συνέως (the Understanding in its utmost power and opulence) *culminates* in Faith, as its crown of Glory, at once its light and its remuneration" (*LS—CC—*46). Cf *Essay on Faith*: "In the five §s preceding we have enumerated and explained the ~~different~~ several Powers, or Forces, belonging or incident to Human Nature, which in all matters of Reason the Man is bound ~~to~~ either to subjugate or to subordinate to Reason. The application of these §s to Faith follows as of its own accord" (*SW & F—CC—*II 843).

[53] The powerful analysis and discrimination of faith that follows to the end of the chapter might be compared with the "Confessio Fidei of S. T. Coleridge" of 3 Nov 1810 (*CN* III 4005). And see above, Frag 1 f 108, f 150.

[54] See above, Frag 1 f 134.

[55] See above, Frag 1, f 41, f 114ᵛ, f 124ᵛ, f 129ᵛ, and nn.

[56] Cf *Essay on Faith*: "The first or most indefinite sense of Faith is FIDELITY: then Fidelity under previous Contract or particular moral Obligation. In this sense Faith is FËALTY. Thirdly, it rises into Fëalty to a rightful Superior. Faith is ALLEGIANCE—the duty of a faithful Subject to a Legitimate Governor. Fourthly: it is Allegiance in active service, Fidelity to the liege Lord under the circumstances and amid the temptations of Usurpation, Rebellion, and intestine Discord. Next, we seek for that rightful Superior, on our duties to whom ~~all~~ our duties to all other Superiors, on our faithfulness to whom all our bounden relations to all other Objects of Fidelity, are founded" (*SW & F—CC—*II 843).

[57] Cf *Essay on Faith*: "we must in-

is fidelity, fealty, allegiance of the moral creature to God,[58] in opposi-
tion to all usurpation, and in resistance to all temptations to ⟨the⟩ placing
any other claim above, or equal with, our fidelity to God.[59]

The Will of God is the last and final claim of all our duties, i.e. on the
supposition that we shall hereafter establish the reality of a supreme
being, or what is tantamount, the existence of any duties at all. To the
will of God the whole man is to be harmonized, alike in commission and
omission,[60] by subordination, or subjugation, or suppression.[61] [*f 20*]
But the supreme Will, which is one with the supreme Intelligence, is re-
vealed to man through the conscience; ~~but~~ and the conscience, again,
consists in an appellable *bearing-witness* to the truth and reality of our
reason. ~~a~~As far, therefore, as the conscience is *prescriptive*, it may le-
gitimately be construed by the term "reason". The terms are in this case
interchangeable. But ⟨considered⟩ in its functions of absolving OR con-
demning, the conscience becomes the consciousness of subordination or
insubordination, the harmony or the discord of the personal Will of Man
to his Reason as the representative of the Will of God[s]. [62] This brings us

---

[s] The following comment is written in pencil on f 19[v] facing this sentence: "Scarcely
true in Expression. The Reason reveals the right, and as the man acts up to it or the reverse,
conscience applauds or blames as the monitor of responsibility."

---

quire after that duty, in which all others
find their several degrees and dignities,
and from which they derive their obliga-
tive force. We are to find a Superior who
is ⟨absolutely⟩ *supreme*, & whose rights
(including our duties) are presented to the
mind in the very *idea* of the~~eat~~ ⟨Supreme⟩
Being ~~and~~ whose sovereign Prerogatives
are Predicates implied in the Subject, as
the essential properties of a Circle are co-
assumed in the first assumption of a Cir-
cle—consequently, underived, uncondi-
tional, and as rationally insusceptible, so
morally prohibitive, of all further Ques-
tion" (*SW & F—CC*—II 843).

[58] Nevertheless, the conception of the
nature of God will also determine the na-
ture of faith, which can vary absolutely
as its object varies, e.g.: "Even while my
faith was confined in the trammels of
Unitarianism (so called) with respect to
all the doctrines of Sin and Grace, I saw
clearly, as a truth in philosophy, that
the Trinitarian was the only consequent
Medium between the Atheist and the An-
thropomorph" (*CM—CC*—I 566).

[59] But such fidelity, fealty, and alle-

giance are not easy. Cf a note of 1825:
"Alas! the desolation from the languor of
my faith in the application of the Faith to
my own Soul; the want of a realizing
sense or Feeling of God personal, of God
as the Father of our Lord and Redeemer;
and the far more deep and clinging real-
ity of my Fears from the Law than of my
Hopes from the Cross" (*CN* IV 5244). Cf
Essay on Faith: "In this sense then, Faith
is—V[thly]—fidelity, fëalty, allegiance of
the moral Creature to God, in opposition
to all usurpation, and in resistance to all
temptations to the placing any other
claim above, or equal with, ~~the~~ our fi-
delity to God" (*SW & F—CC*—II 843).

[60] Cf *Essay on Faith*: "The Will of
God is the last Ground and final Aim of
all our duties: and to this the whole Man
is to be harmonized by subordination,
and submission or subjugation, or sup-
pression, alike in commission & omis-
sion.—" (*SW & F—CC*—II 843).

[61] "Will is *felt* in each, the Reason be-
comes manifest in the Whole—" (*CN* IV
5298).

[62] Cf *Essay on Faith*: "But the Will of

to the last and fullest sense of "Faith": namely, Faith is the obedience of the individual Will to reason—in the lusts of the flesh, opposed to the supersensual (§ 1); in the lusts of eye, as opposed to the supersensuous (§ 2); in the pride of the understanding, or faculty of the finite, as opposed to the super-finite, the mind of the flesh (φρονημα σαρκος), in contrariety [*f 21*] to spiritual truth (§ 3); in the lusts of the Will, as opposed to the absolute and universal (§ 4); and in the love of the creature, as far as it is in opposition to the love which is one with reason, namely the love of God[63] (§ 5).

Thus, then, we may conclude: Faith, in all its relations, subsists in the synthesis of the reason and the individual Will, or the reconcilement of the reason with the Will, by the self-subordination of the Will to the reason.[64] By virtue of the Will, therefore, as the one of its two essential constituents, Faith must be an energy; and inasmuch as it relates to the whole moral man, and is to be exerted in each and all of his component or incident faculties and tendencies,[65] Faith must be a ~~T~~*total*, not a ~~P~~*partial*; it must be a *continuous* and *ordinary*, not a *desultory* or *occasional*, energy.[66] But likewise by virtue of its other essential constituent, namely the reason, faith must be alike a form of knowing, a [*f 22*] beholding; and inasmuch as "to know" and "to behold" are verbs transitive and suppose a correspondent object, it must be a beholding of truth,[67] an intu-

God, which is one with the Supreme Intelligence, is revealed to Man thro' the Conscience; but the Conscience ~~concerning~~ the which consists in an ~~un~~inappellable *bearing-witness* to the truth and reality of our Reason, may legitimately be construed by the term, Reason, as far as the Conscience is *prescriptive*: while, as absolving or condemning, it is ~~one with~~ the Consciousness of the subordination or insubordination, the harmony or the Discord, of the Personal Will of Man with his Reason, as the representative of the Will of God" (*SW & F—CC*—II 843–4).

[63] Cf *Essay on Faith*: "This brings us to the VIth and last and fullest sense of Faith: i.e. Faith is the obedience of the individual Will, ~~from,~~ to the Reason, ~~first~~ in the Lusts of the Flesh as opposed to the supersensual (§. 1.)—in the Lusts of the Eye as opposed to the supersensuous, ~~or~~ i.e. the things seen &c to the invisible &c ⟨(§. 2.)⟩ in the pride of the *Understanding* as opposed to the *infinite* ~~of~~ the

φρονημα σαρκος in contrariety to *spiritual* Truth (§. 3.)—in the Lusts of the personal *Will*, ~~to~~ as opposed to the absolute and universal (§. 4.)—and in the Love of the Creature as far as it is in opposition to the Love which is one with Reason, namely, the Love of God.—" (*SW & F—CC*—II 844).

[64] Cf an alternate formula: "Faith is the marriage of the Will and the Reason: or shall I call it the offspring of that Union?" (*CN* IV 5048).

[65] Cf a marginal note: "Faith is properly a state and disposition of the Will, or rather of the whole Man, the '*I*', i.e. the finite Will self-affirmed—It is therefore the Ground, the Root, of which the Actions, the Works, the Believings, as acts of the Will in the Understanding, are the Trunk and Branches" (*CM—CC*—II 297).

[66] Cf *The Friend*: "But faith is a *total* act of the soul: it is the *whole* state of the mind, or it is not at all!" (*Friend—CC*—I 315).

[67] Cf *Essay on Faith*: "Thus then con-

itive knowledge.[68] And Faith must partake of the nature of an intuition.[69] In the incomparable language of the ~~e~~Evangelist John (whom as we have before said, we quote for the expression, and not for authority or verification), Faith must be a life originating in the Logos, i.e. in the substantial reason that is co-eternal and one with the Holy Will, the which LIFE is at the same time the LIGHT of men.[70] Now as life is here = the sum, or collective, of all moral and spiritual *acts*—in suffering, in doing, and in being—so will Faith be the source and the sum, the energy and the principle, of the fidelity of man to God, by the subordination of his human Will to his reason, as to the sum of all spiritual truths representing and manifesting the Will divine.[71]

[*f 23*] Should it be found that every text in the sacred things in which the word "*Faith*" or ~~some~~ any one of its synonyms, from the first to the last of the canonical volume, falls naturally under some one or other of the senses established in this analysis, ~~and that~~ and these senses being modes only, and applications of, the sense last given, such a correspondence cannot but be admitted as a presumption of its truth—even with those who have yet to acquire a belief in the authority of those writings,

---

clude. Faith subsists in the Synthesis of the Reason and the Individual Will. By virtue of the latter, therefore, it must be an *energy*; and inasmuch as it relates to the Whole Moral Man, & is to be exerted in each and all of his constituent or incident faculties & tendencies, it must be a total, not partial, a continuous, not a desultory, or occasional, Energy: and by virtue of the Former, Faith i.e. Reason, Faith must be a Light, a form of Knowing, a Beholding of Truth" (*SW & F—CC*—II 844).

[68] Cf a marginal notation: "FAITH is but an Act of the Will assenting to the Reason on its own evidence, without, and even against the Understanding" (*CM—CC*—II 277).

[69] That is, it must be immediately present, not deduced. Cf C elsewhere: "All Science derives its reality from immediate, or intuitive Knowlege" (*SW & F—CC*—II 1190).

[70] Cf another formulation: "Christ has been revealed in his identity with the Logos, i.e. as the Substantial personal Reason in whom Life is—the universal communicative Reason 'who lighteth *every* Man'" (*CM—CC*—III 23).

[71] Cf a note on Donne: "Faith i.e. fidelity, the fealty of the finite Will and Understanding to the Reason! = the Light that lighteth every man that cometh into the World, as one with and the representative of the Absolute Will, and to the Ideas—i.e. Truths or rather Truth-powers of the pure Reason, the super-sensuous Truths which in relation to the finite Will and as meant to determine the Will, are moral LAWS, the voice and dictates of the Conscience" (*CM—CC*—II 297). Cf *Essay on Faith*: "In the incomparable expressions of the Evangelist, therefore, Faith must be a *Life* originating in the Logos, or the substantial Reason that is co-eternal and one with the Holy Will, the which LIFE is at [the] same time the LIGHT of Men. Now as LIFE is here the *sum* or collective of all moral and spiritual *Acts*, ~~with~~ in suffering, doing, and *being*: so is Faith the source, ~~t~~ and the Sum, the Energy and the Principle, of the fidelity of Man to God by the subordination of his human Will in all provinces of his Nature to his Reason, as the Sum of spiritual Truths, representing and manifesting the Will of Divine—" (*SW & F—CC*—II 844).

which, though composed by so many different men, in ages so different
and under such different circumstances, do yet contain so uniform a cor-
respondence to the prescript of the pure reason, proceeding as we have
hitherto done, hypothetically only, the actual existence not yet proved,
and furnishing therefore not proofs of the ⟨reality or⟩ realization of any
positions, but merely criteria [*f 24*] for their examination. (That is, while
we are yet in that part of our subject in which we seek to prove not that
this or that is real or realizable, but that this or that alone can be real), or
rather, that what is real can be only known to be such no satisfactory
proof of its being such unless it contain, or accord with, these condi-
tions.)' Our nature is so constituted that in whatever is made known to
us as ideal truth, we cannot but anticipate a correspondent object, either
co-incident with the idea, wherever such co-incidence is not contradicted
by the nature of the object itself, ex.gr. the nature of body relatively to
the idea of a circle, or an approximation to the same. This presumption
will be still stronger with those whose object is to enlighten a belief al-
ready formed, and by rendering it distinct and systematic, to make it a
weapon of defence by persuasion, and to [*f 25*] ensure to it a more reg-
ular practical influence on their own feelings and scheme of actions.

Chapter*"*

On the existential reality of the Idea of the Supreme Being, i.e. of God.

Αγε δη ουν, ειπερ ποτε, και νυν τας πολυειδεῖς
αποσκευασώμεθα γνώσεις και πᾶν το ποικλον της ζωης
εξορσωμεν αφ' ημων, και παντων εν ηρεμιᾳ γενομενοι, τῳ
παντων αιτιῳ πρυσιωμεν έγγυς. Εστω δε μηιν μη μονον
δοξης μηδε φαντασιας ήρεμια, μηδε ησουχια των παθων
ημων ἐμποδιζόντον την προς το πρωτον αναγωγον ορμην·
αλλ' ησυχος μεν αηρ, ηουχον δε το παν τουτο· παντα δε
ατρεμει τη δυναμει προς την του ἀρρητου με τουσιαν ἡμᾶς
ανατεινετω.[72]

' Closing parenthesis inserted
*" The chapter number "IX?" is inserted in pencil

[72] "Come, then, and if ever, let us
pack off multiform knowledge, and let us
banish from ourselves all the variegation
of life and come into the quiet of all
things; let us approach near to the cause
of all things. Let there be for us a quiet,
not only of opinion but also of imagin-
ing, and not a peace of the passive, pre-
venting a drive to the first uplifting, but
a peaceful air and a peaceful all; and let
all things lift us up in unmoved power to
participation in the unspoken."

These are the words of a pagan philosopher,[73] and such the spirit with which he prepares himself and his readers for the August contemplation on which we are now to enter.[74] If on the one side it be a subject of just congratulation that truths both moral [*f 26*] and religious, made known [to]ᵛ but few in the most enlightened nations of the ancient world, and by them received as light from heaven, awful and almost terrible to them from the darkness which it revealed, that truths of which a Simonides despaired,[75] which a Plato deemed scarcely discoverable and still more difficultly communicated, and assuredly not communicable but after a long and earnest discipline or silence and inward stillness[76]—if, I say, it be a rightful ground of exultation that these truths are now the inmates of every cottage and ours ~~almost~~ by birthright, on the other side, it may well bear a question whether the sense of their weight and the comparative depth do not too commonly correspond to the nearness and ~~facility~~ accessibility of the sources from whence they are showered on us. Yet I fear that even this figure conveys a too flattering statement of the fact as it really is, for such is the capacity of the soul, if once its portals be indeed opened [*f 27*] (ἡλιου του υπερουρανιου πυλαι),[77] and so transcendent, and of an interest so inclusive of all other ~~of all other~~ truths and of all other true interests, is the great eternal verity, which is to be its master-light, that wherever it is found accompanied with the indif-

ᵛ Word supplied in pencil on f 25ᵛ

[73] Proclus *Theologia Platonica* (1.5) vol 2 p 64.

[74] C's selection of these moving words as preamble to his own elevation of discourse was a result of the fact that Green had given him in 1820 a rare edition of Proclus: "22 Novʳ. 1820.—Proclus in Plat. Theol. given me by my dear Friend & Fellow Inquirer, [. . .] Joseph Henry Green, Surgeon of Sᵗ Thomas's &c &c—" (*CN* ɪᴠ 4744). Coburn's note is as follows: "Green gave him: . . . *Procli Successoris Platonici in Platonis theologiam libri sex*. Ed with Latin tr by Aemilius Portus. With Marinus's life of Proclus, Pico della Mirandola's *Conclusiones LV secundum Proclum*, and Proclus's *Institutio theologica* [*Elements of Theology*] (Hamburg 1618). In 1807–8 C had made a note 'to hunt for Proclus': See *CN* ɪɪɪ 3276 § 9 and n" (*CN* ɪᴠ 4744n).

[75] Cf C elsewhere: ". . . proofs, which no man could reject, of the being and at-

tributes of God and a future state. It might have been a matter of surprise that the philosophers of old did not arrive at this; that they were extremely puzzled that when Simonides was asked the question, he required day after day to solve it" (*P Lects*—1949— 126; see further 408 n 25.)

[76] Plato, in his *Seventh Epistle*, says that he has not set forth all his doctrines; the subject he seems to consider the most important is not treated: "I certainly have composed no work in regard to it, nor shall I ever do so in future, for there is no way of putting it in words like other studies. Acquaintance with it must come rather after a long period of attendance on instruction in the subject itself and of close companionship, when, suddenly, like a blaze kindled by a leaping spark, it is generated in the soul and at once becomes self-sustaining" (341C–D).

[77] Tr: "the gates of the supercelestial sun". The phrase is from Iamblichus.

ference of customary acquiescence, we must suspect the fact of its being present at all. And, alas! experience supplies too many proofs in all ages of the substitution of a blind feeling—the same, perhaps, with that which results from the sum of our bodily sensations, with a form of words— for that clear apprehension (for this is possible where comprehension, at once by the nature of the gift and the receiver[, is not])[w],[78] for that intellectual beholding which words, indeed, can describe only generally only, or by negative terms, but which is not to be measured by words. For these have done their best and highest if as remembrancers they awaken the dormant ideas in the order most [*f 28*] conducive to the intercommunion of mind with mind, and the philosopher[79] who first spake of deity as the circle whose center was every where and whose circumference nowhere[80]—thus bringing together two images which in all other applications were united and inseparable, but of which one only was predicable affirmatively of the August subject then contemplated— and who on this account brought them together by a negative attached to the one factor, or constituent, and on the other hand [compensated][x] for it by transferring its universality to the affirmative—this philosopher knew indeed that the thought was not imaginable, but who shall dare declare it not intelligible? It is a part of the logic of human nature by which the soul announces its superiority over the senses and the notices of the senses,[81] itself deriving its noblest and most precious possession from the negation of the senses,[82] and like the astronomer who measures [*f 29*] and determines the motion of the solar orb by the vacuities and in-

---

[w] Parentheses inserted   [x] Word supplied in pencil on f 27[v]

[78] C repeatedly relies on the distinction of apprehension and comprehension in theological matters, "For how can any Spiritual Truth be *comprehended*? Who can *com*prehend his own Will or his own Personëity (i.e. his 'I') or his own Mind, i.e. his Person, or his own *Life*? But we can distinctly *ap*prehend them" (Brinkley 385).

[79] An anonymous twelfth-century author, in *Liber de propositionibus sive de regulis theologiae*, generally known and quoted as *Liber XXIV philosophorum* (Book of the Twenty-four Philosophers), and ascribed to Hermes Trismegistus.

[80] On "Deus est sphaera infinita, cujus centrum est ubique, circumferentia nusquam" and its many quotations, see Baeumker 31 n 8.

[81] Cf a beautiful statement in the *Statesman's Manual*: "That, which we find in ourselves, is (gradu mutato) the substance and the life of *all* our knowledge. Without this latent presence of the 'I am,' all modes of existence in the external world would flit before us as colored shadows, with no greater depth, root, or fixture, than the image of a rock hath in a gliding stream" (*LS—CC—* 78).

[82] "The pith of my system is to make the senses out of the mind—not the mind out of the senses" (*TT—CC—*II 179). Again: "The mind always feels itself greater than aught it has done" (*P Lects* —1949—166).

terstices of its ~~light~~ luminous atmosphere, sees by not seeing.* [y] And if the scorner who has skimmed his sciolism[83] from the surface of the mechanic philosophy should retort that the result of knowledge so obtained,[z] as well as an[a] instance,[b] is given us in the poet's "Darkness visible",[84] we must tell him that well it would be for him [c]could he[d] ~~obt~~ make his darkness visible to himself, this being the first condition and evidence of his capacity for light. Herein does the empty intellect differ from the vacant material room,[85] [in] that in the former the capacity is as the recipiency, and the recipiency as the predisposition, and this again according to the immanence of the moral Will in the intellectual power, or its separate subsistence, as with those with whom truth is a matter of choice, and faith a misnomer for a predetermination to hear nothing on the other side of the [*f 30*] question.

These reflections were awakened by a remark which I had myself drawn forth from a theologian by trade by an allusion to the well-known tale of Simonides. "Yes!", replied the good man,[86] "I have often read it in the Spectator, but it always, I confess, appeared to me very absurd; for what can be easier than to combine the three ideas of infinite power, infinite wisdom, and infinite goodness, and nothing less could have sufficed for the creation of the universe, which you know must have had a

* [*Written on f 28*[v]*:*] Mem.: to quote here the sentence from Spinoza Phil. Cartes., from whom M[r] Locke ~~l~~adopted it, which, N.B., surprized me before I found out to whom it belonged.

[y] At this point in the ms there is a series of "X"'s indicating the space where the quotation from Spinoza was to be inserted

[z] The following addition is written in pencil on f 28[v] and marked for insertion here: "is only reached by contradiction"

[a] This word is cancelled in pencil, and the following substitution written above it: "in that"

[b] After this word the following addition is inserted in pencil above the line: "that"

[c–d] ms: he could [*marked in pencil for transposition with pencilled note "transpose" on f 28*[v]]

[83] Shallow knowledge.

[84] Milton *Paradise Lost* I line 63.

[85] The "vacant material room" can be compared to the Aristotelian position (and that of Locke), *nihil in intellectu quod non prius in sensu* [nothing in the intellect which was not first in the senses], and the "empty intellect" with "Leibnitz's qualifying *praeter ipsum intellectum*" [besides the intellect itself] (*BL—CC*—I 141). C was very fond of the Leibnizian amendment (Leibniz's words in his *Nouveaux essais* were actually "*excipe*; *nisi ipse intellectus*"), which reversed the force of the original statement. See *P Lects* (1949) 383; *Logic* (*CC*) 183–4, 226. See below note 365.

[86] It is unclear whether C is here referring to an actual man and conversation, or, as he sometimes does, having a joke.

cause—and then you have the idea of God. What can be clearer and eas-
ier? I should despair of a child of four years old that found any difficulty
in it." Alas! poor child, or rather alas! for us on whom the power of cus-
tom presses ~~with a weight heavy as frost~~

> —with a weight
> Heavy as frost and deep almost as life.[87]

Too often is it thy privilege, if even this be permitted thee by the abund[*f*
31]ance of thy instructor's wisdom, at once to see the truth, and both find
and feel the difficulty. He does not find it quite so easy to infer from a
truth the contradiction of that truth: "and who then made him?" is the
question which many a parent has had pressed upon him, while the eager
eye and earnest grasp of the little querist have shewn with how deep*e*
[an]*f* interest the answer was expected. Is it everywhere? And does it act
every where? What then remains but absolute weakness, and absolute
nothing? If there be no contradiction in self-causation, why extend be-
yond the world? That it is not any necessity of nature, that *g*the resting*h*
in that, the existence of which is known and not supposed by inference,
we have the strongest proof in the undeniable fact [that] all mankind,
with one solitary exception,[88] recognized the world as God, and this in

---

e ms: a deep [*the first word is cancelled in pencil*]
f Word supplied in pencil on f 30ᵛ
g-h The substitute phrase "when we rest" is supplied in pencil on f 30ᵛ

---

[87] Lines 129–30 of Wordsworth's
"Ode: Intimations of Immortality" (*WPW*
IV 283).

[88] The exception is probably Pythag-
oras. C held Pythagoras in unwavering
esteem, even nominating him as the vir-
tual Godfather of his own philosophy:
"In the third treatise of my *Logosophia*,
announced at the end of this volume, I
shall give (deo volente) the demonstra-
tions and constructions of the Dynamic
Philosophy scientifically arranged. It is,
according to my conviction, no other than
the system of Pythagoras and of Plato re-
vived and purified from impure mix-
tures" (*BL—CC*—I 263). Perhaps the
most important element in C's admira-
tion of Pythagoras was that, unlike other
Greek philosophers except Plato, he was
not tainted by pantheism (his thought
"did not in the least partake of Panthe-
ism, but still kept the Deity at a distance
from his works" (*P Lects*—1949—109)).

Another element was wonder that the
palpable genius of Pythagoras shone so
early in the annals of Western culture.
The first man truly to bear the name
philosopher was "Pythagoras, something
like one of the most extraordinary human
beings that has ever astonished and per-
plexed the world" (*P Lects*—1949—97).
Still a third factor was Pythagoras's faith
in human reason: "and thus Pythagoras
commenced a philosophy in the faith of
the human reason, revealed to himself by
purity of moral character, the faith of that
reason in its own dictates. On this plan
he founded the grand system of the Deity
as the *Monas*; not as the one but as that
which without any numbers and per-
fectly distinct from numbers was yet the
ground, and by its will, the cause of all
number; and in the manifestation of the
Godhead he represented it by the famous
triad three, while the world as a dim re-
flex of that was his God in the tetrameter

the rudest schemes of polytheism:[89] the ~N~Parental Night and Chaos of
[*f 32*] Hesiod, no less than in the mysteries of Samothrace.[90] In all alike
a theogony,[91] in all alike

Χαος ην και νυξ· Ερεβους δ᾽ εν απειρυσι κυλπις
~ξυγγ~ Συμμιγνυμενων δ᾽ ετερων ετεροις,
εγενετ᾽ ουρανος ωκεανος τε.
Και γη παντων τε θεων μακαρων γενος αφθιτον.[92]

Or shall we ask our man of ready comprehension to give us help while
we seek by mere reason to combine the term "infinite" with "life", with
"person"? Can he conceive of gravitation as being alive, or connect his
conception of person with space? Can he engender consciousness in that
which per hypothesin[93] is exclusively one and all? For whose self there
is no co-existent, quod una cum se sciendum esset;[94] for whose know-
ledge there is no object? I had said that we might call for help in these
difficulties, but the progress of our enquiry, which is preparatory only to
those helps which our reason needs, should [*f 33*] rather have dictated
the request in behalf of Plato, who even forbade his disciples to apply

---

or the four" (*P Lects*—1949—108–9).

[89] Cf *Aids to Reflection*: ". . . the sen-
sual polytheism, which is inevitably the
final result of Pantheism or the Worship
of Nature; and the only form under
which the pantheistic Scheme—that, ac-
cording to which the World is God, and
the material universe itself the one only
absolute Being—can exist for a People,
or become the popular Creed" (*AR*—
1825—276). Cf John Sterling's report of
C's table talk in 1827: "The ancients
were Spinozists. They could not help
seeing an energy in Nature. This was the
anima mundi sine centro (soul of the
world without a centre) of the philoso-
phers. The people of course changed it
into all the forms that their imaginations
could supply" (*TT—CC*—II 399).

[90] C frequently writes about the mys-
teries of Samothrace, e.g. in the *Philo-
sophical Lectures*: "from the THEURGY
OF THE mysteries of SAMOTHRACE,
founded shortly after Homer, by the
Phoenicians in all probability . . . . A sys-
tem of pantheism it was, but not irreli-
gious . . . . [T]he three first of their di-
vinities answered to the obscure names
of *Axieros*, *Axiokersos*, and *Axiokersa*

. . ." (*P Lects*—1949—321–2). See
below, Frag 3, pp 196–9.

[91] That is, "a generation of the gods".
For the almost universal pantheism of
early Greek thought, except for Pythago-
ras, cf C: "Spinoza re-edified the Panthe-
ism of the old Greek Philosophy" (*CM*—
CC—III 901). Again: "I hold all claims
set up for Egypt as having been the ori-
gin of Greek Philosophy as groundless.
It sprang up in Greece itself, and began
with physics only—then it took in the
Idea of as living cause—and made Pan-
theism out of the two" (*TT—CC*—I
203). Still again: "Pantheism was taught
in the Mysteries of Greece, of which the
Cabeiric were the purest and most an-
cient" (*TT—CC*—I 104–5).

[92] Aristophanes *Birds* lines 693, 694,
701–2. "Chaos and night. In the bound-
less bosoms of Erebus but as one min-
gled with another Ouranos [heaven]
came into being, and Okeanos [ocean]
and Ge [earth] and the unfading race of
all the blessed gods."

[93] Tr: "by hypothesis".

[94] Tr: "in that one must be known
with itself".

the term "infinite" to the unutterable ONE and GOOD as being in its na-
ture unholy and contrary to the essential order, and commanded them, if
they dared at all entrust their conception to words, to think of him as the
Measurer of the Infinite. Nor need I feel shame at a request in which a
Luther[95] would have fervently joined, or at finding a difficulty where
Luther found the insuperable limit of his reason.* Most cordially do I
agree with this mighty minister of truth: without that inward revelation
by which we know ourselves responsible and thus know what no under-
standing can reach, the reality of a Will. ‖In vain should we endeavour
to make up the notion of a divinity out of any materials which the senses
can convey, or the world afford. So general, however, is the prepposses-
sion to the contrary [*f 34*] that it becomes more than merely expedient
not to rest in ⟨an⟩ assertion b̶u̶t̶ if we cannot demonstrate by reason the
existence of God, yet by reason itself to demonstrate its indemonstrabil-
ity.[97] For the most dangerous of all weakness is a false presumption of
strength. It is of the highest importance that we should not be misunder-
stood even in anticipation. So important, indeed, does this appear to me
that I present the final result of my reasoning at the commencement, [so]

* [*Written on f 32ᵛ:*] Quotation from *Luther's Table Talk.*[96]

[95] Of all theologians, C admired Luther most. For a long discussion of Newman's attack on Luther, followed by an affirmation of C's approbation of Luther, see Sara Coleridge's Introduction to the second ed of the *Biographia Literaria* (1847), c–cxxvii.

[96] Elsewhere C speaks of "Luther's table talk, which to a truly philosophic mind, will not be less interesting than Rousseau's confessions" (*Friend—CC—* I 137). Luther's *Tischreden* are not a single work, but collections of utterances taken down at various times by various hearers, and they exist in varying eds, many of them unsatisfactory. For a judicious survey of their cumulative history, see Preserved Smith *Luther's Table Talk; A Critical Study* (New York: Columbia University Press 1907). C used the first English translation by Captain Henry Bell, called *Colloquia Mensalia*, which was published in 1652 and reprinted in 1791. It is difficult to be certain of finding the passage of which C speaks, but it is very probably this one: "Ah, what does reason understand? It can't comprehend how man is made from a drop of blood, how a cherry grows from a blossom, how bone and flesh came into existence. The world is full of everyday miracles, but, as Augustine said with reference to John 6 [.9], because they occur so often these things are deemed of little value. Christ once fed several thousand people with five loaves of bread. What does he do every day? But what happens daily is counted of little consequence. God produces wine from stones and makes butter and bread out of sand. So he once formed man out of the ground, and now he creates men every day out of drops of blood. . . .

"Who can understand anything about these things by means of reason? To be sure, enlightened reason can to some extent understand the Ten Commandments and the religion of the Jews; but articles of faith, like the Trinity and the incarnation of Christ—these don't tally with reason" (*Luther* LIV 377–8).

[97] C may here be obliquely criticising Kant.

that no false alarm may render the enquirer disinclined to undertake the investigation, or make him hold with an unsteady hand the clue which, unfolding as it runs, is to trace the path through the obscure labyrinth into ~~open~~ broad light and champaign. Many may be startled at the position that the existence of the sSupreme Being in any religious sense is indemonstrable, who yet might be brought to ~~welcome~~ see in it a new source of [*f 35*] faith, a new world of harmonies, and above all the transcendent dignity of the doctrine itself, if only they can be ~~led~~ induced to consider that to demonstrate a thing is to establish its antecedent, and thus to construct the thing anew; that what is essentially and in the nature of thought no less than in reality, first, can have no antecedent, and what is absolutely One [can have] no construction. A Neapolitan philosopher,[98] * more than a century ago, has already said "Geometrica idea demonstramus quia facimus; Physica, si demonstrare possemus, faceremus; hinc impiae curiositatis notandi, qui Deum à priori probare student. Metaphysici veri claritas eadem ac lucis, quam non nisi per opaca cognoscimus; nam non lucem, sed lucidas res videmus Physica sunt opaca nempe formata et finita, in quibus metaphysici veri lumen videmus."[100] But long before, Aristotle, the inventor of logic, and to whom ~~we owe the name of~~ metaphysics owes its name[101] but not its [*f 36*] origin, ~~instructed as~~ felt and acknowledged the necessity of a principle deeper than science, more certain than demonstration; for that the

---

* Joh. Bapt. a Vico, reg. eloq. Professor, de antiquissima Italorum sapientia ex linguae latinae originibus eruenda libri tres. Neap. 1710.[99]

[98] The precise passage that follows was quoted in 1811 in Jacobi's *Von den göttlichen Dingen*, with a slightly different introduction: "Lange vor Kant, zu Anfange des achtzehnten Jahrhunderts schrieb Joh. Bapt. Vico zu Neapel: Geometrica ideo demonstramus, quia facimus" down to "veri lumen videmus" (Jacobi *Werke* III 352–3). See M. H. Fisch, "The Coleridges, Dr. Prati, and Vico" *Modern Philology* XLI (1943) 111–22.

[99] The citation is taken verbatim from Jacobi *Werke* III 353 n *.

[100] Tr: "We demonstrate the ideas of geometry because we made them; those of physics, if we could demonstrate we would make—hence of the inquisitiveness of those who strive to prove God *a priori*. The clarity of metaphysical truth is the same as of light, which we do not know except through the opaque; for we see not light, but lucid things. Physical objects are opaque, assuredly formed and finished, in which we truly see the light of metaphysics."

[101] That is, from the treatise called *Metaphysics*. Cf a note on Bunyan: "by 'metaphysics' we mean those truths of the pure Reason, which always transcend and not seldom appear to contradict, the *Understanding*—or (in the words of the great Apostle) spiritual verities which can only be spiritually discerned—/and this is the true and legitimate meaning of 'Metaphysics', μετὰ τὰ φυσικὰ—" (*CM—CC*—I 819). It is generally thought that the name refers merely to the fact that the treatise followed the treatise called *Physics*, but Coleridge's interpretation has been historically inviting.

very ground is groundless or self-grounded is, saith he, an identical proposition. From the indemonstrable flows the sap which circulates through every branch and spray of the demonstration.[102] The concluding truth, which that the reader may see distinct in the clear light of his own understanding and possess in his own right, I would fain [have him][i] to accompany me through the whole process, is this: the[j] dialectic intellect, by the exertion of its own powers exclusively, is suffcient to establish the general affirmation of a supreme reality, of an absolute being, but this is all—[for][k] here the power of the scientific reason stops; it is utterly incapable of communicating insight, or conviction, concerning the existence of a world different from Deity. The very possibility is hidden from the reason. It finds itself constrained to identify, thence to con[*f 37*]found the creator with the aggregate of his creatures, and then, cutting the knot which it cannot untwist, to deny the reality of all finite existence and shelter itself from its own importunate queries in the wretched evasion that of nothing no solution can be ~~conveyed~~ [l]required! Vain Pride of intellect! Mad Narcissus, that in barren Self-love transformest thyself to Form without Substance, Surface without depth, the Object a Shadow, ~~a~~and the subject the Notion of a Shadow! Whence did this Nothing acquire its plural number? ~~Unde hæc Nihili in Nihila multiplicatio, vel rectius transnihilatio?~~ From the senses? But this either confutes the Assumption, or virtually repeating it substitutes the problem itself [. . .] for the Solution of the Problem. In each sense the forms are numberless: & whence the number and the[m] diversity of the Senses?, ~~And what~~ ⟨that⟩ multiply or rather *transnihilate* the absolute Something into this Universe of Nothings? And what is that inward Mirror, in and for which these Nothings have at least a relative reality? Or dost thou wait till Pain and Anguish and Remorse with moody scorn ask thee: And are *we* Nothings?

I have [*f 38*] shown, in another work,[103] that* Dichotomy, or the pri-

---

* [*Written by C on ff 37ᵛ–38ᵛ:*] I had not ~~and~~ ⟨then knowing of,⟩ nor have I now seen, Richard Baxter's *Methodus Theologiæ*; but from the following sentence in his Life (that invaluable Work published from Baxter's own Manuscript

[i] Words supplied in pencil on f 35ᵛ and marked for insertion here   [j] ms: The
[k] ms: but [*correction supplied in pencil on f 35ᵛ*]
[l] The text is in C's hand from this point to the top of f 39
[m] This word is written over another, now illegible

[102] Cf the opening sentence of the *Op Max.*: "In every science something is assumed the proof of which is prior to the science itself" (Frag 1 f 1).
[103] Cf *Logic* (*CC*) 241: "The singular circumstance of this threefold division or trichotomy obtaining throughout the analysis of the mind, and which the founder of the critical philosophy contents himself with noticing as being sin-

mary Division of the Ground into Contraries, is the necessary form of reasoning as long as and wherever the intelligential faculty of Man [?

---

by Matthew Silvester) I cannot doubt that the ⟨merit of⟩ substitutionng ~~of~~ Trichotomy for the then, and alas! ~~still~~ ⟨the⟩ still, prevailing Method of Dichotomy, which forms the prominent excellence[104] in Kant's Critique of the pure reason, belongs to R. Baxter, a century before the publication of Kant's Work.[105] Nay, it appears that the claim of our Countryman rests on a stronger as well as elder [. . .] ⟨plan⟩. For Baxter *grounds* ~~his principle of Method~~ ⟨the necessity of Trichotomy,⟩ as the Principle of Real Logic, on an absolute Idea presupposed in all intelligential Acts: whereas Kant adopts it merely as a fact of Reflection, tho' doubtless as a singular & curious Fact in which he suspects some yet deeper Truth latent and hereafter to be discovered. ~~This perhaps~~ "Having long been purposing to draw up a Method of Theology, I now began it. I never yet saw a scheme, or Method either of Physics or of Theology that gave any satisfaction to my Reason. Tho' many have attempted to exercise more accurateness in dis-

---

gular and worthy of notice, and which he supposes himself to have noticed first, may be found in a much earlier writer, our own celebrated Richard Baxter.*

*It is no more than common justice to this acute and if too often prejudiced yet always sincere, pious, and single-hearted divine, to say that he saw far more deeply into the grounds, nature, and necessity of this division as a *norma philosophiae* and the evils and inconveniences of the ordinary dichotomy when carried from its proper province, that of common logic, into philosophy and divinity than Kant did more than [a] century after. The sacred fire, however, remained hid under the bushel of our good countryman's ample folios." To the statement that Kant "supposes himself to have noticed first", the editor of the *Logic* supplies a note: "Kant does not claim to have noticed it first. For his mentions of trichotomy see *C d r V* 110 (116) and *Critik der Urtheilskraft* Einleitung § ix n."

[104] An "excellence" because it allowed C, along with Fichte, Schelling, and Hegel, to use polarity, by expansion to a three-term thesis-antithesis-synthesis logic, to constitute a dialectical method of philosophical progression. Dichotomy was static; trichotomy engendered true dialectical movement. See Prolegomena x: The *Magnum Opus* and the Principle of Polarity.

[105] In a marginal notation on *Reliquae Baxterianae* C says "Among Baxter's philosophical merits we ought not to overlook, that the substitution of Trichotomy for the old & still general plan of Dichotomy in the Method and Disposition of Logic, which forms so prominent & substantial an excellence in Kant's Critique of the Pure Reason, of the Judgement, &c belongs orignally to Richard Baxter, a century before Kant— & this not as a Hint but as a fully evolved & systematically applied Principle. Nay, more than this! Baxter *grounded* it on an absolute Idea *pre*supposed in all intelligential acts: whereas Kant takes it only as a *Fact* of Reflection—as a singular & curious Fact, in which he seems to anticipate or suspect some yet deeper Truth latent & hereafter to be discovered" (*CM—CC—*ɪ 347–8). To this note C appends another comment: "On recollection I am disposed to consider *this* ⟨alone⟩ as Baxter's *peculiar* claim. I have not indeed any distinct memory of Giordano Bruno's Logica Venatrix Veritatis; but doubtless the principle of Trichotomy is necessarily involved in the Polar Logic: ~~this~~ which again is ~~in~~ the same with the Pythagorean *Tectractys* —i.e. the eternal Fountain or Source of Nature; & this being sacred to contemplation of

weens] to possess within itself the center of its own System: and, vice versâ, that the adoption of Dichotomy ~~on the~~ under the ~~belief~~ supposition of its being the legitimate and only form of distributi⟨ve⟩ Logic, naturally excites and seems to sanction this delusive conceit of Self-sufficiency[107] in minds disposed to follow the clue of Argument at all hazards, and whithersoever it threatens to lead them, ~~as long as~~ ⟨if only⟩ they remain assured that the thread continues entire. And it is now my purpose to evince, that the inevitable result of all *consequent* Reasoning, in which the Speculative intellect refuses to acknowlege a higher or deeper ground than it can itself supply,[108] is—and from Zeno the Eleatic[109] to Spinoza ever has been—Pantheism, under one or other of

---

tribution than all others that went before them, yet I could never see any whose confusion or great Defects I could not easily discover; but not so easily amend. *I had been twenty six years convinced that Dichotomizing will not do it*; but that the [ƒ 38ᵛ] Divine Trinity in Unity hath exprest itself in the whole frame of Nature and Morality." Baxter's Life. Part 3: p. 69.[106]

Identity & prior in order of Thought to *all* division, ~~it~~ is so far from interfering with Trichotomy, as the universal form of Division (more correctly, of distinctive Distribution in Logic) that it implies it.—Prothesis being by the very term anterior to Thesis can be no part of it—Thus in

Prothesis

Thesis   Antithesis
        Synthesis

we have the Tetrad indeed in the intellectual & intuitive Contemplation; but a Triad in discursive Arrangement, and a Tri-unity as a Result.—" (*CM—CC*—ɪ 347–8). See further, Prolegomena x: The *Magnum Opus* and the Principle of Polarity. See below f 247.

[106] Allsop recorded in 1820 that C affirmed that Baxter was "a century before his time, that he was a logician, and first applied the tri-fold or tri-une demonstration ... . He also first introduced the method of argument, that the thing or reason given contains a positive and its opposite ... Baxter tried to reconcile the almost irreconcilable tenets of Calvinism and Arminianism. He more than any other man was the cause of the restoration, and more than any other sectarian was he persecuted by Charles II" (Allsop ɪ 133–4).

[107] Cf a notebook entry: "The evils of Dichotomy are endless" (*CN* ɪv 4784).

[108] Jacobi had argued in his *Briefe ueber die Lehre des Spinoza* that "a being, which has not become, must lie as ground to all becoming; to all evolving (*Entstehenden*) something not evolved; to all changing an unchanging eternal" (Jacobi *Werke* ɪv–1 172).

[109] Not the founder of Stoic philosophy, who was Zeno of Citium. Zeno the Eleatic (*c* 495 to *c* 430 B.C.), was born in Elea, Italy. He was a disciple of Parmenides, whom he accompanied to Athens. Aristotle called him the inventor of dialectic, and he was famed for his paradoxes, which were based on difficulties of analysis of the continuum. His successors, such as Melissos, constituted the Eleatic school of sceptical philosophy. His doctrines were sometimes considered tantamount to those of Spinoza. Coleridge greatly respected him, however: "Zeno's name was ever and ever will be held in reverence by philosophers" (*Friend—CC*—ɪ 438).

its modes:[110] the least repulsive of which differs from the rest, *not* in its consequences which are the same in all and in all alike amount to practical Atheism;[111] but only as it may express the striving of the reasoner himself to hide these consequences from his own consciousness. All Speculative Disquisition must begin with postulates, ~~which the Conscience~~ that derive their ~~might~~ legitimacy, substance, and sanction from the *Conscience*: and from whichever of [*f 39*] the two points the Reason may start, from the things that are seen to the One Invisible, or from the idea of the absolute One to the things that are seen, it will find a Chasm, which the *Moral* Being only, which the Spirit and Religion of man alone can fill up[.] [n]Admirably has the same sentiment been express'd by an extraordinary Mind[112] in a Work written ~~by~~ during the unquestionable period of his life while the author yet posses'd the honour and confidence of the learned and the Men of Science throughout Europe.[113]

> Sciverat quidem, vis rationis, numen dari et omnipotentiam dari, sed quale illud sit, per rationem dictantem non concludere potuit; non [? secus] ac ipsi philosophi quamvis altius et altius iverint, tamen quia τὸ quale in Deo non potuerint per ratiᴏnocinia indagare, hinc sibi τὸ quale finxerant, quod coincideret cum qualitate naturae; et sic unus idemque est fons errorum in populis idolalatris, qui in philosophis quibus natura est idolum; differentia modo intercedit,

[n] The text is in the second transcriber's hand from this point to the middle of f 73

[110] Jacobi had famously concluded that "Jeder Weg der Demonstration geht in den Fatalismus aus" (Jacobi *Werke* IV-1 223)—"every way of demonstration eventuates in fatalism". C, however, who thought constantly about the implications of Spinozism, could (and the present ed thinks he undoubtedly did) have come to this conclusion simply by his own thinking. See *CPT* ch 2–3.

[111] Cf C in a marginal notation: "Pantheism, in whatever drapery of pious phrases disguised, is (where it forms the whole of a System) Atheism" (*CM—CC*—III 1091). "Spinozismus ist Atheismus", said Jacobi in the first of six propositions in his *Briefe ueber die Lehre des Spinoza* in 1787. (Jacobi *Werke* iv–1 216).

[112] E.g.: "I hold, that the religious and the philosophical world are alike indebted to Swedenborg for his not less perspicuous than profound enucleation of the Divine Esse and the Divine Exis-

tere" (*SW & F—CC*—II 831).

[113] Before he devoted himself to the reporting of his visions of heaven and hell, Swedenborg had been a scientist of repute, and a member of prestigious scientific academies. The *Prodromus* or *Outline* is a keen and finely reasoned work on the infinite, and not in the slightest visionary or prophetic. For C's more than merely casual interest (he knew no fewer than eleven of Swedenborg's treatises) see Benjamin P. Kurtz "Coleridge on Swedenborg with Unpublished Marginalia on the 'Prodromus'" *Essays and Studies*; *University of California Publications in English*; *Volume* 14 (Berkeley and Los Angeles 1943). Despite his extensive knowledge of Swedenborg, C rarely mentioned him except in correspondence with his friend C. L. Tulk, who was a wealthy and committed Swedenborgian. See McFarland *Rousseau* 118–19.

[*f 40*] qualis inter crassum et subtile, inter majus et minus plausibile, inter rationem perparum aut nimium exultam.[114] (Eman. Swededenborgii, Prodromus Philosophiae p. 85. 1734.)[o] [115]

I am only too well aware that an attempt to detect error and weakness in the ordinary proofs of truths dear to us beyond all others, and the very dearness of which is itself a presumptive proof of their verity—that an apparent desire to explore the insufficiency of proofs coeval in our acquaintance with the problems which they were meant to solve, and thus associated in our Memory with all the genial and healthful sensations of expanding intellect, cannot but seem invidious and be met with the chill, and the shock, which it had itself occasioned. What, for instance, can be more delightful, more suited to our nature, than the argument from the order and harmony of the visible World, from the general adaptation of means to ends, and of an infinity and intrication [*f 41*] of means and proximate ends, to the one ultimate end of beauty in all, and enjoyment in all, that live? Whatever it may be weigh'd in the gold scales of austere logic and abstract speculation, to the collective man it is irresistible. The proportion of the sexes, the structure of an eye, the correspondence of the object to the sense and of the intermediate powers, as light, and electricity, to both these things struck us like a sensation. The self-evidence of the great Truth that there is a divine Author of an order so excellent seems to us to supersede all detail of proof. We feel the full force, we acknowledge the complete justice of the analogy so beautifully display'd by Bishop Berkeley[p] between the world and a book,[116] and find it as impossible to contemplate the one as to read the other without in-

---

[o] Parentheses inserted   [p] ms: Berkly

[114] Tr: "He knows indeed that there is a Deity; that there is an Omnipotence, but he has been unsuccessful in eliciting the nature of either from the dictates of reason. Much as the philosophers themselves, who after probing the subject with unceasing perseverance, have still been unable to approach by reasonings to the τò *quale* in God; and therefore they have fancied a τò *quale* coincident in qualities with nature. And thus the source of error among the idolatrous vulgar is identical with its source among those philosophers who make an idol of nature: the only difference being what there is between the gross and the subtle, between the more and less plausible, between reason little developed and reason over developed."

[115] The full title is *Emanuel Swedenborgii Sacrae Regiae Maj. Suecicae Collegii Metallici Assessoris Prodromus Philosophiae Ratiocinantia de Infinito, et Causa Finali Creationis; deque Mechanismo Operationis Animae et Corporis.* (Dresdae et Lipsiae, sumptibus Friderici Hekelii, Bibliopol. Regii MDCCXXXIV.)

[116] For Berkeley on the world as a book, see below, Frag 3 pp 299–301 and nn. Cf C in 1795: "The Omnipotent has unfolded to us the Volume of the World, that there we may read the Transcript of himself" (*Lects 1795—CC—94*).

volving the conception of an intelligent Author. The [*f 42*] difference is found not ~~only~~ in any diversity of kind in the languages of the one or the other, but in the transcendent perfection only of that Divine eloquence in which the Heavens declare the Glory of God and the Firmament sheweth his handiwork.[117] One day telleth another, and one night certifieth another—that speech that needeth no translation but the first language of which all others are but the imperfect versions; or there is neither speech nor language, but ~~their~~ voices are understood among them; their sound is gone out into all lands and their Words into the Ends of the World. This method of proof, judged by its practical value and in reference to the ultimate purpose of all proofs, namely that we should all have a firm and lively faith in the existence of God, not that all Men should be enabled to give a philosophic [*f 43*] demonstration of existence, [? ~~deserv~~] deserves and will ever retain its superiority over all other [? ~~At~~] grounds of conviction. First, it is throughout sensuous, free from abstractions, the whole train of reasoning such as might be conveyed in a series of pictures even to the deaf, and want for its completion no other connective but what the Soul, yea, the mere nisus[118] of life, will itself instinctively supply. Hence it is at once lively, affecting, and comprehensible by the meanest capacity. Secondly, it is that proof ~~from~~ in which every other must have begun, and may well, therefore, seem dictated to us by Nature herself, or rather by God in our human Nature. Neque enim negari potest, quin in homine qualites cum que homine, modo rationis usu polleat, sit allud, quod agnoscat. Deum omnipotentem et numen [*f 44*] in omnibus praesens et providum, adeo ut videantur tanquam innatum, et rationis non nimium per *ideas turbatae, aut perparum exultatae vis.[120] Thirdly, this proof is connected in every part of it with

---

* [*Written on f 43ᵛ:*] The Author, here and elsewhere, employs the term "idea", wherein in the stricter language of the Platonist from whom it is borrowed he means the very opposite, namely, the very images, notions, and abstractions of the understanding, in contradistinction of which Plato adopted ⟨the term⟩. ~~if he did not invent~~ He did not, indeed, invent it, any more than Helmont[119] invented the Word "gas", but he gave [it] a new meaning.

---

[117] Ps 19.1.

[118] Tr: "striving".

[119] Jan Baptise van Helmont (1579–1644). Flemish physician and chemist. His works were published in 1648 by his son as *Ortus Medicinae, vel Opera et Opuscula Omnia*. He invented the word *gas* (suggested by Latin and Greek *chaos*) to distinguish aeriform fluids from air.

[120] Tr: "For it cannot be denied that in man as man there are qualities by which he is strong in the use of reason; there may be another that he does not know. I approach omnipotent God, both a divinity present and foreseeing in all things, that he seems as though innate, and an energy not too much agitated by ideas of reason, or at least very little leaping forth."

a sense of the high Wisdom, Providence, and adorable Powers of that Being, the existence of which it sets forth; that fills the soul and has than especial influence over all its highest emotions, or humility, Wonder—Ffeelings which in their highest degree belong exclusively to ⟨the⟩ Idea of God. It is, consequently, far more practical than other evidence can be, even for the philosopher himself, who might yet miss that exactitude which he meets with in the questions of pure science. For it is a scheme of proof which in every instance concentres its whole force, yet in which each instance comes with its own novelty, fresh impression, [*f 45*] and a weight peculiarly its own. Hence there are no bounds to its extent. We follow the physico-theologist, volume after volume, through the Heavens, through the Waters, into the depths of Earth. Each realm of Nature has had its own religious display, and these works are in every language among the most popular. And the [. . .] Delight of adding new instances becomes greatest when theis necessity, as proof, has been forgotten, if indeed it had ever been felt; for the interest is as the Faith, and the light as the Love. Can it then be the purpose of a wise man to evacuate the force, to throw doubt on the sufficiency of such an evidence? As*q* well might he seek to cast a shade on the Sun in Heaven. The Cloud that conceals this, our better Sun, must exhale from the evil heart of unbelief, and rises no higher [*f 46*] than to the unbeliever's own Head. But it is one thing to deny the validity of an argument, and another to determine its true nature, and thus to prevent it from being passed off for a proof of a different kind, for a something which it neither can be nor ought to *r*be, as*s* an argument which addresses itself to the whole man collectively, as an inducement with which each and every distinct faculty of our nature coincides*t* and co-operates—our moral Being on the part of its highest instincts, our understanding by all its analogies, and the speculative reason directly, ⟨indeed,⟩ neutral, yet consequentially and indirectly an efficient ally, first by demonstrating the impossibility of any rational objection, and next by evincing that its dindemonstrableness by mere reason results wholly from its transcendent *u*excellency. In*v* what quarter in [*f 47*] our nature not tenanted by guilt or madness could the inclination to oppose or weaken it arise? But to remind the enquirer that this argument supposes the idea of God already present in the Mind, and the reality of hHis moral attributes to have been already established—to make the student aware that the great book of Nature, in order to ⟨be⟩ read, in order to be a book, supposes all the elements of thought not only to exist in the mind of its reader, but to exist in combination with those

---

q ms: as   *r–s* ms: be. As
t ms: ⟨which⟩ co-incides   *u–v* ms: excellency—in

particular characters, so that to learn is, in fact, a process of reminis-
cence[121]—for the wish to effect this, I say, there are many and impor-
tant motives. We will mention two only for the present—the one, of
which we have, in part, already spoken, is that passage [*f 48*] from The-
ism into Spinozistic Atheism, by no means of unfrequent occurrence
among Men of speculative turn, which very conceivably arises from the
mistaken belief that they had deduced and first obtained the Idea of God,
and the conviction of its reality, from the same causes and Phaenomena
which had awaken'd them to a distinct and, if I may venture the phrase,
a verbal consciousness[w] of the same. Now these Phenomena, taken in
the aggregate, are Nature. What wonder, then, if this constant depen-
dence, or rather this habitual referring, of the Divine Idea to Nature
should at length lead to an identification of the one with the other;[122] if
it should at length appear, what, indeed, it actually would be, had this
been the true ground and origin of the Faith, and a conception abstracted
from [*f 49*] Nature and then personified by that ⟨most⟩ commonest of ar-
tifices, the sudden transformation of an effect into a cause by repeating
the same ⟨number of⟩ facts under the form, and the terms, of [x]agency—
even[y] as the ancients form'd the Naiads from the rivulets, their Driads
from the Mountain, their Aurae ~~from the Bree~~ and Zephyri from the
Gales and Breeze, and an Hemadryad from every Oak. ~~But this ⟨Poly-
theism in general⟩ in effect is Pantheism in its popular side~~[z]

But this and Polytheism in general are[a] in effect the popular side of
Pantheism.[123] The unity ⟨which[b] reason dictates, and which is⟩ indis-
pensable to impersonation, is carried no further than consists with that
plurality which[c] the senses and imagination on their part require.[d] As

---

[w] ms: conscienceness

[x–y] ms: agency. Even

[z] The following comment, referring to this paragraph, is written in pencil on f 48ᵛ: "Il-
lustration quit[e] beside the mark: The Ancients never supposed them to [? create] [? the/
its] rivulet, mountains, &c."

[a] ms: is

[b] ms: with [*correction supplied in pencil on f 48ᵛ*]

[c] ms: with

[d] The following comment, evidently referring to this sentence, is written in pencil on f

---

121 Reminiscence, or *anamnesis*, that
is, that all learning is remembering, is a
powerful doctrine that appears in Plato,
in the *Phaedo* (72e; 76a–e) and the *Meno*
(85d–86b). See below f 246 note 344.

122 I.e., with the result of becoming
pantheism.

123 Cf a note of 1820–1: "did the
Polytheism itself originate in a Panthe-
ism (i.e. God = World + W = G.)—Or
lastly & the opinion to which my own
belief inclines, did it begin in Monothe-
ism (World − God = 0. God − World =
God + World) but soon degenerated into
Pantheism, & thence by means of the ἱρα
γραμματα into Polytheism?" (*CN* IV
4794).

soon as this plurality is rejected, and the reason precipitates or deposits the heterogeneous ingredients supplied by the fancy and the passions, we have, then, in the [ƒ50] first, and more timid, stage, the Anima Mundi of the Stoics,[124] and afterwards, when this too*ᵉ* has been ~~rejected~~ dismissed as a crude ~~a~~Anthropomorphism, ~~and~~ a metaphor,*ƒ* the original of which is itself but a figment of the fancy invented from the same imbecility, and for the same purpose, namely the giving ⟨a⟩ separate subsistence to a unity abstracted from a multitude of effects and then idolized into the cause of the very things of which it was but the generalization and, as it were, the abbreviature, the unity then remaining alone in all its barren and formless dignity.*ᵍ* We have the unica substantia[125] of Spinoza, that mysterious nothing which alone is,[126] and, as well beseems this Phantom set up in lieu of God,[127] [is] invested with the one attribute contrary to creation while it is affirmed to reduce the whole finite creation to a nothing, guarded against all attacks on its rationality by ~~precluding~~

48ᵛ: "Polytheism is not got from Nature at all but from analysis of [? Unity] & personification: of the attributes so obtained. Pantheism is got from nature by simply assuming eternal [? succession], i.e. effects [? without] a cause."

ᵉ ms: to

ƒ The following comment is written in pencil on f 49ᵛ facing this part of the sentence: "Anthropomorphism is *not Anima mundi*[,] has no form"

ᵍ The following comment is written in pencil on f 49ᵛ facing this part of the sentence: "This is beautiful & capable of right application but Coleridge has got off the rails here. He seems to me a little subject to this. Does he lose himself in the inordinate length of sentences & paragraphs, or does the [. . .] of writing break his thread?"

---

[124] C's point is that the Stoics were all pantheists. The phrase *anima mundi* (spirit of the universe) applies to the general position of the Stoics, but is not a technical term in that philosophy—the chief exponents of which, indeed, wrote in Greek.

[125] C attached great importance to the refutation of this formula. Cf a discussion of 1818, which can here be quoted only in its beginnings: "*Spinoza*. Deus est infinita et unica substantia infinitis attributis . . . . In this Spinoza we have an analytic position substituted for a thetic and synthetic. Had you said Res unica cum infinitis attributis is what we mean by God we should have a right to affirm the contrary, for you suppose the correspondent to the term Deus already known to be and the definition is merely your own description of it. If this be a distinctive definition and adequate the subject and the predicate are inter-

changeable, in other words, the definition is purely verbal and still leaves us as before—Unica substantia est unica substantia. So impossible is it O Spinoza even to arrive at a real definition on the assumption of your unicity" (*SW & F—CC*—ı 706).

[126] The conception of substance (οὐσία) was promulgated by Aristotle in his Categories and in his Metaphysics, but it was in Aristotle specifically conceived as involving plurality. For the background of Spinoza's meditations by which he collapsed multiple substances into a single substance, see the chapters in Wolfson called "Unity of Substance" and "Simplicity of Substance" (Wolfson ı 79–157).

[127] "Praeter Deum nulla dari, neque concipi potest substantia"—"Besides God no substance can be granted or conceived" (*Spinoza* ıı 56).

forbidding [*f 51*] all question; for of nothings what solution can be re-
quired?[h] Few, I grant, have been so far able to de-naturalize themselves
as to contemplate the doctrine in the rigid and naked form as it ⟨is⟩ here
represented. ~~b~~But how often have I not ~~heard from~~ ⟨observed⟩ men of ar-
dent Minds, in the early glow of self-thinking and ⟨in⟩ the first [i]efforts
of[j] supposed emancipation from the prejudices of the popular faith,
shrink from the use of the personal as spoken of the Deity, and disposed,
in a more than Poetic interpretation, to substitute for the living Jehovah
the Creator of the Heaven and the Earth

> a sense sublime
> Of something far more deeply interfused,
> Whose dwelling is the light of setting suns,
> And ⟨the⟩ round ocean and the living air,
> And the blue sky, and in the mind of Man:
> A motion and a spirit, that impels
> All thinking things, all objects of all thoughts
> And rolls through all things.[128]
>   Tintern Abbey[k] [129]

Many a Man (I speak not without knowledge)[l] who, lulled with these
dreams and accustomed to interpret the [*f 52*] Divine omnipresence in
any sense rather than ⟨the⟩ alone ~~in the~~ safe and legitimate one—the
presence, ~~th~~namely, of all things to God[130]—has thought himself abun-
dantly religious, yea! hallowing his Sabbath with the loftiest sort of de-
votion:

> ~~w~~When far from boisterous scenes with gentle heart,
> He worships Nature in the Hill and Valley,

[h] Full stop in ms
[i-j] ms: the efforts it [*cancelled in pencil with the correction supplied in pencil on f 50ᵛ*]
[k] The following comment, referring to the quotation, is written in pencil on f 50ᵛ: "What
poor stuff these lines of Wordsworth's are & how utterly unharmonious. Three *ands* in suc-
cession"
[l] Parentheses inserted (following Ward's suggestion on f 50ᵛ)

[128] Though the quotation of the beau-
tiful lines, with their invocation of inter-
fusing and rolling through, softens the
charge of pantheism—which indeed C's
language about his friend is deliberately
trying to do—Boethius is more crudely
direct: to say that "all things are god" is
"an impious assertion" (*quod dictu nefas
est*) (*Boethius* 44).

[129] Lines 93–102 (*WPW* II 262).
[130] As opposed to "the presence of all
things *in* God", which would be panthe-
istic. Cf *Aids to Reflection*: "And this
from having been educated to understand
the Divine Omnipresence in any sense
rather than the alone safe and legitimate
one, the presence of all things to God!"
(*AR*—1825—396).

nNot knowing what he loves but loves it all.
Coleridge's Remorse, Act I.[131]

Be it, however, ~~that the number~~ that the number of such men is comparatively ⟨small⟩, and be it, as in truth it often is, a brief stage, a transitional period in the process of intellectual growth, yet among a number great and daily increasing there may be observed an almost entire withdrawing from the life and personal Being of God,[132] a constant turning of the thought to what have been called the physical attributes, and these too, if ever connected with more than words physically represented, to the omnipresence in [*f 53*] the counterfeit form of Ubiquity, the Immensity, the Infinity the Immutability—a fFate, in short, not a moral Creator and Governor. Admirably has this been set forth by the Philosopher of Koenigsberg.[133] In the position that all reality is either contained *in* the necessary being as an *attribute*, or it exists *through* him as its *ground*, it remains undecided whether the properties of intelligence and will are to be referred to the Supreme Being in the former or only in the latter sense, as inherent attributes or only as *consequences* that have existence in other things *through* him. Were the latter the truth, then, notwithstanding all the pre-eminence which must be assigned to the ETERNAL FIRST from the sufficiency, unity, and independence of his being as the dread ⟨ground⟩ of the universe, his nature would yet fall far short of that which we are bound to comprehend in the idea of God. For without any knowledge or determining resolve of its own, it would [*f 54*] only be a blind necessary ground of other things and other spirits, and thus would be distinguished from the FATE of certain ancient

[131] Cf *Remorse* I ii lines 243–5: "Unfit for boisterous times, with gentle heart/ He worships nature in the hill and valley,/ Not knowing what he loves, but loves it all—" (*PW—EHC*—II 830–1). Cf *Osorio* I lines 244–6: "Unfit for boisterous times, with gentle heart/ He worships Nature in the hill and valley,/ Not knowing what he loves, but loves it all!" (*PW—EHC*—II 529).

[132] For the vital importance of "personal being" see Prolegomena XVI: The Concept of Person. Cf *Aids to Reflection*: "And what has been the consequence? An increasing unwillingness to contemplate the Supreme Being in his *personal* Attributes; and thence a Distaste to all the peculiar Doctrines of the Christian Faith, the Trinity, the Incarnation of the

Son of God, and Redemption. The young and ardent, ever too apt to mistake the inward triumph in the detection of *error* for a positive love of truth, are among the first and most frequent victims to the epidemic *fustidium*. Alas! even the sincerest seekers after light are not safe from the contagion. Some have I known, constitutionally religious—I speak feelingly; for I speak of that which for a brief period was my own state—who under the unhealthful influence have been so estranged from the Heavenly *Father*, the *Living* God, as even to shrink from the personal pronouns as applied to the Deity" (*AR*—1825—395–6). See *CPT* 235, 376 n 69.

[133] I.e. Kant.

philosophers in no respect but that of being more definitely and intelligibly described.*^m*

Kant's vermischte Schriften
§§ 102 and 103[134]

Intelligence—and this only to express the ground of effects analogous to those produced by human intelligence, and what more, indeed, could be strictly and legitimately concluded from the aggregate of sensible objects*ⁿ*—Intelligence alone, I say, excepted, wherein does the notion of God differ from that of gravitation in the understanding of those who represent the Deity not only as a necessary but a necessitated Being, for whom Justice is but a scheme of general Laws necessary to the largest sum possible of the well-being of all, at whatever cost of misery and suffering to many, and for whom [*f 55*] "holiness" and "the hatred of Sin", yea, and "Sin" itself, except as an idle and almost obsolete synonime for "defect" or "calamity", are words without meaning, or metaphorical accommodation to the prejudices of a rude and barbarous age.[135] And yet how is it possible this should not be so, if the idea ~~is~~ wholly originates in the experience of Nature? For what can we infer from natural phenomena but the laws that at once constitute and regulate them. Dr Priestley, therefore, spoke with perfect consistency when, ~~he~~ ⟨having⟩ affirmed that God did every thing, he added, and is every thing;[136] for such is the

---

^m The following comment is written in pencil on f 53^v facing this sentence: "This makes great deal turn upon *in* and *through*. Far too much I take it"

ⁿ The following comment, evidently referring to this passage, is written in pencil on f 53^v: "This seems to me wonderfully poor to come from Coleridge. There is in nature a species of mechanism that resembles human machinery. But it is never *like* so long as nature contains an element of *vitality*—where that pulses Deity is near. So that man who is created [? last] is further from him, & by that nearer to him, as extremes [. . .] [? point]."

[134] *I. Kant's vermischte Schriften. Aechte und vollständige Ausgabe* (Halle, Königsberg 1799–1807). 4 vols. For C's annotations in three different sets of these volumes see *CM* (*CC*) III 316–66.

[135] The phrase "barbarous Age" occurs in the paragraph called "The Verse" prefixed to Milton's *Paradise Lost*.

[136] Cf Priestley: "Nor, indeed, is making the deity to *be*, as well as to *do* every thing, in this sense, any thing like the opinion of Spinoza" (Priestley *Discussion* 253). Cf further: "For any man to have acted differently from what he did, in any given case, he must have been differently disposed at the time, or must have had different views of things present to his mind; neither of which, properly speaking, depends upon himself. For though it does so *immediately*, it does not do so *ultimately*: for since every particular determination depends upon his immediately preceding circumstances, it necessarily follows that the whole chain of his determinations and actions depends upon his *original maker*, and *original circumstances*. And who is our maker but God? or who is it that disposes of us but the same God?" (Priestley *Doctrine* 233).

true and adequate idea of the laws of Nature, or the natura naturans,[137] as distinguished from the natura naturata,[138] though on what pretence the Philosophical theologian annexed the assertion, "but this is not Spinozism", [*f 56*] is no less inconceivable to me than of a Man, having defined a figure as ~~discern~~ described by the circumvolution of a line fixed at one extreme, should then add, "but this is not a circle".[139] If, however, we ⟨d⟩are ~~justified~~ ⟨in⟩ anticipate any result from the known Laws of Association, we may predict that the habitual connection of the idea of God with the laws of Nature, and, for the same purpose, that of ~~explaining~~ accounting for the Phenomena of Nature, in proportion as it estranges the Mind from the personal Will, indisposes[o] it to all those doctrines of religion which either present the Deity to our Minds in the forms of personality, as well as those that rise out of his Personal attributes, and, in fact, to Religion itself, which without a sense of the Divine Personality, ceases to be Religion [*f 57*] and becomes mere [? ~~Theanthropy~~] hypothesis, which, if it were more legitimate and philosophical, might enlarge the intellect and gratify the curiosity, but would inspire neither fear nor hope nor love. The prevention, therefore, of a state of Mind so much more injurious to the moral character than it can ever promise to be serviceable to the Intellectual forms no unimportant reason for detecting any error that has been proved to favor such a state, with whatever truth

---

[o] ms: indispose

[137] Tr: "nature naturing". On C's conception of the old dichotomy between "natura naturans" and "natura naturata" see *P Lects* (1949) 370: "in speaking of the world without us as distinguished from ourselves, the aggregate of phenomena ponderable and imponderable, is called nature in the passive sense,—in the languge of the old schools, *natura* NATURATA—WHILE THE SUM OR AGGREGATE OF THE POWERS INFERRED AS THE sufficient causes of the former (which by Aristotle and his followers were called the SUBSTANTIAL FORMS) is nature in the active sense, or *natura nat-uRANS*."

[138] Tr: "nature natured". This scholastic distinction (used significantly by Spinoza (*Ethica* I 29) and Schelling (e.g. Schelling *SW* III 284; VII 200)) is frequently invoked by C; it differentiates the vital processes in nature from the

actual forms of natural objects. For the scholastic precedence see e.g. Albert the Great's *Summa creaturis* Borgnet XXXIV 403: "some say that there is a *natura naturans* and a *natura naturata*" (Gilson 281). Albert, however, differs from the pantheistic usages of Schelling and Spinoza by conceiving the former term as referring only to God, the latter to created nature.

[139] Cf *Aids to Reflection*: "God (says Dr. Priestley) not only does, but *is* everything. *Jupiter est quodcunque vides*. And thus a system, which commenced by excluding all life and immanent activity from the visible Universe and evacuating the natural World of all Nature, ended by substituting the Deity, and reducing the Creator to a mere Anima Mundi; a spirit that has no advantage over Spinosism but its inconsistency" (*AR*—1825—395).

it may stand in connection; and this, accord⟨ing⟩ly, is the first of the two motives[140] which ~~eoimpells~~ us to exhibit what the so-called proof from the fitness ~~iof not~~ things[141] is not, in order that we may leave it in full and unalloyed ~~possesion~~ possession of that which it is. And this the more when we consider that we deny to it nothing but what is already provided for by more [*f 58*] certain means, including the very degree of civilization which is supposed, in order to the existence of such speculations; whereas, what we ~~would~~ leave to it is as indispensable as the vital Air to the Lungs, which ⌈. . .⌉ ⟨cannot⟩, indeed, from[p] the Air[q] have derived its power of breathing, and yet without it could not continue to breathe.[r] By Reasoning, sayeth the Apostle of the Gentiles, no man arrives at the Idea of God, but that knowledge being given, the things that are seen set forth the Glory of the   .[s] [142] In the like spirit, all the sounder Schoolmen and the first Fathers of the Reformation with one consent place the origin of the Idea in the Reason, the ground of its reality in the Conscience, and the confirmation, reproduction, and progressive development in the order and harmony of the visible world—as far, I mean, as they[t] speak abstractedly from Revelation.

Our second motive [*f 59*] is not unlike the first, and if less important ⌈. . .⌉ ⟨⌈. . .⌉⟩ [? ~~moral~~] ⌈. . .⌉ ~~view is of more~~ in a moral respect, stands, however, in a yet closer connexion with the conveniences of argument. The reasoner, namely, who has taken the assertion of a self-existent Being as ~~demon~~ a truth demonstrably concluded from the Facts of experience, under the acknowledged and universal law of cause and effect, and who, ~~is~~ in consequence, ~~is perhaps~~ during the whole development of his Fancy and Judgement ⟨has⟩ never once suspected any difficulty, or should any start, ha~~ves~~ ~~presented~~ ⟨dismissed⟩ it ~~once under the~~ ⌈. . .⌉ ~~incomp~~ as answered beforehand in the very admission of the divine incomprehensibility—⌈. . .⌉ ⟨such⟩ ~~a~~ Reasoners, and their name is legion, will bring these very difficulties, which had perplexed and (with exception of Heraclitus and Plato, who both referred for their actual faith to a

---

[p] This word is written over another, possibly "rose"

[q] This word is written over another, now illegible

[r] ms: breath

[s] Space left in ms. Ward, writing in pencil on f 57ᵛ, suggests "maker of the universe" as the missing phrase

[t] ms: the

[140] For "motives" see above, Frag 1 ff 55–7 and nn.

[141] More commonly termed the cosmological proof.

[142] Cf Acts 1.20: "For the invisible things of him from the creation of the world are clearly seen, being understood by the things that are made, *even* his eternal power and Godhead".

σΣοφια Θθεοπαραδοος)[143] baffled the Philosophers of Greece, and drove the wisest into Pantheism for their [*f 60*] own creed,[144] and the half scornful, half acquiescent defence of Polytheism for the mass of Mankind[145]—these very difficulties, I say, will they bring to [...][*u*] verbis et syllabis[146] against the holiest, most concerning, and peculiar, doctrines, which by their Nature are incapable of any semblance of proof from the same grounds, or in any similar scheme of deduction, as those in ~~th~~which they mistakenly suppose the true Idea of the Divinity to have been imported into the Mind of Man. In short, no effort, no force of fashion can so confound the inherent distinction of things and of our notices of things[147] as to enable us to contemplate the agency of nature otherwise than in contradistinction from that of a personal Will. Try only to feel grateful to the circulative force that moves the blood in your veins, or to the Laws of Motion which moves the Planets round their Centre, and even to the breeze which moves the vessel towards the appointed Port! No! the Fancy must come in as the mediator; [*f 61*] there must be a spirit on the Breeze, who is not the same as the breeze; there must be an Apollo in the golden car, which, as it traverses the cope of Heaven, forms the Sun to our mortal eyes—the very frequency of the metaphor in poetry, and the fact that the pleasure which we receive in addresses to the Winds, the Mountains, and even to Flowers is owing to our sense that it is a metaphor, i.e. a transition of one kind to a diverse, confirms the truth of my statement. To deduce a Deity wholly from Nature is in the result to substitute an Apotheosis of Nature for Deity. How, then, is it possible that a mind so formed, so educated, should recoil as from a stumbling block, or despise as folly, the total and organized creed of a Religion, the very postulate and precondition of which is an admission of ~~a responsible Will in Man, and thence~~ ⟨a Will good or⟩ evil in itself, and except in relation to which there is nothing in heaven or in earth, without or within, that[*v*] [can] be called either. [*f 62*] That very principle, of which Nature knows not, which the light of the Sun can never re-

---

^u Word crowded into the margin   ^v ms: than

[143] Tr: "a wisdom delivered by God". The phrase occurs in Proclus *In Crat.* p 59P.

[144] Cf a note on Thomas Warton's ed of Milton's minor poems: "Spinoza re-edified the Pantheism of the old Greek Philosophy" (*CM—CC*—III 901). again: "It was by dwelling too exclusively on the Infinite, that the ancient Greek Philosophers, Plato excepted, fell into Pantheism, as in later times did Spinosa" (*C&S—CC*—168).

[145] For polytheism as the popular form of pantheism, see above f 49.

[146] Tr: "in words and syllables".

[147] The distinction insisted upon by Kant, in his conceptions of *Ding an sich* and *phenomenon*.

veal, which we must ~~seek within us and must find within us, what no forms can pres~~ either despair of finding, or must seek and find within ourselves[148]—I speak as only of my own experience, but of my own experience I can truly declare that among the very numerous nominal christians who profess to believe in all ~~parts of~~ the christian doctrines (those only excepted which alone are properly Christian, that is, peculiar to Christianity)[w], I have not met with one, the ground of whose disbelief was not an unbelief in the Creator of Heaven and Earth, the God of Abraham, Isaac, and Jacob, the living Jehovah whose name is I AM!,[149] whose first and ~~in most attributes~~ eEternal Name is in the declaration of that personality, which nature hath not and cannot declare, and of that Being to which Nature does indeed bear witness, as darkness beareth witness to light.[150]

[*f 63*]   Chapter

Of the Origin of the Idea of God in the Mind of Man

Quod verbum non intelligatur quam a rationali homine: nam credere aliquid absque ideâ rei et absque rationis ~~intuitionise~~ est midi memorites retinere vocem omni vitâ perceptionis et affectionis ~~destitul~~ destitutem quod non credere.[151]

The young Bull butts ere[x] yet its horns are formed,[152] the stag-chafer in its worm state makes its bed-chamber prior to its ~~metaphorses~~ ⟨morphosis⟩, exactly as much longer than[y] itself as is required for the length of the horn which is yet to be produced. Through all Nature there is a manifestation of power pre-existent to the product.[153] Scarcely an organ

---

[w] Parentheses inserted   [x] ms: are [*correction supplied in pencil above this word*]
[y] ms: as [*correction supplied in pencil above this word*]

[148] Cf *Lay Sermons*: "That which we find in ourselves, is (gradu mutato) the substance and the life of *all* our knowledge. Without this latent presence of the 'I am,' all modes of existence in the external world would flit before us as colored shadows, with not greater depth, root, or fixture, than the image of a rock hath in a gliding stream or the rain-bow on a fast-sailing rain-storm" (*LS—CC—78*).

[149] Cf C in conversation: "The Personality of God, the *I Am* of the Hebrews is most vividly impressed on the book [of Job], in opposition to Pantheism" (*TT—CC—*I 146).

[150] See Prolegomena XVI: The Con-

cept of Person; *CPT* ch 2; Prolegomena XIX, XX, XXV.

[151] Tr: "That the word is not understood other than by a rational man; for to believe anything from the intuition of the thing is merely to retain in memory a voice in all life destitute of perception and affection, which is not to believe".

[152] Cf *Aids to Reflection*: "The Bull-calf *buts* with smooth and unarmed Brow" (*AR—1825—347*).

[153] Cf *Aids to Reflection*: "Throughout animated Nature, of each characteristic Organ and Faculty, there exists a pre-assurance, an instinctive and practical Anticipation" (*AR—1825—347*).

exists in the higher Animal which had not in some one [or]^z other animal, far lower in the scale, appeared as a rudiment of ambiguous [*f 64*] use, or none, to the possessor. Throughout all Nature there is seen an evolution from within; ~~H~~her process is synthetic throughout; throughout it is the direct ~~p~~opposite to the analytic and reflective processes of the mechanical understanding. ⟨Self-⟩unconscious^a, ~~of itself~~ the man carries on the development of its Animal Being, ~~and all that~~ that organization which places ~~its~~ ⟨the human⟩ in community with the plant and with the mere Animal; and all that arrangement, and that quality of his organs which ~~were~~ ⟨had been⟩ useless or pernicious for a Being not destined for ~~the~~ other, and higher, and even diverse faculties from those of the mere Animal,^{b} ~~are effected~~ ⟨both these he carries on⟩ in the sleep of those faculties, ~~a deep rest~~ in the passiveness of pure sensation.^{c} ^{154} And yet in vain would these rudiments have been formed, in vain [would]^d those powers which, having formed them, reappear as predispositions and instincts, were these not a correspondence prepared in the real present. In vain would the conditions, the possibility, of the [*f 65*] human have been inlaid were not the human, in its full development, already there to meet and to protect it. Only by disproportion of the means to the ends will the babe [survive], abandoned from its birth and suckled in the Forest by the blind and kindly instincts of nature in the Goat or the Wolf. Its eye will remain glazed; its lips, the seat of expression for^e appetite and rage alone. The tongue will utter the sounds of the Ape; the very ear will be deaf to all but the inarticulate sounds of Nature.^{155} Even in its very first

^{z} Word supplied in pencil on f 62^v

^{a} ms: ⟨Self-⟩Unconscious

^{b} The following comment is written in pencil on f 63^v facing this part of the sentence: "Unconsciously man carries on the development of animal [. . .], and that self or [. . .] which places the human being in community both [. . .] and [? within] mere animal."

^{c} The following comment is written in pencil on f 63^v facing this part of the sentence: "This passage wants long study first to [. . .], and secondly to throw it into clear exposition. The meaning is here but it is a muddle as to utterance. Not that a word should be altered except in a note."

^{d} Word supplied in pencil on f 63^v

^{e} This word is cancelled in pencil, and the phrase "will remain to utter" is substituted for it on f 64^v

^{154} See Prolegomena xxx: The Relation of the *Magnum Opus* to C's *Theory of Life*.

^{155} C may in this passage be recalling the famous wild boy found in France just before the turn of the nineteenth century, who, as described by the physician Itard, by being separated from others throughout his formative years had lost the capacity to learn language. See Jean-Marc-Gaspard Itard *The Wild Boy of Aveyron* tr George Humphrey and Muriel Humphrey (Englewood Cliffs, N.J. 1962); Harlan Lane *The Wild Boy of Aveyron* (Cambridge, Mass. 1976). C in 1803 has the phrase "Savage of Aveyron" in his notebooks (*CN* I 1348), and Kathleen Coburn comments: "The 'wolf-child' of Aveyron had been the subject of a book published a few months before this

Week of Being, the holy quiet of its first days must be sustain'd by the warmth of the maternal bosom. The first dawnings of its humanity will break forth in the Eye that connects the Mother's face with the warmth of the mother's bosom, the support of the mother's arms. A thousand tender kisses excite a finer life in its lips, and there first language is imitated from the mother's smiles. Ere yet a conscious*ᶠ* self exists, the love begins; and the first love is love of to another.*ᵍ* *ʰ* The [*f 66*] Babe acknowledges a self in the mother's form ~~one yet~~ years before it can recognize a self in its own. Faith, implicit Faith, the offspring of unreflecting love, ~~ins~~ the antecedent and indispensable condition of all its knowledge: the life is the light thereof. Oh! who can tell the goings on of a mother's heart, or interpret thoughts too deep for Words. When the little Being newly nourished, or awakening from its heaving pillow, begins its murmuring song for pleasure, and for pleasure leaps on the arm, begins to smile and laugh to the ~~motions of its~~ moving head of the Mother, who ⟨is⟩ [? ~~alone~~] is to it its all the World. It knows not what the Mother is, but still less does it know what itself is. If to have put the question and to have returned the answer be to know, the babe knows nothing. But it clings to the Mother and has a right, and an utterable right, to cling to her.¹⁵⁶ Behold, the sweet innocent lies before ⟨thee⟩ on thy Arm, looks up towards thee, and towards thee stretches forth with all its limbs; has the present and yet seeks thee, unutterably thanks thee; and as thou dost [*f 67*] fold it to thy heart and feelest how dear it is to thee, and with a dearness and a love that asks no leave of the judgement, admits of no increase or decrease of*ⁱ* value, and inspires, not follows, even*ʲ* the*ᵏ* forward looking dreams of maternal hope, do not thy hands close as it were of ˡthyself-selves?¹⁵⁷ Thy*ᵐ* Eyes, can they turn from that infant face elseward than

ᶠ ms: conscience [*correction supplied in pencil on f 64ᵛ*]
ᵍ This word is cancelled in pencil, and "of" substituted for it on f 64ᵛ
ʰ The following comment is written in pencil on f 64ᵛ facing this sentence: "very fine"
ⁱ The following correction is suggested in pencil on f 66ᵛ: "from"
ʲ This word is cancelled in pencil
ᵏ The word "far" is written in pencil on f 66ᵛ and marked for insertion after this word
ˡ⁻ᵐ ms: thyselselves? thy

entry: E. M. Itard, *An Historical Account of the Discovery and Education of A Savage Man, and of the First Developments, Physical and Moral, of The Young Savage caught in the Woods near Aveyron in the year 1798* (1802)" (*CN* I 1348 note).

¹⁵⁶ Cf a notation of 1817: "When the little creature has slept out its sleep and stilled its hunger of the mother's bosom / that very hunger a mode of Love, all made up of Kisses—and coos and wantons with pleasure, and laughs and plays bob cherry with the Mother, that is all, all to it—it understands not either itself or its Mother—but it clings to her, and has a right, an undescribable Right to cling to her—" (*CN* III 4348).

¹⁵⁷ The continuing emphasis on the importance of the infant is undergirded

to heaven, and does not the whole heart utter, as with an innate prayer, "our Father that art in Heaven"? Why have men a Faith in God? There is but one answer: the Man, and the Man alone, has a Father and a Mother.[n] All begins in instinct, but do[o] all therefore begin alike? Oh no! each hath its own, and the instincts of Man must[p] ⟨be⟩ human, rational instincts— Reason itself mutely prophesying of its own future advent.

We have said that Man hath from Birth that which is common with the Animal, and that which is especially human. With the Beasts of the Field it possesses the senses, and the sensations, and the desires of self-preservation, and the impulse to pleasure from the pain of its absence. [*f* 68] Beyond the beasts, yea, an⟨d⟩ above the nature of which they are the inmates, man possesses love, and Faith, and the sense of the permanent. As the connexion and the intermedium of both, he possesses reflection and foresight—in other words, an understanding, which is, therefore, a human understanding, not solely nor chiefly from its greater extent than that which the Dog, the Elephant, and the Ant possess, but because it ⟨is⟩ irradiated by a higher power: the power, namely, of seeking what it can no where behold, and finding that ~~it~~ which itself has first transfused, the permanent; that, which in the endless flux of sensible things, can alone be known; which is indeed in all, but exists for the reason alone, for it is Reason. But, by a mystery of the human Soul, the Man may seduce the understanding from the higher Reason, and without forfeiting that great extent and these additional powers which from the Reason, and from the impressions of human love, both from within and from without, it has derived. [*f* 69] As Understanding, it is but the faculty of adapting means to ends, according to varying circumstances. But to what end, or rather, to what ultimate purpose it should itself be directed, remains uncertain. This only is pre-determined, that in one or other of two channels must it flow. It must either develop that which is properly human in man, and the animal Nature, but in subordination, nay, subjugation to his Humanity, or the Animal Nature, to which the human is to be made instrumental only by giving eyes to blind appetite, transform selfishness into self-love and enrich degradation by consciousness[q], intention, and choice— thus differing from the Animal in this alone, that he that hath been made

---

[n] The following comment is written in pencil on f 66ᵛ facing this sentence: "This is first rate argument but would make fools laugh"

[o] ms: to [*correction supplied in pencil on f 66ᵛ*]

[p] This word is written over another, now illegible

[q] ms: conscienceness [*correction supplied in pencil on f 68ᵛ*]

---

by C's understanding that "The Infant is a riddle of which the Man is the Solution; but the Man could not exist but with the Infant as its ante[ce]dent" (*CM—CC*—II 1145).

the Animal which he was not born. If there be an awful moment in the life of Man, it is that in which the yearling babe is seated on its Mother's knee.[158] ~~Shall~~ Full of love and life, shall they be directed to the objects of the senses, so selected as to solicit [*f 70*] the attention and call forth the eager desires, and in those objects to find their destination and their end? Shall the Mother aid in alienating the love of the infant from a kindred form, its own and yet another? Shall[r] it throw the life of the Infant upon objects from which it instantly must recoil, to the bodily sensations of the Infant like echoes from an unreceiving Rock? The gaudy forms that attract its Eye, the delicious fruits which provoke its grasp, can receive and retain no part of the life and love which they attract, that must needs fall back upon the appetites which they are ⟨to⟩ gratify, and finally become connected with the form of the bodily organs which are appropriate to them. They must find their last unity in the self, which is, in truth, no other than the feeling of life, its desires, and its functions, with that image which, being always present to the senses, constitutes[s] the sole person of which the sensual being is capable. [*f 71*] Marvellous, indeed, is the susceptibility of man under the forming hands of Art and circumstance. The whole Animal Nature may be made to have each a temporary existence in him; he may be made to exhibit the pride of the Horse, the [? impotent] rage of [the] Turkey, the Vanity of the Peacock, the servility and Docility of the beaten Dog—and like the dog, for bread and Meat to learn and practise tricks which are against its[t] nature. Sensual enjoyment can beckon him onwards; sensual fear drive him back; and sensual hope re-enliven him. And yet in all this to be indeed an Animal is not permitted to him. The higher part of his Nature remains indissoluble, for it is the very man. But it remains as his avenging demon. It is not the sensual gratifications themselves, as with the animal, who seeks for food when he hungers[u], and when he is satiate sinks to sleep. It is the dream of these, which have obtained a spell-like power over powers, aspirations, and impulses—disproportionate, heterogeneous—that sets [*f 72*] his whole life in motion. Unnatural usurpers of the imagination, not the things but the images of the things, no longer his mere objects, become his Gods, and in their vividness ~~baffle~~ distinguish the self-love in which they commenced. Enslaved by imagination, he may

---

[r] ms: shall   [s] ms: constitute
[t] ms: it   [u] ms: hunger

[158] A startling statement that serves as foundation for C's argumentation about the nature and significance of the mother's relation to the child. Cf the statement elsewhere that Christianity "was associated with our mother's chair, and with the tones of her voice" (*TT—CC*—I 24).

be educated to force his way through fire and blood for one who repays his service with contempt and injury. Nor can it be otherwise. He must become the victim of those powers beyond self which he has alienated and estranged from their rightful objects. Not the mere negation of his true human feelings will be seen; the force and the substance are indestructible, and appear in their contraries. His tendencies upwards manifest themselves in idolatry; his sympathies, in ^vhatred. The^w instinct that seeks for correspondence, and would fain love itself in another, is translated to an impotent craving to verify the possession of power, and derives the assurance from the torments which it is capable of [*f 73*] ^xexciting. He^y becomes loveless as the fish, merciless as the snake that kills by poison, and cruel as the tiger that indulges its lust of destruction ere yet he appeases his thirst and hunger.

^zWe have thus described the results that are to be expected from the cultivation of the animal being by the early direction of the senses to objects which, having no connexion with the beholder but by their qualities as so many stimulants of the animal sensibility—to objects incap⟨ab⟩le of being sympathized with^a—must necessarily never berate, as it were, the attention to the beholder's own body as the one object constantly recurring in the constant change of all the rest, and thus constitute this body the centre, the proper unity, of all else. The image thus potentiated becomes the self, that, namely, ⟨by⟩ which the mind^b represents its own unity in the imagination. This Self is, indeed, a mere phantom, and, like all other images that recur so [*f 74*] constantly as at no one time to attract any distinct and conscious attention, is soon bedimmed into a mere blind feeling—even as pictures degenerate into hieroglyphics, and these again into mere configurations that betray their origin only by exciting a portion of the same feelings as had been habitually associated with the primary forms and the objects represented by them. In other words, the resemblance is felt, not seen, and felt the more because it has ceased to obtain distinct notice. The result will best explain, while it proves, the nature of the process; for, first, it is connected with appetites, either as craving or as gratified, and with such as, during the whole earlier period of the mind's growth, are incapable of being communicated, in which all is received [and] nothing in the same moment given in return. What can the fruit, or the sweetmeat, call to mind in the individual, but that individual's

---

^{v-w} ms: hatred, the

^{x-y} ms: exciting he

^z JHG's hand resumes at this point

^a Dash inserted. An unnecessary "which" is written in pencil on f 72^v and marked for insertion after this word

^b ms: find [*correction supplied in pencil on f 72^v*]

own solitary and incommunicable feelings? or compare a [*f 75*] child ~~es-tranged from~~ ⟨insulated⟩ even ~~at~~ ⟨from⟩ its birth by the high rank or sullen pride of its parents, who had never ~~placed~~ fed at the bosom of a mother— say, rather, who had no mother:

> —that most holy name,
> Which Heaven and nature bless,
> I may not vilely prostitute to those,
> Whose infants owe them less
> Than the poor caterpillar owes
> Its gaudy parent fly—*c* [159]

whose servile nurse, mute and joyless, is forbidden to press its lips with kisses; and finally, one who, instead of playmates, is surrounded with an endless variety of playthings. Compare, I say, a creature thus denatural-ized with the healthful child of a cottage, ~~accustomed~~ whose first play-things were its mother's lap, or father's knee; who had no enjoyment that was not at the same moment seen in the form of another,[160] and thus the latter so inwoven with the pleasures of its senses as to have become their representative, their denominator—I had almost said, their outward ex-istence. Often have I seen a child of two or three years old [*f 76*] seated at the homely table with healthful hunger, and yet incapable of gratify-ing it, because the father had not yet come in, or the accustomed faces of brother, sister, or playmate were wanting.[161] Is it not evident that in the first case there must be soon established a sort of oscillatory move-ment, from the individual to the outward unreceiving object regularly re-turning back as to its only centre, and on the other hand as regular a sal-lying forth of the self to the outward and mere object? In all its after life, its thoughts and its actions, the self, i.e. the phantom by which the indi-vidual misrepresents the unity of his personal being, instead of being the

---

c The following comment, referring to the verse, is written in pencil on f 74ᵛ: "This is very shrewd verse"

[159] "Ode to Georgiana, Duchess of Devonshire" lines 52–7: *PW* (EHC) ɪ 337.

[160] C's arguments here reprise those of his poem "Ode to Georgiana, Duchess of Devonshire" (*PW*—EHC—ɪ 335–8), where the Duchess's poem "Passage over Mount Gothard" elicits motherhood as the font of all feeling for others. The Duchess, reared in luxury and separated from nature, nevertheless in her 24th stanza hails William Tell's action "that first preserved his child,/ Then aim'd the arrow at the tyrant's heart". C asks how, insulated from the lot of mankind, the Duchess could still have such feelings; and his answer is that the experience of childbirth and motherhood acquainted her with pain and with the feelings of the other.

[161] Cf Wordsworth: "Behold the Child among his new-born blisses,/ A six years' Darling of a pigmy size!/ See, where 'mid work of his own hand he lies,/ Fretted by sallies of his mother's kisses,/ With light upon him from his fa-ther's eyes!" ("Ode: Intimations of Im-mortality", lines 86–90; *WPW* ɪᴠ 281).

agent itself becomes the sole motive, and the outward objects at once its means and its representatives, or proxies. Again, by natural reaction, as the objects acquire an interest that does not belong to them, by this ⟨constant⟩ association with the mind and with the feelings, an interest, a false worth which is foreign to their [*f 77*] nature, and, on the other hand, the self borrows from the objects a sort of unnatural outwardness. It becomes, as it were, a thing, and the habit commences of reflecting thereon as on a thing while the things are invested—unconsciously indeed, but for that very cause the more intensely—with the attributes of life and power. In this sort of middle and ambiguous state the essence of superstition consists, in the attributing, namely, of subjective powers and personal agency to ~~the me~~ ⟨the mere objects of the senses, to⟩ objects as objects. Alas! we need not travel to the wastes of Africa for Fetich worshippers—I had been almost tempted to say that the whole constitution of civilized Europe presents the same idolatry, and for the greater part in less imaginative forms. It is the dire epidemic of man in the social state to forget the substance in the appearance, the essence in the form. Hence almost everywhere we behold religion degraded into ceremonies, and then, by the reaction before described, the ceremonies animated into a strange [*f 78*] and unnatural magic. Hence for state policy we have statecraft and the mockery of expedience; for the fine arts, a marketable trade; for philosophy, a jargon of materialism; and the study of nature conducted on such principles as to place it in doubtful rivalry with the art and theory of cooking.

A fearful display, but ~~as~~ necessary ~~a~~ consequence of the first false step in the formation of the human character, and experience is the warrant of its truth. But does ⟨our⟩ nature tempt to this process? No! As sure as ever the heart of man is made tender by the presence of a love that has no self, by a joy in the protection of the helpless which is at once impulse, motive, and reward, so surely is it elevated to the universal Parent. The ~~the~~ child on the knee of its mother and gazing upward to her countenance marks her eyes averted heavenward, while yet it feels the tender pressure of her embrace, and learns to pray [*f 79*] in the mother's prayers and knows this alone, that they mean love and protection, and that they are elsewhere, and that the mother and itself are included in the same Words—⟨indeed⟩ are not there, nor the formal proposition, but the living truth is *d*there. That*e* which the mother is to her child, a someone unseen and yet ever present, is to all.[162] The first introduction to thought takes place in the ~~connexion~~ transfer of person from the senses to the invisible.

d–e ms: there, that

[162] See Prolegomena xix: Mother and Child.

~~and~~ The reverence of the invisible, substantiated by the feeling of love⟨—this,⟩ which is the essence and proper definition of religion,[163] is the commencement of the intellectual life, of the humanity.[164] If ye love not your earthly parent, how *can* ye love your father in heaven?[165]

[*f 80*]   Chapter

On the present general education of man in relation to the Idea of God

> —tu stesso fai grosso
> Col falso immaginar, si che non vedi
> Cio che vedresti, se l'avessi scosso.[166]
> Dante, Paradiso, Cant. 1, St. 30[167]

An attentive observer who watches the intellectual growth of an infant with the combined interests of the parent and the philosopher,[168] where science corrects what the magnifying power of love was necessary to render visible—he, and he only, will detect the formation of a language, while to all others the tones of the child are still inarticulate; and as ~~to~~ the different fragments of the building gleam through the thinning vapour, he will know how to interpret the remaining and thicker mist. As in the patient, retrogressive investigation of organic bodily form, so in the mind nothing will appear [*f 81*] as*f* the first, as beginning, except only the power of communicating itself in each, relatively to an outward contemplator. The acquired, the accessory, whatever has a semblance of increase by apposition, alike in body and in mind, has reference to size, manifestation, action, and reaction. So true is this, indeed, that in the development of the mind, the consciousness itself has the appearance of another. It has been often and well named the mind's eye, if only we consider that it is an eye for the mind no less than [an] eye of the mind. I make this remark for those who have been taught to place the very prin-

---

f The following correction is suggested in pencil on f 80ᵛ: "at"

[163] Cf *The Friend*: "Religion, in its widest sense, signifies the act and habit of reverencing THE INVISIBLE, as the highest both in ourselves and in nature" (*Friend—CC—*i 440).

[164] "Now faith is the substance of things hoped for, the evidence of things not seen. . . . Through faith we understand that the worlds were framed by the word of God, so that things which are seen were not made of things which do appear (Hebrews 11.1, 3).

[165] Cf a sermon of 1795: "But if we love not our friends and parents whom we have seen, how can we love our universal friend and Almighty Parent whom we have not seen?" (*Lects 1795—CC—*352–3).

[166] Tr: "You make yourself dull with false imagining, so that you do not see what you would see had you cast it off."

[167] The lines are also quoted at *CN* iv 4786.

[168] That statement exactly describes C's repeated observations about his son Hartley.

ciple of personal identity in the consciousness, and I would draw their attention to the fact that whatever has its final cause in the consciousness is in no case the essential of the thing, any more than the milestones constitute the essence of a road; but that which size and vividness are in the sensible objects—that, [*f 82*] the means and conditions of consciousness, are in the reflective ~~mechanism~~ processes of the soul. The test is that neither the one nor the other are capable of a mere positive determination; they subsist in relations and comparisons, as a low mountain, a large mole-hill. Hence comes the ~~nece~~ importance of distinguishing the subjective necessity of apprehending an object with a form from the objective necessity of a form in the object, as the ground of its characteristic phaenomena—a ground which, intellectually, we must invest with antecedency and yet, at the same time, contemplate as co-present. But far better would it be, if we could appropriate to each a different term— if, for instance, that which in all changes of manifestation, and the means subservient to it, remains the same and cannot be thought of but as having been that which it is, and the origin of which we can solve only by an act of creation, or at least so far [*f 83*] analogous to it, that it has a similar transcendency to the law of ⟨gradative⟩ continuity, and a similar instantaneity. The nearest illustration ~~in the outward~~ furnished by external things is perhaps that of a focal point in which light and heat become one and effective, while the space continuous with[g] it no more participates of[h] its powers than the parts of the same ellipse the most remote. It were well if this alone were expressed by the word "*Form*", while the impress made by the total superficies of the product of this form were contradistinguished as "*shape*", that word being in its etymon participle passive, the force of which (but, as usual, with its generality diminished and particularized)[i] is still retained in the word [j]"*shaft*". A[k] mechanical shaping is expressed, as in "a marble peach",[169] opposed to the intrinsical and causative form that works ab intra[170] as in the living fruit. If it were possible to imagine not only the external shape to be artificially [*f 84*] supplied by some delusive counterfeit, but by selection and apposition of various substances—excluding, however, all interprenetration— that the taste and touch should be equally deceived, the essential difference would still remain, while to the senses there was a perfect simili-

---

[g] The following correction is suggested in pencil on f 82[v]: "contiguous to"
[h] The following correction is suggested in pencil on f 82[v]: "in"
[i] Parentheses inserted   [j-k] ms: *shaft*, a

[169] The marble peach is a recurring symbol of mechanical shaping as opposed to vital form: "it would be sufficient to ask—why we prefer a Fruit Piece of Van Huysen's to a marble Peach on a mantle piece—" (*Lects 1808–1819—CC*—ii 265). See below f 84.
[170] Tr: "from within".

tude. The shape would contain no proper form, ~~as sure~~ and as surely as ~~an artificial~~ ⟨the natural peach⟩ differs essentially from the supposed artificial one, so surely is there a form not amenable to the senses, and ⟨in⟩ this we must place the principle both of the reality and individuality of each thing that truly *^lis. And,^m* in point of fact, by the intuition of this form, and by its diversity from shape, we actually do determine the reality of the objects of our senses. As far as the mere impressions of the sense are alone in question, the dictum of Berkeley is incontrovertibly true: the sole *esse* of all objects in their *ⁿpercipi.*[171] They*^o* would subsist exclusively in the mind for which they existed, [*f 85*] no ~~more dist~~ otherwise differenced from the same than as the waves from the collective sea.

We will return to the infant that we may apply these truths—but how apply? The very fact with which the chapter commences—namely, that the infant, even in its ⟨in⟩articulate sounds, is copying those of another—proves, if it prove aught, the very contrary of what has been advanced, proves that the child is a passive recipient of forms impressed on it from without. Doubtless, if to imitate, and if the presence of a something imitable, are proofs of a state purely passive—if the mirror can be fairly said to imitate the form of the objects, the rays from which it reflects—we have only to admit that passiveness is the same as recipiency, and recipiency in no essential point different from non-recipiency, for the latter is assuredly implied in the reflection of an *^pobject. And^q* we shall meet with few other difficulties, or none, in our after progress through the scheme of the modern, so-called [*f 86*] corpuscular philosophy, till we reach the conclusion: "Omnia exeunt in mysterium",[172] says one of the schoolmen, but the system now in question begins and ends in a *^rmystery.*[173] *But^s* the mystery consists in the fact of its having been believed and *^tpropagated—a^u* system that commences in contradiction, and concludes in death and *^vnothingness.*[174] *But^w* the compensation, it

^{*l–m*} ms: is; and   ^{*n–o*} ms: *percipi*; they
^{*p–q*} ms: object, and   ^{*r–s*} ms: mystery; but
^{*t–u*} ms: propagated. A   ^{*v–w*} ms: nothingness but

[171] Berkeley had argued, in his *Principles of Human Knowledge* of 1710, that to be is to be perceived: "as to what is said of the absolute existence of unthinking things without any relation to their being perceived, that seems perfectly unintelligible. Their *esse* is *percipi*, nor is it possible that they should have any existence, out of the minds or thinking things which perceive them" (*B Works* II 42). See below note 185.

[172] Tr: "All things end in mystery". C frequently invokes this formula; see *Aids to Reflection*: "*Omnia exeunt in mysterium*, says a Schoolman" (*AR—*1825—135).
[173] Cf *Aids to Reflection*: "*There is nothing, the absolute ground of which is not a Mystery*" (*AR—*1825—135).
[174] That is, the mechanico-corpuscular philosophy. Cf e.g. *Aids to Reflection*: "Let the Mechanic or corpuscular

seems, is more than sufficient, inasmuch as it furnishes you with pictures, right or wrong, for every word that is employed.

So hateful, however, is the whole scheme to my feelings, and so pernicious does it appear to my judgement,[175] that I have not dared venture on its exhibition without having previously entered my solemn protest, without having, as far as in the present stage of the enquiry I could ⟨fore⟩arm[x] the reader against it, by directing his attention to that element of his own nature, and of all that live, the omission of which is at once [*f* 87] the solution and confutation of the doctrines which I am now bound to display in the strongest and fairest light of which they are susceptible. And I dare affirm, that the reader will look in vain for a more plausible statement in the works of the most determined materialists ~~from~~ of France or England.

With few exceptions, few notwithstanding the numerous works in behoof of education founded on the principles of Mr Locke[176] and Drs Hartley,[177] Priestley, Edgeworth,[178] etc.[179]—with a few exceptions, I

---

[x] ms: ⟨fore⟩armed [*the last two letters cancelled in pencil*]

Schemes, which in the absoluteness and strict consistency was first introduced by DES CARTES, be judged by its results"; "in contempt of Common Sense, and in direct opposition to the express declaration of the inspired Historian (Genesis I.) and to the tone and spirit of the Scriptures throughout, Des Cartes propounded it as *truth of fact*; and instead of a World *created* and filled with productive forces by the Almighty Fiat, left a lifeless Machine whirled about by the dust of its own Grinding: as if Death could come from the living Fountain of Life" (*AR*—1825—391–2, 393). Again, of the "mechanic philosophy" C insists: "This is the philosophy of death, and only of a dead nature can it hold good" (*LS*—*CC*—89).

[175] Cf C's passionate rejection, in 1801, of Newton's "corpuscular philosophy": "Newton was a mere materialist— *mind* in his system is always passive—a lazy Looker-on on an external World. If the mind be not *passive*, if it be indeed made in God's Image, & that too in the sublimest sense—the Image of the *Creator*—there is ground for suspicion, that any system built on the passiveness of the mind must be false, as a system" (*CL* II 709).

[176] Locke wrote a treatise on educa-

tion in 1693 called *Some Thoughts concerning Education*. Here and elsewhere he advocated treating children with strictness and severity.

[177] So strong was the associationist tradition of Locke and Hartley that C's benefactor, Thomas Wedgwood, planned a bizarre school where children would be kept in bare rooms, not allowed to go out into nature for fear of contaminating the learning process, and be educated by slowly building up learning structures from controlled external impressions— writing on the white papers of their supposedly empty minds, as it were—after the theories of Locke, Hartley, Condillac, and Priestley. More bizarre even than that, Wedgwood proposed to hire as schoolmaster, of all people on earth, the nature-loving Wordsworth! See David Erdman's long article, "Coleridge, Wordsworth, and the Wedgwood Fund" *The Bulletin of the New York Public Library* LX (1956) 425–443, 487–507.

[178] Richard Edgeworth (1744–1817), British inventor and educator. Visited Rousseau and educated his oldest son in accordance with Rousseau's educational theories. Collaborated with his daughter Maria in *Practical Education* (1798).

[179] That is, of the building of the mind by successive impressions from without.

say, even in the schooled and educated ranks of society, the first three or four years of life have been abandoned to the delusions of nature, and even for the first ten or twelve the preparations for their overthrow have been made rather than avowed an open war. Except the golden rules that the child is to do nothing without a distinct motive, and to hear and read nothing of which he has not, or cannot have given to him, *"clear ideas"*,[180] i.e. figures [*f 88*] or images, and the children of our gentry, like those of their forefathers, and of the inferior classes at present derive their first convictions from their mothers and their nurses—perhaps that philosophy may find an enemy to be conquered, and not languish inglorious for ~~wha~~ want of obstacles on which to exert its prowess. The infant follows its mother's face as, glowing with love and beaming protection, it is raised heavenward, and with the word "GOD" it combines in feeling whatever there is of reality in the warm touch, in the supporting grasp, in the glorious countenance. The whole problem of existence is present as a sum total in the mother: the mother exists as a One and indivisible something before the outlines of her different limbs and features have been distinguished by the fixed and yet half-vacant eye; and hence, through each degree of dawning light, the whole remains antecedent to the parts, not as composed of them but as their ground and [*f 89*] proper meaning, ~~No~~ ⟨no⟩ otherwise than as the word or sentence to the single letters ~~of~~ which ~~it chances~~ occur in its spelling. Let it not be deemed trifling or ludicrous if I say that our modern philosophy is spelling throughout,[181] and its lessons as strange, or, but for the gradual breaking down of the soul by force of habit, and by the very faith which it is intended to subvert—it is as strange, I say, as the assertion is to a child when he is first told than A B is *ab*, or W H O is *who*. Be this, however, as it may, yet for the infant the mother contains his own self, and the whole problem of existence as a whole; and the word "GOD" is the first and one solution of the problem. Ask you, what is its meaning for the child? Even this: "the something, to which my [mother][y] looks up, and which is more than my mother"[z]. The same spirit which beholds the parts in the whole, which knows of no parts as self-subsisting, which acknowledges no connexion between the tree and the ashes which are left when it [*f 90*] has been reduced by fire, nay, which finds a bewildering

[y] Word missing in ms. The editorial insertion follows Ward's conjecture, supplied in pencil on f 88[v]

[z] Quotation marks inserted

[180] An echo of Descartes's enormously influential insistence on "clear and distinct ideas" in his *Discours de la méthode* of 1637. See *Oeuvres de Descartes* ed Charles Adam and Paul Tannery, VI (1965) 18, 33.

[181] In the sense that "the letter killeth, but the spirit giveth life" (2 Cor 3.6).

and, as it were, a spectral terror, a sense of sinking, resembling that which it had suffered or dreamt of as the mother's knees had suddenly given way from under it, in the contemplation of aught as severed from the whole in which it had subsisted. Even as we sometimes dwell on a word that we had just written till we doubt, first, whether we had spelt it right, and at length it seems to us as if no such word could exist; and, in a kind of momentary trance, strive to make out its meaning out of the component letters, or of the lines of which they are composed, and nothing results! In such a state of mind has many a parent heard the three-years child that has awoke during the dark night in the little crib by the mother's bed entreat in piteous tones, "Touch*a* me, only touch me with your finger." A child of that age, under the same circumstances, I myself heard using these very words in answer to the mother's enquiries, half hushing and [ƒ91] half chiding, "I am not here, touch me, Mother, that I may be here!" The witness of its own being had been suspended in the loss of the mother's presence by sight or sound or feeling. The father and the heavenly father, the form in the shape and the form affirmed for itself are blended in one, and yet convey the earliest lesson of distinction and alterity. There was another beside the mother, and the child beholds it and repeats, and as light from light, transferring, not diminishing, carries onward the former love to the new object. There is another, which it does not behold, but it is above; and while the mother's eye is turned upward, the pressure to her bosom is yet closer, and the kiss which her returning lips impress is longer, and a steadfast gaze and a silence had preceded it. The third lesson is given when it has already played round the knee, ~~on~~ which ~~it~~ had before been its only support, and [it] had tottered off in order to follow the outstretched arms that [ƒ92] were to secure its *b*return. And*c* this lesson is the application and, as it were, the synthesis of the two former: the*d* child now learns its own alterity, and ~~as if some~~ sooner or later, as if some sudden crisis had taken place in its nature, it forgets henceforward to speak of itself by imitation, that is, by the name which it had caught from without. It becomes a person; it is and speaks of itself as "I", and from that moment it has acquired what, in the following stages, it may quarrel with, what it may loosen and deform, but can never eradicate—a sense of an alterity in itself, which no eye can see, neither his own nor others. And this is that which thinks on God, which loves and is, therefore, that which is beloved; and its first connexion is, and can be, no other than that invisible to which the mother had lifted up herself. Many, many things perplex the seeking

a ms: "touch   *b–c* ms: return: and   *d* ms: The intellect of the child, not that things live and are beheld, but that aught should be beheld that does not live. Many things, I say, [*f 93*] perplex the child, but never that there is a form to which there is no shape—O! far too often had the maternal warmth been that! That many a night its food and its pillow at the maternal bosom had been. The first doubt is awakened in the mind by that which first awakens, because it implies the strange thought of not having been. It is from the word "*made me*", "*made all*" that the child stands astounded, and oh! who can fathom that depth of being out of which issues that ill-interpreted but awful question, "and who made God?" By cutting asunder the living bond and ~~depen-~~ ~~dence~~ unity in which the soul had stood with the idea of God, all the reality seemed to be endangered, and the words "*Who made* God?" are not, indeed, in full and distinct unfolding, but in their existing, though unevolved, contents, are the same as "Can there be nothing?" and "if God be, surely all must be". The proof of this is to be found in the very efforts which we make, in the very objects [*f 94*] to which we turn in order to ~~satisfy~~ convince, or at least to silence, the little *e*querist. To*f* nothing human do we turn, to nothing that moves and lives, to nothing that even grows—not to the flower, not to the grass before the *g*door. In*h* vain should we ask from forms this confession of death; we must turn to shapes, and even to them not as they are but as they appear to be, to the works of the axe and the saw—and even of these shapes, how many had been like the statue of Pygmalion to the *i*child? And*j* I have ever been not only pleased but affected with an anecdote related of his own childhood by a philosopher in whom the ancient spirit still survived, that the first use to which he turned his knowledge of what lying was to persuade himself that they had been telling him a lie in making him believe that his wooden horse was not *k*alive. And*l* I have myself heard a child of the same age asking passionately, respecting the flowers in the grass, [*f 95*] "But are you sure they are not alive?" But who ever witnessed the least repugnance in a child to the belief that he had a soul, or that his body was his, not he?

[*f 96*]   Chapter

A child derives its first awakenings from life, and life is the immediate and proper unity of all forms, a unity antecedent in the order of thought to the perception of the forms contained or appertaining, and undisturbed

---

e–f ms: querist: to   *g–h* ms: death; in
i–j ms: child; and   *k–l* ms: alive; and

by those forms. It is only in the process of artificial education, though doubtless a necessary, though not necessarily a permanent, result that life itself becomes generalized into the more abstract formula of power. Naturally, all power is recognized as life—in other words, the presence of power in any external object is acknowledged by the human mind in its earlier stage only as far as it conveys the idea of a whole anterior in thought to the parts, and the proper principle of the total form resulting from their combination, i.e. the principle of this combination.[182] It is difficult, in terms of distinct consciousness, to describe impressions that partake of the nature of sensa[*f 97*]tions known as a whole, but only as such. We may, however, venture to say that in the mind of a child, a point having been given as representative of the pre-existing form of a circumference, the child would contemplate without repugnance the circle as generated by ~~the motion~~ a composite motion of the point returning on itself in each moment of its elongation, but never could have chanced on the conception of a number of points composing the shape of a circumference. For why this shape rather than that of a square or a triangle? The supposed atoms, considered merely as atoms, are indifferent to all shapes. There must be a form as the principle of shape, necessarily, therefore, assumed as anterior, this assumption being essential to the conception of cause and effect. But whatever is visible, or rather, whatever is an object of sense as distinct from sensation, is *shape*. The principle, therefore, of shape must be invisible. In the implicit conception ~~of the invisible~~, therefore, of life as unity, as plastic, and as invisible, the human mind [*f 98*] commences. With the awakening of self-consciousness, the first sign or representative of which is not its own bodily shape but the gradually dawning presence of the mother's, the conception of life is elevated into that of *m*personeity. And*n* as particular shape is beheld only in the higher and freer conception of form, so again this form itself, this ⟨antecedent⟩ whole, constituent of its parts, is taken up into and becomes one with the yet higher, or rather deeper and more inward, principle of person. In the child's mind there is nothing fragmentary; its numeration table is truly Pythagorean.[183] The numbers are each and all units and integers, and slowly and difficultly does it exchange this, its

m–n ms: personeity: and

[182] The paragraph reiterates two important Coleridgean emphases; first, the emphasis on "antecedence" and the emphasis on the "whole" as prior to its parts—or, as he says, "anterior in thought to the parts". See e.g. *CN* III 4111n.

[183] In Pythagorean mathematics there were no fractions.

first awakened arithmetic, for that of aggregation, apposition—in one word, ~~as a result~~ of RESULT.*

* [*The following passage, written on ff 98–100 and placed within brackets, is printed as a note in accordance with C's holograph instruction on f 97*[v]*: "The lines following between crochets [ ] to be printed as a Note.—"*] Most noticeable it is, and most worthy a wise man's meditation, that the notion of objects as altogether objective begins in the same moment in which the conception is formed that is wholly subjective.[184] The ~~form~~ shape of every aggregate hath its ⟨sole⟩ existence in the percipient, [*f 99*] and in the percipient ⟨it⟩ results from accidents not determinable by its own powers, as the accidents of local position, distance, the state of its organs, and the sort and intensity of the intermediate agents. Analyze any shape, i.e. the sum of the objective as object of the sense—analyze, I say, this into its constituent parts, and the conclusion is inevitably that of Berkeley. One and all, they are found purely subjective, the~~ir~~ *esse* contained in the *percipi*:[185] and what have we gained by this division of the original identity, this ⟨original⟩[o] co-inheren~~ts~~⟨ce⟩ of ⟨the⟩ object in the subject, ⟨which in an after sense indeed we⟩[p] render~~ed~~ susceptible of distinct consciousness by ~~the~~ instinctively assum~~ed~~⟨ing⟩[q] ⟨the⟩[r] precedence of the ~~former~~ ⟨latter⟩[s] analogous to what is felt in language, where the word is one and the same with the sense, or rather, is received in, and *as* the sense must be [t]distinguished artificially[u] ⟨and⟩[v] by a voluntary act of abstraction in order to be subordinated, but is subordinated in the same instant that it is distinguished—what, I repeat, have we gained by the inversion of this process but ~~in transforming~~ [*f 100*] ~~the rights and dignities of the subject, the~~ ⟨the confusion of Object for Subject, but a delusive⟩[w] *projection* of the subject as[x] object, ~~as by~~ ⟨resembling other of the phantoms⟩[y] ~~the delusion~~ of a concave mirror; and when we have thus ~~disguised and lost for ourselves the consciousness of the subject, when we have~~ brought ourselves to ~~recognize it~~ ⟨mistake it for⟩[z] an[a] object, then to seek for the ⟨corresponding⟩[b] *subject* elsewhere?[c] ~~or rather any where, except alone~~ ⟨~~where~~⟩[d] ~~it can be found.~~ We invent some outward object that is no object to act the part of

[o] Insertion in C's hand [p] Insertion in C's hand [q] Insertion in C's hand
[r] Insertion in C's hand [s] Insertion in C's hand
[t–u] ms: artificially distinguished [*marked with a line for transposition*]
[v] Insertion in C's hand [w] Insertion in C's hand [x] ms: an
[y] Insertion in C's hand [z] Insertion in C's hand [a] ms: as an
[b] Insertion in C's hand [c] Full stop in ms [d] Insertion in C's hand

184 See further Prolegomena XVIII: Subject and Object.

185 In *A Treatise concerning The Principles of Human Knowledge* (1710) Berkeley urged the theory that *to be* was *to be perceived.* C, though he always admired Berkeley (and named one of his sons for that philosopher), was rather severe about the famous formula: "Esse = Percipi: the Sum and Substance of Berkleianism. But it is a mere Assertion in the first place: & 2ndly it is an absurd assertion, i.e. a contradiction in terms" (*CM—CC*—III 916).

[*f 100*] Such is the faith of childhood. And such, too, the creed of the happy boy—must it cease to be that of the youth and the man? It is doubtless a creed of prejudice, for if that which naturally follows from the nature of a recipient, under uniformly present circumstances, may be called instinct, it is the [*f 101*] creed of instinct; but is it delusion? is it grounded in falsehood? So the man of *understanding* asserts. The boy must leave the gentle teachings of its first home and be transferred to the austerer discipline of the understanding. The understanding shall hence-forward be its schoolmaster, and the soul must be weaned by aid of the analytic powers. Hitherto the tree had preceded the conception of the particular tree; the ᵃ sense of the whole tree, that of its trunk and ᵍbranches. Butʰ now its distinct attention must be drawn to all the objects which surround it, and the process of the mind—inadequately, indeed, but not untruly—be thus described: I am surrounded by objects, each of which I have been accustomed [to consider]ⁱ as subsisting in itself; I behold plants, trees, animals. I ascribe to each properties and marks, and by these it is that I distinguish the one from the other. What is not distinct is not at all; every object has its particular determined number of particular determined properties, and ⟨where⟩ ever I hesitate in returning a decisive "yes" or [*f 102*] "No!" to the question "Is it this, or Is it not?", I recognize [it] as result and proof of my ʲignorance. Forᵏ whatever exists is, or is not, this particular something: it is coloured, or it is not coloured; so coloured, or not so; and the moment in which the indefinite presents itself, true existence ceases and the merely notional usurps its place. But this stern and universal determinateness, is it likewise the permanent? Alas! here I have returned the decisive answer: itˡ is, or it is not, this. Theᵐ ⟨An⟩ answer is already inapplicable; a ⟨it is an answer to the⟩ mere echo of a̶n̶ a̶n̶s̶w̶e̶r̶ a voice which is already no more. A new nature

---

a subject ⟨for that which is itself wholly subjective;⟩ᵉ and the deity must be brought in as f̶o̶r̶ the universal painter of t̶h̶e̶ ⟨a⟩ lifeless universal canvas. Yea, consistently, if not well, does o̶n̶e̶ a philosopher of this school commence one of his chapters with the words "On the hypothesis of a God"!ᶠ

ᵉ Insertion in C's hand
ᶠ After the bracket that indicates the end of the passage to be printed as a note, JHG has written "(end of the note)"
ᵍ⁻ʰ ms: branches; but
ⁱ Words missing in ms. The editorial insertion follows Ward's conjecture, written in pencil on f 100ᵛ and marked for insertion here
ʲ⁻ᵏ ms: ignorance; for
ˡ ms: It
ᵐ This word is cancelled in the ms, but a dotted line under it indicates that it was to be restored after "An" had been cancelled in its turn.

has taken place, a new series of determinates, and each of these is that which it is because that which is no more had been determinately that which it was. Every moment is the creature of the preceding: had there been in the preceding moment aught, the least circumstance other than it was, that which now is could not be—it hath no strength in itself, yea, and the strength which made [*f 103*] it that which it is no more, is nothing. We go back with an endless regress, and nowhere does nature present to me aught but what is the mere declaration of an alien strength, and that alien strength gone e'er I can arrest or question it. But is there a strength, then, in the whole; and what I seek for in vain, in the boughs, the sprays, the leaves, shall I find in the whole tree? ~~b~~But what do I mean by that word? Whatever is not throughout determinate, I have rejected as notional, void of true existence: ~~existence and definiteness~~ to be definite is implied in the term "to exist". What, then, are the outlines, in the knowledge of which I may dare attribute true existence to this whole? Before I seek for its strength, I must at least be satisfied that it truly exists. Again, in order to this, I must be able to say, first, what are its parts, and next, what are not its parts. And how shall I determine this? A mere change in the sensations which I receive is no criterion: how different are the sensations, and impressions [*f 104*] received from the trunk, the bud, the leaf, the blossom; yet these prevent not my assertion of the tree as a whole. Is the perception, then, of an interspace, or the sudden transition from seeing to not seeing, a sufficient criterion? But by what right shall I give to one sense, to one sort, or class, of sensations, this right of decision? The tree is still present to me in its odours, in its sounds; and[n] by what right can I ground the positive on a mere subjective negation? But perhaps that which acts immediately on another, and through it on a third, and so on, each again being acted on—in short, the sum of all the agents which are immediate—constitutes[o] the whole; nor may I cease till I arrive at some agent which is not reacted on. But where may I venture to affirm [p]this? What[q] is it that authorizes me to conclude that the unseen existence, in immediate contact with the outlines of those leaves, are in no re~~p~~ciprocity, that they simply act there? By what right shall I deem [*f 105*] the moisture in the cells of the plant a part of the whole plant, and deny it to the gas or fluid which it is at this moment taking up or sending forth? One form alone remains to me that, as each moment contains in itself the whole existence of the moment following, so each particle is that which it is in consequence of its indissoluble connexion with all that co-exists. I can therefore find no whole in nature but nature

[n] ms: And [o] ms: constitute [p–q] ms: this what

itself—all else is but a classification of the accidents of my own mind and senses.

Such, I contend, would be the conclusion that would necessarily follow from every scheme of philosophy that commenced with the assumption of every form of existence as being that which it appears *wholly* in consequence of the existence of some other form, each being to the other cause and effect, and this carried on ad infinitum. It is evident ⟨that⟩ on this supposition there would [be] no greater absurdity in asserting that Westminster Abbey [*f 106*] had given existence to the Paradise Lost than in attributing it to *r*Milton. In*s* the sense of copartnerships, where the partners are infinite in number, it may be said of both; [but] properly and peculiarly, of neither. But on the other hand it is equally evident that the whole scheme is self-contradictory, as well as irreconcileable to the involuntary convictions of conscience and common sense. For first, the scheme manifestly supposes a causative action of each on each, for how otherwise could they all be at once cause and effect relatively to each other?*t* And yet throughout the remainder of the deduction, nothing is taken into the view but the receptivity of actions from without. We begin by contemplating the process of action and reaction by which the different parts of an organ, or the different organs in a one organised body, mutually and reciprocally determine each the form of the other, and all the form of the whole—which whole, however, must be again considered not, indeed, as an effect but as a pre-existing [*f 107*] and causative power, i.e. not, indeed, as a shape but as an active form, the specific principle of a given shape, determining the forms and positions of each and all. ~~It is in~~ ⟨With⟩ this view, I say, the scheme commences; but in the next step this supposed organ or organic part becomes a mere piece of potter's clay, passive to the fingers or the wheel of the potter, receiving shape but ~~repaying it~~ neither making nor modifying the shape of that from which it received it.[186] Nor is this the only fallacy. Not only one of the two original factors, or constituent terms, contained in the primary assumption has been dropped out of the calculation, but that which remains is made to perform its functions. But as these two factors, ~~exist only~~ A and -A, exists only—the one, namely, as A, and the other as non-A—by their opposition, or, as it were, as positive and neg-

---

r–s ms: Milton in   *t* Full stop in ms

186 At Rom 9.21 Paul likens God's power over man to the potter's power over clay. Like Karl Barth, C ascribed great importance to this particular book of the Bible: "I think St Paul's Epistle to the Rom the most profound work in existence" (*TT—CC*—I 387).

ative poles, their functions, which were correspondent opposites as long as they existed severally, become absolutely contra[*f 108*]dictions when taken as united in one and the same act, or agent, or in ⟨one⟩ and the same agent simultaneously. Thus in the instance, or simile, above used, the same piece of clay = A is a mere potter's *"*vessel.[187] Relatively[v] to all around it, as the conjoint causes of that vessel, as distinguished from clay in general, its whole specific being it receives from them passively, even as the sublime statue of Jove, taken abstractedly from the insensate and unindividualized marble quarry, derived its existence from Phidias.[188] But, in the very same moment, the relation only, and that only mentally being changed, this same clay became a potter, this same block of marble a Phidias.[189] In short, at the moment that it is deriving its existence as a pure effect, it is constituting it as an active cause. But if you correct this palpable error and restore to each its lost factor, you in this very act (for to simplify the argument, we will confine the subject to the organic world as that which more obviously [*f 109*] presents the synthesis of action and recipiency) suppose in each an antecedent individuality as ~~both~~ the active as well as passive condition of its specific recipiency. The aconite[190] is nutritious to the goat, and a deadly poison to the sheep. To affirm, therefore, that such a thing is a stimulant, or such a subject a cause, is a senseless proposition, disjoined from the quality of that which is to be stimulated, of that on which the cause is to act, or rather, is to become a cause. Now this individuality, which is as essential to every particular form of integral subsistence, i.e. of every thing, the shape and relations of which are not wholly results of accident, or of laws working

---

[u-v] ms: vessel relatively

[187] See previous note. But C, despite his admiration of the Epistle to the Romans, tended to be critical of the image of clay and potter. Cf *CPT* 192.

[188] "Phidias or Pheidias, c. 500–c. 432 B.C., Greek sculptor, considered the greatest artist in ancient Greece. No original in existence can be attributed to him with certainty.... His greatest achievements were the ATHENA PARTHENON at Athens and the *Zeus* in the temple at Olympi, both colossal figures of chryselephantine workmanship (draperies of beaten gold, flesh parts incrusted with ivory. The *Athena*, dedicated 438 B.C., was the chief treasure of Athens). The *Zeus* was a benignant and majestic bearded figure seated upon a magnificently ornamented throne and wearing a mantle strewn with sculptured decorations .... The *Zeus* was counted one of the Seven Wonders of the World" (*Columbia Encyclopedia* Second Edition 1531). Cf Benjamin Haydon in 1819: "Ah, Phidias, Phidias, grand, great Immortal Creature. The last word I should wish to pronounce in this World & the first in the next, are Phidias! Phidias!" (*Haydon* II 217).

[189] For C, Phidias in human terms represented "almost the summit of conceivable excellence" (*SW & F—CC*—I 670).

[190] A poisonous plant of the crowfoot family, with blue, purple, or yellow hoodlike flowers.

ab extra[191]—a leaf, we will say, as distinguished from a pebble, or the shell of a fish from a fragment of breccia[192] or concrete of shells—is clearly beyond the province of the reasoning faculty. It contains the impossibility of being reduced to the category of cause or[w] relation; for it is [*f 110*] that which, equally with the co-existence of other individuals (all individuality supposes plurality, and all plurality individuality,[x] which is the sense of the scholastic principle "de necessario distinguibili"),[193] is presupposed in order to the possibility of cause or relation. Even the atheists felt themselves obliged to seek for a principle of individuality, which was to be taken for granted as the ground of reasoning which could not itself be explained by reason, in their atoms; and even these did them no service till they had further assumed atoms of different magnitudes and different aboriginal figures. If not, then, in the reason, as the speculative power, then either in chance, which is but another word for avowing a determination not to think at all upon the subject, or in a ~~w~~Will, which, if the total sum and result of these individualities, or simple productive acts, be in the highest degree rational (i.e. ending in due proportion to a common unity)[y], must be One [*f 111*] with reason, though in the order of necessary conception its co-eternal antecedent. But if this absolute Will be the ground, that which is grounded therein must be homogeneous et ejusdem natura[194]—i.e. as ⟨of⟩ an individuality generally, so of each several and (if I may venture an expression in part improper) of each specific individuality, the several and specific principle must be of the nature of a will. And thus nature itself, as soon as we apply reason to its contemplation, forces us back to a something higher than nature as that on which it depends.[195] Spontaneity, for instance, we should not call a Will: we perceive at once its inferiority; but that is of the nature of *Will*, and utterly unintelligible except in consequence of a previous idea of the Will, and that wherever both are found in the same subject, that the one is a result from the other, and, as it were, its offspring, the least reflexion will convince us. The very fingers and muscles of an ex[*f 112*]perienced musician perform the most difficult labyrinths of motion spontaneously, even while the player perhaps is directing his attention to some foreign object, conversing with

---

[w] Below this word, in the bottom margin of f 109, the Greek letters "καπ" are written faintly in ink in an unidentified hand
[x] ms: individuality)
[y] Parentheses inserted

[191] Tr: "from without".
[192] I.e. "concrete of shells"; the word "brescia" indicates the kind or style associated with the city of Brescia in Italy.
[193] Tr: "to be distinguished by necessity".
[194] Tr: "and of the same nature".
[195] The "something higher than nature" precludes pantheism.

the persons near him, or fixing his mind on some movement which is to follow. But who would assert the existence of these habits except as the result ~~of~~and, if I might so say, the incorporation of antecedent distinct acts of will.[196] The same spontaneity in a plant must be referred to some universal will, as the other to a particular Will; for the difference is found not in the spontaneity itself but in the contingent nature of the subject in which it subsists, and this ~~diff~~ again consists wholly in the presence of a particular will in the one case, and the absence of a particular will in the other. The terms "Spontaneity" and "Will" remain untouched in both, and the difference reduces itself to the epithets particular and universal.

[*f 113*] Thus we have seen a system which began in a determination to seek the very truth, and to find it in facts alone, end at last in self-contradiction and [become][z] intelligible [again][a] only upon the supposition of the non-existence of that without which neither the facts themselves nor the power of observing them could possibly exist or have existed. A principle of activity from within, even in its lowest degree of power, even as it manifests itself in a lichen or a fungus, is inconceivable except as [b]spontaneity.[197] And[c] spontaneity is, again, utterly inconceivable except as grounded in a Will, not necessarily, indeed, existing as a Will in the same subject, but yet not mechanically divided therefrom, or as a something made by the Will and heterogeneous from its maker, as the power of a steam engine or a lifeless automaton. But if this be conceded, it ~~must~~ is conceded at the same time that the shape, whether outline or ~~did~~ relative distinctions without intervention of [*f 114*] interspace (if we may hazard the word)—that shape, whether consisting of outlines or inlines, must be of a three-fold nature from three perfectly different causes, and that it must therefore fall under three several kinds: the first, a shape from elanquescence and sensation of the shaping power, such, for instance, as the line described by an arrow, or a rocket in its descent; 2[dly], a shape impressed from without, as that of a clay vessel or of a fluid in the containing vessel, and in this second kind it is mere receptivity as far as the

---

[z] Word supplied in pencil on f 112[v] and marked for insertion here
[a] Word supplied in pencil on f 112[v] and marked for insertion here
[b-c] ms: spontaneity; and

[196] C laid great stress on the importance of "antecedency" in mental progressions. See his strictures on method in the revised version of *The Friend,* e.g.: "We have sen that a previous act and conception of the mind is indispensable even to the mere semblances of Method; that neither fashion, mode, nor orderly arrangement can be produced without a prior purpose, and 'a pre-cogitation *ad intentionem ejus quod quaeritur'*" (*Friend—CC—*I 475).

[197] For a brief conspectus of the conception of organic "activity from within" in Romanticism itself as well as in Coleridge see *RFR* 34–43. See also *TT (CC)* I 258 and nn 6, 7.

shape [? alone/above] is concerned; while the third kind, the outline, or cessation of the power of impressing an image on the eye, is itself an act of power, nay, as far as it is contemplated singly, the pure active constituent of all form—say, rather, it is form itself in the distinction already proposed between form and shape;[198] and as in the second instance we have pure receptivity, so in this we have pure energy, and that the highest in nature, [*f 115*] and that alone by which ⟨it⟩ knows itself or can be made known. For it is equivalent to returning back ~~ton~~ itself before the ~~nadir~~ effluence of its power has lost its intensity in its elongation, these being throughout nature in an inverse ratio, and while yet the mean result of its efflux and reflux, of its extroitive and of its retroitive act, shall be the image or representative product, of the identity of both, i.e. of the plastic nature itself. Now the world is the sum total of all these kinds blended variously in infinite proportions, but still the higher in the scale, the greater the proportion of the third kind is in every thing; the more subordinate and, as it were, connaturalized with the third is the proportion of the second; and the nearer to the minimum, ~~becomes the first~~ and the more accidental and non-essential does the first become. Thus in the organization of the higher animals, the receptivity of influence from without is equipoized by receptivity immediately dependent on the third, or reflex act, and having its whole power and purpose in the [*f 116*] manifestation of the reflex act, and as its necessary condition. Thus the sensibility passes into the muscular power,[199] or that which since Haller[200] ~~has been technically called~~, and at the risk of much confusion from the very different sense of the word in ordinary language, has been technically called "irritability", in order to return again upon itself and to become, i.e., to know or feel itself as Sensibility. The receptivity here is at once the source and the motive, or final cause, and the consequence

---

[198] See above ff 97–8, f 107, ff 113–114.

[199] Note the insistence, which runs throughout the *magnum opus*, on the evolutionary ascent from lower to higher. "There is in the whole chain of being, even in the lowest, though scarcely apparent, an effort at individualization . . . in the next stage, it becomes apparent and separate, but still subordinate; then it is on a par with the nature, which is the lowest state of man" (*TT—CC*—I 82). Again: "one proof of the essential vitality of nature, that she does not ascend as links in a suspended chain, but as the steps in a ladder; or rather at

one and the same time *ascends* as by a climax, and expands . . ." (*TL* 41). On "ascent" as increase in power, see *CN* IV 4517, 4583, 4862, 5150, 5182. Cf App A: "the further we proceed and the higher we ascend" (f 28). See further f 37 and f 70.

[200] Albrecht von Haller (1708–1777), Swiss biologist. Professor of medicine, anatomy, and surgery at Göttingen; first to distinguish and relate muscle irritability and nerve sensibility and show transmission of nervous impulses. Author of *Elementa Physiologiae Corporis Humani* (1757–66). See *TT (CC)* I 111 n 2.

of the reflex act, or of that by which the power places a limit to its own going forth. The act itself is passive only in relation to its own energy, and it energizes in order to become thus self-passive, self-affected, while that proportion of receptivity which belongs to external agency is solely for the purpose of continuing and re-awakening the process of alternation in that higher state in which life—as the identity of sensibility and irritability, but having its distinctive essence and, as it were, its real, though latent, initiative in [*f 117*] the former—passes into the latter in order to return on the former, and thus to make the former the alone proper subject of life, an object to itself.* Add, too, that the influence of the external agent is in all instances mediated by and dependent on the degree and state of the higher. The stimulating substance is no stimulant except as in relation to, and in consequence of, the stimulability.

Still more conspicuous is this truth in the noblest animal, which for that very cause is more than an *e*animal. For*f* the maximum of each lower kind becomes the base and receptive substrate, as it were, of a higher kind commencing, and becomes the positive, and not merely the comparative, maximum, through the irradiation and ~~as it were;~~ may*g*, I say, transfiguration by the higher power, the base of which it has *h*become. In*i* man, I say, this law of proportions becomes fully manifest, and in the strivings of the will to rise, the excess of impressibility, or receptivity of impression from without, not only above spontaneity, not only [*f 118*] above impulse determined by the anticipation of outward objects, but even above that direction of the power more properly called voluntary, which itself predetermines the object by its own knowledge, and previous reflection of that object in relation to itself. Even above this, i.e. the will influenced by the understanding, which still ~~pre~~ supposes a prior state of receptivity in overbalance during the impressions made on the sensations and senses, the man must have an object in himself, an object which he himself has constituted, which is at one and the same ~~time~~ moment the subject and the legislator, the law and the act, of ~~the~~ obedience, the impulse, the motive, and the ultimate end, and in which, therefore, all is*j* energy. And*k* the second principle of shape wholly disappears, and with it whatever in the third kind is borrowed from the second, or, by its proportion being less than all, supposes the coexistence of the second in some proportion, however small, must disappear *l*likewise. Shape*m* itself ceases

---

* [*Written on f 116ᵛ:*] That self-consciousness is neither meant nor necessarily inferred has been already noticed and explained in p. __.*d*

d The space for the page number is left unfilled in the ms
e–f ms: animal: for   *g* A slip for "maybe"?   *h–i* ms: become: in
j–k ms: energy, and   *l–m* ms: likewise; shape

and ascends into form,[201] [*f 119*] "whence the soul receives reason, and reason is her being."[202] This is the ideal of the moral state, the goal, by the approximation to which all ⟨true⟩ progression is predetermined and indicated. The WILL has to struggle upward into FREE-WILL—but observe that Freedom which is impossible except as it becomes one with the Will of God,[203] that ~~Freedom which the Apostle counsels us~~ "perfect law of liberty"[204] which the Apostle counsels us to *look down into* (παρακυψαι) as that which is to be found in the depth and center of the moral being, and which man possesses ~~only~~ not, indeed, but yet is beginning to possess in the effort of emancipating himself from the bonds that prevent it. In Man the Will as Will first appears,[205] enough for him that he hath a Will at all; for ~~in~~ this is the condition of his responsibility, of his [n]humanity.[206] In[o] the ⟨possession of a⟩ responsible Will his creator has placed him, with all means and aidances to boot, to its growth and evolution. With these, in the possession of a Free-Will he is to place himself—that he [*f 120*] may be in the divine humanity even as the divine humanity, that "God may be all in all". ~~How~~ Both how and what we should do are both secondary questions that have no meaning except in reference to the former, incomparably more awful one: namely, what we should be? And on the preposterous derivation of this from the former, in conjunction with the outward consequences by which they are determinable, rests all the schemes of that unchristian epicurean morality[207] which ~~borrow~~ from the gospel itself would patch up the ragged cloak[208] of pagan ethics,[209] in their ⟨basest and⟩ most beggarly form, in

[n-o] ms: humanity; in

[201] For the differentiation of shape and form see above ff 97–8, f 107, ff 113–114.

[202] Cf Milton *Paradise Lost* v 486–7: "whence the Soul/ Reason receives, and reason is her being".

[203] That was the view promulgated by Luther's powerful treatise of 1525, *De servo arbitrio*.

[204] Cf Paul: "where the Spirit of the Lord *is*, there *is* liberty" (2 Cor 3.17); "Stand fast therefore in the liberty wherewith Christ hath made us free, and be not entangled again with the yoke of bondage" (Gal 5.1).

[205] A "will not intelligent is no *Will*" (*CM—CC—*i 355). This insistence decisively differentiates Coleridge's position from the conception of Schopenhauer.

[206] Cf *Aids to Reflection*: "If there be aught *Spiritual* in Man, the Will must be

such. *If* there be a Will, there must be a Spirituality in Man" (*AR—*1825—131).

[207] For extended discussion see Prolegomena iii: The Epicurean and Stoic Background.

[208] For C's subliminal but deep involvement with and opposition to Stoic and Epicurean philosophy see Prolegomena iii: The Epicurean and Stoic Background. This involvement had been going on since the early 1790s. Cf a long description of both Stoic and Epicurean tenets in 1795, with the observation that "Far different from [the Stoics] were the Epicureans yet like them built all their moral Doctrines on the principle of gross self-interest. Epicurus taught that Pleasure was the final Good of Life . . . that there was no Providence—and no future State" (*Lects 1795—CC—*57).

[209] Cf a marginal note: "Since the

order to supersede the Gospel.[210] ~~The single syllable~~ Woful has been their influence; nor is their place so ~~sacred~~ ⟨secure⟩ or imposing as to be sacred from its *p*contagion—taught*q* in universities, quoted and sanctioned by legislators, reduced to action by statesmen, and finally moulding the whole spirit and tendencies of ages and nations. And yet the single syllable BE is [*f 121*] worth a host of them, or rather, let me say, contains in it ⟨truths⟩ from which we may derive an antidote to the contagion from all, and must do so, or we perish.

The scheme of ~~the modern mechanical philosophy~~ ⟨pure mechanism,⟩[211] which under all disguises, tempting or repulsive, christian or infidel, forms the groundwork of ~~all~~ these systems of ⟨modern⟩ moral and political philosophy, political economy, and education,*r*[212] which ~~builds~~ [. . .] ~~derives the mind from the senses~~ by manufacturing mind out of sense[213] and sense out of sensation, which reduces all form to shape and

---

p–q ms: contagion. Taught

r The following word is written in pencil on f 120ᵛ and marked for insertion here: "and"

Revolution in 1688 our Church has been chilled and starved too generally by Preachers & Reasoners, Stoic or Epicurean—first, a sort of pagan Morality, = Virtue, substituted for the Righteousness by faith, & lastly, Prudence, Paleyianism, substituted for Morality" (*CM—CC*—II 291). See Prolegomena III: The Epicurean and Stoic Background and IV: Paley and Morality.

[210] The specification seems to fit Paley especially. Cf *Aids to Reflection*: "I have, I am aware, in the present work furnished occasion for a charge of having expressed myself with slight and irreverence of celebrated Names, especially of the late Dr. Paley. O, if I were fond and ambitious of literary Honor, of public Applause, how well content should I be to excite but one third of the admiration which, in my inmost Being, I feel for the head and heart of PALEY! And how gladly would I surrender all hope of contemporary praise, could I even approach to the incomparable grace, propriety, and persuasive facility of his writings! But on this very account I believed myself bound by conscience to throw the whole force of my intellect in the way of this triumphal Car, on which the tutelary Genius of modern Idolatry is borne, even at the risk of being crushed under the wheels! (*AR*—1825—399–400). See Prolegomena IV: Paley and Morality. But the phrase "supersede the gospel" surely refers to the enmity, from deep in antiquity, of the Epicurean tradition to Christianity. See Prolegomena III: The Epicurean and Stoic Background.

[211] Hartley, writing under the aegis of Locke and Newton, had specifically in 1749 brought mechanism to the fore. In a concluding chapter in the first volume of *Observations on Man* called "Some Remarks on the Mechanism of the Human Mind" he says: "By the Mechanism of human Actions I mean, that each Action results from the previous Circumstances of Body and Mind, in the same manner, and with the same Certainty, as other Effects do from their mechanical Causes" (Hartley *Observations on Man* I 500).

[212] Cf e.g. C in 1821: ". . . the effect & almost universal influence of the Mechanic Philosophy, the Doctrine of Death and cowardly yet boastful Despondence" (*CN* IV 4834).

[213] This specification refers the "scheme of pure mechanism", in all its disguises, back to Locke and the adher-

all shape to impression from without, leads, we have seen, to its own confutation and, scorpion-like, destroys itself, while the tail, ~~infixes~~ turning round in its tortures, infixes the poisoned sting in its head[214]—inevitably leads to it, ⟨I say,⟩ if only it be forced by a stern logic ⟨in⟩to all its consequences.[215] And well were it, perhaps, that this circuit should be taken, and the conviction of the truth [ƒ 122] be at once strengthened and inspirited by a knowledge of the contrary. But alas! how seldom is this the case! In the far greater number of instances the pupil goes but half way, pursues the line of declination far enough to lose sight of the true road, and yet not so far as to be aware of the whirlpool, in the outward eddy of which he is wheeling round and round. The influence of the laws of his country, the acquired nature which comes to every individual born into a state of civilization, custom, habit, imitation, the necessity of preserving a character, the sympathies and supports derived from superior rank and fortune, the consequent absence of temptation—to all of which add, in this country at least, the pressure of our ranks on each other up the whole ascent of the social ladder, with the reserve and watchfulness of demeanour produced from this cause in the higher ranks, and the emulation and even the mimicry awakened in the subordinate classes—add the [ƒ 123] extent and systematic movements of trade, and the interdependence of every species of property (and in ~~the present age all things, powers~~ this age what is not property?—all things and all powers, nay, the very passions, prejudices, and vices of mankind are ~~forms~~ modes of property, or the raw materials out of which it is formed—nay, the man values himself chiefly as a part in the machine), and, lastly, the

---

ents of Locke. Therefore (see Prolegomena III: The Epicurean and Stoic Background) it by the same token refers it to Epicureanism, of which Locke was, according to C, the chief modern sponsor. As C said in 1832, "The pith of my system is to make the Senses out of the Mind—not the Mind from the Senses, as Locke etc" (*TT—CC*—I 312).

214 "The leading differences between mechanic and vital philosophy may all be drawn from one point: namely, that the former demanding for every mode and act of existence real or possible *visibility*, knows only of distance and nearness, composition (or rather juxtaposition) and decomposition, in short the relations of unproductive particles to each other; so that in every instance the result is the exact sum of the component quantities, as in arithmetical addition. This is the philosophy of death, and only of a dead nature can it hold good. In life, much more in spirit, and in a living and spiritual philosophy, the two component counter-powers actually interpenetrate each other, and generate a higher third, including both the former" (*LS—CC*—89).

215 C's constant preoccupation with the threat of mechanism, is, as noted throughout this edition, bound up with his opposition to the tradition of Newton and Locke, and the still older tradition of Epicurus. In his own day it had become a palpable metaphysical presence, as can be seen in Carlyle's powerful essay of 1829, "Signs of the Times".

evidentness of the fact that in such a state of things every deviation from outward integrity must find its speedy, if not immediate, punishment from its mere commercial effect as obstruction and irregularity, so that ere[s] the profit have been received the heavier loss is nigh at hand; and with all these conjoin the almost continual preaching of moral prudence, i.e. of morals on ⟨merely⟩ prudential motives[216]—and we see at once how easily a man may pass through life without a single principle, and never feel the want of it from [*f 124*] the multitude and variety of its substitutes and its counterfeits. The honesty of the community is a fabric in which each is supported by all, as foundationless as a house of cards and, if we extended our view to the proportion of history and measured by ages as we now do by months and years, not proportionally less perishable. ~~Whenever that breath shall visit us~~ But even during the interval, while the ~~nation~~ kingdom is enjoying the blessings which power and wealth can give, while "from the uttermost parts of the earth there arise songs of praise, and glory to the upright nation",[217] dare we on ⟨the⟩ principles ~~which~~ obligatory on all moral beings, and which, as undeniably taught and commanded by the revealed law of God, can alone form the foundations of a Christian community—dare we examine these blessings? Dare[t] we bring out into detail the contents of this prosperity, the particulars into which this most comprehensive generalization is to be [u]resolved? Or, if[v] I may [*f 125*] repeat what I have before said, dare we unmark the bales and cases so marked and look at the articles one by one? Increase of human life, and increase of the means of life, are, it is true, reciprocally cause and effect, and the Genius of commerce and manufactory has been the cause of both to a degree that may well excite our *wonder*. But do the last results justify our exultation likewise? Human life, alas! is but the malleable metal out of which the thievish picklock, the slave's collar, and the assassin's stiletto are formed, as well as the clearing axe, the feeding ploughshare, the defensive sword, and the mechanical tool. But the subject is a painful one, and fortunately the labors of others, with the communications of medical men concerning the state of the manufacturing Poor, have rendered it unnecessary.[w] But religion is our present subject, which relates to the whole only as far as

[s] ms: e'er [*presumably a misunderstanding on JHG's part*]
[t] ms: dare   [u–v] ms: resolved, or if
[w] There is a stray quotation mark in the ms after this sentence

[216] That is, the counsels of Paley. See Frag 1 f 38.
[217] For such a Biblical concatenation of language cf Mark 13.27: "And then shall he send his angels, and shall gather together his elect from the four winds, from the uttermost part of the earth to the uttermorst part of heaven".

it affects and influences the individual, [*f 126*] and which in each individual finds two worlds, the one ~~of~~ infinite ~~importance~~ in extent, and the other of infinite awe and importance as ~~the~~ ⟨its⟩ means and condition. ~~of the other. Have we~~ Do we love our own souls? and have we souls to love? and can we love them ~~without comprehending~~ otherwise than in loving the souls of our neighbours? If we are in good earnest persuaded that a state after death awaits every human being—and that, too, a never-ending state—is it possible to love either our selves or our neighbours without any reference to the immortal and only permanent part of ˣboth? Butʸ if the ~~absurdity~~ impossibility of this be granted, must there not be duties which we owe which especially concern the soul, must there not be relations [between] this immortal creature and the eternal Creator to be an image of whose eternity it was created immortal? And ~~what then are we to~~ in what light, then, are we to regard a system of morals which of the [*f 127*] triple relation acknowledged by our forefathers, viz. our duties to God, our neighbours, and to ourselves merges the first as contained and having no existence but in the two following, and of these recognizes only the least important and perishable portion, and even so yet only in the outward act or deed, while in the source, principle, and ultimate object the last division of duties is alone retained, and the code containing it is in fact and truth no system of morals at all but a scheme of self-love, ~~calculated exclusive~~ enforced exclusively by calculations of pleasure and pain.²¹⁸ It will be said, I am well aware, that the belief in God and a future state is necessary for the regulation of this self-love so that it may produce the greatest possible sum of agreeable sensations to the individual, and to establish a compromise between the self-love of different individuals; ~~But though w~~ and that, therefore, it is our duty to profess this belief. [*f 128*] But though we should grant this, it is not easy to see with what propriety the belief that an irresistible power exists to bribe and threaten us into being happy; or how the belief, ~~of~~ ⟨how⟩ an ⟨immortal⟩ soul, contemplated wholly in regard to and for the sake [of]ᶻ our mortal and perishable enjoyments, or those of our neighbours—and the latter, again, wholly on account of the former ⟨on the plan of "no grindstone, no cheese"⟩ᵃ—can be entitled *Duties* toward God, or *Duties* toward the soul. In the language of common sense, they are surely no more than ways and means of performing the one only duty, namely,

---

ˣ⁻ʸ ms: both? but

ᶻ Word supplied in pencil on f 127ᵛ and marked for insertion here

ᵃ Insertion written on f 127ᵛ and marked for insertion here

²¹⁸ The "system of morals" so described is constituted by the alliance of Paley and the Epicurean tradition. See *Prolegomena* III and IV.

that which ~~we~~ ⟨each man⟩ owes to ~~our~~ ⟨his⟩ own worldly happiness. Alas! and is this the highest honor which can be given to religion, to make it the succedaneum of an idle or inadequate police? And[b] will experience warrant us in asserting that the ⟨practical⟩ result of motives ⟨depends⟩ on their magnitude, and not rather on their intensity? Or that this intensity, again, is not much more certainly producible by their proportion[*f 129*]ateness and present action? Is there not reason to dread that the application to the strongest stimulants of hope and fear will render the mind insensible to the milder and more natural incentives, while they themselves, from the distance and from the very indefiniteness which their own immensity brings with it, and which is too liable to be connected with a sensation akin to that of uncertainty—they themselves may more often act to aggravate the terror that follows, than to disarm the temptation that leads to the commission of crimes? Lastly, has not our recent experience, and an experience too on the most unquestionable proofs—I mean the national schools, consisting of children collected promiscuously from the houses of the poor and ignorant, children, therefore, already more or less contaminated by the habits and examples of their elders—has it not, I say, given practical proof that ⟨to⟩ the social [*f 130*] well-doing of human beings the three most effectual means are the removal of temptation, the maximum of watchfulness, and the minimum of punishment in all its forms, bodily or imaginative? Can any rational and reflecting man peruse the history of Sparta from the time of Lycurgus[219] to Leonidas[220] and retain the belief that it is not in the power of a Government, aided by all worldly motives and all the influences which education and discipline possess, to prevent the subjects[c] from being drunkards thieves, and murderers?

I at least dare not assert this, but still less dare I think ~~so meanly of religion, or that I~~ ⟨the faith that religion⟩ is so wanting in higher objects, or the soul of man so poor in higher capabilities, as that ⟨it should derive from⟩ this ~~should form~~ a⟨ny⟩ necessary or essential ground of its excellence, or its credibility. [d]⟨All goodness is ⟨refluent⟩, circular in its

[b] ms: and

[c] ms: subject

[d-e] This passage, written on f 130[v], is intended as a replacement for the following one, which is cancelled in the ms with a single vertical line: "I know, indeed, that it is the nature of all goodness, having risen, to descend on that [*f 131*] which had been left below, to ~~to take up with it~~ elevate and take up into its own nature the meaner life, in which it had

[219] Traditionally held to be the early (9th century B.C.) Spartan lawgiver who laid down Spartan laws of discipline.
[220] The king of Sparta who in 480 B.C. gave his life, with those of his immortal band of 300, at the pass of Thermopylae to allow the Greeks to organize their successful defence against Xerxes.

movement ~~of flowing back~~ ⟨still as it⟩ ~~ennobles~~ ⟨and revisits⟩ its own source, leaving⟨s⟩ nothing behind ~~which is capable of being elevated~~ but what is incapable of elevation. ~~and even these~~ ⟨And what it cannot elevate⟩ it strengthens and improves. And in this sense religion may be truly said "to lead captivity captive"²²¹ and to strengthen, even for its aliens and enemies, the bonds from which it had emancipated its faithful followers. The energies which mature the blossom stir and kindle ⟨the cruder juices⟩ in the stalk, but it would be strange ~~for this reason~~ to consider this kindly reaction as the proper character and main final ~~cause~~ of the blossom.⟩ᵉ

[*f 132*]   CHAPTER

The perfections of the soul have been divided under two heads, that of ~~assent to~~ ⟨Reception of⟩ the True, and [that of] Election of the Good. These, contemplated in their Idea, are coinherent but nevertheless distinct. Even when they are partially realized in individuals, neither can exist in the total absence of the other; but yet ~~for~~ ⟨in a⟩ practical sense are not only distinguishable but separable, so far, at least, that the preponderance of this or that gives a character to the individual, in whom it is manifested. The tendency toward truth would naturally be allied with the love of the good ~~and is pre~~ ⟨as to its strongest affinity, were he not pre⟩vented ~~only of~~ ⟨by⟩ meaner but nearer interests. As we commenced this work with defining religion as the whole scheme of revealed faith, that it is distinguished from history on the one hand and from philosophy on the other [*f 133*] by being both at the same time, even so may we define it, in its other and subjective form, as an energy operating in the individual soul—that it is the union of the ~~tendencies to truth~~ True and the Good, and yet so as not to confound ~~the one with the other and so that the former shall still be in subordination to the latter~~ the two, yet so as to permit the subordination of the former to the latter—and so that

been born, and to communicate its own positive character to that which had been but the negative condition of its existence. In this sense it may be truly said 'to lead captivity captive', and to strengthen even for its aliens & its enemies the bonds, which it had superseded for its faithful followers. The religion, the cause of which I have proposed to assert, I regard as the flower and crowning blossom of the plant, formed of whatever was most vital in root stem and leaf by the gradual separation and deposition of whatever was earthy and crude. ~~A~~But I know that it is at the same time the seal of its reproductive energies, and sending forth from itself the seeds of the whole plant."

²²¹ Judg 5.12: "Awake, awake, Deborah: arise, awake, utter a song: arise, Barak, and lead thy captivity captive, thou son of Abinoam".

while both are self-subsistent, yet the good alone is self-originated. Truth is indeed a necessary attribute of goodness, but while we must receive the truth for the truth's sake, we love it only because it is *f*good. But*g* the good we love, and elect, because it is good; and we ~~love~~ are capable of loving it with our whole being because we need only contemplate it as realized in its effects to perceive that it is necessarily and eminently true.

This principle of coinherence, [*f 134*] this position that principles that can never be confounded may subsist each indivisibly, one in the other, and so of each we not only may but must predicate the whole, I have in this chapter purposely brought forward in this form preceding in ⟨order to the⟩ proof that they are not of exclusive application to the so-called transcendent mysteries of faith, but are ⟨in kind⟩ in kind, ~~equally implied~~ though not in the same fullness and excellency, implied in every form of intellectual and moral world the moment we have agreed to consider such form as real, or having its ground in some higher form which is *h*real.[222] In*i* short, as soon as we have determined to consider such forms as more than mere generalizations, collective terms used for the purposes of artificial arrangement, and with the inconvenience of having been unhappily chosen inasmuch as the multitude which they represent, and of [*f 135*] which they are to be the common appellative, have another ~~class~~ name belonging to them, collectively as well as singly, thus rendering the former superfluous at the best, but likewise, unless the whole nature of man shall ~~be altered~~ undergo a fundamental change from a philosophy which hitherto has ⟨long⟩ striven, indeed, but hitherto striven in vain—not only superfluous but a source of confusion, ~~by bringing into~~ while the term which ought to express the sum total, and this only, will, spite of ourselves, introduce conceptions and anticipations altogether disparate from, and not seldom incongruous with, the essential character of each of the component facts. As if, for instance, we were to employ the name "Bird" as the collective term of a class of insects, a large number of which had not even wings. ~~But~~

[*f 136*] No man can be more deeply convinced of the truth contained in that often quoted sentence of Thomas à Kempis,[223] "Quis podest tibi

f–g ms: good, but   *h–i* ms: real—in

[222] Another instance of how essential the principle of "coinherence" is to the deployment of the abstractions on which the *Op Max.* depends. For an illustration cf a characteristic statement in App C of *The Statesman's Manual*: "But neither can reason or religion exist or co-exist as reason and religion, except as far as they are actuated by the Will" (*LS—CC—*65).

[223] Thomas à Kempis, originally Thomas Hammerken (1379–1471), German ecclesiastic born in Kempen. Famous as the reputed author of the Christian classic, *De imitatione Christi.*

altâ de Trinitate disputare si careas humilitate unde displiceas Trinitate,[224] ⟨Opto magìs sentire compunctionem quàm scire ejus definitionem,"⟩*j* [225] and no less fully do I coincide with Archb.ᴾ Leighton—it is indeed the main object of the present labour to prove it—that the remarkable mystery of the Son's eternal relation to the Father (and the excellent man might have added, and doubtless meant), the mysteries of the Incarnation, Redemption, and the aids of the Spirit)[226] is rather humbly to be adored than boldly to be explained, either by God's perfect understanding of his own essence or by any other notion. But I cannot but reflect at the same time that the divines who most frequently insist on ⟨the vanity of⟩ all notional reasonings and sensuous analogies as applied to the truths of religion—"vanitas vanitatum et omnia vanitas praeter [*f 137*] amare Deum et illi servare"[227]—that these, from Origen[228] to Thomas à Kempis and to Archbishop Leighton,[229] are the strongest assertors, and at once the profoundest and most eloquent ⟨advocates⟩*k*, of that philosophy which at all times, indeed, but with particular asperity during the last two centuries, it has been fashionable to decry under the name of "Mysticism" ~~for~~ on no better ground that I have been able to discover than that these writers will neither on the one hand attempt to hear with their eyes,[230] nor yet on the other hand allow that

---

j Written on f 135ᵛ and marked for insertion here
k Written on f 136ᵛ and marked for insertion here

[224] Tr: "What good is it to thee to dispute of the high Trinity if thou art deprived of humility, and so displease the Trinity?" (*De imitatione Christi* I i 16, with variation).

[225] Tr: "I would rather feel compunction than know its definition" (*De imitatione Christi* I i 20.)

[226] Cf C in 1833: "The Trinity is the Idea. The Incarnation, which implies the Fall, is the Fact. The Redemption is the mesothesis of the two—the Religion" (*TT—CC*—I 444).

[227] Tr: "Vanity of vanities, all things are vanity, except loving God and serving him." Cf Eccles: "Vanity of vanities, saith the preacher, all is vanity" (12.8).

[227] Origen (?185–?254 A.D.), Church Father, head of the catechetical school in Alexandria, author of many works, including textual studies of the Old Testament. His chief work on Biblical criticism was his famous *Hexapla*, his chief theological work his *De Principiis*, and

his most famous apologetic work, the *Contra Celsum*. C thought "He was too great a man for his Age" (*CM—CC*—II 721).

[229] Robert Leighton (1611–1684), Scottish prelate. Ordained as a Presbyterian. Persuaded by Charles II to become Bp of Dunblane, and sought to harmonize Anglican and Presbyterian teachings. Abp of Glasgow, 1670–4. One of C's favourite theologians, Leighton was "that '*wonderful man*'" (*CL* v 197); "If there could be an intermediate Space between inspired & uninspired Writings, that Space would be occupied by Leighton" (*CL* III 479n).

[230] The oxymoron refers sardonically to what C considered a perversion of religion: attempting to base religion on visual evidence. On the contrary, the sphere of religion consisted in "truths, which the eye cannot see, nor the hand grasp" (f 137). See above: "the reverence of the invisible, substantiated by the feel-

such as will not do this have no sense at all, no appropriate medium for the reception of truth, and of consequence no truth or reference to reality in the structure of their convictions. These above all others, who hold forth with such strength of colouring the weakness of the natural understanding and its necessary perversion when used as an organ of truths which the eye cannot see, nor the hand grasp; [*f 138*] that ⟨if there be a power in man of arriving at truths not derived from the Senses,⟩[*l*] it must be a power proceeding from the union, the focal point, of the entire man, neither merely moral nor merely intellectual nor merely vital or sensitive, but including all *eminentèr*[231] ~~if I may use the language of the older schools; and not~~⟨; and that even this power would be insufficient,⟩[*m*] even this, unless irradiated[232] by a power yet higher—⟨by a power, that is,⟩[*n*] to be partaken of but not appropriated—⟨~~are those who~~⟩ ~~enforce the actual~~ [these] are the masters who enforce most positively the actual existence of such a power, or rather, perhaps, quality, and of such an influence as the source of its irradiation. "Quod verbum non intelligatur quam à rationali homine: nam credere aliquid absque ideâ rei et absque rationis intuitione est modo memoritér retinere vocem omni irtâ perceptionis et affectionis destitutam."[233] But likewise, "quod absque ideis intellectus, et inde rationis [. . .] theoriâ, nulla datur perceptio; notiones enim per se [? similae] [*f 139*] nil nisi umbrae et simulacra cognitionum."[234] The reader is therefore earnestly entreated to dismiss from his mind all suspicion that it is my purpose or pretence to *explain* the mysteries of Faith at all, and least of all to explain them by a transfer of notions, the umbrae et signacula rerum[235] to the nature and proceedings of the Supreme Reality.

For a full insight into the doctrine of ~~i~~Ideas, i.e. of truths ~~having~~ which like the light are their own evidence and the evidence of other things,

---

[*l*] Passage written by C on f 137[v] and marked for insertion here
[*m*] Passage written by C on f 137[v] and marked for insertion here
[*n*] Insertion in C's hand

---

ing of love . . . is the essence and proper definition of religion" (f 79). On the other hand, the visible was associated with pantheism: Coleridge speaks of the Hindus and "their pantheism, or visible God" (Frag 3 f 133); and he says that "the doctrines of the most renowned and orthodox Brahmins affirm positively that what we see is God" (Frag 3 f 129).

[231] Tr: "eminently".

[232] Cf C's earlier statement about

"the Reason as the irradiative power of the Understanding" (f 12).

[233] See above, f 63 and n 151.

[234] Tr: "Apart from ideas of the intellect, and then the theory thought by reason, there is given no perception; for notions similar in themselves are nothing but shadows and signatures of cognitions."

[235] Tr: "the shadows and signs of things".

and for the validity and necessity of this doctrine, I must refer[236] in part
to the preceding chapters on the Good and the True, but chiefly to the
third division of my system of Logic,[237] not wishing to disguise from the
reader that if the arguments and facts there collected have failed in con-
vincing him, either of the reality of ideas, as contradistinguished [*f 140*]
from notions and perceptions—in short, as differenced from both the ab-
stract and the sensuous—or[o] of the necessity of assuming them (the re-
ality of a responsible Will having been pre-assumed, or conceded, on the
ground of consistency),[p] he will find nothing coercive in the train of rea-
soning which is now to follow. And yet, unless the same reader shall
have appeared to himself ~~to have seen~~ ⟨miss⟩ not merely ⟨to miss⟩ the
absence of sufficient proof of the truth, but to see proofs of the false-
hood—even for him the following evolution of ideas will be not indif-
ferent in a future stage of our enquiry, and when the same questions are
considered in relation to a fact, namely the doctrines, the rationality of
which, and not the objective or historic verity of which, it is my present
object to vindicate, were or were not taught by the first teachers [*f 141*]
of revelation, whether they are or are not the literal and obvious mean-
ing of the words used by or recorded of those original teachers. If there
be any, and some writers have professed to be such, who ground their
rejection of the mysteries solely and exclusively on their conviction that
they are not contained, nor the belief of them enjoined, in the sacred writ-
ings, without any reference to the rationality of the doctrines themselves,
nay, who profess that ~~thought~~ their apparent irrationality would not pre-
vent his faith in their truth, if only that truth had been expressly asserted
in the scriptures, or satisfactorily deduced from them—for him this work
can have little interest, and the present investigation none at all. I may,
however, be permitted to express a doubt which I cannot but feel,

---

[o] ms: nor   [p] Parentheses inserted

[236] The statement would seem to in-
dicate that as of this instant Frag 3 was
not yet in existence.

[237] "I hold myself bound to inform
the reader what and what alone I mean
by 'idea'. Those truths, namely (suppos-
ing such to exist), the knowledge and ac-
knowledgement of which require the
whole man, the free will, no less than the
intellect, and which are therefore not
merely speculative, nor yet merely prac-
tical, but both in one, I propose to call
'ideas' .... It will be expedient, how-
ever, to observe that the ideas are not
distinguished from the notions of the
senses, the intuitions of the sense, and
the conceptions and notions of the un-
derstanding by their being referred to an-
other and higher source; for this ideas
have in common with all the truths of
reason. Now though ideas must needs be
TRUTHS OF REASON, truths of reason are
not all necessarily ideas. There are such
that have their source in the speculative
(or theoretical) reason alone, and these
I have termed principles—" (*Logic—
CC—236–7*).

whether such a case had at any time an actual existence, whether, indeed, [*f 142*] it is in the power of any human mind to prevent ~~his views of the rationality and previo~~ the believed irrationality and prima facie improbability of a given interpretation from affecting, consciously or otherwise, his wishes, and with them his judgement in the choice between that meaning and any other that presents itself under more favorable preconceptions.

There are those, however, who readily admit that the common and catholic interpretation would have appeared to them the literal and obvious sense of the scripture texts, supposing that this sense had not appeared to them inconsistent with the main scope of the same or former scripture books, and, above all, incompatible with right reason. Prove to them ⟨both⟩ the harmony ~~of these doctrines~~ and ~~their~~ rationality of these doctrines, and, on their own principles, all objection to the catholic inter-[*f 143*]pretation²³⁸ must cease, with as many [as] make the scriptures, rightly interpreted, the rule of their faith. Now we shall on reflection clearly perceive that to do the one ⟨is to do both.⟩ ⟨For instance, to reconcile the doctrine of the Tri-personality, as deduced from the New Testament,²³⁹ with the unity of the Godhead,²⁴⁰ as enforced in both Testaments, ~~is to do both~~ is to establish the rationality of the former.²⁴¹ For wherein consists the asserted irrationality, but in the supposed incompatibility of Three and One, so predicated of the same subject in the same sense, taken conjointly with the other assertion that there is no second sense possible or representable?*q* *r*⟨~~This is~~ Men of such persuasions form the first of the two classes to which, exclusively, I address myself in ~~theis~~ [. . .] chapter. ~~In~~ The second ⟨comprizes a⟩ class ~~I comprize those men~~ ⟨of ~~men~~ Reasoners⟩²⁴² with whom ~~in point,~~ ⟨on the score⟩ both of intellectual vigour and of fairness in argument, I could enter into ~~the~~

---

q Full stop in ms
r–s Insertion written on f 142ᵛ and marked for insertion here

²³⁸ For C the phrase "catholic interpretation" refers not to the tenets of the Roman Catholic church, but to those of the "universal church".

²³⁹ Tr: "Go ye therefore, and teach all nations, baptizing them in the name of the Father, and of the Son, and of the Holy Ghost" (Matt 28.19). "The grace of the Lord Jesus Christ, and the love of God, and the communion of the Holy Ghost, *be* with you all" (2 Cor 13.14).

²⁴⁰ Cf C in 1832: "What do you mean by exclusively assuming the title of Unitarians?—as if Trinitarians were not necessarily Unitarians—as much as an apple-pie must of course be a pie" (*TT—CC*—I 299).

²⁴¹ The attempt to effect this reconcilement is the final goal of the *magnum opus*. "It is the doctrine of the Tri-unity that connects Xty with Philosophy—gives a *positive* Religion a specific interest to the Philosopher, and that of Redemption to the Moralist & Psychologist" (*CN* IV 4860).

²⁴² I.e. the Deists; "& Deism never did, never can, establish itself as a Religion" (*CN* IV 4860).

discussion ⟨contest⟩ with greater satisfaction and, I confess, with better hopes of the result, if not on their minds, yet on my own—~~I speak of those~~ ⟨I allude to⟩ such ~~were~~ ⟨men as⟩ Lord Herbert,[243] the Earl of Shaftesbury,[244] Algernon Sydney,[245] ~~and probably~~ Harrington,[246] ~~and~~ Halley,[247] ⟨and both the Reimaruses[248] and Mendelssohn⟩[249]; and though less frequent, or less frequently ~~in our times~~ avowed, such there are even ~~now among us~~ ⟨in our times.⟩ ~~I speak of~~ >[s] ~~To such reasoners, and likewise to those~~ ⟨These are the men⟩[250] who, retaining their faith in the existence of ~~an unde~~ Supreme Intelligence, have rejected the christian faith as far as it differs from what they call the light of nature,[251] or natural religion, because the meaning attached to the words of Scripture by the church appears to them [*f 144*] too evidently, ~~and~~ ⟨too⟩ undeni-

[243] Edward, Baron Herbert of Cherbury (1583–1648), "The Father of English Deism". Author of the important *De Veritate* (1624).

[244] Anthony Ashley Cooper, Third Earl of Shaftesbury (1671–1713). He was personally tutored by Locke, and in 1711 published the enormously important *Characteristicks of Men, Manners, Opinions, Times*. The work was influenced by the Cambridge Platonists (Cudworth was Shaftesbury's personal mentor also) and became the chief source for English and continental Deism. Paradoxically, it prefigured important attitudes in Romanticism.

[245] Algernon Sidney (1622–1683), English republican leader and martyr, author of *Discourses Concerning Government* (1698). Cavalry officer on parliamentary side during the English Civil War, but retired (1653–9) on account of Cromwell's usurpation of power. Though he had been a commissioner for the trial of Charles I, he took no part in the trial and was pardoned by Charles II. He returned to England in 1677, but as a consequence of his dealings with Louis XIV in support of Monmouth's rebellion was on discovery of the Rye House Plot convicted of treason and executed. He was much admired by C. See *TT (CC)* I 88 n 14.

[246] James Harrington (1611–1677), political theorist, author of *The Commonwealth of Oceana* (1656), which influenced the Founding Fathers of the American Revolution and was admired by C.

[247] Edmund Halley (1656–1742), English astronomer and polymath, friend of Newton and publisher of *Newton's Principia*.

[248] Hermann Samuel Reimarus (1694–1768), German theologian and early proponent of the Higher Criticism, parts of whose pioneering work on rationalistic theology were published by Lessing as the "Wolfenbüttel Fragments". His son Johann Albrecht Heinrich Reimarus (1729–1814), was also a theologian, and his daughter Elise Reimarus was concerned in the *Pantheismusstreit* between Lessing, Jacobi, and Mendelssohn.

[249] Moses Mendelssohn (1729–1786), German Jewish philosopher and friend of Lessing. Among his numerous works, C was especially versed in his *Morgenstunden oder über das Dasein Gottes* (1785).

[250] C is more gentle with the Deists themselves—or rather with these particular Deists—than he is with their philosophy. Cf *Aids to Reflection*: "The utter rejection of all present and living communion with the Univeral Spirit impoverishes Deism itself, and renders it as cheerless as Atheism, from which indeed it would differ only by an obscure impersonation of what the Atheist receives unpersonified under the name of Fate or Nature" (*AR*—1825—82).

[251] One of them, Abraham Tucker, wrote an influential treatise named *The Light of Nature Pursued* (1768–78).

ably to have been the meaning and intention of the ⟨original⟩ writers, and because Christianity, cleared from ~~all its~~ ⟨these⟩ peculiarities, contains no truths of which they do not find ⟨elsewhere⟩ as stable a ground ⟨of conviction⟩ as the subjects themselves admit.²⁵² ᵗ⟨The Divinity of the Founder, and the mysteries indissolubly connected with his divine character, being once excluded,²⁵³ they deny that Christianity contains any [? ~~doctrines~~] ⟨truths⟩ that can justly, i.e. *appropriately*, be called *Christian*; ~~and~~ ⟨none⟩ not contained in the Religion known by the Light of Nature, as asserted by the Apostle Paul himself, Romans. Ch. II. 6–15:²⁵⁴ in this denial being supported by the majority of the former class, who have styled Christianity a re-promulgation of ~~the~~ ⟨natural⟩ Religion. The additional points, therefore, consist (they argue) wholly of *narrations* of sundry extraordinary Facts, ~~land~~ Incidents, which ~~being~~⟨longing⟩ ~~of~~ to a diverse kind, namely, the Historical, cannot in the proper sense of the word be admitted as *Proofs* ⟨at all⟩ of ᵛ Truths doctrinal, religious, or scientific, and a fortiori not of Truths already established ~~by~~ and having in themselves their own evidence. These narrations, therefore, can only be considered as Testimonies; but which in the ~~preseneet~~ instance require other testimonies—and both the one and the other ~~must~~ ⟨requiring⟩ in order to their credibility, proofs, first of the probability of the Facts themselves; secondly, the ⟨existence & the⟩ possibility (i.e. intelligibility) of ~~the~~ an *occasion* for such facts and of that whatever it be which is implied in or inferred from them—ex. [*f 144ᵛ*] gr. a super-natural Agent, exerting a power on nature, directly or by a personal Delegate. And lastly, a

---

ᵗ⁻ᵘ(p 158) This passage, written by C on ff 143ᵛ–5ᵛ, replaces the following passage, which is cancelled in ink with a single diagonal line: "Or, to speak still more accurately, because, its mysteries once excluded, it ⟨appears to them to⟩ contain no ~~proper~~ addition ~~to religion~~ ⟨at all in respect of⟩ *doctrines* ~~but,~~ ⟨the additions consisting⟩ only of narrations of some extraordinary facts which appear to them to be no proofs at all, but rather testimonies, themselves requiring other testimonies, and both requiring a proof of the rationality of the doctrines, to which these facts stand in the relation of testimony, & of the probability of the facts themselves, ~~to which again they~~ add to which the proof that the narrations of these facts, & in some instances the facts themselves are not susceptible of a natural solution warranted by the common experience of mankind."

ᵛ Carets are written after this word and the next, though there is nothing to be inserted

---

²⁵² These men, Deists all, were admired by C; and that is presumably why he speaks more kindly here of Deism than is his wont.

²⁵³ One of the Deists, John Toland, had in 1696 written a famous treatise called precisely *Christianity Not Mysterious*.

²⁵⁴ These verses, which speak of the righteous judgment of God, conclude as follows: "For when the Gentiles, which have not the law, do by nature the things contained in the law, these, having not the law, are a law unto themselves. Which shew the work of the law written in their hearts, their conscience also bearing witness . ." (Rom 2.14–5).

proof that the *narrations* & in some instances, the Facts themselves ~~to~~ even admitted as identical with the Narrations, are not susceptible of natural solutions, or of explanations warranted by the regular experience of mankind. Independently, therefore, of the ~~express~~ ⌈. . .⌉ ~~of~~ ⟨numerous passages in⟩ the sacred writers, of the intention of which and of its conformity with the literal sense of the words they cannot bring themselves to doubt, the Miracles, ⌈. . .⌉ ⟨nay, the Revelation⟩ itself, as ~~the~~ ⟨the⟩ eminent Miracle, would (they affirm) be senseless & without purpose, unless some other ~~beliefs~~ ⟨Faith⟩ were informed thatn ⟨[? a] Belief⟩ already ⌈. . .⌉ ⟨sufficiently⟩ grounded—that they can find no other than the articles, which in all ages of Christianity have been received as such; and that ~~then they~~ [? enact] ⟨reject⟩ ~~receive because~~ while they are borne out by the former Class, who still cling to the name of Christians, in rejecting these as [? precond] ⟨irreconcil⟩eable with reason, they hold themselves bound in consistency ~~in~~ ⟨to⟩ reject~~ing~~ the remainder likewise (as far as it is exclusively Christian) first, as devoid of all assignable purpose, ~~and secondly as~~ ⟨in respect of⟩ their historic character; and secondly, as superfluous, in respect of proof or testimony—nay, as injurious by diverting the mind from the right & proper sources of ~~religi~~ sober and rational conviction, [*f 145ᵛ*] the reason and the conscience.⟩*ᵘ*

[*f 145*] *ᵂ*How far these men who have been distinguished from the herd of infidels by the name of religious Deists are justified ⟨both⟩ by Reason and ⟨by⟩ ~~itself~~ scripture in their assertion that the truth of a future and retributory state was assumed by the first teachers of Christianity as already sufficiently established, and neither needing or admitting any stronger proofs than it had already received, or by reason that no particular incident, no event occurring in the case of one or more individuals, is in its nature capable of proving a universal doctrine, ("Men", says Maimonides,[255] "may be persuaded by the effect which extraordinary appearances exert on their passions to the reception of re-

---

ᵂ At this point JHG's hand resumes

[255] Maimonides, or Moses ben Maimon, one of the very greatest of all Jewish rabbis. Born in Cordova, Spain, in 1135, and after various travels, including residence in Palestine, died in Cairo in 1204. A polymath, equally adept in law, medicine, philosophy, and theology, he is most famous for his *Dalalat al-Ha'irin—Guide of the Perplexed*, written in Arabic and translated into Hebrew and then into Latin. "Maimonides's major works—major by dint of their un-failing originality, impressive size, and abiding influence—are: the *Commentary on the Mishnah* (*Perush ha-Mishnah*), *Book of Commandments* (*Sefer ha-Mitzvot*), *Mishneh Torah* (also known as *Yad ha-Hazakah*), *Guide of the Perplexed* (*Moreh Nevukhim*)" (Isadore Twersky). C was led to a renewed interest in Maimonides by his friend and mentor in rabbinical studies, Hyman Hurwitz. See *AR* (*CC*) 345n.

ligion, ipsa verò religio non potest confirmari à miraculis."*x* 256 The position would be more defensible had he said, as he probably meant, "quòd religio non potest fundari in miracula.")257 will be the subject of future investigation.258 We have now to attempt a reply applicable to both classes, [*f 146*] and therefore will pave the way by conceding that a testimony in conflict with right reason, that is, where reason interposes its positive veto, cannot rationally be received as testimony; and next, by ~~giving up~~ agreeing to forego, during the present argument, the use of the common distinction "against" and "above" reason. fFor I feel myself constrained to admit that I am unable to understand how any ~~subject~~ question which ~~the reason~~ is brought before the reason in order to the determination of its congruity or incongruity with the same can be called above the reason. To affirm that any given subject is above the reason is to say that reason has nothing to do with the subject; and how this should be possible in any position conveyed or expressed in words, ~~I am as little able to conjecture, as by what other means,~~—of course, therefore, in intelligible words, and therefore [*f 147*] in words corresponding to some forms or other of ~~the~~ [. . .] the perception or the intellect—I am as little able to conjecture as by what other means truths ~~not the objects of the senses~~ distinguished from ~~the~~ phaenomena, ⟨or the objects⟩ of the senses, can be conveyed to our minds, or what other reason we can have for deciding one way or the other if the reason itself be excluded.259 ~~It is~~ But this is, in fact, only one of the countless ill consequences which have fol-

---

x A closing parenthesis was placed here in the ms but never cancelled

256 Tr: "The true religion in itself cannot be confirmed by miracles." Cf C's note of 1807: "Prophetiae veritas non confirmatur miraculis [the truth of prophecy is not confirmed by miracles], is the maxim of Maimonides & all the Jews.—" (*CN* ii 3137). Coburn notes that "Coleridge frequently referred to Maimonides, and is perhaps thinking of, or quoting someone's paraphrase of passages in, *The Guide to the Perplexed* Pt II, e.g. XLVII."

257 Tr: "religion cannot be founded on miracles". It is important to reiterate that for C religion was lodged in reason itself, and that therefore any attempt to prove it by miracles or other "evidences" was not only supererogatory but actually debased its dignity. See Prolegomena vi: The Higher Criticism.

258 This, along with the testimony of Maimonides, constitutes part of C's continuing rejection of Grotius and Paley, and the conception of "evidences" for religion. Cf a letter of 1820, in which C speaks of the "Worthlessness" of "the so-called evidences of Christianity first brought into toleration by Arminius and into fashion by Grotius and the Socinian Divines" (*CL* v 37). On the contrary, for C religion was necessarily implied by the structure of the "Reason and the Conscience".

259 The passage witnesses the confidence C, unlike some theologians, places in the efficacy of reason. He felt that "in every rational being" there is "a somewhat, call it what you will, the pure reason, the spirit, lumen siccum, νοῦς, φῶς, νοερόν, intellectual intuition, &c. &c." (*Friend—CC—*i 491).

lowed from confounding the reason with the understanding.[260] Pious christians, indeed, have escaped these consequences in great measure by attributing whatever there is in man higher than the understanding to the Spirit, which in their by no means unphilosophic vocabulary is the general term comprehending both the ~~praet~~ speculative and the practical reason, and the dependence of both on the Omnipresent Spirit, the [*f 148*] Supreme Reason, which is One with its Eternal Source, the Absolute Will of the Universe.

Waiving, therefore, all these supposed advantages, and cutting off beforehand all means of retreat, I assert not only the perfect rationality[261] of the Doctrine of the Trinity,[262] but that it is Reason itself, and supposed in whatever else is called rational;[263] but in order to this, I have a right to demand that my antagonist should concede to me the existence of a possibility in relation to our comprehension, as ~~distinet~~guished from ⟨a⟩ ~~reality~~ ⟨existence⟩ ~~in reference~~. No wise man would, I presume, have objected to the geometrical demonstration of the properties of a perfect arch, and the continued accession to its strength from every accession to the weight *y*thereon, that*z* no bridge was ever actually built having this property, that no such arch existed, in fact; [*f 149*] and if an unwise man had made the objection, would it not have been a sufficient answer on the part of the philosopher, "I spoke, as a geometrician, of its mathematical possibility, not of its material or historical reality"? Or if the objector rejoined, "But I admit of no mathematical or ideal possibility, of no truth in reason or the idea which is not the reflex, or direct expres-

y–z ms: thereon that

---

[260] "Till this distinction (of Reason & Understanding, νους & φρονημα σαρκος) be seen, nothing *can* be seen aright. Till this great truth be mastered, and with the Sight that is *In*sight, other truths may casually take possession of the mind, but the mind cannot possess them" (*CM—CC*—II 332). Again: "Until you have mastered the essential difference in kind of the Reason and the Understanding, you cannot escape a thousand difficulties in philosophy" (*TT—CC*—I 129). See Prolegomena v: Reason and Understanding.

[261] The supposed irrationality of the Trinity was a chief point of Unitarian attack, and C in asserting Trinitarian rationality was at the same time drawing the battle line against Unitarianism. In Apr 1818 C (*CL* IV 851) recommends Leib-

niz's logical defence of the Trinity (*Defensio Trinitatis per nova reperta logica*) composed against the Socinians in 1669.

[262] "In the Trinity there is the 1. Ipseity. 2. Alterity. 3. Community; or God i.e. the Absolute Will = Identity or Prothesis; the Father = Thesis; the Son = Antithesis; the Spirit = Synthesis" (*TT—CC*—I 77). For a longer description of the Trinity with an expanded discussion of ipseity, alterity, and community see *SW & F* (*CC*) II 1510–12.

[263] This is the crux of C's theology. Cf one of many statements: "Now, I affirm that the article of the *Trinity* is Religion, *is* Reason, and the universal Formula of all Reason—& that there neither is nor can be, *any* Reason, any Religion, but what is or is an expansion of the Trinity" (Brinkley 380).

sion, of some fact in experience, some one of the impressions received through my senses, ~~which when~~ ⟨or their⟩ generalize~~da~~tions by my understanding",[a] I really know of no other reply but one of condolence with the moral or intellectual state of the objector. For what would it avail ~~the~~ to make such a man see that on such a plan there could be no science, no philosophy, no religion as distinguishable from history, or independent of [b]testimony, that[c] either there could be no geometry, or [*f 150*] that it would be no inconsistency to call witnesses into the court to prove a mathematical proposition—what would it avail, I say, when this is the very position asserted?[d] "Yes!" the objector would reply, "that is just what I [e]mean. There[f] is nothing but history." It might be answered, and ~~even~~ with demonstrated⟨ive⟩ force, that even this could not remain, that even history would require a principle of connexion which did not exist in the outward notices or those abstractions which pass on as impressions of real objects or incidents. But the wiser plan, as we have ⟨before⟩ had occasion to remark, is to say, or rather to remain silent, and be content to know that the respondent must make himself a better man before he can be a more intelligent one. We shall be more usefully employed in restating such of our former conclusions that are [*f 151*] now to appear as the premises of what follows. We have begun by supposing the reader's acquiescence in our postulate of a responsible Will, and that therefore that there is a Will, i.e. a something which that word expresses exclusively. We then demonstrated that no meaning not already conveyed appropriately by some other term could be ~~stated and~~ ⟨conceived,⟩ and likewise none that did not deprive the word of all import or directly contradict that sense which, however indistinctly and imperfectly unfolded, permitted the term "responsible" as its congruous epithet or possible predicate. Thirdly, on the assumption of a meaning, which hitherto we have supposed as no otherwise known to us than by the single mark that it ~~is~~ ⟨must be⟩ peculiar to the Will, we proceeded to show exhaustively the different meanings which were not so as being, all and each, already otherwise appropriated, [*f 152*] and then the only sense or definition that truly and exclusively expressed what we ⟨must⟩ mean by the Will if we have any meaning, and what therefore the Will must be, if it be at all.

We then used our best endeavours to make our reader fully ~~conscious~~ aware and distinctly conscious of what he had admitted in admitting the fact of his own responsibility, and with this the reality of a Will as a universal position. We showed to him in this position the germs of almost

[a] Full stop in ms   [b-c] ms: testimony. That
[d] Full stop in ms   [e-f] ms: mean there

all those other positions which he had been accustomed to regard as in-comprehensible, or (to adopt a more familiar and frequent phrase)[g] as utter mysteries, and which, in a certain and rectified sense of those terms "incomprehensible", "mysterious", actually are such. But while we did not disguise this from him—on the contrary, used our best efforts to make him feel and understand the whole weight of the mystery—we displayed to him on the other hand the inevitable consequences involved in the rejection of this postulate, or the denial either of its truth as an idea or of its reality as itself the Ens realissimum.[264] And among these consequences we especially noticed the extinction, or rather the preclusion, of all ideas, ~~whether taken as inceptive or simply regulative~~ with these the sacrifice of all science ~~as contradis~~, i.e. of all sciential truth as con-tradistinguished from contingent and empirical facts. We pursued this subject into the *negative* definition of Ideas, as ~~before of the Will~~ ⟨we had before⟩ done in the instance of the Will. We showed what an Idea could not be, and then attempted to make it evident that its positive sense can be determined only by our conception of Law, in the philo[*f 154*]sophic sense of the term, ~~the~~ "Idea" and "law" being correlative [h]terms. Yet[i] it is equally true that the sense of "law" must in like manner depend on that of "Idea", and therefore that neither term can be made intelligible but in their equal relation to some one higher point[265] which is to be contemplated as the co-inherence and absolute identity of both, that which is at once the Law and the Idea: ~~T~~the law in which all laws have their root and energy, the ~~i~~Idea in which all ideas are compre-hended, and which ~~therefore was revealed~~ the Hebrew Legislator,[266] with surpassing propriety, has represented ~~in the~~ as that which affirms it-self to be because it is, and which is because it affirms itself to be, the "I am in that I am" or, to give a literal version of the original words, "I shall be that which I will be".[267] It needs only to under [*f 155*] stand the na-

---

[g] Parentheses inserted   [h-i] ms: terms—yet

[264] Tr: "most real thing".

[265] Cf *The Friend*: "It becomes nec-essary therefore to add, that there are two kinds of relation, in which objects of mind may be contemplated. The first is that of Law, which, in its absolute perfection, is conceivable only of the Supreme Being, whose creative IDEA not only appoints to each thing its *position*, but in that position, and in conseruence of that position, gives it its qualities, yea, it gives it its very existence as *that partic-ular* thing . . . . We have thus assigned the first place in the science of Method to Law; and first of the first, to *Law*, as the absolute *kind* which comprehending in itself the substance of every possible de-gree precludes from its conception all degree, not by generalization but by its own plenitude. As such, therefore, and as the sufficient cause of the reality corre-spondent thereto, we contemplate it as exclusively an attribute of the Supreme Being, inseparable from the idea of God" (*Friend—CC*—I 458–9).

[266] Moses.

[267] The Hebrew expression is indeed in the future tense. See below, f 225.

ture of correlative terms to perceive, that the only means by which either is definable can be no other than this, that they correspond as the object to the subject; that when we speak of a power acting according to intelligence as manifested in ~~the~~ its outward product and influences, we declare it to be the law of such product, influence, or outward manifestation as the law of the movement of the heavenly bodies; and, vice versa, when we speak of the same as a truth having a necessary existence in the mind or reason of the contemplator, we term it an "Idea", not as an impression or reproduced image of the product, which ~~has~~ ⟨is⟩ already precluded in the negative definition of the term, and which, being passive, is in direct contradiction to the nature of ideas, which are powers [*f 156*] no less than laws, differing from the latter only as subjective and objective, and deriving their apparent dividuousness from the necessities of finite intelligence. ~~We~~ ⟨It⟩ ha~~ve~~⟨s⟩ ⟨been⟩ remarked by us in a former work[268] that it is not of necessar~~ily~~ity that the mind should attain to the idea of the law by experience of the real products, that the history of the sciences, and the science of geometry itelf, establish the contrary. ~~As~~ *j*All objects of sense are in continual flux, and ~~are~~ the notices of them by the senses must, as far as they are true notices, change with them, ⟨while⟩ the Ideas of science ~~while~~ are no otherwise scientific than as they are permanent and always the same. Primâ facie, therefore, ⟨it is absurd⟩ to consider the former as the source of the latter; and hence the first ~~thinkers~~ great speculative thinkers appropriated the ideas to a higher principle than the [*f 157*] faculty conversant with images, ~~and distinguished from the former under the name the reason from the superior or the common na~~ and distinguished the ~~former~~ ⟨superior⟩, and calling the inferior the "understanding", appropriated to the superior the name of "reason". But now the remarkable fact presented itself that the material world was found to obey the same laws as under the appellation of "ideas" had been previously, and independently, deduced, ~~from the reason~~ or rather evolved from the reason;[269] and that the masses act by a force which cannot be conceived to result from the component parts known or imaginable. What then is the ground of this coincidence between reason and experience? between the laws of the sensible world and the ideas of the

---

j There is a stray quotation mark here in the ms

[268] See *Logic* (*CC*) 87.

[269] Cf *The Friend*: "what is the ground of the coincidence between reason and experience? Or between the laws of matter and the ideas of the pure intellect? The only answer which Plato deemed the question capable of receiving, compels the reason to pass out of itself and seek the ground of this agreement in a supersensual essence, which being at once the *ideal* of the reason and the cause of the material world, is the pre-establisher of the harmony in and between both" (*Friend*—*CC*—I 463).

pure intellect? The only answer is that both have their [*f 158*] ultimate ground, and ~~exist~~ are ultimately identified in, a supersensual essence, the principle of existence in all essences and of the essences in all existence, or the Supreme Reason that constitutes the objects ~~what~~ which it contemplates and ⟨then⟩ by the powers thus constituted, viz. the divine Ideas, gives being to ~~all images~~ the whole phaenomenal universe. So far, then, I appear to myself to have left the road firm behind me; and it needs only remind the reader that the original postulate and their concession was that of a responsible Will from which the reality of a Will generally became demonstrable to convince him that ~~if~~ ⟨his⟩ ~~a~~ ⟨there be⟩ responsible Will ~~and that this is as it undeniably is~~ ⟨is⟩ the ⟨essential, indispensable⟩ ground and condition of his Personality,[270] ~~so then in order to~~ ⟨and I obtain the means of at once⟩ demonstrat~~e~~ing the ~~next~~ remaining part of our proposed argument. [*f 159*] For if the reality of a responsible Will, i.e. a Will in a finite being, presumes the being of an absolute Will, the same relation that exists between these must exist between the personality implied in the one and its correspondent in the other. If neither the finiteness in the ~~man~~ one nor the absoluteness in the other case ~~prevents~~ prohibits us from calling the subject by the same name in both, neither can the absoluteness preclude ~~the~~ a personality, inasmuch as this arises from the essence of a Will and not from its contingent degrees, and except as far as we may have associated the conception of limit from without with the term "personality"; and from thence there may arise an expedience to distinguish the same, as predicated of the absolute Will, by some mark of difference which shall at once [*f 160*] express the thing ~~in its e~~ as eminently real, and at the same time the ground and source of all other personality. And this I conceive the term "Personeity" capable of doing. This perfect union of personeity and the absolute Will is, the reader will have already noticed, strongly marked in the Mosaic History, here

[270] See Prolegomena XVI: The Concept of Person, and XVII: The Concept of Will. Will, as repeatedly seen, occupies first place in Coleridge's scale of ultimates, with reason in close proximity in second place, and personality essential to both. For an invocation of other nodes of value and concern in the spectroscopy of C's world of thought, see e.g. *Omniana*, where with reference to a proposal to arrange the human faculties "under the different senses and powers", he lists: "the eye, the ear, the touch, &c.; the imitative power, voluntary and automatic; the imagination or shaping and modifying power; the fancy, or the aggregative and associative power; the understanding, or the regulative, substantiating, and realizing power; the speculative reason ... *vis theoretica et scientifica*, or the power by which we produce, or aim to produce, unity, necessity, and universality in all our knowledge by means of principles *a priori*; the will, or practical reason; the faculty of choice . . . and (distinct from both the moral will, and the choice), the sensation of volition, which I have found reason to include under the head of single and double touch" (*SW & F—CC*—I 333–4).

quoted only as the most ancient documents of the human mind. When the sublime writer is speaking of the supreme Will, he is named Elohim^k, i.e. the self-existent, the strengths or all strengths or efficient powers ~~conceived~~tained in one unoriginated, the Origin and perpetuation of all.[271] But the yet higher revelation he reserves for the Jehovah himself, "I am", and as the consequence of this, "I am the Lord thy God". So that it were no less true and consistent with reason to affirm that the being arises in the personeity [*f 161*] as that the Personality is a necessary accompaniment of the being; for let it not be forgotten that we are at present pledged to no more than to prove that the Will is a possible idea, that we become persons exclusively in consequence of the Will, that a source of personality must therefore be conceived in the Will, and lastly that a Will not personal is no idea at all but an impossible conception. But whatever is true in idea, it can never be proved beforehand that it may not be true in every sense, except as far as it should be predicated of a subject, ~~havin~~ the properties of which are incompatible with those assumed in the demonstration of its ideal truth—as if, for instance, a man should assert the existence of a material bridge in which all the properties of a mathematical arch had been realized. [*f 162*] If, therefore, there be anyone who, admitting the ideal truth of a position, should still persist in asserting its absurdity or self-contradiction in its application to the Divine Nature, he must [. . .] have assumed on his part the corporeality of the divine nature, or he contradicts himself.

"Having once fully admitted the existence of an absolute self-conscious Will or intelligent Creator, we are not allowed to prove the irrationality of any other article of faith by arguments that would equally prove this to be irrational, for it would be the same as to deny the reality of that which we had admitted to be real. Secondly, whatever is deducible from the admission of a *self-comprehending* and *creative* spirit may be legitimately used in proof of the possibility of [*f 163*] any further mystery concerning the divine nature. Possibilitatem mysteriorum (Trinitatis etc.) contra insultus infidelium et hereticorum et contradictionibus vindi~~nco~~; haud quidem *veritatem*, quae revelatione sola stabiliri ~~potest~~ possit,"[272] says Leibnitz in a letter to his Duke. He then adds the following just and important remark: "In vain will tradition or texts of

---

^{k} ms: Jehova Elohim

[271] "Every Hebrew knows that the term *Elohim* is equivocal, designating the deity, the angels, and the rulers governing the cities" (Maimonides 23).

[272] Tr: "vindicate the possibility of the mysteries (of the Trinity, etc.) against the insults of infidels and heretics and in the face of contradictions; not, indeed, the truths which can alone be established by revelation".

scripture be adduced in support of a doctrine, *donec clava impossibili-tatis et contradictionis è manibus horum Herculum extorta fuerit.*[273] For the heretic will still reply that texts, the literal sense of which is not so much *above* as directly *against* all reason, must be understood *figura-tively*, as Herod is a fox, etc."[274]

[*f 164*]   CHAPTER

We have learnt what we must mean by the "Will" if we have any pecu-liar meaning ~~at~~ of a~~ll~~ny kind which that word, and that alone, expresses. And now what do we mean by "Person", ⟨or⟩ "Personality"? It is evi-dently not the same with an individual, nor can it be confounded there-with, those cases only excepted in which the person is already presup-posed, though these cases form so vast a majority of the occasions for using the word "individual" that we feel almost a repugnance to apply-ing it to objects not personal: thus a writer attentive to the finer propri-eties of language would say "a single" ~~sheep or ox~~ in preference to "an individual" ox ~~or~~, sheep, or tree.[^1] His definition, therefore, of the term would be, [*f 165*] "by individual we mean that for which, ~~divided from~~ when not applied to a person, we should say single".

But if we ~~sho~~ may scarcely predicate individuality, still less dare we predicate personality of the single beast or plant. Why not? Of a fox, for instance? Here equally as in a man there is a unity of life in an organized whole. ~~Here as in~~ ⟨Equally with⟩ man ~~we find~~ ⟨the fox ~~pos~~ is found to possess⟩ vital power, instinct, perception, memory, recognition; and as far as we mean by "understanding" the faculty of adapting means to ends according to varying circumstances, it is most undeniable that the fox

[^1]: Quotation marks inserted throughout this sentence

273 Tr: "therefore the key of impossi-bility and contradiction will have been wrested from the hands of these Her-culeses".

274 Cf *Biographia*: "*Possibilitatem mysteriorum* (Trinitatis, &c.) *contra in-sultus Infidelium et Hereticorum a con-tradictionibus vindico; haud quidem veritatem, quae revelatione sola stabiliri possit*" [I am freeing the *possibilitiy* of mysteries (of the Trinity, etc) from con-tradictions, against the attacks of Un-believers and Heretics, not, indeed, the *truth*, which can be established only by revelation]; says LEIBNITZ in a letter to his Duke. He then adds the following just and important remark. "In vain will tradition or texts of scripture be adduced in support of a doctrine, *donec clava impossibilitatis et contradictionis e manibus horum Herculum extorta fuerit* [until the club of impossibility and con-tradiction has been wrested from the hands of these Herculeses]. For the heretic will still reply, that texts, the lit-eral sense of which is not so much *above* as directly *against* all reason, must be understood *figuratively*, as Herod is a fox, &c" (*BL—CC—*I 204).

possesses understanding.[275] Nothing, indeed, as we have fully proved elsewhere, could have occasioned a doubt of the contrary but the unhappy confusion so pregnant in errors between the faculty of the understanding and the gift of reason. [*f 166*] Yet our feelings, which are the representatives and, as it were, the shorthand records of our collective experience—our feelings—when left to their natural course, imply this distinction; for it can only be from the want of one or other or both of two attributes which are not in that same sense wanting in man that we withhold the name of person from the higher order of animals, and these are the Reason and the responsible Will. If we proceed to enquire in which of the two our personality arises, we assume that they are distinguishable, or at least that they are so in that sense in which the question was asked. Now if this be admitted, and if we are to speak of the reason not as it is one with the Will—that is, not of the absolute Will, which is one with the Supreme Reason, but of the Reason [*f 167*] in its relations to the finite and responsible Will—the reply is obvious: it[m] has been clearly demonstrated in a former chapter, in our disquisition on the nature of Faith and Conscience, that Reason is incompatible with individuality, or *peculiar* possession ~~that~~.[n] [276] ~~e~~Each individual must bear witness of it to his own mind, even as he describes life and light; and with the silence of light it describes itself, and dwells in *us* only as far as we dwell in *it*. It cannot in strict language be called a faculty, much less a

---

[m] ms: It

[n] The following incomplete sentence, perhaps intended as a qualification of the preceding sentence, is written in ink on f 166ᵛ: "It would, perhaps, for general purposes be"

[275] C is able to concede *understanding* to the fox while protecting the distinctively human power of mind in the related term *reason*. Cf C's comment of 1801: "It may not be amiss to remark, that the Opinion of Descartes respecting the Brutes has not been accurately stated. Malbranche indeed positively denies all feeling to Brutes, & considers them as purae putae Machines. But Des Cartes asserted only, that the Will and Reason of Man was a Something essentially distinct from the vital Principle of Brutes / and that we had no *proof* that Brutes are not mere automatons. Des Cartes, like Hartley & Darwin, held the possibility of a machine so perfect, & susceptible of Impulses, as to perform many actions of apparent Consciousness without consciousness . . . . Malbranche asserted that Brutes were machines devoid of all consciousness, Des Cartes only asserted, that no one could *demonstrate* the contrary" (*CL* II 695–6). See Prolegomena v: Reason and Understanding. See the succeeding note.

[276] Cf *The Friend*: "In respect of their Reason all men are equal. The measure of the Understanding and of all other faculties of man, is different in different persons; but Reason is not susceptible of degree". "Laws obligatory on the conscience, can only therefore proceed from that Reason which remains always one and the same, whether it speaks through this or that person" (*Friend—CC—*I 190, 192). And see below f 177.

personal property, of any human mind![277] He with whom it is present can as little appropriate it, whether totally or by partition, as he can claim ownership in the breathing air, or make an inclosure in the cope of heaven.

[*f 168*] The truth of this remark may be easily brought home to the conviction by remembering the state of mind in which the pursuit of any pure science, in which the solution, for instance, of any mathematical problem purely geometrical or analytic places us, and then compare it with the state to which we pass in a moral or political contemplation. In a word, try only to reproduce the state of ⟨our⟩ consciousness while we were following Euclid through the 37th proposition,[278] and then the ⟨our⟩ state while we were perusing the pages of Tacitus or contemplating the creations of Milton. Examine wherein the essential difference consists. Is it not that in the one there is the entire absence, the absolute negation, of all conceptions of cause and effect, of all causation final and efficient—or rather, to express [*f 169*] the same truths under a yet higher formula, an absence not only of all succession, i.e. in the objects themselves (the circles, triangles, etc. as distinguished from the successive acts by which we render ourselves distinctly conscious of them)*o*, but likewise of all interagency, or action and reaction coinstantaneous?*p* We should smile at the person who should ask for what purpose circles were equiradial.* We see the full propriety of the phrase "*aeternae veritates*",[280] or may I not say that in this phrase, thus applied, we learn the full *scientific* import of the word "eternal", i.e. not as a mode, or perfection, of time but as that which stands in no relation, that to which time is as inapplicable as the relations of space are to our affections and thoughts. If, then, we have fully mastered the only possible [*f 170*] definition of the Will as that which is essentially causative of reality,[281] we see at once that the whole of the preceding may be comprized in the words, "in the objects of pure science there is no presence of the Will,

* [*Written on f 168ᵛ:*] Vide Kant's Only possible demonstration etc.[279]

o Parentheses inserted   *p* Full stop in ms

[277] C frequently calls attention to this identifying characteristic of reason. See below, f 177.

[278] There is more than one 37th proposition in Euclid.

[279] *Der einzig mögliche Beweisgrund zu einer Demonstration des Daseins Gottes* (1763) (*Kant* II 63–164).

[280] Tr: "eternal truths"

[281] Cf *The Friend*: "all true reality has both its ground and its evidence in the *will*" (*Friend—CC*—I 519–20). Again: "The Will is essentially causative of its own reality" (*SW & F—CC*—I 777); "The Will is that which is causative of its own reality" (*SW & F—CC*—I 778). See also f 243 below.

wherever and as far as the Will ~~is distinguished from~~ ⟨and⟩ the Reason
are not identified. But the absolute Will and the Supreme Reason are
One, and it is the identity of these which we ~~att~~ mean, adoring rather than
expressing, by the term 'God'."[q] Our position amounts, therefore, to the
following: in[r] all purely scientific exertion of the mind there is no ex-
citement of the sense of our [s]individuality. The[t] mind acts, if I may use
so bold yet so appropriate a metaphor, as a verb impersonal. There is nei-
ther agent nor sympathy with any supposed agent: [*f 171*] both agent and
~~act~~ product are lost or contained in the act. The Truths of Geometry are
absolute truths only as far as they are confined to, and have their whole
subsistence in, the acts of the mind; and the mind itself thus contem-
plated is but the general exponent of these acts, combining in one idea
the acts themselves and their source and bond[u]. Individual person, then,
or *a* person, which is A inasmuch as it [is] not B or C—a personality, the
limitation of which is in part from imperfection and privation—is con-
tained exclusively in the idea of a finite Will, which cannot, indeed, be
conceived otherwise than in some relation to a co-present reason, but yet
capable of being conceived in a relation of difference and contrariety to
it. It is evident [*f 172*] that a Will, ⟨and consequently that a personality
such as this,⟩[v] cannot[w] be attributed to God without perverting the term
to idolatry, and not less idolatry from its existing as a supposed monop-
oly because there is but one idol named or admitted in the code.

But here let us pause and ~~examine~~ reflect what it is that we have here
~~neg~~ denied in the preceding paragraph. Let us examine what part of the
position is affected by the argument, and let us be sure that we have not
~~carried~~ driven the negative back over its own bounds into a sphere with
which the ~~h~~argument had no application. In order to this, we must ex-
amine and measure the contents and imports of the words "*such*", for it
is *such* a Will only, and *such* a personality, that [*f 173*] we have hitherto
found incompatible with the Idea of God.

Now it is manifest on the first reflection that these incompatibilities
must be all contained in the limitations or adulterations of the Will, and,
again, that the latter—namely, the adulterations or defects—may for all
logical purposes be reduced under or comprized in the former—namely,
the limitation or deficiency. Were it otherwise, the wiser a man became,
the greater his power of self-determination, ~~the~~ ⟨with so much⟩ less pro-
priety could he be spoken of as a person, and vice versâ, the more ex-

---

[q] Quotation marks inserted   [r] ms: In
     [s–t] ms: individuality, the   [u] ms: band
    [v] Passage written on f 171[v] and marked for insertion here
        [w] ms: such as this cannot

clusive the limits and the smaller the sphere enclosed—in short, the less Will he possessed—the more a person, till at length his personality would be at its maximum when he bordered on the mere animal, or the idiot, i.e. when, according to all use of language, [*f 174*] he ceased to be a *person* at all. Next, then, in what do the limitations, whether defects or deficiencies, consist? What ought we to mean, or rather, ~~mu~~ what must we mean if we ⟨have any⟩ meaning not precluded by the definition of the Will, and ⟨with⟩ the postulate of its reality as so defined (both of which are here supposed to have been conceded)[x]—what meaning, I say, which we can present definitely to our minds, and in accordance with our previous definition and admission of the Will itself, must we attach to its limitations, whether defect or simply deficiency? We say of one moral agent [that] he has an imperfect Will; of another, that he has a corrupt Will. It is plain, then, [*f 175*] that there is a something required in order to perfect the Will which was absent in the first case, and that ~~there is~~ a something in the other case there is a something admitted into the Will which of course ~~therefore is not~~ ⟨is something alien⟩ ⟨(aliegnige-num)⟩[y], or that something has been lost which was the contrary (uni-genum).[282] When a body dissolves or falls abroad in consequence of that vital power which had been its band or copula, yielding to other and lower energies (the so called chemical, for instance)[z] or when some ⟨incompatible⟩ element ~~had escaped~~ has been absorbed and given rise to a new series of combinations—in both these instances—and they most ~~often exist in combintion cor~~ frequently are found in conjunction—the body is said to be corrupted. And so in all other applications of the term "corrupt", "spoiled", or its equivalents. The wine is spoilt [*f 176*] as ~~air~~ wine when, in consequence of the acetous fermentation or other cause, it ~~is~~ has absorbed the acid from the air. In short, the reader may easily convince himself that he never speaks of corruption without implying the absence of something that should have been, or the presence of something that should not. Now what is this something in the present subject? The answer is obvious and exclusive. We know that it is the reason only, the absence of which must in some sense or other be[a] indicated, and that whatever is substituted for the reason ~~opposed or unrecognized~~ and op-

---

[x] ms: what I say must we mean compatibl~~y~~⟨e⟩ with what we mean by the Will, and itself capable of being definitely expressed [*cancelled in ink with a horizontal line*]

[y] Placement conjectural. This word is written in ink at the top of f 174[v] with no indication of where it belongs in the text

[z] Parentheses inserted

[a] ms: must be

[282] Tr: "only-begotten" or "of the same parent".

posed to it, or even not recognized by it, must be considered as alien powers, the presence of which constitutes the corruption of the Will. But here comes the difficulty, if in[*f 177*]deed, after the exposition in the chapter on the nature of Faith and Conscience, a difficulty still remains. The reason is either present or not present. In an eminent sense it is a free gift to us for the Will, indeed, without which it would in the recipient not be reason any more than the light falling on an eyeless face would for that person be light. We have seen too that Reason is insusceptible of being spoken of plurally: there can be no two ʀReasons, for in what way could the one Reason be distinguished from the other but by the negation of Reason, or contrariety to the same?*ᵇ* ²⁸³ If we say a greater or less degree of Reason, we shall be̶ ask ourselves in vain what we mean by the terms. If we use the word "Reason", as the present argument requires, objectively, it is as absurd as it [*f 178*] would be to speak of degrees of certainty between objects a̶s̶ pre-assumed as quite certain. But if we mean to speak subjectively, we are not talking̶ thinking of the mental light that lighteth every man that cometh into the world,²⁸⁴ but of the mental eye which perceives it—that is, we are thinking of that from which the argument requires us to abstract our thought. But more probably we are confounding the two conceptions, the careful distinction of which is the very point in view, the end and aim in this part of our analysis. It is most true that the mental eye must remain a merely potential faculty as long as the inward light is not present, and even so is it with the bodily eye and the outward light, which have supplied us with the metaphor and symbols for the [*f 179*] former. But it is no less true that the eye must be directed to the light, must at least be opened to it, in order for the light to be present for it, and it is this act of self-direction, this act of opening and of receiving, which may be conceived to exist in very different degrees, and likewise to be counteracted or suspended or even suppressed. The moment, therefore, that we distinguish Will from Reason, which we do whenever we speak of not following or disobeying our reason, we in fact imply 1ˢᵗ, thatᶜ the Reason is one and the same in all s̶u̶b̶j̶e̶c̶t̶s̶ m̶e̶n̶, and 2ᵈˡʸ, that the Will on the contrary is not only capable of being conceived of as different, and even as diverse, Wills, but we are under the necessity of so conceiving it in its relation to Reason, [*f 180*] inasmuch as p̶e̶r̶s̶o̶n̶ the Will could not be manifested, even to itself, and therefore could not actually exist without an object.

ᵇ Full stop in ms   ᶜ ms: That

²⁸³ See above, f 166 and note.   below f 223.
²⁸⁴ Cf John 1.9. See above f 178 and

But persons are the only rational objects of a Will in reference to itself as a Will* (no ~~eye~~ I without a Thou, as proved in Chapter __)^d. And if nothing more, yet so much at least has been proved, that individual persons are the result of finite Wills.

It will not, then, be too bold a phrase, should we say that Reason is the presence of God to the ⟨Human⟩^{e} Will independent† of its unity with the divine Will. A Will that ~~can~~ does not contain the power of opposing itself to another Will is no Will at all, and a Reason that did contain in itself a power of opposing a Reason, or of not being one with it, would be no Reason [*f 181*] at all. If the Reader will retrace the different steps of the argument, he will find the conclusion to be that a deficiency of the Will, and likewise a defect, must be both the one and the other in exclusive relation to the ^{f}Reason: that^g in the one case there must be ~~the absence of~~ ⟨wanting⟩ the ACT of ~~being~~ ⟨self-⟩ directed⟨ion⟩ toward the reason, or of opening thereto. But these are acts of the Will, for otherwise the Will would not be concerned therein. In order to make the non-recipiency no act of the Will, we must either ^{h} ⟨suppose the Reason absent. But we have assumed its presence. Add too, that in the absence of Reason the Will itself would cease to be present as far as ~~actual~~ presence is meant.⟩^{i} Thus ⟨in Sleep, where the Reason is withdrawn,⟩^{j} the Will ⟨too⟩ is suspended ~~in healthy~~

---

* [*Written on f 179^v:*] Thus food may be an object of the Will, and a rational object, but ~~not~~ in reference to the life, strength, etc. of the personal ~~Will~~ agent; or again, pleasure is a possible, and possibly a rational, object of a personal agent, but in reference to himself as an appetent and stimulable being. But neither of these has a direct reference to himself as a Will, or, which is the same meaning, to the Will as that which constitutes him a personal, and thence a responsible, being.

† [*Written by C on f 179^v:*] I mean, without necessarily implying—~~and~~ yet of course not excluding its unity with the Divine Will. N.B. What, speaking *metaphysically,* I call Unity, practically and morally would be named Conformity—which latter term, however, in severe propriety of language, is more applicable to the harmony of one finite will with another finite will.

---

^{d} Underscored space left in ms
^{e} Insertion in C's hand
$^{f-g}$ ms: Reason. That
$^{h-i}$ This insertion, written by C on f 180^v, is presumably intended to replace the following passage in JHG's hand, which was never cancelled: "suppose the absence of Reason, which, ⟨however,⟩ we have assumed as *present*, and in the absence of which ~~too~~ ⟨neither would⟩ too the Will ~~would be likewise absent~~ ⟨be present,⟩ as far as actual presence is meant."
^{j} Insertion in C's hand

~~sleep~~.[285] In like manner the corruption of the Will, ⟨or⟩ its [*f 182*] limitation by *defect*, must be an aversion from the reason, a position of itself in an opposite direction. ~~a~~And here there will be no hesitation in admitting that *these* are acts of the Will, and only as such referable thereto ⟨to that Will,⟩[k] or predicable thereof. That the ~~former~~ ⟨same result⟩ is not so immediately seen, or so readily conceded, ⟨in the case of Deficiency as in that of Defect,⟩[l] arises from two causes, or rather from two errors ~~o~~in the mind, the one calculated to remain long undetected, and the other of great pertinacity and apt to hover, if not to adhere, in spite of repeated detection. ~~I mean~~ [m]⟨By ⟨In⟩ the latter error I have in view⟩[n] the necessity of the fancy to frame, or rather to seek to frame, a sort of *substratum* of all acts and powers:[o]⟨and this the Fancy effects, virtually at least, and sufficiently for the purposes of self-delusion, by substituting⟩[p] its own perpetual and constantly baffled *attempts* to produce this supporting [*f 183*] somewhat for the product ⟨or support⟩ itself, ~~and~~ [q]converting, as it were,[r] its own cravings into food. Ipsœa suis desiderus pascitur.[286] [*] The other error, and of more immediate concern at present, consists in the frequent confounding of the reason with the objects to which ~~r~~ ⟨the Reason⟩[s] is applied—⟨in the confusion⟩ of the inward light with the objects beheld in and by that light. ~~The Geo~~ There is no less reason in the first book of Euclid than in the whole six, though the number of truths acquired, and [*f 184*] though the occasions on which the reason is exerted, are many times as great. But these objects, and the power

* [*The following sentence is placed in brackets in the ms and presumably meant be treated as a note:*] For this I will beg leave to refer the reader to my work on Logic and the Glossary of Terms, intended as a psychological and metaphysical appendix to that work, while the application of the ~~pren~~ truths there evolved and explained, to the Will specially, will be found in a more advanced stage of the present work.

[k] Insertion possibly in C's hand
[l] Insertion in C's hand
[m-n] Insertion in C's hand
[o-p] This passage, written by C on f 181[v] and marked for insertion here, is intended to replace the following passage, which he had inserted into f 182: "~~&~~ ⟨and this it effects, virtually at least, and sufficiently for⟩"
[q-r] ms: as it were, converting [*marked in ink for transposition*]
[s] Insertion in C's hand

[285] C characteristically takes note of suspended mental states like dreams and reveries, esp in his theories connected with dramatic and poetic illusion. Of particular pertinence for him was Andrew Baxter's *An Enquiry into the Nature of the Human Soul* (1745), which opposed mechanism and intensively discussed "imperfect states of sleep" (*P Lects*—1949—319) and dream states (see e.g. Beer *Intelligence* 60, 79–81).

[286] Tr: "its own craving is fed."

of adverting to them (in other words, both the knowledge and the faculty) belong to the *Understanding* and to the Sense. ~~oOf~~ ~~which~~ ⟨those,⟩ indeed, ~~the Reason~~ ⟨(i.e. of the Und. and the sense))⟩ᵗ as they exist in man, the Reason and the Will may be a necessary *condition*, but ~~of which~~ neither their amplitude nor their limit, neither their perfection or their deficiency, are affections of the Will, or ⟨do⟩ in any way ~~determininge~~ its character. The frequent occurrence of this distinction in the Jewish and Christian Scriptures, and the importance attached to it, must have struck the most superficial reader, as well as the superior value and worth of those knowledges of which the Will is the proper and immediate Organ. In this [*f 185*] place, of course, I ~~mention~~ ⟨refer to⟩ᵘ the ~~circumstance~~ ⟨Inspired Writings,⟩ᵛ as illustration only—~~and rather~~ ʷ⟨or as furnishing such presumption of truth as ~~in a~~ ⌐. . .⌐ ⟨in such a⟩ ~~subject⟩ˣ~~ ʸ⟨inᵃ subjects ⟨such as this is,⟩ᵇ in which ⟨~~as in the case here~~⟩ᶜ the ultimate appeal must be to consciousness.)ᶻ is ~~fairly~~ derivable from its coincidence with the apprehensions of mankind generally—⟨a coincidence fairly inferred from the general reverential acceptance of these writings.)ᵈ. It was ~~in regard to truth~~ ⟨concerning things⟩ᵉ of highest and exclusive application to the personality—~~truths~~ ⟨things⟩ that interested men only as far as they were persons—that the founder of our religion exclaimed, "I thank thee, O Father! Lord of Heaven and Earth, because thou hast hid these things from the learned and the understanding and hast revealed them unto babes."²⁸⁷ In human law, too, no less, ⟨inquiry is not made concerning⟩ the quantity of knowledge and the degree of intelligence, ~~enquir~~ but whether the individual is a *person* or not; and this is determined by the presence of the Reason in reference to the Will, and of the Will in its bearings on the Reason. The utmost [*f 186*] eminence of the understanding as the organ of knowledge, the greatest conceivable extent ⟨and multiplicity⟩ of knowledge, as the object of the understanding, ⟨if⟩ wholly exclusive of a⟨n individual⟩ Will in relation to a reason not individual, would constitute no personality in the possessor. We should find ourselves incapable of contemplating ~~him~~ such a subject otherwise than

ᵗ Insertion in C's hand   ᵘ Insertion in C's hand
ᵛ Insertion in C's hand   ʷ⁻ˣ Insertion in C's hand
ʸ⁻ᶻ Passage written by JHG on f 184ᵛ and marked for insertion here
ᵃ ms: as in   ᵇ Insertion in C's hand
ᶜ Cancelled insertion in C's hand
ᵈ Passage written by C on f 184ᵛ and marked for insertion here
ᵉ Insertion in C's hand

²⁸⁷ Matt 11.25: "I thank thee, O Father, Lord of heaven and earth, because thou hast hid these things from the wise and prudent, and hast revealed them unto babes." Repeated at Luke 10.21.

as a living machine, an automaton moved by unknown springs, which we might comprize in the term, "Instinct"*—or more truly, we should attempt in vain to conceive such an automaton, because we feel that an understanding so eminent and ample could not exist but in consequence of its participation ~~of~~ ⟨in⟩ the reason and of its actuation by a Will.

ᶠFor the Understanding to become a free discursive power it must be "discourse of reason",²⁸⁹ that is, [*f 187*] potentiated by a power higher than itself. And ~~it~~ ⟨no less⟩ must ⟨it⟩ have received freedom from the Will.²⁹⁰ ~~Without the~~ In the absence of a sun from without, in vain would the ~~ski~~ ⟨ut⟩most skill ~~its~~ ⟨of⟩ horticulture have attempted to make the *almond* re-appear as a distinct kind, and with a name of its own, transfigured to the peach and nectarine—no inapt symbol of the human understanding, considered both in its difference and in its cognation with the understanding of the dog, the elephant, or the ant. There is a difference of degree which could not be attained without a difference of kind received and appropriated, but receivable only from another and a higher source.

Abstractedly, then, from the individual intelligence, we are to treat of personality considered as a thing of degrees; and we [*f 188*] have ᶠdiscovered ʰ⟨1ˢᵗ, thatᵍ there, and only there, where a Reason and a Will are co-present distinctly but in relations either of union or oppugnancy, a personality is affirmed;⟩ⁱ 2ᵈˡʸ, thatʲ it is in the Will itself and not in its limitations, whether of deficiency or defect, that the personality consists, as far as the element of the Will is concerned. On the contrary, we have found that with the increase of these limitations the personality decreases, and that this process may be carried on even to the evanescence

---

* [*Written on 185ᵛ:*] See the last Chapter in the second Volume of Kirby and Spence's Introduction to Entomology²⁸⁸—a dissertation which (and indeed the whole work), tho' I differ widely from the amiable and intelligent Authors' conclusions, I strongly recommend to the Reader's careful perusal.

ᶠ⁻ᵍ ms: discovered, first ⟨1ˢᵗ, That

ʰ⁻ⁱ This insertion, written on f 187ᵛ, replaces the following passage, which is cancelled with a single vertical line: "that it does arise out of the co-presence of a Will with a Reason, or the presence of a Reason to a Will, which may be one with each other, which may be opposed, but cannot be the same. The Reason as Reason is not Will, and the Will may contain the Reason within it, but as the Will is not the Reason. This is the alter et Idem of the highest kind, the ground of all other identity, the origin of all other alterity."

ʲ ms: That

²⁸⁸ William Kirby and William Spence *Introduction to Entomology* (4 vols 1815–26). C was apparently reading the first two volumes of this work in Apr 1822. See *CN* ɪᴠ 4879–96 and nn.

²⁸⁹ *Hamlet* ɪ ii 150.

of the latter ⟨personality⟩ᵏ (in the process of the [ƒ 189] reasoning imag-
ination, at least). For in reality there is too much ground to fear that it is
not permitted to a responsible Will utterly to vanish. ⟨It is too probable,⟩ˡ
that man may precipitate himself into a fiend, but cannot be on a level
with the beast. It follows, therefore, that the essence of Personality is ~~not~~
to be found in ~~any~~ none of those qualities, negations, or privations by
which the finite is diverse from the absolute, the human Will from the
divine, man from God—nay, as we have found these diversities propor-
tionally subtracting from personal perfection, it inevitably follows that
by the subtraction of these diversities, the personality must become more
perfect, and that God, therefore, must be at once the absolute person and
the ground of all personality.²⁹¹ If we hesitated in calling him a Person
when we are with cautious [ƒ 190] reverence speaking of absolute Deity,
it can be only on the ground of his transcendency and inclusive nature—
as if, to take an imperfect and rude ⌐. . .⌐ ~~likeness~~ metaphor (but what
other, on a subject so unique, is ᵐpossible?), weⁿ were thinking of the
root antecedent to the shooting forth of the stem and branches, and hes-
itated to name it the root inasmuch as, by the ordinary use of speech, the
name might convey a false conception of its being such in exclusion and
privation of the other parts, and should thus cast back the eclipsing
shadow of the indigent particulars on the all-sufficient, self-sufficing
basis of their ⟨common⟩ being and the originating cause of their partic-
ular existence. It is enough, however, if, reasoning as the laws and con-
ditions of our nature ~~permit~~⟨rescribe⟩ and the combined necessities of

---

ᵏ Insertion in C's hand   ˡ Insertion possibly in C's hand
ᵐ⁻ⁿ ms: possible?). We

²⁹⁰ Cf *Biographia*: "the free-will, our only absolute *self*" (*BL—CC*—I 114).
²⁹¹ Cf C's marginal note on Jacobi: "Life—the characteristic Epithet of—the *living* God—by which the God of Revelation is contra-distinguished from the Fate and mere τὸ Θεῖον of Greek Philosophy, and the thin abstractions of modern [philosophy].— For it is actu-ally a Fear, almost a Fright, at the Thought that God *lives*—that instead of a logical x y z (which we are compelled by the mechanism of our Reason to pos-tulate, as the ground unconditional of all things, or rather as the one absolute con-dition of unity of Thought—i.e. of Rea-son itself, still however ideal and but an ens logicum et hypotheticum) there is a LIVING God—nay, (to utter the whole Truth so as to prevent the possibility of Mistake, even at the risk of seeming Ir-reverence, in the style of Luther or Zinzendorf), that there is such a person alive, as God.—and that he has a living Son—and that there lives too a proces-sional Person, the Spirit of and from the Father and the Son, and co-equal with both. It is this . . . aversion to a LIVING JEHOVAH GOD, originating in the heart-hardened & soul-blinding Worship of Mechanism, which is the essence of Idolatry & which generates Socinianism, most falsely called Unitarianism, instead of its true name, Unicism" (*CM—CC—*III 76–7).

language and [*f 191*] successive thought ~~prescribe~~ ⟨permit⟩, we have proved that the perfection of person is in God, and that personeity, differing from personality only as rejecting all commixture of imperfection associated with the latter, is an essential constituent in the Idea of God.[292] Once more, let me remind the reader that it is with the Truth of the idea, with the ~~i~~Ideal necessity or tenability of the doctrine, that we are concerned in this, the present stage of our enquiry.

[o]Chapt.

Ideas flowing out of the Divine Personeity.[p]

A great man,[293] to whom an illustrious contemporary attributes every virtue under heaven, puts the question whether the general passion for the corpuscularian or experimental philosophy, which in his time [*f 192*] had already prevailed more than a century, had not smoothed the way for the doctrines of necessity and materialism, with the consequent denial of man's responsibility, of his corrupt and fallen nature, of the whole scheme of redemption by the incarnate word.[q] [294] On the question thus worded, I cannot but remark with pleasure that the arrangement supposes the same order and evolution of the truths of religion as that which has been adopted in the present work. Subjectively, or in relation to the order of conviction, the *responsibility* is assumed as the condition and staple-ring in the chain of the christian faith. This being denied, directly or by a previous disbelief of the necessary inference from the fact [*f 193*] of moral responsibility—namely the Will, and therefore of a power strictly spiritual—the conception of a corrupt and fallen nature is impossible, or rather, the words are without meaning, and of course the whole scheme of redemption becomes equally hollow, first as having no object, and 2[dly]

[o–p] Heading possibly in C's hand [q] Question mark in ms

[292] Cf above ff 159–60.

[293] Berkeley.

[294] Cf *Lay Sermons* : ". . . the following remarks of a great and good man, not less illustrious for his piety and fervent zeal as a Christian than for his acuteness and profundity as a Philosopher: . . . 'Have not the doctrines of Necessity and Materialism, with the consequent denial of men's responsibility, of his corrupt and fallen nature, and of the whole scheme of Redemption by the incarnate Word gained ground during the general passion for the Corpuscularian and Experimental Philosophy, which hath prevailed about a century?'" (*LS*—*CC*—192). See Berkeley *Siris* 2nd ed (1744) 158–60. C's ed notes that "C has replaced Berkeley's sentence on Fatalism and Sadducism gaining grounding during the general passion for the corpuscularian and mechanical philosophy with this remark on necessity, materialism, responsibility, man's fallen nature, and redemption" (*LS*—*CC*—192 n 4).

as having [no] conceivable agent. The last position will be readily conceded, inasmuch as the same reasoning which leads to the absurdity of an incarnate Will, and in fact of a Will at all, will be at least equally effective in evincing the absurdity of the incarnate Word.

Returning to the words above quoted, I think it not superfluous to remark likewise that it is not the phi[*f 194*]losophy to which the philosophic Bishop[295] attributes the doctrines of necessity and materialism, i.e. the denial of Will and Spirit, but to the *general passion* for it.[*] ~~This indeed continues Berkley might have usefully employed some share in the leisure~~ Berkly is far from denying ~~the utility of the experimental~~ that this philosophy forms a useful part of general knowledge, or that it may worthily occupy the principal attention of a ⟨particular⟩ class in the learned world. But when, says he, it entered the seminaries of learning as a necessary accomplishment, and as the most important (he would not have misrepresented the opinion, prevalent in this age at least, had he said the *only*) important part of knowledge, by engrossing men's [*f 195*] thoughts and fixing their minds so exclusively on corporeal objects, it

---

* [*Written on ff 193ᵛ and 194ᵛ, presumably as a note, but with no indication in the text of the sentence to which it refers:*] I do not see, I confess, by what exclusive right a scheme which commences with the assumption of *atoms*[296] can claim for itself exclusively or eminently the epithet of experimental, nor in truth by what right such a scheme can be appropriately called a philosophy. ~~aA~~t least I am unable to discover any other essential distinction between philology, in its most extensive sense as comprehending the objects and the processes of ~~our~~ speculati~~v~~eon, ~~faculties~~ and philosophy, but that the latter term supposes the Will, and therefore the whole man collectively, while the former excludes the Will and refers only to a part of our nature, namely the human intelligence—that only which unites the speculative and the practical, subordinating [*f 194ᵛ*] [the] former to the latter, can be rightfully called a Philosophy.

---

295 Berkeley.

296 C, as pointed out elsewhere in this ed, was wholly opposed to Dalton's contemporary theory of atoms, both on the grounds that they were an assumption that violated the idea of infinity, and that they could not be demonstrated. See Frag 4 f 30ᵛ. C's repudiation of Dalton was bound up with his repudiation of Epicureanism, for atoms formed part of the theory of Epicurus, whom Coleridge strongly reprobated on moral and theological grounds, e.g. "he [Epicurus] taught that the World was formed by the blind play of Atoms—that there was no Providence—and no future State" (*Lects 1795—CC*—157). See Prolegomena III: The Epicurean and Stoic Background. Again: "Leucippus founded the ATOMIC system, or pure Materialism, in direct opposition to the Eclectic philosophy of pure Idealism—and . . . within the next hundred years . . . this SYSTEM was enlarged by Democritus. And during the interval from 322 to 270 years before Christ, it was brought to that state of completion by Epicurus to which it was restored by Gassendi, who was born in a village of Provence in 1592" (*P Lects*—1949—345).

hath, however, undesignedly not a little indisposed them for spiritual, intellectual, and moral matters. The consequence has been that while the sensitive powers, by this constant use of them, have acquired strength, the employment of the mind on things purely intellectual has to most men become irksome. ⟨(rath)⟩ The inference which this genuine philosopher draws in respect of morals—namely, that in order to tame mankind and introduce a sense of virtue is to exercise their understanding, by which he means the cultivation of the mind by contemplations purely intellectual, or what he calls a glimpse of a world superior to the sensible—does not imme we have no immediate concern [with]. But we [*f 196*] may add to the foregoing that in consequence of the neglect of this intellectual discipline among those who stand high and prominent in the eye of the world, thousands form an indisposition to all truths not instantly translatable ⟨referable⟩ into and having no immediate reference to images of sense[297] or so-called matters of fact—who are as ignorant of the experimental philosophy and its results as the merest logician in the days of the old schoolmen. Without the aid of authority, mankind are of themselves too liable and too apt to mistake a clear ⟨plain⟩ or vivid representation for a clear and distinct conception.[298] But when they are sanctioned by that authority, and encouraged to consider this weakness and infancy of their higher nature [*f 197*] as marks of the health and strength of their judgment and common sense, we need not wonder if for mere indisposition they substitute a presumption of the falsehood and uselessness of those investigations which, ʳwhile it strained their faculties, would at once interrupt their self-complacencyˢ and humble their pride.

I have been tempted into this digression by the train of thoughts that pressed on my mind while I was seeking to discover the subjective causes of the aversion to those enquiries which have for the object to bring our ⟨the⟩ moral convictions and our the religious persuasions into harmony with the reason, and to secure for them the acquiescence of the judgement, even where the contemplations truth [*f 198*] itself is such as passeth all understanding—in other words, is either senseless or, if it be

ʳ⁻ˢ ms: would at once interrupt their self-complacency while it strained their unused faculties [*marked in ink for tranposition, the numbers "2" and "1" being written over the respective clauses to indicate their revised order*]

[297] Those "thousands" find their representative in Dickens's Gradgrind. Contrast *The Friend*: "Religion, in its widest sense, signifies the act and habit of reverencing the INVISIBLE, as the highest both in ourselves and in nature" (*Friend—CC—*ɪ 440).

[298] The criterion of the "clear and distinct" had been emphasized for philosophical procedure by Descartes in his *Discours sur la méthode* (1637).

at all, must transcend and consequently disclaim those forms and rules of thinking which find their whole purpose and applicability in the objects of the sense, and derive their whole worth and ~~content~~ reality from their coincidence with sensible impressions, in which coincidence consists what is called Experience. And again, when we ourselves arrange the means, with forethought and definite purpose, for the production of this coincidence, or the determination of the contrary, we name the result experimental knowledge, experience acquired by *experiment. The*[^u] same result, when the means are found in the course of nature, is experi[*f 199*]enced from observation, each having their several advantages and each becoming most perfect when ⟨in⟩ combined⟨ation⟩ with ~~and attested by~~ the other, when the experiment is ~~warranted of general~~ ⟨confirmed, and its expanded⟩ application warranted by observation, and ~~observa~~ the knowledge from observation rendered secure and distinct by the process of experiment. If this be the just sense of these words, we may be allowed to speak of religious experience, but not without considerable violence to language compliment the fashion of the age by pretensions to experimental religion, or an experimental faith, which, where it is more than a mere pretence, is reducible to delusive sensations, and bodily disturbance assumed as parts and tests of a spiri[*f 200*]tual agency, or that very agency which the persons thus deluded have been taught to consider as capable of dividing even the soul and spirit—that is, to raise the individual above his highest individual faculties of understanding, much more to purify his conceptions from the accidents of bodily feeling. This is, indeed, to select the maimed and the sickly from the flock for sacrifice. And yet, unfortunately, it is this mistake, or confusion, which forms the main obstacle to just and religious views and pure intuitions in the one of the two parties into which the ~~world though~~ ⟨majority of the⟩ age may be divided—and this, too, the part ⟨from⟩ which, but for this cause, we might have expected the readiest support and the most favorable prepos[*f 201*]session. I would it were as uncommon, as to every well disciplined mind it is fearful, to hear religionists boast of having sacrificed their reason to their faith,[^299] and set up against a certain pretence and usurpation of the ⟨mere irrational⟩ understanding, and against those who, exulting in their lack and disbelief of all that cannot or will not acknowledge its exclusive laws, may be aptly entitled moths in moonshine—set up, I say, against these a pretence to sensible raptures, trans-

[^u]: *t–u* ms: experiment, the

[^299]: Coleridge was strongly opposed to the doctrine of *sacrificium intellecti* urged by one tradition of Christian theology.

ports of pain or pleasure, and on whom, therefore, their antagonists might no less appropriately, and with equal justice, retort as crickets chirping in darkness, and having for their vital element warmth without light, and this, too, the warmth of the kitchen.[300] The [*f 202*] utter contrast of this habit and of these principles with that individual faith which demands the first fruits of the whole man, of his intellectual powers, therefore ~~command~~ required of us not our sensations but the subjugation always, the exclusion often, and sometimes the entire sacrifice of our sensations and fancies—that full faith in the intelligential, in the power of whom light as well as immortality was brought into the world, the ⟨full⟩ proof of which is given there only where it has been found to expand the intellect at the same time that it purified the heart, to multiply the aims and objects of the mind while it ⟨fixes and⟩ simplifie~~s~~ those of the desires and passions. (Quote on from last line of p. 52, Second lay sermon, to "knowledge", line 6, p. 54).

[*f 203*] Thus it is evident that while the one party reject all truths or assumptions of truth which cannot be brought before the tribunal of the understanding, by which we here mean those rules and powers which have their proper and only objects in ~~the~~ objects of ~~the~~ sense, and the appropriate use of which is in the formation of experience in relation to objects of sense, the[v] other party, admitting the inapplicability of the rules and functions of the Understanding (Αφρονημα σαρκος)[301] to the articles of their faith, renounce equally the cognizance of the Reason, or rather, are, equally with the former party, blind, and adverse to the existence of a Reason as different from and transcending this [w]Understanding. We[x] must, ~~despair~~ as far as either of the two classes is concerned, [*f 204*] abandon the hope of establishing religious Faith on a conviction of the eternal or inherent truth which in part constitutes the religion, and which, in the other part, it is the object and essence of religion to realize. For we cannot too often recur to the definition of religion with which we commenced the present undertaking, namely, that religion is distin-

[v] ms: while the [w–x] ms: Understanding—we

[300] The collocation of warmth without light, and light without warmth, had appealed to C from early in his intellectual career. Cf e.g. a notebook entry of 1799: "Socinianism Moonlight—Methodism &c A Stove! O for some Sun that shall unite Light & Warmth" (*CN* i 467). Again, in the *Statesman's Manual* of 1816: "The light of religion is not that of the moon, light without heat; but neither is its warmth that of the stove, warmth without light. Religion is the sun, whose warmth indeed swells and stirs, and actuates the life of nature, but who at the same time beholds all the growth of life with a master-eye, makes all objects glorious on which he looks, and by that glory visible to others" (*LS—CC—* 48).

[301] Tr: "the mindlessness of the flesh".

guished from philosophy on one hand and history on the other by being both in one—that it unites in its purposes the desiderata of the speculative and the practical being, that its ~~events~~ ⟨acts,⟩ including its events, are truths, objects of philosophic insight, and vice versâ, that the truths in which it consists are to be considered as acts and manifestations of that being who is at once the Power and the Truth, [*f 205*] the Power and the All-powerful, the Truth and the True (ὅ αληθενος και η αληθεια)*[y],[302]* who is at once ὅ λογος και το πνευμα και η ζωη αι-ωνιος*[z].[303]* These hopes I should indeed abandon in no causeless despondence but for the fact that the latter class of cordial, though unreasoning, believers are greatly excusable, first from the absence in later times of any ~~competent~~ vindication of the interests of reason in matters of faith—except, indeed, by those who misapply the term "Reason", and pervert those faculties of discourse ~~(v. p.)~~ ~~(discursio intellectualis)~~ (discursus sive cognitio discursiva)*[304]* as the faculty of reasoning for the purpose of excluding all reasoning and rejecting all the truths that can be seen in the light of reason alone—and 2*[dly]* from the authority and widely diffused influence of the age, an authority and an influence [*f 206*] only not commensurate with the whole of Xristendom, and pervading all classes of society and all processes of education and ~~communication~~ instruction, from childhood to the age when the whole web of the habits and assumptions has been completed—a contexture which it is a task of great difficulty and small hope to unravel, in order with the ⟨natives of the⟩ late discovered African monarchy*[305]* to weave the threads anew into a ⟨better and⟩ more lasting fabric*[a]*. Yet the opportunity of bringing all parts and functions of our nature into harmony with each other, and the thought of finding the common focus, the centre of unity, in religious faith cannot be otherwise than interesting to every soul who is conscious of religious aspirations; and once assured [*f 207*] that these preparatory enquiries end in results which leave all other evidences in full posses-

---

[y] A correctly accented version of the Greek has been supplied in pencil on f 204*[v]*: "ἀληθένων καὶ ἡ ἀλήθεια"

[z] A correctly accented version of the Greek has been supplied in pencil on f 204*[v]*: "ὁ λόγος καὶ τὸ πνεῦμα καὶ ἡ ζωή αἰώνιος"

[a] This word was cancelled in the ms, then underscored with a dotted line to indicate its restoration

[302] Tr: "the true and the truth".
[303] Tr: "the word and the spirit and eternal life".
[304] Tr: "a running to and fro or discursive learning to know".
[305] See Thomas Edward Bowdich (1791–1824), *Mission from Cape Coast Castle to Ashantee, with a Statistical Account of That Kingdom* (1819). Summaries of the mission are given in *Annals of Philosophy* Jan 1818 (XI 9–13), and *G Mag* Dec 1818 (LXXXVIII ii 556).

sion of their former claims, that they loosen no tie, but on the contrary strengthen each severally, and all by combination and insight of their mutual dependence, we may venture to hope that minds thus character- ized will at least afford the following inquisition—~~deduction~~[b] ~~of~~ ⟨into⟩ the mysteries of our Faith considered as philosophic position, and the de- duction of the same from the primary, and therefore indeducible of God as the absolute Will—their friendly wishes, and at least a sufficient por- tion of their attention and of their desire to understand the argument as will be requisite, if not to ~~convince~~ ⟨satisfy⟩ them as to the sanity of ~~writer's~~[c] ⟨my⟩ judgement, yet ~~to inform themselves~~ ⟨at qui⟩ ~~saltem quibus~~ [*f 208*] "at qui illis insanire videar, saltem quibus insaniam ra- tionibus cognoscunt".[306] For the other class, as long, at least, as they re- main of that class, it will be of little import what they ~~profess to~~ reject and what they retain if only they are deprived of the power, even to those who profess ⟨to hold⟩ and believe themselves to hold the entire faith quod semper et ubique at ab ~~omnibus~~ ecclesiâ traditum est[307] as a sanction for the main principle and ground of their infidelity. Deprived of this shield and pretext, it will be sufficient to reply concerning them, rather than to them, that they who scoff at our faith begin by denying their own rea- son. [*f 209*] No man who has convinced himself ~~of~~ ⟨as to⟩ ⟨that⟩ ~~the pos- sible existence of beings~~ beings may exist of which the relations of time and space, as well as those which result from the primary forms of the understanding as applied to things presentable under the relations of time and space, are not predicable—no man who in the terms "eternity" and "omnipresence" means more than indefinite time by the one and indefi- nite diffusion by the other, but must have felt the difficulty of choosing words the least likely to bewilder the judgment of his auditor by the in- trusive associations of habitual fancy. To this difficulty, and the desire of overcoming it, we must attribute the numerical language of the Pythagoreans and the [*f 210*] frequency of musical and geometrical terms in the works of Plato and the Platonists.[308] In the same service, geometry itself was enjoined as the ⟨first⟩ purification of the mind, the first step towards its emancipation from the despotism and disturbing

---

[b] ms: and ~~deduction~~ [*the first word mistakenly left uncancelled*]
[c] ms: the ~~writer's~~ [*the first word mistakenly left uncancelled*]

[306] Tr: "But I am one who may seem to be insane to those, in whose very rea- sons insanity is recognized".
[307] Tr: "that is handed down always and everywhere and by every church".
[308] In a note of 1826 C says that "The Pythagorean Numbers (Numeri numer- antes, Αριθμοι νοεροι και νοητοι) are the Ideas of Plato.—Αριθμοι, Ιδεαι, Νομοι, Δυναμεῖς, νομικοι, are Synon- imes" (*CN* IV 5406). The world of schol- arship generally concedes that Pytha- goras exercised a strong formative influence on the thought of Plato.

forces of the senses. ~~InTo~~ the same end, and as an ulterior measure, tended the discipline of the discursive faculty by the common logic, in order that the pupil, by a precise and intimate acquaintance with the proper powers and forms of the finite, or individual, understanding, might be prepared for the dialectic so highly and mysteriously extolled by Plato[309] as the very wings of philosophy by which we ascend from the conditional to the absolute,[310] from the subjective forms of [*f 211*] humanity and the correspondent objects dependent thereon, each being that which it is, not by any inherent propriety but in consequence of the position of the other as its opposite—ascend, I say, from these to the permanent, the original and ever-originating, to that which is neither object nor subject because it is the root and identity of both. ~~i~~If we examine in what this dialectic consisted, as in the Parmenides of Plato and here and there through the greater number of the Platonic Dialogues, we shall find that it consisted in taking ~~certain premises~~ two positions, each undeniable as the premises—undeniable, I mean, according to the principles of the understanding—on the presumption [*f 212*] that in the understanding the senses and the knowledges obtained by experience and reflexion, all the grounds of truth cognizable by the human being, are contained. From each premise the reasoner arrives and forces his antagonist to follow him by the most legitimate deductions to an inevitable conclusion.[311] In both trains the premises are granted, the deductions are faultless, unclouded by a suspicion of sophistry, and, as we have before said, the conclusion [is] inevitable;[312] and yet they are in direct and exclusive

[309] E.g. *Republic*: "'What, then, will you not call this progress of thought dialectic?' 'Surely.' 'And the release from bonds, I said, and the conversion from the shadows to the images that cast them and to the light and the ascent from the subterranean cavern to the world above" (532b); "Then, said I, is not dialectic the only process of inquiry that advances in this manner, doing away with hypotheses, up to the first principle itself in order to find confirmation there? And it is literally true that when the eye of the soul is sunk in the barbaric slough of the Orphic myth, dialectic gently draws it forth and leads it up" (533C–D).

[310] Cf *The Friend*: "The grand problem, the solution of which forms, according to Plato, the final object and distinctive character of philosophy, is this: *for all that exists conditionally* (i. e. the existence of which is inconceivable except under the condition of its dependency on some other as its antecedent) *to find a ground that is unconditional and absolute, and thereby to reduce the aggregate of human knowledge to a system*" (*Friend—CC—*I 461).

[311] "Plato's works are logical exercises for the mind; nothing positive is advanced. Socrates may be fairly represented in the moral parts, but in the metaphysical disquisitions it is Pythagoras" (*TT—CC—*I 56).

[312] Cf *Treatise on Method* of 1818: "Of PLATO's works, the larger and more valuable portion have all one common end, which comprehends and shines through the particular purpose of each several dialogue; and this is, to establish the sources, to evolve the principles, and to exemplify the art of METHOD. This is the clue, without which it would be difficult to exculpate the noblest productions of the "divine" philosopher from the charge of being tortuous and laby-

contradiction to each other. The inference is evident, though Plato commonly leaves it to his reader's own ^dreflexion: namely,^e either that all reasoning is a mere illusion, and that the simplest [*f 213*] noticing and recording of phaenomena, with the art of arranging the same for the purposes of more easy recollection, constitutes the whole of human knowledge and the sole legitimate object of the human intellect, or [that] there must exist a class of truths to which the measures of time and space and the forms of quantity, quality, and contingent relation are not applicable.[313] And that hence the contradictions beforementioned were the natural and necessary result of the misapplication of an organ to an object, as if a man were to substitute a microscope for an ear-trumpet, or argue on the law of colours from facts obtained by the exercise of the touch. But even this is palliative, and ⟨an⟩ inadequate expression of the absurdity. For the different senses, though different in specie,[314] are not wholly [*f 214*] heterogeneous: there are not only analogies between them, but what Lord Bacon calls common vestiges;[315] their ultimate ~~impressions converge~~ effects converge. But not so with spiritual objects, it being understood that by the term "spirit" in this instance I mean no more than the expression of that which cannot be brought under the measures of Time and Space, ~~Not~~ not by any supposed immeasurable magnitude or innumerable series of successions, but as being wholly alien from the forms of the sense, as space, for instance, in opposition to an inch or a mile, or as the drops in the ocean. In fact the least reflecting minds, if only they have not been hardened by predetermined adherence to a system, find no difficulty in admitting this heterogeneity [*f 215*] in the relations of space, and feel the full absurdity of applying them to their own moral being. There are few indeed who would require any argument for laughing at the question [of] how^f many grains the conceptions and images contained in the mind of Shakespeare ~~were heavier~~ weighed, compared with the sum total of the same in the mind of a ~~stock-jobber~~ coun-

---

^{d-e} ms: reflexion. Namely   ^f ms: How

---

rinthine in their progress, and unsatisfactory in their ostensible results. The latter indeed appear not seldom to have been drawn, for the purpose of starting a new problem, rather than of solving the one proposed as the subject of previous discussion. But with the clear insight, that the purpose of the writer is not so much to establish any particular truth, as to remove the obstacles, the continuance of which is preclusive of all truth, the whole scheme assumes a different aspect, and justifies itself in all its dimensions" (*SW & F—CC—*ɪ 659).

[313] "Plato's works are preparatory exercises of the mind. He leads the mind to see that contradictory propositions are each true—which therefore must belong to a higher Logic—that of Ideas" (*TT—CC—*ɪ 98).

[314] Tr: "in kind".

[315] Phrase not traced.

try *^g*gentleman; or*^h* whether ~~a man~~ Anthony's love of Cleopatra was north west or south east of his respect for Octavia.*ⁱ*

Now to apply this remark. All our prepositions must in their primary meaning express relations of time or space. We have no other words which we can substitute. Our only possible mode, therefore, of conveying our meaning is by [*f 216*] accompanying these prepositions by some word ex~~pressing~~⟨cluding⟩ their sensuous application. ~~Without~~ The idea of time is necessary in order to the conception of a series of causes and effects, but on the other hand a somewhat not successive, a somewhat ~~of~~ which this time measures for beings that can conceive it only in parts and successively is a necessary condition of time. Nay, inasmuch as the succession itself argues a something that, acting successively, remains the same throughout the succession (for where otherwise could the consciousness of this succession originate?) and abstracts*^j* the consciousness, what would be meant by the word *^k*succession? For*^l* it is manifestly ~~a~~ ⟨an existence of⟩ relation, and hath not its being in itself, but [*f 217*] ~~relatively~~ each part in relation to all the others, and all again to some common point—the conscious beholder, for instance, who remains the same throughout—not only, I say, must this be the condition of ⟨time,⟩ ~~it is no less necessarily the g~~ even as the space in the hour glass ⟨is presumed⟩ in the succession of the sands that fall through it, but it is no less necessarily the ground of its time, that which communicates to time all its reality, as far as it is real. Now this, which is at once the ground and the [. . .] ~~again~~ condition of time (and it would be easy, by a similar train of arguments, to apply it to space likewise)—this, I say, then, which is at once the ground and the condition of time and of space is ETERNITY.

As that series which we [*f 218*] contemplate in the idea of time is impossible without supposing some antecedent, or if we say first, yet such as is first, midst, and last but by no means first in relation to any second—but by no means as a link itself, and therefore a part of the chain,[316] and partaking of its indigence and want of a support, or substance not contained in its own idea—~~it follows~~ if, in short, eternity be indispensably supposed in order to the con~~nexion~~⟨ception⟩ of ~~reality with~~

---

^{g–h} ms: gentleman? Or
ⁱ Question mark in ms
^j ms: abstract [*perhaps the phrase "and abstract the consciousness" belongs in the parenthesis*]
^{k–l} ms: succession for

[316] See below f 220 for C's commitment to the metaphor of a chain of reasoning.

~~time~~ ⟨time,⟩ time must in the first instance be brought into some relation to eternity. For if without it, it is not even possible as a conception, much less can it without this relation be rendered the subject of legitimate reasoning. But here comes the difficulty. Whenever we apply the accidents [*f 219*] of time to an eternal, there necessarily arises the semblance either of a contradiction or of an argument in a circle. In natural philosophy this circle is recognized as the law of reciprocal action, so that in every act of bodies that which in the first instance is assumed as cause is by the necessity of ~~reaction~~ ⟨a respondent⟩ action declared to be in the same indivisible moment an effect, and the priority, or [what]*m* we should begin with, is wholly arbitrary, having no ground in the acts themselves which equally suppose and demand each other, but only in the successive* nature of ~~our~~ thought's ~~and~~ language for the human mind. [*f 220*] It cannot, therefore, surprize us that in grammar and in logic we should still find one such circle assumed as the staple of the chain, rightly assumed and legitimately demanded as the only means of letting all the links ⟨that⟩ constitute the chain follow each other in one intelligible line of dependency. We must begin by affirming that AB is absolutely equal to BA, that is, that A is ⟨in⟩ no sense the cause of B in which B is not likewise the cause of A. But this once established, D will become intelligible [*f 221*] as the effect of C, but the cause of E; E the effect of D, but the cause of F; and so on through the whole series. We are compelled by the constitution of our own conscious understanding, and by the very act of reflexion, which is for us the power and the condition of time—I had almost said, which is for us Time—to attribute the relations of cause and effect improperly, and to a transcendent subject, in order that we may have any reality to which the relations of cause and effect in their proper sense can be applied.

We must yield to one argument in a circle at our starting point as the

* [*The following sentence was originally written on ff 219–20 as part of the text and then placed in brackets and keyed with an asterisk to an instruction in JHG's hand on f 218ᵛ: "as a note to the word successive":*] But then this succession of thought, this still recurring resistance, as it were, to the continuous going-forth of our being, which forces us backward, [*f 220*] as it were, ~~toward~~ our center, the result of which is ~~con~~the consciousness of the power resisting, constitutes Time for us̶}̶, so that ~~our~~ the conscious subject, the intelligent "I" in every man, as compared with that of which he becomes conscious, may without extravagance be represented as time in relation to space."*n*

m ms: which [*correction suggested in pencil on f 218ᵛ*]
n The following comment is written in pencil on f 219ᵛ, facing this sentence: "Totally erroneous on his own principles. Surely!"

only way of precluding it ever afterwards, and in every other case. Thus in grammar we begin with the verb substantive, with that which is the identity of being and action, of the noun and the verb; and we regard [*f 222*] the noun and verb as the positive and negative poles of this identity, the Thesis and Antithesis. We say the Identity of these, that which is both in one, not by synthesis in either of its three forms, that is, neither synthesis by juxtaposition or mechanical commixture of the two constituents, nor synthesis by the uniform solution of the one in the other (as, for instance, salt in water)°, nor, lastly, synthesis as a tertium aliquid[317] engendered by the introsusception of the one element in the other, i.e. by proper chemical combination (as, for instance, carbonate of lime from lime and carbonic acid)*P*. Neither, I say, of these forms of synthesis are identity, which can be no otherwise explained than as one containing in itself the ground and power of two as their radical antecedent, or as a point producing itself into [*f 223*] a bi-polar line, when we contemplate the same as anterior to this production and as still containing its two poles, or opposites in unevolved coinherence. Now as the form of language by which we express the act by which we are is properly denominated the verb substantive, we at once see the propriety with which the Hebrew Legislator[318] named that coinherence of act and being which is the ground and eternal power of the universe, of all things, and of all acts, and yet not included in the chain nor the same with the sum total of these, the Absolute I AM.[319] The first great truth, which all men hold implicitly at least and which *q*may be*r* with philosophical propriety called the light that lighteth every man that cometh into the world[320]— the first great truth, which all men [*f 224*] hold implicitly and which it is the highest object and duty of education to render explicit, is comprized in the term "GOD".[321] This unfolded (explicitum) is equivalent to

° Parentheses inserted
P Parentheses inserted
q–r These two words were accidentally cancelled in the ms, then underscored with a dotted line to indicate their restoration

[317] Tr: "third something".
[318] Moses.
[319] Every Coleridgean argument eventually comes back to the Absolute I AM, and its reflection in the human personality. Cf e.g. the statement that "In no other book [than Job] is the desire and necessity of the Mediator so intensely expressed. The Personality of God, the *I Am* of the Hebrews is most vividly impressed on the book, in opposition to Pantheism" (*TT—CC—*i 146). See further *CL* ii 1197.
[320] "*That* was the true Light, which lighteth every man that cometh into the world" (John 1.9). This was one of C's favourite Biblical passages, repeatedly invoked by him to refer to Reason as the expression of the Logos. See e.g. above f 178.
[321] Cf *The Statesman's Manual*: "This primal act of faith is enunciated in the word, GOD: a faith not derived from experience, but its ground and source,

the proposition, "God is self existent and a pure spirit". But in this, its highest acceptation, a spirit means ⟨1ˢᵗ,⟩ a̶n̶ substance having the nature and perfection of an act, and 2ᵈˡʸ, an act substantial, that is, an act having a ground in itself and being its own principle of permanence. I̶We express, therefore, one and the same meaning whether we say in the words of scripture, "God is a Spirit", or with the School Divines, "Deus est actus purissimus", or "God is a most pure act".³²² Now if we join the two positions of self-existence and Spirit, there arises that unique idea which can [*f 225*] belong but to one subject and can therefore be elucidated by no analogy, that the Fathers and the School Divines have struggled to express³²³ by the terms "αυτοπατηρ"³²⁴ and "causa sui",³²⁵ but which is both more sublimely and more adequately conveyed in the Hebrew words "I am in that I am",³²⁶ or rather in the literal translation of the words, "That which I will to be I shall be".³²⁷ For the future, which here involves à fortiori the past and the present, is used as the fittest symbol of an eternal act, to God an all-comprehending present, and to every finite being a future in which nothing past is wanting or left behind. W̶e̶ m̶i̶g̶h̶t̶ ̶t̶h̶u̶s̶ ̶p̶a̶r̶a̶p̶h̶r̶a̶s̶e̶ This sublime enunciation might be paraphrased thus, "The whole host of heaven and earth, from the mote in the sunbeam to the archangel before the throne of glory, [*f 226*] owe their existence to a Will not their own, but my own Will is the ground and sufficient cause of my own ˢexistence. What ͭ I will to be I eternally am, and my Will is the being in which all that move and live, live and move and *have* their being."³²⁸ Let us for one moment review our reasoning and collect

ˢ⁻ᵗ ms: existence; what

and without which the fleeting chaos of facts would no more form experience, than the dust of the grave can of itself make a living man" (*LS—CC—*18).

³²² C repeatedly invokes this statement, which he elsewhere ascribes to Boethius (though this ed has not found it), and which serves as a backdrop to his continuing effort to account for plurality and finitude along with deity. See e.g. *CM* (*CC*) ɪ 232; ɪɪ 1186, *CL* ɪɪ 1195.

³²³ John Taylor Coleridge recorded in 1811 that C "said that during a long confinement to his room, he had taken up the Schoolmen, and was astonished at the immense and acute knowledge displayed by them, that there was scarcely any thing which modern philosophers had proudly brought forward as their own,

which might not be found clearly and systematically laid down by them in some or other of their writings. Locke had sneered at the Schoolmen unfairly" (*TT—CC—*ɪ 9).

³²⁴ Tr: "self-engendered".

³²⁵ Tr: "cause of himself". See e.g. below, f 243.

³²⁶ "I AM THAT I AM—EHYEH ASHER EHYEH" (Exod 3.14) is in fact in the future tense.

³²⁷ Cf a note of 1820: "Be the thing, however, called Identity or Prothesis, this Co-inherence of Act and Being is the I AM THAT I WILL TO BE, of Moses, the Absolute I AM" (*CN* ɪv 4644). See above f 154, note 267.

³²⁸ "For in him we live, and move, and have our being" (Acts 17.238).

the conclusions to which it has conducted us. The Eternal Spirit is tran-
scendent to both time and space, so transcendent that we cannot apply
either the one or the other to the eternal without a contradiction in terms.
But even to finite Spirit it is only in a very modified and inexact sense
that we can apply the one—that is, relations of time—but the other not
at all, or without the grossest absurdity. For it is the conception of a spirit
co-existent with space, or [*f 227*] that which appears in the forms of
space, figure, distance, ⟨place,⟩ and change of place, and yet not an-
tecedent, not, as the Eternal Spirit, antecedent and transcendent to the
same, which renders space ~~an object~~ at all conceivable, or makes it an
object of thought. aAs little as we are capable of conceiving a figure, that
is, a limited space, without the idea of space as limitless, and the subject
to which limit is given, so little could we conceive a limitless space, i.e.
space abstractedly from all ł superinduced limit, without the idea of the
limiting principle, or that positive of which the infinite or limitless is the
negation. Anaximenes displayed no ordinary depth of thought, at so
early a period of philosophy, in referring all things to the finite and infi-
nite as their "principles.[329] [*f 228*] He[v] erred only in confounding the in-
finite with the Supreme Being, an error the enunciation of which consti-
tutes one of the sublimest passages in the writings of Plato.[330] To speak
of north as being south is not more absurd than to ~~give~~ describe Spirit
under any relations of space. Both are contradictions in terms: the one is
an absurdity in sense, and the other logically, or in the understanding.
But not even those forms or conceptions which result from the idea
of time can we without hesitation attribute even to a finite spirit, for

$^{u-v}$ ms: principles he

[329] Only one full sentence of Anax-
imenes (fl 546 B.C.) survives. For citation
and discussion of the various references
in antiquity see Kirk & Raven 143–62.
"Anaximenes' air, too, was indefinitely
vast in extent—it surrounded all things
and was thus described as ἄπειρον, infi-
nite, by Theophrastus" (146); "Yet one
pair of opposites, the rare and the dense,
took on a new and special significance,
and it could legitimately be argued that
all changes are due to the reaction of
these two" (147).

[330] Timaeus asks, "Are we right in
saying that there is one world, or that
they are many and infinite? There must
be one only if the created copy is to ac-

cord with the original. For that which in-
cludes all other creatures cannot have a
second or companion; in that case there
would be need of another living being
which would include both, of which they
would be parts, and the likeness would
be more truly said to resemble not them,
but that other which included them. In
order then that the world might be soli-
tary, like the perfect animal, the Creator
made not two worlds or an infinite num-
ber of them, but there is and ever will be
one only-begotten and created heaven"
(Plato *Timaeus* 31A–B). C writes to
William Sotheby on 10 Sept 1802 that
"Last winter I read the Parmenides & the
Timaeus with great care" (*CL* II 866).

we have seen that for each individual the spirit itself is Time. Time in one sense, namely, as the sense of succession, and in the other sense as the cause of this sense, we must still refer to something that is the opposite to space, or mere extension, and we know no other opposite but is, or [*f229*] is included in, the idea of Spirit. Hence it was that Descartes, who defined matter by extension simply, or that which makes appearance possible, denied to it the attribute of solidity, inasmuch as solidity could be intellectually construed only as resistance; but resistance is an act, and whatever is act is Spirit. It followed, therefore, that body is distinguished from matter on the one hand, and from spirit on the other, by being the synthesis of both. Whatever may be the philosophical merits or demerits of this system of Descartes, it is beyond all suspicion true in logic and mathematics, i.e. whenever we reason either in the forms of the Understanding or of Sense, that all conceivable objects are conceived under the condition of Time and Space as the opposite poles, the [*f230*] former as the point of absolute intensity, or action or power contemplated in relation ⟨to an opposite as⟩ to the subject in which it is to manifest itself, and, consequently, space as the absolute negation of all intensity, as mere extension and absolute non-resistance and mere recipiency. In this sense we say that the ⟨moving⟩ point ~~in measuring~~ generates figure, and in like manner that the minimum of space as measured by time is the [w]Line. But[x] without both Space and time nothing is imaginable, and hence we are compelled to imagine time itelf as a line substituting the minimum of the opposite for its entire exclusion. We have but one other observation to make, namely that the so-called properties of space as manifested by real or imaginary time, or the moving point, contain[y] the principle of [*f231*] all the language of relation in relation to the senses and sensuous fancy.[z] 1st, the minimum of space in the comparative maximum of time gives us the pure conception of length. The maximum of space, the comparative minimum of time, gives us the conception of surface or breadth. ~~a~~And these are proper and primary terms. The language corresponds to an image, and the image is itself a silent language; and ~~But there is yet a~~ we comprize both images in the conception of matter or material appearance—the rainbow, for instance, or a shadow, or a reflexion in a mirror, in contradistinction to a body. Now in order to a body we must suppose or take as placed what we have not the power of placing, a substance to this matter, that which cannot [*f232*] appear as the ground or support, or at all events the anteced-

---

[w–x] ms: Line, but   [y] ms: contains   [z] No punctuation in ms ent cause and condition of appearance; and this it is which we mean by the term *"Depth"*,[331] which is not a property of space directly, as the old logicians clearly saw, who instead of ⟨"length"⟩, "breadth", and "depth" used the terms *"line"*, "surface", and "body". It is, however, though not an image, yet a conception which accompanies all other images, and without which they are mere image: for this, therefore, we need an image as its language or sensuous exponent, and we construct this, the first compound term of the intellect, by placing length relatively to length, or by describing length in an opposite direction to surface, ~~either~~ as ~~dependant from or falling on~~ the perpendicular to the horizontal. This compound image [*f 233*] is the first metaphor of the mind, as the two former are its proper names; and we need not reflect long fully now to understand and feel the cause why, as all language in its very essence is appearance and correspondent to appearances, and all appearances are manifestations of time in space and space in time, we have no other terms of relation but those which we borrow from time, which, itself imaged as a ⟨moving⟩ line, affords us only the simple relation of fore and after, or from space as length, breadth, and, lastly, as rather necessitated by than borrowed from the forms of space, the relations of depth, or upper and under, higher and deeper. Nor shall we seek for the reason why in all language, in speaking of spirit or spiritual objects in contradistinction [*f 234*] from objects of the senses, we prefer words which express the relations of time, which is the analogon of spirit, or of height and depth, which are indeed suggested by the sense, but of which the sensuous expression is metaphorical and, in the strict sense of the word, allegoric. I conclude, therefore, with this simple remark: that if there be those who admit no reality to which the relations of space are inapplicable, for them ~~neither~~ this ⟨and the⟩ following ~~nor the~~ chapters are not written, and can have no *ᵃ*meaning. But*ᵇ* readers of another and more rational description I would place on their guard, that if even body cannot be understood without the use of metaphorical terms, that if the sensuous image which conveys to us the ordinary conceptions of height and depth are metaphorical, how much more so must they be when they are applied to the pure spirit, and the transcendent subjects to which we are now immediately to proceed.

The question which we are now to answer is simply this: of two conceptions that cannot be conceived apart, that is, neither in the absence of

ᵃ⁻ᵇ ms: meaning, but

[331] See "On the Concept of 'Depth'" *SW & F (CC)* I 452–4. Again: "the interpenetration of Length and Breadth = Depth gives the first form of Reality" (*SW & F—CC*—I 560).

the other—of two conceptions, I say, essentially in indissoluble con-
nexion, which must we take as first in the ~~order~~ ⟨process⟩^{c} of intellec-
tion in order to the possibility of the other, ~~T~~these conceptions being the
⟨conception⟩ Will and the conception of Being? The most cloudy gnos-
tic^{332} could not have been ignorant that the existence of a Will anterior
to that of being, in that sense [*f 236*] of the term "anterior" in which a
moment is supposed during which the one is while the other is not, is a
gross absurdity. Infinitely superfluous must it therefore be for us to
protest against any such interpretation, who have so distinctly guarded
against it by disclaiming any proper sense of the terms which are adopted
as metaphors, figures borrowed from the relations of time and space, to
truths, ~~the~~ ⟨an⟩ essential character of which is their transcendency to
these relations. Hence, too, we have laboured, even at the risk of prolix-
ity, to exhibit the arbitrary nature of the terms, or rather, perhaps, the in-
difference which accompanies the choice of one rather than another. It
is, I say, perfectly indifferent in itself, and determinable only by acci-
dental expediency, [*f 237*] whether in speaking of the two co-inherent
elements, A and B, we speak of A as before B, or as anterior to B, or as
deeper than B, or underneath B, or above B, or as inner, or the inmost.
In all alike we mean the same, and each different term or metaphor ex-
presses no alteration in the object but merely the relative position in
which we imagine ourselves to stand to the image or incident, which we
have chosen as the symbol, or allegoric exponent, of the true object.
Have we chosen some evolution ~~of~~ in time, as, for instance, ~~the rainbow
formed by the lig refracted light, or~~ the sun and the solar rays? We think
of the sun as before the rays, the parent before the offspring. If we placed
before our ima[*f 238*]gination the image of a circle and borrowed our
metaphors from the relation of circumference and center, we might speak
of the center as inner or inmost—if, again, of a solid globe, or of the sec-
tion of a globe, it would be perfectly arbitrary whether we presented such
a cone to our eye with the center as its apex, so as to speak of the center

---

^{c} In the ms "process" is written directly above "order" and a horizontal line, which may
have been intended to cancel "order", separates the two words

^{332} For C's knowledge of Gnostic
thought see e.g. *TT* (*CC*) I 35n. The
Gnostics, who in C's time (though not in
ours) were known only in the descrip-
tions of Christian adversaries like Ire-
naeus and Hippolytus, thought the cre-
ator of the world was evil (Plotinus
Enneads II 9, called "Against those who
say the world and its creator are evil",
and generally nicknamed "Against the
Gnostics", asserts the beauty and wonder
of creation against them). Their chief
figures—Valentinus, Basilides, Simon
Magus—conceived complex structures
of distance from the true God, using the
terminology of Christianity itself. For
analysis and a collection of texts see
Werner Forster *Gnosis; A Selection of
Gnostic Texts* English trans ed R. McL.
Wilson (2 vols Oxford 1972–4).

as above the arc, or whether, inverting it, we figured it to ourselves as under, or below, or in the depth.

Let this once be clearly understood, let it once be seen and acknowledged, ⟨that⟩ though the idea of a Will ~~may have~~ ⟨had been⟩ necessary to the idea of being, and though the idea of being is necessarily contained in the idea of Will, yet they are not [*f 239*] the same ideas; for though we cannot conceive of Will without Being, the very paper on which we are writing may remind us that we may conceive of being separately from Will, and to the exclusion of the same.

Our first position, therefore, is that in the order of necessary thought the Will must be conceived as anterior to all, or ~~supportive of~~ ⟨that which supports⟩ the being.[333] And this we may make manifest in two ways: first, we will suppose the contrary and attribute this timeless anteriority, this relative depth, to being. The consequence will be that the Will must be contemplated as ~~produced~~ ⟨a production⟩, a generation, or procession from that being. But this would [*f 240*] destroy the very essence of the Will; it contradicts the essential point of its definition and substitutes the opposites to a Will under the name of Will, for we have seen that no other definition of Will is possible but, *verbally*, "that which originates", and *really*, "that which is essentially causative of reality". But according to this supposition we have not only a reality but all reality under the name of absolute being, ~~standing in the relation~~ antecedent to the Will, standing in the relation of causative thereto, and if not causative ⟨itself⟩, yet assuredly precluding the predicate of original causativeness in any other. On the other hand, there is nothing in the conception of being which is irreconcileable with the conception of product, [*f 241*] offspring, provided only that where we are not treating of finite ~~and exclusive~~ being, or exclusive unity, this be not a consequent ~~in time~~ divisible from its antecedent in time or space. For that ~~the relation~~ even the mere logical relations of cause and effect does not imply any such division we have before shown, and every naturalist discovers as soon as he begins to translate the forms of logic into the correspondent forms in nature, and ⟨among these⟩ to resolve the cause and effect into action and reaction. So far, indeed, ~~of~~ ⟨is the Idea of an⟩ co-eternal consequent from involving any rational inconceivability that all the ancient philosophers who, like Aristotle, asserted a Deity but denied a creation [*f 242*] in time on

---

[333] Cf a letter of 26 Oct 1826: "In the New Testament I have observed that wherever *the Father* is spoken of, not as inclusive of the Word and the Spirit, or as synonimous with the Godhead but *dis-* *tinctively*, the WILL, as the source of Being, and therefore in the order of thought antecedent to Being itself (Causa Sui) is meant—" (*CL* VI 641).

the ground of the communicativeness being an essential attribute of the Deity, admitted this in the far harsher ~~and~~ form ~~of a considered effect~~, for they asserted the world to be a co-eternal effect.[334]

An absolute Will[335]—which, therefore, is essentially causative of reality[336] and therefore in origine [337]causative of its own reality, the essential causativeness, however, abiding undiminished and indiminishable—this is our first Idea.[338]

That of a Will, personeity is an essential attribute,[339] we have cleared from all objections ~~and then proved to be~~ and have traced back to the Will essentially, and ⟨not only⟩ without connexion with any existing or conceivable limits [*f 243*] of the Will, ~~a~~ but that with the increase of defect or deficiency, the principle of person or personal character decreases proportionally, and is consequently perfected in proportion to their removal. If, then, personeity, by which term I mean the source of personality, be necessarily contained in the idea of the ⟨perfect⟩ Will,[340] how is it possible that personality should not be an essential attribute of this Will,[341] contemplated as self-realized (αυτο̷υιος)? The Will, therefore, as ~~a personal~~ being, and because a Will, therefore a personal being, having the causa sui,[342] or ground and principle of its being, in its own inexhaustible causative might: this is our second Idea.

The causativeness hath not ceased, and what shall the product be? All power, and all reality, are already present. ~~w~~What ~~is~~remains, ~~for~~ we must, however reluctantly, yield to the imperfections of human language, both the language of words and the inward discourse of the imag-

---

[334] E.g. Aristotle *Physics* VIII viii–ix.

[335] Cf a note of 1825: "The Absolute Will. *Synomines* or *Appellations*: Abyss βυσσος αβυσσος. Τὸ Ὑπερουσιον. *Asei-*tatis principium ineffabile. *Natura* Dei. Identitas Absoluta. Prothesis absoluta" (*CN* IV 5256).

[336] See above, f 170 n 281.

[337] Tr: "in origin".

[338] Cf C in 1826: "not a week passes, in which some incident or other does not recall to my mind our Saviour's words—No man cometh to me unless *the* FATHER leadeth him. In vain the informing Reason, in vain the inspiring Life, the fecundating Love, if there be not that germ in the *will*, which is the Individual in his essential individuality, which is deeper than all understanding—& till it have been stirred and actualized by that ineffable *Will*, which is the mysterious Ground of all things visible and invisible" (*CL* VI 641). See further Prolegomena XVII: The Concept of Will.

[339] Cf "the *will*, which *is* the individual in his essential individuality" (*CL* VI 641). This central proviso distinguishes C's conception of will absolutely from those of Fichte, Schelling, Schopenhauer, and Nietzsche.

[340] Cf a note of 1826: "Having thus ascended to the Highest, viz. to the Prothesis, i.e. the Personëity of the Absolute Will—there rest awhile" (*CN* IV 5411).

[341] Cf a formula of 1826: "The Personality, the I AM, of the Abysmal Will & Absolute Reason" (*CN* IV 5466). See further Prolegomena XVI: The Concept of Person.

[342] Tr: "cause of itself."

ination and successive thoughts—what, then, remains to be communicated? It must in some high sense be other, and yet it must be a Self. For there is no other than Self (~~which has here the sense of removing~~ the conjunction "than" having here the sense of removing); removing Self, there is no other. How shall we solve this apparent contradiction? The formal algebra of dialectic, or tentative [ƒ245] logic, will instruct us to ~~reply~~ attempt the reconcilement of each by taking both, and the product sought for must be stated as another Self. This, I say, we do ƒin formal science, analogously to the higher processes in algebraic analysis, leaving it for after investigation whether there be any ⟨reality or import⟩ correspondent to the formula, and what that import may be. We must, I say, ~~substantiate Alterity itself~~ proceed as if we substantiated Alterity itself. But if Alterity be a mere abstraction, this is in the first place a contradiction in terms; and in the second place, as the conception could only be abstracted from a plurality or multitude of finites different from each [ƒ 246] other, it would be absurd, as an anticipation of that which as yet must be conceived of as not existing. The alterity must have some distinctive from the original absolute identity, or how could it be contemplated as other? And yet this distinctive must be such as not to contradict the other co-essential term. It must remain in some sense the Self, though another Self. Here again, as throughout, the idea itself, in its transcendency to abstraction and all other, both acts and products of the mere understanding, every where bearing evidence to its own reality according to the reality implied in the ⟨particular⟩ idea,* comes to our aid, and

---

* [*Written on ƒ 245ᵛ:*] The idea of a circle, for instance, compared with the idea of ~~g~~God. Reality is contained in both, though in the first the reality is subjective and mental exclusively while the second affirms an absolute reality. If the expressions of Plato are more than mythical, and if the passages I have in view are not merely ~~are~~ a part of the poetic drapery[343] ~~in~~ ⟨with⟩ which he ~~exhibited~~ clouded a philosophy too lustrous for the unprepared eye of his contemporaries, it must have been inattention to this truth—viz. that realities may be different without ceasing to be reality—which led him to the fiction of prototype circles, substantial and living diagrams in some pre-existent state, our present mathematical figures being the reflexes of these in the troubled mirror which the ⟨rational⟩ souls [ƒ 246ᵛ] were privileged to carry with them in their fall, and the looking on which constitutes scientific knowledges—which therefore, in consistency with this scheme, the divine philosopher entitles "recognitions".[344]

---

[343] Cf C in 1803, that it would be "in the highest degree presumptuous to affirm any thing positively of the Platonic System as there is too much Reason to fear that we do not possess the Key to its Nomenclature; the Works of Plato like the sacred Books of the East keep us in continual doubt what is to be understood literally & what figuratively or allegorically" (*SW & F—CC*—ɪ 140).

[344] Cf a letter of Feb 1801: "Pythagoras, it is said, and Plato, it is known, held

presents us at once with the disti⟨n⟩ctive mark and with the [*f 247*] requisite substance or import. But observe, and never for a moment cease to fix the mind steadily on this truth, that in the idea itself alone must the correspondent sense be sought for. The eye must not move to the right or to the left. All habit of ~~enlightening~~ ⟨supporting⟩ by analogy or^*d* aiding by examples, of relieving by illustrations, must be suspended.* The silence and the solitude which the last-born of ancient philosophy[346] adjured over all nature and all spirits[347] must ~~ha~~ be obtained in the mind before this still small voice can be heard by the soul. From no twilight, and amid no heraldry of multiform and many coloured clouds, can this divine light be born for us. It must divide itself from the [*f 248*] darkness, ~~which more than the soul~~ on which a spirit higher than the individual soul hath descended and made pregnant; and as a birth, and the first day of a new creation, doth the soul contemplate it that doth indeed contemplate it. These words, though authorized and sanctioned by the greatest, wisest, and best of the human race,[348] will, I am but too well aware, appear to the many "the flights of a poet soaring in the high season of his fancies, with his garland and his singing robes about him, yet even for those that consent to sit below in the cool element of prose amongst readers of no empyreal conceit"^*e*, it must appear evident on the

---

* [*Written on f 246ᵛ:*] If it be allowable at all to explain the nature of an idea by that of an image,[345] it can only be by contraries, and we must say that the idea can be beheld in that mirror only in which the reflex is one with the substance, and where the beholder must not turn round ~~(~~or look backward for the original, or ask another ~~as in the instance of his own face~~ whether he beholds it. The infant loving and exulting over its own form and features in the looking glass, as over that of another, is a symbol of the soul in its best and highest states.

---

^*d* ms: of   ^*e* The quotation marks are present in the ms

---

the pre-existence of human Souls, and that the most valuable Part of our knowledge was Recollection. The earliest of these Recollections Plato calls Ζωρυρα", living Sparks, & Εναυσματα, Kindle-fuel. These notions he enforces in the Theaetetus, and the Phaedon, and still more at large in the Menon" (*CL* ii 680).

[345] Cf C in 1801: "By the usual Process of language Ideas came to signify not only these original *moulds* of the mind, but likewise all that was cast in these moulds . . . . Latterly, it wholly lost it's original meaning, and became synonimous sometimes with *Images* simply (whether Impressions or Ideas) and sometimes with Images in the memory" (*CL* ii 682).

[346] Proclus, who was born c 410 and died in 485 A.D.

[347] C is here evidently referring to the Greek passage at the beginning of Chapter X above (f 25).

[348] Though the "greatest, wisest and best of the human race", by the two intensely Platonic footnotes just preceding, may seem to be Plato ("He was a consummate Genius" (*TT—CC*—i 99)), it seems more likely that the words refer to Milton—with the preceding passage

least actual reflection that if [*f 249*] ideas differ in kind from images, abstractions, and generalizations, and are diverse and more than these, nothing less can be declared of them. (He must either deny their existence other than as floating and unfounded words which any man may use in any sense, and which therefore in all correct terminology must receive the same reprobation as that dimmest and vaguest of similes, like any thing meets with among legitimate illustrations.)* In all cases the idea is of necessity presupposed ⟨in the particulars⟩ and stands, therefore, in direct contradistinction to an abstraction or generalization which necessarily presupposes that from which they are abstracted or generalized. [*f 250*] But if this be true of all Ideas, in how awful a sense must it be true of those ideas by which ⟨alone⟩ the being and attributes of the eternal ground and cause are revealed to us. These cannot be but lights, which "being compared with light is found above it, more beautiful than the sun, and above all the order of the stars" (Wisdom Sol. 7C, 29V).[349] And let me be pardoned if I again remind the reader that it is of truth in the idea that it is now, and hitherto has been, my business to treat,[350] and that it has been explained from the commencement that for those only who admit, or at least are willing to assume, the legitimacy of ideas, as far as the possibility⟨le⟩ ~~of any as~~ ⟨truth⟩ of any assumption is [*f 251*] concerned, that these chapters can have force or any merit more than that of a number of figures rightly summed up, but ~~neither~~ ⟨where⟩ the integers ~~of which not~~ and the quotient alike mean nothing. Recurring, there-

---

* [*Written on f 248ᵛ:*] V. Appendix to first Lay Sermon, p. xxxvii.

---

about "darkness, on which a spirit higher than the individual soul hath descended and made pregnant" echoing *Paradise Lost* I 19–22: "Thou from the first/ Wast present, and with mighty wings outspread/ Dove-like satst brooding on the vast Abyss/ And made'st it pregnant." On the other hand, C may possibly be referring not to an individual but to a plurality, or class of individuals. Milton, however, seems the most likely reference.

[349] Cf C: ". . . the Wisdom of Solomon, a work written about a century before the birth of Christ by some Platonizing Alexandrian Jew" (*CL* VI 900). For a more positive reference, cf "Various have been the pictures [of Leucippus, Democritus etc.] given us by Plato, Aristotle and SEXTUS EMPIRICUS, but I know none equal in fidelity and liveliness to that given by a Jewish writer whose work is in the Apocrypha under the name of the Wisdom of Solomon, where speaking of these sophists he said, 'For they said, reasoning with themselves but not aright, Our life is short and tedious and in the death of man there is no remedy; neither was any man known to have returned from the grave.'. . . . 'For we are born at all adventure: and we shall be hereafter as though we had never been . . .'" (*P Lects*—1949—133–4).

[350] This, along with other indications in this section, makes it seem that C is looking towards Frag 3 below, in which he treats in depth of the Divine Idea.

fore, from this digression, we affirm that the idea itself presents the intelligible import which we are seeking, the relation itself that of an infinite fulness poured into an infinite capacity, that of a self wholly and adequately repeated, yet so that the very repetition contains the distinction from the primary act, a Self which in both is self-subsistent but which yet is not the same, because the one only is self-originated. [*f 252*] ~~How can communication be~~ I must not suppose my readers atheists; I know that I may safely presume on their faith not only that God is, but that God is Love.[351] But how can there be love without communication? And how can there be communication without presupposing some other with ⟨(προς τον)⟩[352] ~~than~~ the communicant? And again, how can there be love without life, or communication without act, or an act divine that is not causative, whether as generative, or productive, or creative? ~~This⟩ ⟨Next⟩ therefore ⟨to the self⟩ must be the co-eternal~~ Next, therefore, to the eternal act (which, struggling with words, the ancient theologians have named ~~now the act~~ "Ipseity Aseïty", "Identitas* ενθεσι", "mens absoluta") is the co[*f 253*]eternal act of alterity, or the begetting of the identity in the alterity. Difficult, indeed, or rather impossible is it to render this idea intelligible if we turn from it and in its place substitute any production of thing from thing, or propagation of image from image; but if we pass inward on our mind and know that it is ~~truth of my~~ truth of minds, acts of spirit, and unities transcendent and indivisible of which we are discoursing, we shall discover, where alone it can be found, a meaning, however inadequate, in the terms, utterance of the word, the Word, the word itself, ~~a~~ or adequate expression of the paternal personeity, in the ὅ ων εις τον κολπον τον πατρος, in the which act the ~~father~~ ⟨absolute mind⟩ ~~likewise is~~ [*f 254*] from all eternity personal and ~~the Word~~, therefore from all eternity Father Almighty, and the Word, therefore, in and to whom the mind passeth forth or is uttered, personal, and the only begotten Son of God. Thus the filial Word is the intelligibile et mens altera; the Father, the mens absoluta; but then in relation to the idea of himself, the Intellective Word—he is both the mens absoluta et intel-

* [*Written on f 251ᵛ, the following sentence may have been intended as an insertion rather than as a note:*] As*f* the same writers [. . .] for synonymes or appellations of the absolute will, the abyss, το υπερουσιον,[353] aseïtatis principium, natura dei, prothesis vel identitas absoluta.

f ms: as

[351] "He that loveth not knoweth not God; for God is love" (1 John 4.8).
[352] Tr: "toward this".
[353] Tr: "that which is above being" (Proclus *Theologia Platonica* 3.21).

ligibile reciprocum: as the Father knoweth the Son, even so the Son knoweth the Father. Hence the synonymes for the Logos, namely "αλ-ηθεια και ὁ αληθης",[354] "intellectus ~~communicativus~~ communicatus et se communicans"; and by Philo Judaeus,[355] in writings anterior [to] and certainly independent of the New Testament, the Logos, ~~on~~ which we are anxiously for[*f 255*]bidden to consider as attribute, personification, or equivalent term,[356] is described as "Deus alter et idem".[357]

So far I have proceeded[358] with awe, indeed, but with less fear and apprehension because, though my present purpose is avowedly to prove the possibility and ideal truth of the dogmas ~~of~~ ⟨common to⟩ ~~the Chris-tian faith~~ common to the churches of Christendom, leaving the question of their defensibility both by scriptural sanction and by moral and historical evidences for the other and following division of this work, I could not, however, entirely separate the one from the other, least of all the philosophical from the scriptural sanction,[359] in my own thoughts and feelings, or expect such insulation from the great majority of my readers. [*f 256*] Now hitherto I have felt a spirit of confidence and encouragement from the conviction that every step of my reasoning is capable of confirmation,[360] and will hereafter be confirmed, by express

---

[354] Tr: "truth and the true".

[355] Philo's conceivings of the *logos* were particularly valued by C as hermeneutic tools, because the Jewish philosopher emphasized, as John did not, the same commitment to the dialectic of opposites as did C himself.

[356] Cf C in 1823: "Now when it is asserted, that the Logos of the Evangelist, John, is not the Logos of Philo, the platonizing Jew of Alexandria, it is either intended that they differ as A and B— and in this sense I utterly deny the assertion: or as C and D or (to express the difference by a still more apposite example) as Arius and Athanasius differed concerning Christ . . . —and in this sense I neither deny nor assent, ~~but~~ till the exact amount of the difference is specified . . . . Now if it be asserted that John and Philo differ as A and B, I deny the assertion utterly—or that they differ, as C and D, I in like manner deny the assertion—~~but~~ if they affirm, that John and Philo differ as E and F, or as Athanasius and Arius, I neither deny or admit but wait for the proof—and till then withhold my assent—./—But lastly if they

mean that John differs from Philo, as the Truth and nothing but the Truth from the same Truth ⟨in connection⟩ with sundry impertinences, and without the complemental accessories—to this I fully agree, even on the supposition, that I should see reason to dissent from the former" (*CN* IV 5071).

[357] Cf App D to *The Statesman's Manual*: "the power, by which men are led to the truth of things, instead of appearances, was deemed and entitled the living and substantial Word of God by the soundest of the Hebrew Doctors; that the oldest and most profound of the Greek philosophers . . . were scarcely less express than their scholar Philo Judaeus, in their affirmation of the Logos, as no mere attribute or quality, no mode of abstraction, no personification, but literally and mysteriously Deus alter et idem" (*LS—CC—*95).

[358] That is, in his culminating argument towards the rational defence of the Trinity.

[359] For the belief in the Trinity.

[360] Cf C as early as 1795: "With the Metaphysical Reasoner every fact must

passages of the scriptures taken in their literal sense as well as in the sense demanded by the context. But in advancing to the dogma respecting the procession and distinct self-subsistence, ~~that is~~ or personality, of the Spirit, I have, indeed, the same evidence in my own mind that ~~this~~[g] ~~doe~~ truth of this doctrine is a necessary consequent of the truth of the former; and I know that I have a full and weighty authority in the antiquity and universality of the article [*f 257*] in the faith of the catholic church[361] in all ages, and that not only the article itself but the mode by which it is evolved and made intelligible are substantially the same with the reasonings and representations of the Xristian Fathers of the ~~third~~ ⟨second⟩ [h]century. Yet[i] I dare not pretend to find any such express warrant in the scriptures themselves ~~not~~ (I ⟨do not⟩ mean for the truth itself), the scripture ~~injunction of~~ ⟨authority for⟩ which will be a subject for future investigation), but for the idea under which it will be here represented and the process by which that idea is evolved. For this cause, therefore, I must here once more remind the reader that my present purpose and profession [*f 258*] is wholly and exclusively to prove that it is possible to form an idea self-consistent and consistent with ~~the~~ ⟨all⟩ other truths respecting the Godhead.[362] Nay, more than this, that the idea is so far involved in that of an absolute Will, as the eternal ground of the co-eternal being and intelligence, that the latter being admitted, it is not possible, consistently with such admission, to advance any argument against the rationality of the latter; nor can any reasons be assigned why, seeing that a procession is possible and that the circle is not yet closed, we should not proceed till we ~~find~~ are led to the point from which we commenced, and in the full sense of a plenitude and sufficiency [*f 259*] that precludes all conception of any additional process, find the justification of relinquishing all further attempt.

[g] This word was originally "these", then altered to "this", then cancelled altogether

[h-i] ms: century—yet

---

be brought forward and the ground must be well & carefully examined where the system is to be erected" (*Lects 1795—CC—*95).

[361] C does not mean the Roman Catholic Church, but the "universal" church. E.g. "The present adherents of the Romish church were not Catholics, we are the Catholics. We can prove that we hold the doctrines of the primi*t*ive church for the first 300 years" (*TT—CC—*I 49). Again: "What is the *visible* Catholic Church?—The aggregate of all Christian Churches through the World"

(*CN* III 3872). Still again: "They are not Catholics! If they were, then we are heretics, and *Roman* Catholics makes no difference. Catholicism is not capable of degrees" (*TT—CC—*I 50).

[362] C is careful to emphasise that he is trying to establish the "possibility" of conceiving divine truths. Cf "In what I am to deliver, I have but one end in view, that of presenting an intelligible though not comprehensible, Idea of the possibility of that which in some way or other is, yet is not God nor one with God" (Frag 3 p 5).

~~Self~~ o A supreme, self-originated being hath communicated himself without withholding, and for this act, no recipient being conceived previously thereto, the nearest analogy, and at all events the least inappropriate term and conception that human knowledge and human language contain, is that of *begetting*, and the most expressive relation that of *Father* and *Son*. The Father hath communicated himself absolutely, not, therefore, a shadow of himself; and it would be as gross an absurdity in reason as [*f 260*] it would border on blasphemy in religion to represent the infinite product of an infinite causality as standing in the same relation as ~~a thing~~ the reflex thought of a thing to the ~~hypo~~ thing itself, in the hypothetical processes of a finite understanding. It needs only to examine that fiction of the law of the discursive intellect, if I may so call a subjective necessity arising from the mechanism of the understanding as an instrument of the mental power which we ourselves are able to correct, even as the astronomer corrects and allows for the instruments by which, and the media through which, he observes the movements of the heavenly [*f 261*] bodies, and for the correction of which the higher faculty of reason is given us—we need only, I say, comprehend the process by which the understanding converts the knowledges which it acquires by ⟨means of the⟩ sense and senses into ⟨two⟩ abstractions, the one of which is distinguished by being the direct contrary of the other, and which, as long as they are contemplated as abstractions, are unobjectionable—these are the thought and the thing:[363] the thought engrossing all the transparency, if I may so express myself, the form and intelligibility, and the thing all the substance, whence the mind itself comes gradually to be thought of as [*f 262*] a hollow capacity, a mere comprehension of realities, rather than that which is itself *j*real.[364] The*k* white tablet, the mirror, the empty canvas, etc. are but metaphors meaning the

j–k ms: real, the

[363] Throughout his intellectual career, C was exercised by the problem of the difference between thought and thing, and he considered language itself as reflecting this problem, e.g. he refers to "a mistake, which we have sought to preclude in our definition of Language—namely, that words primarily correspond to *Things*. Consequently, these writers have not perceived that tho' the Things must have existed and in most instances have been seen, prior to their modes of appearance by moving, acting, or being acted on; yet by means of the latter are they first brought into notice, so as to become the distinct objects of human Consciousness—that is, *Thoughts*—and the words *immediately* refer to our *Thoughts* of the Things, as Images or generalized Conceptions, and only by a second reflection—to the Things in themselves. —" (*CL* vi 817). For further musing on the difference between thought and thing see *CN* iii 3605; *CL* ii 1194–5.

[364] Cf C in 1832: "The pith of my system is to make the senses out of the mind—not the mind out of the senses, as Locke did" (*TT—CC*—ii 179).

same,[365] and serving only to disguise that meaning and prevent its grossness from falling abruptly on our consciousness.[366] But if these, even in ourselves, are mere abstractions, having no higher substance, use, or function but that of the plus and minus in algebra—these, I mean, by which we assimilate the thought of a thing to a shadow of a substance, but with the added absurdity of a separately and self-subsisting shadow—and if even in reference to our own finite [*f 263*] being we cannot, without contradiction to all reason, transfer this fiction to our minds or souls, infinitely less dare we attempt it concerning the supreme reality, in whom there is no abstraction, no partial qualities, but who is absolutely. If, then, we designate what we have named, ~~the~~ in imitation of the Jewish Philosopher,[367] the Deus idem et alter,[368] and for the convenience of ~~arg~~ reasoning the infinite product of the infinite causality, ~~the~~ God's co-eternal idea of himself, we recollect that it is the adequate idea, and that if it be not real it cannot express the reality, and therefore

[365] Another example of C's unvarying opposition to all theories that saw the mind of man as a passive receptacle. Locke had used the expression "white Paper" to describe the mind in its pristine state with no innate ideas (Locke 104); before him Aquinas had used the phrase "*tabula rasa*" (*Summa Theologia* I q 79 art 2). In the conflation, "white tablet", C therefore happily sums up his opposition to the entire tradition of Aristotle's view of mind. For extended consideration of the claims of innate (or connate) ideas vs the conception of the mind as a blank tablet, see *CL* II 680, 682, 686. "I do not think the Doctrine of innate Ideas even in Mr Locke's sense of the Word so utterly absurd & ridiculous, as Aristotle, Des Cartes, & Mr Locke have concurred in representing it. What if instead of innate Ideas a philosopher had asserted the existence of *constituent* Ideas" (*CL* II 696).

[366] Cf App E to *The Statesman's Manual*: "all alike pre-assume, with Mr. Locke, that the *Mind* contains only the reliques of the Senses, and therefore proceed with him to explain the substance from the shadow, the voices from the echo: they can but detect, each the others inconsistencies" (*LS—CC*—111).

[367] I.e. Philo Judaeus. For the range of C's involvement with Philo see Woodring's note 23 at *TT* (*CC*) I 34.

[368] But cf a letter of 14 Apr 1816: ". . . the essential meaning of *personality*, from the consideration of which Plato and Philo Judaeus deduced the necessity of a Deus alter et Idem" (*CL* IV 632). In the phrase "*Deus alter et idem*" C may be referring to the God-formula of Philolaus, adduced by Philo in *De mundo opificio*: "himself like himself, different from all others". Though Philo wrote in Greek, the edition of his work by Thomas Mangey in 1742—which was the best edition for a century and a half, and which C almost certainly would have used—contained in facing columns both the Greek text and a Latin translation. The translation does not seem to contain the *idem et alter* formula as such, but it does as it were paraphrase such a formula, whch in itself might accordingly appear to be C's own creation—a gloss, so to speak, on Mangey's Latin (or Philo's Greek), Maney's Latin runs: "*Attestatur mea dicta Philolaus verbis his*: Est, *inquit,* autor & princeps rerum omnium Deus, semper existens unus, stabilis, immobilis, ipse sui simillis, aliorum dissimimlis" (*Philonos tou Ioudaiou ta heuriskomena hapanta* = Philonis Judaei opera quae reperiri potuerunt omnia. Textum cum MSS contulit, interpretation-emque emendavit, universa notis & observatioinibus illustravit

is not adequate. To be the adequate idea of [*f 264*] the father,[369] it must be first substantial as the Father, and consubstantial, or of the same substance, with the Father. Nothing can be wanting that is not excluded by its own nature and in contradiction with the idea itself, but this is a relative Idea. ~~and for this reason~~ ⟨Hence⟩, inasmuch as the term ⟨"Idea"⟩ ~~itself~~ does not ⟨in itself⟩ necessarily involve relation, it becomes comparatively a less fit exponent of the truth which it is meant to convey than those which were used both before and after the Christian era in the works of philosophy as well as in the pages of Scripture—the "Son" etc., the "Word", or even than the term substituted ⟨for "Idea"⟩ by the Apostle, the "*Icon*", εικων του αυρατου θεου,[370] i.e. a [*f 265*] perfect likeness which is yet for that reason not the same, and yet its adequate and consequently self-subsis~~tin~~gent and living representative.

Every reality must have its own form. When, therefore, we contemplate the only begotten of the Father as the Alter in the union of the alter et idem, we affirm that this, namely the alterity, is the *form* of its own reality, and though one with, yet not the same as, the form of the Idem.[371] Instead of the words "Alter et Idem", let us place A = B and B = A, and we then explain our further meaning by saying that B is in A in another sense than A is in B. B is assumed in A; A is presumed in B; or A *being*, B co-eternally *becomes*. I need not warn the reader to exclude all thought of succession in the term "becomes", the employment of which term objectively in the [*f 266*] same sense in which it applies subjectively, i.e. in exclusive relation to the mechanism of the human intellect, forming one of the great errors of the mystics at the close of the s~~fix~~fteenth cen-

---

Thomas Mangey—London 1742—ɪ 24). There "Deus . . . ipse sui similis" might seem to be precisely C's "*Deus idem*", and C's "*Deus alter*" might seem to correspond to "Deus . . . aliorum dissimilis". I am indebted to Frederick Burwick for pointing me to *De mundo opificio* for the location of this formula.

[369] Cf a letter to Thomas Clarkson in 1806: "all *our* Thoughts are in the language of the old Logicians *inadequate*: i.e. no *thought*, which I have, of any *thing* comprizes the whole of that Thing. I have a distinct Thought of a Rose-Tree; but what countless properties and goings-on of that plant are there, not included in my *Thought* of it?—But the Thoughts of God, in the strict nomenclature of Plato, are all IDEAS, archetypal and anterior to all but himself alone:

therefore consummately *adequate*; and therefore according to our common habits of conception and expression, incomparably more *real* than all things besides, & which do all depend on and proceed from them in some sort perhaps as our Thoghts from those *Things*; but in a more philosophical language we dare with less hesitation to say, that they are more intensely *actual*" (*CL* ɪɪ 1195).

[370] Tr: "image of the God".

[371] Cf C in 1821: "The Dyad is the essential form of Unity, the integral *one* would be put half manifest, in a single Pole—the manifested, i.e. realized One, therefore, ipso termino, *exists* in and by self-duplication each duplicate being an Integer, and an Alter et Idem—and the *real* Image of the other" (*CN* ɪv 4829).

tury[372] and in the recent writings of Schelling and his followers, as often as they attempt to clothe the skeleton of the Spinozistic pantheism and breathe a life thereinto.[373] But of this hereafter, when we have compared our doctrine, fully developed, with the closest approximation to the same in ⟨Plotinus and⟩ the most sober of the Neo-platonic writers amongst his followers.

But this divine reciprocation[374] in and by which the Father attributeth his self to another, and the Son beholdeth and knoweth himself in the Father, is not and cannot be contemplated otherwise than as an act—[? ~~or~~] as an [*f 267*] act, therefore, of the divine Will, which is one in both and therefore an act necessarily causative of reality,[375] and, as before, first causative of its own reality. ~~It is if~~ But if real, it is therefore self-subsistent, ~~and we have only to enquire~~; but if self-subsistent, therefore distinct, and having a form of reality which is its own and not the forme of another. We have only then to enquire what this form is, or rather (for this is contained in the idea itself, and arises at the same moment with it) in what terms we shall least inappropriately clothe it ⟨in⟩ words. It has been stated as the act of the Father in the generation and contemplation of the Son, and directed towards the Son. But it is likewise, and simultaneously, as it were, the act of the Son in referring himself, and in him

[372] Cf *Biographia*: "For the writings of these mystics acted in no slight degree to prevent my mind from being imprisoned within the outline of any single dogmatic system. They contributed to keep alive the *heart* in the *head*; gave me an indistinct, yet stirring and working presentiment, that all the products of the mere reflective faculty partook of DEATH. . . . If they were too often a moving cloud of smoke to me by day, yet they were always a pillar of fire throughout the night, during my wanderings through the wilderness of doubt, and enabled me to skirt, without crossing, the sandy deserts of utter unbelief. That the system is capable of being converted into an irreligious PANTHEISM, I well know" (*BL—CC*—I 152).

[373] The statement seems unmistakably to point to the concerns of what is printed as Frag 3 below. Cf C in 1833: "I dread even the appearance of an approximation to the Neo-platonic Proclo-plotinian Scheme & Process.—" (*CL* VI 961).

[374] For "divine reciprocation" C uses

the Greek term *perichoresis*. See below f 268 and note 376; Frag 3 p 37. For a beautiful statement of the conception see below f 276.

[375] This formula, with the reflexive necessity of father and son, and the primacy of the divine Will instead of being, is precisely conceived to avoid pantheism. Cf C in 1826: "our Divines had adopted the foundations of their Faith (which they call Natural Religion) from Paganism—they begin with The Being—Ὁ Ὢν—the necessary legitimate consequence of which is Pantheism . . . . Now St John would have taught them a deeper philosopohy, and the only one compatible with a Moral religion— Θεον = τὸ Θεῖον, the Absolute, or Causa sui—ἑωρακε—i. e. essentially unutterable, deeper than all Idea— . . . —Theos *becomes* ὁ πατηρ by the Act of realizing in the Son—. It sounds paradox, but it is most certain truth, that in order of Thought, under the intrusive form of Time, the Father is a reflex from the Son . . . ." (*CL* VI 537–8).

the plenitude of ~~the Deity~~ ⟨divine⟩ forms [*f 268*] to the Father,[376] and thus directed towards the Father. By what other term can we designate this act but by ~~those of proceeding~~ affirming that it is an eternal proceeding from the Father to the Son and from the Son to the Father, but such procession being in its nature circular, at once ever refluent and ever profluent, the Greek Fathers have entitled the περιχώρησις, or the primary, absolute, co-eternal intercirculation of Deity.[377]

If such, then, be its form as an act, what is then its form as a reality? or self-subsistent? But here we meet with an apparent difficulty: in the two former ideas, that of the Father, or the Will self-realized, and that of the Son, or the Will self-contemplated and realized, and again realized in the supreme Intelligence as the Son, we have ⟨in each⟩ not[l] [*f 267ᵛ*] only an act having its own distinguishable character, but the product of ~~an~~ ⟨the⟩ act as ~~presented to us~~ *being*, in the two forms in which all true being is comprehended: ~~Ego~~ the Idem et Alter; the Supreme Mind and the adequate Idea; an infinite Effect of an Infinite cause (causa sui), which yet being the *infinite* effect, ⌈. : .⌋ ⟨and the⟩ recipient of that full power which has no other definition but that ~~which~~ ⟨it⟩ is essentially causative of reality, is itself causative; and the ~~repeate~~ repeated, or shall we ~~stay~~ duplicated, effect of the eternal, self-causing Source gives the plenary satisfaction, the perfect correspondence, to that infinite causality which without this would have been retracted in itself, ~~and so far limited, and no where absolutely infinite~~ which would be no self inasmuch as this supposes another, and therefore would be neither more nor less than the world in the [*f 266ᵛ*] scheme of Pantheism,[378] i.e. an infinite

---

[l] At this point, having reached the last folio, JHG turned the notebook upside down and wrote the remaining text on the versos from the back of the notebook (ff 267ᵛ–253ᵛ)

[376] Cf a letter to Thomas Clarkson in Oct 1806: "God is the sole self-comprehending Being, i.e. he has an Idea of himself, and that Idea is consummately adequate, & superlatively real . . . . This Idea therefore from all eternity co-existing with, & yet filiated, by the absolute Being (for as OUR purest Thoughts are *conceived*, so are God's not first conceived, but *begotten*: & thence he is verily and eminently the FATHER) is the same, as the Father in all things, but the impossible one, of self-origination. He is the substantial Image of god, in whom the Father beholds well-pleased his whole Being—and being substantial (ὁμοούσιοσ) he of divine and permanent Will, and a necessity which is the absolute opposite of compulsion, as delightedly & with as intense LOVE contemplates the Father in the Father, and the Father in himself, and himself in the Father" (*CL* II 1195).

[377] For this process cf a notebook entry of 1825: "In the mutual affirmation, the Love proceeding from the Father in the eternal pouring forth into the Son, and the Love flowing forth from the Son in the eternal attribution of his Glory, even all Glory, to the Father, the circulation and choral eddying of the Divine *Life*, the eternal Act of Communion . . ." (*CN* IV 5249).

[378] Cf C in 1826: "even the ὁ ὤν, the

power forevermore realized, and evermore absorbed and lost in its infinite product, which product is notwithstanding incapable of being contemplated as an eternal infinity, or as an infinity which is at the same time an absolute unity, but such an infinite as we mean when we apply the terms to the infinity of worlds: an aggregate of finites to which we can attach no end, and to which, indeed, it is impossible that any end should be, for it is an infinite by weakness, not by strength, an infinite formless, as that of space as far as it is infinite, and which ~~the mos~~ wherever and whenever it presents itself as form is no longer infinite. ~~True, the~~ But as soon as the duplication is presented to the mind, and with it the form of alterity, we have only to learn that in this other all others [*f 265ᵛ*] are included, that in this first ~~distinction~~ substantial intelligible distinction (=ὅ Λογος) all other distinctions that ⟨can⟩ subsist ~~indivi~~ in the indivisible unity ⟨(Λογοι θειοι)⟩ contain it, are included, to see at the same moment that under the form of being—that is, under being as not only the essence but as the form of the essence—all is completed, and that the very attempt to pass beyond it is to plunge instantly from light into mere unsubstantial darkness, [. . .] that our words have not only no correspondence in reality but none in idea, conception, image, or act, that is absolute nonsense. [? ~~ro~~]

Now that being in the sense of self-subsistence, or real distinctity, is essential to this ~~procession~~ that proceedeth has been conceded and could not be denied, the principles remaining on which all the former positions ~~had been~~ ⟨were⟩ [*f 264ᵛ*] grounded. And yet it appears no less evident that in another sense or ~~mode~~ ⟨point⟩ of contemplation, the being is not the form of the ~~aet~~ procession, or περιχωρησις,[379] but that as in the former the self-subsistence was the form of the realizing act, so here the act ⟨(το agere)⟩ remains the form of this self-subsistence. We may be allowed in borrowing an illustration from any subject, however humble, provided only we give it as an illustration and not an analogy. In the words ~~po~~ "impero",[380] ~~are~~ "αρχω",[381] we perceive that the import, the essence, if I may so say, is substantive, and hence they are followed by the genitive or dependent case in like manner as the noun substantive, but yet their form is verbal. ~~Now let the for substantive~~ On the other hand, "facies", which with ~~the majority~~ most other nouns of the 5th declension are [*f 263ᵛ*] ~~the same with the participles in each~~ but euphonies of the participles in "ens", "entis", as "res" from "reor", "series" from

supreme Reality, if it were contemplated abstractly from the Absolute Will, whose essence is to be causative of all *Reality*, would sink into a Spinozistic Deity" (*CL*

vi 600).
[379] Tr: "circulation".
[380] Tr: "I rule".
[381] Tr: "I rule".

^m"sequor". The*ⁿ* essential import, originally at least, was verbal, "a mak-
ing", "a writing", and (a frequent use still in North Britain) "a grand" fol-
lowing for attendants, while the form is nominal or substantive. In fact,
the science of grammar is but logic in its first exemplification, or rather
in its first product, Λογος, discursus, discourse, meaning ~~both~~ either, i.e.
thoughts in connexion, or ⟨connected⟩ language, and the ⟨primary⟩ dis-
tinctions of identity and alterity, ⟨of essence and form⟩, of act and of
being, constituting the groundwork and, as it were, the metaphysical con-
tents ⟨and preconditions⟩ of logic.[382] Not so properly, therefore, can the
truths of which we have been discoursing be said to borrow an illustra-
tion from the forms of grammar or the rules of logic, as that these derive
at [ƒ262ᵛ] once their possibility and their import from those primary
truths which, as they are the being of all being, ens entium, so are they
the form of all forms, idea idearum.

What, then, remains but to discover some term which, importing at
once ~~distinct~~ being and act, expresses that the distinct being is the con-
sequent of the act, and therefore expresses ~~the act as the antecedent &
distinguishing construct~~ that of the two constituents the act is the an-
tecedent and distinguishing one, i.e. the form, of the other. Here it seems
as if the circumstances common to all men, and under which the human
mind is every where formed, have guided all men to the same outward
phaenomenon as supplying the aptest exponent and shadow of this
*^o*idea—in*^p* the [ƒ261ᵛ] relation, I mean, of the air to the wind and ~~of~~ the
wind to the air. The wind,*^q* distinguishing and, as it were, individualiz-
ing itself from the air by motion, naturally expresses, we might say in-
stances, being or substance manifesting itself in the form of action, and
having its particular or individual being consequent on the act—this is
the spirit. And hence the act of appropriating the air by ~~making~~ ⟨setting⟩
it in motion ~~in th~~ from or into us, that is, by inspiration and ex- or respi-
ration, has furnished in all languages a name for the act and process of
animal life, and thence for the life contemplated as actual, the *spirit* of
life. Ascending yet higher, the rational acts of the Soul, ~~or~~ those acts, I
mean, which, and which alone, are the same ~~as~~ in all souls and for all,
considered as a self-subsistent, [ƒ260ᵛ] not divided from the soul, and

^{m–n} ms: sequor; the   *^{o–p}* ms: idea. In   *^q* ms: air

[382] Cf C in a long note of Mar 1820:
"Grammar and Logic mutually support
each other. Grammar must have been
learnt in order to the teaching of Logic;
and Logic must have been taught in order
that Grammar may be understood." "In
Grammar the Nomen, or Substantive,
corresponds to the Subject, Object, or
Thing in Logic; and the Verb to the *Act*
of the Logicians" (*CN* IV 4644). See
below, Frag 4 f 38.

~~subsis~~ from its very transcendency subsisting in act, has been ~~in~~ both in the Jewish and Christian churches distinguished from the Soul as the Spirit. Lastly, and in the highest, abstracting our attention from all the imperfections and adulterations, we approach to the perfect Idea in the Holy Spirit, that which proceedeth from the Father to the Son[383] and that which is returned from the Son to the Father,[384] and which in this circulation constitutes the eternal unity in the eternal alterity and distinction—the life of Deity in actu *ʳpurissima.*[385] This*ˢ* is truly the breath of life[386] indeed, the perpetual action of the act, the perpetual intellection ⟨alike⟩ of the Intellectus and of the Intelligibile, and the perpetual being and existing of that which saith "I Aᴍ".[387] To illustrate my [*f 259ᵛ*] meaning, and not in this place as its sanction and authority, I may be permitted to notice that in ~~the language of~~ scripture it is asserted in one place, "the spirit dwelleth in you", and in another, "my Father and I will come, and we will dwell in you", so that the spirit is clearly implied as the unity of the Father and the Son as the act in which the Father and the Son are One; and this, indeed, completes the venerable Tetractys of the most ancient philosophy,[388] the absolute or the prothesis, the Idem,

ʳ⁻ˢ ms: purissima this

[383] "And I will pray the Father, and he shall give you another Comforter, that he may abide with you for ever . . . . But the Comforter, which is the Holy Ghost, whom the Father will send in my name, he shall teach you all things, and bring all things to your remembrance, whatsoever I have said unto you" (John 14.16, 26).

[384] C in 1806 observed that "the Heresy of the Greek Church in affirming, that the Holy Spirit proceeds only from the Father, renders the thrice sacred doctrine of the Tri-unity not only above, but against Reason. Hence, too, the doctrine of the Creation assumes it's intelligibility—for the Deity in all it's three distinctions being absolutely perfect, neither susceptible of addition or diminution, the Father *in* his Son as the Image of himself surveying the Possibility of all things possible, and *with* that Love, which is the Spirit of holy Action (το άγιον πνευμα, as the air + motion = a wind) exerted that Love in that Intelligence, & that Intelligence *with* that Love, (as nothing new could be affected on the divine Nature, in it's whole Self) therefore in giving to all possible Things

contemplated in and thro' the Son that degree of Reality, of which it's nature was susceptible" (*CL* ɪɪ 1196).

[385] Tr: "in the most pure act".

[386] Tr: "And when he had said this, he breathed on them, and saith unto them, Receive ye the Holy Ghost" (John 20.22).

[387] C speaks in 1831 of "that most fundamental truth—that the *ground* of *all* reality, the Objective no less than of the Subjective, is the *absolute Subject*" (*CL* ᴠɪ 877). See further Prolegomena xᴠɪɪɪ: Subject and Object.

[388] I.e. the Pythagorean. The Tetractys, which C sometimes seems to regard as standing even above the Trinity, was a representation of the number 10, formed as an equilateral triangle with four dots or alphas across the base, three above that line, two above the line of three, and one at the apex—a two-dimensional pyramid, in other words. "This diagram, which shows at a glance that 10 = 1 + 2 + 3 + 4, was known to the Pythagoreans as the Tetractys of the Decad, and by it they swore their most binding oaths" (Kirk & Raven 230 n 2).

the Alter, and the Copula by which both are one, and the copula one with them.[389] * But in what did we find the divine necessity of the co-eternal filiation or the alterity? Even in the unwithholding and communicative goodness of the Supreme Mind.[394] Himself being all, he communicated himself to another as to a Self. But such communication is Love, and in what is the re-attribution of that Self to the Communicator but Love? This, too, is Love, filial Love—Love is the Spirit of God, and God is love.[395]

Thus we have the Absolute under three distinct ideas, and the essential inseparability of these without interference with their no less ⟨essen-

---

* [*Written on ff 259ᵛ–258ᵛ, the following passage is placed in brackets and preceded by an asterisk in the ms, as if meant to be treated as a note:*] Hence, however doubtful the authenticity of the seventh verse in the Epistle of John may be,[390] and though, in fact, I have little doubt that it was a gloss originating in a passage of Tertullian[391] and inferred from the text in John's Gospel, the logic of the conclusion remains valid, "for the Father and I are One"[392]—the "hi tres unùm sunt"[393] is an inevitable consequent.

"Observe, however", writes C, "that both the Polar System or Tetractys, and the Tri-une, are necessary views of the same truth, and by no means does either invalidate the practical Reality of the other" (*CM—CC—*ɪ 642). Again, "Tetractys or Tetrad is the form of God, which again is reducible into, and the same in reality with the Trinity" (*TT—CC—*ɪ 289). See Perkins 62–7, where it is suggested that "much of [C's] development of the theme [of the Tetractys] was based on the comprehensive treatment given to it in Ralph Cudworth's *True Intellectual System of the Universe*" (62). See further below, Frag 3 p 166.

[389] In a note of 1818, where C says that "All Physiology, and vital Physiology or Zoonomy by an especial claim, demands the tetradic Logic", he then says that "the universal formula for this highest form of Reason is the following:

Prothesis
Thesis   Antithesis
Synthesis"

(*SW & F—CC—*ɪ 710). See further Prolegomena x: The *Magnum Opus* and the Principle of Polarity.

[390] There are three *Epistles of John*,

and C does not give enough information to identify with certainty that of which he speaks. 1 John 4.7–21, however, virtually explodes with invocations of love and its relationship to God, to Jesus, and to us.

[391] Quintus Septimius Florens Tertullianus (c 155–220 A.D.), Church Father. Born at Carthage. Among his works were *Apologeticum* (in defence of Christianity), *Adversus Marcionem, De anima*, and *De praescriptione hereticorum*.

[392] "I and *my* Father are one" (John 10.30).

[393] Tr: "these three are one".

[394] Cf C in the *Biographia*, speaking of the *magnum opus*: "I do not hesitate a moment in advising and urging you to withdraw the Chapter [i. e. "your Chapter on the Imagination"] from the present work, and to reserve it for your announced treatises on the Logos or communicative intellect in Man and Deity" (*BL—CC—*ɪ 302). We find in the paragraph above the resounding urgency of the rubric "Logos or communicative intellect".

[395] "He that loveth not knoweth not God; for God is love" (1 John 4.8).

tial⟩ interdistinction is the [*f* 257ᵛ] Divine Idea, which, were it possible to abstract so as to remove all assertion of its reality from the mind and to give it, as to the lines, surfaces, and perfect figures of geometry, mental subsistence only, would yet be the most glorious birth of the human soul, a birth reflecting such unspeakable worth and sublimity in the soul whose offspring it was, that it would almost justify us in concluding that reality from the idea, which we had refused to involve in it. For in this idea alone can we render intelligible to our minds that positive unity which is, ~~not because~~ and is affirmed to be, that which it is ⟨wholly⟩ because it is, and not, as in all subjects that only partake of unity, ~~and~~ ⟨each of⟩ which ~~are~~ is A because and inasmuch as it is not B, not C, and so on through the whole series of individuals, whose imperfect [*f* 256ᵛ] unity therefore hath no form of its own, hath no being for its form, but borrows its form from its own opposite and from the opposite of being, from negation or limit, and from multeity. The captive, which is reluctantly constrained in its bonds, is forced to announce the existence of that which hath enthralled it, but with this all-comprehending one, which excludes no true being, we are capable of apprehending, though not of comprehending,[396] substantial truths distinctly subsistent, and yet ⟨one⟩ with the truth and the true, even as the true is one with the good—in the Son only doth the Father love the world,[397] in the adequate idea only doth the supreme mind behold all other forms, which ⟨can⟩ have no form if they have no being, and which have no being except as they are one with that great living Idea [*f* 255ᵛ] which is one with the Father.[398] Whether this doctrine of the living, uncreated truths, the rays of the eternal sun in which the light, radiance, and efficacy of the absolute is contemplated, has*ᵗ* any such moral interest, any such bearing on the practical Will and the intellect in connexion with the practical Will, that is, on our Faith, ~~is~~ ⟨remains*ᵘ*⟩ to be shown. It is sufficient for the present that it is a doctrine derived from the transcendent unity of God no less than from his essential omnipotence, and which cannot, therefore, be inconsistent with that *ᵛ*unity, while*ʷ* on the other hand it seems not possible to deny the doc-

---

ᵗ ms: have   *ᵘ* ms: remain   *ᵛ⁻ʷ* ms: unity. While

[396] For the distinction of apprehend and comprehend, to which C frequently appeals, cf e.g. his comment on Waterland: "how can any Spiritual Truth be comprehended? Who can *com*prehend his own Will or his own Personëity (i.e. his 'I') or his own Mind, i.e. his Person, or his own *Life*? But we can distinctly *ap*prehend them" (Brinkley 385). The distinction is co-ordinate with Jaspers's essential conception of *Das Umgreifende das Ich bin.*

[397] E.g.: "As the Father hath loved me, so have I loved you: continue ye in my love" (John 15.9).

[398] E.g.: "Believe me that I am in the Father, and the Father in me" (John 14.11).

trine without either reducing the idea of God into a formless and hollow unity, or rather sameness, like the unity of space, or into an aggregate of forms with no [*f 254ᵛ*] other unity than the subjective one ~~of sim~~ from the simultaneous beholding of many. Such would be the unity of the universe considered as God.[399] Or, lastly, to an exclusive individuality, that of a Jupiter or a Mars, which is Idolatry. These ends, however, might, I readily grant, be sufficiently provided by the simple statement of the transcendency of the divine unity. This would apply, however, to the doctrine of the Trinity in its common form equally as to that of the uncreated ideas; and in the historical portion of this work it would have been incumbent on us to have begun[400] with the asser-tion of the practical necessity of the Trinity,[401] which, and not its truth merely,[402] would constitute it an article of Faith,[403] for in that portion of our work we must have met with the [*f 253ᵛ*] doctrine[404] of redemption at the very threshold,[405] and with it the divinity of the Redeemer, as positions mutually supporting and requiring each other.[406] But before this, the need and the capability of redemption,[407] and the possibility and, as far as we can, the

---

[399] Cf *Aids to Reflection*: "It would no longer be the God, in whom we believe; but a stoical Fate, or the superessential One of Plotinus, to whom neither intelligence, nor self-consciousness, nor life, nor even being can be attributed, or lastly the World itself, the indivisible one and only substance (substantia una et unica) of Spinoza, of which all phaenomena, all particular and individual things, lives, minds, thoughts, and actions are but modifications" (*AR*—1825—127).

[400] Cf *Aids to Reflection*: "In right order I must have commenced with the Articles of the Trinity and the Apostacy, including the question respecting the Origin of Evil, and the Incarnation of the WORD" (*AR*—1825—247).

[401] Perhaps because "The Trinity is the Will—the Reason or Word—the Love or Life; as we distinguish these three, so we must unite them in one God" (*TT—CC*—I 127).

[402] Cf C in 1810: "The doctrine of Sin & Redemption first authorized by practically necessitating the doctrine of the Trinity—before that Time it was a pure Philosopheme, tho' most beautiful and accurate" (*CN* III 3814).

[403] Cf C: "The Trinity is the only Form, in which an Idea of God is possi-ble—unless indeed it be a Spinozistic or World-God" (*CM—CC*—II 1145).

[404] That doctrine too is an article of faith. In 1830, in a piece called "On the Articles of Faith Necessary to Christians", C says that "Man needs a Redemption, which of his own power he is incapable of effecting, but it hath been offered to Man in, by and thro' the Mediator, together with all the means of finally effecting it to as many, as truly receive the offer.—" (*SW & F—CC*—II 1485).

[405] "For Christianity and REDEMPTION are equivalent terms" (*AR*—1825—303).

[406] Cf C in 1810: "Solely in consequence of our Redemption does the Trinity become a Doctrine, the Belief of which as real is commanded by our Conscience. But to Christians it is commanded—and it is false candour in a Christian believing in Original Sin & Redemption therefrom, to admit that any man denying the Divinity of Christ can be a Christian" (*CN* III 4005). C de-synomized faith and belief; and see "Reflections on Belief" (*SW & F—CC*—II 826–8).

[407] The need and capability were in C's mind long before he had embarked

intelligibility of both are to be enucleated;[408] and we must begin, therefore, with the doctrine of the Ideas[409] as antecedent, but only because ancillary, to the more important truths by which religion rises above philosophy,[410] even that most religious philosophy which,[411] listening in childlike silence in the outer courts of the temple, blended fragmentary voices from the shrine with the inward words of her own meditation.[412]

on serious theological study. As early as Nov 1795 he writes: "Heaven forbid, that I should not now have faith, that however foul your Stream may run here, yet that it will filtrate & become pure in it's subterraneous Passage to the Ocean of Universal Redemption" (*CL* I 168).

[408] Cf *Aids to Reflection*: "The most *momentous* question a man can ask is, Have I a Saviour" (*AR*—1825—243). "The entire Scheme of *necessary* Faith may be reduced to two heads, 1. the Object and Occasion, and 2. the fact and effect, of our redemption by Christ" (ibid. 249).

[409] Cf *Aids to Reflection*: "On the doctrine of Redemption depends the *Faith*, the *Duty*, of believing in the Divinity of our Lord. And this again is the strongest Ground for the reality of that Idea, in which alone the Divinity can be received without breach of the faith in the unity of the Godhead. But such is the Idea of the Trinity" (*AR*—1825—175).

[410] Cf the *Philosophical Lectures*: "in truth philosophy itself is nothing but mockery unless it is considered the transit from paganism to religion" (*P Lects*—1949—224).

[411] "What is Xtianity but divine & pre-eminent Philosophy?" (Brinkley 377).

[412] Cf *The Friend*: "Religion therefore is the ultimate aim of philosophy, in consequence of which philosophy itself becomes the supplement of the sciences, both as the convergence of all to the common end, namely, wisdom; and as supplying the copula, which modified in each in the comprehension of its parts to one whole, is in its principles common to all, as integral parts of one system" (*Friend—CC*—I 463).

FRAGMENT 3

HEHL HM 8195 pp 3–301; the "Divine Ideas" notebook. Inside the front cover of the notebook C wrote, probably between Dec 1820 and Jan 1821, the addresses of Ralph Wedgwood, Thomas Monkhouse, and John Watson: see *SW & F (CC)* 871. Inside the back cover he wrote in pencil, at an unknown date, a quotation he mistakenly attributed to Jeremy Taylor, as in an outline of the *Logic* (*Logic—CC*—284 and n): "In all discourses and intercourses of mankind by words we must agree concerning each others' meaning: and how is this possible, unless we first determine what we ourselves mean by the words we use?— Bishop Taylor (On the Real Presence.)." The ms has been paginated in pencil, presumably by a librarian at the Huntington. The *Op Max* text is written in ink in JHG's hand with occasional corrections and insertions in C's hand. The paper does not appear to be watermarked, although the fragile condition of the ms now (1997) makes examination difficult.

At p 267 in the ms a parenthesis calls for an extract from the *Bhagavadgita* to be inserted into the text. The first leaf of this extract, which was copied out by JG's sometime assistant John Watson (who was also one of C's amanuenses for the *Logic*), is tipped into the ms at p 266, while the second leaf, which includes a transcript of C's commentary on the extract, is preserved at VCL (MS LT 32). In the present edition the complete extract is printed as part of the present fragment, while C's commentary is printed separately in App C below. In the event, much of that commentary, as recorded by Watson, was incorporated verbatim into the text of this fragment; these correspondences are signalled in footnotes.

Muirhead (in his App C) published pp 9–15, 39–43, 123–37, 247–51, and 267–73 of the ms, regularising the spelling and punctuation and omitting cancellations.

DATE. Probably 1822–3. The first two pages of the notebook contain a comment in C's hand on the *Memoirs of the Life of the Rev. Mr. Thomas Halyburton* (10th ed Edinburgh 1797): see *SW & F (CC)* 992–3. If C wrote his comment on Halyburton on 29 July 1822 (as a related note in *CN* IV 4909 suggests), then it is likely that the "Divine Ideas" text, which follows it immediately in the notebook, was written down after that date. The discussion of Indian mythology (pp 261–81 of the ms) must have been written down at the same time as or later than Watson's extract from the *Bhagavadgita*, but that could have been any time from Dec 1820 to Oct 1823 (see the headnote to Frag 1 above). A parenthesis on p 299 of the ms refers to an extract from Berkeley which may be the one that John Watson copied for C into Notebook 30 in 1823 (*CN* IV 5096).

214

[*p 3*]   Chapter

ON THE DIVINE IDEAS

I cannot commence this subject more fitly than by disclaiming all wish and attempt of gratifying a speculative refinement in myself, or an idle presumptuous curiosity in others. I leave ~~it~~ the heavenly hierarchies with all their distinctions, ~~thrones, d~~ "Thrones, Dominations, Princedoms, Virtues, Powers",[1] Names, Fervours, Energies, with the long et cetera of the Cabbalists and degenerated Platonists, to the admirers of the false D~~y~~ionysius,[2] and the obscure students of Cornelius Agrippa.[3] All pretense, all approach to particularize on such ⟨a⟩ subject involves its own confutation: for it is the application of the understanding through the medium of the fancy to truths of which the reason, exclusively, is both the substance beheld and the eye beholding.[4] Or had the evident contra-

---

[1] Orders of angels in the distinctions of the Pseudo-Dionysius. See following footnote. The enumeration is in quotation marks because it comes from *Paradise Lost*, v, line 601.

[2] Pseudo-Dionysius (c 500 A.D.), author of *The Celestial Hierarchy*; for centuries identified with St Paul's convert, Dionysius the Areopagite; hence the name Pseudo-Dionysius. His hierarchies were an elaboration of the henads of Proclus: "The influence which Proclus exercised upon early medieval thought may be called accidental, in the sense that it would scarcely have been felt but for the activity of an unknown eccentric who within a generation of Proclus' death conceived the idea of dressing his philosophy in Christian draperies and passing it off as the work of a convert of St Paul. Though challenged by Hypatius of Ephesus and others, in official quarters the fraud met with complete and astonishing success. Not only did the works of 'Dionysius the Areopagite' escape the ban of heresy which they certainly merited, but by 649 they had become an 'Urkunde' sufficiently important for a Pope to bring before the Lateran Council a question concerning a disputed reading in one of them. About the same date they were made the subject of an elaborate commentary by Maximus the Confessor, the first of a long succession of com-

mentaries from the hands of Erigena, Hugh of St. Victor, Robert Grosseteste, Albertus Magnus, Thomas Aquinas and others" (E. R. Dodds xxcvi–xxvii).

[3] Heinrich Cornelius Agrippa (1486–1535); German physician, theologian, and philosopher; physician to Louise of Savoy (1524–27); historiographer to Emperor Charles v at Antwerp (1529–30); author of *De occulta philosophia* (c 1510, pub 1531), a cosmology based on cabalistic and Pythagorean analyses and magic that helped link him to the Faust legend. C discusses Agrippa at length in the *Philosophical Lectures*: "It is not easy to conceive what that man might have promised himself, would he have preferred common sense to cunning, would he have taken the shorter way of becoming respectable instead of playing the knave and running round that long and weary way of playing the fool. He possessed genius as a poet. He had uncommon acuteness as a philosopher. His remarks, whenever they occur upon the powers of the human mind, are wonderfully applied" (*P Lects*—1949—302).

[4] Cf C in a marginal note: "Strange yet from the date of the Book of the Celestial Hierarchies of the pretended Dyonisius the Areopagite to the Translator, Joannes Scotus Erigena, the Contemporary of Alfred, and from Scotus to the Rev. J[ohn] O[xlee] 1815, not unfre-

diction implied [*p 5*] in the attempt failed in preventing it, the fearful abuses, the degrading idolatrous superstitions, which have resulted from ~~the~~ ⟨its⟩ application to that beautiful yet awful article of the Christian faith, the unbroken unity of the ~~tri~~ triumphant with the militant church, or the communion of Saints, ~~must have~~ form too palpable a warning not to have deterred me even ~~on moral~~ from motives of common morality. In what I am about to deliver I have but one end in view, that of presenting an intelligible though not comprehensible[5] Idea of the possibility of ~~an existence~~ that which in some sense or other is, yet is not God nor One with God. Hitherto, the ~~truths~~ ⟨objects⟩ of which we have been treating (let the inadequateness and impropriety of the term be ~~forgiven~~ felt yet forgiven, or attributed to the inherent imperfections and unfitness of the medium)—hitherto, I say, the ineffable objects have been those of eternity, an ineffable cycle of Will, Being, Intelligence, and communicative [*p 7*] Life, Love, and Action; but without change, without succession. Even such in themselves or in their symbols are the proper subjects of philosophy in its strictest sense, as distinguished from History. In order to contemplate the laws even of nature, in order to refer the phaenomena[6] of the perishable world to a permanent law, we are constrained to consider each ~~as an~~ ⟨minutest⟩ ~~elements~~ as a living germ in which the present involves the future, and in the ~~infinite~~ the ⟨in⟩finite abides potentially. That hidden mystery in every form of existence, which, ~~if con~~ when contemplated under the relations of time presents it-

---

quent Delusion of mistaking Pantheism disguised in a fancy-dress of pious phrases for a more spiritual and philosophic Form of Christian Faith!—Nay, stranger still—to imagine with Scotus, and Mr O., that in a Scheme, which even more directly than ⟨even⟩ the grosser species of Atheism, precludes all moral responsibility and subverts all essential difference of Right and Wrong, they have found the means of proving and explaining the 'Christian doctrine of the Trinity and Incarnation'—i. e. the great and only sufficient Antidotes of the right faith gainst this insidious poison. For Pantheism, trick it up as you will is but a painted Atheism—" (*CM—CC—* III 1083).

[5] C frequently makes a distinction between "apprehend" and "comprehend", and such distinction is essential to any discourse that involves the simultaneous existence of finites and the infinite existence of God. Such matters may be "intelligible"—i. e. rationally possible—but are not understandable, not "comprehensible". The mind may touch them, as it were, but cannot get itself around them.

[6] C (like Berkeley and other eighteenth-century writers) habitually spells the word not phenomena but phaenomena, to emphasize its pre-history in Latin (and Greek) philosophy. The spelling silently re-directs attention from Kant to Aristotle (e.g. φαινομενα και εντελεχαι) and other Greek philosophers. The word φαινομενον, however, is most closely associated with the thought of the Greek sceptics, and it is Sextus Empiricus and others to whom Kant looks for this and other elements in his philosophical vocabulary.

self to the understanding, now retrospectively as an infinite ascent of causes,[7] and now prospectively as an interminable progression of effects[8]—that which when contemplated ~~in space~~ under the relations of space is considered as a law of action and re-action coinstantaneous, continuous, and extending beyond all bound—this same mystery, freed from the phaenomena of time and space and [*p 9*] seen in the depth of real being, no longer therefore a nature, namely a That which is not but which is for ever only about to be,[9] reveals itself to the pure reason as the actual immanence, or (to borrow the term chosen by Bishop Sherlock,[10] to express the same sense) the "in-being" of all in all.[11] Are we struck at beholding the cope of heaven imaged in a dew-drop? The least of the animalcula[12] to which that dew-drop is an ocean presents an infi-

[7] The necessity of extricating "infinite ascent" is what involves C in the evolutionary hypotheses of Schelling and the *Naturphilosophen*. A happier view of ascent is provided by a statement in *Aids to Reflection*: "Thus all lower Natures find their highest Good in semblances and seekings of that which is higher and better. All things strive to ascend, and ascend in their strivings" (*AR*—1825—12).

[8] For descent as opposed to ascent, or as the same matter viewed from a different (and eternal) perspective, cf a notebook entry of July 1826: "Having thus ascended to the Highest, viz. to the Prothesis, i.e. the Personeity of the Absolute Will—there rest awhile, and then commence the descent—1. Thesis = I AM—the Supreme Mind in the form of Will—/the Supreme Will in the form of Reason (Λογος) the union of both in the SPIRIT, or celestial Life—The *chasm*—or apostasy, or the self-position of the Finite—. From this point the duplicity or two sides commences—" (*CN* IV 5411).

[9] Cf Wordsworth: "Our destiny, our nature, and our home, / Is with infinitude—and only there; / With hope it is, hope that can never die, / Effort, and expectation, and desire, / And something evermore about to be" (*Prelude*—1805—VI lines 538–42).

[10] Not Thomas Sherlock (1678–1761), Bp of London. His more famous father, William Sherlock (1641–1707),

was not a bishop but was Dean of St Paul's (as C most certainly knew) and was the author of works some of which were annotated by C. His *Vindication of the Doctrines of the Trinity and of the Incarnation* (1690) led to a charge of tritheism by Robert South, and his *Present State of the Socinian Controversy* (1698) abandoned most of his earlier theological doctrines. C at one point refers to "the oscillatory creed of Sherlock, now swinging to Tritheism in the recoil from Sabellianism, and again to Sabellianism in the recoil from Tritheism" (Shedd V 76).

[11] Cf *Statesman's Manual*: "This same mystery freed from the phenomena of Time and Space, and seen in the depth of *real* Being, reveals itself to the pure Reason as the actual immanence of ALL in EACH" (*LS—CC*—50). To the word "immanence" the 1839 edition adds "or in-being", and a note: "In-being is the word chosen by Bishop Sherlock to explain this sense. See his Tract on the Athanasian Creed, 1827." Thus Sherlock: "Now this intimate Union and *In-being*, when we speak of an essential Union of pure and infinite Minds in a mutual consciousness . . . an universal sensation of each other, to know and feel each other, as they know themselves" (William Sherlock *A Vindication of the Doctrine of the Holy and Ever Blessed Trinity*—1690—52).

[12] The word was used by Leeuwenhoek to describe the protozoa first seen

nite problem, of which the omnipresent is the only solution. If, then, even the philosophy of nature can remain philosophy only by rising above nature, and by abstracting from nature,[13] much less is it possible for the philosophy of the Eternal to evolve out of itself, that is, out of the pure reason,[14] the ~~existe reality~~ actual existence of change, of ⟨the⟩ beginning of that which is, yet before was not, of that which has been and is not, of ⟨that⟩ which is not yet but is to come. The organs of philosophy [*p 11*] are Ideas only, and we arrive at ideas by abstracting from time; and this[a] ~~so true that~~ truth is so obvious that even in popular language we declare it impossible to form any idea of matter or of pleasure or of pain. Yet shall we say that these are not? Is there no history, because history, or the succession of acts and agents and of phaenomena considered as the effects, products or results of acts and agents is not the same with philosophy, though it is grounded on it? Do the mechanical powers—the lever, the pulley, the screw—not exist because they are not the same with the immediate and magical and everywhere present powers without which the~~y~~ ⟨former⟩ yet could not be? The passage from the absolute to the ⟨separated⟩ finite, this is the difficulty, which who shall overcome? This is the chasm which ages have tried in vain to overbridge.[15] If the finite be in no sense separate from the infinite, if it be one with the same, whence proceeded Evil? For the finite [*p 13*] can be one with the absolute, inasmuch only as it represents the absolute ~~truly~~ verily under some particular form. Herein no negation is implied, nor privation, no negation from without; for it is the position of all in the each. But that it is the form which it is, so far from being the result of negation, that even in the less imperfect shapes of the senses, those which proceed from living forms, as [? ~~the~~] in all the objects of the organic world ⟨⟨(take a plant as an instance)⟩⟩, this shape is at once the product, and the sign of the pos-

---

[a] ms: this is

---

through his microscope: "Among these there were, besides, very many little animalcules, whereof some were roundish, while others, a bit bigger, consisted of an oval" (*Leeuwenhoek* 110).

[13] Cf e.g. *The Friend*: "The grand problem, the solution of which forms, according to Plato, the final object and distinctive character of philosophy, is this: *for all that exists conditionally* (i.e. the existence of which is inconceivable except under the condition of its dependency on some other as its antecedent) *to find a ground that is unconditional and*

absolute" (*Friend—CC*—ı 461).

[14] C, significantly, customarily evolves it out of the dialectic interplay of Reason *and* Will. Cf e.g. *Statesman's Manual*: "But neither can reason or religion exist or co-exist as reason and religion, except as far as they are activated by the WILL" (*LS—CC*—65).

[15] Cf a note of 1826: "The *chasm*— or apostasy, or the self-position of the *Finite*—" (*CN* ıv 5411). C is at great pains to overbridge the chasm while still maintaining recognition that it is a chasm; otherwise all solutions are pantheistic.

itive power, of the plant; and a form, or rather a parent shape, proceeding from negation either simply or in connexion with an overpowering impression from without, is found only in the inanimate—the ⟨termination of the⟩ path of the arrow in the air, or the form of the fragment storm-rent from the rock, or of the ~~grain~~ ⟨aggregate⟩ of sand ⟨in the pebble⟩, which the pressure of the ~~tide~~ waters has compressed,[b] and the motion of the tide rounded. But if, on the other hand, the [*p 15*] ~~evil~~ finite here spoken of be separate and diverse from the absolute, we might indeed explain the evil therefrom; but then the question would return, how was the finite possible? I said hastily that from such a finite we might educe the origin of evil: but such a finite were evil! Still the standing room, the δος που στώ,[c] [16] remains unanswered, unattained.

This knot, which we cannot untie, ~~we may cut~~ sundry philosophers have allowed themselves to cut, with what success we shall see ~~her~~ in the conclusion of this chapter, when having fully explained our own system, we shall compare it with that of others who have gone before us: Platonists or Christian Mystics[17] or Spinozists[18] before and since Spin-

---

[b] ms: compression,   [c] ms: ςτώ

[16] Tr: "give me a place to stand" [and I will move the earth] (Archimedes).

[17] C had great respect for "Platonists", as indeed for Spinoza. And in the *Biographia* he renders thanks to the "Christian Mystics": "For the writings of these mystics acted in no slight degree to prevent my mind from being imprisoned within the outline of any single dogmatic system. They contributed to keep alive the *heart* in the *head*; gave me an indistinct, yet stirring and working presentiment, that all the products of the mere *reflective* faculty partook of DEATH, and were as the rattling twigs and sprays in winter, into which a sap was yet to be propelled, from some root to which I had not penetrated, if they were to afford my soul either food or shelter. If they were too often a moving cloud of smoke to me by day, yet they were always a pillar of fire throughout the night, during my wanderings through the wilderness of doubt, and enabled me to skirt, without crossing, the sandy deserts of utter unbelief" (*BL—CC*—ı 152). But C's criticism and ultimate rejection of all these schemes of thought are based on the fact that they are pantheistic and thus op-

posed to all the emphases he held dear. To be sure, in the *Biographia* C flirts longingly with pantheism; immediately following the statement just quoted, he says: "That the system is capable of being converted into an irreligious PANTHEISM, I well know. The ETHICS of SPINOZA, may, or may not, be an instance. But at no time could I believe, that *in itself* and *essentially* it is incompatible with religion" (*BL—CC*—ı 152). By the time of the *Op Max*, however, C had reverted—as multitudinous quotations in this edition show—to a hardened rejection of pantheism or Spinozism. By that time also he can speak of "the errors of the mystics at the close of the fifteenth century" (see above, Frag 2 f 266). For discussion of the formative elements of C's acceptance/rejection ambivalence about pantheism, see "Coleridge and the Dilemmas of Pantheism," *CPT* 107–90. His final and predominating position was "that Pantheism = Atheism and that there is no other Atheism actually existing or speculatively conceivable, but Pantheism" (Brinkley 382).

[18] Cf e.g. C's disparaging alignment

oza. For the present we answer the question thus. We admit the impossibility of grounding the fact of change, the actual existence of evil, and with it all the proper subjects of history, both for evil and for good [*p 17*] (and what indeed is history in its widest extent and grandest sense but the struggle of good and evil, leading towards the [? sal] defeat and the extirpation of the latter by the aiding influence of that good in which there is no evil!). But though the facts, the actual existence, have their beginning and their end in time, yet the possibility may be eternal, that is, without relation to time, and as such it may be an idea, ~~with which philosophy~~ in which, as in ⟨an⟩ appropriate mirror, philosophy might contemplate the desired truth. But here two conditions are required. First, this possibility must be rendered intelligible, it must be found involved in some eternal truth, in the idea of which the mind had ~~before~~ previously rested; and secondly, it must be a *mere* possibility, that which must cease to be eternal in being more or other than a mere possibility. But if we obtain this, we obtain little indeed, and a thin and [*p 19*] insipid*d* nutriment if the gratification of our intellectual powers and instincts were sought or intended; but very much and all that is necessary, nay, all that is expedient or desirable, all that would not in our present state of being be incongruous and detrimental, if the moral interest be the source of the enquiry, and the reconcilement of the moral faith with the reason be the object. First, then, it seems evident that the same reason which has compelled us to ⟨the⟩ conclusion that whatever is distinct in the Deity must be real, substantially distinct, and distinctly substantial—that the same reason, which has led us to admit the self-subsistence of the adequate idea of the supreme mind, must hold equally good of whatever ideas are distinctly contained in that adequate idea, and that these distinctities are both real and actual, as in whom and through whom the eternal act of the Father and the Son, the uniting, receiving, and communi[*p 21*]cating Spirit[19] lives and moves.[20] The Will, the absolute Will, is that which is essentially causative of reality,[21] essentially, and absolutely, that is, boundless from without and from within.[22] This is our first principle.[23]

---

d ms: & insipid

---

of "the Proclo-plotinian Platonists" with "their Spinosistic imitators, the nature-philosophers of modern Germany" (*CM—CC*—III 909).

[19] For C's emphasis on spiritual communication, see above, Frag 2 f 278.

[20] Cf Acts 17.28: "For in him we live, and move, and have our being".

[21] See above, Frag 2 f 170.

[22] Cf a notebook entry: "The Absolute Will essentially causative of Reality (ουσιας) Almight = Θεος. Θεον ουδεις εὡρακε πὡποτε" (*CN* IV 5298).

[23] See above, Frag 2 f 239, f 240, and f 242. "The Will, whose other name is the Good, is the Absolute One pure of the

This is the position contained in the postulate of the reality of Will at all.[24] Difficult, we have never attempted to conceal from ourselves, is it to master this first idea.[25] Nor could it be otherwise, inasmuch as an insight into its truth is not possible; and ~~our~~ we are perforce constrained to the only ~~equivalent~~ succedaneum, the sense of the necessary falsehood of the contrary. We affirm it, ⟨not⟩ because we ~~clearly~~ comprehend the affirmation, but because we clearly comprehend the absurdity of the denial. But in this affirmation it is involved that what is essentially causative of all possible reality must be causative of its own reality.[26] It is not the cause of all reality because it is causative of its own, but it is necessarily causative of its own reality because it is essentially causative of all possible reality. [*p 23*] These, however, are so far one, that being absolute and infinite, such must the reality be: consequently the ⟨absolute⟩ Will self-realized must in its own reality[27] include the plenitude of all that is real as far as it is absolutely real, that is, as far as the reality is actual and not merely possible. Herein lies the depth of the mystery, which without superstitious or slavish fear we may truly call tremendous, and which more or less openly, in words more or less convenient, has been now affirmed and now supposed, in all the great and stirring epochs of the Christian theology:[e] ~~That perilous line on which we pass balancing the soul over a fearful abysm.~~ the[f] narrow isthmus which we have to pass, with atheism on the one side, or a world without a God, and Pantheism, or a world that is itself God;[28] on the one side Fatalism, on the other a sensual Polytheism, as its inevitable consequents. For in the Absolute Will we conceive what [*p 25*] in God ~~and~~ as the ~~s~~Supreme Being, as the ~~Father~~ Divine Person, we could not admit if we dared, for it would involve a contradiction; and we dared not if we could, for it would introduce imperfection into the reality of Deity. For in God,

---

[e] Full stop in ms [f] ms: The

Many, out of whom the Many eradiates as so many iterations of the One" (*CN* iv 5076).

[24] "Will is the xyz or + 0, the Ground of Being, the Suppositum, Timeless but in the Order of Production and Conception, the necessary Pre-suppositum" (*CN* iv 5256).

[25] "An IDEA, in the *highest* sense of that word, cannot be conveyed but by a *symbol*" (*BL*—*CC*—i 156). Again: "one Diagnostic, or contra-distinguishing Mark, appertaining to all *Ideas*, is— that they are inexpressible by adequate words—an Idea can only be expressed

(more correctly, *suggested*) by two contradictory Positions" (Brinkley 291).

[26] For this essential of his scheme, C often utilizes the phrase *causa sui*, borrowed from Spinoza and the Scholastics. See above, Frag 2 f 269, f 225, and f 289.

[27] See Frag 2 f 269; see also f 239.

[28] The two abysses, one on either side of the isthmus, are the same in their unplumbed depths: "it is a matter of perfect indifference, whether we assert a World without God, or make God the World. The one is as truly Atheism as the other" (Brinkley 381).

as God, the absolute Will is absolutely realized;[29] but the actual alone is absolutely real, and the possible, therefore, or potential, as contradistinguished from the actual, and which in all lower than Deity is the opposite pole of the actual (vide Logic Part III)[g] cannot be in God. This Boëthius, the Fathers, and the Schoolmen have expressed in the words "Deus est actus purissimus sine ulla potentialitate".[30] Even so, by parity of reason, whatever is in God as one with God is and can be such only as far as it is actual; but in the absolute Will, which abideth in the Father,[31] the Word and the Spirit, totally and absolutely in each, one and the same in all, the ground of all reality is contained, even of that [*p 27*] which is only possible and conditionally possible [h]alone. And[i] this is indeed implied in the idea and essential conception of a Will, for a Will in which there is no possibility ceases to be a Will absolutely. Hence in speaking of the Will self-realized, which is more than the Will conceived absolutely, we do not hesitate to affirm the necessity of the divine Nature and attributes. Nay, we affirm it, with the clearest insight, that such necessity is the perfection and proper prerogative of God. It is impossible for God not to be God, and it is impossible for a part which is one with the whole to be other than the whole as long as it remains one with the whole.[32] It does not, however, follow that in the part as a part there should not be contained the conditional possibility of willing to be a part that is not one with the whole, of willing to be in itself and not in another; for this is not precluded in the Will, or [*p 29*] in a realization of the Will through and in the Divine Will: it is precluded only by the absolute self-realization of the absolute Will.

We entreat the reader not to be impatient with himself or with us if he does not immediately or speedily comprehend the force of what we have here written. We entreat him rather to proceed onward, and particularly to the statement of doctrines, in which one or other of these ideas have been overlooked, and to the fearful consequences of such oversight, and then to re-peruse ~~our~~ ⟨the⟩ present and preceding passages.

---

[g] Closing parenthesis inserted   [h–i] ms: alone: and

[29] But the "Will, the ineffable Causa Sui, et Fons Unitatis in tota infinita entis sui plenitudine, is evermore and eternally impassible" (*CN* IV 5413).

[30] C frequently adduces this statement, which means "God is most pure act without any potentiality". It is not a mere flourish, but is indispensable to his position (see below, p 40). It enlists an entire tradition of theological realisation. Cf e.g. *CM* (*CC*) II 1186; *CM* (*CC*) I 232; II 1195. See above e.g. Frag 2 f 224.

[31] See above, Frag 2 f 170: "But the absolute will and the supreme Reason are One, and it is the identity of these which we mean, adoring rather than expressing, by the term *God*."

[32] This consideration underlies C's doctrine of the nature of the symbol: "It always partakes of the Reality which it renders intelligible; and while it enunciates the whole, abides itself as a living

First, then, what ~~do~~ conception do we attach to *Idea*? Or rather, as, whatever this conception may be, it must in our present ~~fo~~ scheme of reasoning derive itself from the divine Ideas, what do we wish to convey by this? I know of no other answer than that a divine Idea is the [*p 31*] Omnipresence or Omnipotence represented intelligentially in some one of the possible forms, which are the plenitude of the divine Intelligence, the Logos or substantial adequate Idea of the Supreme Mind; and that as such the Ideas are necessarily immutable, inasmuch as they are One with the ⟨co-⟩Eternal Act, by which the absolute Will self-realized begets its ~~i~~Idea as the other self. Or more comprehensively, since the divine ideas are one with the eternal act by which the absolute Will is causative of its own reality and of whatever is necessarily begotten or proceeding out of that reality.

So far, there is no other difficulty ~~but must~~ ⟨than⟩ attends every contemplation of the Divine Being. An Idea is not simply knowledge or perception as distinguished from the thing perceived: it is a realizing knowledge, a knowledge causative of its own reality;[33] in it is life, and the life is the light of men. And it is this which the eldest Sages of all nations have struggled to express in the various terms of Self-[*p 33*]subsistent Light,[34] living Light, φως νοερον και νοητον, a Light at once intelligent and intelligible, and the communicative medium. The same and similar attributes we find in the sacred writings, no less than in those of philosophers, given to law—there being, indeed, no other difference between law and idea than that Will (or Power) and Intelligence being the constituents of both, in the *idea* we contemplate; the Will or power in the form of intelligence, and in the *law* we contemplate the intelligence in the form of Will or power. Therefore, to suppose God without Ideas, or the realizing knowledge of all the particular forms potentially ~~cont~~ involved in the absolute causativeness, would destroy the very conception of God. It amounts, indeed, to knowing and yet not knowing, since it would be vain to pretend that the supreme mind contemplated the One Idea of its own absoluteness. For either the absoluteness contains in itself the possibility of being in the whole plenitude, or [*p 35*] it does not. If not, in what sense is the absoluteness essentially causative of reality? But if it does, the point is conceded. To say that God knows the universal only, without knowing at the same time whatever is contained in the

---

part in that Unity, of which it is the representative" (*LS—CC—*30).

[33] Cf e.g. a note of 1825: "Pleroma in the Idea—and the Birth of the Distinctities, the Forms, the Infinite in the Finite—yet having their primal essence in Will . . ." (*CN* IV 5233).

[34] Cf C's insistence in this context on light, with his emphasis, in the physical world, on "matter of light". See below, Frag 4 e.g. f 48; and App A frag (*c*) e.g. ff 10ᵛ–11. See further *TT* (*CC*) I 596.

universal, whether as arising out of himself or out of the relations which the involved realities must form and represent to each other, would be, if possible, more absurd than to ~~say of~~ ⟨attribute to⟩ a man perfect insight into a genus with an entire ignorance of its species, i.e. well acquainted with the genus, only not knowing what it meant. Even more absurd, I have said, for when asserted of God it renders the divine Omniscience a mere abstraction under the impossible ⟨ignorance⟩ of that from which it had been abstracted, or a generalization in the absence of all particulars.

So far, therefore, there is no especial difficulty. *This* commences with the consideration of the nature of the reality appertaining to these cases. We see clearly that they must have the eternal truth in which [*p 37*] the possible and the actual are one, and therefore necessity, the essence of which consists in [? ~~it~~] being the union or copula of possible and real.[35] As such, therefore, they are One with God as the περιχωρησις[36] of the Will, the Being, the Intelligence, and the Love. But yet they are this under a particular form, and this necessarily a form of Will, inasmuch as Will is presupposed in Being, and ⟨Being in⟩ Intelligence, and all in Love. That [this] is compatible with the perfect unity of the absolute Will as realized in the Supreme Being and Omniscient Mind, we may conceive from the analogy of the highest intuitions or ideas in our own minds. But we have before affirmed that the idea is a particular form of Will, and that in a sphere which admits only of supreme or perfect reality. But all perfect reality is found in the Absolute[j] only. There[k] follows, therefore, an apparent contradiction: the ideas must be real, inasmuch as they are the Ideas of God and necessarily inferred in the plenitude of the Godhead, and yet no particular form can be real as being [*p 39*] particular. The solution is this. To God the idea is real, inasmuch as it is one with that Will, which, as we see in its definition, is verily Idem et Alter;[37] ~~and~~ ⟨but⟩ to [l]itself the idea[m] ~~it~~ is absolutely real, in so far only as its particular Will affirms, and in affirming constitutes its particular reality to have no true being, except as a form of the universal, and one with the

---

[j–k] ms: only; there
[l–m] Written "the idea itself" and marked with a curved line for transposition

[35] C had from early in his career mused on the nature of necessity, and had passed through a period of declared Necessitarianism: "I am a compleat Necessitarian—and understand the subject as well almost as Hartley himself", he announced in 1794 (*CL* I 137); and he was well aware that necessity figured most prominently in the thought of some of his German contemporaries, most especially in Fichte's *Bestimmung des Menschen* and Schelling's treatise of 1809 called *Das Wesen der menschlichen Freiheit*.

[36] Tr: "circulation". See Frag 2 f 268, f 272.

[37] Tr: "same and other". Though C attributes the distinction to Philo, Philo wrote in Greek. See above Frag 2 ff 254–255.

universal Will. This, however, is the affirmation of Will, and of a particular Will. It must, therefore, contain the potentiality, that is, the power of possibly not affirming the identity of its reality with the reality of God, which is actual absolutely (Actus purissimus sine ullâ potentialitate),[38] or of willing to be yet not willing to be, only because God is, and in ⟨the being of⟩ God, alone. In other words, if the essence of its being be Will, and this Will under a particular form, there must be a possibility of willing the universal or absolute under the predominance of the particular, instead of willing the particular solely as the [*p 41*] glory and ~~plenitude~~ ⟨presentation of the plenitude⟩ of the universal. As long as this act remains wholly potential, i.e. ~~existing~~ ⟨implied⟩ in ~~its opposite as a possible~~ the holy Will as its opposite, ~~pos~~ necessarily possible because ~~it~~ being a holy Will it is a Will, and a particular Will, so long is it comparable with God, and so long, therefore, hath it an actual reality as one of the eternal immutable ideas of God. But in the Will to actualize this potentiality, or as in common language we should say, in the Will to convert this possibility into a reality, it necessarily makes—itself! shall I say?— or rather, *a* self that is not God, and hence by its own act becomes alien from God. But in God all [? ~~absolute~~] ⟨actual⟩ reality is contained:[39] in making, therefore, a self that is not God, ~~the~~ ⟨all⟩ actuality is necessarily *n*lost. A*o* potentiality alone remains, by virtue of the Will, which as Will is indestructible and *p*eternal. A*q* causativeness must remain, for this is the essential of the Will; but it is a causativeness that destroys, which anni[*p 43*]hilates the actual, and in the potential swallowing up all ~~reality~~ actuality, so that the potential as merely potential remains the ~~sole~~ ⟨only⟩ form of ⟨its⟩ reality, ~~it may~~ it is an act that may be said to realize the potential ~~by~~ in the moment of potentializing the alone truly real. What could follow but a world of contradictions, when the first self-constituting act is ~~es~~ in its essence a contradiction? The Will, to make a centre which is not a centre, a Will not the same with the absolute Will, and yet not contained in the absolute, that is, an absolute that is not absolute. But here again I must refer the student to a former admonition, that in the philosophy of ideas our words can have no meaning for him that uses and for him that hears them, except as far as the mind's eye in both is

---

n−o ms: lost, a   *p−q* ms: eternal, a

[38] See above, note 30.

[39] To keep this conception from spilling over into pantheism, C insists that God is "supermundane", above, not in, the world: "the supermundane Personal God—the only-begotten before all worlds" (*CN* IV 5411). Likewise, C follows the Bible in referring to "the God, *in* whom all things are present, even the Son himself and the Spirit, hath no one ever seen" (*CN* IV 5411). The conception of "present to" enjoins an essential separation as opposed to the alternate formulation "included in".

kept fixed on the idea. This must be co-present with the mind, a light kindling the light, or an object supplying the radiance by which it is [*p 45*] itself beheld. If the ray of mental vision decline but an hair's breadth on this side or on that, it is instantly strangled in darkness, or becomes an erring light and its own delusion. No analogy in the usual sense of the word can here befriend us, and even the sensuous images in which the words we use had their origin—and the more sensuous, the less abstract these words are; the more appropriate, the less deceptive—even these become illustrations only as they become symbols and represent the same idea in a lower form, and exerted on a meaner subject. Otherwise they are opake obstacles excluding light, and not veils that soften yet transmit it. A world of contradictions, I have said, commences. The father of self, alien from God, was a liar from beginning and the father of lies. Here the truths of our moral nature are of more avail to us than the powers of our intellectual [nature]. Let us contemplate and endeavour to lay hold of any act of [*p 47*] guilt we find in ourselves, [so] that we can neither deny it to be, and yet when we seek to express its being we discover nothing but contraries, its being's being is contradiction.[40] But with awe we shall perhaps find that a part of our difficulty, a part of the confusion and perplexity which clouds and disturbs the contemplation, is not necessary, nor even attributive to subjective causes that are common to all and arise out of the mechanism or finiteness of the human 'mind, but[s] [arises] from mists from which we ought to clear ourselves, from erroneous associations and passions from which we ought to emancipate ourselves. On this point I have treated at large in a former work, that on Logic.[41] I need only, therefore, refer to the false division which has so long prevailed in the methods of philosophy under the name of Dichotomy,[42] in which the position always begins with two, ~~th~~ a thing

---

r–s ms: mind. But

[40] Cf the conclusion of a poem of 1815(?) called *Human Life; on the Denial of Immortality*: "Be sad! be glad! be neither! seek, or shun! / Thou hast no reason why! Thou canst have none; / Thy being's being is contradiction" (*PW*—EHC—I 426).

[41] This statement possibly dates this fragment as composed around than late 1823—although it may have been still later.

[42] Cf a note of 1820–1: "The evils of Dichotomy are endless; but the greatest & the original is that of seeking an opposite, or antithesis, or counter-position for that which *contains* the opposites as

the germ of a Tree contains potentially the Trunk and Branches, but has none, it substitutes a *contrary* for an opposite, i.e. a mere negation or nothing, which of course can be opposed to nothing— Thus, to Reality they would oppose Non-entity—but Reality can have no opposite, and must therefore be placed thus

Real
Actual   Potential

The Truth, necessity and immense importance of contemplating the Potential as a species of Reality . . . and as its negative Pole, as it were, the actual being the Positive, we may hereafter have occa-

and its opposite.*ʳ* Thus we should have the real, and as its opposite [*p 49*] and co-ordinate the unreal or non-entity, that is, an opposition ⟨in⟩ which there can be no opposite. If, on the other hand, we took the real as the pregnant uninvolved point and the identity of both opposites, and these opposites again as the two poles of the line into which the point produced itself, or in which it unfolded in order to manifest its being, we should see clearly that both alike are forms of that point, and that, therefore, under the idea reality we have to find two opposites, ~~each~~ ⟨both⟩ of which are reality, though each a form opposite to the other. These forms, these opposite poles of reality are the actual and the potential, and the [? ~~habit~~] error against which I am now guarding consists in the habit of substituting for these the false opposition and mere logical contrariety of real and unreal, and thus of considering "the actual" as a mere and perfect synonyme of "real", perfectly commutable words like "swerve" and "deviate", or "daily" and "quotidianal", and in like manner "the [*p 51*] potential" as tantamount, and no more than tantamount, to "unreal" or the mere "non-entity". Without correcting this habit it is impossible that either the present argument, or indeed any reasoning connected with the ideas, laws, or powers, can be intelligible.

Here, as in all other points in which we can neither reproduce the meaning of our words in another's apprehension by presenting the object itself to his senses, ~~and as little~~ nor by directing his attention to an abstraction from any, the only assistance we can yield is that of relating the process by which we ourselves arrived at the conception. Thus I am conscious at present of such and such objects, I am at this moment exercising such or such an act, I am sitting or listening to music with my eyes *ᵘ*closed. Such*ᵛ* images, such acts, such states of affection or passion are actually present; but are the infinity of images, thoughts, acts, emotions of which I have the power [*p 53*] or receptive quality, non-entities? Are they not as really potential as the former are really actual? The amiable Mendelsohn,[43] in his eloquent attempt[44] to re-introduce and vindi-

---

ʳ Colon in ms   *ᵘ⁻ᵛ* ms: closed such

---

sion to show" (*CN* iv 4784). The formulation of the potential as an essential part of reality is of course the signal contribution of Aristotle.

[43] Moses Mendelssohn (1729–1786), German Jewish philosopher and close friend of Lessing. Author of, among other works, *Philosophische Gespräche* (1755), the satire *Pope ein Metaphysiker* (1755), the essay *Abhandlung über die Evidenz in der metaphysischen Wissenschaften*

(1763), *Phädon* (on the immortality of the soul, 1767), and *Morgenstunden* (1785). C spoke highly of Mendelssohn in a letter to Thelwall of 17 Dec 1796 (*CL* i 284). See also *CN* i 377. He annotated copies of *Jerusalem* and *Morgenstunden*. See Alice D. Snyder "Coleridge's Reading of Mendelssohn's 'Morgenstunden' and 'Jerusalem'" *JEGP* xxxviii (1929) 503–17; *AR* (*CC*) 345 n 20.

[44] See Ch xvii ("Beweisgründe *a*

cate the Cartesian demonstration of the divine existence from the invo-
lution of ~~existence~~ ⟨that perfection⟩ in the idea of the ~~divine~~ all-perfect
Being, has however sought a support for this proof from this very con-
templation of potential being. Assuming without right that actual is the
perfect equivalent of real, commutable terms—the one of which, there-
fore, is superfluous—instead of regarding the potential as the minus or
negative pole of that same ~~identity~~ unity of which the actual is the plus
or positive, and yet feeling ⟨with⟩ the same force as we the absurdity of
considering all the futuritions of mind and nature as nothings, he infers
the necessity of an universal consciousness in and for which all these po-
tentials are actual.[45] What portion of truth lies in this view we shall here-
after [*p 55*] point out. At present it is sufficient to detect its inadequacy,
both to the subject itself and to the purpose intended. Grant, for instance,
that all those structures, organs, and functions in a living body which
were neither directly subject to the Will nor existing in the conscious-
ness, all the goings on that continue in profoundest sleep, were [? ~~will~~],
as the Statilians asserted,[46] nothing more than the Soul's potentiality, the
conscious Self in each individual being the actuality, it would doubtless
follow that to an omnipresent mind they would all alike actually present
themselves, but yet, as it should seem, those only that were actually pres-
ent.[w] A But if it be said that this omnipresent consciousness is eternal,
and ~~by its~~ essentially transcendenc~~y~~t to time, yet it is not without per-
plexity or by any direct ~~conclusion~~ ⟨deduction⟩ that we can conclude
thus: A is essentially transcendent to all time, therefore the past and the
future are for him in the present time. Surely in order to [*p 57*] render
this clear and satisfactory, we must prove that the present is no form of
time; and if this were granted, it would still be asked whether the truth

---

[w] Question mark in ms

---

priori vom Dasein eines allervollkom-
mensten, nothwendigen, unabhängigen
Wesens") of Mendelssohn's *Morgen-
stunden, oder Vorlesungen, über das
Dasein Gottes* of 1785 (*Mendelssohn* II
383–92).
   [45] The passage is identified in *CN* IV
4784n as appearing "at the end of Part I
Chap I 'Pure Logic or the Canon', from
Mendelssohn's *Morgenstunden* (Frank-
furt & Leipzig 1790). The quotations
from Mendelssohn (7–8) are sometimes
loosely translated by Coleridge." The
note points to *Logic* (*CC*) 57–8: "In this
point of view 'the total sum of human

knowledge may be represented under the
image of a tree' so as to convey in a just
and lively manner the principle on which
all formal logic rests . . . . 'We shall thus
have a striking image of the relations in
which our conceptions stand to each
other. All individual things, [which]
would answer to the extreme points of
the tree, meet in different species; the
species in kinds or *genera*; the kinds or
genera in classs[es], and finally the
classes unite in some most general con-
ception answering to the trunk or stem'
in this genealogy of logic."

of the difference between past and future, and the difference of both from that mysterious fluxion which connects the one with the other, which certainly exists in finite minds, is or is not present to the universal consciousness as truly existing in beings of finite or ~~pr~~ successive consciousness.[x] If it be answered, No! we instantly fall back into the conceit of an anima mundi,[47] the Indian fancy of a notion of life[48] in which, no one knows how, an infinity of vesicles or bottles of all imaginable sizes were found, each of these shaping the common fluid diversely within its own mound, and as soon as its fragile walls were broken by decay or collision, falling back into the universal element.[49] If this universal be ignorant of the forms produced by these vesicles, it must [*p 59*] be ignorant of the vesicles themselves—that is, by virtue of its penetrancy they cannot exist for it. ~~a~~And thus we should have a true oriental Deity,

> No other than as Eastern Sages paint,
> The God, who floats upon a Lotus leaf,
> Dreams for a thousand ages; then awaking
> Creates a world, and smiling at the bubble,
> Relapses into bliss.[50]

In other words, the absolute universal Thing of Atheism,[51] which, not contented with its own inherent absurdity, the Pantheist has forced into a counterfeit of religion by ~~united~~ ⟨blending⟩ it with contradictions.[52] For in this intense repose of mere universal knowledges, or rather of a one eternal, formless sense of being, exclusive of all alterity, infinite or finite, it is plain that there can be no awaking, and no creation, not even of a bubble.

[x] Question mark in ms

[46] Statilians as a word referring to the adherents of the Roman general and architect Statilius Taurus or his descendant, Statilia Messalina, the third wife of Nero, does not seem to fit the context; but no other use of Statilian has been traced.

[47] See above, Frag 2 f 50.

[48] Elsewhere, C equates the *anima mundi* not with Hindu pantheism but with Spinozistic pantheism: ". . . unless I turn Spinozist or an Anima-Mundi Dreamer—" (*CN* iv 5133). See the previous note.

[49] For C, this is a fundamental image of pantheism: "a Universal God—*all-God* an Oceanic God, Man, Beast and Plant being mere & merely wavelets &

wrinkles on the surface of the Depth" (*CN* iv 5345).

[50] *The Night-Scene* lines 53–6 (*PW* —EHC—i 422).

[51] That is, "the World itself, the indivisible one and only substance (*substantia una et unica*) of Spinoza, of which all Phaenomena, all particular and individual Things, Lives, Minds, Thoughts, and Actions are but modifications" (*AR*—1825—162). For the logical necessity by which a starting point of "thing" or "it is" eventuates in pantheism, see *CPT* ch 2.

[52] "For Pantheism, trick it up as you will, is but a painted Atheism—" (*CM*—*CC*—iii 1083).

But if we reply in the affirmative that there is a knowledge of these finites, that it is a being limitless, comprehending its own limits in its dilatation [*p 61*] and condensing itself into its own mounds, and containing figures, then it must needs be that—in and together with the self-comprehension as the one and infinite—there is a knowledge of the finite, and [of] whatever exists finitely in relation to each finite, and as a knowledge belonging to and under the condition of, the finite. But in this case not only would all things that are have actual reality in the universal mind, but likewise their potential being in relation to the finite would be affirmed in the same act that gave being to the finite, and be included in the product of that act. But this act we have defined as That which is essentially causative of reality, and ~~in reality~~ a form of reality therefore must the potential be, no less, though a far lower form, than the actual. This idea of the reality of the potential and the necessity, as far as it extends, ~~of~~ ⟨that⟩ ~~the same thing should be~~ of predicating both ⟨the actual and the potential⟩ of one and the same [*p 63*] subject, namely that its being is actual as far as it is in the being of God and potential in relation to itself as particular existence—~~and~~ ⟨to which ʸ(if we may be allowed to anticipate a truth, the proof of which will be given in another place) let us add⟩ᶻ the awful consequence, that whatever actually is, even for ourselves, is thus wholly and solely by the presence of the Deity to the mind, and that sense itself, ~~lik~~ as if it were an opake reason, is possible only by a communion with that life which is the light of man, which lighteth every man that cometh into the world,[53] and without which the solar light would be ~~without the rays that fall on the impassive rock the~~ ~~s~~ a contradiction in thought, a powerless power, a light that is darkness—this idea, next to that of the Will, or rather with it, is the great master key, not only of all speculative sciences, physical as well as metaphysical. Without a clear apprehension of this truth, and such as the mind can rest on with inward quiet, even the conception of the absolute Will as conveyed [*p 65*] logically in the definition so often repeated is neither safe nor worthy the name of an idea. It is true that the Will does indeed contain in itself power and intelligence, but not as the synthesis of the two, but as the identity of both. We cannot generate the idea of the Will

---

ʸ In the ms the parenthesis is placed before "to"
ᶻ The inserted passage is written on p 62 and marked with a caret for insertion here

[53] "That was the true Light, which lighteth every man that cometh into the world" (John 1.9). Cf the words of Jesus: "Then spake Jesus again unto to them, saying, I am the light of the world; he that followeth me shall not walk in darkness, but shall have the light of life" (John 8.12). C, however, customarily equates the light of the world not simply with Jesus but with reason. See above, Frag 2 f 178 and f 223.

by adding the conception of power to that of Intelligence, or of Intelligence to that of Power.[54] These, indeed, the Will must contain; but in order for these to be the Will, a somewhat, not contained necessarily in either, that is to be essentially causative of reality, must be added. But this is the essence of the Will itself, and of course it cannot therefore be added, but must be preconceived. We cannot, therefore, constitute the Will, for we must presuppose it in the commencement of the attempt. Hence we must ~~not~~ say that Might and Intelligence are essential to the Will, or that they are of its essence, but not its essence. For that it is absolutely its own essence is the great ⟨sole⟩ distinctive [*p 67*] predicate of the Will. Now here is what was with no unseemly fear and inward trembling named the abyss or abysmal mystery, that there is in the causative Allmight of God (who shall dare utter it? or if he feel permitted, in what terms shall he utter it? Shall he say a more than God, or a less than God, and yet more in the sense other, a somewhat that God did not realize in himself; for the real containeth both the actual and the potential, but in God as God by the necessity of his absolute perfection there is no potentiality).[a] When, therefore, we speak of the Will as the ground of the divine existence, from which it indeed would be more wise to abstain, or when we meet with it in the mystic passages of writers of deserved name and undoubted piety, it will be highly expedient to bear in mind that the words are used prolepticè or by anticipation,[55] i.e. the Will contemplated after we have ~~assumed it~~ [*p 69*] beheld its self-realization, as the necessary being, ens entium,[56] or Supreme Mind. And thus considered distinctly from the intelligence, as again realized in its own form, as the co-eternal idea of the Supreme Mind, and thus considered as the representative alterity of the being ~~to~~ which ⟨is⟩ the eternal form, ~~or~~ ⟨i.e.⟩ self-manifestation of the Divine Will, and of which the Will is the eternal essence. Then, contemplating the power not indeed as the Will but yet as a power of the Will, and therefore a causative power, we give birth in our minds to an idea which is not the same with that ~~of~~ which we express by the verb substantive "*Is*", though it is implied in the great I Am and it is that which we express by the word "*Have*", and

---

[a] Closing parenthesis inserted

[54] Cf a marginal note: "*Will* is incapable of distinction or division: it is equally implied in 1. vital Being. 2. in essential intelligence, and 3. in effluent Love or holy Action. Now Will is the true principle & meaning of *Identity*" (Brinkley 202).

[55] The conception of *prolepsis* or anticipation was associated with the thought of Epicurus, and its invocation here is another testimony to the subliminal concern with Epicureanism throughout the *magnum opus* (see Prolegomena III: The Epicurean and Stoic Background).

[56] Tr: "being of beings".

not ill even on this account entitled a "Verb auxiliary", as by its aid we are enabled to express the idea presented to us in the mirror of the reason without offence to the religious feelings, even the most scrupulous. [*p 71*] For who would hesitate to admit that God *hath* an infinite power,[57] and that in the fulness of his Wisdom and Love, he produceth that which could not be saved[b] in him, but which he is not. Now such are all beings that are not absolutely God, either as the absolute being or mind, the absolute idea and word, and the absolute act, or the spirit of Love and Holy Life—all, therefore, in whom the potential necessarily co-exists as alternable with the actual. And this by virtue of the Will, which is the common essence of all; for all are as realizations of the Will, and yet not exempted from potentiality by being in their own forms or necessarily absolute. If, therefore, we speak of the ground or the nature of Deity, we nevertheless abjure the rash and dangerous expressions that the depth begetteth the paternal Deity, or that a Not-Good, which yet is not Evil, a Not-Intelligent, which is not the contrary of Intelligence, is to be con[*p 73*]ceived before the evolution of the Good and the Wise, which however disguised ~~be~~ it may be by false analogies and words that excite emotion rather than convey thought or distinct meaning, is little better than the Night and Chaos of Hesiod and the Greek Sophists that followed him. The ground is not to be called God, ~~but it is~~ much less God the Father; it is the ⟨abysmal⟩ depth (βυβος αβυβος)[c] ~~the~~ ⌈. . .⌋ ~~abysm~~ of the eternal act by which God as the alone causa sûi[58] affirmeth himself eternally. The depth begetteth not,[59] but in and together with the act of self-realization the supreme mind begetteth his substantial idea, the primal Self, the adorable *I am*, its other self, and becometh God the Father, self-originant ⟨or ~~if~~ lest this word should lead to the conception of a Beginning, self-existent, self-caused⟩[d] and self-subsistent, even as the Logos or Supreme Idea is the co-eternal Son, self-subsistent but begot-

---

[b] ms: save   [c] A mistake for "βυθός ἄβυσσος", "bottomless abyss"
[d] The inserted passage is in C's hand

[57] As opposed to "*is*" an infinite power". See below, p 109.

[58] Tr: "cause of himself". See Frag 2 f 225 and f 269.

[59] Cf the paragraph that follows with C's note on Böhme: "The Depth begetteth not, but in & together with, the Act of Self-realization—the Supreme Mind begetteth his substantial Idea, the primal Self (I AM) its other Self, and becometh God the Father, self-originant and self-subsistent even as the Logos or Supreme Idea is the co-eternal Son, self-subsistent but begotten by the Father—while in the mutual and reciprocal act of Self-attribution, the effusion and re- fundence, the inspiration and respiration of Love the Son is Deus alter et idem/ and these words express the Triunity—Deus, Alter, Idem—i.e. Deus: Deus Alter: Deus idem in Patre et in Filio, per quem Pater et Filius Unum sunt, qui et ipse cum Patre et Filio est unus Deus" (*CM— CC—*I 694).

ten by the Father, while in the mutual act of self-attribution the effusion and refundence, the in[*p 75*]spiration and respiration of divine Love, the Son is (or may I innocently say of the eternal that hHe becomesth?) Deus alter et idem,[60] and these words express the Tri-unity: the*ᵉ* Deus, the paternal; the Filius, the Deus alter; and the Spirit, the Deus idem in patre et in filio per quem pater et filius unum sunt, qui et ipse cum patre et filio est unus Deus.[61] Whatever is else, and in that sense more than this, we must say of it that God hath or possesses it, as far as it is one with God and willeth itself to be one with God, and willing affirmeth as the divine instrument its actuality as God's and not as in itself.[62] And yet if we say that there is an innocent and a true sense in which these ideas, living spiritual and substantive in the eternal idea, may be called uncreated forms and eternal truths, powers, and intelligences, we shall speak not only truly but scripturally. "For I have said ye are Gods [*p 77*] and all of you the begotten of the Most High. But ye shall die like men, and shall fall like one of the princes[63]—that is, so far as my Will gave you being, I gave you actual being, and begot you in the only begotten, begotten before all creation, and while your Will was one with my Will, ye were my offspring, the children of the most *ᶠ* High. But*ᵍ* there is a possibility of a Will that is not a Holy Will, and that ye will to be by your own Will; and hence there is a futurity, a fearful futurity, a change which cannot be without destruction of that actuality which ye would but have transferred to another source, without a fall proportioned to its height."[64] Nor will it be little in favour of this paraphrase, with many of my readers, that the only begotten, who came among us to renew in us by the aid of his might the power and high privilege to be the Sons of God, did himself especially refer [*p 79*] his*ʰ* unbelieving persecutors to this very passage, when they took up stones to stone him, because in declaring himself to

---

ᵉ ms: †The   *ᶠ⁻ᵍ* ms: High: but   *ʰ* ms: the his

[60] Tr: "God other and the same".

[61] That is to say, the Trinitarian formula is satisfactorily accounted for by the simple consideration of *alter et idem*, with God as the paternal or *idem*, the Son or *Filius* as the *alter*, and the Holy Spirit as both God in the Father and in the Son, through which father and son are one, all three constituting one God. The Latin words mean: "God the same in the father and in the son through whom the father and the son are one, who himself is one God both father and son". See above, Frag 2 ff 263–9.

[62] The emphasis on "having" or possessing" precludes the pantheistic emphasis of "being".

[63] Cf Psalm 82.6–7: "I have said, Ye *are* gods; and all of you *are* children of the most High. But ye shall die like man, and fall like one of the princes."

[64] Cf *Table Talk* 1 May 1830: "A FALL of some sort or other—the creation, as it were, of the non-absolute—is the fundamental postulate of the moral history of man. Without this hypothesis, man is unintelligible; with it, every phenomenon is explicable. The mystery itself is too profound for human insight" (*TT—CC*—II 79).

be the Son of God he had made himself equal to the Father.[65] "If our Lord reasoned there hath been even in yourselves, or in your forefathers, who were like yourselves, ground for the infinite wisdom to ~~declare~~ address you as Gods because the Sons of God, and this while he beheld them as mortal creatures and fallen spirits, surely ye may conclude that he whom the Father hath sent to call you forth from this mortality, to raise you from this fall, must needs be of that rank which may consistently not only with truth but humility be named by him the Son of God. For how can he, who is necessarily as well as essentially the Son of God, take you up into his own nature to be once more Gods or deiform spirits, and the offspring of the Most High,[66] [if not that] in him only [*p 81*] in whom ye were begotten can ye be regenerated?"[i] Any other interpretation of these words I cannot admit as compatible with ordinary reverence for Christ, though but as an inspired Teacher, for to what does the Socinian gloss [j]amount?[67] It[k] is, say they, a mere argumentum ad hominem.[68] ~~if the Scripture~~ "If a writer of scripture ventured to call the mere receivers of a former and less important mission Gods, and you take no offence at the passage, on what ground of equity can you be indignant with a missionary himself, and with higher credentials than Moses, because he had called himself the son of God?" The coolness with which this comment passes over the fact that an inspired writer, speaking in the person of God himself, had declared those mortals to have been in their ~~primary~~ origin Gods and the offspring of the Most High, and that therefore those words must, if the prophet [*p 83*] were indeed inspired of God, be true and pregnant, might almost provoke a smile; for if the words ~~were~~ ⟨did⟩ indeed convey a truth, then the passage remains a correct and forcible argument of the divinity of Christ, drawn by himself from the former nature even of Man. And if not, the argument would really amount to this: "It is very true I spoke somewhat bombastically and ~~with~~ ⟨an⟩ indiscreet⟨ly⟩ ~~metaphor~~, but there was a former prophet and inspired writer who set me the example and ~~talked~~ ⟨ex-

---

[i] Full stop in ms   [j-k] ms: amount; it is

[65] Cf John 10.30–6.

[66] Cf Acts 17.28: "For we are also his offspring. Forasmuch then as we are the offspring of God, we ought not to think that the Godhead is like unto gold, or silver, or stone, graven by art and man's device."

[67] The Socinians, to whom C often refers, were the forerunners of the Unitarians of his own day, and by C considered not to be true Christians, in that they denied the Trinity and the Godhead of Christ. The name comes from their first theorist, the Polish theologian Faustus Socinus, and his work *De Christo servatore*, in the 16th century.

[68] Tr: "argument to the man".

pressed⟩ still more ~~laxly~~ ⟨inappropriately*[l]*⟩." An argumentum ad homi-
nem, indeed, but such a one, ~~indeed~~ ⟨methinks⟩, as instead of arresting
the shower of stones would assuredly have exasperated it into a tempest.

I have said, and cannot too earnestly impress it on the reader's mind,
that the Eternal existence of the Divine Pleroma or the Logos[69] as one
with the eternal, [*p 85*] all-comprehending Idea of the Supreme Mind is
not asserted by me and [is] to be contemplated by none for the gratifica-
tion of any speculative interest;[70] nor*[m]* [is it to be] contemplated at all
but with awe and, as it were, by a passing glance admitted between the
wings with which the ~~Se~~praph Meditation veileth her countenance as she
kneels before the glory of the mystery—or as if we had been placed in
a cleft of the rock and veiled with the hand while the glory passed by,
which *[n]*in the*[o]* instant of its removal permitted us to catch a glance of the
skirts and train of the Divinity. Further than will suffice for preserving
our conception of the divine nature from evaporating into a mere ab-
straction, further than is rendered necessary as an inevitable consequence
of the only view of the divine Being which is consistent in itself and ~~free~~
~~f~~ equidistant from superstition on [*p 87*] the one hand and pantheism
on the other, we have no sanction from within or from without for
concerning our thoughts, much less our fancies, therewith. Under what
forms the possibility of such a state may be represented, the reader ~~in-~~
~~nocently~~ may derive an innocent amusement in learning from an inter-
esting pasage in the 8th book of Plotinus's 5th Ennead, in which he speaks
of the Host of Ideas ⟨or the Eternal Life⟩ in the Logos[71]—~~Αιω~~ Ëon
(Ἀιων) or Truth (v. Epist. I John, Chap. V, Verse 20[*]): "It is a tranquil
life which they that dwell ~~in God~~ ⟨therein⟩ possess, and Truth is their
Mother and Nurse and Essence ⟨(ουσια)⟩ and Nourishment. And they
see all things as far as they are in Essence and themselves in others. For

[*] [*Written on p 86, facing the parenthetical biblical reference on p 87. The
slight misquotations ("Truth" for "true", "the Son of God" for "his Son Jesus
Christ") suggest that the words were supplied from memory:*] "We are in him
that is the Truth even in the Son of God. This is the true God and Eternal Life."

---

[l] ms: inappropriate   *[m]* ms: or   *[n–o]* Written twice in ms

[69] See Prolegomena xiv: The *Mag-
num Opus* and the *Logos*.

[70] This statement is highly abstract,
but in its implication it connects directly
with C's most urgent practical concern.
Cf a note on Edward Irving: "Christ has
been revealed in his identity with the

Logos, i.e. as the Substantial personal
Reason in whom Life is—the universal
communicative Reason 'who lighteth
every Man', & therein constitutes the
proper Humanity" (*CM—CC*—iii 23).

[71] That is, in the long passage quoted
below.

all is transparent, and there is nothing dark nor resisting; but every one to every one is perspicuous ~~and all to every one~~ ⟨even to the inmost⟩, and all things to every one: for it is light to light. For every one has all things in himself and again beholds all things [*p 89*] in every other. So that all things are every where, and the all is all, and every thing all, and the ~~splendour~~ ⟨glory⟩ infinite. But every thing is more eminently some one thing, and yet all things fairly shine in every thing"[72]—which, and more that follows, amounts only to our former definition of a divine Idea, that it is a representation of the universal under the eminence of ~~a particular~~ some form in particular.

We, however, are morally and religiously interested with two points only. These are the reality of the existence of distinct beings in the plenitude of the Supreme Mind, whose essence is Will and whose actuality consists in their Will being one with the Will of God. That this is compatible with the perfect unity of the absolute Will, we are assisted in conceiving by the analogy of the predominant thoughts or Ideas [*p 91*] in our own minds. Yet in speaking of these distinct Beings as particular forms of ~~Will~~ existence, there ⟨would⟩ ~~arises~~ an apparent contradiction if we had meant to assert that these forms of eternal being were actual as particular forms. But we teach the very contrary of this. To God each form is real, inasmuch as it is the necessary offspring of a power, the essence of which is to be causative of reality or the absolute Will. And again, to God each form is actual, because and as far as it is one with the Will of the Father or the ~~personal Wills~~ ⟨Will and Spirit⟩ of the Deity, which we have proved to be verily idem et alter,[73] at once the source of identity and alterity, and ⟨of⟩ the unity in both. But for the distinct form itself, it is real, indeed, inasmuch as a Will is its essence; but it exists actually, inasmuch only as its [*p 93*] particular Will affirmeth (i.e. constitutively willeth) its self to have no actuality, no true being, other than as a form of the universal, being mind and spirit and one with the universal Will. In this sense only do we assert the actual existence of the Eternal Life, and in this we are interested because without supposing this actuality it would be impossible to conceive a transition out of the same into any other *p*state. Under*q* any other condition, *r*such existence would be*s* incompatible with the Eternal. This, then, is the first point, and one

p–q ms: state: under
r–s Written "it would be such existence" and marked with a curved line for transposition (the "it" left uncancelled)

[72] Plotinus *Enneads* 5.8.4.
[73] Tr: "same and other". This fact, it must be reiterated, provides the dialectical basis that eventually extricates the rationality of the Trinity.

of which, simply because it is an eternal truth, the Idea itself can be the only direct evidence. The next point is the possibility of a fall from this state, a ceasing to be eternal, a transition into the temporal. A The possibility, I say, for as in the eternal there can be no direct evidence but the idea, as light is the [*p 95*] only evidence of light, so of the temporal or historical there can be no other proof but the fact. The binding conception, therefore, between both must be the possibility of the fact. Not the possibility simply—for that which is fact, i.e. real, must be possible, and needs no proof, but of its possibility in connexion with the idea of the eternal—but the possibility of an eternal becoming temporal. Now this possibility, I say, w̶ might be eternal, and it is this alone which we are interested to establish. ⟨The interest of⟩ T̶the former b̶e̶i̶n̶g̶ ̶i̶n̶v̶o̶l̶v̶e̶d̶ ̶i̶n̶ ⟨is derived from⟩ this as t̶h̶e̶ ⟨its⟩ n̶e̶c̶e̶s̶s̶a̶r̶y̶ condition, o̶f̶ ̶t̶h̶i̶s̶ inasmuch as in order to prove a change from A, we must prove both a prior existence as A and a possibility of becoming otherwise. Now we have said that the host of heaven refer their being, with all its attributes and glory, to the eternal source, and that to the going-forth of the all-comprehending I AM the answer [*p 97*] and the seal of bliss is a willing "Thou alone art and we in Thee". But this is an answer of a being whose essence is Will, of a being that in joy and love freely willeth to be one with the universal Will. But this is not possible; there is no meaning in the words if there be not a potential Will of the contrary, that is, if there be not a possibility of willing its actuality in its Self and not in God. There must be, if the actual Will be a Will, a potentiality of willing the universal under the predominance of the particular, instead of willing the particular solely as the glory and presentation of the plenitude of the distinctions of the universal. For it remains the peculiar and incommunicable attribute of God as the universal being to be pure act without all potentiality. But in the particular beings included as the necessary offspring of the all-comprehending Self, as long as the [*p 99*] Will of affirming another Self remains merely possible, or in the technical language, the expediency and uses of which as instruments of reasoning, we shall have increasing proofs as we proceed—as long, I say, as the Will of Self in Self, which appertains to the Eternal Center alone, remains wholly potential, existing only to be precluded, existing only to furnish the joy and the triumph of the Will that is one with the Will of God, so long is the form of being compatible[t] with the Eternal, and the partaker of Eternity.

This, then, is our second point. It must be eternally possible for all forms of being not absolute and universal to will itself for its Self. It must

---

[t] ms: is compatible

be possible to will a Self that is not God. But in God all Good is, and to will the contrary of Good is to will Evil. But in Will alone causation in-heres.[74] To will Evil, therefore, is to originate [*p 101*] Evil. But the pos-sibility once established, the fact of its existence is the only proof of its ~~having ceased to be only possible~~ actuality. And here it is that the light streams in on the subject and reveals the importance of the distinctions which the imperfect powers of language have compelled us to convey, in words that must needs appear at the first perusal and prior to a distinct insight into their importance, thorny, prolix, and wearisome. Evil ex-ists.[75] This is a proposition which we cannot be called on to substanti-ate, it being included in our first postulate as a truth, the denial of which would render the whole religion purposeless and the whole series of ar-guments by which we might assert and vindicate its claims a baseless structure—or a series of positions, which might have been true but that the premise from which they all alike flow [*p 103*] is false, and the ob-ject to which they all tend non-existent and impossible. Evil, then, ex-ists. It is not eternal, therefore had an origin. It did not originate in God, who is verily and eminently the Eternal. And yet prior to*u* Evil, there was nothing not eternal.[76] Now ~~if we would prove this~~ should it be asked for

u ms: than

[74] See above, Frag 3 ms pp 21, 55; Frag 2 f 170.

[75] Cf a notebook entry of 1803: "To return to the Question of Evil—woe to the man, to whom it is an uninteresting Question—tho' many a mind, overwea-ried by it, may shun it with Dread/ and here, N.B. scourge with deserved & lofty Scorn those Critics who laugh at the dis-cussion of old Questions—God, Right & Wrong, Necessity & Arbitrement—Evil, &c—No! forsooth!—the Question must be new, *new spicy hot* Gingerbread, a French Constitution, a Balloon, change of Ministry, or which had the best of it in the Parliamentary Duel, Wyndham or Sheridan, or at the best, a chemical The-ory, whether the new celestial Bodies shall be called Planets or Asteroids— &c—Something new, something *out* of themselves—for whatever is *in* them, is deep within them, must be *old* as ele-mentary Nature. To find no contradiction in the union of old & novel—to contem-plate the Ancient of Days with Feelings new as if they then sprang forth at his own Fiat—this marks the mind that feels the Riddle of the World, & may help to unravel it" (*CN* I 1622).

[76] C wrestled perpetually with this topic. Cf a line of speculation in Dec 1823: "The Will, whose other name is the Good, is the Absolute One pure & eradiates the Many, out of whom the Many eradiates as so many iterations of the One. The Will, which is *Evil*, would be the Many utterly without the One; therefore *not* the Many but a striving to originate the Many by the destruction of the *One*/. But the One is essentially indestructible: even to destroy the appearances of the One, it must be of the One in the Many, and therefore by the destruction of the Many in the One. It therefore contradicts itself, in one and the same Act (or rather strife) willing to originate & to destroy. Self-contradiction is its essence—it is a Lie & the Father of Lies from the begin-ning. Evil is antipathy to the One; but the One is the Being of the Many. It destroys therefore the possibility of its own Being—and Self-destruction *is* its essen-tial Tendency" (*CN* IV 5076).

what reason we should be anxious to establish our minds in a full con-
viction of the truth of these positions, it is only necessary to consider
what must be true if these are not. First, if there be no Evil there is no
Guilt, no rightful punishment, no other distinction than Pain and Plea-
sure. But this once granted, the greatest of evils must immediatedly re-
sult, a world of Pain bodily and mental, torture of body unconnected with
crime past or present, and remorse for guilt without guilt, a refinement
of cruelty beyond the power of earthly tyrants, the affliction of the in-
nocent by the loss [*p 105*] of the consciousness of innocency. In short,
the old Epicurean argument will return on us with irresistible force, so
irresistible that the supposition of any satisfactory reply thereto is not so
properly inconceivable as most conceivably and glaringly absurd. If
there be no Evil but Pain or physical Evil, this is clearly a calamity in
the ~~poor~~ ⟨guiltless⟩*ᵛ* victim; and ~~of the causer we must~~ *ʷ*⟨for this very
Reason supposes *Evil* in the Causer or Inflicter, if able to have prevented
this Calamity. And thus the ~~Argument~~ ⟨Conclusion⟩ contradicts and sub-
verts ~~itself.~~ ⟨the Premise:⟩ For it⟩*ˣ* necessarily follows that ~~it~~ ⟨this
Cause⟩*ʸ* either could not prevent it, and was therefore not omnipotent; or
could (i.e. had the power, if it had ⟨possessed⟩*ᶻ* the knowledge~~)~~ how to
apply it) but did not know how, and was therefore not omniscient; or
lastly, it both could and knew how, but *would* not, and was therefore
not all-good, therefore not *ᵃ*God. For*ᵇ* an almighty, all-wise, all-good
Being is the Idea of God, the sole legitimate meaning of the word. But
if not God, that is, a divine, intelligent, self-comprehending [*p 107*]
Will, ~~therefore~~ ⟨then it must be⟩*ᶜ* either a Demoniacal Will[*] or no Will

[*] [*The text that follows, which was originally written as part of the sentence
on p 107 and then placed within parentheses (possibly by C), is here printed in
accordance with C's holograph instruction on p 106: "this Parenthesis to be
printed ~~a~~ as a note":*] For*ᵈ* the scheme of Manicheism[77] is too palpably absurd

ᵛ Insertion in C's hand
ʷ⁻ˣ Insertion in C's hand. Running out of room on p 105, C continued the passage, from
"And thus" to "For it", on the facing verso (p 104) and marked it for insertion after
"Calamity"
ʸ Insertion in C's hand
ᶻ Insertion in C's hand
ᵃ⁻ᵇ ms: God: for
ᶜ Insertion in C's hand
ᵈ ms: for

77 Referring to the teaching of Manes
(c 215–275 A.D.) that flourished in the
late third and fourth centuries, and that
claimed Augustine as an adherent for no
fewer than nine years. Manicheism was
based on a dualism and absolute opposi-
tion of light and darkness, which resulted
in a dualism and separation of good and
evil but also a dualism of divinity.

at all, a mere fate, or the blind first-mover of an immense machine, or a generalisation of the machine itself, a Deus Multitudo[78] with no higher unity than a heap of corn or a pillar of sand, the architecture of a whirlwind. Again, then, the ~~argument~~ ⟨proposition⟩ recurs unweakened: that Moral Evil *is*—an Evil which is the *sting* of calamity, an Evil from which all ⟨else⟩ that is or can be *called* Evil, derives its Evilness, either as a necessary consequent of that evil or by its continued presence [e]therein. And[f] this necessity, too, must be such as does not [*p 109*] arise out of its superiority to any power that might attempt its removal, but an essential necessity, from the absolute contradiction of the removal ⟨of the consequent⟩ during the continuance of the antecedent to the goodness, holiness, and wisdom of God, so that to will ~~the same~~ ⟨it⟩ would be the very same as for God to will ~~that~~ himself not to be God. But this is one among the numerous and important advantages of the principle ~~ion~~ which our whole system has been built, that the Will is ~~a~~ higher and deeper than Power, for it is that which God eternally *is*, whereas of power, yea, even of power infinite, taken in itself and abstractedly, we must say that God *hath* it, and hath it in himself and of himself, rather than that he *is* it. And this again amounts to little more than that the ⟨Supreme⟩ Will is an idea incapable of abstraction. We not only cannot think of it abstracted from Intelligence and Love as real, [*p 111*] for this would apply equally to the idea of ~~the~~ [. . .] an unbounded *power*; but we cannot think of it at all, which cannot truly be said of the latter, i.e. of power as [g]power. This[h] necessity, therefore, I repeat, is a necessity superior to power, for it consists in the ⟨ab⟩ ~~impossibility~~ absolute incompossibility of its contrary with that which is the ground, ~~and~~ cause, and condition of all possibility and all reality—and therefore of necessity itself. For necessity is the identity or co-inherence of the possible and the real. Once more, then,[i] Evil ⟨is⟩, and with it its necessary consequence~~ts~~.[79] *With* it, I say, and as long as *it* continues, and *for* it, though it were but for its removal! Now

---

when applied to the absolutely first to need any confutation here, if indeed, ~~of which~~ ⟨of which⟩ I am more than doubtful, there ever was such a faith to be confuted except in the confutants' own fancies.

[e–f] ms: therein: and   [g–h] ms: power—this   [i] ms: th~~e~~n

[78] Tr: "God throng".

[79] C's emphatic reiterations were at least to some extent conditioned by harsh realisations occurring in the course of his own misery-ridden passage of life. In his youth no such emphasis prevailed. In 1795 he had said: "Reasoning strictly and with logical Accuracy I should deny the existence of any Evil, inasmuch as the end determines the nature of the means and I have been able to discover nothing of which the end is not good. Instead of evil, a disputable word, let us use Pain—" (*Lects 1795—CC—*105).

our next position is that it began, that it had an Origin. ~~therefore was not eternal~~ I do not mean a cause or ground or principle, for rather as far as we speak of the *actual* exclusively, the very contrary is the truth; [*p 113*] and when I call it originant, originative, or original (and I use these words only to give them their right sense, and because they are the terms which the Schools of Divinity have appropriated to this purpose, and because they have been fearfully misunderstood—even in those schools—and confounded with "aboriginal" and "hereditary")—this evil is original,⁸⁰ or had a beginning, therefore was not eternal, and yet as having begun must of necessity have had* an antecedent. But here the Eternal alone is present. And it has been demonstrated that Evil could not originate in God, therefore in the eternal in some sense in which it is not God. But again, whatever is actually eternal is such only as God, or as one with God, therefore in an eternal which is not eternal actually,ʲ therefore in an eternal possibility or potentiality. But [*p 115*] this we have shown to be contained in the idea of the divine Plenitude, in the absolute necessity of the difference of the particular from the universal, of the dependent from the absolute, they being all forms of the Will, and having Will as their essence and subsistence.

And here let me entreat the earnest inquirer not to take offence at words where the intended sense is blameless, and where the words, though capable of offence and therefore to be avoided in a popular work in which the affections and our practical nature are addressed and not, as is here the case, the speculative intellect especially, though in behoof of the affections and for a future practical interest, and where, therefore, it is most expedient to give to each important term its own precise and peculiar import, by [*p 117*] having so done to abide by the same through-

* [*Written on p 112:*] I use the preterite or past tenses for the sake of ⟨being⟩ more easy⟨ily⟩ intelligibility⟨le⟩. A truth would have been equally expressed had I used the present tense "originates" or "begins", "As in Adam we all die", etc. But this would have been combining two difficulties in one, and the reader has been already put on his guard with respect to the imperfections of language, which if they compelled us to expressions of time when we were treating of the Eternal alone may well ~~excuse our~~ necessitate the same on subjects in which the temporal is concerned, and yet in relation to the Eternal.

ʲ Written "actually eternal" and marked with a curved line for transposition

By the 1820s, however, life and thought had driven him to the emphatic avowals above.
⁸⁰ Cf *Aids to Reflection*: "... the Mystery of Original Sin will be either rejected, or evaded, or perverted into the monstrous fiction of Hereditary Sin, Guilt inherited" (*AR*—1825—293).

out, even at the risk of jarring with the associations or senses connected with the same word in the more frequent, though laxer and less proper, use of the same. On this occasion I refer more expressly to the term "*uncreated*". There is a sense of the word "Creature" which includes whatever is not God, or Very God of Very God, and in this sense I do not use the word,[81] save only when I apply it to God or the Tri-unity. ~~For as it~~ As applied to all else, or other than the Father, the Son, and the Spirit, however glorious, I denounce it as sacrilege and idolatry. But there is a sense of the Word "created"—and this too by the Creeds of the Church, and the Councils, and by Sᵗ Paul, in the original Greek at least—in which the terms[k] "*created*" and "*uncreated*" simply express that which had a beginning in time, that which, not having been, became [*p 119*] or began to be. So that not only in the disquisitions of philosophy and the books of Plato and the Platonists but in the writings of the New Testament, the Creature or the Creaturely as simply such, or ⟨now⟩ denominated and now derived, from things that are not ⟨as in⟩.[l] Thus[m] ⟨too⟩ Augustine tells us that out of nothing was the world created,[82] itself being almost nothing, i.e. το μη οντος ov. In this sense "created" is opposed to "begotten" and "proceeding", and if it ~~were neces~~ followed necessarily from the use of "uncreated" that therefore the ideas or living powers were begotten or proceeding, I might still vindicate myself by the authority both of the church and scripture, as long as I did not imply, as long as I [*p 121*] heedfully guarded against, the position that they were begotten for them-

---

[k] ms: term
[l] ms: (I Cor. Chap. I, where the Apostle, speaking of our restoration to things eternal by the ministry of the Creatures, expresses ~~it~~ ⟨the sense in words⟩ that God has chosen, yea, even the things that are not) [*cancelled in ink with vertical lines*]
[m] ms: thus

[81] That is, "uncreated".
[82] E.g. "omnia quae fecit, quia ex nihilo fecit, mutabilia sunt" (P[atrologia] L[at.] 42, 551); "ita ut creatura omnis sive intellectualis sive corporalis . . . non de Dei natura, sed a Deo sit facta de nihilo" (P[atrolog.] L[at.] 34, 221) (quoted in Gilson *Augustine* 313 n 2; 336 n 13). C may well have in mind, however, the statement "Mundum e nihilo creavit ipsum paene nihil" (*CM—CC*—I 645). George Whalley's note to that is as follows: "'He created the world from nothing, it being almost nothing.' The meaning of C's 'Well might Augustine say, on the emanative plan' [which precedes C's quotation of the Latin] is ambiguous. He evidently has in mind Augustine *Confessions* 12.8, as misquoted in Sir Walter Ralegh *History of the World* (1677) 3 (see *CN* II 3088 and n) tr LCL: 'But all this whole was almost nothing [*prope nihil*], because hitherto it was altogether without form; but yet there was now something apt to be formed. For thou, Lord, madest the world of a matter without form; which being next to nothing [*paene nullam rem*], thou madest out of nothing; out of which thou mightest make those great works which we sons of men do wonder at.' By substituting 'the world' for 'matter without form', Ralegh—and C—have distorted Augustine's meaning" (*CM—CC*—I 645 n).

selves, or were self-subsistent: for these belong exclusively to the be-
gotten Son, and who therefore in this, its highest and most proper sense,
is assuredly the only begotten. Even before all time, the Sons of the Most
High were Sons of adoption only, though eternally adopted, yet having
their Sonship [. . .] only in the only-begotten, and through him and for
him. And if we said that they were formed by him in himself, we should
not speak amiss if thereby we better distinguished these adopted Sons of
Glory from "the begotten, the Only-begotten Son",[83] the eternal Heir of
all Glory, in whom all the rest have their title, their Sonship, derived from
and dependent on his. Thus explained and thus guarded, I say too little
in affirming that it ought to minister no occasion of offence, for it not
only interferes with no attribute of God and the Trinity, but is [*p 123*]
the opening to the view, first of his holiness and ~~self~~ absolute self-suffi-
cience and ineffable goodness, and then of his Wisdom and Love and In-
finite Mercy.

Do we then affirm that a change can take place in the plenitude of the
divine Idea, a change in the Eternal, a diminution in the Infinite, or rather
in the measure of the Infinite? We recoil from the thought, and abhor it.
What do I say, though? That it cannot be, for how can the adequate Idea
of the Supreme Mind abide, and aught that is contained or involved
therein cease to be? Rather, therefore, be it said that we recoil from the
attempt to think that which would have appeared a blasphemy, could we
see through the ~~opacity~~ ⟨"dense opake"⟩[84] of the ⟨intervening⟩ absurdity.
To borrow an illustration of spiritual [*p 125*] truths, above all of ~~such~~
spiritual truths so unutterably transcendent, from the most glorious ob-
jects of the senses, or the most subtle and refined forms of the material
world, is not without peril.[n][*] But I will venture to anticipate those
higher views of the material world, which I trust will be opened out in

[*] And[o] the more perilous from the prevailing, and in fact the only tolerated
system of philosophy, which has rendered it difficult even for the sincerest seek-
ers after truth to emancipate their minds from the habit of considering all bodies
as a concrete ⟨aggregate⟩ of corpuscles, serving as a basis, or cushion for the in-
sertion of I know not what properties—which, however, when questioned are
but streaming aggregates of other corpuscles which nevertheless need the same

----

[n] The rest of the sentence is enclosed in brackets and keyed with an asterisk to an in-
struction in JHG's hand on p 124: "to be printed as a note"
[o] ms: and

[83] Cf John 3.16: "For God so loved
the world, that he gave his only begotten
Son, that whosoever believeth in him
should not perish, but have everlasting
life."
[84] The phrase is not, as might be sup-
posed, from Milton. Nor is it from
Spenser, Shakespeare, Dryden, or Pope.

the following section of this work;[86] and after the example of the inspired prophets no less than of the ⟨ancient⟩ sages, whose philosophy approached nearest to the doctrines of inspiration,

> ~~w~~We'll try to borrow from the glorious sun
> A little light to illustrate this act,
> Such as he is in his solstitial noon,
> When in the welkin there's no cloudy tract,
> For to make gross his beams and light refract.
> Then sweep by all those globes that by reflexion
> His long small shafts do rudely beaten back,
> And let his rays have undenied projection,
> And so we will pursue this mysteries retection.[87]

~~An impo No less impos~~ Not more impossible is it to conceive the ~~focus~~ ⟨sun⟩ ~~lux et lumen~~ sun, the tri-unity of the focus lux et lumen,[88] to be in all its splendour and yet rayless [*p 131*] than to conceive the spiritual

---

process and must, in spite of the theorist's reluctance, be contemplated in the same light with the larger atoms, [*p 127*] from between which they are supposed to be effluent. The understanding, indeed, soon feels that it is trifled with, that the difficulty is deferred without being diminished ~~as~~

> as mother's dear
> In pleasance from them do their children share,
> That back again they may recoil more near,[85]

and that if the subtlest atoms do at last act by their properties and not by contact, even though contact itself could[*p*] be conceived efficient otherwise than by some property, there can exist no pretext in reason why the original body should not produce a correspondent effect by its own power—though the reason, I say, is baffled, and even the understanding feels itself trifled with, yet the fancy is ~~peopled~~ disturbed, crowded, and eddying, and ~~interferes~~ troubles the intellective power, rendering it exceedingly hard to contemplate any form of the senses [*p 129*] in that purer light in which alone the corporeal can become a fit symbol of the spiritual.

p A slip for "could not"?

85 Henry More *Antipsychopannychia* "The Preexistence of the Soul" verse 7 lines 6–8 (var).

86 Perhaps a substantial indication as to the proper placement of what in this ed is entitled Frag 4.

87 Henry More *Psychozoia* II verse 7 (More 19). C has changed the opening: "Then let us borrow" to "We'll try to borrow".

88 The three words are all synonyms of light. C needs three words, because he will use the image of the sun ("the spiritual sun") as an adequate symbol of the Trinity.

sun without its effluence, the essentially causative Will without its co-eternal products.[89] As long as the rays are part of the glory, radiant distinctly but without division, so long are they one with the sun, and such must be from eternity to eternity. But these spiritual rays are themselves essential Wills and have their causativeness, which is One with that of the Divine Will as long as they are rays of the Sun.[90] But if we could conceive any number as separated from the solar orb and no longer a prolongation of its effluence, strangled in clouds and borne anew as it were in rainbows and the phantoms of the air, would there be for this any loss or change in the sun or in the solar sphere? But to what purpose do I adduce this symbol if the reader beholds and contemplates it in the spirit of the corpuscular system, [if] the ⟨utter⟩ differences will overlay the shadowy [*p 133*] and less than poetic likeness, and ~~pl~~ set into the ferment the sensuous imagination and the correspondent functions of the understanding, which it is our main desideratum to keep at rest, silent and under a veil? But if it be requisite that the enquirer should learn to contemplate the sun itself as a reflex power, as a form revealed to us by the shape[91] which it impresses on the recipient sense, which therefore ~~mimics an~~ is an effect in us of the sun rather than the sun itself, then we have the same difficulty to overcome, the ~~same~~ task remaining the same and the mere articulable sounds altered. I have no other answer to this objection but that I have found it a help in my own mind to use this image as the philosopher of Nola[92] had done before, as a mental diagram for the fixing [of] the attention and the ordonnance of the [*p 135*] memory—as, in short, the best, most comprehensive, richest, and most flexible organ of a memoria technica. And this, the sun, with its profundity

[89] The image of the sun shedding its light but not being diminished was a favourite image by which Plotinus explained how the One could be causative of the world.

[90] As early as 1794, in his poem *Religious Musings*, C had said that "the Great Invisible" was "by symbols only seen" (*PW*—EHC—I 109 lines 9–10); and this action involved "a peculiar and surpassing light" (line 11).

[91] For C's desynonymising of form and shape, see Frag 2 f 98, f 107, ff 113–14, et passim. See also *CN* IV 5295.

[92] Giordano Bruno. The life and system of Bruno, along with those of "Jacob Behmen, George Fox, and Benedict Spinoza", was the fifth of the sections of the proposed *magnum opus* communicated to John May on 27 Sep 1815, and to Daniel Stuart on 7 Oct 1815 (*CL* IV 590, 592). C said in 1819 that his "History of Giordano Bruno" was halted because a certain person would not lend him books of Bruno's writings (*CL* IV 926). He lists Bruno among those who possessed "great Genius and original Mind" (*CL* IV 938), and he calls Bruno "one of my great Favorites" (*CL* III 127). C was spurred and reinforced in his admiration by a luminous appendix on Bruno, from which C lifts actual phrases, attached to the second ed of Jacobi's *Ueber die Lehre des Spinoza* in 1789 (Jacobi *Werke* IV–i 7–10, IV–ii 2–46). See *CPT* xxxiii.

of forms and forces, of lights and shadows, will not fail to present, and without ~~danger~~ ⟨risk⟩ of error, if only the main difficulty have been once thoroughly apprehended, and in that very apprehension overcome and disarmed, though not removed. It is enough to have seen that it is a difficulty which arises out of our nature, and while that nature remains, must remain with it; that it arises out of that department of our nature, which hath no jurisdiction over the subjects on which we are at present discoursing; that the faculty out of which the ⟨difficulty⟩ springs, and the difficulty itself, therefore with it remains, ~~nor~~ nay, will be active.*q* ~~the eye remains gazing~~ While*r* the ear is deeply listening [*p 137*] to some sweet harmony from an unknown distance, the eyes will gaze thitherward, even though ~~we~~ ⟨it⟩ should have been ascertained that it was the music of the air, such as travellers are said to have heard in Ceylon and Sumatra, produced by the motion of currents and counter-currents, the glancing fingers of electric fire in the higher atmosphere. This difficulty is that in ⟨the extrication of⟩ which we have been so long engaged, that potential duplicity of being which we have proved to be of necessity involved in all particular forms contained in the universal or absolute idea, ~~b~~of all Wills contained in the adequate offspring of the absolute Will, of all subsistencies living in the absolute self-subsisting life. This duplicity cannot be rightly deemed or called a self-duplication, for of all subsistencies, subsisting in and as one with the eternal mind (νοῦς) there is no self other than the ⟨self of the⟩ great I AM ~~tha~~.[93] But the power (potentia) here asserted [*p 139*] is the power of losing that, of substituting a self that is not God, a center in that which cannot be other than peripheric. Neither can we say that this god-less self, this false and contradictory self, a lie from the beginning and the father or fountain of all lies, is begotten, for what is begotten is consubstantial with that of which it is begotten; nor yet proceeding, for that which proceeds must be convirtual with its source and proceed only to return, the circle of the fountain which is everywhere stream, of the stream which is in every point fountain; nor yet can we say that it was made, for of that which is made the component parts pre-exist, and the composition alone is given: ~~or There rem~~ shall we dare, then, say *s*"create"? But*t* to create is to call into ac-

---

q ms: active, as   *r* ms: while
s–t ms: create but

[93] See *Logic* (*CC*) 85: "If then we elevate our conception to the absolute Self, Spirit, or Mind, the underived and eternal "I Am", then and herein we find the principle of being, and of knowledge, of idea, and of reality; the ground of existence, and the ground of the knowledge of that existence, absolutely one and identical; both are alike adequately expressed in the term "sum quia sum", "I am because I affirm myself to be". See further *CL* II 1197; Frag 2 f 243, f 223.

tual being that which actually was not; the τα μη οντα are exclusively the proper subjects of creation. There remains only [*p 141*] the term "to will", or "to cause", or "to will causatively". The potential, still a form of reality, though its negative role, and therefore a form of Will, willed itself to be actual under impossible *"*conditions. For*ᵛ* to be actual was to will its subsistence to be in God, and the power of willing otherwise existed potentially, by necessity ~~of the~~ ⟨in a⟩ ~~Will on~~ part of a Will, and part because it was a particular Will. It could not but be, because the real was, and the actual was, but in all particular forms the actual could not be without the particular. The result can be no otherwise expressed, as far as it can be at all expressed, than that a self became, which was not God, nor One with God. The potential was actualized, ~~but~~ ⟨yet⟩ not as actual, but by a strange yet appropriate contradiction as potential. Thus the actuality became merely potential, and yet not subordinated to this [*p 143*] actualized potential, but existing only in the eternal actuality as a power, and in the ⌈. . .⌉ false self only as the possible subject of that actuality. Here, preeminently, is it indispensable to keep the idea steadfast before the mind in the first formation of the distinct senses attached to the several component terms, and should it exceed our power to fix the idea through the whole process of the reasoning, to ~~accommodate~~ ⟨reason⟩ nevertheless by the terms with that kind of assurance of faith with which the algebraist places his signs, ⟨letters,⟩ and cyphers, his ~~polar axioms~~ + and − and ∨ etc. in their due places, drawing out ~~of~~ the thread of its calculus, now emerging into light and now hidden in the cylinders of the machine. Happily, there is but one thing necessary for us to believe with a full insight, namely that such an origination of self must have been eternally possible. [*p 145*] That it became, the fact itself has proved, and the glory, the wisdom, the omnipotence, and the infinite love of God, unassailed, unapproached, we have learnt ~~on the dictate of reason rather as reason itself~~ from reason; that it is a legitimate idea that Evil may be, as experience proves that it is; that it was not nor cannot be eternal, ~~that yet it~~ and therefore had an origin; that it did not originate in God, or in the Will of God as God, or in the absolute Will as absolute, nor even in the particular eternal as eternal; but that ~~it~~ ⟨Evil⟩ was and ⟨is⟩, in the strictest sense of the words, self-originated, self-originant. The false Self and Evil differ but as essence and form, as cause and effect— differences that exist only for the abstracting and dividing understanding but, contemplated absolutely, must be represented in a fearful sense αυτομητηρ,*ʷ* αυτουιος.[94]

ᵘ⁻ᵛ ms: conditions for   *ʷ* Possibly a slip for "αὐτόματος", "self-willed"

[94] Tr: "father of itself, son of itself".

[*p 147*]   Chapter

Before we proceed to state the necessary result of an Evil thus originated, supposing it abandoned to itself, uncounteracted and unassisted, or [to state] the conceivability of any such aid or counteraction, and, lastly, the effects and the process which would designate and accompany this combat of Good and Evil as far as they can be rendered subjects of ideal insight—that is, be found involved in the preceding ideas, partaking of the same conceivability and necessity with them, so that each successive act and manifestation should in the first instance arise out of the preceding and yet ~~throw back~~ render the prior steps additionally intelligible, so that our whole progress should be a repetition of two positions: AB is conceivable and ideally necessary, because it is the idea which ~~alone~~ ⟨we⟩ necessarily [*p 149*] form of our primary postulate A, with the assumption and concession of which we have commenced our series of evidence. But in B a third in like manner is contained. This is the nature of the first position. The second ˣis thatʸ C, thus evolved out of B, shall either increase the sphere of our comprehension respecting B, either positively or indirectly by clearing up some apparent contradiction in the ~~former~~ constitution of the idea. As when, for instance, two contradictory positions, both of which are contained in the same idea, are possible only under such a condition. But this condition is ⟨necessarily⟩ contained in the idea, inasmuch as that which is true cannot consist of contradictory components. Before, I say, we proceed to this, it will be no uninteresting nor unserviceable digression, if we compare our system hitherto concerning the Deity [*p 151*] and the possible origin of Evil consistently with the idea of God, with ~~that~~ ⟨some⟩ schemesᶻ of preceding philosophers that shall seem to bear the nearest resemblance to the present, and from which, at first sight, it might have the appearance of having been borrowed.⁹⁵ ~~In this light I know of~~ For this purpose I know of no one having the same claims with the doctrines of the Eclectic ⟨G or Egypto-Grecian⟩ Philosophy,⁹⁶ or more definitely the Dogmas of Plotinus.⁹⁷ It

---

ˣ⁻ʸ ms: is: That   ᶻ ms: scheme

⁹⁵ The schemes of "preceding philosophers" that C chooses to refer to in the discourse that follows—Plotinus, the Samothracian deities, the Cabbalists, and the Hindus—might at first glance seem entirely discrete; but they are linked by the fact that, first, they all assert a form of trinitarian thinking that C wishes to separate from the true Trinity of Christian theology, and that, secondly, they are all a form of pantheism. Cf a letter of

23 May 1818: "We owe it at least to the most venerable of all sciences [theology], that it should first be heard.... How can we do this, but by an examination of all the Systems . . . that have been taught or received as scientific Theology?"—and the first of the systems he then mentions is "the Pantheism of India" (*CL* IV 863).
⁹⁶ Of the Eclectic philosophy C says elsewhere: "It is very difficult to speak

has, indeed, been long familiar with the learned to affirm or deny the identity of the supposed Platonic Trinity with that of the Christian Church;[98] and if it were reasonable to found ~~an op~~ a decision on so momentous a subject on a single fragment of Speusippus,[99] and this comprised in one short sentence,[100] I should be inclined to the *a*affirmative. But*b* I am well aware that however well calculated a single passage

a–b ms: affirmative: but

accurately of the opinions of a sect whose great pride was to combine and reconcile all the truths of the other philosophies that had appeared in the world, in that very instance presenting itself as the mimic of Christianity and pretending to do what had been really done by Christianity; and the more difficult is it because, as their predominant features, according to themselves, were in the union of Pythagoreanism with Platonism, it becomes doubly perplexing to us who are not really well acquainted with what Platonism was" (*P Lects*—1949—237).

[97] Plotinus, though he achieved his philosophical maturity in Rome, came from Egypt and underwent his formative philosophical training there.

[98] Henry More, for instance, as preliminary to his *Psychozoia*, which is the first part of his *A Platonick Song of the Soul*, said in 1647 that "*Ahad*, *Æon*, and *Psyche* are all omnipresent in the World, after the most perfect way that humane reason can conceive of. For they are in the world all totally and at once every where. This is the famous Platonicall Triad: which though they that slight the Christian Trinity do take for a figment; yet I think it no contemptible argument, that the Platonists, the best and divinest of Philosophers, and the Christians, the best of all that do professe religion, do both concur that there is a Trinity" (More [B7]: "To the Reader, Upon the first Canto of PSYCHOZOIA"). Cudworth, again, in the *True Intellectual System of the Universe* in 1678 speaks explicitly and at length about the Platonic Trinity and says in part that "the *Generality* of the *Christian Fathers*, before and after the *Nicene Council*, represent the *Genuine*, *Platonick Trinity*, as really the

same thing with the *Christian*, or as approaching so near to it, that they differed chiefly in Circumstances, or the manner of Expression" (Cudworth 621). He says that "we cannot but take notice here of a Wonderful Providence of Almighty God, that this Doctrine of a Trinity of Divine *Hypostases*, should find such Admittance and Entertainment in the Pagan World, and be received by the wisest of all their Philosophers, before the times of Christianity; thereby to prepare a more easie way for the Reception of Christianity amongst the Learned Pagans" (625).

[99] Greek philosopher (d 339 or 338 B.C.), nephew of Plato, and selected by him as his successor as head of the Academy (347). Only a fragment of one of his works, *On Pythagorean Numbers*, survives. See Guthrie v 457–69. According to Diogenes Laertius, Speusippus left behind "a vast store of memoirs and numerous dialogues", and after listing some thirty titles, he says that "They comprise in all 43,475 lines" (*DL* I 379, 381).

[100] J. R. de J. Jackson notes that "C refers to the fragment in *P Lects* Lect 5 (1949) 175. It is quoted in Tennemann III 9n from Stobaeus *Eclog. Physic.* I c 3 p 38: 'the Nous is not the same as the One or the Good, but has a nature of its own'. C's version in *P Lects* runs as follows: 'I refer to the passage in which we are told that the intelligential powers, by the Pythagoreans and Anaxagoras called the *Nous* (the *Logos* or the *Word* of Philo and St. John) is indeed indivisibly united with, but yet not the same as the absolute principle of causation, THE PATERNAL One, the super-essential Will ...'" (*Logic*—*CC*—33 n 2).

might be to confirm other [*p 153*] proof, it would be highly unsatisfactory if advanced as the proof itself. The writings of Plato are indeed still extant and sufficiently voluminous, but independent of Plato's own assertion in an epistle, the authenticity of which I see no reason for doubting, that he never has nor ever would commit to writing his convictions on this subject,[101] the ~~origin of~~ mysterious nature of the Supreme Being and the origin of Evil in consistence with the admission of a perfect Goodness—independently of this, I say, I have long convinced myself that it was no part of Plato's aim or purpose, in the works which he made public and which are still extant, to teach or unfold his own philosophy, or indeed any philosophy in the strictest and Platonic sense of the word.[102]

My own convictions on this subject, with their grounds consisting, I willingly confess, for the greater part [*p 155*] in hints or incidental observations found in the Platonic dialogues which appear incompatible with the doctrine either of emanation or expansion (as the two flaws, one or the other of which prevent any resemblances of the Christian Trinity found in the Greek Philosophers later than Plato and his immediate successors,[103] Speusippus, Xenocrates,[104] and Polemo, or in the Theolo-

---

[101] Plato *Epistles* VII 341B–344D.

[102] Cf *Philosophical Lectures*: "the works of Plato contain the opinions of Socrates, but they by no means convey the opinions of Plato. I do not mean that they convey different opinions but they do not convey the peculiar opinions of Plato" (*P Lects*—1949—156). Plato himself said, in the *Phaedrus* and in two of the *Epistles* (supposing them genuine), that no one should commit true philosophy to writing. This distinction between what are called the *exoteric* and *esoteric* doctrines of Plato must be a major factor in any attempt to assess his thought. True philosophy, Plato apparently believed, was a living thing educed only from dialectic conversation, e.g. "no dead discourse, but the living speech, the original of which the written discourse may fairly be called a kind of image" (*Phaedrus* 276A).

[103] For the immediate successors then specified—"Speusippus, Xenocrates and Polemo"—cf *Philosophical Lectures*: "Therefore I say that Plato united the elder philosophers with the philosophy of Socrates, and this is proved to us

not only by the little which the ancients record of Xenocrates, namely that with the Socratic words he united the Pythagorean, but by both Xenocrates and Speusippus, and likewise by two other followers who have been recorded, CRANTOR and POLEMO who following that, maintained: firstly, the immortality of the soul, as the best and worthiest ground of hope . . . THE finite nature of the material world as the proximate cause, but by no means as the absolute origin of pain and imperfection in the world; and, lastly, the reconciliation of man, and . . . of the whole creation, with the Deity, as the only remedy of these evils" (*P Lects*—1949—176–7).

[104] 396–314 B.C. The successor to Speusippus as head of the Platonic Academy (339–314). He left Athens with Aristotle shortly after Plato's death, and did not return until Speusippus was no longer in the ascendant. As C says in *Philosophical Lectures*: "we may derive from Xenocrates, Speusippus's successor, the proof of another assertion which I hazarded, namely, that the true idea of Plato's genius and system is to be found

gyies of Persia and Hindostan, from being more than verbal resem-
blances, or apparent resemblances),[c] [are] strengthened, however, by the
positive assertion of a distinctness of the Good as well as of the Intelli-
gent from the Absolute Source. These belong to another work, and can
form no link in the chain of evidence attempted in the present. At all
events, the conjecture will with more propriety be introduced in the his-
torical part, either ~~as determin~~ in aid of the argument for the ~~early~~ exis-
tence of this doctrine in the earlier and even [*p 157*] patriarchal church,
or among the known and probable causes that predisposed the more cul-
tivated portion of the pagan world to the acceptance of the christian faith.

With still ~~more~~ less hesitation may the statements of the Jewish Cab-
bala in the purest state,[105] with the grounds for its existence before the
christian era, and likewise the numerous passages bearing on this article
of faith[106] and the doctrines connected with and presupposing it, be re-
served, both ~~for~~ ⟨as parts of⟩ the historical evidence and still more for
hermeneutic purposes, as determining the true sense of the christian
scriptures considered as historical documents. I pass at once, therefore,
to the ~~Graeco~~ Aegypto-Graecian school, or the Alexandrine Philosophy,
taking for my guide and authority the immediate disciple of Ammo-
nius,[107] the founder of this school, ~~and beyond all~~ [*p 159*] ~~comparison
the greatest~~ the first who reduced its tenets to writing, and beyond all
comparison the profoundest philosopher[108] and the ⟨most⟩ important
work of which the school is entitled to boast. And here, instead of se-

[c] Parentheses inserted

---

in the union of Pythagoras with Socrates"
(*P Lects*—1949—176). For discussion
of Xenocrates see Guthrie v 469–83.

[105] For the fullest utilisation of C's
considerable knowledge of the Cabala,
see Tim Fulford *Coleridge's Figurative
Language* (London 1990). See esp C's
discussion in *Philosophical Lectures*,
where in speaking of Johannes Reuch-
lin's service to Hebrew studies and his
recommendation of the Cabala, he says:
"What the origin of the Cabala was I
cannot pretend to tell you precisely. I
know it is commonly said that it began
from the 10th century or even later in the
middle ages. This appears to me utterly
unlikely. At least I find the references to
it so strong in the works of the first cen-
tury . . ." (*P Lects*—1949—299).

[106] I.e. the Trinity. C was firm in his
opinion that the Cabala must be ac-

counted a form of pantheism, and that
therefore it could not in any way be
aligned with the Christian Trinity, which
was precisely the remedy to pantheism:
"the Cabbalistic Theosophy is pantheis-
tic: and Pantheism, in whatever drapery
of pious phrases disguised, is (where it
forms the whole of a System) Atheism,
& precludes moral responsibility, and
the essential difference of Right and
Wrong. . . . It is not therefore half a
dozen passages respecting the three first
Proprietates in the Sephiroth, that will
lead a wise man to expect the true doc-
trine of the Trinity in the Cabbalistic
Scheme" (*CM—CC*—III 1091).

[107] Ammonius Saccas (d after 242
A.D.), Alexandrian philosopher, the
founder of the Neoplatonic school and
teacher of Plotinus.

[108] I.e. Plotinus.

lecting the passages in which a divine Trinity is asserted, much less enlarging their number from works later than the time of the Emperor Julian,[109] the authors of which purposely coloured their language and selected their terminology with the view of setting up a religion of philosophy, now as a rival of Christianity and now as including the christian faith, I will give the substance of their ~~opinions~~ ⟨principles⟩, or rather the grounds and primary principles on which their doctrine rested, and there in ~~the original~~ ⟨its fundamental⟩ and inherent diversity from the doctrines evolved in the preceding chapters, a diversity which no succeeding approximations [*p 161*] to the language of the catholic church,[110] nor real resemblance to the arguments and explications of the catholic article, as ~~in~~uttered in the writings of the Fathers can remove or [? ~~mystify~~] diminish. In opposition, then, to the ~~assertion~~ position laid down, or neglectful of the warning given by Speusippus, the most faithful organ of original Platonism,* they established their first principle, their ~~princip~~

[*] [*Written on pp 160, 162, and 164:*] ᵈτον νουν ουτε τῳ ΕΝΙ ουτε τῳ ΑΓΑΘΩ αυτον ιδιοφυη δε. The order, therefore, of the Hypostases (τῶν ιδιφυων) in the ~~Supreme~~ ⟨Godhead⟩ , according to Speusippus, was Τὸ῁΅ΕΝ, tha̶t̶⟨e⟩ ~~source of Unity, the~~ One as the source of Unity and Ground of all Being; Ο ΝΟΥΣ; and το ΑΓΑΘΟΝ—the latter answering to the Sophia, the name appropriated to the Holy Spirit by the Fathers, as the divine ⟨Unity, Being &⟩ i̶Intelligence in communicative Act—even as we say in common life, the Good only are Wisd̶o̶m̶⟨e⟩—i.e. Wisdom is distinguished from Intelligence by *Goodness*, i.e. by beneficent *Act.ᵉ* I by no means, however, assert that Speusippus had given a positive character or, as it were, an intelligible content to the idea of the Το ῁΅ΕΝ. More than an algebraic mark standing for an un[*p 162*]known⌈. . .⌉quantity, the position alone of which is determinable, it may have been ⟨more⟩ yetᶠ ~~different from it~~ far short of a full Idea. What the founder of the Critical Philosophy[111] has entitled Schemata[112] or Outlines, determining the extent but not, or only partially, denoting the contents, would perhaps be nearest the truth. He saw certain attributes, the το ὑπηρούσιονη,ᵍ[113] for instance, but did not see that these

---

ᵈ⁻ᵉ Possibly in C's hand   ᶠ ms: and yet
ᵍ A slip for "τὸ ὑπερούσιον" "the supraexistential"

---

[109] Julian the Apostate (c 331–363), Roman Emperor (361–363), enemy of Christianity and publicly declared adherent of paganism.

[110] By "Catholic church" Coleridge meant the "universal" church, not the Roman Catholic church.

[111] Kant.

[112] The schema is a variant of imaginative function; it is a mental synthesis in the imagination divorced from a specific image. When we pass beyond the

specific images we do not cease to think; the continuation rather takes place as a schematism: "It is schemata, not images of objects, that underlie our pure sensible concepts. No image could ever be adequate to the concept of a triangle in general. . . . The schema of the triangle can exist nowhere but in thought" (*Kant* IV 101). For discussion see McFarland *Rousseau* 221–4.

[113] Tr: "the above being".

absolutum primum,[114] in the idea of the Good; their second in Mind, ὅ ΝΟΥΣ; and their third they called the ΨΥΧΗ,[h] soul or life. That these, considered not in themselves but as manifested in the world, coexistent in unity, is a doctrine ~~which~~ of most frequent occurrence in Plotinus and still more as applied to the different orders of the gods in Proclus; but that the Deity, the Supreme Godhead, existed as a Trinity in Unity neither appears nor was indeed possible without the grossest inconsequence, as will appear by the definition which [*p 163*] these writers give both of the νους and of the ψυχη, not to add that such an idea is precluded by the doctrine of emanation under whatever form presented.

The use of negation or negative positions in the presentation of ideas and conceptions, whether in the primary development of the thought or in exciting and assisting the mind of another to repeat the process, is twofold. First, as preparative (προ καθαρτικον), as in giving directions to a traveller whose immediate object lies beyond a heath where there are many paths and the one which alone he is to take is dim and unknown to him, we first describe the others in succession, each by some appropriate mark and still ending with "Now this you are not to take" or "None of these are your road", then proceeding to describe the one in question positively, that is, by its proper characters, ~~we can~~ ⟨if it be in our power so to do⟩. If not, we must leave him to find them out by himself, or to give [*p 165*] up the object he had in view—content with having saved him in the one case from going astray, and in the other from wasting or risking the waste of his time and strength. Such is the first use of negation. Its second use we may distinguish ~~by~~ as determinant, where for the most part the negation is partial only, as disjunction conjunctive, as when, in describing the predominant hue of the opal or the occasional opalescence of the horizon at sunset, we may say it is not a green but an intervening or combining hue, or both colours in one.[115] Now this ap-

---

were united and realized in the idea of an absolute Will. Of course, the advantages from this more just view of the subject were negative, but not therefore unreal or of small magnitude. fFor to this we may attribute the superior modesty and temperance in dogma and deduction of the first Academic School, and their freedom from the error of making the difference between Good and Evil to consist in degree only, and Vice with all its consequences pure negations in the abstract, but in fact mere diminutions and, as it were, rarefactions, of Virtue. An error at all times injurious, but if carried into its close and legitimate consequences, sub[*p 164*]versive of all morality and all ⟨true⟩ religion.

[h] ms: PSYXH

114 Tr: "first absolute".
115 On the two uses of negation com-   pare a parallel statement of 1822: "The
   use of Negation or negative positions in

plication of negatives is of highest utility in all reasoning in which we proceed by antithesis, or what I have elsewhere called the logic of Trichotomy, or still more accurately, adopting both the principles and the terminology of the eldest Pythagorean school, the Tetracτtic.[116] This takes place when we have to speak of the indifference, punctum indifferentiae,[117] of two ex[*p 167*]tremes, ex. gr. in the magnet, ~~in~~ ⟨likewise in cases [of]⟩ neutralization, ~~or~~ whether in the proper sense of the term, ex. gr. in water as the neutral product of oxygen and hydrogen, or where a positive tertium aliquid[118] results from the union of two opposites, as the salts from the combination of acids and alkalis, or in combination ~~by~~ ⟨with⟩ an overbalance of one component; and lastly, and if possible, of still more indispensable use in the treatment of radical powers, which I have elsewhere compared to the point unproduced, to the positive unit contemplated as ⟨not⟩ yet unfolded, and which ⟨first⟩ manifesting itself in two opposite, corresponding forces, each ~~of which~~ supposesing the other and both presupposing their common root. In short, we find the convenience in all instances, and the necessity in many, when we have to form or convey a distinct conception or clear ideas of ⟨indifference, of⟩ synthesis, or of ~~a~~ prothesis, by which last I here mean the identity of any [*p 169*] two, not their union or equilibrium.

Now in this second use it is evident that some positive idea must be either given previously, or else furnished by and, as it were, reflected from the negative positions themselves. ~~Or else~~ Where this is not the case, the result can be only a negative idea, which in truth is a contradictory phrase, tantamount to no idea at all of the particular subject in question. Let us apply these remarks to the first principle of the Plotinian Trinity.[119] We are told that this first principle "Non proprie dici posse, aut *efficere*, aut *cogitare*: imò, ne *esse* quidem".[120] We must not affirm of it that it either acts or does or thinks, nay, we dare not say even that it is.[121] Now if this is not a description of nothing, it is necessary

---

the presentation of Truths, whether in the primary developement of the Thought, or in exciting and assisting another Mind to repeat the process, is two fold. First, preparative. . . . Second, determinant, where the negation is partial only . . . . This is of highest utility in the Logic of Antithesis . . ." (*SW & F—CC*—II—1035).

[116] For the mutual implication of polarity, trichotomy, and the "Tetractic" see Prolegomena x: The *Magnum Opus* and the Principle of Polarity. See also, Frag 2 f 277.

[117] Tr: "point of indifference".

[118] Tr: "third something".

[119] For Plotinus's trinity, see *Enneads* 5.1: "The Three Initial Hypostases".

[120] Tr: "Not properly to be called possibility, or effect, or thinking: more deeply, not even being".

[121] Cf *AR* (1825) 162: "the superessential ONE of Plotinus, to whom neither Intelligence, or Self-consciousness, or Life, or even *Being* may be attributed".

that some positive should be given, either in ~~the~~ as implied in the distinguishing name or in its definition, but in [*p 171*] order to the distinguishing ⟨in the first place⟩ it must not ~~then~~ be a mere repetition of the question: thus [to the question,] "Who wrote the Iliad?" it is no answer to *ⁱ*say, "The writer"; or*ʲ* [to the question,] "Who was the first poet?" to answer, "The man who first successfully attempted poetry". ~~Neither can it add any positive contents to an affirmation of the first principle~~ Neither can it form any positive reply to a question concerning the first principle, that it is designated as the first. *ᵏ*Nor will the defect be removed in this instance, though to the first we should add the word "*cause*",* for independent of other objections, of which the ambiguity of the term and ~~the~~ ⟨its⟩ deficiency in objective truth being not the least, yet this again forms part of the question, which is, "What idea shall we form of the first as the necessary condition of all others?" But secondly, the pretended characteristic must not be a mere generalization or abstraction common to a multitude of subjects, unless there ⟨have⟩ been some other conception afforded, by aid of which it becomes possible to contemplate the same for itself independent of and, as it were, anterior to the ⟨general⟩ application of the same. ~~to~~ Now can this be said of the term "Bonum", "αγαθον", or "the Good"? Assuredly the conception of goodness taken simply and singly implies a given direction of a power, or the directing [*p 173*] act itself, and in all cases suggests the accomplishment of any act or process ~~eons~~ morally considered. It is indeed some objection to the term, as used by Plotinus and his*ˡ* successors, that "the Good" and "the Useful or Advantageous", "Utile sive Commodum", is confounded with "the Good", and in the non-removal of this confusion, which, it must be confessed, is the grievous error of the Socratic morality,¹²² as

[*] [*Written on p 170:*] Note. In the true and only philosophical sense, *cause* is a subordinate form of the human understanding under the more comprehensive term of "reciprocal action", by which we reflect on all things as a chain of antecedent and consequent, each prior link becoming a cause relatively to that which follows, and the first cause still remaining a link of the chain, though a first link. The very epithet of a first cause as applied to the Supreme Being is borrowed from the Cosmotheism of the Pagans, with whom God was One with the world, either as the world or as a component part of the same, imagined, or rather tried to be imagined, as ~~at once~~ ⟨always⟩ co-existing yet always prior.

<hr>

ⁱ⁻ʲ ms: say the writer: or
ᵏ This sentence is written on p 170 and marked for insertion here.
ˡ ms: its

122 Cf   *Philosophical   Lectures*:   to think deeply of that which men ought
"There is a greater defect . . . . He began   really to exist in and to pursue. He seri-

given both in Xenophon[123] and in the dialogues of Plato.[*] Had Plotinus extricated himself from this labyrinth, the investigation of the Good would necessarily have led him to the same truth as it has been the object of this work to establish and [q]explain. But[r] as it now stands in his works and in ~~those~~ the books of the Alexandrian Philosophers without exception, the term is a mere reverential epithet without any substance

[*] *The following passage is written on pp 172 and 174 and keyed to the text at this point with a large "N", which presumably stands for "Note":*] There are not, indeed, wanting passages that prove the occasional and apt—at times it might seem, successful—effort of this great, good man[124] to rise into a purer idea. But he appears to have attempted it by denying the distinction rather than pursuing it to its proper results—and what is most unfortunate, the passages in which the bliss essential to Pleasure, Ἡδονη, and even from Happiness, ευτυχια, ευδαιμονια, by the term "ευπραζη"[m] as the identity of well-being and of well-doing, is[n] inconsistent with the reasoning adopted in all the investigations into the nature and formation of virtue and vice, the latter being evidently reduced to mere error. The strongest and most decisive proof, however, of the obscurity and unsteadiness of the Socratic conversations on this point is afforded by the fact that not only the Epicureans but ~~the~~ [? [gr]] Aristippus,[125] whose scheme was of more undisguised sensuality, no less than the Cynics and the Stoics ~~with~~ laid claim to the authority of Socrates and believed himself[o] to have received his[p] [*p 174*] fundamental principles from his [Socrates's] mouth.

> [m] A slip for "εὐπραξία" or "εὐπραγία", "well-doing"
> [n] A mistake for "are", if the intended subject of the clause is "passages"
> [o] ms: themselves　　　[p] ms: their
> [q-r] ms: explain: but

ously proposed to himself and to his fellow-citizens the question, what is the *summum bonum.* . . . Now here there does certainly appear in the Socratic doctrines a considerable vacillation. Socrates . . . says, 'I devote to the furies the man who first made the distinction between the useful and the honorable;' but it was not a man that made the distinction—it was human nature that had made it" (*P Lects*—1949—149).

[123] Greek historian (c 431–c 352 B.C.), disciple of Socrates. In addition to his famous *Anabasis*, he wrote an account of the life and teachings of Socrates called *Memorabilia*, and a dialogue, *Symposium*, representing Socrates as the chief figure. Xenophon's portrait of Socrates is important as both a confir-

mation and, in its differences, a counterweight to the portrait put forward by Plato. Cf *Philosophical Lectures*: "But had this regarded any essentials of Socrates's doctrines, had there been anything in the doctrines of Plato contrary to them, Xenophon would have noticed and resented it, and this not having been done I think we may fairly rely on the works of Plato as containing the true opinions of Socrates" (*P Lects*—1949—156).

[124] I.e. Plotinus.

[125] Greek philosopher (c 435–366 B.C.), studied under Socrates, and accompanied Plato to Sicily. Founder of the Cyrenaic school of hedonism, which taught that pleasure was the main goal of life. Epicurus was accused of appropriating his doctrines.

to which it may be *ˢattached. For*ᵗ which conception can we possibly affix to a Good, inde[*p 175*]pendent of being, intelligence, and action, of a Good, quae nec *efficit*, nec *est*?[126]

From this principle, however, emanates (we are not told how—it should seem in strict consequence by its own efficiency, which, however, would destroy ~~the propriety as~~ its conceivability as second)ᵘ [127] a second principle, the Νοῦς, ⟨Mens,⟩ or Mind. Now in what relation can we place the Νοῦς to the Ἀγαθόν[128] so as to give substance and propriety to the conception "second"?[129] There is no priority in the thought, or rather we should conceive of the Mind, of an intelligence knowing the nature of being and action, as presupposed in the good, and in any other relation as effect—for instance, how can it stand in this, when we are forbidden to conceive of the antecedent as efficient? In vain would we fly for refuge to metaphors and describe the mind as the simulacrum or mirror of the good, if there have been nothing in[*p 177*]serted in the latter ~~idea~~ that accounts for the being and existence of the former. Nor is this the only evil. We are told repeatedly that this second is inferior to the first. Nay, in yet stronger language, that it is worse. Now let us grant for a moment that notwithstanding we are forbidden to attach any efficiency to the first principle, we should yet place the conception of Power as a basis under the form of the ~~g~~Good. This *power* must of course be conceived as infinite or absolute. But if so, where shall we find the ground ~~E, Ea~~ ⟨in⟩ what way shall we acquire an insight into the possibility, of an inferiority, a diminution, nay, a deterioration, in the effect[130] or, if you will, the offspring? Assuredly an infinite power must have an infinite effect, and this in truth has been the strong and valid objection of the Peripatetic Philosophers against those who asserted a beginning of the world: that an infinite power necessarily producing an [*p 179*] infinite effect with infinite velocity, the power and the product could in no

---

ˢ⁻ᵗ ms: attached; for   ᵘ Parentheses inserted

[126] Tr: "which neither *effects* nor *is*".

[127] The scheme of Plotinus is precisely a system of emanation, that is to say, it rests on the image by which the sun's rays shed their effluence without the sun itself being altered in size or diminished in brightness.

[128] Tr: "good".

[129] A necessary but perplexing question. The burden of C's argument throughout this run of discourse is that where the Christian Trinity has three factors of equal and reciprocal importance, the Plotinian trinity is one of gradated steps and therefore radically unequal in its factors.

[130] Actually, Plotinus does supply an answer. Cf a commentator: "Often, though not always, Plotinus describes emanation as a necessary ... process, somewhat like a point of absolutely intense light which emits a cone of light without any loss of its own substance. As the cone of light expands in volume, it grows dimmer, finally passing into complete darkness" (Merlan 473).

wise be distinguished, no, not even in thought, except by a fraud of the imagination, substituting images, or rather the general impression from images, of finite causation. I have said, "or, if you will, the offspring", and ~~such~~ words conveying the same meaning are occasionally used by Plotinus. Evidently, however, used as metaphors, being generally preceded by ⟨words expressing⟩ some other form of production, and accompanied with a parenthetic ᵛ("or if I may so say", for instance) theʷ Νοῦς is said to im-mane, and elsewhere, passively to be im-maned or evolved or, as it were, progenitum, a progeny of. Secondly, we know from the writings of Philo-judaeus that the words "born", ⟨"generated",⟩ etc. had been long familiar in the schools of Alexandria and are taught by the mythology of India, that in the first instance, at least, they were not used intentionally as metaphors [*p 181*] or as mere aids to the imagination. ~~As m~~Mere metaphors they became, when as in Plotinus there is nothing in the antecedent which could render the terms expressive of a real relation, when, as before observed, there is an endeavour to convey an abstract of cause and effect by accumulating the different modes of production, and leaving to the reader the task of generalizing the whole.

But if in the mere ~~idea~~ abstract conception of power we can find no ground of its limitation, is it to be found in the conception which is given as the form of this power, the distinction or character? Is it to be found in the conception of the Good? But how should this be possible when we are told both by the old and the new Platonists that in the Good there is no withholding?

In no way, therefore, has the poste[*p 183*]riority of the Νοῦς to the first principle been rendered intelligible. No idea has been presented, in which ~~a~~ ⟨a⟩ distinct⟨ness⟩ ~~sense~~ and propriety of the particular position is contained, or from which it can be evolved. The same remarks are applicable in a still more obvious and palpable character in the third principle, the Ψυχη,ˣ anima, life, or ʸsoul—theᶻ two latter senses being confounded in the Greek word, and no attempt made by the writer to prevent, or even avoid, the consequences of the equivocation. Still less do we find any ~~distinct~~ character given by which the obscure fact of life, quod datur, non intelligitur,[131] is rendered intelligible, which yet it must be before it can be legitimately ~~distinguished~~ denied of the Αγαθον[132] and the Νοῦς,[133] or distinguished from them, if the two former principles are intended for more than general terms, the products of the

---

ᵛ⁻ʷ ms: (or if I may so say) for instance the   ˣ ms: Pψυχη
ʸ⁻ᶻ ms: soul. The

[131] Tr: "that is given, not understood".

[132] Tr: "good".

[133] Tr: "mind".

abstracting and generalizing understanding, and mere logical entities. Well! this third principle, however, [*p 185*] flows or springs out of the Νους in the same way as the Νους flowed or sprang out of the Αγαθον? And even as the Νους is more imperfect than the Αγαθον, so is the Ψυχη[a] lower and worse than the mind. To use the words of Creutzer[134] in his edition of Plthe chapter concerning beauty,[135] "Sic ut mens imperfectior ipso bono est, sic anima mente est deterior. Atque cùm anima sit mentis ratio (λογος) et aptus[b] (ενεργεια): tertia illo[c] loco abest à summo bono: utque hoc nullius entis indiget, eo quod ipso sit superius, mens autem indiget boni: sic anima rursùs indiget mentis, estque adeò anima mentis quaedam imago obscurior. Est porrò vita actusque anima non minus quam intellectus, sed tamen debilior intellectu. Videt quoque anima pariter atque mens, sed lucidius haec, obscurius illa."[136] We need quote no more to convince the most inattentive reader that though there are three mentioned, yet in no one of the three is there to be found [*p 187*] aught that could entitle it to the name of a principle, and still less any bond of ⟨a⟩ unity that means more than mere connexion. Need it be said that the word "God" or "Deity" in its philosophic sense is wholly incompatible with comparative debility, obscurity, and progressive deterioration; or where these qualities can be predicated of a subject, to call it God is to affirm of the same thing that it is and that it is not? A frag-

---

[a] ms: Ρψυχη   [b] Creuzer: actus   [c] Creuzer: illa

[134] Cf C's invocation: "a man of great learning, Creuzer" (*P Lects*—1949—120). Friedrich Creuzer, professor at Heidelberg, was at the centre of the Romantic ferment in Germany. His editions of Plotinus and his *Symbolik und Mythologie der alten Völker, besonders der Griechen* were of great effect in the developing emphases of the Romantic movement. Actually, his youthful discovery of Plotinus communicated its enthusiastic effect in letters and conversation well before formal eds appeared. Despite his enormous classical learning, however, his editing technique was careless (particularly for Plotinus, who presented great textual problems), and it was destructively criticised by the Homeric scholar Voss. See *Der Kampf um Creuzers Symbolik; eine Auswahl von Dokumenten* ed Ernst Howald (Tübingen 1926).

[135] *Plotini liber de pulcritudine . . . adjecit Fridericus Creuzer* (Heidelberg

1814) xcvi–xcvii. Of this volume C writes to J. H. Bohte, a bookseller, on 27 Feb 1819: "Creuzer's Plotinus you will set down to my account, which shall be settled whenever you express the Wish" (*CL* IV 923). The "chapter concerning beauty" is *Enneads* 1.6, which was Goethe's favourite among the *Enneads*.

[136] Tr: "Thus as mind is less perfect than is the good itself, so is spirit less than mind. And as the spirit is the reason (*logos*) of the mind, and act (*energeia*), a third thing is absent in that place from the highest good: and this is lacking in no being in that in which it is superior to it; mind, however, is lacking in the good: So in turn the spirit is lacking in the mind, and then the spirit is a certain obscurer image of the mind. Further, the spirit is the *life and act* not less than the intellect, and yet weaker than in the intellect. Likewise the spirit sees equally with the mind, but the latter more lucidly, the former more obscurely."

mentary Deity, a diluted Godhead, a reflected and re-reflected Supreme, a rainbow with its secondary rainbow, or at best a borrowing from other systems, a substantiation of the Plotinian God, a sun with its two parhelia of unequal b~~l~~rilliance! But not only is that unity wanting which is indispensable in the conception of a divine Trinity in which each is absolutely God, but even the unity in its lowest sense as the negation of interspace [*p 189*] or chasm is now ~~missing~~ obscure, as we may fairly infer from the frequent and favorite metaphors of Imago, Simulacrum, Reflexion, Shadow; or, where present, is purchased by a perfect confusion of the Deity with the Universe. And still the objection ⟨with⟩ which ⟨we⟩ began ~~with the first~~ recurs in its full force, and each stage of the process renders it not more applicable, but only more glaring. What are we to conceive by an infinite power under the fatal necessity of gradu-al~~ly~~ exhaustion, and which at each successive step becomes feebler and worse, from the Super-ens[137] to the Verè-ens,[138] from the Verè-ens to the Non-verè-ens,[139] thence to the Non-verè-non-ens,[140] and last of all to the Verè-non-ens,[141] vice, matter, and utter nothing?

I will not detain the reader with the objections which might be made to the composition of the ψυχη as made up of the λογος and ενεργεια, when neither of the components ~~parts~~ have been found [*p 191*] or explained in either of the preceding ideas, or how, by the mere combination of the general conception *Energy* with a rhythm of intellect, the simple idea of Life can be produced, or whether this rhythm or proportion be a movement of the mind in itself or a movement produced in the ενεργεια by the mind as acting distinctly and à supra?[142] Or whether in both cases the energy is not presupposed, ~~and consequently~~ which, if it be, it cannot, of course, be added as another and integral factor. But it is of great importance to notice and to impress the necessary moral results of this system and of all ~~possible~~ systems, real and possible, in which the being and nature of God and the World are explained on the hypothesis of emanation.[143]

It is self-evident that on this scheme Good and Evil are distinguished each from the other by no positive difference, but by a mere difference in degree; diversity (difference of kind)[d] there exists none, [*p 193*] nor can exist. Nor is this all: either the idea of guilt is absolutely denied, and

---

[d] Parentheses inserted

[137] Tr: "above being".
[138] Tr: "truly being".
[139] Tr: "not truly being".
[140] Tr: "not truly not being".
[141] Tr: "truly not being".

[142] Tr: "from above".
[143] Pre-eminently the system of Plotinus, but also that of Proclus, and even of Porphyry and Iamblichus.

with it, therefore, responsibility, and all the religion of the world, its hopes and its emotions, or by a strange absurdity the crime, the Evil, increases as the guilt [e]diminishes. For[f] it is clear that an evil, whether positive or negative, accompanied with energ~~ies~~y and intellect, only not perfect, will ensure a greater condemnation in respect of merit or demerit than tenfold that mass with obscure light, [. . .] an encumbered intellect, and an energy in its last dying vibrations. It would be superfluous to add how wholly unexplained, or rather in what utter opposition to this scheme is the fact that to the noblest and most intellectual creature alone do we attribute guilt or the possibility of guilt, or in what contrast the scheme stands with that old and widely diffused idea which is found as the basis of all religions [*p 195*] that are more than local superstitions or traditions blended with allegory: the idea, I mean, of an Evil Spirit, inferior only to God in Power and Intelligence.

Thus, that the Alexandrian philosophy from Plotinus to Proclus[144] bears no other resemblance to the doctrine respecting the tri-unity of the Deity, or the unity of the Tri-personal God, than what it derives from the phrases borrowed by these philosophers from the Jewish and Christian Church, or the imperfect traditions of the earliest ages, is evident. It is evident that the resemblance of the doctrines is merely verbal. Whether more than this is true of the esoteric philosophy of Plato himself[145] and

---

[e–f] ms: diminishes, for

[144] Greek Neoplatonic philosopher (410?–485 A.D.), follower of Iamblichus and Plotinus, opponent of Christianity, head of Plato's Academy at Athens (c 450). His chief works were *Elements of Theology* and *Platonic Theology*, but he also produced commentaries on Plato, a compendium of Aristotelian philosophy, and treatises in mathematics and astronomy. C studied him carefully, and E. R. Dodds used as a kind of epigraph to his edition of *The Elements of Theology* a statement by C in 1810: "The most beautiful and orderly development of the philosophy which endeavours to explain all things by an analysis of consciousness, and builds up a world in the mind out of materials furnished by the mind itself, is to be found in the *Platonic Theology* of Proclus" (E. R. Dodds xxxiii). The statement pertains as well to C's own procedure in much of the *Op Max*, e g: "As we are still within the bounds prescribed by the mind, exerting its powers, unaided, on such facts alone as are found within its own consciousness" (Frag 2 f 1).

[145] Cf C elsewhere: "I have spoken of the unwritten dogmata of Plato, of those which he would not publish and which were peculiarly, and which alone were, his own. A strong light, I say, is let in upon the sacred recesses of this interior doctrine, at least a component part we may say, which in addition to a few others from a few other sources will almost suffice for some future Cuvier . . . in metaphysics to make up the whole system and reproduce the Platonic philosophy for us as it then existed. The fragment has been preserved by STOBAEUS. I refer to the passage in which we are told that the intelligential powers, by the Pythagoreans and Anaxagoras called the *Nous* (the *Logos* or the *Word* of Philo and St. John) is indeed indivisibly united with, but not yet the same as the absolute principle of causation, THE PATERNAL

of his immediate successors may perhaps be rendered more or less probable, but cannot be proved. In like manner, ⟨respecting⟩ certain tenets that seem to bear on this doctrine, in the scanty records of the Samo-thracian mysteries,[146] it will be sufficient to say that they are parts of [*p 197*] a system clearly pantheistic,[147] of a system in which the *World* is God.[148] The resemblance, therefore, must be superficial only, not to add ~~what implies~~[g] ~~indeed to the Alexandrine scheme, likewise~~, that as the Alexandrine scheme in its later and most systematic exposition affirms a Triad of Trinities, so the Samothracian gives us a double Trinity, the inferior and the superior, giving a priority to the former—a consequence inevitable in a pantheistic scheme in which *in*distinction must of necessity be antecedent to *dis*-tinction, the imperfect strivings to the consummate form, the chaos to the kosmos, ~~Ŧthe~~ [h]αξειρος, αξιοκερσα, and αξιοκερσος (whom we are instructed by Varro[149] to identify with the Ceres, Proserpine, and Pluto),[i] to ~~Pluto, Proserpina, and~~ [? ~~Vulcan~~] ⟨~~Ceres~~⟩ the Jupiter, Bacchus or Minerva, and Apollo. Still, however, the

---

[g] An "ap", left uncancelled, is written above the "im" in "implies"
[h–i] This phrase is written on p 196 and marked for insertion at this point; parentheses inserted

---

One, the super-essential Will" (*P Lects*—1949—175).

[146] Though records were scanty, the Samothracian mysteries had great currency in antiquity.

[147] Cf C in 1830: "Pantheism was taught in the Mysteries of Greece, of which the Cabeiric [i.e. the Samothracian] were the purest and most ancient." (*TT—CC*—I 104–5).

[148] In an address to the Bavarian Academy of Sciences in 1815, immediately published at Stuttgart and Tübingen as an essay called *Ueber die Gottheiten von Samothrace*, Schelling discussed the significance of the Cabiric deities of Samothrace called Axieros, Axiokersa, Axiokersos, and Kadmilos, identified respectively with Demeter, Persephone, Hades (Dionysos), and Hermes. He rejected the idea that they could be explained by emanation, which was a trope of descent; tr: "the downward-proceeding, ever more self-attenuating emanations of a highest and superior deity. . . . Therefore the idea of emanation seems suited neither for the interpretation of ancient mythology in general, nor for the interpretation of Samothracian mythology in particular". What these deities represented, Schelling on the contrary argued, was rather a trope of ascent; tr: "Representation of unsolvable life itself, as it progresses in a sequence of ascending steps from the deepest into the highest, representation of the universal magic and of the everlasting theurgy in the whole universe, through which the invisible, indeed, the super-actual is continually brought to revelation and actuality, that was the deepest meaning of the holy, revered doctrine of the Cabiri" (*Schelling SW* VIII 359, 368).

[149] Marcus Terentius Varro (116–127 A.D.), most learned of the Romans (*doctissimus Romanorum*, in Seneca's description), friend of Cicero, enthusiast for Greek philosophy. He wrote, among many other works now lost, *Antiquitates rerum divinarum et humanarum*. Cf C's note of 1825: "Varro's Opus Grande Rerum Divinarum et Humanarum—Ah! that is a Loss!" (*CN* IV 5232).

resemblance in certain points, but more especially in respect of the Cadmeilos or Mercury as the Mediator of the two systems, is*j* so striking as almost to compel the belief in some connexion between the Samothracian and a purer doctrine, however [*p 199*] the latter may have been mutilated by tradition or transformed by adaptation.[150] Now if it can be made evident—and it is only necessary to retrace ~~our steps~~ the grounds and process of our argument, only necessary to know what the doctrine is to make it evident that it never could have originated in a scheme of pantheism, and that it has neither meaning nor practical application in such a system, the very principles of which, negative as well as positive, it must contradict, and itself evaporate into mere abstracts, generalizations, or allegoric symbols.

It ⟨only⟩ remains, therefore, that the doctrine must have existed previously to the great apostacy[151] of the pantheists,[152] that it must have been the received form of Monotheism with those who united both personality and positive infinity, i.e. absoluteness, in their idea of the One God,

j ms: are

[150] C, ever warring against pantheism, is trying to substitute his own anti-pantheistic speculation for the speculation that Schelling had produced on the topic of the meaning of the Samothracian deities. By C's counter-interpretation, the deities become a typological witness to the Christian Trinity. Cf a marginal notation: "The ancient Mystae were so far Pantheists, that they made the lowest first, the highest posterior—prima quia inferiores, ultimi quia supremi. So Varro, himself the reformer of the Samothracian rites. If we however take the whole in the order of *manifestation* not of Power & Being, the system is then susceptible of a safe and orthodox interpretation—The 3 first Cabiri are physiological Deities, Gods of Chaos—then comes the caller forth, the *Word*, Hermes, Mercury—then appear the supreme Triad, in which the Hermes appears again as Apollo or Minerva—" (*CM—CC*—II 575).

[151] The "great apostasy" was the substitution of polytheism (which C defined as pantheism) for monotheism: "the last and total Apostacy of the Pagan World, when the faith in the great I AM, the *Creator*, was extinguished in the sensual polytheism, which is inevitably the final result of Pantheism, or the Worship of Nature; and the only form under which the pantheistic Scheme—that, according to which the World is God, and the material universe itself the one and only *absolute* Being—can exist in a People, or become the popular Creed" (*AR*—1825—276). Cf C in 1830: "I hold all claims set up for Egypt as having been the origin of Greek Philosophy as groundless. It sprang up in Greece itself, and began with physics only—then it took in the Idea of a living Cause—and made Pantheism out of the two" (*TT—CC*—I 203).

[152] Cf C in a marginal note: "The Samo-thracian Mysteries contained the Patriarchal Faith & Expectations disfigured by their forced combination with Pantheism or the Worship of Nature—the eight Cabiri were as follows:—Axieros, Axiokersos, and Axiokersa, the infernal Trinity—or dim Personeities of the Chaos in the throes of self-organization—corresponding according to Varro to Pluto, Vulcan and Proserpine—4th the Camillus, or Cadmilus, the Mercury of the Greeks, or Mediator between Hades and the World of Light" (*CM—CC*—II 582–3).

with all for whom God was neither the Homeric Jove on Olympus, with ⟨the Gods⟩ his dim Elders ⟨G̶o̶d̶s̶⟩ and ⟨the Gods his⟩ ambitious Juniors at the same table, [*p 201*] nor yet the Jupiter est quodcunque vides[153] of the Philosophic Roman,[154] and that it had become so interwoven with those traditions and traditionary anticipations, those prophetic dreams of the Eastern world, so widely diffused as to have made it the policy— perhaps the necessity—of the founders ⟨or framers⟩ of the new system to retain the appearance at least; and while they did away [with] all sub-stantive and inhere[nt] distinctions, ⟨to substitute⟩ their cruda [? indis-taque] moles[155] ⟨to cast⟩ their ⟨own indistinguishable⟩ hyle[156] in the moulds and abstracts taken from the t̶r̶u̶e̶ ⟨earlier⟩ faith.[157]

We are, I am aware, encroaching on the historic portion of our en-quiry. But it was expedient and indeed requisite to prove the perfect in-dependence of the view here given from that which the terms used in its exposition would almost inevitably suggest to the learned reader, before we could with propriety undertake the examination of those other views which either rejecting or not pretending to include the doctrine of the [*p 203*] Trinity—either, I say, rejecting it, a̶s̶ ⟨both⟩ a̶n̶ ideally and in fact, or receiving it wholly on the authority of revelation—have yet a̶t̶t̶e̶m̶p̶t̶e̶d̶ asserted the existence of a God as demonstrable, and have a̶t̶t̶e̶m̶p̶t̶e̶d̶ given what they at least considered as the demonstration and sufficient proof. Now this, of course, is equivalent to the position, either that it is possible to prove the existence and attributes of a being without any cor-responding idea of the same, or that there is an idea of God, and that a true idea, which does not contain and which is not contained in the idea of the Tri-une God. But if we look a little nearer into this subject, we shall perceive that all these positions are included in the conception of demonstrating the supreme Being in the strict and proper as well as ety-mological sense of the word "*demonstrate*". For that, the evidence of

---

[153] Tr: "Jupiter is whatever you see".

[154] The "philosophic Roman", for C, would most likely be Cicero. But here it is possibly Seneca. The statement seems clearly a sentence from Stoic pantheism and is similar to what Seneca frequently says. For the pantheism of all the Stoics see Frag 2 ff 49–50. C in 1819 com-mented of the Stoics in general that "throughout they confounded God and Nature" (*P Lects*—1949—219).

[155] Tr: "crude [?and indistinct] mass". The second word was presum-ably supposed to be *indistinctaque* ("and indistinct").

[156] Tr: "matter".

[157] As this long discussion attests, C was deeply interested in the Samothra-cian deities and their meaning. In addi-tion to his knowledge of Schelling's trea-tise, he annotated a work by George Stanley Faber *A Dissertation on the Mys-teries of the Cabiri; or the Great Gods of Phoenicia, Samothrace, Egypt, Troas, Greece, Italy, and Crete* (2 vols Oxford 1803) (*CM—CC—*ii 573–585). See further *CN* iv 4839, 5069 f 23 and nn; *CN* iii 4385; *TT* (*CC*) i 105, 557; *CM* (*CC*) i 616, 659, 665, 678; *P Lects* (1949) 89, 321–3.

which is contained in itself or in its own idea, is not said to be demonstrated, but gives [*p 205*] the ground of demonstration. But on the other hand, if ideas or truths known by their own light are above demonstration, [then] ~~notions abstracted and~~ conceptions, whether more or less general, formed from the notices of the senses ⟨respecting⟩*k* or objects of the sensible world are *below* it. If it be possible to demonstrate the existence of the Deity, there must be a corresponding science; and as the sciences must fall under one or other of the two heads, those which have intuitions or things in relation to time and space, or number, measure and motion for their objects, the επιστημαι*l* αισθητικοι,[158] or those which have the conceptions of the understanding, and the knowledges obtained by reflection for their subjects, or the επιστημαι*m* λογικοι,[159] the science in question must be either (if I may [be] permitted to speak by analogy from Geometry and Geology)*n* ~~a~~ ~~Theopasy~~ ⟨Theometry⟩*o* or a theology. *p*We will, however, include both in the latter term and proceed to inquire whether there does [or] can exist a Science, i.e., a system or chain of knowlege, [? ~~and~~] whether grounded on principles of speculative Reason or on facts of Experience, that may claim the title of Theology, or a Science, & therefore have knowledge or theoretic insight for its proper and immediate Object, and this a science concerning God.

In a work like the present it is, I trust, unnecessary for me to add that I use the terms "*speculative*" and "*theoretic*" in their primary and most general meaning, [*p 209*] that is, in contradistinction from the acts and experiences of the Will and what has been recently called the *Practical* Reason,[160] the proper object of which is not Truth (speculari, intueri, in-

---

k Insertion in C's hand

l A slip for "ἐπίσταμαι"

m A slip for "ἐπίσταμαι"

n The parenthesis, in C's hand, is written on p 204 and marked for insertion here

o Insertion in C's hand

p This sentence, in C's hand, is evidently intended as a replacement for the following one, which is cancelled in ink with a single diagonal line: "But as I ~~know one in~~ am acquainted with one instance ⟨only⟩ of the former, the pretence of proving God by a direct and sensible intuition of God, as distinguished from [*p 207*] inference or deduction, though I shall not omit this theory but on the contrary give it the lead, still it will be sufficiently intelligible if I say that the enquiry will resolve itself into one question: Is there a *Theology*, or Is a science, a logical knowledge, which ~~is~~ ⟨may⟩ therefore ~~entitled~~ claim the title of Theology, possible?"

[158] Tr: "sensible perceptions".

[159] Tr: "rational perceptions".

[160] I.e. by Kant in the *Kritik der reinen Vernunft*, where "speculative" reason is set against "practical" reason— the latter concerned with the moral (e.g. *Kant* III 518). The concern with "practical" reason was developed fully in the *Grundlegung zur Metaphysik der Sitten* (1785) and in the *Kritik der praktischen Vernunft* (1788).

telligere)[161] but Being and Action. It may not, however, be superfluous to remark that there is a force in the greek termination λογια, i.e. επιστημη λογικη,[162] which is not ~~possessed by our or the latin *Science*~~ contained in the term itself of our "*Science*", inasmuch as the object of a Science is not merely to know but to understand that which we know, one knowledge in connection with or dependence on another logically, that is, according to the forms and rules of the understanding. The question, therefore, may be thus stated: Is there a knowledge of the existence and attributes of God which ~~the understanding~~ can be reduced to the conceptions of the understanding, and which the understanding itself could deduce from [*p 211*] reflexion on ~~itself~~ its own processes or ~~fr~~ on the notices obtained elsewhere~~?~~, the universal principles of Reason, namely* the principium identitatis, that [of] de non contradicendo, and that of the sufficient ground being presumed. If such a science exist, it must be true

---

* Note. 1. The principle of identity: Whatever is, is, or A = A.[163] 2. The principle of contradiction: The same thing cannot be said to be and not to be at the same time.[164] 3. The principle of the sufficient cause: Quicquid pendet, pendet ab aliquo.[165] All three are evidently analytic judgements. The reader will observe that I have translated Causa sufficiens by "the sufficient ground", not "cause", [? ~~or "causation".~~] judgements*q* concerning causation being all and of necessity synthetic. See Logic Sect. II.[166]

q ms: Judgements

[161] Tr: "mirroring, contemplating, understanding".

[162] Tr: "rational knowledge".

[163] In his *Logic*, C, speaking of "the celebrated principles or rather principle of contradiction and identity" says: "The principle of identity is 'A = A' or, if we prefer the refinement of the *Wissenschaftslehre* (Fichte has so called his peculiar system of idealism), 'if A = A, then A = A', and the principle of contradiction that 'A is [not] not-A'. Both amount, as we have seen, to the position 'A is', and even this supposes an assumption of the latter word 'is' as either one and the same with A, so that 'A is' really means no more than a tautological repetition of 'is, is', or in other words a mere and simple assertion of being universally, or that something must be" (*Logic—CC*—87).

[164] "The principle of contradiction is: *impossibile est idem simul esse [ac non] esse*—well this is a good definition of

the impossible but is it therefore a principle? If it be a *princeps*, that which is to go before, there ought to be something that should follow; but what is to follow in the present instance? How can we arrive from this negative to a positive? Through another negative? As whatever is not *ens* and *non ens* at the same time is possible[?] But the rule that two negatives make a positive is grammatical, not logical. Besides, even this is not to be inferred immediately, for it requires an intermediate position, viz. that the contrary of the false is true. Both of them may be entitled axioms but neither of them can be named a principle. The rival position, the *principium identitatis*, is in fact two positions. First, 'whatever is, is'. Secondly, 'what is not, is not'" (*Logic—CC*—89).

[165] Tr: "Whatever depends, depends on something".

[166] Cf *Logic*: "For had the distinction between synthetic and analytic judg-

that without presupposing the idea of God, the mind can either find ~~or deduce its~~ 〈his〉 existence ~~intuitively~~ 〈by the sense〉 ~~or demonstrate it by construction,~~ 〈by construction of intuition〉 ~~or deduce it conclusively by reason of its~~ [? ~~conception~~] by the sense, i.e. intuitively, or by constructing the intuitions of sense, or deduce it conclusively by the understanding as a legitimate conception.

What is more or other than this may be philosophic truth or 〈a〉 Philosophy ~~a science~~, but that it cannot be called science will be ~~best shown~~ evident to all who know what is philosophy.[167] [*p 213*] Now what philosophy is, can, methinks, be known only by having and producing it. For unless it be present with other things as either in[r] them or out of them, how can we learn wherein it differs from them? And if this remain unknown, how are we to learn what it is and what it has in common with them? But we are ~~finite~~ beings of finite intelligence. We see in part and know in part,[168] as the very word "*learn*" may suffice to remind us, and it seems clear that as I must learn before I can know, so I[s] must know before I can understand. The understanding does not give the knowledge materially, for it is by placing some knowledge under ~~its~~ 〈any〉 given series of conception as their common support that we are said to understand this or that subject. Now these supporting knowledges [*p 215*] may be themselves dependent, and be unintelligible, except some other be placed under them. Not only each several science must have its postulates and presumed knowledges, but all the sciences must suppose a something common to them all, by virtue of which they are all alike sci-

[r] ms: as in   [s] ms: so that I

ments been present to their [the metaphysicians, metaphysical divines of the dogmatic philosophy] minds, they could not have thought of deducing the principle of the sufficient cause from the principle of contradiction and identity, on which alone the truths of the common logic rest, as both their ground and their condition. They must have seen that the principle of contradiction is the adequate ground of analytic judgments only, or identical propositions, as they are more commonly named by our English metaphysicians, but that a cause implies a synthetic judgment or a position resulting from the conjunction of two subjects. Yet on this mistake rest all the pretended scientific demonstrations of the Divine Existence and all other fundamental truths of religion and of morality; an attempt and an assumption that has been injurious in more ways than one" (*Logic—CC*—206-7).

[167] Cf a note of 1816: "Science is not Philosophy, but the organ of Philosophy. The Object of Science is Truth merely, or clear Knowing: the Object of Philosophy is Knowlege in subordintion to the Good, as the unum scibile, Truth for the sake of THE TRUE—that is, God and all other realities as in God" (*SW & F—CC*—I 448).

[168] Cf Paul: "For we know in part, and we prophesy in part. . . . For now we see through a glass, darkly; but then face to face: now I know in part: but then shall I know even as also I am known" (1 Cor 13.9, 12).

ence substantively,[169] that is, I mean, where the knowing is accompanied with a something known, and that something not the mere forms of the knowing itself. This common support, without reference to which the sciences could merely possess a formal import—that which is possessed by logic relatively to the forms of the understanding, and by the pure mathematics relatively to those of the sense, we may call the ground of the reality of our knowledge. And again, however, by means of reflection, abstraction, [*p 217*] and generalization, we may separate the subjects of the sciences from each other, as physics from zoology, chemistry from crystallography, *etc. Yet* in fact matter and life, body and form, and to comprize all in one, object and subject do, in fact, co-exist so inseparably—we might even say, coinhere[170]—that it is not in our power to ask for a ground of the reality of the One, which was not at the same time the ground of the reality of all the rest.*v*

*§§.*w* The sciences are distinguished by their subjects, and these again either in nature or the objects of the senses collectively, or in the human mind in relation to nature and to its own forms and functions. In other words, there are as many sciences as there are sorts of knowledges contained in one or other of the two most comprehensive kinds: 1st, the knowledges acquired by perception and sensation, [*p 219*] and those acquired which the mind acquires by its own acts and experiences; and in all alike the knowledge becomes a science in consequence of its being deducible from its first principles, whether original or borrowed from the results of some higher science.*x* We know the colours of the rainbow, but though we should assume the certainty of the knowledge derived from our senses (and, as facts of the senses, they assuredly are certain†),

---

* [*Written by C on p 216:*] To be considered, whether the matter of the 5 leaves preceding may not be abridged & superseded by this §§.—

† [*Written on p 218:*] Note. Lessing in one of his comedies introduces a simpleton who has just been seeing the wonders and diableries of a pretended ma-

---

    t–u ms: &c, yet   *v* A square bracket is placed here in ink, possibly by C
    w The sections symbols are in C's hand   *x* Colon in ms

[169] Cf *Logic*: "The understanding is the substantiative power, that by which we give and attribute substance and reality to phenomena and raise them from mere affections and appearances into objects communicable and capable of being anticipated and reasoned of. . . . The proper and immediate substance, or hypostasis, is the understanding itself . . . the understanding is the substantiative power. The substantiative power is its essence. . . . Therefore we said that the understanding hath a twofold character. It gives and it attributes substance" (*Logic—CC—*239).

[170] "Most noticeable it is, and most worthy a wise man's meditation, that the notion of objects as altogether objective, begins in the same moment in which the conception is formed that is wholly subjective" (Frag 2 f 98).

no^z one would call this a scientific knowledge. In order to this there must be a dependency, a connexion, and of course a something, whether fact or conception, the evidence of which is assumed and conceded. Even where, as in the Optics of Sir I. Newton, or rather in that part of the Newtonian optics which relates to colour, the premises ~~depend on~~ ⟨are derived from⟩ experiment, the facts must have been proved before the scientific reasoning [*p 221*] begins. In reference both to the process and to the result or product of any science—and as far as the knowledge is scientific—there is no difference in the character of the premises. Whether self-evident, or the evident result of some other science grounded on self-evident truths, or prepared for the occasion by observation or ~~investigation~~ ⟨experiment,⟩ the premises ~~are alike data~~ occupy the same place and exercise the same function as premises of a science. For if they were not ~~preconceded~~ ⟨(et postulata et preconcessa)⟩[172] demanded on the one side and preconceded on the other, the science could not have commenced: it would have perished in the birth.

The sciences are more or less particular, more or less ^{a}universal. But^b in hastily passing through the catalogue of their ~~char~~ several names as derived from their ~~immediate~~ ⟨characteristic⟩ aims and objects, we discover one character [*p 223*] common to all, namely that they are either abstracted from the objects of experience or inferred in the act itself by which the experience is made and reasoned on. Equally clear is it that as far as the act and form of contemplation and deduction can be divided from the object or matter so contemplated and deduced, the only inference is that of the faculty or ground of the agency. And this too from a

---

gician, which have^y left him so sceptical respecting the evidence of his senses that, speaking of a blazing fire, he exclaims, "This fire does not really burn, it only seems to burn; but it does not really seem, it only seems to seem."[171] Now there might be some pretence for the first scruple, but the second contradicts itself. What seems, must really seem. Every phaenomenon, as a phaenomenon, is of the highest possible evidence.

^{y} ms: has ^{z} ms: But no
$^{a-b}$ ms: universal; but

[171] Cf *Logic* 218: ". . . the same absurdity as that of the simpleton in one of our old plays, whom the poet introduces fresh from the wonders and sight-baffling sights of a pretended magician and which have left him so doubtful respecting the evidence of his senses, and so proud of his newly acquired scepticism, that speaking of a blazing fire he exclaims 'This fire does not really burn; it only seems to burn; but it does not really seem, it only seems to seem.'" The incident occurs in *Die Matrone von Ephesus*, first published in Lessing *Theatralische Nachlass* (Berlin 1784). For a supposed ghost, C substitutes "pretended magician" and his "wonders and sight-baffling sights".

[172] Tr: "both demanded and preconceded".

necessity of the human mind, according to which I cannot conceive an effect without a cause, or act without a power, or an act of power without presupposing an agent. Whether, however, ~~of the human mind, or an absolute~~ this necessity be absolute or only relative, resulting from the nature of things in their essences and universal grounds, or ⟨merely⟩ from the constitution and limitation of the human faculties re[*p 225*]mains undecided. As far as the reasoning is concerned, whether by deduction, conclusion, or demonstration, ~~the question cannot be pro point~~ this is a point which cannot even come into the question. That without which we cannot reason must be presumed ~~in order to~~ as the ground of the reasoning. Now, then, I look round and try in vain to discover a vacant place for a science, the result of which is to be the knowledge and ascertainment of God, i.e. of the reality and existence of the Supreme Being— ~~namely~~ the*c* conditions being such as were stated when the question was first proposed by us, namely, in the absence or rejection of the ideas as the datum.[173] The doubt respecting the possibility of such a science was expressed ⟨so far⟩ conditionally, i.e. unless the idea was taken as the ~~praemissum~~ datum,*d* and the result [*p 227*] ⟨as the da⟩ anticipated and ⟨pre-⟩contained in the premise. I called on opponents who, rejecting ~~all innate ideas~~ the doctrines and existence of Ideas altogether, deny the idea of God inclusively. Nor does it follow that therefore they reject all principles of reason, or all self-evident truths, or even the existence of innate conceptions as far as these are equivalent with a determinate faculty in the mind, enabling and predisposing it to contemplate objects in certain determinate relations to itself, such as the universal conceptions of quantity, quality, and of relation itself, that are presupposed in the assertion of all particular quantities, qualities, and relations. Even these, I say, may be admitted as antecedent to every particular application or limitation of the same, or resolved into generalizations and representative conceptions, abstracted and generalized [*p 229*] from the particulars, and therefore, of course, posterior to them. The difference is great in itself and gives rise to two different schools or sects of philosophy, but it does not bear on the present point. For I have elsewhere shown, and now refer* to the work and passage, that though all ideas must be truths of reason, yet truths of reason are not all, or necessarily, ideas.[174] And no better instance can be given of the reason, on which the distinction rests, than that which we are at present discussing, the Idea of God. ₐAn idea, I re-

---

* [*Written on p 228:*] Note. See last chapter of Judicial Logic.

c ms: ⟨on⟩ the   d ms: & datum

[173] Tr: "given".   [174] See *Logic* (*CC*) 237.

peat, implies the reality of ~~the thing~~ that to which it corresponds as well as its ~~f~~own formal truth—and more than this it would be superfluous to repeat, the subject having been treated before and elsewhere so much at large, and in addressing an antagonist with whom I am reasoning [*p 231*] on the assumption of their non-existence.

An idea, then, being thus contradistinguished alike from the forms of the sense, the conceptions of the understanding, and the principles of the speculative reason by containing the reality as well as the peculiar form of the truth expressed therein,[175] and likewise by ~~having its~~ ⟨its⟩ source ⟨being⟩ neither ~~in the~~ ⟨exclusively⟩ speculative nor ~~in the~~ ⟨exclusively⟩ practical, neither in the reason without the Will nor in the Will without the reason, A and the existence of ideas in the human soul being altogether denied, it remains to be shown in what other way a science of God can be conceived to exist.[e] In fact, if ~~it~~ ⟨the idea⟩ were admitted and pre-assumed as a datum, it would be a ~~very unusual sense of the word~~ strange and unauthorized use of the word to term the knowledge so derived a science or a scientific proof. At the utmost it could amount [*p 233*] to no more than a logical exposition, or an analysis, or a series of exemplifications of the same truth, ~~each of which~~ as if a man should demonstrate the essential properties of the triangle in a vast succession of diagrams, and in all imaginable varieties of size, and colour, and relative position: each would have the force of all. Add, too, that this sense is expressly excluded in the definition of the term, according to which the challenge was hazarded. We have seen that the sciences either respect the formal truth alone, or else assume the reality in their premises as a datum. Now the very thing to be proved in the present instance is the reality, that is, the positive existence, self-subsistently and not merely in and for the mind, as in the pure circles etc. of geometry. If not from the idea, ⟨from⟩ what other source? And, vice versâ, if the reality be not presumed, from [*p 235*] whence shall we derive the conception? In astronomy, the reality ~~th~~ expressed in the premise is derived from observation, that is, from the notices of sense, and the form from the sense itself, o~~f~~r the relation of the things to the mind of the contemplator generally. We know of what we are speaking, and before we begin to reason concerning them. If we are asked, "Of what are you about to reason?" we could point to this or that, or refer to some phaenomenon of outward or inward experience; and having thus determined the subject matters, we say it is these which we wish to understand.

[e] Question mark in ms

[175] Cf the definitions of Idea at *Logic* (*CC*) 236–7.

Let us suppose, then, that instead of any particular class of phaenom-
ena such as supply the subjects of chemistry, ~~or~~ mineralogy, ~~or~~ astron-
omy, ~~etc. etc. or~~ of psychology, zoonomy, etc., etc., we took the sum
total, and that the universe was the subject which we proposed to [*p 237*]
understand, and that its reality was contained, of course, in that of all the
single facts composing it. Now whatever the suppositions were that en-
abled ⟨us⟩ to understand this, or (more accurately speaking) by which
this was understood, the result, it is evident, would be the science of the
f universe. The*g* supposition itself could not possibly be the result. Need
I say that to suppose (su⟨b⟩pponere) is to put one thing under another or
others so as to give stability to that which is superposed (superpositis) in
some given direction and relation? Or that an hypothesis is a sub-posi-
tion in relation to the human mind, so that ~~well~~ ⟨when⟩ I can commence
and arrange any series in co-incidence with the forms of my mind, I say
I understand them?—a word which will give the same meaning whether
I take the verb "stand" neutrally or actively. ~~i~~In both cases the mind it-
self is the actual [*p 239*] hypothesis.[176] I either use "stand" for "make to
stand", and then say, "I place such and such a conception under these",
and in so doing make my own faculties and the reality implied in them
the support of the former and the pledge of their consistency, or I take
my whole being collectively and declare that it supports, that its reality
and order is one ~~and the sa~~ with that of the phaenomena which it stands
under or understands.[177] Need I say further that in ~~order to suppose~~ all
sub-positions, a *po*sition is implied, that that which communicates a re-
ality, strength, support, must itself possess it, and can give no more than
what itself possesses? For the phaenomena I have the evidence of my
outward and inward sense. Of there being more than the forms of ~~the~~ ⟨my
own⟩ mind singly and exclusively, I have the proof [*p 241*] of my sen-
sibility and the comparison of my senses with each other, with my past
experience, and with the experience of other men. But in what manner
shall I derive either from the phaenomena, or from their congruity with
the forms of my understanding, or from the affections of my sensibility
by which I ~~rely~~ am determined to identify these phaenomena with ~~a~~ self-
subsistents other than my mind, any other result than what the process
itself expresses? It is, indeed, abundantly more easy to show that we all
of us in fact do attribute an alterity and ~~accompanying~~ ⟨a proper⟩ reality
to phaemomena in consequence of their co-existence with certain affec-
tions of our own sensibility than to ~~prove~~ ⟨explain⟩ by what right we do

f–g ms: universe: the

[176] I.e. sub-position.   [177] See above, f 106.

this on theoretical premises and by arguments derived mediately or immediately from the understanding alone. For in order to this it would be necessary to prove [*p 243*] that the order and whatever else establishes the congruity of the phaenomena with the forms of the understanding were not caused by the understanding, even as the symmetry of the fragments seen in the kaleidoscope is caused by the kaleidoscope itself[178]— difficult, I mean, unless a something be presumed, which can be fairly deduced neither from the ~~facts~~ evidence of the senses nor the abstractions which the understanding forms from its own processes and substantiates for itself as its own constitutive faculties from the acts inferring and generalizing the corresponding faculty. For we are bound not to forget [that] this very notion of faculty, property, and the like, is itself a product or facture of the understanding, ~~wholl~~ not less mechanical than that of a luminous circle that arises from the eye in the rapid rotation of a single point, and which ⟨a child or⟩ an ignorant spectator might naturally consider as the luminous [*p 245*] body itself and the cause of the light of which under the given circumstances it is the necessary effect. And I greatly fear that ⟨in⟩ ~~any presumption~~ whatever shall be thus presumed, though such presumption is altogether precluded in the terms of our challenge, will be found either to imply the idea of God, or rather to pre-suppose and be grounded on that idea, or to prove nothing at all in relation to his existence.

The ~~shortest~~ most satisfactory way, however, of settling the question will be that of stating and examining the different supposed or asserted proofs. ~~n~~Not that from this only the impossibility of any scientific proof could be deduced: in[h] addition to this we must show à priori that all possible proofs must from the nature of the human mind be one or other of a ~~certain~~ number that can be previously defined and characterized. Then, [*p 247*] if we can prove that the failure in each particular scheme, taken as an example of each, is not attributable to any fault on the part of the reasoner which some following reasoner might correct, but to the very nature of the proof itself, we shall have amply demonstrated our position: that ~~a~~ ⟨there is no⟩ speculative proof, no properly scientific or log-

[h] ms: we in

[178] See J. R. de J. Jackson's note: "C first mentions the instrument in 1818 (*CN* III 4411), hard on the heels of its appearance. See *Description and Method of Using the Patent Kaleidoscope, Invented by Dr. Brewster* (1818)—an attempt to market the device—and David Brewster *A Treatise on the Kaleido-* *scope* (Edinburgh 1819). In 1818, S[ara] H[utchinson] called it 'entirely the plaything of the Adults' (*SH Letters* 144; see also 140 and 142), and Shelley mentions the rage for it in Italy (*The Letters of Percy Bysshe Shelley* ed Frederick L. Jones—Oxford 1964—II 69)" (*Logic—CC*—163).

ical demonstration possible. In other words, that the idea of the Godhead is the true source and indispensable precondition of all our knowledge of God. That, consequently, all that is true and valuable in any of the so-called proofs and demonstrations consists of expositions of this idea, or the different means by which the understanding is enabled to exemplify this idea in all its experiences, whether inward or from without, whether derived from the sense and the senses or by reflexion on itself and on its own operations. Nor is this all—[*p 249*]we must add the ⟨theoretic⟩ purpose answered by thus exemplifying the idea ⟨of God⟩ ~~in addition to~~— the moral one of awakening the conscious attention of the soul to this great idea, with the emotions ~~appertaining~~ ⟨inseparable from⟩ its ⟨due⟩ contemplation—which, so far from the idea or knowledge being deduced or concluded from any or all the particulars of sensation and reflexion, is that of deriving these as components of a world (τοῦ κοσμου and not τοῦ χαιοῦς)[i] [179] from this idea. [j] The Reason* as the living source of living ⟨and substantial⟩ verities presents the Idea to the ~~understanding~~ individual mind and subjective intellect, which receives and employs it to its own appropriate ends, namely to understand thereby both itself and all its objects—receives it, I say, uncomprehended [*p 251*] by it to comprehend ~~all things~~ ⟨the universe⟩, the world without, and the yet more wonderful world within.

[k] In this attempt to exhaust all the *possible* schemes[180] on which the Deity if demonstrable at all, must be demonstrated, I shall begin with the one, which is so far a *mere* possiblity, that I know no ~~manner in which~~ ⟨example of its⟩ adoption. This scheme would be expressed in the asser-

---

* [*Written by C on p 248:*] I here use the word in its highest ~~sense,~~ ⟨as well⟩ as most comprehensive Sense—and not ~~to answer the~~ ⟨for the mere⟩ Collectæneum of *theoretic* principles or of ⟨such⟩ speculative truths as are accompanied with the sense of ⟨unconditional⟩ necessity and absolute universality.

[i] A mistake for "τοῦ χάους" (Attic spelling). Perhaps JHG misheard C, or perhaps C confused the genitive form of the noun "τὸ χάος ("chaos, unformed matter") with that of the adjective "χάϊος" ("genuine, true")

[j] ms: The Reason in that highest sense, in which the speculative is united with the practical, not the reason, as the mere collective of necessary & universal theoretic principles; but [*cancelled in ink with a single diagonal line*]

[k-1] These two sentences, in C's hand, are evidently intended as a replacement for the

[179] *Kosmos* and *chaos* are opposed terms in Greek cosmology, defined each by its opposite—the former implying order and the latter disorder.

[180] In his attempt to "exhaust all the *possible* schemes" C in this fragment devotes most attention to the Plotinian and the Vedic traditions. That among other possible schemes these receive such prominent attention is not solely because they each present a trinitarian conception that competes with the Christian Trinity, but also because they are close in other ways.

tion—We have a *pure* sensuous *intuition* of God—or—We know God
by the *sense*, as distinguished from the *Senses* or bodily organs of
Sense—in the same way as we ~~know~~ ⟨behold⟩ mathematical figures,
~~Lines~~ ⟨ex.gr.⟩, the Point, Line, Triangles, Circle &c of pure Geometry.¹
But as it is certain that nothing but mathematical forms, geometrical or
arithmetical, are ~~the~~ objects of the sense in [*p 253*] this acceptation of
the word, and as it is equally clear that these are ⟨entitled⟩ objects only
~~from their~~ because they may be confidently anticipated in all men at all
times, but have their sole subsistence in the ~~subject~~ mind ~~itself~~ or sen-
tient faculty itself, this scheme would commence with a contradiction.¹⁸¹
We ~~seek~~ ⟨ask for⟩ the real ground of all other reality, which is again dis-
tinguished into subjective and objective,¹⁸² or the reality of the mind and
the reality out of the mind, and a portion or derivative of the one di~~vivi~~-
sion is offered to us as the ground of both—an absurdity not less than if
in speaking of a tree that had divided itself into two main branches, we
should assign a spray of the one as the common trunk of both. As, how-
ever, this scheme has never to my knowledge been seriously advanced
by any sect or individual, the confutation is superfluous, or excusable
only ~~on the plea~~ in a systematic arrangement ~~in which it is desirable to
exhaust~~ [*p 255*] ~~all the~~ framed on the principle of exhausting the terms.

There occurs, indeed, in the Rabbinical writings a position which may
be regarded perhaps as belonging to this scheme, namely that God is
space.¹⁸³ But candour requires us to consider this as a symbolical ex-
pression, and that the Hebrew sages meant no more than that Space was
a symbol of God's omnipresence and infinity, or that Space and Time
were the two modes or general forms under which ⟨alone⟩ the human
mind could contemplate external and successive existence, and that the
ultimate object, corresponding to these forms, was God's Eternity and
Omnipresence. In any other sense the position would be absurd. For

following sentence, which is cancelled in ink with an "X": "It is evident that ~~the~~ ⟨any⟩
knowledge of God, not pre-existing in the Idea, must be derived either directly from the
Sense or the Senses, that is we must know God by seeing him, either mathematically, as
in the instance of geometrical figures, or physically as we see feel &c external objects"

¹⁸¹ Though C says he knows no ex-
ample of this theory's adoption, in fact it
is rather close to Jacobi's view whereby
reason directly intuits God. See Prole-
gomena v: Reason and Understanding.
¹⁸² Cf e.g. C in 1818: "And first I af-
firm the eternal Ground and substance of
that, which as accommodated to the
Non-absolute becomes the Law of the
Identity and Antithesis of Subject and
Object" (*SW & F—CC—*I 783).
¹⁸³ Cf C in 1803: "The Hebrews
called God 'Space.'—" (*CN* I 1379). C's
conjecture here is wide of the mark. The
"God is space" remark may well have
been recalled from something he heard
from his friend Hyman Hurwitz, who
was his guide in Rabbinical studies.

Space is either taken as ~~an~~ outward⟨ly⟩ ~~reality~~, possessing an objective reality and a subsistence independent of the sentient faculty—~~and~~ in which case it would aggravate the necessary consequences of this hypothesis by applying it to the [*p 257*] Divinity, and the ~~positio~~ words would be tantamount to the assertion that God is a something having all the properties of nothing. But if Space be considered as one of the two universal forms of the sentient faculty in man, the ⟨exposure of the⟩ position in this sense is ~~expressed~~ ⟨contained⟩ in ~~the preceding paragraph~~ that of the scheme first mentioned. That which has no subsistence but in the faculty of a finite mind is asserted to be itself—the subsistence of the universe, material and intellectual.

The second scheme is so monstrous that it may well excite wonder to find it ~~not unsupported~~ exemplified in any existing creed or profession. And such ~~we might have~~ as would have excused the confident anticipation

> That of such doctrine never was there school,
> But the heart of the fool,
> And no man therein Doctor but himself.[184]

This scheme of theology ~~that we~~ is contained in the assertion that we see God with our eyes—"Jupiter est quodcunque vides".[185] [*p 259*] And this not in that sense which the Latin sentence might be made to convey, giving to the verb substantive an active or transitive force—"Jove gives being to whatever we behold", or the world of sense has no ~~true reality~~ other than a communicated reality. Now the doctrines of the most renowned and orthodox Brahmins affirm positively that what we see is God as much as a tower or a tree is a tree or a tower, notwithstanding the different shapes and magnitudes which it may assume for different beholders according to the distance, the perspective, etc. Nay! these very delusions, which collectively they entitle Maija, are no delusions but just and proper forms of God, no more divisible or even distinguishable from his being than the form of the human race can be thought of separately from the essence or the ⟨so-called⟩ accidents of a body from the body itself. For these ~~very~~ ⟨several⟩ percipients with all their several modifications, [*p 261*] mental and organic, the distance, the perspective, are all God, in whom there is no gradation of degrees, but all is equally real and equally unreal.

Few things are more calculated on the first reflection to surprise a

---

[184] Milton *Samson Agonistes* lines 297–9.   [185] See above, note 153.

Christian who has seen the Brahman Theology in its true light than the admiration which writers of undoubted learning and believers of unquestionable sincerity have expressed respecting it and its asserted approaches to the doctrine as well as to the sublimity of the Hebrew Scriptures. This, however, is, I am persuaded, an effect of that excessive attention to the physical attributes of the Deity above the intelligential, inasmuch as the former, viz. ~~the~~ Omnipotence and Omnipresence, are treated of in a certain sense as the substance of the Deity, as God himself, and the intelligence as an adjunct or property. At all events, I am disposed to regard it as resulting from the habit of contemplating the physical attributes of God [*p 263*] with a concession of his intelligence to the exclusion of this personality and the consequent bedimming of the moral. Hence I have found myself justified in discussing this subject more at large than its own intrinsic character merited,[186] and the more so because in the present relations of Great Britain to Hindostan the eulogies of Brahmanism,[187] which are most familiar in that rank of life from which individuals are selected for commanding and influencive situations, may exert, and in fact have exerted, on measures and questions of no trifling interest ⟨both moral and⟩ political. As to many of these, more especially to the admirers of the late truly admirable Sir W. Jones,[188] the strong terms of reprobation with which I have introduced the subject will appear paradoxical,[189] I would first earnestly request

[186] That is to say, the pantheism of the Hindu writings, and not their intrinsic merit, generates C's attention. Cf his assertion that "the Pantheism of India" is "in *kind* the *same* as it is = to the Fetisch worship of the African" (*CL* IV 863). Cf an even more explicit note of 1818: "Shall we begin with sense? The African's Fetisch and the Brahman's Pantheism (see Bhagavatgeeta, p. 90–3)" (*SW & F—CC*—I 606).

[187] In the MS Green sometimes spells the word "Brahminism" and sometimes "Brahmanism", with the related words "Brahmin" or "Brahman". It is not possible to know which form C, orally dictating, had in mind; but either would be permissible, although they refer to somewhat different things. "Brahmins" were the priests of Hinduism; "Brahman" referred to the divine force and underlying reality of the universe.

[188] Sir William Jones, English orientalist and jurist (1746–94). While serving as judge of the high court of Calcutta, he mastered Sanscrit (among many other languages), and by his translations set in motion the enormous flood of Romantic orientalism. For comprehensive discussion of the larger aspects of the phenomenon of Romantic orientalism, see Raymond Schwab *La Renaissance orientale* (Paris 1950). See also A. Leslie Willson *A Mythical Image: The Ideal of India in German Romanticism* (Durham NC 1964).

[189] Despite C's scorn for the lack of sophistication in the translation of the *Bhagavad-Gita* from which he quotes, the reprobation most primarily stems from his distaste for the pantheism of the Hindu writings. Cf a statement about Sir William Jones: "In Sir W. Jones's VIth Diss., that on the Persian's (Vol. 1, p. 203 of Dissertation &c relating to the Arts, and Literature of Asia) we have the most pleasing account of the Pantheistic Scheme of Theomonism of the Persian

their serious attention to the following extract from a work[190] which the Brahmins believe to contain all the grand mysteries of their religion, and which the enlightened [*p 265*] translator of the work himself considers as calculated to bring about the downfall of Polytheism by withdrawing the mind of the idolaters from each particular image to the One God present in all. I would further entreat him to ~~re-peruse the~~ ⟨turn back to this⟩ ~~extracts~~ after his perusal of the observations, which will be found in a following page, on Pantheism in its purest and most intellectual form, that, namely in which it exists in the Ethica of Benedict Spinoza.[191] After such preparation, I must leave it to his own judgement to answer the question, whether ~~in addition~~ to all these consequences ~~of~~ ⟨from⟩ the system there must not be added in the Brahman or sensual Pantheism[192] the realization of these consequences on the ~~mind~~ spirits of the holders of the doctrine, ~~W~~whether the logical consequences of Spinozism must not, from the nature of man, be the practical results of Brahmanism,[193] which so far from removing Polytheism, not only involves it as a [*p 267*] strict consequent as soon as ever any other race of intelligences beside the human is admitted to exist, but by the constant and extreme sensuality in the representations of their Ἕν καὶ πᾶν,[194] or World = God or God = World, must inevitably engender the craving after it.[195]

---

and Indian Philosophers. But here, as in Europe, the System is either the same as religious Idealism, = the Berkleian Scheme: or subject to all the odious consequences of Spinosism, such as the indistinction of good and evil, or moral and physical, of God and blind Fate—" (*CN* iv 4737).

[190] The *Bhagavad-Gita*.

[191] Cf C's wistful statement about Spinoza's thought in the *Philosophical Lectures*: "it was pantheism, but in the most religious form in which it could appear" (*P Lects*—1949—385). For C's alternation between love of Spinoza's character and mind, and alarm at his pantheism, see *CPT* 187–9.

[192] At one point C aligns three forms of pantheism—or "Spinosism"—that of Spinoza, that of the "Brahmans", and that of Schelling: "Spinosism in all its forms, ἐποπτικοῖς (as in the Hindu Polytheism) η νοητικοῖς (as in Spinoza's own works), or in both conjointly (as in Schelling and his followers) is principally and eminently forbidden in the 2nd Commandment, and the same Veto is

implied in the first" (*CN* iv 4671).

[193] Cf a notebook entry: "Thou shalt not worship God *under* any image— thou shalt not hold God to be the substrate of Nature or immediate invisible Cause of the phaenomenal World or of any single Phaenomenon, for it is an 'I' that is alone the Lord God—and *him* thou shalt personally worship" (*CN* iv 4671). For a detailed argument that Spinoza and the Vedas urge the same philosophy, see S. Melamed *Spinoza and Buddha; Visions of a Dead God* (Chicago 1933).

[194] Tr: "one and all". The Greek phrase, *hen kai pan*, largely due to Lessing's use of it in his conversation with Jacobi, was in common currency in the Romantic era as the symbolic rubric of pantheism. It originated in Stobaeus as a phrase describing the Eleatic philosophy of Meslissos. See *CPT* 341–2 n 13. See further Prolegomena xxv: Pantheism and Evolutionary Materialism: The Meaning of the *Magnum Opus* with Respect to Coleridge's Own Time.

[195] Cf *Aids to Reflection*: ". . . the

*ᵐ*Extract f*ᵐ* the Brăgăvăt-greētā of Dialogues of Krĕĕshnā and Arjŏŏn.—¹⁹⁶

I behold, O'God! within thy breast, the Dēws assembled, and every specific tribe of beings. I see Brăhmā, that deity*ⁿ* sitting on his lotus-throne; all the *Rĕĕshĕĕs* and heavenly Ŏŏrăgăs. I see thyself, on all sides, of infinite shape, formed with abundant arms, and bellies, and mouths, and eyes; but I can neither discover thy beginning, nor middle, nor again thy end, O universal Lord, form of the universe! I see thee with a crown, and armed with club and Chăkră, a mass of glory, darting refulgent beams around. I see thee, difficult to be seen, shining on all sides with light immeasurable, like the ardent fire or glorius Sun.*ᵒ* Thou art the Supreme Being, incorruptible, worthy to be known! Thou art prime supporter of the universal orb! Thou art the never-failing and eternal guardian of religion! Thou art from all beginning, and I esteem Thee*ᵖ* Pŏŏrŏŏsh. I see thee without beginning, without middle, without*�q* end; of valor infinite; of arms innumerable, and the sun and moon thy eyes; thy mouth a flaming fire and the whole world shining with thy refracted glory! [*f 1ᵛ*] The space between the heavens and the earth is possessed by thee alone, and every point around: the three regions of the universe, O mighty spirit! behold the wonders of thy awful countenance with troubled minds. Of the celestial bands, some I see fly to thee for refuge; whilst some, afraid, with joined hands sing

---

ᵐ Here the following parenthesis appears: "☞ (Here comes in the annexed Extract of three pages, ending with the words 'I am anxious to learn thy source, and ignorant of what thy presence portendeth.')." This refers to an extract from the *Bhagavadgita* made by John Watson, the first leaf of which (written on both sides) is tipped in at p 266 of the ms, and the last leaf of which (which includes a commentary by C printed in App C) is preserved in VCL (MS LT 32). Substantive variations from the printed text of Wilkins are recorded in the textual notes below.

ⁿ Wilkins: Deity
ᵒ Wilkins: sun
ᵖ Wilkins: thee
* q* Wilkins: and without

---

sensual polytheism, which is inevitably the final result of Pantheism or the Worship of Nature; and the only form under which the pantheistic Scheme—that, according to which the World is God, and the material universe itself the one only absolute Being—can exist for a People, or become the popular Creed. Thus in the most ancient Books of the Brahmins, the deep sense of this Fact, and the doctrines grounded on obscure traditions of the promised Remedy, are seen struggling, and now gleaming, now flashing, through the Mist of Pantheism . . ." (*AR*—1825—276–7).

¹⁹⁶ From the trans of Charles Wilkins: *The Bhagavat-geeta, or Dialogues of Kreeshna and Arjoon; in eighteen lectures; with notes. Translated from the original, in the Sanskreet* (London 1785) 91–2.

forth thy praise. The Măhărshĕĕs, holy bands, hail thee, and glorify thy name with adoring praises. The Rŏŏdrăs, the Adĕĕtyăs, the Văsŏŏs, and all those beings the world esteemed good; Ăswĕĕn and Kŏŏmar, the Mărŏŏts and the Ooshmăpās; the Găndhărvs and the Yăkshăs, with the holy tribes of Soors, all stand gazing on thee, and all alike amazed! The worlds alike with me are terrified to behold thy wondrous forms gigantic; with many mouths and eyes; with many arms, and legs, and breasts; with many bellies, and with rows of dreadful teeth! Thus as I see thee, touching the heavens, and shining with such glory; of such various hues, with widely-opened mouths, and bright expanded eyes, I am disturbed within me: my resolution faileth me, O Vĕĕshnŏŏ! and I find no rest! Having beholden [*f* 2] thy dreadful teeth, and gazed on thy countenance, emblem of time's last fire, I know not which way I turn! I find no peace! Have mercy then, O God of Gods! thou mansion of the universe! thouʳ Sons of Dhrĕĕtărashtră, now, with all those rulers of the land, Bhēēshmă, Drōn, the son of Sōōt, and even the fronts of our army, seem to be precipitating themselves hastily into thy mouths, discovering such frightful rows of teeth! whilst some appear to stick between thy teeth with their bodies sorely mangled. As the rapid streams of full flowing rivers roll on to meet the ocean's bed; even so these heroes of the human race rush on towards thy flaming mouths. As troops of insects, with increasing speed, seek their own destruction in the flaming fire; even so these people, with swelling fury, seek their own destruction. Thou involvest and swallowest them altogether, even unto the last, with thy flaming mouths; whilst the whole world is filled with thy glory, as thy awful beams, O Vĕĕshnŏŏ, shine forth on all sides! Reverence be unto thee, thou most exalted! Deign to make known unto me who is this God of awful figure! [*f* 2ᵛ] I am anxious to learn thy soursce, and ignorant of what thy presence here portendeth.—

There is[197] in almost all the Sanscrit philosophical and religious writings, as far as they have fallen under my notice, a character which, it seems to me, might be plausibly accounted for on the supposition of childish intellects living among gigantic objects, of mean thoughts and huge things—living Lilliputs among inanimate Brobdignags. Thus their Pantheism, or visible God, God proved to them ⟨not from but in and by⟩

ʳ Wilkins: the

[197] Cf App C for another (presumably   extract.
earlier) version of C's comments on the

the evidence of their senses, ~~seems to me a natural result of an imbecile understanding in a languid and relaxing~~ [*p 269*] ~~climate~~ taken in conjunction with the languor of a relaxing climate and the lulling influences of a deep, sombre and gigantic vegetation, seems to me a natural result of an imbecile understanding ⟨producing indistinction⟩ half from indolence and half ~~for amusement~~ ‌intentionally by a partial closure of the eyelids, and when all hues and outlines melt into a garish mist, deeming it unity.

The translator of the Bagavat-Geeta[198] finds in the story of churning the ocean for the fourteen jewels a wonderful affinity to—Milton!![199] I could not, I confess, ⟨help⟩ inferring from this remark that taste does not resemble the wines that improve by a voyage to and from India. fFor if there be one character of genius predominant in ~~the Paradise lost~~ ⟨Milton⟩ it is this, that he never passes off bigness for greatness. ~~But~~ Children never can make things big enough, and exactly so is it with the poets of India.

[*p 271*] It would be more than we are entitled to expect of the human mind if Sir W. Jones, Mʳ Wilkins,[200] etc., great and good as we know them to have been, had not overrated the merit of works,[201] the power of understanding which is of such rare occurrence and so difficultly attained. In the present instance there is an additional excuse—an excuse which ~~almost justifies~~ more than acquits the judges, though it cannot prevent the reversal of their decision; for ⟨to⟩ the writings in question, ~~are hung~~ all the ~~prin~~ notions, images, and feelings which are best calculated to excite that obscure awe that lies midway between religion and superstition hang and encluster. ~~Their supposed~~ ⟨received⟩ ~~survival from a re-~~

[198] Charles Wilkins.

[199] In the Wilkins trans, n 78 on page 145 says: "The story of churning the ocean for what are called *Chowdă Răttăn*, or fourteen jewels, is of such a curious nature, and in some parts, bears such a wonderful affinity to Milton's description of the war in heaven, that the Translator thinks it will afford the reader an agreeable contrast to the subject of this work." Cf *Philosophical Lectures*: "Now this is said, and it is published by the authority of the East India Company I find (for which certainly we are much obliged to them, for it is a very interesting poem) but with a declaration 'I should not fear to place in opposition to the . . . 1st and 6th [Books of our own Milton, highly as I venerate the latter, the English transla-tion of the Mahabharat.'] That however is a piece of taste" (*P Lects*—1949—129).

[200] Charles Wilkins (later Sir Charles Wilkins) (1749–1836), British orientalist. He was the first Englishman to gain a command of Sanscrit, and Sir William Jones attributed his own study of Sanscrit to Wilkins's encouragement. He collaborated with Sir William Jones in the founding of the Asiatic Society of Bengal, and founded a press for the printing of Oriental languages, for which he was responsible for designing many of the typefaces. In 1785 he published a translation of the *Bhagavad-Gita* that was the chief source of C's knowledge of the poem.

[201] Cf App C.

~~mote antiquity, and their asserted.~~ Their undoubted antiquity is so great,[202] and the antiquity claimed for them at once so daring and so visionary, that we might almost say "liber ipse superstat",[203] the book itself walks like a ghost of a [*p 273*] departed world. ~~t~~There is a superstition involved in a survival so contrary to the ordinary experience of mankind. I have myself paid this debt of homage[204] on my first presentation to these foreign potentates ~~under the introduction~~ by aid of the great linguists above mentioned. But having so done, I sought to purge the sight with the euphrasy of common sense, and took a second and more leisurely view before I put the question to myself, "~~a~~And what then have I seen?" ~~What are these pote~~

What are
These Potentates of inmost Ind?![205]

Shall I confess the truth? Their next neighbour of the north, the temple-throned infant of Thibet with the Himālā behind and the cradle of the Ganges at his feet, conveys to my mind an impressive likeness, seems to me a pregnant symbol of the whole Brahman Theosophy. Without growth, without production! ~~a~~Abstract the enormous shapes and phantasms, the Himālā, [*p 275*] the Ganges of the fancy, and what remains? A baby! The personality and the additional mystery of secondary self-impersonation, metamorphoses, incarnations—these and all the attri-

---

[202] There are three fundamental clusters of doctrine in Hindu theology. The oldest is contained in the *Vedas*: "The literary expression of the Aryan religion is found in a substantial number of hymns, probably dating, in more of less their present form, from 1400 B.C. to 800 B.C. These were arranged in three collections, to which a fourth was later added, and of which the most important is the *Rg-veda* ('Royal Knowledge')." Somewhat later (800–500 B.C.) emerged the *Upanishads*: "The *Brahmanas* show that, in the settled period after the Aryan invasions, there was increasing elaboration of ritual. . . . From this preoccupation with ritual there emerged a desire to explain its inner meaning, and this is one main concern of the *Upanisads*. They try to answer in various ways the question 'What is *Brahman*?' (the sacred power implicit in ritual performances). *Brahman* came to be thought of as the power sustaining the whole cosmos. . . . The

knowledge of the essential meaning of ritual was identified with knowledge of the self. These strands of thought were intertwined in the famous equation which forms the most influential point of Upanisadic teaching—*Brahman* is the self (*atman*)." The third cluster is the doctrines of the *Gita*: "In the three centuries or so after the compositions of the classical *Upanisads*, there was considerable development of theistic ideas, and these were synthesized with Brahmanic and yogic concepts in the most famous religious writing of the Indian tradition—the *Bhagavad Gita* ('Song of the Lord'). It is one book of the immense poem the *Mahabharata*, which together with the *Ramayana*, the other great Hindu epic, has had enormous influence on popular religion and thought" (Smart 1–2).
[203] Tr: "the book itelf survives".
[204] Cf App C.
[205] Source not traced.

butes of persons—dance in and out like wandering flashes or motley
aliens from a distant country, the mutes of the show, ~~often enough to call
forth,~~ [? but/that] ~~and without even the semblance of an attempt to re-
solve,~~ often enough to ~~awaken~~ ⟨remind⟩ us of their incompatibility with
the doctrines of omneity and infinity, which are the constant theme and
the philosophic import of the Indian theology, but without even an at-
tempt to resolve the riddle. ⟨These impersonations or Avatars⟩*[s]* ~~These
impersonations and *avatars* are so evidently allegories,~~ ⟨betray them-
selves as fables (μυθοι),⟩*[t]* half verbal and built on accidents of language,
and half symbolical, though nothing can be more obscure and conjec-
tural than their direct interpretation.
[u]~~These allegories~~ ⟨impersonations or Avatars⟩ ~~b~~Being ⟨therefore⟩, evi-
dently allegorical, and the allegory physiological or physiogonical, not
historical—on the contrary, plainly intended as the antecedents of all
history, moral and natural—the personal drapery, instead of drawing the
mind to a the conception of any true personeity in the real agent, or sub-
ject, veiled hidden under this veil, tends rather to preclude it.⟩ [*p 277*]
Nay, the omneity, ~~as far as it is attended by any shadow~~ which alone
could cast even the ~~unsta~~ unsubstantial shadow of unity, is everywhere
falsified into omniformity, so that the system so strangely eulogized and
even assimilated to the mysteries of the christian faith is essentially and
in fact Atheism in the form of Polytheism.[206] If I consider the work from
which the preceding extract was made—and this work is a fair specimen
of the most ancient Indian Mythology in general—if,*[v]* I say, we consider
it as poetry,[207] it labours under the mortal disease common, with few ex-

---

[s] Insertion possibly in C's hand

[t] Insertion possibly in C's hand

[u] This sentence, written on p 276 and marked for insertion here, is evidently intended
as a replacement for the following one, which is cancelled in ink with a diagonal line: "But
the sense of these allegories being physiological, or if I may be allowed the term, physio-
gonical; [*p 277*] not historical, the personal drapery, instead of conveying any conception,
of ~~the~~ ⟨a⟩ true personeity, as the ultimate correspondence."

[v] ms: If

[206] Part of the reason for C's attack
on "Brahmanism" in this chapter was not
only its great prestige in contemporary
German thought (see "Introduction" to
this fragment), but also the fact that In-
dian philosophy presented a Trinity—
the *Trimurti*—which, like that of Ploti-
nus, could be seen as a competitor to the
Christian Trinity that C was so exercised
to vindicate. The connecting of C's ob-
jections to Indian theosophy with Sto-

icism and Epicureanism shows how per-
vasively the latter formations underlay
the entire spectrum of cultural manifes-
tations against which he warred. See Pro-
legomena III: The Epicurean and Stoic
Background.

[207] Quoting the same extract in the
Philosophical Lectures, C had called the
Bhagavad-Gita a "great poem of India"
(*P Lects*—1949—127).

ceptions, to all Indian poetry, the attempt to image the unimageable, not by symbols but by a jumble of visual shapes helped out by words of number—a strange conjunction of a cold and arbitrary arithmetical [*p 279*] process with a delirious fancy which excludes all unifying imagination, or rather all imagination, which is essentially *Vis unifica*.[208] It is remarkable that the Greeks gradually removed this rude scheme of figurative representation from their higher Deities, and retained it only in their inferior Titanic and, as it were, uncivilized Deities: Argus, Briareus, Geryon, etc. Thus in the preceding extract the men sticking between the teeth of the omniform Kreeshna[209] is worthy of Rabelais![210] But if we are, as our present subject demands, to receive it as Theosophy, Theology, Ethics or all in one, I find little more than the endless repetition of the old εν και παν[211] a system, which, taken as the ground of a system,[212] is either a barren truism or a most fruitful *w*falsity. Or*x* if we are to form our judgement by the Ethics, and take the ethical consequences as the criterion of the Theology, we shall find ourselves on the same point, for the morals are in the first place equivocal at the best—and not seldom abominable and worthy only [*p 281*] of a Mexican Priest-

w–x ms: falsity: or

[208] C always insisted on the unifying power of the imagination as opposed to the merely aggregative power of fancy. Thus, his first enunciation of the distinction between imagination and fancy, in 1802, refers to "Fancy, or the aggregating Faculty of the mind—not *Imagination*, or the *modifying*, and *co-adunating* Faculty" (*CL* ii 865–6).

[209] Cf *Philosophical Lectures*: "Thus as I see thee, touching the heavens, and shining with such glory; of such various hues, with widely-opened mouths, and bright expanded eyes, I am disturbed within me; my resolution faileth me, O Veeshnoo! and I find no rest! Having beholden thy dreadful teeth, and gazed on thy countenance, emblem of Time's last fire, I know not which way I turn! I find no peace! Have mercy then, O God of Gods! thou mansion of the universe! the sons of Dhrutarashtra, now, with all those rulers of the land, Bheeshma, Dron, the son of Soot, and even the fronts of our army, seem to be precipitating themselves hastily into thy mouths, discovering such frightful rows of teeth! whilst some appear to stick be-

tween thy teeth with their bodies sorely mangled" (*P Lects*—1949—128).

[210] François Rabelais (c 1483–1553), author of the great comic novel *Pantagruel* (1532) and *Gargantua* (1534).

[211] This statement decisively identifies the entirety of Hindu philosophy and theology—certainly in C's perspective—as pantheism, for *hen kai pan* is the talisman of pantheism.

[212] In a note of 1820 C says: "All consciousness begins in the distinction between Subject & Object . . . to evolve the former from the latter leads inevitably to Materialism & to Hylozoism, & thence to Spinosism, and to evolve the latter from the former, is Idealism, and thence to Pantheism—& thence to Spinosism. . . . Thus both Fichte and Schelling . . . have evolved as their ground position the same doctrine, as Swedenborg, & Boehmen . . . thence the distinction between the primary and the empirical Self—and thence inevitably of the former with God, and the final to Ἐν και παν, the fatal Serbonian Bog of all Mysticism!" (*SW & F—CC*—ii 829–30).

hood—and in the second place bad or good—they have no imaginable connexion except where absolute apathy[213] is extolled as the summum bonum,[214] both in the Epicurean sense as Happiness and in the Stoical as Virtue.[215] Of Life I have found one feeble hint, but of Love, ~~as the sour~~ without which as the source, life itself has no religious bearing nor any intelligible genesis—of Love, the idea of life, and without which life is an unintelligible fact (datum non intellectum),[216] not a single one.

Lastly, if we allow the assumption of a dependent multitude of parts, and if the word "God" merely expresses the necessity of a something without which this dependence would not have been possible, in this sense the question, whether there be a God, involves or rather supersedes the answer. To take a trivial but yet just illustration, it would be tantamount to the question, whether Richard's [*p 283*] son had not Richard for a *y*father. But*z* a living, personal, and not merely contemplable but adorable God and creator—this is the question, and to this, instead of finding any direct or affirmative answer in the Brahman Theology, I can discover only a continued and restless attempt to establish a negative by the substitution of the world itself, or rather of a phantasm reflected from it in the optic cylinder of a dreaming fancy.

⟨First, the quotation from Warburton[217]—then⟩*a* [218]

---

y–z ms: father; but

a The insertion, in C's hand, replaces the following passage, which has been cancelled in ink with a single vertical line: "Before we proceed to the next point, let me be permitted, with Warburton, to regret the existence of one serious obstacle to the communication of truth. (Here quote the words from the Divine Legation &c.) It is not easy to calculate the degree of assistance which the modern Socinians have derived from this weakness of

[213] It is not entirely clear what C has in mind here, because the Stoic philosophy alone made "apathy" the moral goal of meditation.

[214] Tr: "highest good". The phrase characteristically appeared in Stoic argumentation, e.g., "summum bonum est convenienter congruenterque naturae vivere" (Cicero *De finibus* III 9). But it was used in other contexts as well, e.g., Boethius: "beatitudo est summum naturae bonum ratione"—"happiness is the highest good of a rational nature" (*Boethius* 75).

[215] One of the fullest discussions of the rival claims of Stoic and Epicurean views of the highest good is that offered by Cicero's *De finibus*, but there is also extensive material in his *De natura deorum*. For C's discussion of the rival claims see *Lects 1795* (*CC*) 156–7.

[216] Tr: "given not understood".

[217] William Warburton (1698–1779), controversialist and Bp of Gloucester. His most famous work was *The Divine Legation of Moses* (2 vols 1737–41), where he upheld the divine origin of the Mosaic law against the Deists. C used the *Divine Legation* extensively in the background of his theological lectures in 1795 (see *Lects 1795—CC—* 87, 112n, 113n, 116nn, 117n, 119n, 122, 133n, 135n-6n, 154, 211 and n).

[218] Warburton's *magnum opus* is so vast, so Cudworth-like in its encyclopedic classical learning (the work first appeared in 1737) that one can have no confidence in selecting the passage C might have had in mind here. He does, however, elsewhere point to a passage,

To this ~~weakness~~ inconvenience the present subject is ⟨more particularly⟩ exposed ~~in a still greater degree~~. The instances of the adaptation of means to ends, and the pre-established harmony of things, are so beautiful in themselves, so admirably suited to the purposes of meditation, and so irresistibly ~~remind~~ refer the awakened soul to the perfections of the great Creator and Governor of the World—they are so eminently fitted to excite the tenderest, noblest, and most elevating notions of humanity, and lastly, they are so universally intelligible, they [*p 291*] speak so directly to the heart as scarcely to need the intervention of the understanding as the interpreter, that it is impossible even to seem to ~~detract from~~ ⟨question⟩ their weight and worth in any relation without giving of-

the imagination. It is in vain ~~to repeat that~~ ⟨for⟩ the defender of the peculiar [*p 285*] doctrines of Christianity to repeat that he is shewing not what any given evidences, historical or moral, are as parts of an organized whole; but merely what they would be, if detached from the rest and presented as the only proofs:—not what the ~~facts~~ incidents related, and the morals prescribed, in the books of the evangelists are in themselves; but what they would be, taken without any reference to the pre-existence of the redeemer in his divine character, before Abraham and under the [. . .] veil of Moses, and with the denial of the doctrine of redemption itself, any otherwise than as all good examples ~~are of~~ have a saving, & metaphorically, a redemptive influence—it is in vain, I say, to urge that we are speaking exclusively of the force which these incidents & these precepts could be expected to have on a learned and pious Jew, if brought forwards as [*p 287*] proofs of a new & necessary revelation and of a religion, entitled to supersede the religion delivered on Mount Sinai, or even on a pious Deist, who had found in the clear intimations of his own reason & conscience, and in the consent of the whole human race, with exceptions so few as to justify him in striking them out of the calculation as monstrosities, this consent too ripening into full confidence in proportion to the greatness & goodness of the individuals, evidences subjectively sufficient to produce as high a degree of faith in the doctrine of a future state as any historic evidence was calculated to produce. No! these evidences, these incidents, have been so habitually associated with the awe & admiration which indeed, in their ⟨true and⟩ proper state of coherence, they deserve & may justly demand, that the feelings of the hearer will not endure them to be otherwise characterized, even on the supposition of what they would be, if plucked live asunder [*p 289*] from the living & ~~only~~ organized body to which they belonged. It is even, as if in reasoning against the doctrines of gross materialism, the philosopher were to present a human eye, which not himself, but his opponent had detached: the ordinary beholder contemplates with horror, what he still involuntarily ~~confuses &~~ continues to call by the name of that, which it had been."

and that passage appears to fit well with what he seems to want in this instance. Thus in a note of 1816–17 he says of Warburton: "quote his remark in his Preface to the Divine Legation concerning the slanders, to which a man makes himself obnoxious by removing *rubbish* from *Churches*" (*CN* III 4322). The remark is as follows: "What do our directing Ingineers advise you to, in this exi- gence? . . . Keep within your *strong holds*. Watch where they direct their battery, and there to your old mud walls clap a buttress. . . . If, in the mean time, one more bold than the rest, offer to dig away the rubbish that hides its beauty, or kick down an awkward prop that discredits its strength, he is sure to be called by these men . . . a secret enemy or an indifferent friend" (*CN* III 4322n).

fence, without the risk of awakening suspicions and unkindly feelings against the supposed detractor. Not without difficulty will he convince even the most candid of his auditors that he is no less sensible than others of the value and beauty of these facts, or of their close relation with and their direct bearing on the idea of God and the truth of his existence; and that if any difference there be between them and himself, it is confined to this point: whether this idea results or is fairly deducible from the phaenomena that are the basis of these several judgements concerning the reciprocal fitness and harmony of things, or whether on the contrary these judgements do not presuppose the idea, whether ⟨by its light⟩ the phaenomena are not [*p 293*] themselves first read and interpreted ~~by its light~~?

*b*To place my views beyond the risk of being misunderstood, I will first extract from the Minute Philosopher of Bishop Berkeley the passage in which the proof à posteriori of the existence and attributes of the Supreme Being is presented ~~not only~~ in the happiest and most beautiful form it has hitherto assumed, declaring at the same time that ~~I consider the argument~~ the premise being assumed, the deduction and conclusion are both unobjectionable and convincing. I shall then have only to examine the premise in order to exhibit the true nature and value of the proof; and if it should appear that it in no wise contravenes my position, but on the contrary implies it, and it being fully understood on the other hand that this position (namely the pre-existence of the [*p 297*] Idea in the human mind), the proof is by me admitted to be no less conclusive on the intellect than it is persusasive for the affections. I shall then be allowed, I trust, without giving pain or occasion of scandal to the weakest consciences to expose with freedom the insufficiency and confusion in the reasoning of those who deny and even deride the doctrine contained in the premise, and pretend to the power of begetting the idea, or rather the idea itself—or, in the language of M*r* Locke, of conveying it into the mind by the force and instrumentality of the same reasonings as they be-

---

b ms: Now I have already stated in general that I ~~challenge~~ deny the possibility of deriving the idea of God from any foreign source. I deny the possibility of conveying the conception & belief of the Supreme Being, in the first instance into any mind, in which it did not previously exist, or by any other means, than by awakening that idea in the mind, so that the knowledge resulting from the attempt can be fairly said to have been ~~deduced~~ given and not rather evolved & brought into distincter consciousness. In pursuit of this I have shown that we cannot discover God by our senses, that we cannot see God: and I have now to prove that neither can we discover Him by means of the Understanding, working on materials ~~furnished~~ supplied by the senses, or from the facts of its own ~~powers~~ ⟨forms⟩ & functions, nor by any judgements [*p 295*] which it is entitled to form in consequence of the congruity of the phaenomena of the senses with these its own forms. [*cancelled in ink with a single vertical line*]

lieve demonstrative of a real existence in perfect correspondence to the idea.[219] Nor let it be regarded as the mark of a disposition to decry authority, or an insensibility to the merits on which it is founded, if I use this honest freedom, not only unabashed by the great celebrity of the Author[220] whose work I have selected as the Text book of my comments, but even impelled to use it with the greater boldness from the [*p 299*] popularity of the book and the strong and wide influence attached to the name of the writer.[221] I confess that, with all possible deference for both, I ~~am te~~ have been often ~~tempte~~ reminded by this attempt of those insects ~~described by our naturalists~~ whom nature has favoured with peculiar instruments or organs to which our naturalists ⟨have given the name⟩ of *ovipositors*, by means of which they cannot only insinuate an egg novum et omnino alienum[222] into the living body of other insects, but can involve it at the same time with the necessary means of ~~its~~ exciting and sustaining its evolution. (Here insert the Extract from Berkeley.)[223]

~~Here then~~ The reasoning, we see, ~~proceeds on the s~~ commences with

---

[219] C's point is that "Idea" is intrinsic in the structure of the mind, not introduced from without—it cannot, "in the language of Mr. Locke" be a the result of a "conveying . . . into the mind". On the contrary, Idea is "not but another word for *a fancy*, a something unreal"; on the contrary, it is "the most real of all realities, and of all operative powers the most *actual*" (*C&S—CC—*18).

[220] It is not entirely unambiguous who the author is. It might be Berkeley, whose work is certainly being used as a text; or it might, on the contrary, be Locke, whose language has been invoked in the previous sentence. One suspects that it is the latter, because of the negative suggestion contained in statements such as "decry authority" and "unabashed". C admired Berkeley as much as he despised Locke.

[221] For C's inveterate hostility to Locke, cf e.g. a statement of 1815: "But till Logic be studied in good earnest, and the whole system of Lockian Pseudo-psychology subverted, there is little chance of the philosophic Truth being listened to" (*SW & F—CC—*I 401).

[222] Tr: "new and entirely foreign".

[223] Although no extract from Berkeley is included in the *Op Max* mss, and C does not specify which passage he has in mind, it may be the one he had John Watson copy from *Alciphron: or, the Minute Philosopher* Dialogue 4 (2nd ed 2 vols 1732) I 145–7 (*B Works* III 155–8) into Notebook 30 in 1823 (*CN* IV 5096; the conjectural date for this entry, Dec 1823–Jan 1824, is too late, as Watson had already left for Germany on 11 Oct 1823: see headnote to Frag 1). The participants in the extracted part of the dialogue are the theist Euphranor and the freethinker Alciphron. The text is from *CN*, omissions from the source being supplied in square brackets: "Euph: No wonder, we cannot assign a time beyond our remotest memory. If we have been all practising this language, ever since our first entrance into the world: If the author of nature constantly speaks to the eyes of all mankind, even in their earliest infancy, whenever the eyes are open in the light whether alone or in company: It doth not seem to me at all strange, that men should not be aware that they had ever learned a language begun so early, & practised so constantly, as this of vision. And if we also consider that it is the same throughout the ⟨whole⟩ world, and not, like other languages differing in different places: it will not seem unaccountable, that men should mistake the connexion between the proper objects of

and grounds itself on the position that there exists a legitimate analogy between the world of the senses and a ^cbook. And^d we are fully per-

^{c–d} ms: book: and

sight & the things signified by them, to be found in necessary relation, or likeness: or, that they should even take them for the same things. Hence it seems easy to conceive, why men, who do not think, should confound in this language of vision the signs with the things signified, otherwise than they are wont to do, in the various particular languages formed by the several Nations of Men—

[It may be also worth while to observe that Signs, being little considered in themselves, or for their own sake, but only in their relative Capacity, and for the sake of those things whereof they are Signs, it comes to pass, that the mind often overlooks them, so as to carry its Attention immediately on to the things signified. Thus, for example, in reading we run over the Characters with the slightest regard, and pass on to the meaning. Hence it is frequent for Men to say, they see Words, and Notions, and Things in reading of a Book; whereas in strictness they see only the Characters, which suggest Words, Notions, and Things. And by parity of Reason, may we not suppose that Men, not resting in, but overlooking, the immediate and proper Objects of sight, as in their own Nature of small moment, carry their Attention onward to the very things signified, and talk as if they saw the secondary Objects? which, in truth and strictness, are not seen but only suggested and apprehended by means of the proper Objects of sight, which alone are seen. *ALC*. To speak my mind freely, this Dissertation grows tedious, and runs into points too dry and minute for a Gentleman's Attention. I thought said *Crito*, we had been, told the Minute Philosophers loved to consider things closely and minutely.]

Alc. [That is true, but in so polite an Age who would be a mere philosopher? There is a certain scholastic Accuracy which ill suits the freedom and ease of a well-bred Man. But, to cut short this Chi-

cane,] I propound it fairly to your own conscience, whether you really think that God himself speaks every day & in every place to the eyes of all men? Euph: That is really & in truth my opinion: and it should be yours too, if you are consistent with yourself, and abide by your own definition of language. Since you cannot deny that the great mover & author of nature constantly explaineth himself to the eyes of Men by the sensible intervention of arbitrary signs, which have no similitude or connexion with the things signified, so as by compounding and disposing them to suggest and exhibit an endless variety of objects differing in nature, time, & place thereby informing & directing men how to act with respect to things distant & future, as well as near and present. In consequence, I say of your own sentiments, and concessions, you have as much reason to think the universal agent or God speaks to your eyes, as you can have for thinking any particular person speaks to your ears. Alc. I cannot help thinking that some fallacy runs throughout this whole ratiocination, though perhaps I may not readily point it out. Hold! let me see! In language the signs are arbitrary, are they not. Euph: They are. Alc. And consequently they do not always suggest real matters of fact. Whereas this natural language, as you call it, or these visible signs, do always suggest things in the same uniform way, and have the same constant regular connexion with matters of fact: whence it should seem, the connexion was necessary, and therefore according to the definition premised it can be no language. How do you solve this objection? Euph. You may solve it yourself by the help of a picture, or a looking-glass. Alc. You are in the right. I see there is nothing in it. I know not what else to say to this opinion more, than that it is so odd and contrary to my way of thinking, that I shall never assent to it."

suaded that ~~the more this notion is pursued in detail~~ the more the comparison between the two is carried into detail, the more steadily the particulars of each are referred to their [*p 301*] essential forms, the more perfect the analogy will be found, the more clearly will the differences ~~seem~~ be discovered to be either apparent only, or inessential—at all events, not more or greater than the nature of analogy permits and requires, for nihil simile est idem.[224] But as the analogy of the world to a book, the Homer's Iliad for instance, such must be that of the book to the world. Whatever is essentially true of the book must be true of the world. ~~We can~~ What we affirm or deny of the one must be affirmed or denied of the other.

[224] Tr: "nothing similar is the same".

FRAGMENT 4

VCL S MS 29, "Say Vol. I" (*L&L* B1); wms "John Hayes | 1815 [*and*] 1816".
This is probably the earliest of the three clasped vellum notebooks together cat-
alogued as S MS 29, and is identified as Vol I by Charles A. Ward in pencil on
the unfoliated verso facing f 1. The text is written in ink in JHG's hand (with oc-
casional corrections in C's hand) on ff 1–92 and 193–4, ff 93–192 and 195–8
being blank. (On Ward, who briefly owned the ms of C's *Logic*, see *Logic—
CC*—xxxiii–xxxiv.)

DATE. 1819–21. A reference on f 8 to "the growth of a tulip in 1819" suggests
that year as the *terminus a quo* of the fragment's composition, while ff 77–83
draw upon notebook entries assigned by Kathleen Coburn to the period 1820–
1: see *CN* IV 4775–6 and nn. The list of chemical symbols on ff 193–4 is very
similar to one in a notebook entry of June 1819 (*CN* IV 4555).

[*f 1*] We may lawfully introduce a digression[1] here as an assistance to
our own imagination, as long as we employ it to no other purpose than
that of reproducing the equilibrium of judgement, which had been de-
ranged by previous prejudices in favour of familiar theories—as long as
we use the detection of their falsehood merely to counteract the sense of
improbability, which should attach to the ideas substituted because new
and strange, and, lastly, as long as we keep ourselves aware that it is a
digression or diversion, and no part or link of our constructive reason-
ing.

The pre-existence of a material state, but above all of organic
phaenomena, to the existing antithesis of sun and planet will to every
mind familiar with the works and educated in the schools [*f 2*] of mod-
ern physics and physiology appear so startling as to become for a time a
proof either of the falsehood of any scheme in which such a position
forms a part, or that the scheme was intended, and to be interpreted, not
objectively or scientifically, but in a subjective sense, just as we speak
of the rising and setting sun. Before, therefore, we examine into our right

---

[1] This is not the first of the sections of
the *Op Max* that begins with a declared
digression, and the phenomenon is in-
dicative of the circumvolving argument
that typifies the work. It also points to the
likelihood that this fragment follows
App A in sequence of argument, and per-
haps in sequence of composition as well.

as derived from reason to pre-condemn the said position as utterly im-
probable, if not impossible, we are bound to put the previous question:
by what right of reason have we received the opposite position as prob-
able, if not demonstrably true?

Is the solar system, in its present astronomical state, eternal? This is
contradicted indirectly by all that we know of Geology. If we suppose,
as is clearly implied in the grounds on which the asserted impossibility
of material organisation prior to the present relations of the centre and
its peripheric bodies, that the present order of things is the product of the
present state of light and gravitation, surely it borders on contradiction
to affirm that a state of universal fluidity should be the result of [*f 3*] the
same relation in the same proportions. The body of the earth has been
aptly called the great archive of the past. Stratum below stratum, each
seems to have its own history distinct from that of the foregoing; all unite
their suffrages against the conception of their having been formed in one
⟨and the same⟩ moment or epoch, and all alike declare in the most intel-
ligible language that their formation has been successive. Whithersoever
this may lead us, and however long our journey may be, it must still stop
infinitely short of an eternal time, waiving[a] even the metaphysical ab-
surdity that seems involved in the combination of time with the predi-
cate of eternal. We must needs, therefore, anticipate some point which
is either a beginning or the re-commencement of a cycle. But in order to
this, a cycle must be shown, a tendency, at least—that something which,
in the smallest arc of a circle, distinguishes the returning from the
straight line. And at last we arrive at the same difficulty, multiplied by
its recurrence at every intermediate change which we before noticed:
namely, that ~~effect~~ ⟨different states,⟩ and a succession of different states,
should be the effect [*f 4*] of the same agents in the same proportions of
agency. Instead of this, then, if we suppose with Buffon,[2] Schelling,[3] and
others that the planets etc. were exploded from the sun,[4] we have then to

---

[a] ms: waving

[2] Georges Louis Leclerc, Comte de
Buffon (1707–88), French naturalist; au-
thor, with others, of *Histoire naturelle*
(44 vols, 1749–1804), completed by
Lacépède. Cf Laplace: "Buffon is the
only one I know who has attempted,
since the discovery of the true system of
the world, to trace the origin of the solar
system. He supposes that a comet, by
falling into the sun, expelled a torrent of
material which reunited into globes of
various sizes and at various distances;

these globes, after cooling and becoming
opaque and solid, are the planets and
their satellites" (q in Whitney 141).
[3] Schelling discussed the planetary
system at length in 1802, in Sect 8 of his
*Fernere Darstellungen aus dem System
der Philosophie* (*Schelling SW* IV 450–
508).
[4] Cf C in a marginal note on Steffens:
"Schelling & all others have attempted to
explain the multeity (ex. gr. the Planets
of the Solar System) out of the Unity (ex.

ask whence came the sun, and during what time did it exist before and without these explosions? If by an internal change it became explosive, such a change supposes a beginning as the first link, and this too a law opposite to all our experience and destructive of all the conditions of experience, viz. a principle of self-destruction—and this too under forms, which if at all conceivable, can be conceived only as *b*instantaneous. For*c* what was capable of remaining by the law of self-preservation could alone remain, and what was not bound to that which remains can never be described as properly belonging to it during any determinable time. For if so, this time must contain some causative power not involved in the term time, as time; but no such power is afforded by the theory, or can be imagined, otherwise than by the contradiction of the former hypothesis by which the discontinuance of these explosions, and the fact that there remains a sun, was to be accounted for. The [*f*5] whole, then, would be reduced to the purely subjective principle: that the One is prior to the Many—a principle true only as far as we contemplate the world subjectively, i.e. as manifestations of mind deriving their being from mind, in short, as long as objectivity itself is but a form of the subjective. From the point of view, however, on which these theorists have placed themselves, the principle is not merely false by misapplication, but rendered null by the perfect equivalents of the contrary position— and this in the very next breath, as it *d*were. For*e* the sun must have been accumulated from the many in order to have presented a unity afterwards to be dispersed or divided, for a unity prior to all multeity is in the very terms declared eternal; and, in the present instance, this argument presses still more strongly, for this anti-planetary sun is not only a factitious unity but a compound formed by a compulsory aggregation of heterogeneous parts, incapable of remaining as parts in consistence with the *f*unity. And*g* after all, what is gained? Whatever difficulty there may exist in the present state of the planets[5] is not overcome, but merely transferred: [*f*6] the very same effects must have existed as effects prior to the moment in which they began to act as causes. Lastly, ⟨with⟩ little right can that school [? ~~because/concede~~] reject any position on the score

---

b–c ms: instantaneous; for *d–e* ms: were; for
f–g ms: unity; and

---

gr. the Sun) by successive or simultaneous explosion. Now I take the reverse, and explain all out of the Multeity involved in each, and presupposed as the conditions of its existence. This goes thro' the whole—the Earth *rose* in it's present position" (*CM*—*CC*—v 266).

[5] For C's more than merely casual interest in celestial phenomena see "Draft of a letter on Comets" *SW & F* (*CC*) I 766–9.

of its improbability, i.e. the absence of analogous experience or comprehensible causation, which itself begins by an assertion certainly unsupported by any experience seemingly contradictory to it (in the lax sense of the word "contradictory", at least, and as much so as when we should say it would be contradictory to experience that the sun would not rise tomorrow), and assuredly incomprehensible inasmuch as it involves, without explaining the assertion, that a power existing as a part should overcome the whole of which itself is a part. Now in order to effect this, they must show an essential difference between some power that manifests itself as explosion, from the projectile power necessarily assumed of the whole unit, in order to explain the possibility of its motion in an ellipse around the body towards which that unit is at the same time gravitating. With good hopes should we behold them attempting this investigation in good earnest, for whatever the [*f* 7] particular result might be, it could not but tend to emancipate the imagination from that tyranny of the visual and the palpable over the reason, of that domination of death over life and living power[6] in which the whole theory originated, and from which source alone the stream continues to be fed.[7] We finish our digression, therefore, with this one remark, that as surely as reason is reason, and man a partaker thereof, nothing can be more improbable than the assumption of effects as causes that preclude all cause [and] substitute for an eternal, which they dare not predicate of any one thing, an everlasting, which belongs to none, which will not predicate the eternal of aught besides, or allow aught of which the eternal can be predicated but the hollow phrase of an infinite series multiplied ad infinitum by an infinity of changes, proceed sine die[8] giving themselves[h] the lie, and find a solution by multiplying its necessity in order to establish its hopelessness.

---

[h] In the ms "itself" was written above "themselves", then scratched out

[6] It was "life and living power" and the theory of form based on organic growth, which had become increasingly prominent with the investigations of Leeuwenhoek in the 17th and Bonnet in the 18th centuries, that provided C with an arsenal of thought to use against mechanism. Cf, almost at random, a remark of 1817: "Most significantly, my Lord, did the ancients name the object of Physiology the Genesis, the φυσις, the natura rerum—i.e. the birth of things. They searched after, and recorded the *acts* of the world: and the self-subsistence, yet interdependence, the difference yet Identity of the forms they express'd by the symbol of begetting. With the Moderns, on the contrary, nothing grows; all is made—Growth itself is but a disguised mode of being made ..." (*CL* IV 761).

[7] Cf e.g. *Biographia Literaria*: "... an indistinct, but yet stirring and working presentiment, that all the products of the mere *reflective* faculty partook of DEATH" (*BL—CC—*I 152).

[8] Tr: "without date".

[*f*8]   Of all the theories grounded on the corpuscular philosophy, in the corpuscular scheme, and acknowledging no powers but mechanical and chemical, the latter again mechanically contemplated, it is evident, and at present we believe generally admitted, that they are all alike incapable of explaining life and organisation.[9] Now the datum[10] in all mechanics is weight or gravity, and impact in connexion with gravity. Let these be assumed as prior, and as far as they are concerned, life and organisation are miracles, i.e. they are effects or consequents with an heterogeneous antecedent which neither is nor can be conceived as being their cause. The assumed priority, therefore, would at best be but an historical accident, with no more causative connection than the age ⟨birth⟩ of George the Third ⟨in 1750⟩ to the growth of a tulip in 1819.[11] Yet, still, life and organisation are not merely co-present with the laws of the so-called inanimate matter; they are undeniably connected, and apparently, at least, in a constant [*f*9] interchange of *i*being. We*j* must, then, condemn ourselves if, another road lying open, we leave it wholly untried: that the one certainly does not lead to the object proposed is rather a presumption that the other *k*may. We*l* are certain that the planetary mechanism, contemplated mechanically and as inanimate, cannot causatively explain life and organisation: let us, then, examine whether we may not be more successful in reversing the order of priority, namely, whether in life we may not find the conditions of universal organisation, and, again, in universal organisation the conditions and the solution of mechanism. This, then, is our present problem.

That we shall be more successful in the latter attempt, in part at least, is certain, for we shall avoid that transgression of the laws which we ourselves had established as conditions of the possibility of a *m*philosophy. For*n* first we shall not commence with an abstraction,[12] but this we

i–j ms: being; we   *k–l* ms: may; we   *m–n* ms: philosophy; for

[9] This, in C's hope, was the strongest bastion against the Newtonian rigidities of the "mechanico-corpuscular" scheme. Cf *Aids to Reflection*: "I am persuaded . . . that the dogmatism of the Corpuscular School, though it still exerts an influence on men's notions and phrases, has received a mortal blow from the increasingly *dynamic* spirit of the physical Sciences now highest in public estimation" (*AR*—1825—387). See Prolegomena xxx: The Relation of the *Magnum Opus* to Coleridge's *Theory of Life*.

[10] Tr: "given".

[11] The date of 1819 assumes special interest as a possible indicator of the date of composition of this fragment.

[12] Cf a letter of 31 Jan 1819, where Coleridge says of his *"magnum opus"* that he had been working with four postulates: "That the System should be *grounded*. 2. That it should not be grounded in an *abstraction*, nor in a *Thing*. 3. That there be no chasm or saltus in the deduction or rather production. 4. That it should be bonâ fide progressive, not in circulo—productive not barren—"(*CL* iv 917).

should have fallen into in asserting the priority of mechanism as at once instanced in and dependent upon the [*f 10*] "Mechanique celeste".[13] In order to see this, we need only reduce the term "Mechanism" to a higher formula, as the action of all, as either the result or the aggregate of the actions of each considered as the components of the aggregate, or the efficients of the result. If we assume that the actions of each are component, and the all the sum of the aggregate, we have then clearly a mere generalisation, the unity and sole reality of which is in the mind generalising; but if as efficients of a result, the result is of course posterior to the efficients, and we have as evidently transgressed by a saltus,[14] having namely leaped over and passed unnoticed the nature and degree of the efficients, each in itself, which, by the hypothesis itself, is the sole objective ᵒreality. Recall,ᵖ too, our former remark that from mechanism to organisation, i.e. from shape as the forma formata[15] to form[16] as forma formans,[17] there is no progression possible; and we shall find, first, that by taking the priority of mechanism, we bona fide bid adieu to our whole attempt, which demanded the constant [? ~~adherence to~~] ⟨coincidence with⟩ three conditions, each and all of which we should here have violated: namely, that we should have [*f 11*] reasoned on and from an abstraction or generalisation; secondly, have moved per saltum[18] instead of continuously; and lastly, have come to a full stand, or to a retrogressive movement, instead of progression. Unless, therefore, some third term shall be discovered, neither a degree of mechanism nor of organisation, nor yet superior in scale to the latter, and ceasing to be a degree by becoming a new and higher kind—in short, as long as mechanism and organisation exhaust the calculus as its only conceivable terms— then, and so long, we have a proof positive, though not indicative or explanatory, of organisation as anterior to mechanism:[19] either A or B must be first; B cannot be, therefore A is.

To the preceding proposition I can conceive but one objection, namely a denial of our assertion that whichever be the prior state, M or O, they are indissolubly connected, and by a connexion for which we know no

ᵒ⁻ᵖ ms: reality; recall

[13] The *Traité de mécanique céleste* (1798–1825) was the masterwork of the great French mathematician and astronomer Pierre Simon Marquis de Laplace (1749–1827). He was more popularly known for his *Exposition du système du monde* (1796). For a discussion of his activity and opinions, see Whitney 133–54.

[14] Tr: "leap".

[15] Tr: "form formed".

[16] For C's desynonomisation of shape and form see Frag 2 f 98, f 107, ff 113–14.

[17] Tr: "form forming".

[18] Tr: "by a leap".

[19] This contention, as frequently noted, was of great importance to C (as to Jacobi), "for the philosophy of mechanism . . . in every thing that is most worthy of the human Intellect strikes *Death*" (*CL* IV 575).

other exponent but that of cause and ^{q}effect. In^r opposition to this, it must be maintained that they are pure co-existents, [*f 12*] without connexion or inter-agency, or that they are co-efficients of the same dignity; but this is scarcely worth answering, for it can neither be based in any ideal necessity, and it is in direct opposition to the known fact. It refers to no principle à priori, for then a definition must be given of mechanism, separating it as a power per se from those of the objects on which it is ^{s}exerted. In other^t words, we must conceive some real being under the name of "weight", for instance, perfectly independent of all ponderable matter: à posteriori, it is so far from drawing even a semblance of confirmation from our experience that experience itself would become impossible on the presumption. If there be on earth a truth, it is that the modifications of quantity, figure, colour, etc. are causally connected with quality or power ab intra;[20] and, again, that quality ⌈. . .⌉ is in myriads of things antecedent to the determinate quantity, while nowhere do we find any proper form of quantity not resulting from some quality, but taken [*f 13*] as sole and independent the antecedent of a determinate quality. In other words, quality may, and in many instances must, be conceived independent of quantity, but quantity can never be conceived but as a consequent of quality. If this quality be so far universal that the quantity in any given object—a stone, for instance—contribute but an infinitesimal part of the sum which acts in and on it, we call this [the] power of mechanism.[21] Where, on the contrary, the object supplies from itself a ⌈. . .⌉ definite and preponderating portion of the quality which it manifests by its quantity, and the modifications thereof, i.e. size and figure, we deem it a power of organisation. In both instances alike, in the order of thought and nature, quality is not merely antecedent to quantity, but causally antecedent. Should a scruple suggest itself, derived from the properties of mathematical figures, it will be sufficient to recollect that if these figures be taken as pure theorems or productive acts of the imagination, the quantity here is quality manifesting itself. [*f 14*] It is wholly aloof from magnitude and whatever else is ^{u}passive. But^v if we conceive it as corporeal, i.e. as having size and existing by comparison and varying co-portionality to the sensation of the percipient, it falls under the antecedence of quality as modified in [the] § concerning quality as the power of mechanism; unless where it falls under the second head, i.e. whether the object be a needle or a thorn.

Well, then! that organisation in the sense here determined is ante-

$^{q-r}$ ms: effect: in $^{s-t}$ ms: exerted in, other $^{u-v}$ ms: passive; but

[20] Tr: "from within".
[21] C is here formally engaged in "laying the foundation Stones of the Constructive or Dynamic Philosophy in opposition to the merely mechanic—" (*CL* IV 579).

cedent to mechanism, we appear to have demonstrated.[22] It remains to show the form and process of this antecedence. That an act of ~~the ef~~ each efficient must be contemplated anterior both to an effect, of which it is but a co-efficient, and to an aggregate, of which it is but an infinitesimal component, it remains that we should determine what this act is and by what necessity it becomes: in order to this we must determine what is meant by the singular number, by the "An" efficient as a part, indeed, but yet "A", that is, one part—in other words, [*f 15*] what is comprised in the term "integral part". Again, in order to this we must recollect the subject matter on which we are discoursing, the point on which our philosophy is now standing. Waiving[w] the question whether the term "integral part" would be applicable either to the divine plenitude or the state designated as chaos, it suffices that it is not to these that we now apply it, but to a state in which the law of polarity has commenced by means of two contrary powers united in the same subject, and manifesting the unity by opposition.[23] These powers, in their most comprehensive forms, we have recognized and already explained as multeity and unity.[24] The answer to the question, therefore, is easy, as the state itself of which we are now treating is not wholly real nor perfect, but fluxive and by participation only, so neither can the term "integral part" be taken as otherwise than participial and fluxional. From the chaos it derives the principle multeity, below number.[25] But it is not this, for we have passed out

---

[w] ms: Waving

[22] This, as previously emphasised, is one of the most compelling insistences in C's entire philosophical agenda. Cf a statement of 1817: "it is not of a dead machine that I speak" (*CL* IV 769).

[23] See Prolegomena X: The *Magnum Opus* and the Principle of Polarity. Cf from among many possibilities, *The Friend*: "the antithesis of Truth and Being is but the result of the polarizing property of all finite mind, for which Unity is manifested only by correspondent opposites" (*Friend—CC*—I 515 n 3); "a law which reigns through all nature, the law of polarity, or the manifestation of one power by opposite forces" (*Friend—CC*—I 479); "It is the idea of the common centre, of the universal law, by which all power manifests itself in opposite yet interdependent forces . . ." (*Friend—CC*—I 511).

[24] The reference is possibly to the dis-

cussion of multeity in App A. In *Theory of Life* C speaks of the possibility of having "borrowed a scholastic *term*, and defined life *absolutely*, as the principle of unity in *multeity* . . . " (*TL*—1848—42). Again, in 1822: "But both this (the analytical) and the former (the synthetic) are functions of unity. It is the Unity in Multeity which constitutes both the primary and the reflex Act" (*SW & F—CC*—II 1006). For an important application to aesthetics, cf *The Principles of Genial Criticism*: "The most general definition of Beauty, therefore,—that I may fulfil my threat of plaguing my readers with hard words—Multeity in Unity" (*SW & F—CC*—I 372).

[25] Cf App A: ". . . in the plenitude we had Number ⟨above⟩ multeity so in the contrary state we have a multeity alien from number . . ." (f [3]).

of chaos: from the [*f 16*] divine love, as indivisibly distinct in the divine plenitude, we derive the principle of unity. But it is not that principle, but an exponential generated by the influence of that principle on and upon the multeity.[26] It follows, therefore, inevitably, that of an integral part no other than a flowing yet gradative definition can be given, analogous to the integration obtained in the higher mathesis by the extremes of the differentials.[27] Wherever ~~the mult~~ and in proportion as the multeity is seen in consequence of the preponderance of the unity, we have there an integral part, ⌈. . .⌉ an integer absolute subsisting only in approximation.

We find in Aristotle two axioms, each, taken in itself, of full and equal evidence, yet ~~the~~ ⌈. . .⌉ ⟨each⟩ apparently in direct contradiction to the other; and in the conciliation of this seeming contradiction we ~~may~~ shall assuredly obtain some guiding principle in ~~the priority~~ arranging the priority of the two great classes of phaenomena, the *o̶Organic* and the *Mechanic*.[28] The first [*f 17*] of these axioms is: "In every true whole, the whole is prior to its parts"; the second: "The parts constituting the whole are necessarily prior to the whole so constituted". It is clear that both in the term "Whole" and the term "Parts", there must lurk a double meaning. Let us take an instance: I draw a circle which I suppose to be formed by a point so moving forward as at the same time to be ~~return~~ tending to return upon itself, or, which would be equivalent, an ⌈. . .⌉ indefinite number of points placed on the imaginary line, which the point in the former line would have described. If we take these as physical points, it is evident that they existed as such prior to the appearance of the line; but it is equally evident that the circle-line must have pre-existed, in its idea, in the mind of the describer, or no reason could be assigned why these points, indifferent to all figure, had not constituted a triangle, or square, or simple straight line equal to the circumference of the circle. As phys-

---

[26] "In Nature there is a tendency to repeat herself so as to attempt in each part what she had produced in the Whole/ but with a limited power and under certain *conditions*. In this, the only scientific, View Nature itself is assumed as the Universal Principle of Life, and like all other *Powers* as contemplated under the two primary Ideas of Identity and Multëity—i.e. alternately as one and as Many. In other words, exclusively of *degree*, or as subsisting in a series of different intensities" (*CN* iv 5464). The different intensities are well represented by

what Schelling calls *Potenzen*. What C calls "Multeity" Schelling calls *Vielheit*.

[27] Cf a note of 1826: "the Idea in the form of Multëity, viz. Life as existing in a gradation of different intensities from a minimum to a maximum" (*CN* iv 5446).

[28] In "arranging the priority of the two great classes of phaenomena" C, as noted throughout this ed, placed the hopes of life in the organic, and found death in the mechanic. The organic-mechanic opposition ran throughout his thought. See, for a famous instance, *Lects 1808–1819* (*CC*) i 495.

ical points, therefore, placed by a force ab extra[29] so as to constitute a circular⟨le⟩ [. . .], they, called parts by anticipation, necessarily pre-exist [. . .] relatively to the circle. [*f 18*] It follows, therefore, that the second axiom is an universal truth of mechanics, or of bodies acting on each other by impact. But on the other hand, that as parts of that circle, namely as mental phaenomena, they pre-supposed the circle, deriving the very principle of their constituency by which they first became Parts of that particular character from the idea = Circle. The only question, therefore, is what we are to understand by the term "Idea", or by the circle having mental pre-existence. Is it merely notional, purely subjective, like perspective forms in looking at a panorama? Or a mere result of memory conjoined with imitation? Not the latter, assuredly, for this would be a mere evasion by assigning as the cause of A another A, differenced from the former solely by a powerless position in [x]time, the[y] circle first perceived justifying the same question with the same force as the thousandth, though enriched by the memory of all the preceding 999. We must come at last to one or the other of two solutions: a circle pre-existing in mind, or an efficient and yet eternal necessity of a nature negatively defined as not mind. We see at once that the latter are mere words without [*f 19*] meaning, or mean only the striving and the self-frustration of the thought attempting to make a phaenomenon, as a phaenomenon, its own reality—like a monkey tormenting itself by alternately[z] looking at and behind a looking glass. In short, it is a blank confusion of an effect determined as a mere effect, with a cause considered as a productivity separated from the product. The former, therefore, alone remains; and striking out the useless interpolations of memory and imitation as so many zeros put before a figure, we find ourselves, [. . .][a] as before, constrained to have recourse to a circle in the mind. The other question may not seem of such easy solution: what this mental circle is to [b]be. For[c] if, indeed, it be notional and purely subjective, it can have as little claim to a place in a system of construction, material, corporeal or spiritual, provided only it be real, as the verbal definition of a fluid would have in the extinction of a fire or the circumvolution of a wheel. At least, whatever objections may be suggested to invalidate this assertion, e.g. the assumed influence of our thoughts and fancies on the Will, [*f 20*] must acquire all their force at the cost of the hypothesis by declaring what was assumed as merely notional to be the contrary, and in-

---

[x-y] ms: time. The   [z] ms: alternate
[a] Approximately seven words cancelled   [b-c] ms: be for

[29] Tr: "from without".

stead of notion must substitute a self-subsistent soul, self-determined in a given direction. If, therefore, we are to make any use of Aristotle's first axiom and to find any power not mechanical, we must establish the reality of this idea, namely, both in the mind and in nature equally objective (objective in mind and subjective in nature),*d* *acting* in the world of the senses yet not as an object of sense, and *being* in the world of the *e*intellect—not*f* as a result of sensation, or ⌈. . .⌉ ⟨unsubstantial⟩ product of *g*volition. It*h* must have all the essential attributes of reality: namely, ~~reality~~ ⌈. . .⌉ it must be self-actual and having a being [? ~~above~~] prothetical to either of the two modes of existence within the mind; and as out of the mind, as proved by the constant correspondence which in either it has to the other where it is not contemplated as Idea, it presents itself as law; where not as law, ever as Idea, or that which cannot be conceived of in the subjective other than as objective, [*f 21*] or in the objective otherwise than as *i*subjective. In*j* the Soul it must exist as a nature, in Nature as a soul; and that this is even so, the very properties of curves, circles, etc. in mechanics themselves utterly unaccountable by mechanics, is a demonstration as irrefragable as it is obvious. Thus in the construction of an arch, neither the materials nor any force exerted by the component stones or masses of the arch produce the properties of an arched bridge except as far as they are derived from and ⌈. . .⌉ pre-assumed in the figure itself. It appears, therefore, that in order to the verification there must be a power acting in an opposite direction to that which is supposed in the science of mechanics, and contradistinguishes mechanical force, and which, considered as opposed to the mechanic, is as a power ab intra[30] to a power ab extra,[31] and again as a power anterior to and causative of the phaenomenon, viz. figure, quantity, ~~of~~ extension, etc., to a power caused by and in immediate dependence on the phaenomenon. Thus we find in every body the capability of presenting a [*f 22*] mechanic power which, if we cautiously consider, we shall discover to be properly material, matter being defined [as] "that*k* which appears only or hath its existence ὅλως εν τῷ φαινεσθαι"[32]—which, again, we shall find equivalent to the definition of matter, "phaenomenon imponderabile".[33] And secondly, we shall find a power properly spiritual, spirit being properly defined as "that*l* which cannot appear in itself, either not at all or as manifested in another". And as a corollary

---

d Parentheses inserted *e–f* ms: intellect not
g–h ms: volition it *i–j* ms: subjective in
k ms: "That *l* ms: That

[30] Tr: "from within". [32] Tr: "wholly in what appears".
[31] Tr "from outside". [33] Tr: "unweighable appearance".

we may annex that every body, as a phaenomenon ponderabile,[34] pre-supposes in order to its existence both a mechanical force appertaining to it and a spiritual power, as the supporter of the force and the ground of its conceivability. But as it follows from these definitions that not every phaenomenon is ⟨needs be⟩ corporeal, so doth it follow that it is not absolutely necessary for every spirit to be so—in other words, that though "Body" implies both matter and spirit, yet neither "matter" nor "spirit" supposes[m] any logical necessity of their co-existence as body. And again, that though matter were adequately defined "δια του φαινεσθαι",[35] [f 23] or "phaenomenon imponderabile", which (as long as we conffine[n] our discourse to the subponenda, or prothetica) is the same as "phaenomenon sine pondere", yet, I say, that though this were an adequate definition of matter, it does not follow that the weight, or rather the principle of ponderability, would be an adequate definition of spirit. The reason of this difference is obvious: that which is known to us only as being extraneous is exhausted in the term "appearance", but that which is proposed to us as what is defined only negatively, viz. but which cannot appear, may and probably will be susceptible of many positive definitions, among which the power of weight or gravity may be only one [o]species. And[p] so, in fact, we shall find it to be, for a power may be opposed to another, which is exclusively ab extra by its having a transcendency to the same, viz. by its being equally ab intra and ab extra, and truly neither properly because both inclusively. Or it may be conceived of as an ab intra directly and pecu[f 24]liarly opposed to the ab extra, and between these, viz., a power universal as far as respects the relations of space, and a power which must be conceived of as acting centrally in relation to a given space—[q]sundry sorts of powers, all alike spiritual and yet having, if we dare so express ourselves, different dates of conceivable origination, evidenced by different results and events in the great history of the world, by which that succession which we know philosophically must be under the condition already established or con-ceded, at least in the apostasis[36] and anastasis[37] and which yet cannot be, if not distinguishable is distinguishably peopled.

We have in a former stage[38] exemplified this in the powers of astrin-

[m] ms: suppose
[n] On f 22[v] "confine" is written in pencil facing this word
[o-p] ms: species; and
[q] Dash inserted. The syntax is difficult, and it is possible that the words "in relation to" were intended to begin a new sentence

[34] Tr: "weighable appearance".
[35] Tr: "through appearance".
[36] Tr: "standing away from".

[37] Tr: "rising again".
[38] The implication is that C com-pleted more of the scientific section of

gency, contraction and dilation, in the compound power of amassment, and even in the centrifugal and centripetal powers as the prae-supposita of gravitation.[39] Try for a moment, in imagination, to explain the phae-nomen<del>e</del>a of cohesion by the old fancy of <del>H</del>hooks and eyes,[40] con[*f* 25]fining ourselves solely to the material figuration, and we shall see at once the necessity of integrating the material figure by a something, the positive attributes of which we find ourselves in the first instance com-pelled to designate by a negation in which we place an actual opposition. Suppose a hook to be lifting up a fish: how does the hook withstand the weight, or the dragging down, or pulling this way and that way of the ʳanimal? Ifˢ we answer, "by its cohesion", it is clear that we must not ex-plain this cohesion again by hooks, but that we must assume a power al-together ἑτερουγενους[41] from the hook as that particular figure—a

---

ʳ⁻ˢ ms: animal if

---

the *magnum opus* than appears here. The reference could possibly be to the dis-course contained in App A below, where such matters as amassment and astrin-gency receive considerable discussion. If that is the case, and if it be also the case that the present fragment should, as sug-gested above, be dated as belonging to the year 1819, then the so-called Opus Magnum printed in the appendix would stem at latest from that year and possibly from the preceding year.

[39] C's continuing involvement with gravitation in this run of argument is dic-tated by two realities. The first is the ob-vious role that gravity plays in physical reality, and in the generation of any cosmogony whatever. The second—and this it is that accounts for the special per-sistence of gravity's invocation here—is that gravity was the primary datum and, as it were, the "cutting edge" of Newton and the mechanico-corpuscular school. Cf C's statement in *Philosophical Lec-tures*: "Sir Isaac Newton, contempla-ting the abstracts of material bodies as weight, mass, and motion and the condi-tions of a perfect theory as far as bodies are considered exclusively under the conceptions of weight, mass, and mo-tion, he made the bodies mathematical, for he contemplated them under those conditions only which he could state ab-stractly and as parts of a definition. From this arose his hypothesis of gravity, and from this again finally the law of gravi-tation, and thence forward neither theory nor hypothesis were further regarded. Nothing but the law was at all paid at-tention to, with the law dwelt power and prophecy, and by exclusive attention to the law it has been that late disciples of Sir Isaac Newton, [La Place] and others, have removed all the apparent difficul-ties in the theory of gravitation and turned them into the strongest confirma-tions of the same" (*P Lects*—1949—360). Gravitation, as the universal power of the Cosmos, fulfilled the role of God, but since gravitation had neither con-science, nor consciousness, nor will—in a word, person—in its conception, its apotheosis by the Newtonians and Laplace made it virtually an anti-Christ to C.

[40] The invocation of the old fancy of "hooks and eyes" in adjacence to an ex-planation of "the phaenomena of cohe-sion" correlates with C's language to Southey in 1809 about "all the connec-tions of logic, all the hooks and eyes of intellectual memory" (*CL* iii 254). Epi-curus and the "interlinking" of atoms (Long & Sedley 46) would seem to stand behind both collocations.

[41] Tr: "of another nature".

power which cannot be conceived as superinduced upon the hook, but which, bearing an opposite relation to all we conceive in the term "extra"[42] and "ab extra",[43] we know no better way of expressing than by the term "ab intra",[44] though meantime a certain perplexity in our imagination, a certain inability to light and settle upon any one point, instructs us that we have not used a nomen verè [*f 26*] proprium,[45] and yet that it is something more than a metaphor. The difficulty is irremediable, but the solution is to be found in the heterogeneity of the power, which therefore disimpropriates the term "intra" relatively to "extra", these being opposites ejudem generis,[46] and that we are speaking of a power not in space but yet in relation to space, and actualizing the attributes which suppose an existence in space, as figure etc. We see, therefore, already two species of spirit, the one opposed to the extraneous only because it is distinguished from it as comprehending it, or as at once comprehending and transcending it, or as a universal is opposed to a particular. Such a power we suppose Gravitation to ᵗbe. Theᵘ other, where a particular is opposed to a particular when a power by its own product gives the attribute of direction, which, again, may be conceived as ᵛtwofold. Forʷ the power, which by its effect or product gives the condition of a determinate direction relatively to some other power, may be conceived as having its limit common to it and its antagonist by ~~balance~~ equilibrium, and which limit, therefore, is the [*f 27*] effect of both, in which case are necessarily homogeneous and differenced by the direction, or else the limits are themselves the products manifesting as limit, generally, indeed, a finiteness, and, as it might seem, an absence, inasmuch as it admits an addibility of ˣpower. Butʸ as far as those limits are determinate, not limit in general but those particular lines of limitation, they attest the energy of the producing power. Strange would be the confusion between the extreme points of an outstretched arm which stops at a given point of space because it could get no further, and the beautiful outline of the fingers in themselves; and yet beneath the invisible cap of abstraction, or reduction of a thing to a mark of calculus, it has been allowed to pass muster in Hegel,[47] Oken,[48] and others, nay, to be the basis of ~~tha~~ system

ᵗ⁻ᵘ ms: be the   ᵛ⁻ʷ ms: twofold for
       ˣ⁻ʸ ms: power but

[42] Tr: "outside".
[43] Tr: "from outside".
[44] Tr: "from within".
[45] Tr: "name truly fitting".
[46] Tr: "of the same kind".
[47] Georg Wilhelm Friedrich Hegel (1770–1831), German systematic philosopher. C annotated some of Hegel's *Phänomenologie des Geistes* because of its pantheism, but was not enthusiastic about what he read.
[48] Lorenz Oken (1779–1851), German *Naturphilosoph*, follower of Schelling and progenitor of the protoplasmic

of the universe. Or take the peoints of an arrow, or rocket, at the exhaustion of its power of ascent, or the line described by its fall, and we never dream of classing it with the segments of a leaf—nay, the truth is that in the latter instance the line of limit is altogether positive and ^{z}energic. As^a far as the produc[$f\,28$]tivity is concerned, the want or defect of energy is to be found wholly in the matter of manifestation. We shall find little difficulty in accepting the truth of this (and a distinct insight is not wanted in the present stage of our ^{b}progress). Where^c we trace precisely the same configuration in leaves of very different magnitude, language itself instructs us to say there is a deficiency in the materials. Thus, then, we have already got, as equally though differently contradistinguished from matter, Spirit as universal, and relative only by the relativeness of something else compared with its own irrelativeness, and Spirit particular, or rather limitary, determined by its antagonist and homogeneous with it. And both these powers, though spirit as opposed to Matter, yet revealing themselves *materially* and, in so doing, constituting body, are conceivable only in relation to Matter as Phaenomenon, i.e. they not merely need matter in order to manifest their existence, but they cannot be conceived of—I do not say merely not imagined, for that is involved in the definition of matter, but they cannot even be thought of except as the [$f\,29$] actualization of matter, except as integrated thereby into Body—in short, except as body and in relation to Body. And no less evident is it that, adverting to the principle of multeity, and in it to the forms of all and part, the All will distinguish a power which the parts possess not as partial or several, but as contained in the All, as when water is aerated, the drops partake of the gas not as drops, but as drops of that aerated water. So again, è contra,^{49} the globular form belongs to the drop as a drop, and is lost as soon as it passes into a drop in the stream. Now the former of these powers properly constitutes^d the science of statics, while the latter constitutes^e that of Mechanics onat the one esinde^f and Chemistry on the other end, and hence we see a full solution of the fact that mechanical power always presupposes statics as its universal and actualizing principle, or, in other words, all mechanical

---

$^{z-a}$ ms: energic as $^{b-c}$ ms: progress where
^{d} ms: constitute ^{e} ms: constitute
^{f} The terminal "e" was mistakenly left uncancelled in the ms

---

basis of life. Cf C: "... the best and cheapest Natural History in existence—viz. Oken's in three thick Octavo Volumes, containing the inorganic world, and the Animals from the Πρωτόζωα, (Animalcula of Infusions) to Man—" (*CL* v 422).

^{49} Tr: "from the other side".

power, as power, supposes Spirit[50]—but as mechanical, it supposes Matter of equal necessity. The spirit, therefore, must be that which is most opposed to Matter, as infigurative, and universal, as opposed to the contrary extremes[g] [*f 30*] as characteristic of matter, viz. figure, and particularity, and multeity. Thus, for instance, remove from any machine its particular figure, and it ceases to be a mechanical and becomes a statical power. But, vice versâ, the matter, which constitutes the power mechanical, must, in order to this union, be a form of matter most opposite to the form of spirit: it will be in the highest degree relative, even as its spirit is altogether irrelative in itself; and, above all, it will be the result of the very power to which it is at the same time, and for that very reason in opposito, i.e. it will be a whole constituted by its parts.* ~~which yet~~

* [*Written on f 29ᵛ and presumably intended as a note:*] But yet that these parts exist as constituents of a Whole compels us to refer to some other and superior Whole by which they had been and are constituted. It is just difficult, and yet in sound Logic as requisite, to explain an Atom as a World; or rather, an Atom is a contradiction in terms, except it to be rescued by such an acknowledgement of its uselessness as would be contained in the limitation, an Atom as far [as] our senses or power of division extend.[51] I say that this is useless, because the standard to which it refers has no one of the properties of a standard from its being different in each individual, and perhaps in each different experiment, though made by the same individual—and again, because an atom, as the sensible product of one such experiment, has no conceivable application as the factor of any scientific calculus.[52] Where it appears to have, as in Dalton's

[g] Written over another word, now illegible

[50] Cf a note of 1816 called "Consciousness and Self-Consciousness": "Now all Power is but Will realizing itself in Act, of which Being ... is the product—" (*SW & F—CC*—ɪ 429). C continues to argue for the priority of spirit against the tradition of the "mechanico-corpuscular" philosophy.

[51] C properly discriminates between so-called "atoms", which experimental and theoretical science constantly divides and re-divides, and true "atoms"—i.e. axiomatically undividable quantities—which are an absurdity. Epicurus, like his predecessors Leucippus and Democritus, posited atoms in part to counter Zeno the Eleatics's infinite divisibilities of the continuum (see e.g. Long & Sedley 41).

[52] The intensity of C's attack on atoms is largely generated by their role in the thought of Epicurus, even where Epicurus is not named; for Dalton's new theory precisely replicated the Epicurean threat of antiquity. With regard to that intensity, cf a letter of 28 July 1817: "What matter is it to the World, it will be said,—of what consequence can it be to society at *large*, that the Physiology alone taught or tolerated at the present day sets out with a pure fiction, an ultimate particle to wit? that it proceeds with a blank miracle, i.e. the causeless & therefore praeternatural Hardness or infrangibility of these corpuscles, with an Apotheosis of death, by virtue of which the insensate moats are elevated into Demiurgic atoms, indivisible & yet space-comprehending minims, that are at once the stuff, the tools, & the workmen

~~originate in and though by constraint must acknowledge as its causative~~
~~antecedent parts constituted by the whole or a Whole anterior to its parts~~
Thus in order to construct a machine, we conceive it as an aggregate of
parts, and put together those parts so as to make the [h]machine. But[i] that
there are parts for us to put, but that there are parts capable of forming
a Whole, or still more precisely and nakedly, that the multeity hath
~~becom~~ been actualized into Parts, we require an impartible substance, [*f*
31] ~~an One o~~ το αυτο, communicative of unity to the το αλλο. On the
other side we have Chemistry, or chemical power, where the union be-
tween power and chemical is not produced, as in the former instance, by
direct opposition, but by a [j]disparateness. Thus,[k] for instance, here is no
ab extra which attributes an intra to its antecedent in order to ~~oppos~~ be
conceived in opposition to that antecedent, and another ab extra con-
trarient by *direction*, but *essentially* homogeneous, in order to realize [l] it-
self. Neither[m] [n] is it[o] opposed as particular to universal, relative to irrel-

---

theory,[53] it will be found a mere synonym for "Weight", as opposed to "Exten-
sion"—in short, a clumsy fiction to evade an explanation of the different specific
gravities of such chemical substances as the chemists have not yet succeeded in
decomposing. An atom, therefore, cannot be justified, even on the ground of a
chemical element,[54] for the latter refers to ~~an~~ determinable fact that depends on
the simple question, "Has it or has it not been done?"

[h-i] ms: machine but   [j-k] ms: disparateness thus
[l-m] ms: itself; neither
[n-o] Written "it is" in the ms and marked in ink for transposition

---

of the material Universe" (*CL* IV 758).
Epicurus, in his *Letter to Herodotus*, had
said blankly that the atom (*atomos*) was
"indivisible and unchangeable". "It fol-
lows that the first beginnings must be in-
divisible (*atomous*), incorporeal entities"
(*DL* II 571).

[53] John Dalton (1766–1844), English
chemist and physicist. Among his many
important achievements, he arranged a
table of atomic weights (1803) and was
the first to give a clear statement of
atomic theory (1803–7). Published *A
New System of Chemical Philosophy*
(1808–27). The youthful C, according to
the industialist Robert Owen, visited
Dalton in Cambridge on several occa-
sions (*TT—CC*—I 392 n 4); and see
John Unsworth "Coleridge and the Man-
chester Academy" *Charles Lamb Bul-*

letin ns no 32 (1980) 149–58. On C's re-
jection of "Dalton's Theory" see *TL*
(1848) 51 n 1.

[54] From antiquity onward, true atoms,
that is, absolutely irreducible physical
magnitudes, were opposed—certainly by
the critics of Epicurus—because they
contradicted the conception of the infi-
nitely small. Leibniz, for instance, was
opposed to the possibility of true atoms,
as was Descartes. Cf C's note of 1819:
"Atoms.—If understood and employed
as xyz in Algebra, and for the purpose
of scientific Calculus, as in elemental
Chemistry, I see no objection to the ~~as-~~
~~sumption~~ Fiction not overweighed by its
technical utility. But if they are asserted
as real and existent, the Suffiction (for it
would be too complimentary to call it a
Supposition) is such and so fruitful an

ative, as in mechanics; and though equally with these it supposes the statical power* ~~yet~~ as its base, not as its positive principle, as a necessary ~~pre-~~condition, not as its immediate causative antecedent. That ab intra which hitherto has been but suppositious, formed by reflex, and potentiated only in anticipation (being in truth no more than the offspring of relation in the intellectual construction of a circle on a plane*P* surface, and consequently no more than relative length) now appears to *realize* itself, and wedding [*f 32*] itself, as it were, in that moment to the form of depth which in like manner had hitherto been but another relation of length, ~~awakens~~ gives no determinate product, indeed, to the efforts of conception, but rather an uncertain quantity, or fluxion, between the magnitude A, out of which it has passed, and a magnitude into which it is passing— ⟨gives⟩ a something which, in the very nature of the thing, can be only expressed by metaphor, which the Theorist who rejects the metaphor, because metaphorical, must (supposing him consistent) deny Chemistry to be Chemistry. He must make it ~~a species~~ either ~~of~~a part of mechanics or a part of Zoonomy. For in chemistry we no longer find (characteristically and prominently, I mean) Power opposed ~~by~~ ⟨to⟩ the matter which it is actualizing, but Power opposed ~~by~~ ⟨to⟩ Power, and the Matter, or Phaenomenon, as the inactive product. In the Mechanics the activity of the Matter hides and disguises the universal Power which it supposes and demands of all the powers that may exist in the bond of the universal power, a submersion in that universality, and, relatively to the mechanism [*f 33*] itself, an indifference. They are either subservients to quantity, or equal to nothing. For not only are the *qualities* by which bodies are differenced, not only are the *qualitative* differentials, I say,

* [*Written on f 30ᵛ:*] It does not in the same way presuppose it. I mean, it supposes the statical power.

P This word was originally "sphere", then the letters "pl" were written over the "ph", the "s" being mistakenly left uncancelled

absurdity that I can only compare it to a Surinam Toad crawling on with a *wartery* of Toadlets on its back, at every fresh step a fresh Tadpole. The contradictions, which it involves, were exposed by Parmenides, 460 years A.C., so fully as to leave nothing to be added. An atom is a body which contradicts the constituent character of a Body, namely, that which fills a space, ~~for~~ and consequently must have the relations of Space, viz. two Poles and the point of bisection" (*CN* IV 4518). It must be reiterated that C's emphatic rejection of atoms was part of his larger rejection of the Epicurean revival of his day, augmented by the corpuscular theory of Newton. See Prolegomena III: The Epicurean and Stoic Background, et passim.

indifferenced, but even the *quantitative*, as Cohesion, act only as the conditions of the manifestation of weight and figure.

But the chemical powers do the very contrary. Instead of a relative indifferencing with co-existence, instead of permitting a co-existence with an indistinguishable ~~subserviency~~mersion in the common power, viz. Gravity, or a quantitative distinction measured by the subserviency to the figure and direction, i.e. to the mechanics—instead of all this, I say, no co-existence is *q*permitted. The*r* powers destroy each other in the act of becoming some new power which may either manifest itself as a positive power or as a copula of properties derived from the entire suspension—what we might perhaps venture to call an intussusceptive equilibrium, or chemical neutralization. Instead, too, of a submersion in the universality, or common power, the Chémique asserts its equality with the Statique—nay, its rights of seniority—and exercises no less sovereignty over the latter [*f 34*] than the latter (the Statique)*s* had exercised over the *t*Méchanique. Even*u* as the Statique constitutes Matter into Body generally, so does the Chémique constitute Gravity as particular Gravity.[55] As we must conceive realized Weight in order to the incorporation of matter, so must we seek for a power to realize this weight. For as far as the sensible world is concerned and Statics are considered mechanically (in the Méchanique céleste), as the mechanical Whole presupposes its parts, so must the statical Whole, or total Gravity presuppose the specific Gravities of its components. We need not seek, in the weakness of our antagonists, substitutes for direct proof: we have it as the legitimate offspring of our own idea, but as a mere illustration we will refer to the attempts which have been made to realize universal Gravity ~~asin~~ ~~ait~~s universality—we refer to the Newtonian Aether,

q−r ms: permitted the   *s* Parentheses inserted
                           t−u ms: Méchanique even

[55] When contemplating C's continuing play with the French words "mécanique", "chémique", "statique", one should keep in mind that he read little French. He confesses to the Beaumonts in Sept 1803 that he is "but a wretched French Scholar" (*CL* II 994), and that situation, because of his dislike of the French Enlightenment and of Revolutionary France, never changed. The *Mécanique céleste*, because it consisted mainly of mathematical equations, could not have been actually read by C, and the deficiency of his knowledge of French adds further certainty to that fact. In that context, his insistence on conducting his argument in terms of French words reveals itself as more a device of dissociation from the greatest of French mechanists than as a warrant of control over French texts. As another device of dissociation (displacing his own guilt) C charged that the *Mécanique céleste* was "an unprincipled Plagiarism" from Kant's *Allgemeine Naturgeschichte und Theorie des Himmels* (1755) (*CL* IV 808).

[which] under all its names and disguises cannot be better defined than as a power which in every point of space is at the same time penetrating and resisted.^{v} We may refer likewise to the curious fact that in all the cosmogonies hitherto constructed, the ~~prod~~construction of the system, and of each planet's [$f35$] relations to the center, and the production of the planet in itself, as of our earth geologically considered, have been completely out of sight and hearing of each other.[56] In the one system, the planet, with all its inherent gravities contained and hidden in the sum of its cosmical ~~gravity~~ attraction, is formed, or exploded, and the specific gravities themselves are taken for granted; in the others there is a chaos, the resolution of which into specific gravities constitutes the very mass ~~that is to be exploded~~ which the former had exploded. Nor, indeed, was it possible that the two systems could be united either by subordination or co-ordination, for in order to give a moment's plausibility to the combinations and precipitations of the chemical chaos, it is necessary to suppose it per se, the causes of each whole as instituted—as the results, the specific gravities, must have been posterior, therefore, to the explosion of their aggregate from the solar mass of which they had been a ^{w}part. And^x yet to have been a mass at all, the mass must have had its specific gravity relatively to the sun, so that whichever way we move, the second step contradicts the former, and, in the words of the com[$f36$]manding officer in an Irish regiment of volunteers, we move right about to the left and advance backwards—which, if I may be forgiven for a momentary relaxation, might suggest a solution of that part in the Bramin Mythology which represents the world raised up out of Chaos on the horns of a bull—at least I know no better, half word, half pun, half image, for the expression of so notable a dilemma.*

* [*Written on f35^v:*] It has always appeared probable that the picture language and hieroglyphics both of Egypt and of India are in part verbal, i.e. that the figures as often may refer to the sound of the name as to the properties of the animal or thing.[57] But this would lead me far, too far, however curious the subject

---

^{v} A caret appears here in the ms as if to indicate an insertion, but without any text to be inserted
$^{w-x}$ ms: part, and

[56] C's linking of discourse about the planets and their formation to the "earth geologically considered" would seem to be a response to a question by the *Naturphilosoph* Heinrich Steffens: "What if the history of the formation of the earth coincided with the history of development of the planetary system?" For the conflicting theories of Steffens and Eschenmayer on these matters, see the long discussion at *CN* IV 4640n, with corollary notice of G. H. Shubert and others.
[57] C overrated his credentials for speaking on such subjects: "I have for some time worked hard in Egyptian Antiquities, & if I do not delude myself,

Let us, then review the position on which we stand. We have a power causatively determinant of Body, viz. both of the matter and of the spirit. It contrasts the Méchanique and the Statique, specifies the figurability and the weight, and yet it supposes the Statique already coexistent as its basis, as an inferior, while on the other hand the Statique, to any conceivable mechanical relation, presupposes it as its determinant; and yet, though there appears a mutual necessity, there is no mutual production, so that we might establish a cycle in which each was alternately producent and product—a something is yet to be conceived which, explaining the Chemique, may perfect the circle and constitute a period, or intercirculation, like a new power [which] shall open [*f 37*] it anew. Well if we leave off in each period with an increased light, and the relative morning end the day which the evening began.

Need we wonder[y] that ~~the circle remains~~ our curve still ~~cir~~ refuses to return on itself, that it is still parabolic instead of an ellipse, when we reflect that the very condition and prime element of calculus is wanting? When we reflect that all manifestation or objectivity supposes not only that which is manifested,[58] but likewise a That to which it is manifested, an Object without a Subject is a contradiction.[59] If we take the term

---

might be: the prevalence of punning and the modified nature and dignities of the pun itself in the early periods of language amongst the sacerdotal nations. Suffice at present a reference to the Apocalypse and the scientific puns of the ancient Cabbala.

---

[y] Mistakenly cancelled in ms

---

have the means of *quashing* the *deduction* at least which certain half Infidels have drawn from Champollon or what's his name's decypherings. . . . My Belief, grounded on no slight evidence, in addition to that of common sense & the *Harmony* of Historical Experience, is: that all Inscriptions, Hieroglyphics, &c earlier than Moses are ancient Forgeries—that the wisest Ancients were well acquainted with these pretended Kings &c & regarded them as mere Egyptian Lies—&c &c—In short, my researches with the light of English Common Sense have rendered me a sturdy Anti-Egyptian & a very sceptical Hindostanist. S. T. C." (*CL* v 442). J. F. Champollion, who deciphered the Rosetta Stone in 1821, published *Précis du système hieroglyphique*

in 1824.

[58] "All consciousness begins with the distinction between Subject & Object" (*SW & F—CC—*II 829).

[59] C invoked a form of the same consideration in refutation of Spinoza: "Spinoza, at the end of his life, in his last letter, seems to have gained a glimpse of truth. He begins to suspect his *premiss*. His Unica Substantia is in fact a mere Notion, a *subject* of the Mind and no *object* at all" (*TT—CC—*I 98). See further Prolegomena XVIII: Subject and Object. Cf a note of 1825: "there must be a double correspondence of the Object, to the Subject producing as well as to the Subject in which the Idea is to be re-produced" (*SW & F—CC—*II 1314). Cf a passage of 1824 entitled "The Subjective

"Subject" in its lowest, i.e. most indeterminate sense, as Spirit or the Manifestable, the contradiction is palpable because it is a contradiction both in terms and the [z]imagination. But[a] no less shall we find that this spirit itself becomes contradictory, except as far as it contains in itself its own dative, its own "to whom" it is manifested, or supposes it in some other. But even ~~here it is~~ in this latter case the res manifestata,[60] as opposed to matter as the merè manifestans semper alterum manifestans,[61] cannot retain the name "Spirit" [*f38*] in any other form than as we suppose it to be an aggregate or sum total of powers which must all, though in endless difference of degrees, be at once nominatives, objectives, and datives relatively to each other. Strange as this phraseology may appear, I can find no more commodious preventive of circumlocution and repetition; and indeed if language be, as it is, the offspring and epiphany of the human soul, it cannot be surprising that the elements of grammar should supply the most appropriate metaphors for the elementary forms of human reasoning,[62] and the science of words, elaborate expressions for the science of thought.[63] But above all must the philosopher be on his guard against the delusion which arises out of his own communication of thought. This he cannot effect but by words or language. But all language is utterance, i.e. Outer-ance, and [b]with ~~o~~Outness[c] [64] the imagination necessarily associates a sensation of reality more or less faint, and it requires all the caution of reason to prevent this sensation from passing itself [off][d] for a sense. This is especially applicable in the present stage [*f39*] of our progress: we have been both compelled and entitled to employ and consider the universal, the principle of ponderability—I mean, ens staticum[65]—as the realizing unity by which

---

[z-a] ms: imagination but   [b-c] ms: with~~o~~Outness
[d] Insertion supplied in pencil on f 37[v]

Nature of Objectivity": "is not this a hint, that Objectivity is itself Subjective? That Spirit, i.e. potential Mind, *is* whatever is? . . ." (*SW & F—CC*—II 1187).

[60] Tr: "thing manifested".

[61] Tr: "purely manifesting, always manifesting the other".

[62] Cf *Treatise on Method*: "Grammar brings us, naturally, to the Science of *Logic*, or the knowledge of those forms which the conceptions of the mind assume in the process of reasoning" (*SW & F—CC*—I 675–6).

[63] C more than once asserts this view. See e.g. Frag 2 f 273 for grammar as implicit logic.

[64] C frequently uses the word "outness" which was used before him by Berkeley. Cf a note of 1808: "All minds must think by some *symbols*—the strongest minds possess the most vivid Symbols in the Imagination—yet this ingenerates a *want*, ποθον, *desiderium*, for vividness of Symbol: which something that is *without*, that has the property of *Outness* (a word which Berkley preferred to 'Externality') can alone fully gratify/ even that indeed not fully—" (*CN* III 3325). See Owen Barfield's chapter called "Outness" (Barfield 59–68).

[65] Tr: "a standing thing".

the multeity is raised into figure and relation, and thus, relatively to the Mechanique, it (the Statique) stands as the substance to the form, as the current to the direction. But here we must interpose the Sabbatical moment—we must gather strength by a renewed prostration within the Holy of Holies, and with cleansed eye refuse to behold any true unity but in the Deity, any true and essential distinction except in that divine Unity.[66] Out of this, the Alpha and Omega, we can find no attributes but those of Allness and Multeity—and as long, therefore, as we speak of that which is not God, we can comprehend no other Allness which is the reflex and Symbol of unity but that which is derived from the multeity—become conceivable as component parts.[e] An Allness that in its Unity is the causative principle of its comprehended distinctions would be = God, and herein we discover the [*f 40*] cause of the oscillation of Newton, and of the schism amongst his followers:[67] the one party shrank from the notion of contemplating Gravity as God, and from its gross Pantheism and moral death, the necessary accompaniments of such a contemplation. For either this deified Gravity is different from Mind, and opposed to it, or it is the same, and comprehensive of it: the former implies a copulation of blasphemy the most terrific, and superstition the most gross. God becomes the Idol, and the Idolater becomes God: the latter is less shocking, and for that reason more pernicious, as it either destroys all distinction of right and wrong, guilt and holiness, good and evil, or attributes them promiscuously to the Deity. Scared by the perception, or repelled by the presentiment of these consequences, the one party sought a refuge in a material aether, and thus afforded the triumphal moment of successful[f] confutation to their antagonists by detection of the absurdities exposed by us in our yesterday's disquisition. All of which, however, are reducible [*f 41*] to the one abysmal absurdity of attributing causative of the distinctions which it comprehends to a material Allness, to an abstraction which can be referred to no noun substantively, and to none adjectively, but either at the loss of the unity or of its totality, for such is the term "Omneity". ~~There is one other~~ It is derived neither from verb nor from substantive, and we must either refer it to the singular "Omne",

---

[e] Dashes inserted in this sentence   [f] Written over another word, now illegible

[66] Cf a letter of 12 Jan 1818, where C classes himself among "*Christian Philosophers*, in whose mind there are but four main classes of Truth—God. The living tri-une God. The alienation from God and the reconciliation to him in the Word & through the spirit—" (*CL* IV 809).

[67] Especially prominent among the "followers" of Newton was Laplace, who specifically said that the purpose of his *Mécanique céleste* was mathematically to reduce the known phenomena of the world to the law of gravity ("la gravitation universelle"), and to complete the investigation of the planets, satellites, and comets begun by Newton (Laplace I [Preface] A).

which signifies only "each", or from the plural "Omnia", which represents the subternumeral confusion of "each" infinitely repeatable, or more accurately, assumed without repetition as indefinitely repeated.

But the same reasons which deny all self-subsistent reality to the universal, relatively to the particular, apply with no less force to the specific, relatively to the universal. The universal has no significance but as the sum of the specific, but the specific will be found to have as little significance, unless it be in some way or other substantiated by the existence of the individual. But even so, the individual must present to us some power, some prin[*f 42*]ciple of actuality, in order to preserve the significance of the particular universal and specific, even in that state of acknowledged insufficiency in which they have been presented by us. This part of our argument is difficult and subtle: we have seen the Méchanique, which to the Statique bears the relation of particular to universal, yet not so as that its Idea is exhausted in that relation. We have seen, I say, the Méchanique acknowledge a causative antecedence in the Statique, yea, in the very act of antithesis thereto, deriving from it a Unity. And yet we have seen with equal clearness that the Statique can have in itself no Unity but that which is implied in Totality, and refers to a higher Unity which is in its components—which, again, would be a contradictory term in any higher sense than that of effect, or participation. Suppose, for a moment, that the component parts or integers of any given mass were all of the same specific gravity: it is clear that the mass itself must either be contemplated as a mere cumulus,[68] and, consequently, that either it becomes itself a specific gravity[*f 43*]—ceases of course to be considered as a Whole, and becomes a part relatively to some Whole—or that the term "specific" in the expression "parts of specific gravity" has no meaning or application relative to the mass composed, but ~~are~~we have simply mere parts of a mere cumulus. ~~It follows then that the Méchanique~~ But what if, instead of a cumulus, we were to conceive a whole composed of the specific gravities? I answer, try to conceive it, and you will find it utterly impossible to conceive a specific whole that is more than a cumulus, formed by parts that are not specific, i.e. differential relatively to each other. The old philosopher,[69] the

[68] Tr: "piling up".

[69] Anaxagoras. C was rather unenthusiastic about this philosopher, whom he seems to have regarded as tainted by the proximity of his thought to atomism. "Then rose Anaxagoras who in many respects resembled our own Locke" (*P Lects*—1949—145). He observes that Anaxagoras attempted to reconcile the discordant views of the Eleatics and of Democritus, but "so lame was the system of the world which he brought forward that not only Aristotle, but Plato himself complains of him that his *Nous*, or supreme reason, was a mere hypothesis to solve a few impossibilities but never

founder of the scheme of Homieomery,[70] constructed a heart of little hearts and a liver of little livers, but he never ventured to make the blood out of hearts or livers, still less a body, and least of all a body out of little bodies.[71] In short, all mechanical ~~holds~~wholes suppose parts relatively differenced, and all that have more than relative existence imply a more than relative difference of the component parts, though the semblance of [*f 44*] the contrary will, from the imperfection of language as much as from any other cause, present itself to us in the transitional states from the lower to the higher—in crystallization, for instance, but of this in its own place. It follows clearly, I[st], that[g] the keystone ~~it~~of ~~our~~the arch is not to be found in the specific, and II[dly], that[h] it must be found in the individual, the sole remaining term, though under what condition, whether as inherent in the individual, or as participated by it, we do not at present [i]see. We[j] know only that the very lowest, and each in its turn above it, is something more than it could be ~~either~~ of itself, and, consequently, that hitherto each is more than it could be either of itself or by virtue of its immediate antecedent. In short, we require more than a principle of subordination to account for the subordination itself, and this subordination, again, is insufficient for the solution of the problem, unless a something be added in which the subordinates are equal, some common flash which courses down all the links and by its coinstantaneous presence [*f 45*] to all, indifferences the subordination which it does not destroy—nay, which it requires for its own manifestation. We have only to add that this individual must be One with the required sense of the subject: it is an X which is to supply a proportionate subject to the hitherto objective, as well as an individual to realize the specific and the universal. Our direction, pathless as the region before us appears, is designated by the relation in which we first perceived, by our want of a correspondent we wanted, the dative of manifestation, and saw that both our objective and nominative cases were such by anticipation of this dative. Our Problem, therefore, will be the same as to discover in an identity a recipience of alterity which shall, however, be indifferenced in that identity, so that it shall be altered without ceasing to be identical, and, vice

---

[g] ms: That   [h] ms: That   [i–j] ms: see we

---

introduced when he could do without it" (*P Lects*—1949—146).

[70] Anaxagoras himself did not use that word, but early commentators on him did. See Kirk & Raven 386–7.

[71] Aetius said that "Since, therefore, the nourishment contains parts that are like the things which it produces, he called them homeomeries and said that they were the first principles of existing things . . ." (Kirk & Raven 388n).

versa, remain identical without ceasing to be continuously altered. But this, however, we must so limit that neither the identity nor the alterity shall be demanded in any higher sense than may be [*f 46*] attributed to that which is not God.

For some time past—for too long a time, I fear—we have been lengthening our journey by turning wide from the direct pursuit of truth in order to combat error. The field has been worse tilled because we have been ploughing with the sword in our hand. Something too anxious we have likewise been in the extrication and establishment of ⟨our⟩ Terminology, and it may be some time before we can place ourselves again in the current of Intuition. We must attempt to reproduce the constructive state by no violent means, lest, as occurs in the missing of a name, we exhaust the power of recollection in the effort. We began with the Spirit as the Spirit of Love and of Communication, and even in this we obtained, both for that first stage and for all future stages of the process, the privilege and rightful power to stand at equidistance[72] from the opposite errors of the mechanic materialist and of the pantheist.[73] For by the first act of the Spirit as Spirit, we had communicated to the Multeity such a participation of Unity as sufficed to effectuate the conception of omneity without [*f 47*] involving the notion of an aggregate, or the preconception of parts. But, then, with exactly the same clearness, and as contained, indeed, in the same intuition, we saw that this conception of an all might, and would, be the substance or subject of Power generally, but never could be employed in the intellectual construction of any power in particular—as Attraction, Repulsion, or Gravitation—and this we have explained at large in our first disquisitions on ~~Cha~~Aether and the transition of Chaos into it.[74] This epoch we will designate by the terms "Unity", "Indistinction", "Omneity". The next epoch began the Articulation of the

---

[72] Such standing at equi-distance was in largest terms adopting the role of Paul against the Stoics and Epicureans (Acts 17.18–32), the former of whom were absolute pantheists and the latter atomists or mechanic materialists.

[73] Contrast this defining statement with its counterpart in Frag 3 above: "the narrow isthmus which we have to pass with atheism on the one side or a world without God, and Pantheism or a world that is itself God" (p 23). Pantheism, as one side of the abyss, is a constant in both statements; but the statement in the present fragment narrows the abyss of

"atheism" to "the errors of the mechanic materialist". The external world as presented by pantheism was alluring, but the external world of the mechanic materialist was not: "the Mechanic or corpuscular Scheme", instead of "a World created and filled with productive forces by the Almighty Fiat, left a lifeless Machine whirled about by the dust of its own Grinding" (*AR*—1825—391, 393).

[74] Cf App A: ". . . Darkness is 1st *Chaos* that is before the separation of Light—2d In the separation it becomes Aether" (f 62).

breath, Spiritûs; it superinduced Distinction, the possibility and condi-
tion of the conception of parts—that is to say, not parts in the corporeal
sense, for this were an anticipation had it even respect to a truth, and such
an anticipation as would destroy that portion of truth which actually ex-
ists for the ~~philosopher~~ intuition in the corpuscular philosophy, or the
doctrine of Atoms. We should have spoken of Distinction following the
Spirit of Union, and then interpreted [*f 48*] our words by the contrary
sense, Division without Distinction: not parts, therefore, but relations we
must seek for, and these we found in Light.[75] We obtained an Outward
and an Inward. In what sense, and as not yet supposing an Outness or an
Inness, we must refer to our disquisition on this subject. Suffice at pres-
ent that we found the necessity of conceiving a Matter of Light[76] and a
darkness, and the conception of the same as divided the one from the
other. The Aether as actualized could not strive outwardly, and by this
striving realize itself as matter of Light, but it must at the same time
strive inwardly (i.e. the blind self-seeking by which, in actualizing the
potential, it had originally potentialized the actual and become Chaos);[k]
and this striving likewise must realize itself as matter of darkness, but
yet *potential* only. And in relation to ⟨the matter of⟩[l] Light, therefore, as
representing the actual,[77] it must be conceived as the opposite of matter,
viz. Vacuum, Addibility—in short, all the forms of the Potential as [*f
49*] merely potential.[78] And yet, on the other hand, in relation to the
Light itself, as the very act, the true superinducent of Distinction, and

---

[k] Closing parenthesis inserted
[l] Passage written on f 47ᵛ and marked for insertion here

[75] The past tense in "we found" is
perhaps generated by a priority in the
discussion of light in App A frag (*c*) ff
2ᵛ–3, 7–12ᵛ, 18ᵛ–27ᵛ, 29ᵛ–32ᵛ. The
great emphasis on light may well derive
primarily from Schelling, for in the *Ideen
zu einer Philosophie der Natur* of 1797
(which C read in the second ed of 1803),
the second chapter is entitled "Vom
Licht" (85) and the third, "Ueber die
Lehre der Naturphilosophie vom Licht"
(113).

[76] C takes the phrase "matter of light"
from Schelling, who uses the expression
"Materie des Lichts" (*Schelling SW* II
385). Schelling does so because he has
argued (382, 383) that light, despite its
speed, is in fact matter.

[77] To realise how C, both from Bibli-
cal predisposition and personal experi-
ence, was prepared to accord light the
most honorific status in his view of the
natural world, it is well to note that in
1820 he uses Aristotle's word for the ac-
tual (*entelecheia*) in referring to light:
"But *in Life* Light must be the En-
telechie, the central Point, that takes up,
& is not taken up—The Word is *Light*—
in it is *Life*—and this Life is the Light of
man—The divine Cycle cannot be more
adequately expressed, from Light to
Light thro' Life—" (*CN* IV 4678).
[78] The tenacity with which C here
pursues the subject of light is prefigured
and as it were dictated by a powerful
declaration in App A frag (*C*) ff 7–7ᵛ.

therein of Actuality et vice versâ.[*] But in relation to Light itself,[81] this Darkness must be construed emphatically as Matter, or possible manifester of Light, and further our expressions cannot reach. Light is opposed to matter as darkness, or the matter of light is opposed to darkness as the utter absence of manifestation, and in either case from the very conception of light[82] this opposition can only be construed as a division.[83] Our next step procured for us a ~~g~~Gradation; and from the contrary powers of the Word in the Spirit and of the Chaotic principle, ~~teach~~ new act of the former evoking a new ~~tendency~~ manifestation, or at least tendency, in the latter, we obtained the conception of Interjacency, and therein a second involute of Antithesis, an XY which differed from the Aether in the ordonnance of its [m]forms. The[n] Aether could not be con-

[*] [*Written on f 48*[v]*:*] N[ote]. For we are here in some measure within the divine sphere, and speak of Light as the act of the divine Word,[79] but within that sphere[80] all forms of production must of necessity be construed reciprocal, that being our only exponential of the Eternal.

[m-n] ms: forms the

[79] Cf a letter of Sept 1817: "And God said—Let there be *Light*! and there was *Light*. And God divided the *Light* from the *Darkness*—i.e. Light from Gravitation . . . the two Poles of the material Universe are established, viz. Light and Gravitation" (*CL* iv 771).

[80] See the foregoing note. Cf a letter of September 1817: "I am attempting to trace the Genesis, the φύσις, the *Natura rerum*, the Birth of Things" (*CL* iv 769).

[81] At this point, C begins (or possibly continues) a persisting commitment to theorisation about light, which runs through the discourse in App A below as well. The background to this activity was not solely Newton's *Optics*, but German *Naturphilosophie* also.

[82] The "very conception of light" was for C not simple and intuitive, but a conception of ornate *naturphilosophische* ramification. Cf a letter to Tulk of 12 Jan 1818: "We may now proceed to the second of two primary Poles of Nature, namely LIGHT. This too must be bipolar: and as the antithesis of Length, must correspond to breadth—instead of the magnetic *axis* we must take hemispherical *Surface*-lines, the Representatives of which we select as East and West—the East, as Contraction, Particularization, Fire, Oxygen, negative Electricity: the West as dilation, Universalization, Water (= ὕδωρ ἐν ὕδατι), Hydrogen, positive Electricity. And this permit me to call the Noun *adjective* of Nature.—The first is the line of Substance, the second the surface-lines of Existence, or Modification.—Or take the one as Magnetism, neg. and pos.— and the *real* Synthesis will be Galvanism, or constructive Chemismus.— And with these, I aver, and with these only, all known chemical facts may be solved—" (*CL* iv 808).

[83] See e.g. a long and turbid *naturphilosophische* note that as late as 1825– 6 fancifully mixes theological with hopefully scientific schematism: "The Opposite (n.b. not the Contrary) I would call the Nadir. As in the former Darkness (i.e. Gravity, as the Unific inhibitive Power) at once hides and represents itself in a Form of Light, as the distinctive exhibitive Power; so in the latter Light penetrates the Mass—to lose yet represent itself in a form of Darkness.— I. Σκοτος παμπρωτον—the Potential Identity of Light and Darkness. The *all in each* (Tohu Bohu) of Moses.—Chaos. II

templated in the same relation as Matter and as Vacuum, though the darkness [*f 50*] might be considered now as vacuum and now as matter—in either way, however, the conception of absence and ~~potentiality~~ the mere potential predominates. Subtle as it may appear, we had to preserve the Antithesis, and yet reverse its constituent conceptions; the XY was to stand in a full opposition to the matter of Light as far as it was Light, but only in an opposition of Degree, as less to greater, This to That, to the Matter of Light. Here, as in all parts of our Philosophy, the constructing explains the construction: this XY stands in a different relation to Light from the Aether, in proportion, therefore, as the Aether, relatively to Light, is a vacuum consequently unresisting, the XY must be conceived as in some degree resistant; but only in some ^{o}degree. In^p some other view, therefore, it must needs be contemplable as non-resistant and, anticipating the construction of act on potentiality as motion in space, we may say permeable. In like manner, too, we must take its resemblances to all of which it is an intermediate:^{q} to the Aether ⟨as Vacuum⟩^{r} it shall appear as Plenum, while in some opposite relation it must appear a Va[*f 51*]cuum to a Plenum, but both the one and the other relatively and comparatively, for the sphere in which we are constructing is actualized only as far as it is a world of Relations and Gradations— its true reality is not in itself. Now review the terms of the construction and observe whether, in the simple and child-like language of the ~~patriarchal world intellect~~ ⟨senses⟩, we could express it otherwise, ⟨when by distance converted into an object of sight,⟩^{s} than^r [*f 52*] "Heaven" or

$^{o-p}$ ms: degree in

^{q} No punctuation in ms

^{r} Written on f 49^v and marked for insertion here

^{s} Passage written on f 50^v and marked for insertion here

^{t} ms: as a Firmament in the midst of the Waters i.e. the Matter of Light that which has distinction of Relation but no distinction of Parts and let it divide the waters from the waters i.e. the necessary conception of interjacency while the waters i.e. indistinctions are distinguished by their relation to the firmament the only relation possible. As many times as ~~the Multeity in combination~~ the midterm of the multeity as combination with the transcendent Oneness and super-numeral Distinction shall compell us to repeat that of which we know only that it cannot be conceived as numerically but One so often must we repeat the Other in one vast circle the Firmament as a lesser [*f 52*] and whatever is most actualized in the center or nucleus. We mention this digressively only not as if in all the stages

Σκοτος δυναμικον, Vis Tenebrarum, Vis *Massifica*, or Gravity, as the Positive Pole of Creation. III. Lux Lucifica, Λογος λεγομενος, the distinctive manifestative Power—whence Utterance, Song, Articulation in Nature—the Negative Pole. IV. Corpus, Tenebrae substantiatae, Gravitas γινομενος. V. Lux materialis—ρημα εκδοτον. VI. Lumen seu Forma Lucis et Phaenomenon. VII. Umbra, seu Corporis Forma et Phaenomenon—The pure phaenomenon of Body, as far as it is not Light—" (*CN* IV 5290).

"sky", and this again the dignified terms of what, contemplated in proximity, we entitled the "Air". That not merely the relation of the Atmosphere, but likewise its properties and attributes from its secondary antithesis and resemblance to matter as the matter of light, and to aether as the matter of darkness, will be shown hereafter. Our next stage presented us with the construction of the Solid and the Fluid, the former of which we would exchange for the term "Firmamental", of which we saw thus much: that both were contained in the matter of light, both, therefore, opposed to the aether, and both disparate from the air.

[*f 53*] Indistinction cannot be actuated by the Spirit so as to be indistinction with unity—in other words, raised into unity, but yet so far retaining its former nature, i.e. indistinction as still to be without distinction of parts—this, I say, cannot be, but that in the succeeding ~~moment~~ and alternate moment the multeity must be actuated by the Logos[84] so as to be Multeity with distinction, or Multeity realized into the semblance of distinction. It is not necessary for us to determine the mode of succession, yet it seems anticapable that we shall finally adhere to an alternation, in the first place comprehending in its sphere each the All, this followed by an oscillation, and the period concluded by the separation, so that the twofold act of the Logos in the spirit, following that of the Spirit as Going forth and preparing for the Logos, shall give not only locality, first to water and secondly to *"*earth. But*ᵛ* let it not be forgotten that throughout our whole scheme, our progress is still retroactive in the preceding period: for instance, we had con[*f 54*]stituted an air that is an XY, having a relation which through all stages shall remain the essential characteristic of Air, viz. as the common mean between the matter of darkness, or Aether, and the matter of light; but we by no means suppose this Air the present *ʷ*atmosphere. So*ˣ* when, in the present instance, we affirm an existence given to water and to earth, we bind down the meaning of these terms to a simple correspondence to their constituent causes, as the present earth's to metals, and the series of metals[85] to the metallity—so the fluids of the present epoch to the fluid here opposed to the

---

of creation this were the one and only form but as being *a* one form of most easy construction to the human imagination & for that reason adopted as the representative of all by the philosophic lawgiver of the Hebrews. [*cancelled in ink with horizontal lines*]

ᵘ⁻ᵛ ms: earth but
ʷ⁻ˣ ms: atmosphere so

[84] Cf a letter of 1818: ". . . uniting thy energy with the Holy *Word* (Logos in the same sense as in John I.i. = intelligential Energy, distinguishable (tho' not separable, even in thought) from the energic WILL)" (*CL* ɪᴠ 884). For the systematic rather than merely fortuitous impact of this word see Prolegomena xɪᴠ: The *Magnum Opus* and the *Logos*.

[85] The phrase "series of metals" is from Steffens.

firmamental—and leave it to a future period to enrich this view by trac-
ing the analogies of water and metal first to figure and secondly to *ʸ*light.
But*ᶻ* least of all, in the separation of the dry land from the waters, would
we be suspected of favouring the scheme of chemical precipitation, a
scheme the most extravagant in its assumptions, yet the most barren in
its results, of all the many absurdities [*f 55*] into which the whole con-
tinuity of nature and thought has been crumbled down by modern *ᵃ*analy-
sis. Neither*ᵇ* fluids nor solids, earth nor*ᶜ* water are data with us, but, like
all products of living powers, mutually call each other forth and never
can exist in separation but by the intervention of the series in which they
have modified each other.

Here we must already notice ~~and bring into distinct conception~~ the im-
portant distinction between two kinds of modification: *ᵈ*⟨the later and
higher being that in which opposite powers co-exist, each in the other,
yet in each under such a predominance of one power as to permit us to
call the product by its name, but not really to contemplate it otherwise
than, as it were, a mid state, on tiptoe in the act of "about to pass" into
the other. Thus the blood in animals: and thus in affirming one product,
ex.gr. it is a solid = the containing coat, we are compelled the next mo-
ment to conceive this solid itself as constituted by fluids, i.e. made up of
veins and arteries. It is truly a phantom of separation, which seems every
where and yet no where realized. The former and lower, on the other
hand, is⟩*ᵉ* ~~the first and lower being~~ that in which two opposite ~~action~~
powers or states, having alternately passed into each other, and again
separating with an intermediate oscillation, shall leave each on the other
an impression of the former state, or an *impression* ~~where~~ ion the one,
the nature of which is compatible with retention, and a *change*, at least
a relative and temporary exhaustion, in the other. Thus the tendency to
figure, which in its first stage of existence supposes a counteraction from
its opposite, i.e. we must add continuity, which may be called the pro-
plasma, or preconception, of the fluid to the point, in order to con[*f
56*]ceive the line; but the point, here being the active, and the continu-
ity, or actualized space, being the passive, the line henceforward be-
comes the ground ~~of~~and exponent, or specific character, of the firma-
mental, as opposed to the fluid—and, again, the fluid, refusing all
distinction of parts by figure, in ~~fly~~eeing and retiring from figure consti-
tutes the drop, or globe, which is the perfection of *ᶠ*figure. And*ᵍ* the sta-

ʸ⁻ᶻ ms: light but
ᵃ⁻ᵇ ms: analysis neither [*emended after Ward's suggestion in pencil in the ms*]
ᶜ ms: or [*corrected in pencil*]
ᵈ⁻ᵉ Passage written by C on f 54ᵛ and marked for insertion here
ᶠ⁻ᵍ ms: figure: and

lactic is the true characteristic of the fluid, and not of one kind of fluid from another, as in the language of naturalists hitherto, who have chosen to call the air and gases fluids generally without any such comparison of the differences with the points of identity which could justify them in making it a species of one kind, rather than the compound result of two or more, either in balance or preponderance. The drop, therefore, or sphere is the first and proper opposition of the figureless [h]⟨(i.e. in the figurated: for the continuity has taken up into ⟨itself⟩ the impression of the figurative in the prior intermodification of the Point, and the Continuum, in the prægenesis of the *Line*)[*]⟩[i] to the figurative ⟨in the Figure⟩[j] of the fluid to the firmamental.[k] [*f 58*] [l]Whichever way we take it, the first and simplest act of the primal oscillation, and of all its returns, which must be distinguished from a following higher and more potentiated oscillation—[m] [*f 59*] [n]⟨Again, then, we must place the globular in ⟨productive⟩

[*] [*Written by C on f 55[v] as a separate paragraph beneath the parenthesis to be inserted into the sentence on f 56:*] N.B. the *power* of the Figureless is in the Drop, itself the perfection or consummation of Figure: the *power* of Figure, or the Figurative, in the Line.

[h–i] Parenthesis written by C on f 55[v] and marked for insertion here

[j] Insertion in C's hand

[k] ms: (But as it is likewise subject to the common law anterior to Depth by which as in a plain circle there is a relative outward and inward or a going forth from and a returning to and as in [*f 57*] the present instance we have begun with the more potentiated inward or depth as swallowing up ~~all figures~~ the forms of figure—so we must not forget to contemplate it in its going forth against figure or continued destruction of the line by an infinite production of opposite lines if we take the point during its generation of the line as counteracted or drawn back proportionally to its propulsion which is an act of the true inward we have of course the curve as the result superficially and really the globe but if we conceive it instead of being drawn back simply departed from by a going forth in every other direction we have as necessarily the form of breadth presented to us. And this too namely the seeking after breadth or the tendency to find a level becomes a second characteristic of the fluid if only we combine with it its inherent incapacity of figure except by coercion or outline ab extra i.e. from the firmamental. Now what the banks of a lake present to our eye viz. a level breadth deriving outline wholly from an alien and rival this same in all the end[*f 58*]less degrees and repetitions which the numberless proportions of the primary indistinction & multeity each to the other in the necessary co-existence of both must produce we shall find rendered permanent in ⟨& from⟩ the oscillation as above stated so namely the firmamental becoming the basis shall give fixity to the act of the fluid the fluid again shall supply the breadth its own secondary character no longer however as at variance with length but as a potentiation of the same if we said that it ~~supplied a unity~~ as the actualized distinction supplied a unity to the points here regarded as the representative of the actualized multeity and in this unity both a freedom and a conversion of the dissenting acts to consentients we should have expressed the same meaning and have come somewhat nearer to the mode of thought and language prevalent with our chemists and naturalists. [*cancelled in ink with a single vertical line*]

[l–m] This passage, at the bottom of f 58, is not cancelled in the ms, but was probably supposed to be

[n–o(p 324)] This passage, written in JHG's hand on ff 58[v]–61[v], replaces the conclusion

antagonism with the line, and the genesis must evidently be Breadth; but in the oscillation we are compelled to find a twofold form of the genesis, the one representing the moment in which the lineal is predominant over the globular, the other that in which the globular is predominant over the ^{p}lineal. The^q latter will correspond to breadth with density, and in its own nature, as long as it is not circumstantibus ~~counteractive~~ contrà-actum,[86] and inasmuch as it must partake of the power of ☉ (centrality) even antecedent to the higher potentiation of ⊕ as consequent on ⊘ by some form of tenacity or adhesiveness, as distinguished from proper cohesion—the former corresponding to superficial depth, and anticipating as well as recalling the opposition of light to gravitation (> to ⊕), and that the lineal is the proper genesis of the former, we shall not only expect that which, indeed, is involved in a realized superficies, viz. Thinness, or tendency to the lamellar structure, but likewise transparency, or the transmission of Light ✶ to its rejection. Though it must still (the abiding genesis still remaining in the firmamental, [$f\,59^v$] and of course partaking of the ○ by a double right, for it is not so properly ✶ centrality (☉) as to the predominance of the globular in the lineal) be susceptible of combining in ⟨a⟩ different relation the opposite to the transparent, viz. the lustrous, as well as the appearance of this in consequence of the transparency permitting a transmission of rejected, i.e. reflected >. We shall not be surprized, therefore, among the earliest of those productions which are within the mystery of Light as revealed in the present order and epoch of the world, as in the granite or primary mountains we find in the granular quartz the correspondent to the g~~r~~lobular or central, but still bearing evidence of its other parent by its tendency to crystallize, which, again evoking an act of the opposite power, becomes at the same time transparent, or balanced, as it were, between both, in part transparent and in part lustrous, or, by another modification, according to the proportion and directions of the creative powers, translucent. Its hardness, we shall hereafter find as fully solved by its relation to light. Again, in the Feldspar,[87] where the pure silica [$f\,60^v$] ap-

---

of the original parenthesis, which is written at the top of f 59 and cancelled in ink with a single vertical line: "of which we shall treat hereafter—the results of this primal act of the oscillation I say must manifest their parentage by assimilations to the characters of the constituent agents and patient. But an assimilation rendered imperfect and as it were internally contradicted by the reluctance of the latter and in this anticipating or taking it retrospectively bearing witness to the after-separation of the two)."

$^{p-q}$ ms: lineal the

[86] Tr: "counteracted by circumstances".

[87] An aluminum silicate, usually glassy and moderately hard, found in igneous rocks.

pears as alumina and co-exists with it—though under its predominance
we have the character of Breadth in its manifested state as breadth of Den-
sity, but containing still the power of breadth in both its forms, or rather
in such combinations as both may co-exist under all the degrees of the
predominance of either, as in the following [? schistous] evolutions.
Lastly, in the Mica we find all the constituents of the superficial breadth,
the lamellar[88] thinness capable of an approximation to ideal superficies,[89]
to which the human power ~~can find~~ ⟨cannot find⟩ nor the mind imagine
any last bound. The transparency etc. will occur of themselves. How
closely the after formations correspond to this view, especially in the dis-
appearance of the one or the other of these three substances, how the gran-
ite itself becomes modified by the occasional evolution of the fourth form,
the Hornblende,[90] we may hereafter have occasion to describe more at
large, though in no part of our work shall we proceed beyond a demon-
stration of the powers and their relations to each other, the knowledge to
which contains the principles of Mine[*f 61*ᵛ]ralogy. For we are not
labouring as mineralogists but as philosophers.⟩ᵒ

ʳOne other relation, and still elder, has yet remained untouched, and
cannot, indeed, be fully expanded till the next stage of our progress. I
mean the relations to Light.[91] The truth I seem to myself to have mas-
tered, but I shrink from the difficulty of explication. [*f 60*] We have al-
ready contemplated matter as matter of light, the primal state of the earth
succeeding to the first ~~distinctiv~~ lucific act of the Logos, the matter of
darkness, or the Aether, and the air as the intermediate term. But here we
have to distinguish the matter of Light itself as acting by the rejection of
Light, or the reception thereof. By the rejection of Light, I mean only
that the tendency produced by this lucific influence may, from the prav-
ity of the agent (material), viz. by the original apostatic self-seeking, be-
come a nisus[92] to division without that distinction which necessarily im-
plies a community, or the existence of another in the self, as another and
yet equal to self. This would, of course, produce, in consequence of
Light, a contrariety to ˢLight. Notᵗ less real than mere indistinction, it

ʳ This sentence is preceded in the ms by the following one, which is cancelled in ink
with a single vertical line: "We shall ~~find~~ expect to find therefore in the earliest products
the representatives of the Depth or globose as in the Quartz of the Breadth as in the Feldspar
and of the Line in conjunction with the above described presence of unity in the tendency
to crystallize while the separation itself aided by ~~the result~~ a quality implied in the globose
will necessarily present a show or suggestion of precipitation."
ˢ⁻ᵗ ms: Light not

88 Referring to a thin plate or layer
89 A surface; outer area.
90 A dark-coloured silicate found in
granite and other igneous rocks.
91 Cf *CN* ɪv 5290.
92 Tr: "pressure".

would be a virtual rejection of Light, as particularity devoid of Distinctiveness. The other contrariety would be the positive indistinction, or absence, of particularity, or distinguishable parts ⟨as⟩ such: for instance, for illustration's*u* sake only, we might [*f 61*] contemplate the hypothetical Caloric differing from the former as the absorptive extinction from the rejection of Light. Now we must conceive a number of intermediate gradations between these as the extremes. aAnd ~~these~~ ⟨here⟩ again ⟨we⟩ must remember that as the primal element was ~~alternately~~ ⟨now⟩ ~~all~~ fluid, ~~and all solid~~ ⟨now solidescent,⟩ then oscillated⟨ive⟩, and lastly separated, this separation, the epoch under which we exist must be regarded as a part or diminuendo of the oscillation, and the separation, ⟨therefore,⟩ as comparative and phaenomenal only. At all events, we shall find, as a necessary gradation, a state in which the light shall be not so absorbed as to exclude a partial result—the contractive tendency, for instance—and on the other hand a state in which the contractive, being disarmed by the dilative—in chemical language, the oxygen by the hydrogen—Light shall be virtually rejected, i.e. admitted but not received, and all this still imperfectly, as being states of a not yet wholly ceased oscillation, so viz. that the transmission of light may still be accompanied by a reflection of [*f 62*] the same, and the reflection of light ~~have~~ ⟨be⟩ rarely, or in the first conception never, so perfect but that, in its lower form at least, it shall have been received not, indeed, as Light, or the power of distinction, but as the hybrid offspring of Light as division, or the tendency to Division, by contraction with the various results which complicate balances and counteractions will necessarily bring into existence.*v*

---

u ms: illustration

v ms: Now I say review the preceding positions re-combine them and then construct that result which would follow from the least complicate form of counteraction and then examine whether the substance called primitive granite does not display a surprizing coincidence in the purest metals only dare we look for an approximation to the ideal antithesis to Light the lustre which is the perfect opposite of the transparent in the first and simplest actions we must necessarily imagine asuch a reception of Light or rather such a coercion by light as shall at least suffice [*f 63*] to drive inward, zurückzuerzwängen, the metalleity for agreeable with our hypothesis which has not yet supposed a solar agency and consequently no surface relative to solar radiance we can conceive no situation in which a portion can be placed which shall either peculiarly expose or wholly exempt it from the influence of Light or the aërial products of light a far more complex sertable of actions and counteractions would be requisite to render imaginable such specific surpluses should exist in the greater part as to effectuate a total exclusion in the remaining portion in other words it must not be in the eldest granite that we can expect a reduction of the metals but still the mica remains as attesting metalleity by its lustre and filling up the explanation of the components of granite, the dense quartz, the breadth of the feldspar, the lustre of the mica, the hardness of all while the ⟨formal⟩ simplicity of the mass attests the simplicity of the productive action, more complicate actions [*f 64*] being still expressed by variety of total form, and sameness of the component matter. [*cancelled in ink with a single vertical line*]

[*f 64*] We will conclude this the fourth great division of our anastatic process, the metastasis, or transition, of chaos into aether being taken as the first[93] by a distinct recapitulation and specification of the powers hitherto evolved, in the order of their birth and epiphany, that so we may not, by too long and continued an attention to the products, fall under the idolatry of the senses, the consequence of which is the passion for death, and the reward a dead palsy of intellectual life,[94] and choosing darkness for light, turns the light itself into darkness and science into a pompous sepulchre of truth.

Ist Mere potentiality (= ϕ, i.e., chaos philosophicum).[w]

II. The same actualized. Offspring: Aether: Darkness as the positive $\maltese$ and possible basis of Light: Materia prima: Indistinction in actu: Multeity in posse: Principium continui vel ipse continuitas (hebraically, the faces of the waters, or indis[*f 65*]tinctities made to become *a* face and *an* indistinction).

III. Verbum lucificum: Lux = $>$: the Multeity actualized, but in union with the already actualized indistinction, i.e. Continuity, yet so that the one shall be the ground of the other, this the apparent, that the supposed. Offspring: Matter of Light.

IV. As the conjunction of 2^{d} and 3^{d}. Here commences the retro-action of the second on the first as the first, the result of which must be contemplated distinctly, tho' not separatively, from the second. In the ϕ the $\int$ or imperfect $^{N}|$ = the polarity is within and below the $\bigcirc$, i.e. we have the mere possibility of polar power if a something not contained in the ϕ be superinduced. The true poles are the apostatic Will and the metathetic, or redemptive, spirit and Word—in plainer words, the creaturely Self and the Divine Word. But as the patient here is a Will, the patiency must itself be a form of action; but as it is a mere Will of potentiality, this would be impossible without supposing a preparatory impregnation by which the patiens[95] might become an Ens[96] [*f 66*] at all, or a Subject under any form. This having been effected by an act of Free-grace, an overflowing of the Love in the descent of the Spirit, all following acts

---

[w] Closing parenthesis inserted

[93] The Boehmesque wording here, and in the four enumerations below, recalls that of the Extended Plan of 1828. See Prolegomena XIII: The Transformations of the *Magnum Opus*.

[94] C repeatedly uses the trope of "death" in conjunction with the "mechanico-corpuscular" philosophy, materialism, or any variation of the standpoints of Locke and Newton. In this fragment alone see above, f 40.

[95] Tr: "enduring thing".

[96] Tr: "thing". For the play between *patiens* and *ens* cf App B frag (*b*): "the preparatory Impregnation, by which the Pati*ens* became an *ens* at all, or a *Subject* under any form".

must be regarded as influences on the subject which suppose a conflu-
ence on the part of the subject—a confluence but not an harmony, not
an entire intussusception of the influence by the subject, or perfect sur-
rendering of the latter to the former, for this were the last great end: the
established Stasis,[97] not the Anastasis. But as the Materia subjecta, taken
as a unit, is itself the counterpole to the divine influence, there must be
the possibility of an Act *in* the subject, having such a nature for the
ground of its possibility that it cannot counterflow without confluence.
Now this is effected, 1st, by a nature containing a contradiction essen-
tially, which contradiction we have already exhibited in the two con-
traries indistinction and multeity as both and equally necessary attributes
of one and the same nature, and 2dly, by the ineffable distinction in the
transcendent [*f 67*] unity of the Spirit and the Word, and the correspon-
dent Distinctness-in-unity of their influence, the first offsprings of which,
as we have seen, are the actualizations of the Indistinction and the Mul-
teity, which so actualized, and in all the after degrees of their potentia-
tion, are the real poles in omni creato.[98] Hence it is evident that there is
no possibility of resisting either influence but by assisting the other. It
cannot resist the word but ~~it must in so far submit itself to the spirit~~ by
subjecting the principle of multeity to that of Indistinction, and thereby
allying itself in fact with the influence of the spirit, or the divine princi-
ple of communion, and so vice versâ. Hence, therefore, we have a three-
fold polarity:^{x} 1st, that^y of the Creaturely and the Divine Will; 2^d, the^z
Indistinction and the Multeity in the Creature itself, which, having been
actualized by the spirit and the word, constitute it existentially, i.e. are
both the creature and its properties as A Being. 3^d, the^a result of the dis-
tinction of the divine influences in the creature, partaking therefore of
the [*f 68*] Creature's essential self-contrariency, or the opposite acts by
which, in resisting THIS, it of necessity allies itself with THAT—attests
on the one hand the Divine Father by still appearing to the contempla-
tion as Acts Superinductions, which the substantiating Imagination
⟨now⟩ personifies into Agents and Superinducents, and now concretes
into Effects and Superinducta, while on the other hand it betrays the crea-
turely mother by the disturbance of that divine unity in which both in-

---

^{x} Full stop in ms ^{y} ms: That
^{z} ms: The ^{a} ms: The

[97] In the Extended Plan of 1828 (see
Prolegomena XIII: The Transformations
of the *Magnum Opus*), "Division the
First" was "*Stasis*", which then sub-
sumed the following: "Commences with
the Absolute Actuality, essentially caus-
ative of all Reality—2. The Tetractys,
and Tri-unity—3. The Pleroma. 4. The
Eternal Possibilities, which the Supreme
Good demands as possible but forbids to
be willed as actual".

[98] Tr: "in everything created".

fluences are One, yet not the same, and thus adulterating each to the production of a tertium aliquid[99] = the influence shorn of its beams by the creaturely ingredient, for instance, Division as the adulterative Residuum of Distinction. I need not add that in reality no one of these poles can exist but as variously modified by all, and that the necessary results are Predominance, Subjugation, Alternation, Oscillation, Gradation, Appearance, Latency, and Common Effect—the latter in a twofold form, viz. Equilibrium of Two and Inequality of Two on a common base as a Third.

We may now count them.

[*f* 69] I. Abduction from the Self, as manifesting the being drawn toward the true center, as ✕, the self-seeking or tendency to the false and fantastic centre in the opposite direction. These are realized Poles, and manifested in the Creature = Vis centrifuga ✕ Vis centripetalis.

II. The actualized Indistinction ✕ Multeity. Offspring in the Creature or the realized Poles, Attraction ad extra. Appropriative Attraction, or Astringency, as ✕ separative Self-projection, or Volatility.

III. The influx from the Light, with the Spirit as ✕ by the creaturely: Conjunction: Offspring or realized Poles, Particularization, Contraction as ✕ Omneity, Dilation. § Of these Six opposites,[100] the two first, the Centripetal and Centrifugal, are the ordinant Powers. The two last, Contraction and Dilation, are the modifying, and the two middle are the Substantiative.[101] The two first belong to Wholes, or the mass; the middle two, to the components or constitutents of the mass; and the two last, to the differences superinduced on the said components. The play and changes of these form the physical contents of the history [*f* 70] of the Cosmogony. Thus, for instance, there exists in the co-existence of Volatility with Astringency, as the positive and negative poles of the same subject, no sufficient cause for the preponderance of either: it could neither fly abroad nor where, in other words, it would be unmanifestable and = 0. But this preponderance is obtained when it is modified by one or other of the other two polarities. We will suppose the modification to be by the contractive power: now to modify is of itself, in a certain degree, to counteract, though by a still higher degree of counteraction to A than to B, or vice *b*versâ. Let*c* Z and X be taken as direct antagonists,

---

b–c ms: versâ let

99 Tr: "a third something".

100 Compare the "six opposites" nominated here to the "six Opposites" in App B frag (*d*) f 154.

101 Cf the statement in App B frag (*d*) f 154: "The Play and changes of these six Opposites, the two first being the Ordinant Powers, the two last the Modifying, and the middle two the substantiating give the contents of the History of the Cosmogony".

corresponding to Astringency and Volatility, i.e. / and $\cdot\cdot$., and let Y, the power of contraction, counteract Z = ½, but X = 2: it is evident Y becomes a potent though indirect auxiliary of ^{d}Z. If^e to this we add the centripetal force in its primary form as $\odot$, we shall have an additional auxiliary to Z, and the result will be $\frac{\cdot\cdot}{/}$ = Cohesion. (This Steffens[102] would express as the essential declination of the magnetic axis, or line of being, to the electrical or hemispherical line [*f 71*] of becoming.) It is evident, however, that the $\cdot\cdot$. is subjugated, not destroyed, though co-exced, and restrained from actual separation, or self-projection, by the predominance of /.^{f} It^g is still present, and must manifest itself in some way or other; but this it cannot do substantively, for it is absorbed in cohesion: it must exist, therefore, as a power, and thus we have the power of repulsion. But again the /, though predominant in the formation of cohesion, yet that being formed, the / likewise is taken up into it and, equally incapable of manifesting itself substantively, or in self-subsistence, must likewise manifest itself as a power, viz. the ~~power~~property and power of attraction;[103] and as these cannot manifest themselves in the same outward act, they must alternate as we see them in the magnet.[104] A secondary superinduction of the contractive power, or cohesion, would constitute hardness, the contractive power still remaining subordinate to the cohesion, and therefore appearing as a property of the same. And here we may observe the endless transitions of the form of ⟨one⟩ polarity into that [*f 72*] of another,[105] manifesting the sameness of the subject in all,[106] for here the negative pole of the third polarity, which in its own character is properly active, becomes, by being taken up into the second polarity, i.e. the indifference of / and $\cdot\cdot$. = Cohesion, a prop-

---

$^{d-e}$ ms: Z: if ^{f} Full stop inserted
^{g} ms: it

[102] Heinrich [né Henrik] Steffens (1773–1845), Norwegian physicist and philosopher, disciple of Schelling, professor of mineralogy at Halle (1804–6, 1808–11), and of physics at Breslau (1811–32) and Berlin (1832–45). Of all the *Naturphilosophen*, except for Schelling himself, C relied most upon Steffens.

[103] The emphasis on matter as incorporating a dualism of attractive and repulsive force was the highly influential contribution of Kant, in his *Metaphysische Anfangsgründe der Naturwissenschaft* of 1786 (*Kant* IV 511). It inaugurated the whole of *Naturphilosophie*'s defining emphasis on an all-pervading dualism, opposition, and polarity.

[104] The magnet was the central physical reality of *Naturphilosophie*, and from its contemplation emanated all that philosophy's self-confidence. For C's contrast between "electricity and MAGNETISM" in cultural history, see *SW & F* (*CC*) I 642–3.

[105] Cf Schelling's general observation that all forming occurs through "metamorphosis or dynamic evolution" (*Schelling SW* III 61).

[106] Cf *CL* IV 790: "Unity can manifest or reveal itself only by opposite Poles". See in general Prolegomena x: The *Magnum Opus* and the Principle of Polarity.

erty of the same, while the / and ⋰. themselves, which are properly con-
stituent and resting, become ⟨active⟩ powers, viz. Attraction and [h]Re-
pulsion. But[i] if we increase the counteractive influence to a given ex-
tent, it will then master and embody itself in the cohesion, and appear in
its own form—at first the astringent power, though now subordinate, yet
still predominant over the ⋰. as the co-subordinate, and the contraction
will appear as particularisation in the phaenomenon of Rust, Friability,
Brittleness, etc., etc., etc., according to the proportions of the terms em-
ployed. But it is evident that a still greater exertion of the counter-active
power, by counteracting the ⊙ no less than the /, will become a power-
ful, though indirect, ally to the ⋰., or the self-projective [*f* 73] power,
but in so doing will have attained its maximum, and thereby call forth its
own opposite pole, that of [j]Dilation. And[k] hence we see that the self-
projective cannot subsist but in alliance and co-presence with the Dila-
tive. We may illustrate this by comparing a cloud in the atmosphere with
the atmosphere itself: in the cloud the self-projective power has mastered
the indifference of the contractive and dilative—I mean the phaenome-
non correspondent thereto, or Water. In the atmosphere the self-projec-
tion, as potentiated by the maximum of the contractive power, has called
forth the dilative, and a new indifference appears, viz. that of air, in
which we find a higher dignity than that of water, upon the principles ex-
plained in the preceding disquisition, viz. a co-inherence of the one in
the other without the entire destruction of both in a third—analogous to
the fluid and solid of the organized body in a yet higher dignity. Hence
we see the reason of the confusion in the language of naturalists hitherto,
now designating the air as a fluid, and then [*f* 74] again describing it as
an infinity of particles having repulsion without attraction, i.e. as self-
projection, or the minimum of continuity, which is directly destructive
and not the opposite but the contrary of the fluid which supposes the co-
hesion, or /, as its predominant constituent under the mastery of the dila-
tive, the liveliest instance of which in melted iron or other coherent met-
als in a state of flux. Thus we can neither think of the air as a fluid, but
we are instantly obliged to modify our terms by the counter-assertion of
its volatility; and the only possible form in which we can reconcile the
contradiction is not to make them both and neither, for this, as we shall
hereafter show, would be the same as to affirm its organization, in the
ordinary application of that word in animal or vegetable life—but this
being precluded, to conceive the one in the other, the volative in a dila-
tive, the ∨ representing the central points, the other the circumjacent ex-

pansion, and hence, too, of conceiving the air to be that in re[*f 75*]ference to aether, which earth and water are in reference to air—or the intermediate term, as before explained, between the matter of light, and aether as the matter of darkness. Need we wonder, then, that in so many speculations concerning the air, the chemists on the one hand should introduce as a distinct [? ~~somewhat~~] fluid their Caloric, while the writers on Acoustics as warmly plead for the introduction of an aether, both the one and the other as the menstruum, or fluid cement, of their realized atoms. Now to recur to our example, in the change of the terraqueous into the atmospheric, there must be a given point common to it with the opposite change of the atmosphere to the terraqueous, so that a high cloud would differ from the atmosphere by the substitution of .∴. as the puncta centralia,[107] i.e. the third or modifying polarity assuming the character of the second, or substantiative, instead of the ⌈. . .⌉ ∵. curbed in by the .... with ∼ ~~but~~ for the inter- and circumjacencies. Now this common point must necessarily appear as a virtual conversion, in the one case, of the [*f 76*] *n*∵. into $\overset{h}{\sim}$, and in the other, of the $\overset{h}{\sim}$ into *n*∵., the truth of which, forced upon us by so many facts of meteorology, no better reason for doubt has been assigned but that certain men are unwilling to acknowledge that nature may be a better chemist than themselves, or the too common quid pro quo of human egoismus, "I cannot do it, ergo it cannot be done".

It is sufficient if we have sufficiently illustrated the nature of the actions and passions of the six poles: the application in detail, as far as the detail is requisite for our purpose, will be given each in its own place. We must now take up the chain of our disquisition at the last link: III. The going forth of the Word, or descent (condescension) of the distinctive viticulative power in the spirit on the Aether. The action of Time on Space. Of realized Time or ~~the~~ > on realized space or aether. The results of this in the production of an Outwardness and an Inwardness, a matter of Light, and the Aether becoming, in consequence, the [*f 77*] matter of darkness; for the Aether minus Light is the only possible antithesis of the Aether + Light, and the air as the intermediate term, have been already amply explained in preceding disquisitions. ᵇBut the latter part of this, the fourth ⟨great⟩ period in our scheme week of creation,[108] differing

---

107 Tr: "central points".

108 The "scheme week of creation" is an especially vivid testimony to C's concern to coordinate his scientific schematisms with the account of cosmogonic origins in Genesis. Though C was well aware of Bacon's warnings about mixing religion and science, e.g. "in every age Natural Philosophy has had a troublesome adversary and hard to deal with; namely, superstition, and the blind and immoderate zeal of religion" (*Novum Organum* I § 89), his need to harmonize his various interests led him to ignore

from Moses numerically only in consequence of our reckoning the actualizing of ~~aether~~ chaos into Aether as our first day, will perhaps admit of a clearer development, and may seem the more to require it, as it is to lead us on the yet unattempted part of our progress. ~~I am mainly solicitous therefore~~ I mean the further potentiation of the matter of light, and its separation into the fluid and firmamental, with the consequent retro-action on the air: $\odot$, $+ \odot$, $- \odot$, $\varnothing$, $\oplus$. I am mainly solicitous, therefore, that in this stage of our ascent,[109] which may be aptly termed our first great landing-place,[110] and before we attempt the second flight, σζ~ τα μεν φυτα τα δε τυχον και φυτοειδῆ—we should have thoroughly mastered [*f 78*] the elementary natures, the primary physical powers, the Divi et Numina cosmoplasta,[111] with especial reference to the fluid and the firmamental, still more austerely μορφη και το αντιμορφων,[112] so, namely, that we should not only possess distinct conceptions of their genesis and proprieties, their hostilities and alliances, direct and indirect, but by repeated presentation of the same to our mind in various forms, and even in various synonyms, have rendered them clear as well as distinct—in short, alert, manageable and ready at the first call. Now we cannot commence better[113] than by calling out the two leaders who for a

---

these warnings. See *SW & F (CC)* I 794–5: "On the Scientific Appositeness of the Creation in Genesis", also pp 790–4 preceding. See further *CN* III 4418.

[109] The conception of stages of ascent willy-nilly forces C to produce a scheme of evolutionary rising in competition with that of Schelling and his army of *Naturphilosophen*. For extended examples of C's commitment to ascent, see Prolegomena XXX: The Relation of the *Magnum Opus* to Coleridge's *Theory of Life*, and Frag 2 above: "the maximum of each lower kind becomes the base and receptive substrate, as it were, of a higher kind commencing, and becomes the positive, and not merely the comparative, maximum, through the irradiation and, may I say, transfiguration by the higher power, the base of which it has become" (f 117). Cf a statement of 1828: "Life has an ascension toward Mind" (*SW & F—CC*—II 1427). See App A f [29] and f [70].

[110] C here avails himself of a term and conception first utilised in *The Friend* in 1818, where there is "The Landing-Place or Essays Interposed for Amusement Retrospect and Preparation"; "The Second Landing Place" (with the same subtitle); and "The Third Landing-Place or Essays Miscellaneous" (*Friend—CC*—I 127–61, 339–69, 525–80).

[111] Tr: "divine and spiritual shapers of the world".

[112] Tr: "form and anti-form".

[113] Cf the paragraph that follows with this note of 1820–1: "Now we cannot perhaps commence this Muster and Review better than by calling out the two Leaders of the File, who for a long time past have not appeared before us in their own names—I mean, SPACE and TIME. And this too will have the additional advantage that it will recall and impress anew the varince [sic] between our system and the Schellingian; that the points, in which we differ, are not merely momentary but essential, and that the Difference therefore amounts to Diversity. Let me not, however fail to declare that in the several Works of Heinrich Steffens, especially in his Beytráge zur innern Naturgeschichte der Erde, the Spirit

long time past have not appeared before us in their own names: I mean Space and Time.[114] And this, too, will have the additional advantage that it will recall and impress anew the variance between our system and the Schellingian, and prove that the points in which we differ are not only momentous but essential, and the difference therefore = Diversity. Let me [*f 79*] not, however, fail to declare that in the several works of H. Steffens, especially in his Beiträge zur innern Naturgeschichte der Erde, the spirit within me bears witness to the same spirit within him— but that in him the line of its circumvolution was begun from a false centre and with too short and undistended a compass, forced thereby usque ab initio,[115] to close too early on itself, and thus leaving his familiar genius imprisoned within the magic circle of its own describing.[116]

Still, among all the real or verbal definitions of Space and Time hitherto given, Steffens's seems to me the clearest and simplest, and that which most breathes the spirit of the old Ionic school,[117] viz. Space = the[l] form by which the infinite is taken up into the finite; Time = the[m] form by which the finite is taken up into the infinite.[118] I object, however, to the phrase "Infinite" on account of its habitual association with Magnitude—in short, with Exceedingness—not to mention its being a too frequent synonyme of the absolutely per[*f 80*]fect, or [n]God. Besides[o] this, the definition is distinguished from real, not, indeed, as a merely

---

[l] ms: The   [m] ms: The
[n-o] ms: God: besides

---

within me bears witness to the same Spirit in him—but that the Line of its Circumvolution was begun from a false centre and with too short and undistended a Compass, forced thereby usque ab initio to close too early on itself, and thus leaving his familiar Genius imprisoned within the magic Circle of its own describing" (*CN* iv 4776).

[114] Cf C in 1817: "In the science of Relations I take the Self-affirmance as the Unity, the Self-affirmedness as the Omneity, and find in Time the appointed Symbol of the former, while in Space I find the symbol of the Latter—and then making them common measures each of the other deduce the Genesis of Length, Breadth, and Depth—as the symbola generalissima of all physical Science" (*CL* iv 762).

[115] Tr: "right from the beginning".

[116] For a long and detailed criticism

of the specifics of Steffens's position see *CN* iv 4662. In another note C says "my plan comprizes Oken's & Steffens's without the fictions of the one or the deficiencies of both" (*CN* iv 4719).

[117] Cf a notebook entry of 1820–1: "Still among all the real or verbal definitions of Space and Time, given by the Natur-philosophen, Steffens's seems to me the clearest and most simple, and breathes most the spirit of the old Ionic School, the genial Spirit of Anaximander and Parmenides—" (*CN* iv 4776).

[118] Cf Steffens: "die Form, durch welche das Unendliche in das Endliche aufgenommen wird, ist der *Raum*, durch das Erkennen mit der Zeit identifisirt. . . . Die Form, durch welche das Endliche in das Unendliche aufgenommen wird, ist die *Zeit*, welche durch das absolute Erkennen mit dem Raume identifisirt wird" (Steffens *Grundzüge* 13).

verbal definition, but yet as purely formal and unpregnant. To me it would convey a more clear conception to say that in the generation of a line, that which supplies the fluency is Space,[119] and that the fluent is Time; or Space is that which gives the continuity to the point, and time That which superinduces the point on the continuity, the synthesis of both being motion. As preferable, however, to Steffens's, yet in perfect harmony with it, I adopt the following: Infinito finiendo τo infinitum finibile est spatium, τo Finiens est Tempus, actus quo finitur infinitum est motus, et productum est figura.[120]

All this is well and good as far as it goe⟨s;⟩*p* but Steffens will not stop here.[121] hHe*q* takes it up pick-a-back and carries it over the boundaries into an alien country; ⟨transfers it⟩*r* from the quiet realm of geometry ~~and passing off a~~ ⟨into that of Physiology—thus brings a⟩*s* mathematical theorem ⟨into a combination with a substantial agent⟩*t* ~~and then~~ [*f 81*] ~~bringing them together~~. ⟨Thus⟩*u* he draws with a slate pencil on the *thought* of a slate, and connects the members of a syllogism with real whipcord, i.e. his *"time"* is actual, his "space" a mere term for the power implied in the act; or his "time" is a verb transitive with an = 0 for its accusative case. But space actualized must react as co-agent with time, at once its spouse and its antagonist,[122] for Time is the spouse qui laedit in am-

---

p Insertion in C's hand   *q* The capital letter is in C's hand
r Insertion in C's hand   *s* Insertion in C's hand
t Passage written by C on f 79*v* and marked for insertion here
u Insertion in C's hand

[119] Cf to the end of the paragraph, a notebook entry: "In the generation of a Line, that which gives the continuity to the Point, is SPACE: that which superinduces the Point on the continuity is time: the Synthesis of both MOTION.—Sp: = the Base; T: + the Epibase; Motion, the Act of Union; the Line, the Product—or lastly, The Fluent, the Fluibility, and the Fluxion—and ask V'ridè which *he* likes best. In infinito finiendo, τò Infinitum finibile est Spatium, τò Finiens est Tempus, Actus quo finitur Infinitum est Motus—et τò Productum est Figura—" (*CN* IV 4775).

[120] Tr: "In the giving bounds to the boundless, the limitable limitless is space, the limiting is time, the action by which the limitless is limited is motion; and the product is shape".

[121] Cf, to the end of the paragraph, the following, in a notebook of 1820–1:

"All this is well—and good as far as it *goes*. But Steffens will not stop there; but takes it up *pick a back* and carries it over the boundaries into another Country— from the quiet realm of Geometry ⟨in⟩to the Domain of Dynamics, and passes off a mathematical Theorem for a physical Idea, and so doing he ~~employs~~ draws with a slate pencil on the *Thought* of a Slate, and ties the members of a Syllogism together with with ~~a~~ real Whipcord—i.e., His Time is actual, his Space a mere term for the power implied in the act, or his Time is a verb transitive with an O for its accusative Case" (*CN* IV 4775).

[122] Cf, to the end of the paragraph, a notebook entry of 1820–1: "But Space actualized must re-act, as the co-agent with Time—its antagonist as well as its Spouse—*laedit in amplexu*—subjected but not destroyed, and subjected too as a

plexu,[123] Space as one subjected but not deprived of all power— and in this instance, too, ⟨subjected⟩[v] not as the wife to the husband, but as a mother to the common offspring of both,[124] viz. to figure, in whom both exist and continue to exercise a modified influence, Time as the power of figure, Space as the power of the *fFigureless,*[w] εν αμορφῳ το αντι-μορφον; Time ⟨most revealed⟩[x] in the lineal, Space in the globose. That these are the twin offspring of both, in the mysterious war-and-love embrace of productive nature, implies that both parents exist virtually in both the rival twins, yet so that this, viz. time as the power[y] [*f 82*] of figure, nisus figurativus[125] το επιμορφουν,[126] shall preponderate on the one in linea sive longitudine,[127] and that, viz. Space, as the nisus ὅ αντι-μορφους[128] fugacitas à longitudine,[129] shall preponderate in the other, globus σαγμα.[130] And thus, again, in the second generation, ⟨viz.⟩[z] the offspring of the lineal opposed to the globular, ⟨i.e.⟩[a] in breadth. *Time* ⟨is⟩[b] predominant in superficial ⟨breadth,⟩[c] *Space* in dense breadth, or ⟨in⟩[d] breadth with *Density. But space, ⟨were it an⟩[e] *actual* ⟨somewhat,⟩[f] [131] must by the very definition actuate itself, i.e. be causative of its own reality; but ⟨this is not the Case. Therefore⟩[g] as its actuation is not by its own power, the self-actuation is itself an effect—the ignorance or denial of which is the πρωτον ψευδος[132] of the Naturphilosophie, and converts

* [*Written on f 81ᵛ:*] N.B. Density is Depth + Breadth—for who would call a spider's web hung perpendicular to the ground, or the spokes of a slender wheel, dense?

[v] Insertion in C's hand   [w] The capital letter is in C's hand
[x] Insertion in C's hand
[y] The bottom corner of the leaf is torn and repaired with tape, without loss of text
[z] Insertion in C's hand   [a] Insertion in C's hand
[b] Insertion in C's hand
[c] Insertion in C's hand, the word crowded into the margin
[d] Insertion in C's hand   [e] Insertion in C's hand
[f] Insertion in C's hand
[g] Written by C on f 81ᵛ, and marked for insertion here

mother to her ~~Son~~, children, the common offspring of both, ⟨namely in Figure,⟩ ~~and~~ in whom both exist and continue to exercise a modified ~~power~~ influence, he as the Power of Figure, ~~in Her~~ she as the *Power* of the Figureless, i.e. ως το αντι-μορφον—he in the Lineal, she in the Globular" (*CN* IV 4775).
[123] Tr: "who wounds in embracing".
[124] Cf, to the end of this paragraph, an almost identical notebook entry of

1820–1: *CN* IV 4775 ff 82–82ᵛ.
[125] Tr: "figurative striving".
[126] Tr: "the extra-formed".
[127] Tr: "in line or longitude".
[128] Tr: "striving against form".
[129] Tr: "flight from length".
[130] Tr: "covering".
[131] Cf, to the end of this paragraph, *CN* IV 4775 f 83.
[132] Tr: "first falsehood".

Nature, or the phaenomenal world, into a blind Godhead playing at Cat's cradle with himself for the thread.

The result, however,[133] as far as our present argument is concerned, remains the same. Space and Time are realized, but realized space we have shown to be equal to *Aether*, realized Time = ⟨to⟩[h] Light. Hence a new series of powers [*f 83*] co-eval with the preceding and co-agents in their products, yet differing from them ⟨preceding⟩[i] by the successiveness of potentiation implied in the distinctive power, acting on a creaturely subject. Hence ~~viz~~ the Aether ⟨appears⟩[j] in its first power as vis continui,[134] in its second power ⟨as⟩[k] Fugacitas à lineâ,[135] in the third as Centrality ⊙, in [the] ⟨(4th as ⬕ , and in the (5th as ⊕, etc. And though the lineal and the globular are the primary Forma formantes[136] ⟨if we⟩ consider them as Subposita,[137] Surface and Density are the primary Formates Formae formatae when we speak of posita; ~~et~~ and the lineal and globular first appear, i.e. pass into phaenomena in the successive evolution of figures, according as the □ and > are potentiated in the threefold polarity, viz. the Substantiative, the Modifying, and the Ordinant. 1st, the[l] Substantiative ⟨~~appears~~ is⟩[m] the □ = / and ⋱... 2d, the[n] > modifying as .... and ∿. 3d, the[o] Ordinant □ + > as + ⊙ and − ⊙, [p]⟨the + ⊙ centrifugal and − ⊙ centripetal⟩.[q]

Suffice at present that the lineal predominates in the elementary forms of crystallization, the [*f 84*] globular in the Dense and Massive (I mean what the German crystallographists call "DERB"), and in the integral masses, i.e. the disappearance of the lineal in the indifference of both, i.e. of the lineal and globular. This, of course, must be really true, according to the degree of independence, that is, according to the greater or less actual integrity of the said masses. Now as the planetary masses are ⟨wholly⟩ integral ⟨and⟩ relatively integral, relatively to the other planets, i.e. their mutual dependence, in that degree in which it exists is neutralized as interdependence, and of course in ~~the~~ a very slight degree af-

---

[h] Insertion possibly in C's hand
[i] Insertion in C's hand
[j] Insertion in C's hand
[k] Insertion possibly in C's hand
[l] ms: The
[m] Insertion in C's hand
[n] ms: The
[o] ms: The
[p–q] Written by C on f 82v and marked for insertion here. In the ms the symbols are placed directly above the adjectives

[133] Cf, to the end of this paragraph *CN* iv 4775 ff 83–83v.
[134] Tr: "power of continuing".
[135] Tr: "flight from line".
[136] Tr: "forming form".
[137] Tr: "things placed under".

fects their several integrities, while all alike are dependent and have the nature of subordinate parts relatively to the sun. We might already anticipate that their motions must form ellipses, and it is worthy of notice that Copernicus[138] might have found in the idea of his own system, and have apodictically deduced from the hypothesis of the sun's centrality, a rectification of his error in asserting [*f 85*] the perfect circularity of the planetary orbits.[139] But it is not allowed, perhaps, to the imperfection of human nature to detach itself at once from the preceding state: like a bird that by arduous effort has loosed itself from a bird-lime twig, part of the viscous fetter will still adhere to its feet and plumage and ~~render~~ its flight ~~wobbling~~ unsteady,[r] now here the flight of Copernicus was lopsided by the relics of the Aristotelian figment in which that great man had confounded, almost to the nature of a pun, the term "celestial" in its sense of imperishable, eternal, perfect, with the vulgar use of the word as space not contained within the utmost limits of the earth's atmosphere, or the ~~supposed~~ higher line supposed as sublunary.

An attempt to give, in this stage of our progress, the completed genesis of all that is now contained in the M ~~as~~—µ (= firmamental and fluid) would be utterly inconsistent with the distinctive form and evolution [*f 86*] of our philosophy, which acknowledges the reality of succession, and consequently ~~acknowledges~~ supposes a retroaction in every new production, a potentiating resilience, as ~~preceding and~~ at once preparing and being one with every act of projection. The Naturphilosophen, with whom all manifestation is in fact illusion, and whose cosmical history is but a coherent story of subjective and so far necessitated fictions, have

---

[r] ms: and unsteady

[138] Nikolaj Kopernik (1473–1543), Polish astronomer, first conceived the heliocentric system that overturned the Ptolemaic system of conceiving the relation of the earth to the sun. Author of *De revolutionibus orbium coelestium* (1543). In praising Kepler, C says "How often and how gladly does he speak of Copernicus! and with what fervent tones of faith and consolation does he proclaim the historic fact that the great men of all ages have prepared the way for each other, as pioneers and heralds! Equally just to the ancients and to his contemporaries, how circumstantially, and with what exactness of detail, does Kepler demonstrate that Euclid copernicises— ὡς πρὸ τοῦ Κοπερνίκου κοπερνικίζει

Εὐκλείδης!" (*Friend*—*CC*—ɪ 486.) C was fond of evoking the phrase; e.g. "Kepler would demonstrate that Euclid Copernicised, or had some knowledge of the system afterwards adopted by Copernicus, yet of this there is little proof; and certainly for many ages after Euclid it was the universal opinion, that the earth was the fixed and immoveable center of the universe" (*SW & F*—*CC*—ɪ 679).

[139] It was Copernicus's successor, Kepler, who mathematically demonstrated that the orbits of the planets were not perfect circles but ellipses, though he did so with great perplexity; his age interpreted the disappointing discovery to be the result of the Fall of Man, which had distorted all perfection.

done otherwise. The result is as might be expected. The whole is in truth but a scheme of the logic of the human imagination—not how things *came* to *be* so, for this is precluded by the *"always"* as our only representative of the term *"eternal"*, but how *we* come to contemplate this "always," and evermore the same in all the differences of succession and relative extraneity. Of course, in addition to the inherent barrenness of the scheme (for the asserted offspring are all contraband, and brought into the palace of philosophy from the homely cottage of empiricism, as in the old tale of the warming-[*f 87*]pan), [it] leaves the subjective itself, and the necessity of contemplating the world in flux, colour, and limit, ~~itself~~ unexplained and inexplicable. No! we shall deem ourselves amply rewarded for our toils, and invoke philosophy by the additional attribute of the munificent, if, at the close of the system, and when all the powers that now are have been duly evolved, each in its own branch in the tree of philosophic genealogy, the great pedigree of the world, we shall have been able ⟨to refer⟩ each class of phaenomena to a law praeestablished ab antè,[140] and thus have demonstrated the possibility of organizing all the sciences into a living and growing body of knowledge. Thus we have already deduced the powers which are constitutive of quartz, feldspar, and mica as the components of granite; but till the course of our scheme has potentiated the $\odot$ and $\oslash$ into $\oplus$, and in so doing have realized a full antithesis of $\oplus$ to $>$, in consequence of which, however, $\mathrm{L} >$ itself must stand forth in a different [*f 88*] form from that which it possessed as $> \maltese \square$, we could by no means attempt the solution of granite mountains, which must fall within the sphere of the ordinant polarity. Again, we must be content for the present in showing the increased play of the .... powers and their coincidence with the gradual appearance of primitive $^s\backslash$ and^t incombustible $/_\mathrm{c}$, the necessary excitement, i.e. through the maximum of the eo .... of its revealed $\maltese$ $\sim$ by the increased combination of the $\overset{h}{\sim}$ with the $/_\mathrm{c}$, the metalloid $\ominus$ or balance of both powers by the $\odot$ as the common basis and subjugator of both in the increasing manifestation of Kali, as in Basalt, etc., ^{u}etc. In^v the commencing and increasing reduction of metals, and the imitative arborescence of the imperfectly reduced or metallic ores, we find on all sides an approximation—may we not venture to say, a preparatory yearning after—and a presensation of a new triumph of $>$, but yet a tri-

---

$^{s-t}$ An uncertain reading. The virgule differs in form from C's symbol for carbon or attraction (i.e. /), corresponds to no other symbol in his glossary on ff 193–4, and is written over the "a" in "and", possibly to indicate that the word was to be cancelled
$^{u-v}$ ms: &c—in

140 Tr: "from before".

umph of $>$ [f 89] contained in the embrace of $\square$, and which, when the full emancipation of $>$ shall have potentiated $\square$ into $\oplus$,^{w} will appear as the power of $>$ within the sphere of $\oplus$, otherwise expressed as $\oplus$ under the power of $>$, even as sound, for instance, may be referred to $>$ under the power of $\oplus$—but still by no gradation in all this, I say, we find ourselves celebrating, as it were, prophetic vespers on the eve of vegetable life. But as the evening doth by no gradation pass into the new morning, but is divided from it by its own night, so here by no gradation, no mere addition or composition of powers already evolved, can these pre-adaptations of nature to vegetative life actually become vegetation—for this a new actualization of the potential will, i.e. of the will of the re-ascending apostacy, is required, which, again, is not possible but by a new Going forth of the word in the Spirit, a new product of the great original polarity, the ⟨Creaturely⟩ Self and the Divine Love. [f 90] Even so, in the ⟨early⟩ appearance, primitive though junior, of the crystalline marble, we find the $\cdot\cdot$. under the predominance of /—produced because the $\cdot\cdot$., has coexisted⟨ing⟩ with the /, must by the law of alternation *appear*, but having appeared remains as a prisoner in chains, manifesting no formative dispositions, exhibiting few varieties, and none in the nature of productive evolution, as if it were a something that waited for a distant day, for the ascent of a star as yet below the horizon, in the culmination of which it should assume the same aptitudes and predispositions as the components of granite, or rather the whole series—which, beginning in silica and alumen, ends in the stone-coal—exhibits in the present eve. And what if, in the dawning of life to which our eyes are now looking forward, we should discover a form of life bearing a similar analogy to vegetation as here the primitive marble bears to the carbonic silica and alumina, [f 91] and even to the other, more enigmatic magnesian earth, in which we contemplate the nitrogen, under a similar predominance of ...., as the contractive power that, as ⟨in⟩ the primitive lime of the $\cdot\cdot$. to the / by the auxilium of the ..... This is certain, that what in the anti-vital products would appear as the unvarying self-unmodifying must in the products of life appear as the perishable impermanent—a something, in short, which, like the lime in the former instance, appeared only to assert its future appearance in its own rank, and in addition to this, in the latter case (that of the vital products), to assert the superior dignity of that rank by a present though evanescent priority. An onward look of prophecy will not misbeseem us at this moment of

---

^{w} The symbol appears to be an amalgam of the symbols for gravitation ($\oplus$) and weight ($\triangle$)

our subject, in which we are to pause with the "prophetic soul of the whole world, dreaming of things to come".[141] We shall recommence with that new [*f* 92] and distinct energy by which we, if not leap, yet stride into the world of light. ǂLike Orpheus, the command is that we keep our eye steadily toward the light that is to come, lest like Orpheus, looking backward on the phantom⟨atic⟩[x] though prophetic semblance of life which is behind us, and endeavouring ⟨to produce⟩[y] the reality out of the phantom itself by an intensity of our own contemplation, we lose the one forever, and leave the other forever a phantom. Such, it appears to me has been the proceeding of Schelling and of a yet more Orphic mind, H. Steffens.[z]

[*f 193*]	Glossary of Terms employed in the Dialogues de Finibus et Methodo Philosophiae[142]	
/	Carbon	= Attraction—Magnetism. North ideally. N. by N.E. really. Fixity.
∴	Nitrogen	= Repulsion as the *power* of separative projection + Magnetism. South ideally. S. by S.W. really. Volatility.
....	Oxygen	= Contraction. − Elect. East. Particularization. N.B. ∴ when disting. from Chlor. or Iodine.
~	Hydrogen	= Dilation. + Elect. West. Universalization.
⊙	Centrality.	Involution of each in each or 4 = 1 and then 1 + 4 = 5. Pan the 5th Numen and 3[d] Deity ⟨N.B. as Quality ad intra⟩,[a] the offspring of the two Deities / and ∴ with their Numina .... and ~.
⊕	Gravitation. N.B. as *property* or *Power* ad extra.	
⊕̸	Weight. Specific Gravity.	
▢	Ether. Actualized Space.	

[x] Insertion possibly in C's hand
[y] Insertion in C's hand
[z] Ff 93–192 are blank
[a] This passage is written in the left margin and marked with a brace to indicate its place in the sentence

[141] Cf Shakespeare: "Not mine own fears, nor the prophetic soul / Of the wide world, dreaming on things to come . . ." (*Sonnet* 107 lines 1–2).

[142] A very similar but not quite identical listing, under the same title, is supplied in *CN* iv 4555.

Glossary of Terms employed in the Dialogues de Finibus et Methodo Philosophica.—

1. Carbon = Attraction — Magnetism North ideally. N. by N.E. really. Fixity.

... Nitrogen = Repulsion as if *power* of seperative projection + Magnetism. South ideally. S by S.W. really. Volatility.—

.... Oxygen = Contraction.— Elect. East. Particularization N.B. ... when diffring from Chlor: or Iodine.

~ Hydrogen = Dilation + Elect. West. Universalization

☉. Centrality. Involution of each in each or 4=1 and then 1+4 = 5. Pan the 5th N. =men, ∠ 3rd Deity. the offspring of if two Deities. 1 and ... with their Numina .... and ~

N.B. as Quality ad extra)

⊕ Gravitation. NB as *property* or *Power* ad extra

Ⓐ. Weight. Specific Gravity

☐. Ether. Actualized Space

>. Light.

☰ Caloric.

3. First leaf of the "Glossary of Terms" from fragment 4 in Joseph Henry Green's hand. VCL S MS 29 Vol I f 193. Victoria College Library; reproduced by kind permission

∪ Sulphur

◠ Phosphorus

⋰ Chlorine

⋱ Iodine

Alkalies. Triangles with y apex
upward & the Initial
following. –

Earth Triangles with the apex
downward with the Initial
following. – NB. Seldom used
the name (or the initial where
it is the only metal begin-
ning with that letter) being
as brief or briefer. –

. Metal.. Metalleity ○ Metals collec-
tively or indefinitely OO or O↓

▽, △ and O↓ = the Earths, Alkalies
and metals. –

V Oxyds Ṽ Chlorides V̇ Iodides

◇ Acids x◇ Cloric acids
i◇. Iodic acid.

⦂̇ Water ⦂⦂ Fire ⸫ Air

λ Logos πγ Spirit γ maker ʃ life

Σ Body σʃ organization

σʃ∼ Vegetation σʃ..... Animality,
animalization

3. Mechanism 8 Chemical compound
or product 𝕏 Neutralization
Balance. 8 Predominance.
Thus Water is 𝕏 Coal 8. The
latter always supposing a Third

>	Light.
≡	Caloric.
[ƒ 193ᵛ] ⌄	Sulphur.
⌒	Phosphorus.
..ˣ..	Chlorine.
..ⁱ..	Iodine.
Alkalies.	Triangles with ⫽ apex upward and the Initial following.
Earth.	Triangles with the apex downward with the Initials following. N.B. Seldom used, the name (or the initial where it is the only metal beginning with that letter) being as brief or briefer.

Metal, Metalleity. ○ Metals collectively or indefinitely. ○○ or ○s
△, ▽, and ○s = the Earths, Alkalies, and metals.

∨	Oxyds.	ⱴ̌	Chlorides.	ⱴⁱ	Iodides.
◇	Acids.	x◇	Chloric acids.		
		i◇	Iodic acids.		
~̈	Water.	·∴·	Fire.	˙/.	Air.
λ	Logos.	πν	Spirit.	γ	matter. ζ life.
Σ	Body.	σζ	organization.		
σζ ~	Vegetation.	σζ....	Animality, animalization.		
3.	Mechanism.	8	Chemical compound or product.		
		𐊭	Neutralization, Balance.		
		-8-	Predominance.		

Thus Water is 𐊭, Coal -8-. The latter always supposing a third [ƒ 194] something, or common base, of the two opposite Numina, independent of the *primary* co-existence of the four in each, under the predominance of the one placed first, or rather singly. Thus / is / ˙∵. .... ~ under the predominance of /, and so with the rest.

Observe, ∧, and so ∨, means oxyds generally, without special reference to oxygen. .... used simply thus means the power generally, and includes Chlorine and Iodine as well as oxygen. But oxygen as a stuff or Element of the laboratory is signified by ..ˣ..

Marks of Relation already explained, q.v.

APPENDIXES

APPENDIX A

VCL S MS 28 ("Magnum Opus"). These fragments consist of three pocket note-books (two disbound), all contained in a brown envelope inscribed on the back in ink: "The recently found scraps of Op. Mag. One seems a continuation of a Scrap marked 'A', the other may fit in someplace, I do not know, but has a pencil note of S.T.C. on inside cover. | A. H. B. Coleridge." (In fact the note does not appear to be in C's hand: see the headnote to Frag (*b*) below.) Because these fragments are much more lightly punctuated than those of the main text, the emendation of the texts has had to be correspondingly heavier. Full stops are inserted silently wherever capitalisation clearly indicates the beginnings of new sentences, but less certain emendations are, as in the main text, recorded in the textual notes.

(*a*) Disbound notebook containing a single unsewn gathering of 12 leaves, 185 × 115 mm; wm "Ruse and Turners | 1820". The text is written in ink in JHG's hand, with occasional corrections in C's hand. The first eight leaves are lettered A-H at the top and centre of each leaf.

DATE. 1820 (the wm date) or later.

[*f 1*] It is a FACT that there are certain doctrines, commandments, precepts, and narratives which collectively are ~~held to be~~ received as true and of divine ~~origin~~ authority by the Greek, Roman, Anglican, Evangelical, and ~~r~~Reformed churches. We ~~are entitled to~~ ⟨might indeed, in the ordinary allowance of words,⟩*a* assume that they are received by the whole christian world, the one exception under the name of "Unitarianism" being too insignificant ~~at all events as~~ ⟨in number and⟩*b* too recent ⟨in⟩ origin to invalidate the rule in any calculable degree. ~~and~~ ⟨Add, that⟩*c* its professors having never been acknowledged for a christian church by any body of ~~men~~ ⟨Christians⟩*d* having [. . .]tian*e* authority.* [*f 2*]

* [*The following sentences, written as part of the text but surrounded by parentheses and preceded by an "X" in the ms, are printed as a note in accordance with C's holograph instruction at the bottom of f 1: "X. To be printed as a Note at the bottom of the page":*] Note. At all events not prior to the partial re-

a Insertion in C's hand   *b* Insertion in C's hand
c Insertion in C's hand   *d* Insertion in C's hand
e The beginning of the cancelled word is obliterated by a hole in the ms

347

*h*These doctrines etc., as common to all christians, ~~taken~~ collectively constitute the CHRISTIAN RELIGION,*i* the following being the sum: that there is one only God who is the Father, Son, and ~~the~~ Holy Ghost as the Creator, so the Preserver and Governor of the Universe; that Man ~~has lost his~~ ⟨fallen "quem longissima" from⟩*j* original rectitude has become corrupt in ⟨his own⟩*k* nature, and yet so as to remain a responsible being; that for the redemption and restoration of fallen Man, God was manifest in the flesh [*f 3*] the eternal Son, very God of very God and One with the Father, uniting the human with his divine nature and submitting to the death of the cross; that he rose from the grave and became our Redeemer, Mediator and Judge; ~~lastly~~ that previous*l* to this manifestation of God in the flesh (the so-called Incarnation), there were preparatory dispensations as parts of the same great process, namely, the patriarchal, the mosaic, and the prophetic; ~~dispensations~~ and lastly, that this same process is still carrying on by reading and hearing of ~~the~~ ⟨certain⟩ scriptures, by the aids of the Holy Spirit, by the general dispositions of Providence, and by the continued intercession of the Redeemer, through whom there is forgiveness of sins and everlasting life for as many as receive the Lord Jesus in Love and Faith, manifesting both by obedience to his commandments. [*f 4*] To these tenets we may ~~add~~ ⟨subjoin⟩*m* one ⟨other⟩*n* article of belief, at least, of universal acknowledgment, that all the above tenets are either contained in ~~or undeniably~~ ⟨may plainly be⟩ inferred from *certain books* ~~which together are entitled the Bible as~~ consisting of two parts written in two different languages ⟨and entitled⟩*o* the

---

peal of a statute of William and Mary by the british legislature. No such acknowledgement, it is clear, [*f 2*] was here *intended* by parliament, though it may and doubtless will be deduced from the words of the bill—the power of drawing such an inference ⟨and attracting the public attention to their sect⟩*f* being, indeed, all that the petitioners, the unitarians aforesaid, either meant of wanted. It needs not the spirit of prophecy to foresee that ~~the~~ ⟨our⟩ legislators sooner or later will find reason to ask themselves what their predecessors ~~could have meant~~ ⟨did intend⟩ by granting such a petition in a form susceptible of such an inference.*g*

f Insertion in C's hand
g Question mark in text
h–i Numbers written in the ms over the words of this passage indicate how they are to be arranged. The original arrangement is as follows: "These doctrines &c, ~~taken~~ collectively constitute the CHRISTIAN RELIGION, as common to all christians,"
j Insertion in C's hand
k Insertion in C's hand
l The following comment is written in pencil on f 2*v*, facing this word: "Q*y* previously"
m Insertion possibly in C's hand
n Insertion possibly in C's hand
o Insertion in C's hand

old and new Testaments. That these books are themselves possessed of divine authority is likewise a ~~common~~ belief common to all the churches of Christendom, but as the exact sense in which this acknowledgement is to be understood—whether under *any* limitations[p] and with *what,*[q] again, by what criterion the judgement is to be guided in the particular application of such limitations—are questions in which the learned among the different christian churches are far from being agreed, [r]⟨we have therefore not included this Tenet ~~in~~ ⟨among⟩ the Universals of Christianity.⟩[s] The~~y~~ ⟨churches⟩ are, however, unanimous that nothing con[*f 5*]fessedly contradictory to these scriptures can be a *true* part, while the protestants assert further that nothing which is not contained ⟨in them⟩ expressly or by clear implication can be a necessary part of the christian religion. But as our object ~~is~~ at present ~~to~~ ⟨concerns⟩[t] the Faith common to all, and as the opinions last stated ~~concern~~ ⟨belong to⟩ the differences between one church and another, ~~we have no present concern with them~~ ⟨it is enough that we have thus simply mentioned this circumstance⟩.[u] In the present work the Scriptures must find their place among the proofs and documents of Christianity, and must of course undergo the same examination ⟨as other less venerated Reliques of former Times⟩.[v] We should otherwise be guilty of ~~the same~~ ⟨a similar⟩ vicious circle in reasoning as our protestant divines have objected to the defenders of the roman church: namely, that the church of Rome is paramount and infallible because the scriptures assert it, and the scriptures [*f 6*] are infallible, or what means the same, that certain books are especially and exclusively ⟨sacred⟩[w] Scriptures, because the church has so determined ~~it~~. Even so we should say such and such tenets are divine, for they are contained in the scriptures, and certain books are exclusively *scripture*, because they contain such and no other tenets.

[x]⟨As our subject leads us especially to the books of the New Testa-

[p] ms: limitations?

[q] ms: *what?*

[r–s] Passage written by C on f 3[v] and marked for insertion here

[t] Insertion in C's hand

[u] Insertion in C's hand

[v] Insertion in C's hand

[w] Insertion possibly in C's hand

[x–y](p 351) This passage, written by C on ff 5[v]–7[v], replaces the following sentence on f 6, which is cancelled in ink with a single vertical line. The conclusion of the sentence, at the top of f 7, is not cancelled but clearly should have been, and hence is included here: "Whatever other evidence is given of the scriptures themselves supposes the prior enunciation & acceptance of the Christian Creed or Essentials of Faith, and therefore at once places the scriptures in the rank ~~to~~, which we have allotted to them; namely not among the primary articles of faith, but with the proofs of their existence as articles of Faith, consecutive on an antecedent proof of their own authenticity; ~~ans~~ or at least documental validity,

ment, we may here remark that all the proofs, brought in support of their *authenticity* and of the high worth and authority thereby attached to their contents, suppose the prior enunciation and acceptance of the Creed: ~~or~~ [? ~~Essentials~~] ⟨i.e. of the *primary* articles of⟩ Faith above given. The Books themselves, therefore, can neither be included in the number of *primary* Articles, nor admitted even among the *primary* Proofs of these Articles. For first, their own *authenticity* must be established by its own proper proofs. But the mere establishment of their authenticity will only suffice to determine the [? ~~day~~] ⟨age⟩ and date, ~~in~~ ⟨at⟩ which such and such Doctrines were already known and taught as Articles of Christian Faith: and that⟨us⟩ of course, to prove them *primary* articles. In other words, the *Authenticity* (we take the word here in its narrowest sense ᶻ⟨and here are speaking of *external* evidence exclusively)—the *authenticity*⟩ᵃ of the Books establishes in the first instance only the *chronology* of the Doctrines. If their validity, as documents, is to extend beyond this point; if they are to prove that ~~these~~ ⟨certain⟩ Doctrines are *essential* as well as [*f* 6ᵛ] *primary* Articles of Faith, and to evince the obligation of receiving them as such; and if in justifying these higher claims we are to keep clear of a suspicious *Reciprocatio principii*, in which the Competence of B. is affirmed on the authority of A, the competence of A. having been received on the authority of B; some testimony or facts equivalent to such testimony, supplying proofs or presumptions at least of the circumstances and characters of the Writers drawn from other sources than the Writings themselves, must be adduced in the *first* instance. This done, we may then consider the New Testament as a collection of contemporary yet separate works by several and independent Authors, each of whose⟨m⟩ may furnish available evidence in behalf of the others, subject to no greater caution than would be required in weighing and collating the testimony of *any* six or seven ⟨contemporary⟩ Historians and Advocates, of presumptive Respectability, who were the professed Partizans of the same Cause. But what and how great the Drawbacks from or Accessions to the weight of their authority, from the character of the Cause itself—this is a question, the solution of which comprizes the more important Half of the *internal* [*f* 7ᵛ] Evidence: and that part too which is one and the same with the internal evidence of the Religion itself, negative and positive.ᵇ The absence of self-contradiction

---

and on a pre-determination of their own character and the nature of the [*f* 7] proof, which they afford."

   ᶻ⁻ᵃ Passage written by C at the top of f 5ᵛ with the following instruction: "(last line but 5, after the word 'sense' insert:"

   ᵇ A mark appears here in the ms as if to indicate an insertion or note, but without any text to be inserted

and of whatsoever contradicts the self-evidence of *Reason* ~~and~~ or the imperative Laws "written in the *Heart*" of Man, as the main contra-distinguishing mark of our Humanity; and vice versâ, the excellent fitness of the Credenda to those excellent ends, the *Idea* of which, inherent in the Reason, is brought into consciousness and bear witness to the [. . .] coincidence ~~in the doctrines~~ ⟨of and correspon⟩dency of the doctrines, in the moment ~~that the Conscience~~ ⟨awaked from without⟩ ~~prescribes their realization~~ that, the latter having been once intelligibly announced, the Conscience, awakened from without or from within, prescribes their realization as the Maxim (= regula *maxima*) or uppermost Rule of ~~Act~~ Will and ~~Will~~ Deed.)[y] [*f7*] The unthinking, and those whose belief does not rise above acquiescence and amounts to little more than the absence of denial or perhaps the absence of all disposition to any enquiry, can f rest in the gross quid pro quo of making the scripture their religion because they [. . .] have learnt that their religion is contained in the scripture. Whatever may be pretended to the contrary this notion reduces all actual distinct belief to one only article: the veracity and infallibility of certain men named as the writers of certain books—nay more, it removes all rational and discriminate admiration of the books themselves, for in order to this some characters of excellence must be found in the contents themselves, rendering the cause of their infallibility credible; but whatever is adduced to justi[*f8*]fy this necessarily supposes grounds of the truth and excellence of the doctrines etc. independent of their being found in the scripture and forming, therefore, a most important part the so called *Internal* of the Evidence of the scriptures themselves. We may safely appeal to those at all likely to be our readers whether a work being presented to them, containing gross contradictions to the dictates of their conscience—whether, for instance, if the parts of the Koran enforcing despotism authorizing a sensual polygamy here, and promising sensual delight hereafter, [or] all the mythological books of the Brahmins, with their accursed laws respecting the Brahmin class and that of the Parah, were presented to them as inspired writings—they would condescend to wait for any outward evidence in support of the assertion, at least with any other [*f9*] view than that of gratifying the wish of learning, if possible, at what time and under what circumstances so palpable and infamous an imposture could have been passed on the belief of men. The result, then, [is][c] that the credibility of a religion must necessarily depend in the first instance on a rule pre-established in the *mind* of the individual, the truth or falsehood of which rule is ⟨pre⟩assumed and presupposed in the religion itself and constitutes the point from which it proceeds.

[c] Word inserted in pencil

Thus S Paul ~~has~~ decides that no man can be supposed to receive a reli-
gion as coming from God, and therefore, of course, neither the written
nor oral records of its articles and their derivation, unless he is pre-con-
vinced of the religion and attributes of God. Much, therefore, as this part
of the subject has been hitherto neglected ⟨previous⟩ ⟨preconditionally⟩[d]
to [*f 10*] any rational examination of the christian religion, ~~there must~~
~~be premised~~ we must ~~previously~~ determine first, and as far as ~~the~~ history
and philosophy are concerned, what the necessary postulates or as-
sumptions are from which the examination must proceed, and as far as
the religion refers to the moral and religious being, what state of mind
the examinant must bring with them to the enquiry, the denial or absence
of these being tantamount to a rejection of the whole beforehand by de-
nial of the premises παντος[e] γαρ λογ⟨ισμ⟩ου κριτον τι ὅ λογος των
λογσμων αρχη.

[*f 11*]   CHAPTER 2$^{\underline{d}}$

In our last we endeavoured to shew that the sacred scriptures require a
proof for their own admissibility as evidence in order to their becoming
supports of the other parts of the edifice of Faith. They may be pillars,
they may be the main beams of the preserving and sheltering roof, but
they cannot be the foundation. It would be sufficient, however, to re-
member that the authenticity and the definite character of each several
book and then of the whole collectively are (it is admitted on all hands)
parts of the problem, and cannot therefore be taken as the first step of the
solution, or the contradictory proof. It is very possible, indeed—and
such, we trust, will appear to be the fact—that they conjointly with the
other [*f 12*] articles of christian belief (in other words the scriptures and
their contents) interpreted as in the preceding chapter may supply a very
impressive both argument and evidence, on the principle of correspon-
dence, and thus produce that final effect which the contemplation of har-
monious parts conspiring to a consistent beneficent whole never fail to
produce on minds that are themselves well constituted and who there-
fore know in the highest sense of the word, that of ultimate knowledge
or facts of consciousness, that the strongest support, which it is possible
for a moral position to possess, is that it cannot be denied without plac-
ing the denier in a state of self-contradiction. We therefore purposely
guarded our assertion by confining it to the first step, to the introductory
proof. The same reasoning will[f]

---

[d] Word written by JHG on f 8^v and marked for insertion here   [e] ms: παντοσ
[f] Text breaks off here

(*b*) Account book in marbled paper covers, containing a single sewn gathering of 22 leaves with printed vertical columns, 177 × 110 mm; wm "C WILMOTT | [*device*]". The text, in sections numbered 10–17, is written in ink in JHG's hand on both sides of ff 1–21. Inside the front cover the following note is written in pencil in an unidentified hand: "The objective [? entitled] is that point where subjective & objective become identified, matter mind—to [? whether] they have exponents of One & the same is that great object [. . .] investigation. I rest in the hope & faith that such may be demonstrated—The interpenetration of the whole being of all we perceive, understand or hope." Below this is another note in the same hand: "Creech's Lucretius—". (Lucretius is quoted on f 13 of the present fragment, but in Latin, not in Thomas Creech's translation, which C read in *Anderson's British Poets*: see *CM—CC*—I 51, 82.) F 22 is blank except for two sums (both correct) written in pencil, one on each side of the folio, in an

	£	.	s	.	d
	16 . 16	1	0	6
unidentified hand, possibly JHG's:	3 3 and	2	3	4 R
	19 . 19	7	10	3
		10 " 14 " 1

DATE. 1820s?

[*f 1*]   (10)

13. And the ~~World~~ ⟨word⟩ went forth from God, even God the Word: "Let there be Light." That Light was as the consequent of the going forth of the Word upon the apostacy as now placed by the antecedent act of the Spirit between the Chaos and the Cosmos which we have designated by the term "Aether", but could it not have arisen out of the powers already awakened? In order to see the contrary let us review those powers. To begin from the first apostatic power the Will to realize Self, used for the purposes of logical exposition as a power, may be designated "ATTRACTION NIHILATIVE"—‡in seeking to realize the potential it pontentializes, i.e. reduces to mere potentiality the Real. Without this potential it could not be truly a Will, yet with it, otherwise than as merely potential, [*f 1ᵛ*] it cannot really be. This state as an inanition of intelligence, and therefore only negatively intelligible, as necessarily unintelligible we know not how to represent but as a dark striving a blind anguishing lust without subject or object merum pravum, das blosse böse, the substance that still casts the shadow death as the *ᵍ*involutes. We*ʰ* have seen the two contraries multeity and utter indistinction, and we

ᵍ⁻ʰ ms: involutes we

have learnt all that can be learnt of their nature by seeing at once and with equal force the necessity and the incompossibility of their co-existence, and found that we had but antedated our own state of mind as often as we have strove either to deny or affirm the Atoms, or the infinite divisibility of matter as the materia of body. [*f* 2] As in the plenitude we had Number ~~without~~ ⟨above⟩ multeity, so in the contrary state we have a multeity alien from number; and as in the former the essential numbers existed wholly as intelligences in unutterably perfect distinction, so in the latter we have utter indistinction the mere residuum, which, self-precipitated, is incapable of being taken up into it, becoming intelligible even in the present state only as far as it is not presented, that is, only as far as it is contemplated in a substitute.

14. In this state it has received its first fluxion of restored reality by the presence of the divine Love, the Self, the phantom which can be conceived of as the desire only to appropriate that which cannot be [*f* 2ᵛ] except as it is in another—is so far realized as to constitute the second power, or ATTRACTION APPROPRIATIVE. Multeity transfigured into the equilibrium, and the indistinction into an aether in which the ~~resistance~~⟨pulsion⟩ is the correlative of each attraction, and both exhausted each by the other, presents an unresisting *material* of attraction and repulsion: more than this cannot be conceived from the act of the divine spirit as love without introducing arbitrariness and confusion, for what more could Love do than to give an interpenetration whi~~ch~~le yet it preserved the identity, and to realize the mighty intercirculation each in all and all in each—but this would be to create the Deity with the plenitude. It would exist not [*f* 3] intellectually for us, but verbally only, as if we gave to an echo perfect identity with the sound and at the same time a numerical difference—we should but repeat the same idea twice and call the repetition two ideas before the most distant approach could be made even to the shadowy symbol of the divine ⁱplenitude. Weʲ must have seen the indistinction compelled into distinctness, but in the agency we affirm and involve the necessary presence and energy of the Logos; but ~~to~~in affirming the presence of the Logos carefully, let as guard against the phantom of a somewhat supervenient, the possible object of a consciousness distinct from the consciousness itself, or of a perception distinct from the sense. The presence of the Logos is one and the [*f* 3ᵛ] same with the sense of distinctness as far as it~~s~~ [? ~~presen~~] is relatively present, for again must we remember that this intelligence is a Will: no blind power that is evil were all, or none in itself always, all because it is relatively that for

---

ⁱ⁻ʲ ms: plenitude we

each alone by which each and all become intelligible. Hard, indeed, it is for a finite intellect to conceive, though it were but negatively and altogether impossible to express the truth of the eternity as coexistent with the perception of the eternal in Time and Space. Yet the great movements of the celestial bodies system within system, the birth and the death of worlds and how every moving space still presumes a space relatively immoveable, every measured point a time, that is, [ƒ4] measured itself as time, a wider time relatively unsuccessive while both of time and space, the cycle of motion present, as in a symbol, all successions at once— these contemplations best aid us in apprehending that which itself comprehends us, which is presented to us in every act of perception as an inevitable condition but an impossible consequence, yea, even as to the different climes of this planet, the relatively immoveable sun is at once dimly awakening the dark into twilight, dawning, rising, risen, climbing, meridional, descending, and setting—even so must we conceive the agency of the Logos as ⌈. . .⌉ parcelled out, as it were through the expansion, and divided in the [ƒ4ᵛ] long successions of developments and ages. In the logos itself the succession could not be, for he is the eternal; but neither in the materia could succession be utterly alienated from the logos, for succession presumes distinction, and the logos is essential distinctness, the number of all numbers.ᵏ

[? ~~15~~] The preceding caution is most necessary even when the full plumage has grown and we are strong on the wing, denizens of higher air and familiar to the solar blaze—still this will remain necessary, for as "to wonder with perplexity like one self questions in a dream (= το θαυμζειν) ⟨is the beginning⟩, so to wonder as one adoring is the end of philosophy (το θαμβειν)".* Be it therefore fully understood [ƒ5] that to

---

* [*Written on ff 5–5ᵛ after the asterisk and indented from the left margin:*] ~~15~~ As one who sees now close upon him and in the next instant at a far distance an ever-moving light wonders and, looking around him, beholds its reflection on all objects, yet seemingly partaking of all their hues, which yet it seems to give and evermore turns to the far distant light, which though endlessly shifting its position attracts him as the source from which all the reflections proceed with such perplexing and questioning [ƒ 5ᵛ] wonder, philosophy hath its beginning "δια γαρ το θαυμαζειν οι ανθρωποι και νυν και το πρω τον ηρξαν το φιλοσοφειν". But again as the Epoptes who has passed through all the grades from imperfect to distinct vision lies at length prostate before the glory from whence all light proceeded, and, his head enclosed within the skirts of the glory, worships the vision itself in itself and no longer as reflected from the visible, he

---

ᵏ In the right margin after this paragraph a capital "R" has been written backwards in ink in an unidentified hand

this §, as often as we speak of degrees and successions in the divine agency, whether we have remembered to insert or have omitted to add the word *"Relatively"*.

[*f*6] 15. If we would ask, therefore, where, relatively to the creature, we shall determine the first agency of the Logos, impelled, as it were à tergo by the truths already demonstrated and unbribed, uncorrupted by any anticipation of that which we wish to have explained and which we foresee as requiring a solution for this, would be to preclude all hope of establishing a law by overlaying it in the first struggles of intellection by hypothesis and *l*theory—if,*m* we repeat, faithful to these laws of pure constructive Dialectic, we enquire for the first form of the agency of the Logos, we must needs seek for that which in the Logos constitutes the kind (if we may dare so to dignify this word),*n* both as exclusive [*f*6*v*] of all degrees in the filial Godhead as accompanying all relatively to us, and relatively likewise specifying the least and, as it were, rudimental degree. But this is *Distinction*, in the creature ⟨therefore⟩ a sense of distinction; but again it is a sense of distinction according to which the creature is ~~then~~ supposed to *o*be. Now*p* we have supposed it in that state which we have denominated "ATTRACTION APPROPRIATIVE", in which in the realized attempt to constitute a self it would have another, not as the other but as itself; but in this we have found the attempt, not, indeed, as before in the chaotic state self baffled, but baffled by all balancing and, as it were, neutralizing all. In seeking Self, it*q* [*f*7] has been fleeing from self, and its flight suspended not from within, for it is still as in a dream fleeing, but from without, and thus once more lost in an equal, though in another indistinction. The sense of distinction, therefore, can be no other than the reverse of this act, a recalling of the flight as it went forward to seek itself: it must now re~~tre~~⟨coil⟩ inward; and in these acts of the Spirit, indeed, the outward and the inward have first their full creaturely meaning, the*r* preparation having been made by the act of the spirit in the genesis of space as the praesuppositum of outward and inward. But I know no more appropriate name as exponent of this act than that of ATTRACTION ASTRINGENT.

---

loses himself in το θαμβειν εστι τελος του φιλοσοφειν. θαυμαζοντας φιλοσοφουμεν φιλοσσοφηζαντας θαμβουμεν.

l–m ms: theory If
n Parentheses inserted
o–p ms: be now [*an uncertain reading: "now" may have been intended as the last word of the previous clause*]
q In the bottom margin of this folio a "3" is written in ink
r ms: The

[ƒ7ᵛ]   (16)

Of no ordinary kind are the difficulties which press upon us, whether we consider the complexity or the diversity of the acts which are to be the forces by which we are to work in the construction of nature: for 1ˢᵗ, though the agents be not only different but diverse and even contrary, yet the immediate agencies must still be conceived in the same subject; and while on the one hand there is a simultaneity which we cannot conceive but in the form of succession, on the other there is a simultaneity which we cannot even conceive as successive, and yet by the nature of words are compelled so to express ourselves. Again and yet more formidable is the difficulty [ƒ8] arising from the manifold nature of the relations, all of which must still be borne in mind—the relation to the divine Will in its own Holiness and Absoluteness to the influence of the divine Will in the creaturely Will, both as divine and as creaturely, and lastly the relations of the creatures in the multeity each to the other under all the conceivable relations of Space and Time. Yet these relations are perforce interdependent, and thus let in on us a new train of difficulties— the various degrees, I mean, of Reality from the ~~ends~~⟨s⟩ verè ens, or the absolutely actual to the Non-Ens non ~~verè~~ ⟨omninò omnino⟩ Non-Ens, or the merely potential of which we would yet cannot predicate non-entity only because the causation of the absolutely actual can never utterly cease or [ƒ8ᵛ] end in nothing. Thus ~~where~~ the subjects being interdependents, and all alike praesuppositious, where shall we find the point which is to predetermine any one position as the determinant of all? We have, indeed, the divine influence, but still as creaturely, and the immediate agents are ⟨influenced⟩ creatures, indeed, but yet creaturely. ˢWhile if we assumed a compulsive influence on ⟨and⟩ of the creature this must preclude it shᵈ seem all other agency be too vast to admit of associates and the result would be the baffling of our whole attempt put an end to all philosophic enquiry ~~whether~~ ⟨with an⟩ est quia sic Deo placitum est. And to this we might submit if it were indeed religious, but religion forbids us ~~tour~~ transference [of] the inalienable [ƒ9] attribute "I am in that I am"—nay, the Godhead itself, for by no dialectic arts shall we ever be able to distinguish the position, "God does all things exclusively", from the densest Pantheism, for "God is all things and all things are God". It will be enough for us at present to have made ourselves distinctly conscious of these difficulties to recollect that some of them have already in some part been surmounted, and, as the light has dawned, to

---

ˢ The absence of necessary words in this sentence (which makes punctuating it impossible) suggests that it was written down hurriedly from C's dictation

feel a trust that it will continue to rise as we continue to toil onward on our journey, and lastly to fix our attention on the fact already demonstrated: that[t] the divine influence does exist and must be considered as one of the cosmoplastic ~~infl~~ forces, and that this divine influence is the [ƒ9ᵛ] influence of the Logos, consequently of distinction itself, in whom and from whom all other distinction in heaven and in earth derives its Esse or its Posse, and consequently that relation, yea, an ⟨omni-⟩central and all-predetermining relation, must exist either in its Esse, as in the Plenitude, or in its Posse, or in the transitional state from the Posse to the Esse as a tendency in the cause and an approximation in the effect.

We recommence our progress, therefore, with the exemplification of this in the completion of the ⌈. . .⌉ idea of Gravity. We have already deduced from the influence the κοινον τι, not as good and divine but as evil divinely compelled into a symbol and image of [ƒ 10] the good. From this and from the evil in its own remaining nature, we have deduced the necessary co-existence both of the centrifugal and of the centripetal forces, and when we last ended we needed nothing but the circumference in order to fix the center, to fill the area, and consequently to compleat the idea of gravitation as one indeed in itself, but composite relatively to its causative antecedents. We have seen the influence of the divine distinction acting in the Self-Will as Self and for self, though by the inherent contradictoriness in all acts proportionately as they partake of Self, we have seen it baffling its own object and lost in the κοινον τι instead of becoming all as the all-appropriative [u]center. But[v] as surely as the influence is [ƒ 10ᵛ] divine, so must it in an equal measure create a direction that is divine; and having condescended to become, as it were, disguised and connatural with the Self, so must it compel the Self to work in it, and this alone suffices. At every point in the generation of the line centripetal or centrifugal, convergent or divergent, in every moment of the act of production a counter act ⟨co-exists⟩, modifying the former and yet incapable of neutralization or of neutralizing (for the reality of both is the God, in the one the God incarnate, in the other the God επιφανης, or super-apparent)—the result of which must necessarily be a motion cycloidal. For again observe that we are not speaking of two lines but of one and the same [ƒ 11] subject where, the forces divided among two or more several participants we ~~might deduce and~~, these of course, therefore, finite and exhaustible powers, we might deduce either Rest or a movement diametrical. But being forces of one

---

[t] ms: That   [u–v] ms: center but

Subject, nothing remains but the line having a tendency at once to flee from and, fleeing, to return upon itself, and yet from the other equally necessary products, and as far as the conditions of multeity ⟨as far as⟩ realized by the distinctive[w] act during several subjects must be conceived, existing in their severalty with that degree of ever-promising yet never fixable reality which belongs to it; and therefore, as far as these severals are several, the straight lines must likewise be [*f 11*ᵛ] conceived as remanent. aAs far only as each has its real being in the others, or in other words, as the all of a multeity partakes of a whole, so far only can the circular motion be manifest. ~~Circular~~ Cycloidal form and cycloidal motion can appertain, therefore, to masses only, and though a mass be there, must be conceived an inherent tendency to such form and movement. Yet only in certain masses can it appear, namely in proportion to the degree and permanence with which each has its being in the other. But this is what we mean by ˣ*Organization*—theʸ abstraction, therefore, of organization, because its indefinite minimum. The tendency to gravity, or the act of Amassment, is a tendency to organization; and [*f 12*] at that point in which the tendency is matured into an apparent cycloidal form or movement, it is organisation in its minimum, and in this sense whatever may be predicated of a part appearing as a whole gravitated and gravitat~~ed~~ing to is predicable of Organization, and vice versa, the difference ever arising out of the degrees. In this sense only can we rightly understand and accede to the position of those philosophers who affirm the World organic, while at the same time we are equally instructed to guard against those extravagancies which, neglecting degrees and forgetting that, though organic, it is the minimum of organization, have raised it from a material mass to an all-perfect animal, yea, [*f 12*ᵛ] to a God among Gods. Having thus orientized our map and determined its different bearings with some thin outlines of its largest realms, we must return in order to fill it up; and our next investigation, therefore, will lead us back to the first twofold results of the act of contraction as modifying and modified by the attractive or appropriative force, namely the first gathering together as one and the first ejaculation, or occupation, of ⟨unfilled⟩ space, in which and in order to which we shall, if any where, discover the necessity and the nature, or genesis, of specific Gravity, and determine how far we may be enabled ⟨to evolve⟩ the apparently diverse elements without the all-explaining, because all sup[*f 13*]posing, doctrine einer ursprünglichen Diversität gewisser Grundstoffe.

ʷ Written over another word, now illegible   ˣ⁻ʸ ms: *Organization.*—The

(17)

[*]The point to which we have deservedly directed our watchful and almost fearful attentions has been hitherto, and must still continue, so to admit the divine influence as not to exclude the agency of nature, and on the other hand so to appropriate an agency in nature as not to convert it into self-sufficeingness and divinity. fFor our aim has been solution of the great problem by deductions from antecedents conditional or causative, and whether we turned [*f 13ᵛ*] God into the world or the world into God, this aim must have been baffled, for in both all antecedence is preprecluded, and even that analytic process which may give greater distinction, though no increase, to our knowledge, [and] may conduce to the clearness of our On-look, can in no way communicate Insight—even this analytic process, I repeat, must begin with mere facts unintelligible without containing any ground of their unintelligibility, inasmuch as, being many, they would be incapable of being resolved into One, for in the One only can the mind rest satisfied as rightfully incomprehensible because containing in itself the perfectly intelligible necessity of its incomprehensibility. In other words, the absolutely first [*f 14*] can have no plural as the first, and cannot therefore be predicated of the many. The truth, therefore, must be somewhere in the interstate between both these errors, and in determining the self-justifying proportion of these agencies, we have felt and made ourselves deliberately aware that the great difficulty of our whole task subsists. It does not meet us here, now, for the first time, and the principle, therefore, by which we have before encountered it, and with seeming success, must once more be submitted to a fresh test of its applicability. We took that essential characteristic attribute of the divine agent which, without consideration of degree or specific nature in the material to be influenced thereby, was inseparable [*f 14ᵛ*] from the admission of the agency in all cases, and again of this very attribute we restricted ourselves to that idea which was the necessary accompaniment of its presence merely as its presence—that which was common to all possible objects and cases. Thus as the condition of the metastasis, or transition, we took the divine will as the spirit as Love, and we sought for that essential of Love which is universally involved in the conception, and we found this in a Going forth, in an act of appropriation—not

[*] [*The following quotation is written in three rows along the left margin of f 13, perpendicularly to the beginning of the text of § 17:*] (Lucret. Liber II)

Id facit exiguum clinamen principiorum,
Nec regione loci certa, nec tempore certo.

that this was by any means an adequate exponent of Love; on the contrary, that which is left unsupplied is incomparably more important than that which is brought forward. But we remembered that the Spirit [*f 15*] of Love had been already defined for us; that the subject then before us was not properly speaking the Spirit of Love, but the influence of that spirit on the Love-less, and consequently partaking ⟨only⟩ o̶n̶f that essential accompaniment of love of which the agency of love was the indispensable condition of its having *z*existed—but this being granted, could*a* yet be conceived to exist without love, or even to have its immediate cause and antecedent in the contrary principles of Self lust. The spirit of love goeth forth still to find and to constitute its self in another as another, the prochoresis which saith "et alter" and the perichoresis which again refers the alter to the "idem". In the contrary state the self will of itself, merely and [*f 15ᵛ*] helplessly potential, yet in the first nascent reality communicated to it, or rather in it—this self will too goeth forth and to appropriate, but not by the constituting of another as itself, but in order by destruction of the alterity, to appropriate for itself. Thus we were able intelligibly to introduce the divine agency without at once substituting a new material, which we should have done by accepting the presence of the divine Will in the plenitude of its energy, therefore as the sole agent, and therefore again as both material and agent—an identity, in short, of the operans and the operatum, the opus operans of a self-perplexing Pantheism. Instead of creation and a world we should have substituted the eternal act [*f 16*] by which the divine Will is evermore self-perfected.

The same form we adopted in the first introduction of the divine Will as the Logos, or intelligens and intelligible distinction, ὸς νουν και νουμενος νοητα ποιει. As equally with the former presence of the divine Will, it too, like the former, must have been a realizing presence; as an accessional act of the divine Will, it must have been followed by an accession of reality; as the Logos, and so far distinguishable from the preceding act, this accessional reality must partake of distinction, yet inasmuch as both are the ineffable unity of the divine Will, it is impossible that either should [*f 16ᵛ*] contravene the product of the other, and lastly, with respect to both alike our immediate subject, neither the Spirit nor the w̶Word in their own proper being, but the influences of the same on a material self-alienated and contrarient. What, then, in that accompaniment of the idea of the divine distinction which, inseparable from that idea, is yet capable of being conceived as co-existing without the

z–a ms: existed (but this being granted) could

plenitude of that attribute to which it is nevertheless perforce adherent?*b* In the plenitude itself it is form, yea, forms numberless above number that distinguishes without dividing, individualizes without disturbance of unity, and appropriates without exclusion each every where, and every where [*f 17*] all in each "εφολοφυης*c* μερισμος και αμειριστος".*d* Here the "αμειριστος" is the incommunicable characteristic of the Logos as God, or the divine alterity, the "μερισμος" is the characteristic accompaniment in the *e*divine. We*f* have the intelligible limit, but at once voερον και νοητον, intellectual at that the same time that it is intelligible. Remove, therefore, from the idea of a comprehension that in every form of alterity includes the whole as the identity—remove whatever is incommunicably divine and we have in its nascent and conditional quantity Distinction proportional to the *g*eExclusion. But*h* an exclusive comprehension is the *i*same—with a contraction a limit that appropriates by rejection [*f 17v*] is a tendency to division, for it is a self-separation, and the division and the separateness are as actual, and likewise as unreal, as the self which divides and separates—as far as the self alone should be considered, they must, like that self, be merely potential, a*j* perpetual act of annihilation;*k* as far as that self is influenced and proportionally realized by the source of all *l*reality, so far must these too be real, and the medium is given us in all the different degrees of subjective reality, and like these varying from the flitting phantasm to the ⌈. . .⌉ phaenomenon common to all material beings as far as they remain material.*m*

In these principles we have [*f 18*] hitherto succeeded in the intellectual construction of the attractive and contractive forces, of the centripetal and centrifugal, of the vibrating straight line, its introition and extroition in the Self-will, and the center as the κοινον τι determined by the circumference as the continual process of the redemptive and revocative influence. We have clearly seen likewise that the κοινον τι can never become the identity, of course can never be self-sufficing, but must still suppose its reality else where, the very essence of the Self-wills being μερισμος, partition, and consequently it being the necessary predicate of them that they can never constitute other than a part which may relatively and in a secondary sense be called [*f 18v*] a whole but never can be the Whole. Again, we have seen that the Self-Wills, in proportion to the grade of their realisation, have become realizing, for this is the

---

b Question mark inserted   *c* This word written again at the top right corner of f 17
         d Quotations marks in ms   *e–f* divine we
    g–h eExclusion but   *i–j* In the ms this passage contains no punctuation
    k Colon in the ms   *l–m* In the ms this passage contains no punctuation

essence of Will—[n]even in the apostacy it realised its own destruction indestructibly. They must therefore have realized their own struggles and opposition, though with some correspondence to the low degree of their reality, and the exponent of this we find—and only there can find—in the ideas [of] transitory, temporary place—in short in the ever-varying forms [? as] Auseinanderheit. It followed, therefore, that the process partaking at once of the divine and of the apostolic must have been progressive, not co-instantaneous; amassment must [*f 19*] have preceded amassment and struggle have counteracted struggle in order to the [. . .] production of an equilibrium relatively permanment. But there is yet another necessary predicate of the multeity involved in its essential contrariety to the plenitude, viz. that the idem still excludes the alter, that B β cannot be $\alpha = aA$ and because it is B—this is the law announced by Leibnitz and implied in the adage "quicquid est simile non est idem", or "no two things can have the same predicates". [. . .] We have now but one other recollection to make in order to be prepared for the next step in our ascent, but this is indeed a subtle form of thought, hard to be fixed, [*f 19ᵛ*] though it is easy to see into the impossibility of its being otherwise—I refer to the unsubstantial, unactual, merely potential nature of the Self in the Self-will. The Will is indeed imperishable, unchangeable, but the Self neither is or can be aught but a phantom, a mere subjective phaenomenon in the proper product of guilt realizing itself by delusion, and to the contemplation all our ideas of matter [o]correspond. We[p] predicate a oneness only conditionally, relatively, transiently, almost arbitrarily;[q] that which now appears as many, we see by the inherent tendency of appropriation to lose each, the Self which it [? proe] tended to aggrandize and to be fused into. [*f 20*] One which remains One till, the copulative act overpowered by an opposite force, it contracts again into an innumerable multeity yon mass of iron fluid—who shall say what [r]point is[s] different? who, in any point in the minutest filing of the mass congealed, shall point out any mark of oneness which does not apply equally to the whole mass of the melted metal?[t] Or let the contractive power have acted throughout on that filing so that it shall be an axyd throughout—who shall count, whose imagination shall follow its ineffable multeity to an ultimate part which is no longer a relative whole?[u]

[n] Dash inserted
[o-p] ms: correspond we
[q] No punctuation in ms
[r-s] The numerals "2" and "1" are written above these words, probably indicating that their order is to be reversed, though the reversal makes no sense
[t] Question marks inserted
[u] Question mark inserted

Now if we combine these two principles first—the Leibnitzian law of [*f 20ᵛ*] exclusion by ~~pr~~ occupation, or the material incompatibility of alterity with identity, and 2^*dly* the changeable form and extent of Self, the nature of which may likewise be deduced from the necessity of the co-existence of two powers, the nature, namely, of the multeity and ⟨that of⟩ the divine influences—both, tho' in very different forms and degrees, realizing and effective—by combining these we arrive at an insight into the nature, causes, and necessity of specific gravity in general. We see that general gravitation and specific gravity necessarily presuppose each other: it remains for us, therefore, to try whether with any proportionate success we can particularize both. That there must be many masses, we [*f 21*] know; that these masses, because different, must have specific gravity, we see; and we see no ground but rather a presumption to the contrary that each mass sh^d not contain differentials as its components, and yet maintaining their differences for themselves, though equalized imperfectly in the common gravitation, or the specific gravity of the mass itself. This must therefore form the subject of our next enquiry. We have an indeterminate determination. We have now to seek for a determination of the determination, eine Bestimmung der Bestimmtheit, and in this we shall find, if any where, either as consequent or accompaniment, [? all] the other imaginable diffe[*f 21ᵛ*]rences of matter corporealized.

(*c*) Disbound notebook containing three sewn gatherings, 37 leaves, 183 × 115 mm; wm "C & S | 1815". The text, in sections numbered 18–20, is written in ink in JHG's hand on boths sides of ff 1–33, ff 34–7 being blank.

DATE. No earlier than 1817 (the year C met JHG), probably 1820s.

[*f 1*]   (18)

In our last disquisition we deduced the necessity of Specific Grav~~itaty~~ in general, or rather we shewed that all gravitation was of necessity *relative*, and of course the same mass, the gravitation of which relative to its own parts was general gravitation, was specific relatively to some other body; and we may now further observe that this is the only sense in which we can understand the old paradox of a circle ~~whose~~ the center ⟨of which⟩ is every where and its circumference no where. But understanding it with the correction of the quid pro quo in which most of these paradoxes originate, viz. its being predicated of the divine Being when in fact it expresses only the inherent imperfection of matter, and is predicable only of the material world. Indeed we may almost venture to establish it as a general rule that every position in any degree intelligible [*f 1*ᵛ] which yet the mind as impelled to express by a contradiction in terms belongs to the multeity or its products, the transfer of which to the deity constitutes the first, midst, and last of the errors of Pantheism in both of its two forms: Theocosmism, according to which God is the world, and Cosmotheism, according to which the world is God.

In order to elucidate the particular necessity, in order, as it were, to apply specifically the general necessity of specific gravity, in order to substitute for the position "something of the kind must be" a reason why it is so as it is in any particular system, we must leap back a few spaces, viz. to thate point of contraction, the one result of which alone we have been evolving. We have seen the actual and the potential changing places, the actual seeking to find a staple, as it were, [*f 2*] or centre of reality in a Self, and by that very act becoming potential, which under the universal influence of the all-realizing Will must give some proof of reality, namely manifestation, and yet from its own inherent imperfection can manifest itself only as a striving, the permanence of which, itself never more than merely relative and comparative, is not self-supplied but wholly dependent from without or on another—such is Gravity. But on the other hand, and as a necessary consequence of the first, the potential becomes actual, and yet the position [. . .] is difficult and perplexing, not so much from its subtlety as from the nature of words (a position, therefore, which being, to borrow a phrase from Sᵗ Augustine, being silent we understand, but seem to be grasping at the air as soon as we attempt to communicate)—but yet, I say, the inter[*f 2*ᵛ]change is such that it is still the actual which becomes potential, while vice versa, that which becomes actual is still and retains the character of the potential. Thus our conception of ⟨material⟩ presence of substance, as still found in Weight, and with this are linked the appearances of contact and all approximation. The relations, therefore, of distance and of all extroition, not supposing the change or removal of the former, fallᵛ under the category of light in its widest sense. The truth of this we may prove to ourselves experimentally when we say that the sun sends forth its confluence, gives outwardness and distance to its potentiality: we have the conception "Light"; but if we should say, with the Newtonians, that myriads of corpuscles are shot forth ejaculated from the sun instead of light, we immediately ask where the light comes from [*f 3*] by which they are rendered visible, instead of light—we have particles whose visibility presupposes light, and therefore become the very problem of which they were to be the solution. In the same manner a small degree

---

ᵛ ms: falls

of self attention will convince us that we employ a substitute and not a synonyme when, instead of saying, "how sweetly that rose smells", we should exclaim, "what a prodigious number of particles of smell have flown off from yonder rose". In the latter case we find that we have not moved a single step forwards, that "a particle of smell" are words without meaning, and if we correct the phrase into "odorific particles", the problem remains unchanged in its essentials, and we need only generalize the term "rose" and the term "particle" into the higher formula "odorific body" to find that our position would stand thus: we[w] do not smell [$f3^v$] an odorific body because it is an odorific body that we smell, for it is self evident, first, that what ever difficulty adheres to the notion of smelling a rose, or a rose being odorific, must equally apply to the smelling a particle, or a particle being odorific; 2dly, that[x] in both cases alike we are at last constrained to apprehend it as a *potence*, or [? act] quality, of something becoming extroitive without becoming substantial, or self-substantiated, and this is what we meant by the potential becoming actual without losing the character of potentiality. Here, however, two cautions may not be altogether superfluous: first, that our position is wholly unconcerned with and unaffected by the experimental facts by which the odorific substance may be separated from other substances with which it had co-existed, whether organically or by juxta[$f4$]position, for these substances so separated (as, for instance, the civet from the civet cat)[y] stands in place of the former terms—whatever we have said of the rose, we have to repeat totidem verbis of the rose water or attar of roses—2dly, that[z] the whole concerning which we treat is[a] relative, and that A is never so far opposed to B but that whatever is predicated of the one within[b] a new relation becomes[c] predicable of the other, yea, as in the plus and minus of electricity, or in the acid and alkalies of chemistry, each is both. Illustration (Hyd. + sulphur). But by the latter caution we resume our argument, namely by an inference or deduction which the too exclusive habit of contemplating all things in Trichotomy, as Thesis, Antithesis, and Synthesis, has it should seem withdrawn from the contemplation of some recent and active philosophers. [$f4^v$] From the relatively interchangeable and amphoteric nature of all material objects considered as actual or potential, there arises the necessity of contemplating them as at the same time gradative, ~~an~~ or susceptible of degrees which in their own nature et secundum legem continui ought to be

---

[w] ms: We   [x] ms: That
[y] Parentheses inserted   [z] ms: That
[a] ms: are   [b] ms: with in
[c] ms: become

infinite, but here as every where an infinite under the form of multeity, consequently an infinite below number; and this, in fact, seems the defect of the Leibnitzian reasoning, that his system did not comprehend the origin and true character of the merely potential, in consequence of which he ever speaks of continuity as actual, whereas it is no case predicable but of and in proportion to the potential of the Deity or the [d]plenitude. We[e] can never affirm it without at the same time affirming its contrary, ex.gr. ολοφυης μερισμος and μεριστος. We must therefore contemplate this [*f* 5] as actualized by number or the power of number, and in the continuity thus counteracted, in the multeity so far realized, seek for the mixed nature of [f]degrees, herein,[g] perhaps, following the course of the Pythagorean School in their doctrine of living and causative numbers. Let us, then, recollect the material ⟨which we have⟩ separately prepared: we have relative Opposites, each of which not only contains potentially the quality of the other, but ⟨may⟩ actually exert it at the same time if only under a different [h]relation. We[i] have likewise a ground of continuity, but this in the potential only; as the potential we have likewise a ground of distinction from the influence of the essentially actual: positive discontinuity cannot arise, for how could discontinuity arise from continuity? Still less could it arise from the divine logos, who is indeed all distinction, but eternally [*f* 5ᵛ] and indivisibly One; and the result must partake of both, can only be semblance of discontinuity, discontinuity relative to the Self, the distinction of which as the εσθλον τι is the pravity—derived, therefore, from the reality—[j]gives to it by the act of the Logos, and yet a living and articulated connexion a distinction without intervacuity, or total division in relation to the whole. Now whatever is distinct and at the same time participant is, and gives the definition of, a *Degree*. The interchangeable thesis and antitheses of the material world must necessarily contain a range of intermediates: these cannot be infinite, for that would either be the plenitude or the continuity, in both cases destructive of the conception of Degree, and in both cases alike contra Hypothesim. Nothing remains but determinate number, for which no other reason can ever appear [*f* 6] assignable but the numbers themselves, inasmuch as these are the divine influence and the representatives of the divine power, not contemplated in its own perfection but as a self Will so influenced. The number there being = the Logos, to ask any other reason would be the same as to ask a reason for Reason itself.

[d-e] ms: plenitude we   [f-g] degrees. Herein
[h-i] ms: potential we   [j] Dashes inserted

(19)

We have never been suffered to forget that we have a twofold agency scarcely more diverse relatively to the agents than inseparable in the act itself, ⟨the agency of⟩ each being in a certain sense the condition of the agency of the other. These are the Eternal and the Temporal, or successive, and both must have their correspondents or exponents in a true system of philosophy. To the Eternal belongs Science; to the Successive ⟨belongs⟩ History, [*f* 6ᵛ] while the Synthesis of the two is Philosophy under the preponderance of intellectual activity, and Religion relatively ad totum hominem. But as the "qui bene docet bene distinguit" is a truth likewise cogent, the scientific and historic, though co-ordinate, in fact must alternate in the exposition. Our first division, which we have entitled "Stasis", ~~as~~ ⟨and elsewhere⟩ the "Plenitude", is both eminenter comprehending but likewise transcending both. The second, ~~wei~~.e. the Apostasis, is for us purely historic, the possibility by [? ~~and~~] which is the scientific part having been established in the first. With the Metastasis commences the historical condition of the Historic, and the ~~philosophic~~ ⟨scientific⟩ condition of the future scientific. With the Logos as the distinctive influence, the historic for itself appears as the necessary antecedent to the scientific as the realizing principle of science, which without that history must have begun in and with mere abstractions, or with generalizations [*f* 7] that deceptively conceal the à posteriori in the forms of the à priori. The genesis of Light, its separation from darkness, the formation of the Aether, the arising of the Powers of Attraction, the Centrifugal, the Centripetal, general and specific Gravity, together with the origin of the circumference ~~and~~, the center with the convergence and divergence of the lines that actualize the area, are all so far historical that they are all alike successive, though still retaining as the bond and property common ~~to~~ both to the Historic and to the scientific, as both appertaining to a system of Philosophy, namely the quality of Productiveness; for ~~these~~ it treats of "the generations of the heaven and the earth and the days in which God the mighty One created them". Now, then, the scientific must ascend the chair and provide for intelligibility of the following History by laying its foundations and furnishing its implements by the evolution of the [*f* 7ᵛ] Possible and first of the first created, namely Light. We have traced it successively from 1ᵏ Outwardness, 2 Potentiality, 3 Potentiality actualized—from these in conjunction with the results, the necessity of which was involved in the act and the con-

---

ᵏ This and the following two numbers are superscript in the ms, but lowered here to avoid being mistaken for footnotes

dition and antithetic accompaniments of the act of contraction, we educe Space, which in itself represents the correlative or objective conception of ⟨pure⟩ Potentiality. But Light, we have seen, is Potentiality actualized, yet so as to return its native essential and specific character as potential: if, therefore, it must be present in space without being space, it must have relations to space, and yet it cannot, in the corporeal sense of the word, be said to fill it without ceasing altogether to be potential—the only conceivable is that of penetrating space without filling ⟨it. And⟩[m] what more, we may ask, can the adherents[n] of the Newtonian corpuscular scheme intellectually mean by the picture of Light as incomparably less than [*f* 8] the smallest interspaces ⟨between the component particles⟩ of the densest and most cohesive masses? This, then, we must take as the 4th power of light, or shall we say with more severe accuracy, the 5th which; nor will it repent us on so important a subject again to re-enumerate these attributes:

~~Light~~ Attributes of Light by Opposition

1st, Light as opposed to Darkness, i.e. Distinction ⌈. . .⌉ ⟨opposed to⟩ the Multeity.

2^d, Outwardness per se not as but as the conditional antecedent of ~~an Outward~~ ⟨Outness⟩, i.e. intervention of Space between surfaces as opposed to an inward, an in-ness ~~being a~~ necessarily being a mere imagination as incapable of material realization. The second, then, outwardness as opposed to Inwardness.

3dly, And as far as it relates to the material, it is Potentiality as opposed to Actuality, but [*f* 8^v]

4^thly, and in its relation to the realizing power of the divine distinctive influence, it is Potentiality actualized, in opposition to actuality potentialized (v. last Disquisition).[o]

5^thly, And as the consequence of the former, in conjunction with the accompaniments and conditions of the former, it is the penetration of space in equal opposition both to space, i.e. mere potentiality, and to the filling of space, i.e. corporeal actuality.

6^thly, Self-projection, as opposed to the Vis Inertiae, this is proved first by light's being a primary power which in order of thought is antecedent to all the powers, that only excepted which is baffled by equilibrium, namely the Aether, but this being, therefore, as far as it is the material of all, παν ὑλη, the prima nuda mera[p], the Panhyle—[*f* 9]materia to which all schemes of philosophy have either come or led—is merely passive, [and] consequently no ⟨active⟩ power can be attributed to it without a contradiction in terms

7^{ly}, If ⟨spontaneously⟩ self-projected, it must likewise possess an analogous, or rather correlative, power as the exponent of its energy in alterum, for a realizing power, as hath been already demonstrated, must exist proportional to the reality by the essential nature of ~~the~~ Will; but the Self expresses at once an act and object of the minimum of reality, [so] that, therefore, by which the alterity is re-introduced as the contrary direction to the former must express a proportionally greater reality, and therefore a proportionally greater realizing power, though in part—or it may be on the whole—it should produce an equilibrium to itself by powers which, in consequence of its existence, arise in its opposite. As the correlative to the αυτο ενεργεια, [$f9^v$] it possesses, therefore, the power of evocation ab altero which we here take, ~~f~~thus generally [? ~~will~~] [. . .] deferring the statement both of the "What" is evoked, the "How", and the modification. It is sufficient for our present purpose that evocation is and alone is the antithetic co-existent of spontaneous projection as attributes of the same agent, in proof of which we are required only to point out the amphoteric, or attribute which is the common essential of both—now this is manifestation, but ~~that which~~ A having its essence in B, which is likewise the essence of C, and being yet differenced from C by relation, only finds in C its correlative.

9^{ly}, By the law of continuity + distinction, as explained in our last disquisition, arises the necessity of Gradation, but gradation is two kinds: 1st, it^q is applicable to the products of [$f 10$] two opposite powers, these products partaking of each in ~~diff~~ all realizable proportions—th~~ie~~ese, therefore, we shall represent by a perpendicular line, or the line of longitude, and entitled "*grades of subordination*". Or the gradation may consist of the distinct attributes of One Power which, [? ~~omitting~~] ⟨resigning⟩ the ⟨here⟩ ambiguous term "Degree" or "Grade" to the former, we shall simply term "Co-ordinates". Whatever,therefore, are co-ordinates of Light must be conceived of as attributes, and will be found indeed contained in, and if I may so express it, the historic acts of the attributes already enumerated. As this, therefore, is, as it were, the Anastomosis belonging equally to the scientific which has constituted the business of the present Disquisition, and of the Historic which is to follow, we shall make it a Disquisition of itself.

---

^{q} ms: It

[*f 10ᵛ*]   (20)

We recommence with the character which Light acquires by its opposition to the κοινον τι, or tendency toward the center, which, being in all, can therefore be in none, i.e. can be conceived of only as a Place borrowing all its power from a tendency that can never be perfected, for in the place itself the power altogether ceases, having indeed become evanescent in its nearer approaches. This, as the opposite of Light, we have designated as the "Actual potentialized": Light, therefore, as its opposite must be the "Potential actualized". But it will be convenient for a more orderly insight to go farther back—now the first opposite of Light is Darkness, from which it is separated, but Darkness is, 1ˢᵗ, *Chaos*, that is, before the separation of Light—2ᵈ, inʳ the Separation* it becomes Aether—3ᵈ, inˢ the act of separation in which it is Outwardness without Outness, it divides into the matter of Light and Aether, the latter being equally contradistinguished from Light and [*f 11*] Matter as matter *of*— in other words, it is opposed to Light as Darkness, and it is opposed to the matter of Light, as matter indeterminateᵗ to a determinate matter.

Yet as the actual, namely the material, of the phaenomenon in its antithesis to the φαινον, though the actual potentialized, the matter of Light itself must have a correspondent realization. Now this can be no other than a plenum ~~from~~ unresisting from its passivity, i.e. its potentialization herein contrarient to the plenitude, or active plenum, unresisting from interpenetration. Now the unresisting and passive plenum is Aether which, therefore must not only have pre-existed as the conditional material of Light, but must co-exist with it as the matter of Light—it must co-exist, I say, with Light and with matter as the matter of Light, consequently it must exist as separate and Aether per se ~~for it is~~. Now this, again, is imaginable only as aetherial interstate and circumjacency. SPACE is common to this Aether with whatever else hath Potentiality; but interstate it has [*f 11ᵛ*] not, but IS. It IS the space which it constitutes but not fills.

It follows, therefore, that Light in its very first Power (= Light (1)ᵘ negatively causes Amassment by production of circumjacency. Its second act, therefore (= Light (2),ᵛ which has been shewn to be the force of contraction, is inter-distinctive and can only have its effects sub-phaenomenalized by a partial transfer, as it were, of the circumjacens, a

* [*Written at the bottom of f 10ᵛ:*] The state immediately antecedent which is a condition of the separation.

ʳ ms: In   ˢ ms: In   ᵗ ms: in determinate
ᵘ Superscript number in ms   ᵛ Superscript number in ms

subtraction therefrom and translocation of the subtracted to the circumjectum. But this, again, involves the necessity of a correspondent division—correspondent, I say, because the Aether itself, or the circumjacens, may be filled but can never be thought of as destroyed; and on a mistaken view of this truth rests the doctrine of a v[. . .]^w as the necessary condition of motion.

But this interdistinction is another, or additional, act of realization. In order to the clear intellection of which we must speak our former proofs that both the attractive power which belonged to matter in the conjoint reali[f 12]zation and baffling of which, ⟨the [? Chaos]⟩ became Aether, and which by the genesis of Light and of the consequent contractive force became astringent or attractive ad intra—we must recall, I say, the position that this attractive ~~power~~ force and the contractive are forces of the same power as the immediate agent, although that it is a power having these forces to the influence of an agency altogether diverse. From this too we deduced ~~the~~ two forms in which ~~alone~~ the co-inherence of ~~the~~ each in the other and the opposition of each to the other can be balanced and represented, namely Alternation, whenever each is taken in its totality as the opposite of the other, and Gradation, when both are conceived either as equal or under the predominance of some one. Again, when we conceive either of any two opposites in its totality, it can yet not remain in any form of absolute simplicity, for it is essentially relative and therefore modifiable according to its relations. Now this mark of the multeity, which in the language of the Mystics [f 12^v] would be called its "Mother", we can only, as hath been before shewn, designate as co-ordinates, and hence arises a new form, that of Subordinates differing from degrees in this point. ~~That we conceive~~ Let the subordinate be X, let Z signify the one opposite in its totality, and Y the other. Now when X expresses the ~~cha~~ essential character of Z, but under the predominance of and procession from Y, X is the subordinate of Y, for we do not here conceive any mixture of Z and Y, but the striving of each totally to express its Self as the whole—for instance, Gravitation is co-inherent in Light, and Light in Gravitation, and the attempt to manifest this co-inherence constitutes subordinates, even as the revealing of the muteity in the unity hath constituted co-ordinates.

Thus, then, we have a fourfold form: 1st, Alternation—2^d, Gradation, or varying proportion—3^d, Co-ordination—and 4th, Subordination. We ⟨may now⟩ return to our ^{x}subject. The^y attractive and contractive are forces of One Power; they must therefore [f 13] have, or appear in, the

---

^{w} Word obscured by an ink blot $^{x-y}$ ms: subject the

form of Alternation. But it is in Alternation, which necessarily partakes of both the forces, and therefore belongs to the second form, or that of Gradation materially considered, and is alternate, as the word itself implies, under the necessary form of Time or Succession from the moment that the first force became real by the production and realization of the second: neither can be conceived wholly without the ^{z}other. When,^{a} therefore, we say that the attractive must now alternate in consequence of the contractive, having arrived at its maximum of energy, we mean that the attractive commences its predominance, subordinating but not excluding the opposite ^{b}power. But^c the attractive + contractive, considered as simply balanced, or rather interpenetrated, will give as the conception of Cohesion generally, which equally implies the body's cohering, which presupposed contraction, or tendency to individualization and the cohesion of the [$f\,13^v$] bodies, which of course is an attraction appropriative each of the other as a tendency to overcome that of individualization. If, now, we take this secondary power as the force of cohesion, and subordinate to it while we add to it the force of contraction, so that the result shall be the opposite of the contractive, as is here required, we shall have the force of Dilation. On the other hand, if we reverse this process, and uniting subordinate, the cohesion, to the contractive, we shall have the repulsive, the force of repulsion, not ad alterum as a power extra se, in opposition to the appropriative attraction, which latter has been the ground of many errors, but, if opposite at all, to the attraction which in consequence of the genesis of contraction has assumed the form of astringency, i.e. attractio intra se non ad extra. The two proper opposites, or primary roles, are Attraction and Contraction; the other powers are rather disparate than opposite, and if opposite, yet not to the primary but to the secondary [$f\,14$] and composite powers. Thus the repulsive is the predominance of the contractive, but yet not the domination, but as it were a precedent or governor limited by its subject, which limitation, however, could not be conceived of as enduring, for the greater would altogether suppress the lesser were it not further modified by the co-existence of an opposite state in which the lesser exists as the ^{d}superior. But^e as hath been shewn, what ~~coincidence~~ exists with, yet not as existing in, can only exist in difference of time or in difference of place, and if not in the one, therefore in the other. We may now proceed to the HISTORY, and find that the alternation which corresponds to the Contraction must necessarily be an act of Dilation, or of the dilative force. But this dilative force is not, as hath been demonstrated, the proper

---

$^{z-a}$ ms: other when $^{b-c}$ ms: power but $^{d-e}$ ms: superior but

Opposite of the contractive, for it is not a primary pole and cannot therefore be directly opposed to a primary pole. It^f must therefore [$f14^v$] partake of the properties supposed and presupposed in the contraries in so far it partakes of the contractive as contractive, that is, counteracts the astringency; and in counteracting the same, it therefore opposes the constitutive of astringency, namely that of seeking itself inward, or the centripetal power; and in partaking of the contractive, it partakes likewise of that power which was the antecedent occasion of the contraction, namely the tendency towards another, or the centrifugal power. If, therefore, we combine with these a power of cohesion with its antecedents, as far as they are found in the attraction or the ⟨appropriative⟩ tendency ad intra, we shall arrive at a product in each property of which all the component forces are characterized, and which, therefore, from the nature of human language we cannot describe accurately without approaching to contradictions; for [$f15$] it must go forth, and yet it must remain, and it can only go forth as far as it ^{g}remains. It^h must increase the attraction appropriative and dead to destroy the interspaces, the results of the contractive force, and yet it must diminish the cohesive power in proportion as it increases the continuity; it must at once constitute and yet counteract the particularity; it must be characteristically appropriate, with a tendency to become and, as it were, to merge itself in the common. In short, it can be only understood as the union, or rather as a tertium aliquid, arising from the union of the κοινον τι and of the opposite, or circumferential, powers. It is a product, too, of powers, and yet a power in itself: as a power it cannot be a phaenomenon, and yet as a product it must be conceived as a something having powers as a subphaenomenon. All these properties are presented to us [$f15^v$] in the Element, or whatever other name we may choose, of Warmth. And in this, which may well be called the first-born of light and the aetherial darkness, must be supposed to exist, wherever the parents exist—it is the subelement, or the intermediate, between the elementary forces and the materiae determinatae, or elementary products of the elementary forces. But on the present step of our ascent we must trace it as a ~~power~~ ⟨co-ordinate⟩ of light inasmuch as^i

---

^{f} ms: it

$^{g-h}$ ms: remains it

^{i} The text breaks off here, and the following parenthesis has been inserted in pencil in the same hand as the note written inside the front cover of the notebook containing Frag (*b*) (see the headnote to that fragment): "(n.b. *Spirit, Love*)"

[*f 16*]   *Recapitulation*, or Catalogues of Acts and their Results.

1̶ˢᵗ   I

α) Lust of Attraction, i.e. of Intussusception of Alterity into a Self. The blind striving of a part to BE as a Self, and yet to HAVE the whole in and belonging to itself. The perpetual act of Self-destruction by essential contraction in the act of Self-affirmation.

β) Result—As a faint attempt, yet the best in our power to ~~convey~~ suggest an apprehension of confusedness at once without unity and without interdistinction, we pluralize the result under the name of "Attractions appropriative" blankly and essentially potential.

γ. Result (2.ʲ το αλλογον, αζωον. αθεον. Το ανυ του ενος, αναριθμον, ανταριθμον. Multeity with privation of number: CHAOS.

                                       II

α. Inceptive Actualization by the prae-realizing momentum of the [*f 16ᵛ*] divine Will as divine, i.e. essentially causative of reality.

β. Result. Inceptive transition from confused Allness to integral parts, the rudimental embryons, as it were, of distinguishable Self-Wills.

γ) In and with this momentum, and not as a different act, but yet to be distinguished in it rather than from it, the equal communication of One through All by the divine Will as Love, Life, the Spirit.

δ) Result as combined with β. Inceptive transition from boundless multeity to Totality.

ε) Result (2.ᵏ Inception of communicability, i.e. ⟨(1 ground or antecedent possibility⟩ of action, recipiency, and reaction.

ζ) Result (3.ˡ We had here to seek for some property of love and of the Spirit which could not but be in whatever the influence of the Spirit acted, and we found this as Attraction appropriative actualized in each in the form of a GOING-FORTH, for the προχωρησις is, as it were, the outward [*f 17*] character of the Spirit.

η) Result (4.ᵐ But this influence in the subject of the influence must be modified by the nature of the subject. iIn the present case it must be such as can be conceived of as belonging to an apostate Self-Will, a blind coveting an uncoiling and distending enmity, and thus we now, for the first

---

ʲ Superscript in ms   ᵏ Superscript in ms
ˡ Superscript in ms   ᵐ Superscript in ms

iline, recognize the necessity and origin of the existence of two opposite tendencies in the substratum of one Power. This, however, is not yet Polarity itself but the ground of Polarity, as indeed whatever is spoken of in this division, namely the Metastasis or μεθοδος, is transitional and preparatory.

θ) Result (5.[n] The self-Will as the material subject must be conceived of as impelled by Love, as a Power diverse therefrom and not as properly partaking of its inwardness, namely of the Love of Love. It is actuated by the Spirit, but not transmuted or dis-selfed. Heterogeneous from the Spirit, it partakes only of the direction of the Spirit: it is the dry leaf that [*f 17ᵛ*] moves through and with the motion of the air, but can neither inhale nor assimilate it. The spirit of God moved *upon* the surfaces of the indistinctions. The total result, therefore, of the twofold and diverse agency is intelligible only as a Going-forth against.

ι) Result (6.[o] But the same direction with the same force, the same in kind and the same in degree, is communicated to all. In the very moment, therefore, that the powers are actualized, they are balanced and thus suspended and, as it were, entranced. Hence, totally and exhaustively acting in the construction and continuance of the equilibratio, they can [? stand][p] only in the relation of other passiveness to whatever is not comprehended in the Equilibrium. Observe, however, that we speak of a relative negation, not of a pure vacuity of power, not of utter privation. It is not, as it was in the Chaos, essentially potential and unactual, but an actuality alter per alterum, or [*f 18*] antedating a metaphor from space; it is an actuality potentialized ab extra, and therefore fitliest characterized as the material of appropriative attraction.

κ) The conjoint Result is the μετακοσμησις of Chaos, the γενεσις of the AETHER

λ) The Chaos became Aether, and the capacious and capable Aether was the work of God, the Spirit. It was the breath of God breathed on the closed eyelids of the darkness; it was the precursive hush that, brooding the restless spasms of the death-throe into the smoothness of sleep, made the death and the darkness parturient to the fiat of the heavenly Lucia. (*Corollary to Section II.*) Spiritus non desinit esse spiritus, articulatus licet atque etiam in articulatione inter Alia quasi verborum, complet spiritualiter et consiliat. The divine breath went forth before the Word, but the Word is not without the breath, but still accompanying, still followeth [*f 18ᵛ*] that which through and from it proceedeth evermore. And this important Truth we will bear in mind throughout our future progress, that

---

[n] Superscript in ms   [o] Superscript in ms   [p] Word crowded into the margin

the functions of the Word are distinguishable from those of the Spirit, but not separable, much less in opposition.

Section III

α) The Word went forth from God in the power of Distinction.

β) Result (1.*q* Outwardness as constituting and opposed to the conception and volition of Inwardness, but Outwardness without outness: as far as this moment is concerned, even as in all time and in all creaturely states, the inwardness is not In-ness but a vain striving toward the same, and in the highest evolution of the Selfish Powers a phantom, but a phantom self-necessitated.

γ) The inward existed only in the striving of the Will: that which is relatively only to this Striving outward is actually the Whole, but by combining, as in Section [*f 19*] II θ, the effect and the subject of the act, we obtain ~~in~~

δ) Result (2.*r* The matter of Light: Light as Matter and matter as Light.

ε) This Outward, we have said, is the actual whole, the actuality of the whole, but there was an opposite striving, and this the striving of a Will that had been suo determinato gradu realized, therefore, by the definition of Will, proportionally realizing. It must realize, therefore, but in this case it can only realize the potential. In constituting its reality it must by the same act ~~p~~totally potentialize it. But again, a reality from which all the Attributes of reality are withdrawn by anticipation—withdrawn and not merely held in suspense or frustrated, pro tempore et quam diù causa frustrantes in actu manent is the same as a reality that exists only in the conception ~~as~~, but in that conception as necessary, not only necessary as a conception but objectively, and yet again without any mark or [*f 19ᵛ*] or constituent of the objective or the actual, though it were only, as in Aether, an actual potentialized. We must find, therefore, a correspondent to a contradiction, a something that has all the character of nothing, a something whose whole being is in its cause; and this will be found to be the same as SPACE. Space therefore is the Result (3.

ζ) Light we have seen as the power of Distinction. But without a total re-willing of the Apostacy and its result, the Chaos into the divine Plenitude, which ⟨act⟩ we have demonstrated in our first Disquisitions to be the same as Annihilation, and that Annihilation impossible from the essential nature of the Will—the light must exist in opposition to a somewhat, which therefore must remain as the opposite of Light, for the ef-

---

q Superscript in ms   *r* Superscript in ms

fects must be correspondent to the causative agents. A total absolute distinction would not be [. . .] ⟨light⟩ but the power of light, the more than light, for [*f 20*] "the glory of God would lighten it and the lamb be the light thereof ".[s] But if not a total distinction, it must be a distinction *from* as well as in, and in this sense, and as the exponent of this truth, we will use (whether or no we so interpret) the words of the Mosaic Cosmogony, that the Word of God divided and separated the Light from the Darkness. Before the separation the Darkness was Chaos; as the immediate antecedent of the separation it became Aether; the actual separation, therefore, could only have been from the Aether. The Aether separated itself, the part became Light, the other part remained Aether. Strictly, therefore, may it now be called the remainder or residuum of Light. It follows, therefore, that we have as

η. Result (4.[r] Amassment as the consequence of Light and Aether, and the necessary opposition of one to the other. We may state the result, therefore, as twofold: the Circumjacens as ~~the~~ appropriate to the Aether, and the Circumjectum, [*f 20*[v]] or mass, as appropriate to the matter of Light. For the Light itself is not Deity, but the product of the Divine Influence in the Creature, and so must it ever be till the Creature or Natur— the terminations in both designating the future—the potential shall have be~~ca~~ome actual; total, Act.

θ. The attraction appropriative was a Going-forth with the Spirit, but yet against the Alterity. But blindly, indistinguishably by the force of the evil essence, the power of distinction has been superinduced, the outward has been opposed to the inward, and the phantom Self, or in-ness, hath been transferred to the latter. The appropriative attraction must therefore follow the transfer, and returning, the essence and the power have [? changed] or reversed the direction. It is still a Going and a Going in hostility, but it must be a Going from an hostile fleeing, enoying, [*f 21*] withholding. In other words, it is distinctly ⟨an attraction⟩ self-appropriative, and this we may aptly name "Astringency", or "astringent attraction".

Section IV

α. Thus we have the self-conversion of the appropriative into the astringent attraction—this in consequence of the Inwardness, which Inwardness had its occasion in the Outwardness, this Outwardness finally being specifically caused. Henceforward we will confine the term "Attraction"

---

[s] Closing quotation mark inserted   [r] Superscript in ms

to the appropriative Attraction and designate its opposite, namely Astringent Attraction, by the single term "astringency".

β. But as these are opposite forces of the same agent, we must for this cause only suppose a point of indifference or balance.

γ. But hard and especially obscure as the conception of Multeity is, purely potential as the ground of individuation is, as far as the unassisted agency of the individual is ⟨alone⟩ contemplated and phan[*f 21ᵛ*]tomastic, and mutable as the form of Self is and ever must be, having no reality but in the striving of thereafter—dark and difficult, I say, as these forms and tendencies are, yet their agency has been demonstrated as necessary, and their participation in every act incapable of being excluded. [? A] Self without Multeity, if the words meant anything, could be applicable only to God as the Divine Plenitude. But equally contradictory and baffling, still, we find a multeity without any form of Individuation, even as a Distinction OF, i.e. ab altero et diverso et quasi ab extra, without some form of individuation as the result or correlative. To apply this to § β.

If we begin with the conception of an individuum we find in the opposite forces of the individuum itself a mid-point, or balance of indifference, but in these very forces, in the grounds and conditions of their opposition, gradations, and alternation, we find that we have already contemplated the individuum as participial of multeity in itself, while that it is capable [*f 22*] of remaining for a moment—as far, namely, as it does remain—we have presupposed a multeity ab extra.

δ. Comprize, therefore, with the act and results of the individuum those of the multeity, both in and without that individual, and then in this ⟨moment of⟩ equilibrium, this mid-point of indifference of attraction and astringency, we shall have formed the genesis of *Cohesion*. Observe, too, that whatever varying conditions that may rise up before us in future shall have differenced the extent or gradation of the forces themselves, will effect an equal difference in the point of indifference, and we shall have so many sorts ~~of co~~ or degrees of cohesion.ᵘ In other words, the necessity of the multeity as the ground of the law of continuity pursues and overtakes us every where—in the lowest asylum we are driven to one state lower, nay, the more intense the ⟨creaturely⟩ unity or principle of individuation is, the more intense becomes the necessary act of its potentiality—the more intense, I say, [*f 22ᵛ*] the diversity of its poles, i.e. of its multeity. That which was the mid point of the line A——B, con-

---

ᵘ This sentence, which in the ms is unpunctuated except for the full stop, may have been intended as two sentences, the second beginning, "The extent or gradations . . ."

templated by itself, immediately becomes a line D——E, with F as the mid-point corresponding to the C, which it was in relation to A and B. The mid-point itself is essentially gradative, and Cohesion, without altering its common nature, is conceivable in all ⟨the⟩ forms of grades that are possible between the pure Idea ~~of individu~~ of an ultimate part and of an Allness exclusive of parts, the pure ideality of which is proved by the perfect sameness in substance in both. For a mere Atom, which is yet material, is nothing but a finite Allness, and vice versâ, a finite Allness is nothing but an ultimate part.

ε. Here we must endeavour to remove a difficulty which was probably owing in some measure to an oversight or insufficiency of a former disquisition. First of all, we had unnecessarily thrown in an occasion of perplexity by antedating the genesis of space [*f 23*] as a something having the attribute of nothing: this certainly should have waited for the genesis of the reflex, or self- distinctive power. As long as our objects were exhaustively employed in materializing, we should have found a full adequate in the Aether. 2^(DLY), we^v did not, perhaps, dwell sufficiently on the merely inceptive and fluxional nature of the act of the Spirit. Too much, perhaps, did we dwell on the distinct and previous character of this operation, so as to subject ourselves to a delusion of the imagination, as if there were a separability as well as a distinctness of the act of the Spirit from that of the Word—in short, as if they were successive units and two actions ~~as well as two acts~~ instead of a twofold act. Hence arose a question: why, the whole of Chaos having become Aether, was not the whole Aether in like manner transformed or potentiated into matter of light? why was the matter of light (= lux phaenomenon) [*f 23*^v] separated from the darkness?^w Observe, we do not ask for the final cause, but for the efficient necessity; we seek for an insight into the absurdity and impossibility of the transformation of the whole Aether into the matter of Light. And we now proceed with better hopes to cope with this problem when, instead of taking the Chaos as total Aether, and then the Aether as transformed partially into light, we conceive of it in the Aether, and the light as formed out of the Chaos, so that the operation of the Spirit in the formation of the Aether is co-incident with the distinctive act by which the light was separated from the Aether. In the order of thought we give a priority to the act of the Spirit from the necessity we are under of conceiving form as either involved or superinduced, and in both cases presupposing a materia, a substance, and likewise because in the matter of light itself, as well [*f 24*] as in the Aether, we presume a something participant of both

---

^v ms: We   ^w Question marks inserted

ζ. This will become still clearer when we recollect that the Lux lucifica is evocative as well as distinctive, and distinctive because evocative. ~~Hence~~

η. Hence we have in the first place three forms of agency contained in the act of light (lucific act) as realized in a diverse materia: 1st, the^x evocation, which can only be represented by its contrariety to the former creaturely or self-seeking direction. If that former be a fleeing back in upon the self and relative to that self be the actual, then ⟨the⟩ power of moving, or being influenced to move away from, Self and to a center out of Self (which we know is realizable only as a return to God, but which in the present stage of our enquiry must, relatively to the creature, be^y confined to the notion of a center out of itself, i.e. ad extra, as in opposition to ad intra)—then, we repeat, this [$f24^v$] power^z must be opposed to the former as the potential, but this power is called into act by an influence of the Divine Will, which is essentially realizing. We have, therefore, as hath been demonstrated in a former Section, a potential actualized which we behold in full correspondence in Light (lux phaenomenon). The opposite, of course, can be no other than the actual potentialized, and of this, again, we have the full correspondent in the Aether; and we now see that ~~in~~ the very act of potentiating of Chaos into the Aether supposes the co-instantaneous separation of the light. So that in one point of view we may truly represent the Chaos as disparting into Light and Aether, and yet, with a more scrupulous accuracy demanded of us by the order of thought, conceive the Chaos as passing into Aether inclusive of Light potentially, and then of the [$f25$] Light actualized and separating from the Aether. We shall do best, therefore, as we have now done in taking both.

θ. The deductions are most important, for, first, it is evident that we must take a mid-point which is to the Light as Aether, so far as it is potential and future, and yet again to the Aether as Light, inasmuch as it is the act of passing into light, counteracted and hereby made successive by the opposite tendency and restraining influences à diversis, even as (to use a familiar illustration)^a the boiling water is passing into steam but compelled to pass successively by the superincumbence of the atmosphere. This, therefore, is the matter of Light, and the distinction between Light and Darkness. And the ground, therefore, of all Distinctness as Light itself is the cause. This is the first Deduction.

ι. The second and equally momentous deduction is that the matter [f 25^v] of light necessarily supposes an amassment relatively to itself, and

---

^{x} ms: The ^{y} ms: must be ^{z} ms: this power ^{a} Parentheses inserted a circumjacency relatively to the Aether. The matter of light becomes the circumjection, the Aether the circumjacens.

κ. The third Deduction is that there is a necessary proportion of the circumjectum to the circumjacens, of the mass to the Aether.

λ. And 4^{LY}, from whatever cause we may be able hereafter to evince the necessity of a plurality of masses—as, for instance, from the inherent non-reality of a partial center, or if we may dare so to express ourselves, from the essential relativity of all matter by virtue of its essential multeity—in these acts and tendencies we must find the place of the laws of motion and distance, which must all alike be finally reduced to the reciprocal relations of the mass and the Aether.

μ. Every where as we proceed [*f 26*] we find the same form in various realizations or genitures: thus the plurality of the masses is inferred from the gradations and opposition of the multeity to the unity. We cannot increase or intensify the unity—as, for instance, in the idea of mass—without instantly necessitating an alternate and counterbalancing act representative of the multeity. But as we must necessarily meet with this subject, viz. the plurality of the masses in a more advanced stage, we content ourselves at present with having pointed out the place in which the laws are to be found, without attempting to evolve the laws themselves.

v. We have constituted Cohesion as the punctum indifferentiae, indifference-point, of attraction and astringency. Now if we take the astringency per se, comprehending in our view, as before, the instances of multeity and the relations of the circum[*f 26ᵛ*]jectum to the circumjaciens, we obtain in the fulness of the idea the force of Contraction.

ξ. The contraction, therefore, is not Light, nor can Light be designated as a contractive power: it is a cause and a condition of such agency as produces the contractive force, and contraction may more properly be entitled among the results of light than its immediate effects.

o. On the contrary, though, Light as the distinctive power is by the reaction of the astringency the occasion of Contraction, yet as the evocative power (v. § ζ) it forms a similar union of alliance with the attraction, as, in its distinctive character, it had done with astringency. Conceive, therefore, the Attraction which is a Going-forth of itself acted on by the evocative power which, as it exists in the materia evoked, will appear as propulsion ab intra, and we have immediately the [*f 27*] Dilative force or power of Self-dilatation.

π. But, again, if we conceive the contractive force as predominant over the attraction, so that the astringency shall convert the Going-forth into a fleeing from, so that the potential shall be actualized as potential, and we have a necessary circumjacens in which the Aether, influenced by the evocative power, participates of light—that is to say, it is the same power as the Dilative, but instead of being contemplated, as in the individual, it is conceived as an aetherial inter ens—or the circumjacency becoming a multeity of interspaces between the products of astringency, and this compleats the idea of the Repulsive force or force of Repulsion.

ρ. Hence we see the difference and the likeness of the forces of Dilation and Repulsion: we perceive that they are disparates, not Opposites or Poles, and that [*f 27ᵛ*] the true and only Opposites are the forces of Attraction and Contraction—and again that the contractive force differs from the astringent only as far as the astringent is conceived under the forms of Relativity and Multeity ad alterum quasi ab extra. In our next Disquisition we shall seek the forms which must necessarily follow on any given amassment of the matter of Light under the combined or alternate and successive forces of Light and Aether, of Attraction and Contraction, of Dilation as the subordinate of Attraction and Repulsion, and Repulsion as the subordinate of Contraction.

[*f 28*] We have never entertained a hope so disproportionate to our powers as to plough the field with a single *ᵇ*furrow. We*ᶜ* ⟨were⟩ well aware that the team must be many times turned in to the same parallel, but our object was to have provided one line measuring the whole extent as a mark and as a means of connexion. To vary the metaphor—if we can but pass a road, however narrow, through the wilderness. though the objects seen from thence to the right or the left of the road lie within a narrow compass, it shall be sufficient for us if only the road itself is without a chasm, or with such only as a plank can over-bridge by the plank, we would understand those instances in which the particular mode and form may be unknown, but yet the perception be clear that in some form or other it must have been. The farther we proceed, the higher we ascend, for our journey is [*f 28ᵛ*] anastatic: the higher we ascend, the wider and more commanding will be our view. § We have so far proceeded as to have mastered at least a general view of the powers and forces which are to be our instruments, and have provided a faithful interpreter in the deduction, and consequently in the nature, of these powers; but ⟨in⟩ the process of their operation historically, we must be content to be still less minute, in the trust that we may take a something less inadequate view when we re-trace the ground more at leisure, because with more confidence, with more enlarged powers, and those too refreshed and exhilarated by having reached a goal placed at a sufficient distance from the

ᵇ⁻ᶜ ms: furrow we

starting point to secure us that we are in the right road. We have seen that Light involves Amassment, Amassment a Circumjacency, and that both are inconceivable except under the assumption of Plurality, i.e. of many masses, many circumjacencies, and consequently Interjacencies.

[*f* 29] As long as we contemplate the action of Light within the luminous mass either as allied with or as counteracting, now Attraction, or the Going-forth, or Astringency, or the Fleeing-in-from, we find ourselves confined to the secondary forces Dilation and Repulsion. These, however, are disparates, not opposites: the principle of Opposition is to be sought for only in the primary powers of Attraction considered, as in the phaenomenon of Expansion and Astringency, as Contraction, or seeking a center in itself. If, therefore, we conceive the first act, for in the application of time to acts necessarily synchronous our choice is indifferent—if, I say, we take the dilation of the luminous mass as the first act of the light combining with the expansion, we necessarily suppose a recession of the Self from the Self, which, however (and this of the last importance to be borne in mind), it is not the denying or abandonment of Self, but still a self seeking differenced from the opposite by its [*f* 29ᵛ] direction only even as the effort to appropriate the alterity by destruction of the Self of others is grounded in the same principle as the effort to secure the Self from being appropriated by others lessened or lost. It is fated that the act of dilation should be progressively followed by a lessening of the sensible Self, which we behold symbolized in the language of the senses by the phaenomenon of ᵈThinness. Asᵉ long as Self be the object and Self-seeking the Sphere, so long we must extenuate in proportion as we expand. It follows, therefore, that with the act of dilation there must now co-exist, and now alternate, the contrary act of Constriction. If these acts, however, were in each total, and these Totals merely alternative, there could be no progress, no connexion between the two; for in the A being present, B would have ceased to exist—consequently no intermediate, no gradation, and, lastly, no test of multeity. But neither the multeity co-existing as the opposite to the divine [*f* 30] Unity, nor the Totals [. . .] because Totals capable of co-existing and therefore of being opposites, it is evident that we should have changed our subject and have substituted some other we know not what in its place. By virtue, therefore, of the same law of multeity by which we have established the plurality of masses, we must infer both acts as co-existing; but as by the law of time or the necessity of successive existence in the finite, the two opposites cannot exist as two and as opposites in the same subject at the

ᵈ⁻ᵉ Thinness as

same moment, and yet they must co-exist in order to be opposite, they must therefore exist in different subjects and, by an extension of the same law, constituting, therefore, different places. For place, indeed, expresses nothing more than the relations which any one determinate sphere of agency bears to other and different spheres—as^f soon as we contemplate them under the form of Space, i.e. supposing ourselves as conscious beings, [$f\,30^v$] for the contemplators or in reference to the Aether or actual potentialized, when we strive to conceive of the object in itself, prior to the imagination, what, then, is the result of these inductions? Evidently^g this: that while one part of the mass was moving in one direction, another part would be moving in the opposite; that this, however, could not appear or be as if the total mass were divided into two halves, each fraction exerting the same act in the same intensity, for this would to all intents constitute two masses, and could not be conceived without a corresponding interjacency. And this, it is possible, we may see cause hereafter in certain cases to assume; and that it may be found contained in the fact and phaenomenon of projection, which yet were we in any sense or at any one moment to conceive as universal or total, would ipso facto bring back again the Chaos, or uncounteracted multeity. We must therefore have a right to conceive of these opposites as taking place in one mass [$f\,31$] remaining one mass. But this we cannot do otherwise than under the form of gradation, it being indifferent whether we contemplate it as a gradually increasing dilation from one given point, or a gradual condensation toward any given point. Where that point will be must be determined, or rather included, in the figures in which any mass is capable of existing, and this again must depend on the powers, or rather the moment of evolution in which we suppose each mass to be— if, for instance, we were to conceive that moment to be purely lineal, it would be one as when we contemplated the unity in the minimum of the multeity and differenced from it, or made creaturely by its polarity alone. Other, again, would the range of figures be if we assumed the resurgence of the multeity and the opposite powers in consequence as existing at the same moment in different subjects, which would bring with it of necessity some form of breadth [$f\,31^v$] or surface as the exponent. Again, another range of other figures would result when we had arrived at the product of the centrifugal and centripetal powers as Gravitation, and the consequent commencement of a pure opposition of Gravitation to Light, and vice versa. Various, too, must the forms be which arise from the co-existence of these in their reconciling media as well as in their actions

---

^{f} ms: As ^{g} ms: evidently

and reactions as separate, though co-existing. They, in truth, would form a science in itself of immense extent, which, should it ever be grounded or taken up into pure intellection with no other residuum than what is involved in the diversity from God, such would be the Philosophy, or rather the philosophized science of Geometry. And all the vast and stately edifice of the present Geometry well worthy to be the pride of the human soul awaits only the descent of the glory [. . .] to become at once the temple and the [*f 32*] Shekinach of the divine humanity. Much we might even now do, but that it would delay us even to the exhaustion of our forces, till in our labors on the road we had expended the powers of progression. Here, therefore, as elsewhere, it is sufficient that we, as the masters of the divining rod in their progress over metalliferous souls, make a mark where the rod has signified a mine, but leave the opening of it to the labours of successive ages We may just hint that the forms and the apparent inertness of the problematic cometary bodies manifestly present to us a stage and conditions of figuration altogether different from the solar or planetary masses, and that the same idea will be either the guiding or the proceeding light, should science hereafter render the laws of formation of meteoric bodies generally, whether cloud or fire or meteoric consolidation or whatever may be contained [*f 32ᵛ*] in the gradation of these. In sundry comets the whole has been transparent so far that either no nucleus has been observable, or a nucleus which did not exclude the light of stars of the second magnitude. No sensible influence could be traced either of the comet on the bodies by which it passed, or, vice versâ, of the bodies on it. These, therefore, we are compelled to contemplate as little more than breadth or surface at the utmost, but as a commencing state of depth or subtler-amassment. In others the nucleus as condensed to an opacity yet still could not have reached to that point in which the gravitating power is full-born, as is evident from the fact that a nucleus calculated as of greater magnitude than the planet Jupiter passed at a perilous small distance from the moon without the least disturbance of its motions, but most of all from the small proportion which even here to the enormous extent of its dark, [*f 33*] of its luminous atmosphere and of its tail, or fan-like expansion For we ~~shall~~ ⟨have⟩ seen in ~~our next~~ ⟨a preceding⟩ disquisition that at a given degree of condensation, a new form of the divine agency must become manifest, and that the result of this, in addition to the former, is Gravitation, and consequently a spheroidal figure. What we have now, then, to do is to make it evident that no one mass considered in itself could contain the power of progressive self-formation independent of its relations; that these as generalized under the name of "place" must contain the determination of its changes; that, therefore, we have no right to consider comets as growing worlds any more than the aurora borealis etc., but yet that they may present to us a formation under conceivable circumstances which, being known, might enable us to infer other formations under other circumstances according to the conceivable ^{h}differences. And^i this, I trust, we shall be able to [$f\,33^v$] effect, as far as our present purpose demands, in our next disquisition, in which, having determined the locality—or in the phrase of the Schoolmen, the *"ubi"*—necessary for the genesis of Gravitation, we shall find in that genesis the birth, likewise, of the [. . .] elements under ~~those~~eir unchangeable forms, which no revolutions of chemistry can by any possibility lessen or multiply.

$^{h-i}$ ms: differences &

APPENDIX B
Unassigned Manuscript Fragments

The following four fragments, all in C's hand, cannot be identified with certainty as part of the *Op Max*, but they are sufficently closely related to Frags 1–4 in subject-matter to justify being included in the present edition rather than in *SW & F*. The dates of these fragments are uncertain, but the limited evidence available (see the headnotes to Frags (*a*) and (*b*)) suggests that they could have been written about the same time as the major *Op Max* mss, i.e. 1819–23. The texts were transcribed by Heather Jackson from the original mss, and her transcriptions were then checked by Nicholas Halmi against photocopies of the mss.

(*a*) BM MS Egerton 2801 f 84; wm "[ ]19".

DATE. 1819 or later. The paper bears the second half of the wm date 1819.

Introduction to the Organon, or Logic of Ideas, more properly *Noetic*.—

The Love of THE GOOD is rare ~~as rare as the Counterfeits are numerous.~~ ~~But~~ ⟨but⟩ rarer still is the Love of THE TRUE! ~~and of this too~~ ⟨each⟩ ⟨Both as rare, as their⟩ ~~the counterfeits are many. What the genuine Character is, in either case, and the vaildity of~~ ⟨on what grounds⟩ ~~our assertion that it is,~~/Both inversely to the number of their counterfeits. ~~And~~*ᵃ* ~~in either~~ These are hard words—~~assertions~~ ⟨but⟩ not hazarded without a deep conviction of their truth.

(*b*) BM MS Egerton 2801 f 123; no wm. On the verso C has written: "D. of Winchelsea / Wrangham / R. Sharp Esqre".

DATE. 1819–20? If this fragment is contemporaneous with the list of names on the verso of the ms, then it may have been written around the time of DC's arrival in Cambridge in May 1820. C wrote to his friends Francis Wrangham and Richard Sharp about securing a fellowship for DC: *CL* IV 948–52 (to Wrangham 28 Sep 1819), V 54–5 (to Sharp 13 Jun 1820).

We will conclude by a distinct recapitulation and specification of the powers ~~or~~ in the order of their birth and epiphany.—1. Mere Potential-

---

ᵃ In the ms a lower-case "a", not cancelled, is written above the cancelled capital "A"

388

ity (= φ: i.e. ~~0 philosophicum~~ ⟨0 nil, vel chaos phi⟩losoph$\underline{\omega}$v) actualized. ~~into~~ ⟨Offspring:⟩ Ether. (Darkness; materia prima, indistinction in actu, multëity *in posse* = *the faces* of the *waters* or indistinctities made to become a face of an indistinction; princium continui, vel ipsa Continuitas.) 2. Lux lucifica. The Multëity actualized in consistency with the actualized Indistinction, ⌈. . .⌉ ⟨or⟩ Continuity, but so that the one shall be the Ground of the other, *this* this *apparent*, or distinguished, that the *supposed*. OFFSPRING: Matter of Light.

Ist and 2nd Here commence the retro-action, of the second on the first *as* the first, the result of which must be contemplated distinctly tho' inseparably from the second. In the $\oplus$ the | or imperfect $^N|_S$, = the polarity is within and below the $\bigcirc$: i.e. we have the mere possibility of polar power, if a something not contained in the $\oplus$ be superinduced. The true Poles are the Apostolic Will and the metathetic Spirit and Word—the creaturely Self and the Divine Love. But as the patient here is a will, the patiency is itself a form of action—with the one exception of the preparatory Impregnation, by which the Pati*ens* ~~was~~ became an *ens* at all, or a *Subject* under any form. This having been effected by an Act of *free Grace*, by an overflowing of the Divine Love in the chatachoresis or descensive Procession of the Holy Spirit, all following Acts are Influences *on* the Subject, which suppose a *con*fluence on the part of the subject, but not an *harmony*, not an entire intussusception of the Influence into the Subject, or perfect surrendering of the latter to the former—for this ⟨is⟩ the *consummation*, the last great *End*, the re-established *Stasis*, not the Antistasis. There must therefore be the possibility of an *act* IN the subject, ~~it being at the same time kept in mind~~ ⟨we not forgetting meantime, that⟩ the Materia Subjecta taken as a unit is itself the Counter-pole to the divine Influence; and it again, it must^b

(*c*) BM MS Egerton 2801 ff 130–1; a single unwatermarked sheet folded in half to make two leaves, each approximately 180 × 110 mm.

DATE. 1819 or later?

[*f 130*] ⟨~~Prospectus~~⟩^{c}

I

§§ *Lust* of Attraction by intussusception of Alterity into the Self⟨.⟩ ~~or~~ †The blind striving of a Part to be a Self and yet to *have* the Whole, in and ~~for~~ ⟨*belonging*⟩ to its Self—The perpetual act of Self-destruction by

---

^{b} The ms ends at this point
^{c} Written perpendicularly to the rest of the text, and cancelled

~~the~~ essential Contradiction in the self-affirming Will.—Therefore, we may call it *plurally* (so best as to convey the *confusedness*, without unity ⟨and yet without interdistinction⟩ Attractions Appropriative in ~~its~~ blank potentiality = ^{d}Chaos: Multëity^e with privation of Number: Tò ΑΛΟ-ΓΟΝ, ΑΖΩΟΝ, ΑΘΕΟΝ.

II.

α   Inceptive Actuality by the free realizing Moment of the divine Will, *as* divine.

β   The result = inceptive *transition* from ~~Multëity~~ ⟨confused allness⟩ to integral parts, the ⟨rudimental⟩ embryos (as it were) of distinguishable Self-Will—

γ.   In, with and ⟨as⟩ the same, momentum, the inceptive *transition* from the boundless Multeity to Totality by the ⟨equal⟩ Communication of One thro' All by the divine Will, as Love, Life, the Spirit.

[*f 130^v*] δ. Result (1.^{f} Inception of Communicability, i.e. of Action, Receptivity, and Re-action.

ε. Result (2.^{g} Hence the Attraction appropriative actualized in each, as *a going forth* (for this is that property of Love and of the Spirit, which cannot but be where the *influence* of the Spirit ~~is~~ ⟨acts⟩; but yet it is ⟨as⟩ a *going forth against*, for it is the Apostate *Self-Will*, ~~that~~ ⟨it⟩ is ~~blind~~ a blind coveting, ~~and altogether~~ ⟨an uncoiling and distending⟩ enmity which is the materia or subject ⟨of the influence. It is still the Self-will, actualized, ~~not actuated by the efficiency~~ not actuated by the Spirit, not transmuted, sanctified⟩ and which is impelled by Love ⟨or *dis-self'd—*⟩^{h} but doth not partake of its inwardness; still heterogeneous from the Spirit it partakes only of the *direction* of the Spirit. It is the dry Leaf that moves ~~in~~ ⟨with⟩ the motion of the moving Air, but neither inhales nor assimilates its vital inwardness. "The Spirit of God moved *upon* the *surfaces* of the Indistinctions."

ζ. Result (3.^{i} But the same direction with the same ⟨force⟩ is communicated to all. In the very moment therefore that the forces are [*f 131*] actualized, they are balanced and their actuality is entranced as it were, in the equilibrium. Hence totally and exhaustively acting in the formation and continuance of the Equilibrium, there remains only a mere passivity to whatever is not comprehended in that equilibrium. Yet it is not utter privation, ~~but~~ or vacuity of Power, but a relative Negation. It is not, ⟨as

---

in the Chaos⟩ a mere potentiality ⟨in essence,⟩ but an actuality poten-
tialized ⟨ab extra:⟩/ it is not indeed Appropriative Attraction, but it is the
Material thereof.

η. The conjoint Result is the metacosmesis of Chaos, the Genesis (or Be-
coming) of the ETHER.*j*

θ. And the capacious and Capable ETHER was the work of God ~~in his
Spirit~~ the Spirit, as the Spirit singly. It was the Breath of God breathed
on the closed Eye-lids of the Darkness, the ~~preordinative~~ ⟨Brooding and⟩
Hush, that ~~struck a Sleep in~~ ⟨smoothing⟩ the ~~universal~~ ⟨convulsive⟩
Death-throw⟨oe⟩[*f 131ᵛ*]—~~made~~ Sleep—⟨into the smooth-made Death
and the Darkness⟩ parturient ~~of Light and Life~~ at the voice of the heav-
enly Lucina.

§§ 1. ~~But the~~ At Spiritus, ⟨articulatus licet,⟩ non *Spiritus* esse desinit /
atque etiam in articulatione interstitia quasi verborum complet spiritu-
aliter et conciliat. The ~~Spirit~~ ⟨Breath⟩ goeth forth before the Word; but
the Word is never without the Breath, but ever accompanying ever fol-
loweth that which ever more proceedeth thro' and from the Word. There-
fore, henceforward and throughout our future progress let it be borne in
mind, that the agency and functions of the Word are distinguishable from
those of the Spirit, but not separable, much less in opposition to them.

---

k~~1. Attraction appropriative, equal in each, and therefore by the balance
= O in all—~~*l*

(*d*) BM Add MS 34225 ff 153–4. 220 × 180 mm. The second folio has been
mended with a strip of paper (152 × 177 mm) attached below the text. Neither
the original folios nor the additional strip is watermarked.

DATE. 1819 or later?

[*f 153*]   2

an act of such a nature, i.e. having such a nature for the ground of its pos-
sibility, that it cannot counterflow without Confluence. Now this is ef-
fected, ⟨first⟩ by a nature containing a contradiction as its essence, which
contradiction we have found in the two contraries, Indistinction and Mul-
teity; and 2ⁿᵈˡʸ by the ineffable distinction in the transcendent Unity of
the Spirit and the Word, and the correspondent distinctness in unity of
their Influence, the first Offspring of which, as we have seen, is the ac-

---

i Superscript number in ms   *j* Word written in large letters
k–l Written upside down at the bottom of the page

tualization of the Indistinction and Multeity, which so actualized and in all the after grades of their potenziation becomes the *real Poles* in the ~~Omn~~ omni creato. Hence it is evident, that there is no possibility of resisting either influence but by assisting the other. It cannot resist the Word but by subjecting the principle of Multeity to that of Indistinction, and thereby allying itself in *fact* ~~tho' not in~~ with the influence of Communion/ and vice versâ. Hence therefore we have a three fold Polarity— First that of the Creaturely ~~to~~ and the divine Will: second, the Indistinction and the Multeity in the creature itself, and which as actualized by the Spirit and the Word [? ~~of~~] constitute it existentially, i.e. are both it and its properties: thirdly, the result of the distinction ~~in~~ of the divine Influences in the creature, and partaking therefore of its essential ⟨self-⟩ contrariancy, in the opposite acts by which resisting *this* it allies itself with *that*; *ᵐ*attests on the one hand,*ⁿ* ~~their~~ divine ~~Parent~~ ⟨Father,⟩ by still appearing *acts*, *superinductions*, ~~and~~ (so indeed as to render it natural for the human ~~mind~~ ⟨imagination⟩ to represent them to itself ⟨now⟩ as Agents, ⟨&⟩ superinducents, and now as Effects and superinducta) and on the other hand the creaturely *Mother* by the disturbance of the Unity ⟨in which both Influences are one, yet not the same,⟩ ~~and the adulteration~~ and by adulterating each so that a tertium aliquid shall be the product, having ~~that of~~ the Influence ~~struck out~~ ⟨"shorn of its⟩ beams" by the creaturely ingredients. Thus Distinction is the phantom of Division, &c.—I ~~n~~ scarcely need [*f 154*] add, that in reality neither of these ~~six~~ Poles can exist, but as variously modified by all—and that the necessary result is, alternation, oscillation, predominance, subordination, gradation, latency, appearance, ~~equilibrium~~ ⟨common effect⟩ from equilibrium as of two, or of inequality of as two on a common base as a third.—We may neither count them—1. The drawing toward the true Center, or abduction from the Self ⚹ the Self-seeking, or tendency to a fantastic Centre in the opposite direction.—Offspring in the Creature, or realized Poles, the vis Centrifuga ⚹ vis centripetalis.—2. The actualized & variously potenziated Indistinction ⚹ Multeity. Offspring in the Creature or realized Poles, Appropriation, or Astringency ad extra ⚹ Separative Self-projection or Volatility. 3. The *Light* with the Spirit, ~~or~~ ⟨the influx⟩ *from*, opposed by the creature⟨rely⟩ Components—Offspring, ~~of~~ or realized Poles, Contraction, Particularization ⚹ Dilation, Omneity.—The Play and Changes of these six Opposites, the two first being the Ordinant Powers, the two last the Modifying, and the middle two the substantiating give the contents of the History of the Cosmogony—as far as the *physical* is concerned—

ᵐ⁻ⁿ C originally wrote "on the one hand attests" and then marked the words for transposition

APPENDIX C

John Watson's Transcript of Coleridge's Commentary on the *Bhagavadgita*

VCL LT 32. The ms, a single unwatermarked sheet folded in half to make two leaves, consists of the conclusion of John Watson's extract from the *Bhagavadgita* and a transcript of C's commentary on the extract. Because the quotation from the *Bhagavadgita* (ff 1–1ᵛ) is printed complete where it is called for in Frag 3 p 267, only C's commentary (also in Watson's hand) is printed here.

DATE. 1820–3. Watson was JG's assistant from c Dec 1820 to Oct 1823 (see the headnote to Frag 1 above).

There is in all the Sanskreet writings I have yet seen (excepting some parts of the Sacontalá) a character wʰ I can only account for on the Hypothesis of childish intellect living among gigantic objects mean thoughts and huge things—living Lilliputs and inanimate Brobdignags! So too their Pantheism seems to me a natural result of an imbecil understanding producing indistinction by half closed eye-lids, and when all hues and outlines melt into a garish mist, deeming it *Unity*! Children never can make things *big*ᵃ enough. I was impressed in the same manner, when I read Cary's translation of the Raman-ana.

It would have been more than human, if those great and good men Warren Hastings, Sir W. Jones, C. Wilkins, etc. had not overrated compositions, the power of ~~reci~~tading which is so rare and attained with such difficult~~y~~ies: the writings themselves too venerably beclustered by all the notions, images, and feelings lust calculated to excite that obscure awe which lies between [*f* 2] Religion and *Superstition*. Liber ipse *superstat* Perque umbras unus; est [. . .] umbra Deum. We too will pay our de~~p~~bt of homage in our first presentation to these foreign Potentates; but having once payed it we must purge the sight with the euphrasy of sober sense, and purpose to answer the question which the *Government at home* expects from our mission, viz. ~~w~~What sort of *men* are these ancient Potentates of "inmost Ind"? Their neighbour of the north the temple-throned infant of *Thibet* with the Hĕĕmālăy behind and the cradle of

---

ᵃ This word appears to have been written over another, now illegible

the Ganges at his feet—this more than *It* yet less than *He*, this το αει βρεφος, seems to me their Brachycryptograph of Brahmen Theosophy, without growth, without production! Abstract[b] the enormous shapes and phantasms, and what remains? a Baby! The personality and the additional mystery of secondary self-impersonation, i.e. person Self-personifying—these dogmata and all the attributes of Person dance in and out like wandering flashes, often enough to call forth but without even an attempt to resolve their apparent incompatibility with the Omneity and Infinity which are the constant theme [*f* 2ᵛ] of the Indian Theology. Nay, the humanity is every where falsified into Omniformity (in this respect far below Spinosism) so that the system is essentially Atheism in the form of Polytheism.

If I consider the work as Poetry; it has the mortal Disease of all Indian poetry: the attempting to image the unimageable, not by symbols but by a jumble of Images helped out by ⟨words of⟩ number—a delirious *fancy* excludes all unifying *Imagination*. The men sticking between the teeth is worthy of Rabelais, and a good mockery of Claudian. But if I am to think of it as Theosophy—I find more than the ordinary repetitions and circles of common Ἐν καὶ πᾶν-ism, a system which is either a barren Truism or a most fruitful falsity, while the morals, equivocal at the best, have no imaginable connexion with the Religion, expect where absolute apathy (the function of the extreme East and west of Stoicism and Epicureanism) is extolled as the highest. Of life there is one feeble hint, of Love not one.

---

[b] ms: abstract

INDEX

Abp = Archbishop   Bp = Bishop   ed = edited

Works appear under the author's name; anonymous works, newspapers, periodicals, etc are listed by title. Subentries are arranged alphabetically, sometimes in two parts, the first containing general references, the second specific works (collected editions appearing at the end of this second part).

Birth and death dates are provided when they are known, but birth dates of persons now living are not given.

COLERIDGE, SAMUEL TAYLOR (1772–1834)

I POETICAL WORKS   II PROSE WORKS   III LECTURES   IV MARGINALIA
V NOTEBOOKS   VI COLLECTIONS AND SELECTIONS   VII MAGNUM OPUS

I POETICAL WORKS

II PROSE WORKS

III LECTURES

IV MARGINALIA

V NOTEBOOKS

development
  early plans xci–iii, xcvii–cv, ccxxiv; Extended Plan c–v, 326n93, 327n97; foundations xli–iv; incompleteness cliv–ix; non-publication cxliii–lvii; outlines xcix–cv, cxxiii; and C's life cxi–iv
Glossary/symbols 340–3
philosophical/cultural background
  conservatism clxiv–ix; Epicurean/Stoic philosophies xliv–ix, 144–6, 144n207– 8, 145n210, 145n213, 178n296, 285; evolutionary materialism clxix–xx, clxxv–xxx; genre clix–xiv; mysticism lxxx, 284n212; natural science lxxx–ii, ccxxi; *Naturphilosophie* lxxxi–vi; pantheism clxix–xvii, clxxx; polarity lxxxv–xc; Romanticism lxxxi–ii, cxix– xx, clviii–ix, clxx–xxi, clxxxi; system lxxv–xxxi, clxxxi–ii, cciii, 3n1
proposed content/treatises xciii–vii, 302n38
  Constructive Philosophy xciv; defence of Articles of Church xcvi; Dynamic Philosophy xciii–iv; Estesean Methodology cii–vi; history of Christianity xli; history

of Philosophy xciv; Logos xcv, xcviii, cvi–xi; Logos Agonistes xcvi; Logos Architectonicus xciv; man and the probable destiny of the human race xcii, xciii; Pantheists and Mystics xciv–v; Science of Premises xcv; Spinoza/Spinozism xcvi; St John's Gospel xciv–viii; system of logic xciv; transcendental Philosophy xcv; Unitarianism xciv
Proposed Preface 3
proposed titles xlii
  Assertion of Religion ci, cliii–iv, ccxxvii, 48n133; Eidoloclastes xcii, xcviii; Estesismos xcix–c; Logosophia xciii, xcviii–ix, cvii, cxxx, cliii, ccxxiv, 100n88; Philosophy of Epochs and Methods c
relation to other works
  Aids to Reflection cxcvii–ccvii; *Essays on the Principles of Genial Criticism* xcv; *The Logic* ccxxii–ix; *Philosophical Lectures* cliii–iv, clxxxviii–cxcvii, ccxiv–v; *Theory of Life* ccvii–xxii, 332n109; Wordsworth's *Recluse* lix, ccxxix–xxxv

Jacobi, Friedrich Heinrich (1743–1819) lxiii–vii, lxiii*n*117, cxxxvi, 275*n*181, 278*n*194
on I and Thou cxli; on personeity cxxxi; on the soul cxv; on system clxxxi *Briefwechsel* cxli*n*487; *David Hume über den Glauben* lxiv*n*126, lxv–vi; *Jacobi an Fichte* lxv; *Ueber die Lehre des Spinoza* lxv, clxxii, 107*n*111, 245*n*92; *Von den göttlichen Dingen* lxv, 103*n*98; *Werke* ed Friedrich Roth and Friedrich Köppen lxiii*n*118–20, lxiv*n*121–2, lxiv*n*126, lxv*n*127–30, lxvi*n*137, cxxxi*n*445, 103*n*98–9, 106*n*108, 107*n*110–11, 245*n*92
Jacobinism clxiv, clxv
Jaeger, Werner (1888–1961) *Paideia: The Ideals of Greek Culture* tr Gilbert Highet xci*n*249
Jahagëan system cii
Jahn, Johannes (1750–1816) lxxiii
Janus *see* Jahn, Johannes
Jaspers, Karl (1883–1969) *The Philosophy of Karl Jaspers* ed Paul Arthur Schilpp xliii, cxxxviii, clvii, 211*n*396
Jerome, St (c 342–420) xlvi
Jewel, John (1522–71) *Apologia Ecclesiae Anglicanae* 50*n*144
Johannine Logos cx, cxi, cxv
Jones, Sir William (1746–94) 277, 277*n*188–9, 281, 393
Julian the Apostate (Flavius Claudius Julianus) (331–63) 252, 252*n*109
Junghuhn, Friedrich clxxviii
Jupiter est quodcunque vides 264, 276
Justin Martyr, St (c 100–c 165) lxxi

Kaleidoscopes 273, 273*n*178
Brewster on 273*n*178; C and 273*n*178; Shelley and 273*n*178
Kant, Immanuel (1724–1804) xlv, lvi–xii, lxv, lxvii, lxxxiii–v, lxxxiii*n*204, xci, cxvi, cxx, cxxiv, cxli, clxvi, clxxii, clxxxv, ccxxviii, 47, 102*n*97, 104*n*103, 114, 118*n*147, 216*n*6, 252, 252*n*111
on categorical imperative 58*n*166; C on 40*n*109; on good will 41–3, 41*n*112, 41*n*114, 42*n*116–17; Jacobi on lxiii, lxiii*n*117, lxiv*n*122; on moral law within lii; on personal identity cxviii–ix; plagiarism from clvi; on self-love 29*n*70; as Stoic xlv; on system lxxvii, clxxxi; on thesis/antithesis/synthesis xc; on wellbeing 41*n*114, 42; on will cxx

Die Grenzen der Sinnlichkeit und Vernunft lvii*n*88; *Grundlegung zur Metaphysik der Sitten* 39, 58*n*166, 265*n*160; *Kritik der praktischen Vernunft* cxx, 40*n*109, 105, 105*n*105, 265*n*160; *Kritik der reinen Vernunft* lvii*n*88, lviii, lxi–xii, lxxvii*n*174–5, lxxvii, xc, cxviii, cxx, clxvi, ccxxviii, ccxxix, 105, 105*n*105, 265*n*160; *Logik* clxxxi*n*649; *Metaphysische Anfangsgründe der Naturwissenschaft* 329*n*103; *Gesammelte Schriften* lvii*n*87–8, lviii*n*90–1, lix*n*93–4, lxn98, lxn100–1, lxi*n*104–5, lxi*n*107–8, lxii*n*109, lxii*n*111–12, lxxvii*n*176–7, lxxxix*n*235–8, cxix*n*365–6, cxxiv*n*413, clxvi*n*580, 29*n*70, 40*n*110, 41*n*112–3, 44*n*122, 58*n*166, 59*n*167, 65*n*184, 168*n*279; *Vermischte Schriften* xc, 115, 115*n*134
Keats, John (1795–1821) clviii
on double touch 30*n*71
Letters 30*n*71
Kelber, Wilhelm *Die Logoslehre von Heraklit bis Origenes* cxin320
Kepler, Johannes (1571–1630) 337*n*138–9
Kernberg, Otto cxxxi
Kielmeyer, Karl Friedrich (1765–1844) lxxxiii
Kierkegaard, Søren Aabye (1813–55) clxxxi
Kirby, William (1759–1850), and William Spence *Introduction to Entomology* 175*n*288
Kirk, Geoffrey Stephen, and John Earl Raven *The Presocratic Philosophers* 315*n*70–1
Kittel, Gerhard (1888–1948) ed *Theological Dictionary of the New Testament* tr Geoffrey W. Bromley cixn313–16
Knight, Richard Payne (1750–1838) *Analytical Inquiry Into the Principles of Taste* 44*n*124
Knights, Lionel Charles (b 1906) "Coleridge: The Wound without the Bow" 23*n*53
knowledge of existence 66, 66*n*187, 67
Kohut, Heinz (1913–81) cxxxi
kosmos/chaos 274*n*179
Kurtz, Benjamin P. "Coleridge on Swedenborg" 107*n*113

labour exploitation, Paley on lii
Lamb, Charles (1775–1834) xci
on *Aids to Reflection* cc